CHIDUSHIM ON PARSHA

Sefer Shemot

Rabbi Bernard Fox

Edited by
Rabbi Eliezer Barany

Table of Contents

Preface	3
Shemot	4
VaEyrah	51
Bo	81
BeShalach	122
Yitro	169
Mishpatim	212
Terumah	255
Tetzaveh	298
Ki Tisa	322
VaYakhel	356
Pekuday	388

Preface

It is with the help of *HaKadush Baruch Hu* and with tremendous joy that I can present the collected writings of Rabbi Bernie Fox on the *Parsha*. Those familiar with his writings know how invaluable a *melamed* – teacher – he is. He disseminates *Torah* so clearly and helps others develop in learning and a love of *Hashem*. For those unacquainted, I can share with you a glimpse of what you're about to experience.

He articulates complex details in a way that is accessible to even casual students and helps guide them through the mazes of multifaceted issues. These books convey brilliant teachings that provide foundational lessons; allowing the reader to properly learn the *Torah*, delve into the *Talmud*, understand the *Rishonim*, and advance their own *Talmud Torah* abilities. The reader will gain broad knowledge on a myriad of topics while also diving deeply into specifics, thus enabling a substantial understanding of a verse and its surrounding topic. I write this with the idea that the reader will be prepared for how deep and comprehensive these writings are and also to instill the sense of excitement about what is in store, that I always feel when I read the Rabbi's thoughts and ponder his natural prose style. Studying these writings will allow one to truly approach *Kol HaTorah Kulo* – the entirety of Torah.

On a personal note, I am deeply grateful and honored to be able to share these lessons. Rabbi Fox's writings transfixed me from the very first analysis I read of his; a piece he wrote on *Megilat Ruth*. He established an appropriate approach to understanding the *Rishonim* on the text and allowed for a grasp of the text itself. Since then, I have learned answers to longstanding questions, have better understood passages in the *Torah*, have expanded my learning skills and have grown to love *Talmud Torah* even more! Compiling the Rabbi's writings has been a labor of love which has sustained me from start to finish.

It is my hope, in sharing his collected writings, to be able to be *Marbitz Torah* – disseminate *Torah* – and to help others experience the same enhanced love of learning that I did and which so many of Rabbi Fox's *Talmidim* –students, have.

With tremendous gratitude,

Eliezer Barany

Shemot

"These are the names of the Bnai Yisrael that came to Egypt with Yaakov, each man and his household." (Shemot 1:1)

This pasuk introduces Sefer Shemot. Nachmanides, in his introduction to Sefer Shemot discusses the theme of Sefer Beresheit and this Sefer. He explains that the theme of Sefer Beresheit is creation. He acknowledges that this assertion raises a question. It is true that Parshat Beresheit describes the creation of the universe. Parshat Noach is a continuation of this discussion. Hashem destroyed the world through the Deluge and then reconstructed it. At the end of Parshat Noach the Dispersion is discussed. This event was crucial in forming the various peoples and societies. However, beginning from the end of Parshat Noach the theme seems to change. Avraham is introduced. From that point forward, the Sefer deals with the forefathers. In short, only a small portion of the Sefer seems to deal with creation. How can this be reconciled the Nachmanides claim that the entire Sefer is an account of creation?

Nachmaindes explains that the account of the lives of the Avot the forefathers is also a description of creation. These events tell of the creation of Bnai Yisrael. The theme is still creation. In other words, first the Sefer begins with the creation of the universe. Then, it continues with the description of the formation of the Jewish people. Nachmaides seems to imply that these two aspects of creation are related. The implication is that the creation of a nation that will receive the Torah is central to the purpose of the universe. The revelation of the Torah is essential to the completion of the universe. Nachmanides further elaborates on Sefer Beresheit's discussion of the formation of Bnai Yisrael. He explains that the account of the lives of the Avot provides many illusions to the events that would occur to their descendants. In other words, many of the experiences of the Avot were harbingers of Bnai Yisrael's future. According to this assertion, the Avot were not merely the ancestors of the Jewish people. Their lives presaged the experiences of their descendants. In a sense, their lives and experiences formed the future of Bnai Yisrael.

This thesis appears to be somewhat mystical. However, it does not need to be explained as a mystical concept. Perhaps, Nachmanides maintains that the Almighty used the lives of the Avot to provide guidance to Bnai Yisrael. An example will clarify this concept. Avraham went to Egypt in order to escape famine in Canaan. In Egypt, Sara was taken by Paroh. Hashem punished Paroh. Paroh released Sara. Avraham and Sara returned to Canaan. Nachmanides explains, based on the Midrash, that these events served as a precursor to the experiences of Bnai Yisrael. Avraham's descendants would also be confronted with famine. At Yosef's behest, they would descend to Egypt. They too would be persecuted by Paroh. However, eventually Paroh and the Egyptians would be severely punished. Bnai Yisrael would be redeemed. The nation would return to the Land of Israel. What is the function of this precursor? Avraham's experiences offered hope to Bnai Yisrael. The nation knew that their forefather Avraham had also suffered at the hands of the Egyptians. He too was in an apparently hopeless situation. However, the Almighty miraculously saved Avraham and redeemed him from his suffering. Avraham's experiences offered hope to the Jewish people. The redemption of Avraham proved that they too could depend on the salvation of Hashem. Based on this example, we can explain Nachmanides' thesis.

The Almighty provides counsel and hope to Bnai Yisrael through the experiences of the Avot. Through the lives of the forefathers, Hashem instructs Bnai Yisrael. The people can study the experiences of their ancestors. These events offer hope and guidance to the nation. According to Nachmanides, the theme of Sefer Shemot is redemption. The Sefer begins with the redemption of the Jewish nation from Egypt. However, this rescue from persecution was not a complete redemption. The Sefer discusses the receiving of the Torah and the building of the Tabernacle. Nachmanides explains that these events were part of the process of redemption. The redemption was not complete until the Tabernacle was constructed and the Divine Presence rested among Bnai Yisrael. These comments seem to contradict Nachmanides' position on the importance of the Land of Israel. Nachmanides maintains that the Torah is fundamentally designed to be observed as a comprehensive system. It governs individual action and also national behavior. The Torah only realizes this design when the nation is in the Land of Israel. In other words, the Torah is designed for observance in the Land of Israel. Clearly, Nachmanides maintains that the Land of Israel is central to the observance of the Torah. Therefore, it would seem that the redemption was not complete until the nation entered and captured the Land of Israel. Yet, Nachmanides asserts that the redemption was completed in the wilderness! The presence of the Almighty in the camp of Bnai Yisrael completed the redemption.

It seems that Nachmanides maintains that there are two aspects to redemption. Redemption is both a personal and a national experience. On a personal level, redemption occurs through establishing an intimate relationship with the Almighty. This relationship can occur in the Land of Israel and also in exile. The nation that left Egypt was able to achieve this intimacy with Hashem while still in the wilderness. They attained personal redemption. However, national redemption cannot be achieved in the wilderness. National redemption requires the complete implementation of the Torah. This only occurs with the possession of the Land of Israel. This resolves the contradiction in Nachmanides. Sefer Shemot tells the story of the redemption. The generation of the wilderness achieved complete personal redemption when the Divine Presence descended within the camp. However, Nachmanides maintains that, as a nation, the redemption process was only completed with the occupation of the Land of Israel and the complete implementation of the Torah.

"And these are the names of the Bnai Yisrael that came to Egypt. Each man with his household came with Yaakov." (Shemot 1:1)

The passage above is the opening of Sefer Shemot. Sefer Shemot deals with the bondage of Bnai Yisrael in Egypt and their eventual redemption. The commentaries on the Torah have various views regarding the reasons for Bnai Yisrael's bondage. Many share the view that is was a punishment for some wrongdoing. However, they differ widely regarding the specific failing that engendered the bondage a persecution in Egypt.

Nachmanides maintains they crucial incident that led to the exile and persecution of Bnai Yisrael in Egypt occurred early in Sefer Beresheit. Avraham was confronted with a famine in the land of Canaan. In response to this famine, Avraham abandoned the land of Canaan and descended to Egypt. Nachmanides maintains that Avraham sinned in his decision to leave the land of Israel and seek refuge in Egypt. Nachmanides asserts that Avraham also committed a second sin. While in Egypt, Avraham denied that Sara was his wife. He claimed that she was his sister. Avraham engaged in this deception, in order to protect himself from the Egyptians. He feared that in order to seize Sara, the Egyptians might murder her husband, but as her brother he would be safe from harassment. According to Nachmanides, Avraham should have relied upon G-d's providence and assumed that he would be protected.[1]

The Talmud teaches us in Tractate Taanit that it is prohibited to rely upon miracles. Each individual is required to exercise common sense. We may not endanger ourselves needlessly with the hope of being saved by a miracle.[2] Why, then, did Avraham sin by traveling to Egypt and claiming that Sara was his sister? Both of these decisions reflect Avraham's determination to provide for his own safety, without relying on Divine intervention.

It seems that Hashem intended to demonstrate, through Avraham, a fundamental concept of the Torah. The Almighty is the Creator of the Universe. He is aware of all the intricate details of His creation. Furthermore, He will intervene with nature on behalf of His devoted children. Towards this end, G-d endeavored to demonstrate, through Avraham, the effects of His Providence. He made Avraham wealthy and mighty; He protected him from all harm. Because of this relationship, Avraham should have stayed in the land of Israel. He would have been protected, and unharmed by the famine. Similarly, upon entering Egypt, Avraham should have acknowledged Sara as his wife. His frank honesty in the face of danger would have been rewarded. G-d would have protected Avraham from the aggression of the Egyptians. Remaining in the land of Israel and declaring Sara as his wife would have served as a demonstration G-d's Providence, in the most dangerous of situations, over his beloved.

In short, it is prohibited for a person to rely upon a miracle. However, Avraham had a unique mission. The Almighty wished to demonstrate His Providence through Avraham. Because Avraham abandoned the land of Israel and protected Sara though deceit, he denied Hashem the opportunity to demonstrate His influence over nature on behalf of Avraham.

Nachmanides then demonstrates a remarkable set of parallels between Avraham's experiences in Egypt and those of his descendants.

Avraham was confronted with a famine. He descended to Egypt to survive. Bnai Yisrael was confronted with famine and descended to Egypt to survive.

The Egyptians took Avraham's wife – Sara. The Egyptians attempted to kill all the male children Of Bnai Yisrael but wanted to take the women of Bnai Yisrael for themselves.

Hashem intervened to save Avraham. He punished the Egyptians. Hashem intervened to save Bnai Yisrael and punished the Egyptians.

Finally, the Egyptians send Avraham away and he left with great wealth. The Egyptians send Bnai Yisrael away and they left with great wealth.

Nachmanides explains that this parallel occurred through design. Avraham sinned in descending to Egypt and in claiming that Sara was his sister. Instead, he should have relied on Hashem to save him from famine and danger. Nachmanides asserts that Avraham must have been guilty of wrongdoing – albeit accidental. Otherwise, he would not have experienced this misfortune. Finally, Nachmanides adds that Bnai Yisrael's exile to Egypt was also caused by Avraham's error.

---

[1] Rabbaynu Moshe ben Nachman (Ramban), *Commentary on Sefer Beresheit* 12:10.
[2] Mesechet Taanit 20b.

Abravanel agrees that Nachmanides' basic reasoning is valid. The experience in Egypt seems to be a punishment. This implies the commitment of a sin. However, he objects to ascribing this sin to Avraham. He insists that we do not have the right to ascribe a wrongdoing to Avraham that is not explicitly indicated by the Torah. Instead, he maintains that the sin was committed by the *Shevatim*. The brothers sinned in selling their brother Yosef into bondage. The Torah does identify their behavior as a sin.

Like Nachmanides, Abravanel offers proof to his thesis by outlining the various parallels between the sin of the *Shevatim* and the punishment experienced by Bnai Yisrael.

The *Shevatim* sold Yosef into bondage in Egypt. Their descendants experienced bondage in Egypt.

They threw Yosef into a pit. Their male descendants were thrown into the river.

The *Shevatim* caused Yosef to enter bondage. Yosef caused them to descend to Egypt and eventually, their descendants entered bondage.

They were caring for flocks and Yosef came to assess their work with these flocks. They descended to Egypt in order to provide their flocks with pasture.

It is interesting that although Nachmanides and Abravanel both assume that some sin led to the exile and bondage in Egypt, they differ on the specific sin. Abravanel rejects Nachmanides' thesis because it requires that we attribute wrongdoing to Avraham by inference. He argues that although we have the authority to explain and interpret the Torah, we must work within strict perimeters. We cannot ascribe a sin to the *Avot* – the forefathers – that is not explicitly stated in the text of the Torah.

This is an interesting dispute. It seems that Abravanel's criticism of Nachmanides is reasonable. Nachmanides is making remarkable and drastic inferences at the expense of Avraham! Why was Nachmanides not sensitive to Abravanel's concerns?

Perhaps, the basis of this dispute lies in understanding these two Sages' perspectives on the purpose and theme of the Torah's narrative. It seems reasonable to assume that even Abravanel would agree that the Torah is not a set of biographies. There is no attempt in the Torah to provide a comprehensive biographical sketch of Avraham or any of the *Avot*. However, Abravanel does maintain that the Torah wishes to provide us with a characterization of Avraham and the *Avot* that is fundamentally complete. Our identity as Bnai Yisrael is linked and built upon the foundation of our understanding of the *Avot*. The image and understanding presented in the Torah of Avraham and the other *Avot* contains the basic information that we are to integrate into our fundamental understanding and image of these individual. Based on this understanding of the Torah, Abravanel argues that the Torah would not exclude information that is needed to understand these individuals. We cannot assume that the Torah's characterization of Avraham is misleading or incomplete in a fundamental manner.

In contrast, Nachmanides is willing to assume that the Torah's explicit treatment of the *Avot* is incomplete. This suggests that Nachmanides has a somewhat different understanding of the intent of the Torah's narrative. It seems that according to Nachmanides, the Torah is primarily concerned with outlining the unfolding of Hashem's providence over Bnai Yisrael. In this narrative the *Avot* are key characters. But they are characters in a narrative that is not primarily about them. It is about Hashem's providence. From this perspective it possible to assume that the explicit picture that is communicated regarding the *Avot* may not be comprehensive. The Torah describes Avraham's actions and decisions. It outlines the impact of these actions on the future of his descendents. This is relevant to the narrative of Hashem's providence. However, it is not essential to this objective for the Torah to explicitly evaluate Avraham's behavior.

And *these* are the names of the sons of Israel, who came into Egypt with Yaakov; every man came with his household. (Shemot 1:1)

Seeking Connections

1. Sefer Shemot's strange opening

Sefer Shemot opens with the above passage. The passage begins with the phrase "And these are the names". The use of the word "and" suggests that this passage is a continuation of previous material. In other words, this passage continues some previous discussion in the Torah. What is the discussion that is continued with the first passage of Sefer Shemot?

And Yosef dwelt in Egypt, he, and his father's house; and Yosef lived a hundred and ten years.

And Yosef saw Ephraim's children of the third generation; the children also of Machir the son of Menasheh were born upon Yosef's knees. (Beresheit 50:22-23)

2. The rapid growth of Bnai Yisrael in Egypt

Rabbaynu Avraham ibn Ezra offers a response. The response presents some problems. However, it provides an interesting contrast to some of the other responses that will be considered. He suggests that this passage is connected to the closing passages in Sefer Beresheit. In those passages, the Torah concludes its discussion of Yosef's life. It explains that Yosef lived one hundred ten years. Although he was the second from the youngest of his brothers – only his brother Binyamin was younger – he predeceased his brothers. Nonetheless, he had the opportunity to witness the emergence of three generations of his own descendants. He was alive for the births of his great-grandsons. The final passage of Sefer Beresheit describes Yosef's death, his embalming, and his placement in an – *aron* – a burial casket that would remain in Egypt until the return of Bnai Yisrael to their homeland.

The implication of these passages is that Yosef was blessed with experiencing the emergence of three generations of descendants. This might suggest that this blessing was unique to Yosef and not shared by his brothers. Sefer Shemot addresses this issue. It tells us that Bnai Yisrael descended to Egypt as a small clan composed of seventy individuals. However, it quickly grew. The group that entered Egypt and the generations that followed them bore many children. The clan quickly grew into a nation.

According to Ibn Ezra, Sefer Shemot begins with the word "and" to connect its opening passages to those at the end of Sefer Beresheit. Through making this connection, the Torah corrects the impression made by the final passages of Sefer Beresheit. Yosef was not unique.[3]

And they took their cattle, and their goods, which they had gotten in the land of Cana'an, and came into Egypt, Yaakov, and all his descendants with him; his sons, and his sons' sons with

---

[3] Rabbaynu Avraham ibn Ezra, *Extended Commentary on Sefer Shemot*, 1:1.

him, his daughters, and his sons' daughters, and all his descendants he brought with him into Egypt. (Beresheit 46:6-7)

3. The antecedents of exile

In Ibn Ezra's approach, the word "and" creates a connection between two sets of passages – those opening Sefer Shemot and those closing Sefer Beresheit. Rabbaynu Yitzchak Abravanel suggests that the word "and" connects more than two short sets of passages. It communicates a much broader connection between the narratives of the first two books of the Torah.

According to Abravanel, the word "and" communicates that the events in Sefer Shemot should be understood as a direct result of those in Sefer Beresheit. The final chapters of Sefer Beresheit describe the development of the brothers' resentment toward Yosef. It describes the brothers selling Yosef into bondage. Yosef eventually emerges as the virtual ruler of Egypt and saves his family from starvation. He brings his father, his brothers, and their families to Egypt and he cares for them. Sefer Shemot describes the descent of Bnai Yisrael into bondage and the eventual redemption of the Jewish people. According to Abravanel, the word "and" communicates to us that the bondage and redemption of Bnai Yisrael that are described in Sefer Shemot are the consequence of the events in Sefer Beresheit.[4]

4. Egypt and the process of nation building

The difficulty with Abravanel's suggestion is that the Torah is communicating a message that is self evident. Any reader understands that the conflict between Yosef and his brothers, the emergence of Yosef as leader of Egypt, and the measures that he took to save his family from famine led to the descent of Bnai Yisrael into bondage. What is the Torah communicating to us by specifically drawing our attention to this sequence of events through its use of the word "and"?

Perhaps, the answer is that the Torah is providing the solution to a mystery. The narrative of Sefer Beresehit leaves the reader with a question. This narrative strongly suggests that the events described are not just the result of human intrigue, conflict, and good fortune. The narrative is describing the hand of G-d operating behind a veil. Hashem manipulates events and leads the brothers, by means of their conflicts and experiences, toward a specific end – the exile of the Jewish people from the land of their fathers to the land of Egypt.

However, the narrative does not provide an explanation for why this exile was necessary. When Sefer Beresheit ends, the reader is left with this unsolved mystery. But then Sefer Shemot opens with the word "and". This word alerts us that indeed our sense that part of the story was left untold is correct. Now the story will continue. In this continuation of the narrative we will discover the solution to the mystery.

The specific solution is not clearly and overtly stated. However, Sefer Shemot does describe a process of nation building. A small clan becomes a great nation. How the suffering and bondage of Egypt effectuated this transformation is not explicitly stated. The reader must study the story, contemplate it, and seek the specific answers. However, the word "and" tells the reader that herein lies the answer. It invites the reader to study the material and find the answers.

---

[4] Don Yitzchak Abravanel, *Commentary on Sefer Sehmot*, 1:1.

And G-d created man in His own image, in the image of G-d He created him; male and female He created them. (Beresheit 1:27)

5. Two books with a single theme

Ibn Ezra suggested that the word "and" connects two sets of passages. Abravanel suggested it connects major portions of Sefer Beresheit and Sefer Shemot. Rav Naftali Tzvi Yehudah Berlin – Netziv – suggests that the word communicates an even more extensive connection between Sefer Shemot and Sefer Beresheit.

We are accustomed to referring to the five books of the Torah as Beresheit, Shemot, VaYikra, BeMidbar and Devarim. However, the Sages had other names that they used when referring to the books of the Torah. One of these Sages – BaHaG – uses an alternative name for most books of the Torah. For example, he refers to Sefer VaYikra as the Book of Priests. This name reflects the content of the book. Much of the content deals with laws that are related to the duties and obligations of the *kohanim* – the priests. However, BaHaG refers to Sefer Shemot as the second book of the Torah. In other words, instead of assigning it a name of its own, he identifies it as second to Beresheit in the books of the Torah. According to BaHaG, why does this book of the Torah not deserve its own name?

Netziv explains that the designation as second book of the Torah communicates that together with Sefer Beresehit it composes a single story told in two parts. Sefer Beresheit and Sefer Shemot are to be understood as a single narrative. What is their unifying theme?

Netziv responds to this question by quoting numerous statements of the Sages. However, rather than reviewing these statements, let us consider the overall narrative of Sefer Beresheit. The sefer opens with the account of creation. The account gives special attention to the creation and early development of man and woman. Only human beings are created in the image of Hashem. The human being is endowed with unique intellectual capacity and free will.

As the narrative continues, it emerges that Hashem has expectations of humanity. We have freedom to choose but not all of our choices are deemed by Hashem as appropriate. Eventually, one individual – Avraham – emerges who uses his wisdom and desire for understanding to find Hashem. Hashem enters into a relationship with Avraham and makes a covenant with him and his descendants.

The theme that emerges is that the universe has a design. That design relates to the human being. The human being is its most fundamental component and humanity has a mission. This mission is to seek understanding and to enter into a relationship with Hashem.

When Sefer Beresheit ends, this mission has not been achieved. Only a few individuals have reached the exalted goal that underlies creation and gives it meaning. However, overall, humanity lives in darkness. The creation narrative is an uncompleted story. All of the characters have been introduced but the plot has not unfolded.

Netziv explains that Sefer Shemot completes the creation narrative. The Jewish people are redeemed from Egypt and they arrive at Sinai. They experience revelation. This is not only the story of the emergence of the Jewish nation. This narrative is also describing the fulfillment of human destiny. Bnai Yisrsel stood at Sinai and experienced revelation not only as a people but also as the agents of humanity.

According to Netziv, BaHaG refers to Sefer Shemot as the second book of the Torah in order to communicate that its story completes the Sefer Beresheit narrative. It describes the arrival of humanity at its destination. At Sinai a journey initiated by Adam and Chavah comes to its end. Creation finds meaning and purpose.[5]

According to the view of Netziv, the word "and" that opens Sefer Shemot communicates to us that we are not beginning a new story. We are reading the second part of the creation narrative that began unfolding in Sefer Beresheit.

6. Living a meaningful life

Netziv's view has enormous implications regarding how we chose to live our lives. Not all choices are equal. They are differentiated not only by their impact on our happiness, but also by their meaningfulness. Some choices are consistent with the design of creation; others are not. Sadly, much of our attention and energy is devoted to considering and weighing the impact of our decisions on our happiness. Less attention is devoted to considering the challenge of living a significant and meaningful life.

For many of us our values and our religious life are secondary to our professional commitments and our other passions. Our relationship with Hashem is relegated to the time available for it and is far down our list of priorities. However, according to Netziv, this relationship is the fundamental source of creation's meaning and it is our mission as human beings to embrace this relationship.

However, we are each endowed with the capacity to make choices and thereby, to make changes. We must believe in ourselves. We must believe in our capacity to be different than we are and to become more than we are at the moment. When we embrace this faith in ourselves, we embark on a lifelong journey of authentic growth.

And the children of Israel were fruitful and had many children. And they multiplied and became very mighty. And the land was filled with them. (Shemot 1:7)

Avraham's prophecy of his descendants' exile and oppression

The opening *pesukim* of Sefer Shemot list the sons of Yaakov. The Chumash explains that Yosef and his brothers died in Egypt and that in Egypt in exile, Bnai Yisrael grew into a large and mighty nation.

Rabbaynu Ovadia Sforno explains that during the lifetime of Yosef and his brothers, Bnai Yisrael emulated the example of these *tzadikim* – righteous individuals. The people were committed to lives of truth and morality and their descendents emulated them. However, with the passing of these inspirational characters, the behavior of their descendants began to deteriorate. This moral corruption was responsible for their bondage. In other words, Bnai Yisrael became enslaved to the Egyptians as a consequence of their abandonment of the values of their ancestors.

Sforno does acknowledge that the exile of Bnai Yisrael was the realization of a Divine decree upon the Jewish people. It was predetermined. However, this decree did not include bondage and suffering. The suffering of Bnai Yisrael in Egypt was a punishment for the sinful behavior of the people.

---

[5] Rav Naftali Tzvi Yehudah Berlin (Netziv), *Commentary Hamek Davar on Beresheit, Intro.*

Sforno's position presents an obvious problem. Earlier, in Parshat Lech Lecha, Hashem revealed to Avraham that his descendants would be exiled to a foreign land; they would be oppressed in that land, and finally, they would be redeemed. This prophecy was a reference to the exile in Egypt. This prophecy seems to contradict Sforno's contention that the oppression experienced by Bnai Yisrael was not preordained. If the bondage and oppression was not predetermined, how could Hashem tell Avraham that his children would suffer Egypt?

Sforno explains that Hashem's message to Avraham does not indicate that the fate of the people was preordained. They sinned of their own volition and this behavior caused the bondage. Hashem knows the future with complete clarity and through means we cannot understand. Hashem's knowledge does not imply preordination.

This explanation reconciles Hashem's message to Avraham with Sforno's contention that bondage and suffering were not preordained. However, the answer gives rise to a further question. Why then did Hashem share this information with Avraham? If the bondage and oppression of Bnai Yisrael were not preordained, why did Hashem include these elements in His description of the nation's future?

Sforno responds that this message was given to Avraham for transmission to his descendants. The prophecy would serve as evidence that the suffering of the people was not merely an arbitrary nuance of fate. Hashem had revealed to Avraham that this punishment would occur. Because of this revelation, the people would know that their suffering was not the result of chance events. They would know that Hashem was aware of and had foretold their oppression. This would lead them to search for the reason for their suffering and hopefully to the realization that the deterioration in the nation's relationship with G-d was the basis for the bondage. This would suggest a means to end the suffering. Repentance could save the people. Without the message transmitted through Avraham, the people might conclude that they were the victims of political or sociological forces and that repentance could not help. Avraham's prophecy disproved this assumption.[6]

And there arose a new king over Egypt, who knew not Joseph. (Shemot 1:8)

Making Room for Hashem

Raban Shimon ben Gamliel says: On three things the world stands – upon justice and upon truth and upon peace. (Tractate Avot 1:18)

1. **Appreciation of others' kindness to us as a central Torah value**

Our Sages tell us of the importance of acknowledging kindnesses performed by others from which we benefit. If we benefit from a kindness, we are obligated to acknowledge it. This kindness may be a meal provided at a time of need. It may be a sensitive word or gesture. A kindness may be the offer of a ride to some event. The form of the specific kindness is not relevant. Regardless, the recipient must acknowledge it.

Various mitzvot of the Torah are predicated upon this principle. The obligations to honor our parents and teachers are expressions of this principle. Also, it is notable that the obligation to acknowledge a received kindness is not impacted by whether the person performing the act had a selfish motive. We need not investigate the motives of our parents in having children in order to determine whether we are obligated to honor them. Every child has the obligation to revere one's

---

[6] Rabbaynu Ovadia Sforno, *Commentary on Sefer Beresheit*, 13:13.

parents regardless of the purity of the parents' motives for creating a family and for supporting and raising children.

2. Appreciation of others as a social catalyst

It is easy to comprehend the practical importance of this ethic. Our Sages observe that the world rests upon justice, truth, and peace. In other words, in order for a society to function it must be governed by justice. Also, peace and goodwill must exist among its members. Of course, economic and social interaction requires commitment to honesty. Peace and goodwill only exist among individuals who acknowledge one another's kindnesses. The benefactor, whose kindnesses go unrecognized and unacknowledged, will sooner or later reconsider his benevolence.

3. Paroh's forgetting Yosef leads to his denial of Hashem

However, the midrash on Parshat Shemot deals with this issue from a completely different and startling perspective. The Torah tells us that a new king arose in Egypt who did not know Yosef. Of course, this is a difficult statement to understand. How could this new king be unaware of Yosef's rescue of Egypt from the ravages of famine? How could this new king not be aware of the decades of service and wise counsel that Yosef provided to his predecessor?

The Talmud responds that the passages should not be understood in a completely literal fashion. Instead, it is describing an attitude and manner of behavior. This new king conducted himself as if he did not know Yosef. Of course, he knew his nation's recent history. He was aware of Yosef's remarkable contribution to creating the Egypt he now ruled. However, the new king chose to ignore Yosef's contribution. He chose to act as if Yosef had not existed.[7]

As the Torah's narrative continues, it explains that this new king initiated a policy of severe oppression and genocide against Bnai Yisrael. Eventually, Hashem reveals Himself to Moshe and tells him that the time has come for Bnai Yisrael's redemption. Hashem sends Moshe to Paroh with instructions to appeal to him to moderate the treatment of Bnai Yisrael. Moshe asks that Paroh allow Bnai Yisrael to travel into the wilderness and serve Hashem. Paroh responds that he will not grant this request. He asserts that he does not know of this Hashem to whom Moshe refers. The Sages comment that Paroh's denial of Hashem is directly connected to his previous denial of Yosef's contribution to Egypt.[8]

This seems to be a strange claim. Paroh was an idolator. He accepted the Egyptian gods but not Hashem. His response to Moshe is understandable. His religious perspective differed from Moshe's. Why should he abandon his beliefs and replace them with Moshe's? How was this denial of Hashem related to his prior denial of Yosef's contribution to Egypt? The Sages' response is profound. However, before it can be appreciated, other issues must be considered.

And he said to his people: Behold, the people of the Children of Israel are too many and too mighty for us. Come, let us deal wisely with them, lest they multiply, and it come to pass, that, when there befalls us a war, they also join themselves with our enemies, and fight against us, and ascend from the land. Therefore, they set over them taskmasters to afflict them with their burdens. And they built for Paroh store-cities, Pitom and Raamses. (Shemot 1:9-11)

4. Paroh's campaign against Bnai Yisrael and its motives

---

[7] Mesechet Eruvin 53a.
[8] Rav Menachem Mendel Kasher, Torah Shelymah vol 3, p 20

Earlier in the parasha, the Torah explains that this new king did not know Yosef. The Torah explains that this king slandered Bnai Yisrael, questioned their loyalty to Egypt, and persecuted them. Clearly, there is some connection between his denial of Yosef's role and the persecution that this king initiated. What is the connection?

One possibility is that the persecution would have been impossible if the king recognized Yosef's role in the salvation of Egypt. He would have been unable to justify the persecution of the family of Egypt's rescuer.[9] However, there is another possible connection worth considering. Perhaps, Paroh's persecution of Bnai Yisrael was an expression of his determination to deny Yosef's role in preserving Egypt. Paroh recognized that as long as Yosef's family and descendants remained honored members of Egyptian society, they would serve as a reminder of Yosef's enormous contribution to Egypt. If Paroh was to succeed in erasing the record of Yosef's work, he needed to also eliminate this reminder. With this objective, he set out to remold his people's perceptions of Bnai Yisrael. He began by recasting Bnai Yisrael as foreigners of questionable allegiance to Egypt. He then dehumanized them by gradually reducing them to servitude. He then took his final step in his strategy of erasing Bnai Yisrael. He initiated a policy of genocide.

This interpretation of the pesukim suggests that Paroh was obsessed with forgetting Yosef and eliminating the evidence of his accomplishments. This obsession went so far as to motivate an attempt to destroy any remnant of Yosef's people. What was the basis of this obsession?

5. Paroh's vendetta against Yosef and its motives

Paroh resented that the Egyptian people's survival and prosperity was the result of the genius and abilities of a foreigner – Yosef. He regarded Yosef as an affront to the honor of the Egyptian people and an insult to the throne. The king of Egypt had been helpless to save his own people and instead had been compelled to rely upon the aid of a foreigner to rescue Egypt. This suggested to this new king the limits of his own power and capacity. He intensely needed to believe in his own mastery of his fate. However, as long as the memory of Yosef persisted, he was forced to acknowledge that even the king of Egypt is a limited mortal, unable to control his fate, and helpless to insure the welfare of his people. For a king who wished to be regarded as a deity,[10] this was an intolerable admission.

Now, the comments of our Sages can be considered. They explain that one's failure to acknowledge the kindness of others inevitably leads to denial of Hashem's kindness. They cite Paroh's denial of Yosef's kindness and Paroh's subsequent denial of Hashem as evidence of their proposition.[11]

6. Self-pride prevents one from appreciating others

Based upon the above analysis of Paroh, the profound insight of the Sages can be understood clearly. What internal force renders a person insensitive to the kindnesses received from others? What prevents the recipients from feeling appreciation? Our Sages are suggesting that the cause is often an unwillingness to acknowledge one's own limitations and frailty. A

---

[9] Rabbaynu Yosef Bechor Shur, Commentary on Sefer Shemot 1:8.
[10] Rabbaynu Shlomo ben Yitzchak (Rashi), Commentary on Sefer Shemot 7:15.
[11] Rav Menachem Mendel Kasher, Torah Shelymah vol 3, pp 20-21.

person who acknowledges all that others do for him, will come to realize that virtually every accomplishment is not a consequence of one's personal resourcefulness, but the result of the combined contributions of many others.

We are each small, helpless individuals. All that we achieve is through our participation in a vast enterprise in which we are a beneficiary. The most powerful ruler depends upon others to feed, and cloth himself. He requires the assistance of others to educate and provide for his children and family. Alone, he cannot protect himself from an insignificant organism. A bacteria or germ may suddenly enter his system and without proper medication he will be incapacitated or even die. Each of us is completely dependent upon others. Our personal humility is a function of our recognition of our degree of dependence upon others. Recognition of our dependency is demonstrated and reinforced in our consciousness through our acknowledgment of all the benefits that are bestowed upon us by others.

If we do not acknowledge the endless kindnesses from which we benefit, then we quickly succumb to Paroh's malady. We begin to delude ourselves. We exchange humility for self-pride. We begin to imagine that we are the masters of our fate. Once one succumbs to this malady, then there is no room in one's consciousness for Hashem.

And Paroh said: Who is Hashem, that I should hearken to His voice to let Israel go? I know not Hashem, and moreover I will not let Israel go. (Shemot 5:2)

7. Paroh rejected the idea of a Creator and Sustainer of all existence

This point can be clearly understood by again considering the comments of the Sages. Paroh responded to Moshe that he did not know Hashem. Why did Moshe's reference to Hashem evoke such a sharp response from Paroh? Paroh could have simply refused Moshe's request that the people be permitted a brief interlude in which to serve Hashem. Why did Paroh feel compelled to deny Hashem?

By referring to the god of Bnai Yisrael as Hashem, Moshe communicated a message to Paroh regarding the nature of Bnai Yisrael's perception of its god. The god of Bnai Yisrsel – Hashem – is not a local deity or a member of a community of deities. Moshe proposed the existence of a single G-d. This G-d is the cause of all existence. He is Creator and Sustainer. Everything exists solely by virtue of His will. All that we are and that we have is an expression of his boundless beneficence. For a king who fashioned himself as a potentate and virtual god, this was a completely untenable proposition.

If we succumb to the sedition of our own egos, then we too will inevitably alienate ourselves from Hashem. We may continue to imitate service to Him, to perform the expected religious rituals and devotions. However, in our hearts there will be no room for Him.

8. Creating a place for Hashem in our lives

In conclusion, we must be vigilant in our acknowledgment and appreciation of others. We must take care to take notice of the kindnesses we receive. This is crucial for the health and vibrancy of a community. By appreciating one another and acknowledging kindness, we encourage cooperation and mutual assistance. These are the basis of any community.

Moreover, by acknowledging and appreciating others we open our hearts to Hashem. We reinforce our cognizance of our own finitude and we build humility. Personal humility is the foundation upon which rests our appreciation of Hashem and our devotion to Him.

"And a new king arose that did not know Yosef." (Shemot 1:8)

This passage introduces the initiation of Bnai Yisrael's subjugation in Egypt. Our Sages disagree on the meaning of this passage. Rav understands the *pasuk* literally. The previous king died and a new king assumed authority. Shmuel disagrees. He argues that a new king did not come to power. The existing king changed his policies. He is called a new king because of this reversal.[12]

Both of these interpretations are designed to explain the sudden change in the Egyptian king's attitude toward Bnai Yisrael. However these explanations share a problem. The *pasuk* describes a reversal. Bnai Yisrael were invited into Egypt. They were given autonomy and treated with respect. Suddenly, this changed. Paroh and his government began sponsoring the persecution of Bnai Yisrael. What caused this sudden change? The *Chumash* provides one hint. It comments that this new king did not know Yosef. Rav and Shmuel argue over whether this king was newly appointed or merely established new policies. Bur regardless of the interpretation, the implication of this hint is clear. Bnai Yisrael were treated well by the Egyptians in deference to Yosef. Once the Paroh and the Egyptians forgot Yosef, the persecution of the Jewish people began.

However, this hint does not provide a complete explanation of the change in treatment.. In order to appreciate the limitations of the *pasuk's* explanation, some introduction is required. The Egyptian people respected Yosef. Understandably, they were grateful to him. He had saved Egypt from a destructive famine. It follows that this gratitude extended to Yosef's family. The Egyptians' regard for Yosef had tremendous impact on their treatment of his family. Generally, immigrant populations can expect little tolerance. Persecution of alien minorities is common. As long as Yosef was alive, his family was spared this treatment. Furthermore, the Egyptians treated Bnai Yisrael with a respect that sometimes bordered on awe. This is most apparent at Yaakov's death. The Egyptians accompanied Yaakov's children to Canaan in order to honor Yaakov. The respect showed by the Egyptians was so grand that the people of Canaan were deeply impressed.[13] In short, the treatment Bnai Yisrael received was the opposite of the norm for immigrant groups.

This raises two questions. First, why were the Egyptians so devoted to Bnai Yisrael? True, Yosef had saved Egypt. Certainly, the Egyptians were obligated to treat his family fairly. But the respect of the Egyptians for Yosef's family went far beyond this requirement. What motivated the Egyptians? Second, as our *pasuk* explains, the Egyptians eventually forgot Yosef's contribution to their country. It is understandable that this would lead to a cessation of the deferential treatment received by Bnai Yisrael. However, this is not what happened. The Egyptians initiated a policy of persecution. What caused this extreme change in the Egyptian attitude?

Nachmanides asks a related question in Parshat VaYigash. In that *parasha*, Yosef reveals himself to his brothers. He urges Yaakov to settle in Egypt with his family. In Egypt, he can protect them from ravages of the famine. The Torah comments that Paroh and his servants were pleased with this idea.[14] Why did Paroh and his government wish Yosef's family to settle in

---

[12] Mesechet Eruvin 53a.
[13] Sefer Beresheit 50:11.
[14] Sefer Beresheit 45:16.

Egypt? Nachmanides responds that Yosef created somewhat of an embarrassment for the Egyptians. He was a freed prisoner and a former servant. These are not the usual credentials for a prime minister. The Egyptians were far from comfortable with this situation. Now, the Egyptians discovered that Yosef was a member of a prestigious family. His brothers were regarded, in their land, as princes. This solved the Egyptians' problem. Yosef's brothers added to his credibility. He was worthy to serve as prime minister. He was a member of a distinguished family! The Egyptians were eager to receive Yosef's family. They were the proof of Yosef's worthiness to hold a high position.[15]

Nachmanides' insight has far-reaching implications. The honor the Egyptians bestowed on Yosef's family was not an expression of love or appreciation. The Egyptian's did not overcome the prejudices that are generally felt towards foreigners. However, these feelings were suppressed. The Egyptians needed to elevate Bnai Yisrael in order to preserve their own self-respect! This explains the Egyptians unusual deference towards Bnai Yisrael. It was not motivated by gratitude. It was an expression of self-interest.

This need only existed as long as Yosef lived. With Yosef's death, the Egyptians no longer needed to venerate his family. Now, all the suppressed prejudices emerged. Bnai Yisrael received the same treatment typically offered to the Jewish people in foreign lands. The persecution of Bnai Yisrael began!

"And a new king arose that did not know Yosef." (Shemot 1:8)

Sefer Shemot discusses the suffering of Bnai Yisrael in Egypt and their eventual redemption. Our passage introduces the events that led to the enslavement of Bnai Yisrael. The Torah tells us that a new king arose over Egypt. This king did not know Yosef. He was not familiar with Yosef's contribution to the salvation of Egypt from famine and to the creation of its great empire. The apparent message of the passage is that this king did not feel indebted to Yosef, his family, or Yosef's descendants. Any favor that previous rulers had shown towards Bnai Yisrael was replaced by antipathy and prejudice.

Rashi comments that Rav and Shmuel suggest alternative interpretations of our passage. Rav explains that this king was literally "new." Shmuel disagrees. He suggests that the king was new in his conduct. He put in place new policies – specifically towards Bnai Yisrael.[16]

Both the interpretation of Rav and the alternative offered by Shmuel present problems. Rav explains that he understands the passage in a literal sense. The simple meaning of the passage is that a new king occupied the throne. However, there is a problem with this interpretation. The passage contains an extra word! There is no reason to refer to the king as "new." The passage could merely have stated that a king arose who did not know Yosef. It would be obvious from this statement that he was new. Only a new king could be ignorant or unappreciative of Yosef's contribution to Egypt.

Shmuel's interpretation provides an explanation of this seemingly superfluous term. The passage refers to the king as "new" because he is only new in his conduct and behavior. But, Shmuel's interpretation ignores the simple meaning of the passage. It seems that Shmuel is

---

[15] Rabbaynu Moshe ben Nachman (Ramban), *Commentary on Sefer Beresheit* 45:16.
[16] Rabbaynu Shlomo ben Yitzchak (Rashi), *Commentary on Sefer Shemot* 1:8.

asking the reader to interpret the passage in a manner that is completely inconsistent with its obvious and clearly stated meaning.

Gur Aryeh and others respond that Rav and Shmuel are not arguing over the actual historical event. They both accept that simple meaning of the passage. The "new" king was a newly appointed monarch. However, both are bothered by the term "new." Why is this term included in the passage? If a king arose who did not know Yosef, obviously he was new! By referring to this monarch as "new," the Torah is communicating a message about him. Rav and Shmuel differ on the message.

In order to understand Gur Aryeh's explanation of the dispute between Rav and Shmuel, we must consider our passage more carefully. Although our passage is short, it communicates three points: First, the passage tells us that a king arose. Second, the passage relates that the king was – in some sense – new. Third, the passage tells us that this king was not familiar with Yosef. Obviously, these three points are presented as elements of a single passage because they are related. However, what is the precise nature of the relationship?

Before we attempt to understand the relationship between the three elements of the passage, let us identify the fundamental unifying message of the passage. Then, we can consider the relationship between the various elements within the context of the overall message.

The basic message seems obvious: Bnai Yisrael entered Egypt as a favored, privileged minority. In a relatively short span of time they lost their privileged status and became persecuted, enslaved, and eventually, subjected to genocide. The Torah explains how this shocking transformation occurred. The Torah tells us that the first step towards this transformation was somehow related to a change in the ruler of Egypt.

Now, let us reconsider the three elements of the passage. There are two possible understandings of the structure of the passage: The first option is that the first portion of the passage explains the second. A king arose. This king was "new." Because he was new, he did not know Yosef. In other words, he was not bound to the policies and behaviors of his predecessor towards Yosef's people. This is Rav's understanding of the passage.

However, the *pasuk* can be understood differently. It is possible that the second portion of the passage explains the first. The first portion of the passage tells us that a king arose and that this king was – in some sense – new. The second portion of the passage explains the nature of the king's novelty. He broke from the policies of his predecessors in his treatment of Yosef's family. This is Shmuel's understanding of the passage.

In other words, both Rav and Shmuel agree that a king arose and that his attitude towards Bnai Yisrael was very different from his predecessor. However, they differ on the reason behind this change in attitude. Rav argues that this king's rise to the thrown represented a new era and a break with the past. He was not bound to the policies and practices of his predecessors. He implemented his own policies.

Gur Aryeh suggests that Rav seems to be describing a deposing of the former monarch and his dynasty rather than the succession of a monarch within a dynasty. A monarch who continues the dynasty of his predecessors is committed to implementing his predecessors' policies and basic outlook. However, when a king is deposed and his dynasty is replaced, the new ruler owes no loyalty to the policies of the past. Instead, he may be tempted to distinguish himself from the previous rulers of the overthrown dynasty. He does this by breaking with the past and establishing a new – perhaps radically new – path. According to Rav, this king's attitudes towards Bnai Yisrael were a consequence of his disavowal of the past and his need to strike out on a new path that would be uniquely his.

Shmuel seems to describe a king who continues the rule of an established dynasty. In general, he is devoted and loyal to the status quo. However, this king was "new" in a single, important respect: He initiated a new set of policies towards Bnai Yisrael.

In short, Gur Aryeh suggests that Rav and Shmuel agree that a king arose who veered drastically from pervious polices towards Bnai Yisrael. Yet, they disagree on the reason for this sudden change of course. Rav argues that the change was occasioned by political upheaval. A king arose who was completely new and disassociated from the policies of the previous king. Shmuel suggests that this ruler succeeded his predecessor in a normal political transition – without chaos or upheaval. He had no reason to not continue the policies of his predecessors. Nonetheless, in one area – his treatment of Bnai Yisrael – he differed drastically from the kings who preceded him.[17]

Let us consider Rav and Shmuel's positions more carefully. According to Rav, it may not be meaningful to consider the causes or roots of the new king's hatred or persecution of Bnai Yisrael. This king had no commitment to past policies. He represented political change. It is not surprising that this ruler would succumb to simple xenophobia and prejudice towards a privileged minority. Furthermore, Bnai Yisrael may have served as a convenient scapegoat to be blamed for the inevitable setbacks and failures that accompany political upheaval.

However, according to Shmuel, this new king, in most respects, was devoted to established traditions, mores and values. Why in one area did he depart from tradition? Why persecute Bnai Yisrael?

It seems reasonable to look for an explanation in the immediately preceding chapters of the Chumash. The closing chapters of Sefer Beresheit deal with the final years of Yaakov's life. Yaakov asks Yosef to bury him in the land of Canaan. Yosef agrees, but Yaakov is not satisfied. He asks that Yosef pledge himself with a vow and Yosef complies. Nachmanides is concerned with Yaakov's demand that Yosef provide a vow. It is unimaginable that Yaakov would not trust Yosef! Why was his solemn commitment not adequate? Why did Yaakov demand a vow? However, Nachmanides notes that a subsequent event provides the explanation of Yaakov's behavior.

Yaakov dies and Yosef must now fulfill the pledge he made to his father. Yosef asks Paroh for his permission to leave Egypt and bury his father in Canaan. He tells Paroh that he is bound by a vow. Paroh allows Yosef to travel to Canaan. But Paroh also indicates that the vow is a factor in his decision; he is not willing to require that Yosef violate a vow made to his father. Apparently, Yaakov foresaw that Paroh would resist Yosef's request. Therefore, Yaakov did not require a vow from Yosef because he did not fully trust his son. Yaakov demanded that a vow because he recognized that this vow would help overcome Paroh's resistance. Yosef understood his father's design. He agreed with his father's assessment and in petitioning Paroh, he noted that he was bound by a vow to fulfill his father's wishes.

---

[17] Rav Yehuda Loew of Prague (Maharal), *Gur Aryeh Commentary on Sefer Shemot* 1:8.

However, Nachmainides acknowledges that his interpretation raises an obvious question: Yaakov assumed Paroh would resist his wishes to be buried in Canaan by Yosef. Yosef agreed with this assessment. Both seem to have foreseen some obvious issue that would incite Paroh to refuse Yosef's request. What was this issue? Nachmanides suggests two possibilities. However, let us focus on the first of these responses. Nachmanides suggests that Paroh might not have had any objection to Yaakov's burial in Canaan. However, Yaakov wished Yosef to take charge of the burial and personally execute his wishes. Yaakov and Yosef predicted that Paroh might object to Yosef's leaving Egypt to travel to Canaan and would instead insist that Yosef charge his brothers with this mission.[18]

Nachmanides' explanation seems incomplete. He tells us that Yaakov and Yosef correctly anticipated that Paroh would resist consenting to Yosef leaving Egypt and traveling to Canaan. However, he does not explain the reason Paroh would resist this reasonable request. Let us consider the obvious possibilities.

Perhaps Paroh was afraid Yosef would not return. He relied on Yosef's council and administrative skills. He could not take the chance that Yosef might abandon him. Yet, this is not a reasonable explanation: When Yosef, his brothers, and a delegation of Egyptian dignitaries traveled to Canaan to bury Yaakov, Yosef and his brothers did not take their possessions and were not accompanied by their young children. Certainly, Paroh had more than an adequate number of hostages to assure Yosef's return.

Perhaps Paroh was concerned that Yosef's return to Canaan would inspire in him a desire to return to his ancestral home. He would return to collect his family and belongings and would then lobby Paroh to allow him and his family to return to their homeland. Of course, Paroh could resist granting Yosef's wishes. But he would risk losing Yosef's full support and assistance. The difficulty with this explanation is that Paroh even resisted the removal of Yosef's body from Egypt.[19] This seems to indicate that Paroh was not merely guided by the practical need to retain Yosef's services. He did not want Yosef to be associated with Canaan – not in life or even death!

It is not that difficult to imagine Paroh's concern. Yosef had tremendous authority. In practical terms, he was the actual ruler. In order to hold his position, Yosef was required to speak, dress, and generally conduct himself as an Egyptian. Yosef's imitation of an Egyptian was compelling enough to convince his brothers. Why was this masquerade required? Apparently, the Egyptians preferred to think of Yosef as one of their own people. They were not eager to acknowledge that they were ruled by a foreigner – one whose true allegiance was to a different homeland!

Yosef's masquerade as an Egyptian – or, at least a naturalized citizen – was successful until his family came to Egypt. The emergence of his family must have created some controversy. But, Yosef could reasonably argue that his entire family had transferred its allegiance to Egypt. The death of Yaakov and Yosef's burial of his father in Canaan belied any claim of uncompromised loyalty to Egypt. Egypt was reminded of Yosef's roots and his connection with a foreign homeland.

Let us return to our question on Shmuel's opinion: What brought about the regime's change in attitude towards Bnai Yisrael? What motivated the regime to deny and renounce

---

[18] Rabbaynu Moshe ben Nachman (Ramban), *Commentary on Sefer Beresheit* 47:31.
[19] Rabbaynu Shlomo ben Yitzchak (Rashi), *Commentary on Sefer Shemot* 13:19.

Yosef's contribution to Egypt? Perhaps, Yosef's emergence as an alien from a foreign homeland was the root cause of this change. As long as Yosef was regarded as an Egyptian, the Egyptians could accept his leadership. But once events revealed to them that Yosef's allegiance was complicated and equivocal, the Egyptians came to resent him and their dependence on the foreigner. It is not surprising that this resentment led to eventual denial of Yosef's contribution to Egypt.

And Bnai Yisrael was fruitful, swarmed, multiplied, and became very mighty. The land was filled with them. And a new king arose over Egypt who did not know Yosef. And he said to his nation, "Behold, the nation Bnai Yisrael is many and mightier than us. Let us take wise counsel, lest they become many. And it will be that when war will occur it, too, will join our enemy, do battle with us, and ascend from the land." (Shemot 1:7-10)

Optics and Consequences

1. **A population explosion**

The above passages discuss the antecedents to the enslavement of the Jewish people in Egypt. They describe the explosive growth of Bnai Yisrael and Paroh's response. Why did the expansion of the nation's population provoke Paroh's fears and his extreme response?

Let us consider a related issue. The Torah tells us that "the land was filled with them". To what land does this refer? Did the Jewish people overrun the Land of Egypt? If this is the case, then it is difficult to understand how Paroh succeeded in subduing the largest component of his country's population. Rabbaynu Avraham ibn Ezra responds to this question. In Sefer Beresheit, Yaakov and his family arrived in Egypt. Yosef negotiated their settlement in the district of Goshen. According to Ibn Ezra, the district of Goshen was now filled with the members of the family.[20] If Bnai Yisrael was contained within the district of Goshen, why was Paroh fearful?

The passages explain that Paroh did not trust Bnai Yisrael. He questioned the loyalty of Yaakov's descendants. Was this simply a result of their number? A careful reading of Paroh's message to his nation is revealing. Paroh refers to Yaakov's descendants as "the nation Bnai Yisrael". Paroh was the first person to describe Yaakov's clan as a nation! In other words, Yaakov's descendants are no longer a family residing in Goshen. They fill its borders! They have grown into a nation.

Now, Paroh's fear becomes clearer. Yaakov's descendants had grown from a family into a nation – so large it filled the borders of Goshen. A foreign clan can be contained within the fabric of the host nation. But an alien nation has its own unique identity. As a nation, it has its own culture, interests, and goals. These interests and goals may be different and even compete with those of its host nation. Paroh expressed his fear to his people. "Bnai Yisrael is a nation. These people are not members of our nation. They have their own national agenda. Can we trust them, or will these Jews pursue their own interests at our expense?"

And they placed upon it tax-officers to oppress them with their burden. They build storage-cities for Paroh – Pitom and Ramses. To the degree they oppressed them, they multiplied and expanded. The Egyptians were tormented by Bnai Yisrael. And they subjugated Bnai Yisrael with rigor. They made their lives bitter with arduous labor – with mortar and bricks, and every

---

[20] Rabbaynu Avraham ibn Ezra, Commentary on Sefer Shemot, 1:7.

sort of work in the field. All the labor that they forced them to perform was arduous. And the king of Egypt said to the Hebrew midwives – one's name was Shifra and the name of the second [was] Pu'ah. He said, *"When you birth the Hebrew women and you see [the infant] on the labor-stool, if it is a male, kill him. If it is a female, sustain her."* (Shemot 1:11-16)

2. Paroh's response

The Torah describes the measures taken by Porah in response to his fears. It is not completely clear from the passages whether these measures were instituted simultaneously, or sequentially.[21] Also, what was Paroh's strategy? How did his measures address his fears?

Ibn Ezra explains that the answer to the second question is found in these passages. The passages explain that despite the measures taken by Paroh, Bnai Yisrael's population continued to grow. Ibn Ezra explains the all the measures implemented by Paroh shared a single objective. His goal was to arrest population growth.

Ibn Ezra further explains that Paroh's initiatives were sequential. As each failed, Paroh instituted his next measure. First, Paroh levied a labor tax. He required that Bnai Yisrael provide workers for state projects. His objective was to disrupt family life and thereby, procreation. When this failed, he authorized his ministers and the Egyptian people to subjugate the Jews and to oppress them with grueling labor. He reasoned that exhausted slaves would not procreate. When Bnai Yisrael's population continued to expand even under these trying circumstances, he implemented his policy of genocide.[22]

3. Introduction of genocide

The final step in the above passages is Paroh's program of genocide. The program had two stages. In the above passages, Paroh directs the Hebrew midwives to kill the male children they deliver. The midwives disregard Paroh's directive. Paroh responds by enlisting the Egyptian people as his agents. They are to seek out Jewish male infants and drown them. Why did Paroh initially seek the cooperation of the midwives?

Ibn Ezra explains that Paroh did not want to openly promote genocide. His preference was to clandestinely implement his program. He attempted to enlist the midwives to covertly kill the male infants at birth.[23] Nachmanides – Ramban – provides important details. The midwives would kill the infants but claim that the babies had died in childbirth.

Ramban further explains that Paroh implemented a covert plan because he was not confident that the Egyptian people were prepared to tolerate a formal program of genocide. Enlisting the general population into this program would take time, planning, and an organized propaganda operation. When Paroh's covert plan failed he was forced to take the steps required to transform the Egyptian people into agents of genocide.[24]

---

[21] It seems from the passages that some measures were sequential. He levied a labor tax. Then, he intensified the required labor. However, did he implement genocide as a new measure or simultaneous to the intensification of the labor?

[22] Rabbaynu Avraham ibn Ezra, Commentary on Sefer Shemot, 1:13.

[23] Rabbaynu Avraham ibn Ezra, Commentary on Sefer Shemot, 1:16.

[24] Rabbaynu Moshe ben Nachman (Ramban / Nachmanides), Commentary on Sefer Shemot 1:10. Ramban explains that Paroh initially levied taxes upon Bnai Yisrael. Ideally, he would have attacked with his army. However, his own people were not prepared to accept this

And the midwives feared the L-rd. They did not do as the king of Egypt told them. They sustained the children. (Shemot 1:17)

The defiance of the midwives

The above passage describes the brave defiance of the midwives. They refused to participate in Paroh's wicked plan. However, the Torah adds, "They sustained the children". This phrase suggests that their defiance extended beyond disobeying Paroh's orders. They took positive measures to assure the survival of the children they delivered. What were these measures?

Ibn Ezra offers a surprising and amazing response. The midwives became more conscientious in their work. They approached their responsibilities with an enthusiasm and commitment that was previously lacking.[25] In other words, before Paroh attempted to enlist them, these midwives had not made their best effort on behalf of every child. After Paroh attempted to make them his agents, they became more scrupulous in and committed to their work.

This interpretation of the passage raises questions. First, why were the midwives initially less diligent in their work? Second, how did Paroh's actions motivate them to a higher level of commitment? Ibn Ezra does not discuss these issues.

4. Responding to misery

It is unlikely that the midwives were intentionally careless in their work. It is more likely that internal forces undermined their commitment. To understand these forces, one must imagine oneself in their situation. The Jewish people were oppressed. They were subjected to terrible suffering; their lives were miserable. The midwives were charged with bringing infants into a world in which they were doomed to share the fate of their parents – endless suffering and misery. The ambivalence produced by this situation is understandable. This ambivalence undermined their commitment. They continued to do their work, but their vigor and efforts were not maximal.

How did Paroh's efforts to recruit them change their attitude? This is difficult to know. However, apparently, Paroh's approach to them evoked their self-awareness. They became aware of their behavior – that they were not doing their best work. Can we better understand this sequence? How did Paroh's approach to them produce a heightened self-awareness?

5. Paroh's recruitment

Perhaps, the midwives were responding to a troubling mystery. Why did Paroh approach them? How could he believe that they would act as his agents in the murder of their own children? What did Paroh observe in them that suggested they would participate in his repulsive scheme? These questions provoked introspection. Suddenly, these midwives became aware of

---

unwarranted savagery. These comments imply that before Paroh succeeded in enlisting the Egyptian people as his agents of genocide, he was required to drastically reshape attitudes toward the Jews.

[25] Rabbaynu Avraham ibn Ezra, Commentary on Sefer Shemot, 1:17. See his comments. He recognizes that his interpretation of the phrase is remarkable. It is a harsh critique of the midwives' initial behavior. He defends his position by arguing that it is the only reasonable interpretation the passage's closing phrase.

their ambivalence and its effect upon them. They realized that Paroh had studied them. He had observed their work. He recognized they had given up hope for a better future. They bemoaned the outcome of their efforts – another life doomed to misery. His observations suggested to Paroh that these midwives might be susceptible to his coercion. They might be forced to become his agents. When they realized that their own behavior had created the "optics" that invited Paroh to approach them, they immediately rejected their ambivalence and applied themselves to their work with renewed vigor and commitment.

This analysis reminds us to be mindful of how we present ourselves to others. This applies to us as individuals and as a community and nation. For example, we wish to be respected as Jews. To achieve this, we must take care to display our Jewishness proudly. If we demonstrate a willingness to compromise our Jewishness or fail to demonstrate pride in our identity, then we invite our enemies to attack us.[26]

And Bnai Yisrael was fruitful, swarmed, multiplied, and became very mighty. The land was filled with them. And a new king arose over Egypt who did not know Yosef. And he said to his nation, "Behold, the nation Bnai Yisrael is many and mightier than us. Let us take wise counsel, lest they become many. And it will be that when war will occur it, too, will join our enemy, do battle with us, and ascend from the land." (Shemot 1:7-10)

Optics and Consequences

6. **A population explosion**

The above passages discuss the antecedents to the enslavement of the Jewish people in Egypt. They describe the explosive growth of Bnai Yisrael and Paroh's response. Why did the expansion of the nation's population provoke Paroh's fears and his extreme response?

Let us consider a related issue. The Torah tells us that "the land was filled with them". To what land does this refer? Did the Jewish people overrun the Land of Egypt? If this is the case,

---

[26] Thank you to my friend Rabbi David Twersky for sending me a link to an interview with Israeli Nobel Prize winner Israel Aumann https://www.youtube.com/watch?v=ZkPBOrqEDHs&feature=youtu.be. Professor Aumann objects to the manner in which the term Palestinian is used. The term is used to refer to the Arab population of the area that was known as Palestine during the Mandate period. Prof. Aumann points out that his wife is as much a Palestinian as any Arab. She has the papers to prove that she was a resident of Palestine during the Mandate period. Jews who lived in Israel under the Mandate have as much claim to being Palestinians as Arab residents. It is completely inappropriate and inaccurate to reserve the identity of Palestinian for Arabs. He explains that this use of the term also undermines Israel's legitimacy. It implicitly cedes that the only people with an authentic link to Palestine are its Arabs. Jews are foreigners who have transported themselves to Israel and colonized it. This concession invites Arabs to assert their claim as Palestine's sole legitimate people.

Prof. Aumann's comments are another example of the idea developed above. The midwives' behavior invited Paroh to approach them. Use of the term Palestinian to refer exclusively to Arabs and the implicit concession in this usage, invites our enemies to deny the legitimacy of our historical attachment to the Land of Israel.

then it is difficult to understand how Paroh succeeded in subduing the largest component of his country's population. Rabbaynu Avraham ibn Ezra responds to this question. In Sefer Beresheit, Yaakov and his family arrived in Egypt. Yosef negotiated their settlement in the district of Goshen. According to Ibn Ezra, the district of Goshen was now filled with the members of the family.[27] If Bnai Yisrael was contained within the district of Goshen, why was Paroh fearful?

The passages explain that Paroh did not trust Bnai Yisrael. He questioned the loyalty of Yaakov's descendants. Was this simply a result of their number? A careful reading of Paroh's message to his nation is revealing. Paroh refers to Yaakov's descendants as "the nation Bnai Yisrael". Paroh was the first person to describe Yaakov's clan as a nation! In other words, Yaakov's descendants are no longer a family residing in Goshen. They fill its borders! They have grown into a nation.

Now, Paroh's fear becomes clearer. Yaakov's descendants had grown from a family into a nation – so large it filled the borders of Goshen. A foreign clan can be contained within the fabric of the host nation. But an alien nation has its own unique identity. As a nation, it has its own culture, interests, and goals. These interests and goals may be different and even compete with those of its host nation. Paroh expressed his fear to his people. "Bnai Yisrael is a nation. These people are not members of our nation. They have their own national agenda. Can we trust them, or will these Jews pursue their own interests at our expense?"

And they placed upon it tax-officers to oppress them with their burden. They build storage-cities for Paroh – Pitom and Ramses. To the degree they oppressed them, they multiplied and expanded. The Egyptians were tormented by Bnai Yisrael. And they subjugated Bnai Yisrael with rigor. They made their lives bitter with arduous labor – with mortar and bricks, and every sort of work in the field. All the labor that they forced them to perform was arduous. And the king of Egypt said to the Hebrew midwives – one's name was Shifra and the name of the second [was] Pu'ah. He said, "When you birth the Hebrew women and you see [the infant] on the labor-stool, if it is a male, kill him. If it is a female, sustain her." (Sefer Shemot 1:11-16)

7. Paroh's response

The Torah describes the measures taken by Porah in response to his fears. It is not completely clear from the passages whether these measures were instituted simultaneously, or sequentially.[28] Also, what was Paroh's strategy? How did his measures address his fears?

Ibn Ezra explains that the answer to the second question is found in these passages. The passages explain that despite the measures taken by Paroh, Bnai Yisrael's population continued to grow. Ibn Ezra explains the all the measures implemented by Paroh shared a single objective. His goal was to arrest population growth.

Ibn Ezra further explains that Paroh's initiatives were sequential. As each failed, Paroh instituted his next measure. First, Paroh levied a labor tax. He required that Bnai Yisrael provide workers for state projects. His objective was to disrupt family life and thereby, procreation. When this failed, he authorized his ministers and the Egyptian people to subjugate the Jews and

---

[27] Rabbaynu Avraham ibn Ezra, Commentary on Sefer Shemot, 1:7.
[28] It seems from the passages that some measures were sequential. He levied a labor tax. Then, he intensified the required labor. However, did he implement genocide as a new measure or simultaneous to the intensification of the labor?

to oppress them with grueling labor. He reasoned that exhausted slaves would not procreate. When Bnai Yisrael's population continued to expand even under these trying circumstances, he implemented his policy of genocide.[29]

8. Introduction of genocide

The final step in the above passages is Paroh's program of genocide. The program had two stages. In the above passages, Paroh directs the Hebrew midwives to kill the male children they deliver. The midwives disregard Paroh's directive. Paroh responds by enlisting the Egyptian people as his agents. They are to seek out Jewish male infants and drown them. Why did Paroh initially seek the cooperation of the midwives?

Ibn Ezra explains that Paroh did not want to openly promote genocide. His preference was to clandestinely implement his program. He attempted to enlist the midwives to covertly kill the male infants at birth.[30] Nachmanides – Ramban – provides important details. The midwives would kill the infants but claim that the babies had died in childbirth.

Ramban further explains that Paroh implemented a covert plan because he was not confident that the Egyptian people were prepared to tolerate a formal program of genocide. Enlisting the general population into this program would take time, planning, and an organized propaganda operation. When Paroh's covert plan failed he was forced to take the steps required to transform the Egyptian people into agents of genocide.[31]

And the midwives feared the L-rd. They did not do as the king of Egypt told them. They sustained the children. (Shemot 1:17)

The defiance of the midwives

The above passage describes the brave defiance of the midwives. They refused to participate in Paroh's wicked plan. However, the Torah adds, "They sustained the children". This phrase suggests that their defiance extended beyond disobeying Paroh's orders. They took positive measures to assure the survival of the children they delivered. What were these measures?

Ibn Ezra offers a surprising and amazing response. The midwives became more conscientious in their work. They approached their responsibilities with an enthusiasm and commitment that was previously lacking.[32] In other words, before Paroh attempted to enlist them, these midwives had not made their best effort on behalf of every child. After Paroh

---

[29] Rabbaynu Avraham ibn Ezra, Commentary on Sefer Shemot, 1:13.
[30] Rabbaynu Avraham ibn Ezra, Commentary on Sefer Shemot, 1:16.
[31] Rabbaynu Moshe ben Nachman (Ramban / Nachmanides), Commentary on Sefer Shemot 1:10. Ramban explains that Paroh initially levied taxes upon Bnai Yisrael. Ideally, he would have attacked with his army. However, his own people were not prepared to accept this unwarranted savagery. These comments imply that before Paroh succeeded in enlisting the Egyptian people as his agents of genocide, he was required to drastically reshape attitudes toward the Jews.
[32] Rabbaynu Avraham ibn Ezra, Commentary on Sefer Shemot, 1:17. See his comments. He recognizes that his interpretation of the phrase is remarkable. It is a harsh critique of the midwives' initial behavior. He defends his position by arguing that it is the only reasonable interpretation the passage's closing phrase.

attempted to make them his agents, they became more scrupulous in and committed to their work.

This interpretation of the passage raises questions. First, why were the midwives initially less diligent in their work? Second, how did Paroh's actions motivate them to a higher level of commitment? Ibn Ezra does not discuss these issues.

9. Responding to misery

It is unlikely that the midwives were intentionally careless in their work. It is more likely that internal forces undermined their commitment. To understand these forces, one must imagine oneself in their situation. The Jewish people were oppressed. They were subjected to terrible suffering; their lives were miserable. The midwives were charged with bringing infants into a world in which they were doomed to share the fate of their parents – endless suffering and misery. The ambivalence produced by this situation is understandable. This ambivalence undermined their commitment. They continued to do their work, but their vigor and efforts were not maximal.

How did Paroh's efforts to recruit them change their attitude? This is difficult to know. However, apparently, Paroh's approach to them evoked their self-awareness. They became aware of their behavior – that they were not doing their best work. Can we better understand this sequence? How did Paroh's approach to them produce a heightened self-awareness?

10. Paroh's recruitment

Perhaps, the midwives were responding to a troubling mystery. Why did Paroh approach them? How could he believe that they would act as his agents in the murder of their own children? What did Paroh observe in them that suggested they would participate in his repulsive scheme? These questions provoked introspection. Suddenly, these midwives became aware of their ambivalence and its effect upon them. They realized that Paroh had studied them. He had observed their work. He recognized they had given up hope for a better future. They bemoaned the outcome of their efforts – another life doomed to misery. His observations suggested to Paroh that these midwives might be susceptible to his coercion. They might be forced to become his agents. When they realized that their own behavior had created the "optics" that invited Paroh to approach them, they immediately rejected their ambivalence and applied themselves to their work with renewed vigor and commitment.

This analysis reminds us to be mindful of how we present ourselves to others. This applies to us as individuals and as a community and nation. For example, we wish to be respected as Jews. To achieve this, we must take care to display our Jewishness proudly. If we demonstrate a willingness to compromise our Jewishness or fail to demonstrate pride in our identity, then we invite our enemies to attack us.

"And the king of Egypt said to the Hebrew midwives, one who was named Shifrah, and the second, who was named Puah. And he said, "When you deliver the Hebrew women, and you see on the birthstool, if it is a son, you shall put him to death, but if it is a daughter, she may live." And the midwives feared Hashem. And they did not do as the king of Egypt had spoken to them, but they enabled the boys to live. And the king of Egypt summoned the midwives and said to them, "Why have you done this thing, that you have enabled the boys to live?" And the midwives said to Paroh, "Because the Hebrew women are not like the

Egyptian women, for they are skilled as midwives; when the midwife has not yet come to them, they have given birth." And Hashem benefited the midwives, and the people multiplied and became very strong. And it took place when the midwives feared Hashem that He made houses for them." (Shemot 1: 15-21)

Sefer Beresheit describes the immigration of Bnai Yisrael to Egypt. Bnai Yisrael were invited to Egypt by Paroh. They were honored and valued by the Egyptians. Sefer Shemot describes the persecution of Bnai Yisrael in Egypt and their redemption from bondage. The opening chapters of Sefer Shemot explain the transformation in the attitude of the Egyptians towards Bnai Yisrael.

The Torah explains that this transformation was predicated on fear. The Egyptians observed the growth and vigor of Bnai Yisrael. Also, they did not fully trust the loyalty of Bnai Yisrael. With these two factors combined, the Egyptians were concerned that if their nation was attacked or invaded, Bnai Yisrael could not be depended upon to rally to the defense of Egypt.

The persecution of Bnai Yisrael had a specific goal. It was designed to break the nation and eliminate it as a threat. The persecution developed in stages. It began with the levying of taxes. It then evolved into outright persecution and bondage. Finally, Paroh attempted to put into place a program of genocide.

Initially, this genocide was designed to be covert. Paroh met with the Jewish midwives who served Bnai Yisrael. He directed them to murder any Jewish males they delivered. The midwives did not carry out these instructions. Instead, they continued to perform their duty as midwives and applied all of their skills to successfully deliver Jewish children. Paroh challenged the midwives and asked them to explain their refusal to fulfill his instructions. The midwives explained that they had no opportunity to obey Paroh's instructions. Whenever they were called upon to facilitate a delivery, they discovered that the child had already been delivered by the mother. Any opportunity to covertly murder the child was lost.

Paroh seems to have accepted this explanation. Hashem rewarded the midwives. The description of the reward is vague. The Torah tells us that Hashem made houses for them. Rashi quotes the Talmud in explaining this reward. He explains that the "houses" to which the Torah refers are the families of the *Kohanim, Leveyim*, and the family from which David descended.[33]

As a consequence of this failure, Paroh implemented a new plan. He instructed the Egyptians to implement genocide. He authorized and instructed his own people to seize and kill all newborn Jewish males.

There are many interesting elements in this narrative. First, it is notable that Paroh seems to have accepted the midwives' excuse for their failure. It is surprising that he did not suspect them of undermining his plan. We would expect that rather than accepting their explanation, he would have punished them. Why did the midwives believe that their explanation would be accepted? Why did Paroh accept this explanation?

In fact, the passages are somewhat vague in describing the midwives' explanation. There are two elements to their explanation. The second element is clearly stated; the midwives explained that they had no opportunity to carryout Paroh's instructions. When they came to the home of the expectant mother, the child had already been born. However, the first element of

---

[33] Rabbaynu Shlomo ben Yitzchak (Rashi), *Commentary on Sefer Shemot* 1:21.

their explanation is less clearly stated. The passages tell us that the midwives told Paroh that Jewish women are not like their Egyptian counterparts. They are *"chayot."* The meaning of this term in this context is not obvious. Certainly, it is meant to describe some trait of Jewish women that enabled them to birth their children without the assistance of a midwife. However, what is the precise trait to which the term *"chayot"* refers?

The above translation adopts the position of Rashi and many others. According to Rashi, the midwives explained to Paroh that Jewish women are skilled midwives; they do not require the services of other midwives in order to deliver their children.[34]

Rabbaynu Avraham ibn Ezra suggests a more literal explanation. The root of the term *"chayot"* is *chai* – life. According to Ibn Ezra, the midwives explained to Paroh that Jewish women are endowed with a tremendous life-force or vigor. Because of their strength and vigor, they do not require the services of a midwife.[35]

Based on Ibn Ezra's explanation, we can understand the midwives' reasoning in offering their excuse. The midwives presented an explanation that perfectly corresponded and reinforced Paroh's own prejudices regarding Bnai Yisrael. Paroh and the Egyptians feared Bnai Yisrael. Their fear was based upon the perception that Bnai Yisrael were different than themselves. They believed that Bnai Yisrael were stronger, possessing more vigor and energy. The midwives appreciated the power of this perception and they constructed their explanation to perfectly correspond with the Paroh's perceptions. Paroh may have been disappointed in the failure of his plan. But undoubtedly, he was pleased that his perceptions regarding Bnai Yisrael were confirmed.

Another issue that should be considered is the reward received by the midwives. Hashem's rewards are not arbitrary. They correspond with the act or virtue that they acknowledge. What is the connection between the reward received by the midwives and their efforts on behalf of Bnai Yisrael?

This question can be answered on two levels. Geshonides suggests a simple explanation. The midwives were devoted to their people. They were willing to risk their lives in order to protect and assist Bnai Yisrael. This devotion is an essential quality of a leader. The leader must be dedicated to the welfare of his nation. In other words, the devotion of the midwives was an inspiring example of a trait required in a leader. Therefore, the midwives were rewarded by being selected as progenitors of the leadership of Bnai Yisrael.[36]

However, Gershonides' explanation takes on a deeper significance if we consider an important insight provided by our Sages. Rashi explains that Paroh's implementation of a program of genocide was motivated by a specific concern. He had been told by his astrologers that a redeemer was to soon be born to Bnai Yisrael. Paroh knew this redeemer would be a male. His plan of genocide was devised to deprive Bnai Yisrael of their redeemer.[37]

Based on Rashi's comment, Gershonides' explanation is even more compelling. The midwives were specifically instrumental in undermining Paroh's plan to deprive Bnai Yisrael of

---

[34] Rabbaynu Shlomo ben Yitzchak (Rashi), *Commentary on Sefer Shemot* 1:19.
[35] Rabbaynu Avraham ibn Ezra, *Commentary on Sefer Shemot*, 1:19.
[36] Rab. Levi ben Gershon (Ralbag), *Comm. on Sefer Shemot*, (Mosad HaRav Kook, 1994), p 3.
[37] Rabbaynu Shlomo ben Yitzchak (Rashi), *Commentary on Sefer Shemot* 1:16.

leadership. They were rewarded by being chosen as to be the progenitors of Bnai Yisrael's leadership.

The most disturbing element of this narrative is that it seems that the courageous efforts of the midwives were a failure. As a result of their refusal to carryout Paroh's instructions, he implemented a general, public policy of genocide. He ordered the Egyptians to murder all newborn Jewish males. It seems that the refusal of the midwives to participate in Paroh's plan only resulted in a more widespread and intensive program of genocide.

Gershonides offers a brilliant insight into this issue. He explains that the nurturing of a child from among Bnai Yisrael who would develop into a redeemer of his people was not a simple proposition. Bnai Yisrael were a nation of slaves. They had been humbled and humiliated by servitude. Their pride and self-image had been destroyed. How could one of their offspring be expected to rise above these attitudes and develop the courage, knowledge and self-confidence required to achieve prophecy and assume a role of leadership? How could a member of this oppressed nation ever challenge the authority of Paroh?

The redeemer – Moshe – was able to become a prophet and leader because he was raised in the household of Paroh as the king's adopted grandson. How did this occur? Moshe's parents attempted to hide and protect Moshe from the Egyptians' program of genocide. Eventually, they could no longer hide him. They placed him in a basket among the reeds at the shore of the river. Paroh's daughter discovered Moshe. She realized that he was a Jewish child. She was overcome with compassion for this innocent child and she took him under her protection and raised him as her own.

This is a remarkable series of events. However, it is clear that Paroh's own efforts to subject Bnai Yisrael to a program of genocide were the antecedents of these events and laid the groundwork for their occurrence.

Paroh's genocide program forced Moshe's parents to place him in the river in the hope that he would be discovered and sheltered by a compassionate Egyptian.[38]

However, it should be noted that the refusal of the midwives to participate in Paroh's program was also essential to the unfolding of the events that led to Moshe's development. Paroh attempted to enlist the cooperation of the midwives in order to conduct his program covertly. His preference was to not publicly declare a policy of genocide. This suggests that he recognized that some Egyptians would not condone or support this program. Furthermore, those members of the society that were the most intelligent and open-minded would be the most likely to oppose Paroh's efforts.

Paroh's daughter was one of these intelligent and open-minded individuals who could not accept Paroh's program. She was overcome by compassion for this Jewish child who was destined to be murdered for reasons she could not accept. She acted on this compassion and saved the innocent child. Paroh could not oppose or refuse his own daughter. He allowed Moshe to be raised as a member of his household.

In short, the resistance of the midwives forced Paroh to publicly declare a policy of genocide. This cruelty evoked the compassion of his daughter. She acted on this compassion, rescued Moshe, and raised him in the king's household.

---

[38] Rab. Levi ben Gershon (Ralbag), *Comm. on Sefer Shemot*, (Mosad HaRav Kook, 1994), p. 6-7

"And the woman conceived and she gave birth. And she saw that the child was good and she hid him for three months." (Shemot 2:2)

Parents often sense that their children come preprogrammed. Children seem to be predisposed to certain behaviors and attitudes. Is this perception accurate? Are we capable of molding our children? To what extent can we influence their development? This week's parasha provides some insight into this issue.

One of the topics discussed in this week's parasha is Moshe's early development. Moshe was born during a period of severe persecution. Paroh had decreed that all male babies born to Bnai Yisrael should be drowned. Our pasuk tells us that Moshe's parents saw that their child was good and decided to take desperate steps to save his life. Our Sages ask two questions on this passage. First, the passage tells us that Moshe's parents saw that he was good. The Torah does not waste words on the obvious. Virtually, every parent thinks his or her baby is beautiful. Even if others think the infant has been a little shortchanged in natural beauty, this is rarely the perception of the baby's parents. So, what is the point that the Torah is making in telling us the Moshe's parent believed him to be beautiful?

Second, the Torah implies that because Moshe's parents were so moved by his goodness they decided to hide him. Does this mean that other parents who were not so moved willingly offered their children to the Egyptians for execution? Certainly, this is not the case! There is no doubt that all parents did their best to try to save their newborns from the Egyptians!

Nachmanides raises and answers both of these questions. He explains that the Chumash does not intend to tell us that Moshe's parents were impressed with his beauty in the same manner as other parents. In the case of other parents, this impression is based on the internal feelings of the parents. Their love for their offspring generates their conviction in the beauty of the child. As we have pointed out, because the source of the judgment is internal, it may have no objective basis in the external reality of the child's actual appearance. In contrast, Moshe's parents – Amram and Yocheved – based their evaluation of Moshe's goodness on objective evidence. The Torah tells us that they saw he was good. The Torah is telling us that they saw objective evidence. The Chumash is not interested in revealing the exact nature of this evidence. Our Sages suggest various possibilities. For example, in Tractate Sotah, the Sages suggest the Miryam – Moshe sister – received a prophecy that Moshe would save Bnai Yisrael.

Nachmanides further explains that although all parents must have tried to save their newborns from the Egyptians, Amram and Yocheved resorted to desperate measures. For example, they attempted to hide Moshe in the river. They were moved to resort to these schemes because they knew that Moshe was special. Therefore, they had reason to hope that Hashem would intervene and cause these measures to succeed.[39]

Nachmanides' insight not only explains our passage but it also answers other questions on our parasha.

"And the child matured and she brought him to the daughter of Paroh and she was a son to her. And she named him Moshe – for from the water I pulled him." (Shemot 2:10)

---

[39] Rabbaynu Moshe ben Nachman (Ramban), *Commentary on Sefer Beresheit* 2:2.

The daughter of Paroh rescues the child from the river. She adopts the child as a son. She names him Moshe. This name is derived from the phrase, "I drew him from the water." This name – Moshe – is name by which the child will be known throughout the Torah. Did not Moshe's parents provide him with a name? Why is Moshe known by the name that he received form the daughter of Paroh and not by the name he received from his true parents?

Our Sages tell us that Moshe's parents did give him a name. It was either Tov or Tuvya.[40] Both names are derived from the word tov – good – and refer to Moshe's parents' initial impressions of their child.

Now that we know Moshe's original name, we can understand its replacement. The initial name refers to the Amram's and Yocheved's recognition that their child was special and different. This recognition was the basis for their unusual plan to save him. Paroh's daughter renamed the child Moshe. Apparently, she chose this name because her experience of saving the child from the river created a maternal bond. Because of this bond, she adopted the child and he was raised as a prince in the home of Paroh. So, Amram's and Yocheved's desperate plan succeeded wonderfully. Not only was Moshe saved, he was rescued from bondage and raised as royalty. This confirmed Amram's and Yocheved's conclusion that the boy was special and that Hashem's providence would work on his behalf. To Paroh's daughter the name Moshe represented her bond to the child. But to the reader of the incident the name alludes to the act of providence that forged a bond between a condemned infant and a princess. The name Moshe is a specific expression of the providence represented by the name Tov. So, the Torah did not replace the infant's original name with a completely new name. Instead, it expanded on the theme of original name with a new name that communicated the same idea of providence over the child but with far more detail.

In short, the Torah is telling us that it was part of this providential plan that Moshe grow and mature in the house of Paroh. Why was this important?

"And it was in those days and Moshe matured. And he went out to his brethren and he saw them in their burdens. And he saw an Egyptian man strike a Hebrew from among his brothers."
(Shemot 2:11)

Moshe matures and he investigates the condition of his brothers – the Hebrews. He observes an Egyptian man persecuting a Hebrew. Our Sages note that the passage opens by telling us that Moshe had matured. The previous passage opened with the same phrase. Each phrase refers to a different periods in his life. Yet, each describes Moshe as mature at that moment. At which point did Moshe actually become mature?

Nachmanides explains that maturity occurs in stages. In the prior passage the Torah is telling us that Moshe had reached an adequate level of maturity to be brought to live with the daughter of Paroh. In our passage, Moshe has further matured. He is now interested in his brothers and their travails.[41]

This is a simple and obvious explanation of the passage. However, Rashi offers an alternative explanation. Rashi comments that the first passage refers to physical development. When Moshe was physically mature, he was brought to the daughter of Paroh. However, he was

---

[40] Mesechet Sotah 12a.
[41] Rabbaynu Moshe ben Nachman (Ramban), *Commentary on Sefer Bereshit* 2:11.

not yet prepared to assume responsibility as a member of the royal household. Our passage tells us that Moshe has matured emotionally and was now ready for responsibility. He had been appointed to supervise Paroh's household.[42]

Rashi's explanation is not unreasonable. However, it seems much more speculative than the simpler explanation offered by Nachmanides. Why does Rashi prefer his explanation over the more obvious interpretation?

> "And he looked in each direction and saw that there was no one there. And he struck the Egyptian and he hid him in the sand." (Shemot 2:12)

Moshe decides he must save his brother from the Egyptian. He will have to kill the Egyptian. But Moshe does not act impulsively or rashly. First, he carefully inspects whether he is being observed. Once he is certain that he is alone, he kills the Egyptian and hides his body.

The Torah describes in detail Moshe's precautions to avoid detection. Nonetheless, in the next passages Moshe discovers that he was observed. And these observers are eager to inform against him. Moshe realizes that he must flee Egypt.

What is the message in this juxtaposition? What does the Torah tell us by juxtaposing a description of Moshe's precautions with his discovery?

Perhaps, the Torah is pointing out that Moshe was not discovered because he was impulsive or careless. On the contrary, Moshe took every possible precaution. Nonetheless, he was discovered. The implication is that providence was again at work. Providence decreed that Moshe was raised in Paroh's home. Providence now decreed that he leave that home. Why was it now time to leave?

Let us return to an earlier question. Why was it important for Moshe to be raised in Paroh's house? Gershonides explains that this upbringing helped prepare Moshe for his future mission. Egypt was the most advanced culture of its time. The Egyptians had the most advanced knowledge of science. In Paroh's home Moshe would learn from the most accomplished of Egypt's scholars. He would be exposed to the most advanced thinking of the age. This would help prepare him intellectually for his role as leader of Bnai Yisrael. However, he would also prepare emotionally. In Paroh's home he developed as a free person and as a member of the royal family. Paroh was familiar to him. This relationship would be invaluable. Paroh would not be able to overawe Moshe. Moshe would be able to stand up to Paroh.[43]

However, Moshe's development in this environment also posed a danger. Moshe could forget his origins. He was in danger of becoming an Egyptian. The bond between Moshe and his adopted family had to be severed at the appropriate moment – after Moshe had gleaned from the environment the maximum benefit but before he assimilated. According to Rashi, Moshe appointment over the royal household was this moment. Once Moshe assumed a position of authority, his identity was endangered. At that moment, providence again intervened to break the bonds between Moshe and the royal family.

---

[42] Rabbaynu Shlomo ben Yitzchak (Rashi), *Commentary on Sefer Shemot* 2:11.
[43] Rabbaynu Levi ben Gershon (Ralbag), *Commentary on Sefer Shemot*, (Mosad HaRav Kook, 1994), pp. 6-7.

In other words, Rashi is suggesting that Moshe must have matured in some way that precipitated Hashem's intervention and Moshe flight. He suggests that the maturity that Moshe reached was in his position as a member of the household. Rashi contends that once we interpret Moshe's maturity in this way, we can appreciate the connection between Moshe's maturity and the crisis that immediately follows and culminates in Moshe's flight.

The Torah position on the importance of environment upon children is very clear. The Torah maintains that these influences are crucial and help shape the personality of the child. The Torah's account of Moshe's early life describes Hashem interfering with natural events in order to carefully shape this environment and then reshape it.

And an angel of Hashem appeared to him in a flame of fire from within a bush. And he saw that the bush burned with fire but the bush was not consumed. (Shemot 3:2)

Moshe's Spiritual Journey

1. Moshe's first prophecy and its remarkable message

Parshat Shemot opens with a description of the enslavement and persecution of Bnai Yisrael by the Egyptians. Then, the Torah introduces Moshe. The Torah describes the circumstances surrounding his birth and his rescue from death by Paroh's daughter. Moshe attempts to defend his people from the cruelty of the Egyptians and to promote greater harmony among Bnai Yisrael. As a result of these efforts, he kills an Egyptian task-master who is beating a Jew. He is forced to flee Egypt and resettles in Midyan and becomes a shepherd for his father-in-law Yitro.

Moshe is caring for his flock when he encounters an angel of Hashem. This angel presents himself as a flame burning in the midst of a bush. Amazingly, the fire burns intensely within the bush but the bush is not consumed.

This encounter introduces one of the most significant moments in the history of humanity. In this encounter, Moshe will be directed by Hashem to lead Bnai Yisrael out of Egypt and into the Land of Israel. Moshe will be commanded to communicate specific messages in Hashem's name to his people and to Paroh. He will be told that he will perform wonders and miracles and that he will lead the people to Sinai where they will serve Hashem.

Hashem had spoken to the Patriarchs but he had not selected them to act as His spokesperson. Neither had He appointed the Patriarchs to perform wondrous miracles on the scale of those that would be performed by Moshe. In other words, this encounter introduced a relationship between Hashem and Bnai Yisrael and a degree of Divine revelation that had never before occurred.

And Moshe said: I will now turn and I will see the great vision – why the bush does not burn. And Hashem saw that he had turned to see and He called to him from the bush and He said, "Moshe." And he said, "I am here." (Shemot 3:3-4)

2. Moshe's response to his first prophecy and its significance

Perhaps the most interesting element of this encounter is the Torah's description of the events that took place immediately after Moshe observed the wondrous flame and bush. The Torah describes these events in remarkable detail. Upon seeing the flame and bush, Moshe says to himself that he will turn and study this great vision and explore the phenomenon. In other words, the Torah points out that Moshe made a very conscious and intentional decision to look at the bush and flame more closely and to study it. Why is this detail of the encounter so important?

The Torah's detailed description continues. The Torah explains that when Hashem saw that Moshe had turned to look more carefully at the flame and bush, He addressed Himself to Moshe. In other words, the Torah wishes to communicate that Moshe's first prophecy and communication with Hashem required that he turn to the bush and study it. Hashem only addressed Moshe when and because He saw that Moshe had turned to the bush and sought to better understand it. Why did Hashem only address Moshe after he turned to more carefully study this wondrous phenomenon? Why was Moshe's response essential?

Rabbaynu Avraham ibn Ezra explains that Moshe's encounter with this flame and bush was the first of the wonders with which he would be involved. It was a precursor to the other miracles that he would perform.[44] Hashem initiated this first prophecy with this wonder as evidence of the Divine revelation that would occur in Egypt. Through Moshe, Hashem would perform other remarkable wonders that would confirm His sovereignty over the universe and His relationship with His prophet Moshe.

Rabbaynu Ovadia Sforno explains that the Torah is communicating an important lesson regarding prophecy and the prophet's relationship with Hashem. The prophet is not a passive instrument in the process of prophecy. Instead, he is engaging in seeking knowledge and understanding. Prophecy is a response to the prophet's quest for enlightenment. The Torah explains that Moshe's response to his observation of the bush and its flame was essential to the prophecy. He was moved to understand the wonder and to uncover its secrets. Hashem called to Moshe and spoke to him only in response to Moshe's pursuit of wisdom and understanding.[45]

3. **According to the Midrash, the bush appeared to Moshe in a vision**

Maimonides and many others disagree with Ibn Ezra's interpretation of the Torah narrative. Unlike Ibn Ezra, they contend that Moshe did not see an actual bush and flame. Moshe experienced a prophetic vision.[46] The vision of the bush and flame were intended as a parable. Moshe was presented with this parable and invited to contemplate its meaning.

The Midrash Rabbah sides with Maimonides' position. The Midrash observes that Moshe said, "I will now turn and I will see the great vision – why the bush does not burn." The Midrash assumes that Moshe was not speaking to himself. He was addressing himself to the other shepherds that were with him. The Midrash continues and explains that none of the other shepherds accompanied Moshe to look more closely at the bush. They did not see the bush that so fascinated Moshe.[47] The bush and its flame existed only in his mind. The other shepherds could not share his prophetic encounter.

Rav Yosef Dov Soloveitchik Zt"l points out that this interpretation is supported by the passage that introduces the encounter. The passage states: And an angel of Hashem appeared to

---

[44] Rabbaynu Avraham ibn Ezra, Extended Commentary on Sefer Shemot, 3:3. 2. 3.
[45] Rabbaynu Ovadia Sforno, Commentary on Sefer Shemot 3:4.
[46] Rabbaynu Moshe ben Maimon (Rambam) Moreh Nevuchim, volume 3, chapter 45.
[47] Rav Menachem Mendel Kasher, Torah Shelymah vol 3, p 124.

him in a flame of fire from within a bush. The pasuk specifies that the angel appeared to Moshe and to no other.[48]

This interpretation of the passages presents a new problem. If Moshe's encounter with the bush and its flame was a prophetic vision unfolding in his mind, then what is the meaning of the Torah's description of his response? What is the significance of Moshe turning to the bush and announcing his attention to investigate it? Why does Hashem suspend His communication with Moshe pending this awaited response?

In order to answer this question it is important to again recognize that the prophecy that awaited Moshe would communicate astounding news. Hashem would reveal to Moshe that He was poised to enter into a unique relationship with him, to fulfill His promise to the Patriarchs that He would redeem their descendants and give them possession of the Land of Israel, and that He would perform wonders and miracles that would reveal His sovereignty to Bnai Yisrael and humanity. In short, this prophecy would require that Moshe envision, understand, and embrace a radically different view of reality.

In his comments on these passages, Rashi explains that when Moshe said, "I will now turn" he was saying, "I will turn from here and approach there." What does Rashi intend to communicate in this elaboration upon Moshe's words?

On the third day he lifted his eyes and he saw that place from a distance. (Beresheit 22:4)

And Avraham said to his lads: Remain here with the donkey and I and the lad will go there. We will prostrate ourselves and we will return to you. (Beresheit 22:5)

4. Avraham and Yitzchak's journey to the site of the Akeydah

The above passages are found in the Torah's account of the binding of Yitzchak – the Akeydah. Hashem commands Avraham to take his son Yitzchak and to offer him as a sacrifice upon a mountaintop that Hashem would reveal. Avraham and Yitzchak journey forth in search of the mountain selected by Hashem. They are accompanied by two companions. According to our Sages these companions were Avraham's servant Eliezer and son Yishmael. On the third day of their journey Avraham sees in the distance the mountain selected by Hashem.

How did Avraham know that this mountain that he saw in the distance was the site selected for the Akeydah? The Midrash explains that Avraham observed that a cloud hovered over the distant peak. He asked Yitzchak, "My son, do you see what I see?" Yitzchak responded, "Yes." He asked their companions, "Do you see what I see?" They responded, "No." When Avraham heard their response, he concluded that they could see no better than their donkey. He immediately instructed them, "Remain here with the donkey."[49]

What does this Midrash intend to communicate? Rav Soloveitchik explains that Avraham and Yitzchak were prepared to embark upon an intense and exalted spiritual journey. Yishmael and Eliezer had been their companions on their arduous journey – to this point. However, the spiritual mountain that they would now climb was beyond the ken or capacity of these two faithful companions. They could neither envision the objective – the distant mountaintop – nor master its ascent. Why? They shared the vision of the donkey. Like the donkey, they understood and lived in a material reality. They could not break free from the shackles of their material

---

[48] Rav Yosef Dov Soloveitchik, recorded lecture on Parshat Shemot.
[49] Rav Menachem Mendel Kasher, Torah Shelymah vol 1, p 781.

conception of reality and embrace the spiritual aspirations and vision of Avraham and Yitzchak. Eliezer and Yishmael had traveled as far as they could. They could proceed no further.

Now, Rashi's comments can be understood. Rav Soloveitchik explains that Moshe understood that in order to understand the message of the bush and its flame, and to enter into this prophetic communion with Hashem, he must turn aside. He must leave the path he has walked and take a different path that will bring him to the bush. This means that he must turn aside from his accustomed manner of perceiving the reality. He must be prepared to adopt a completely new perspective and redefine the realm of the possible. Moshe's engagement in the prophecy can only proceed through his shedding of his previous notions. He must study and consider the vision of the bush and the prophecy unfettered by these comfortable, familiar, but obsolete notions.[50]

"And He said, 'Do not come close to here. Remove your shoes from your feet. For the place upon which you stand is holy ground." (Shemot 3:5)

Moshe has his first prophetic vision. He sees a bush that is completely aflame. But the bush is not consumed. Moshe begins to contemplate the meaning of this strange vision. A voice calls to him from the bush. The voice instructs him to remove his shoes before approaching closer. He is treading upon sanctified ground.

What is the meaning of this command? Many of the commentaries choose a similar approach to interpreting this element of the vision. Moshe is preparing to consider the meaning of the burning bush. The voice instructs Moshe that some form of preparation is needed before he can proceed. This preparation is related to the sacred meaning of the vision.

Gershonides explains that the Almighty was directing Moshe to seek the inner meaning of the vision. Shoes protect our feet from the ground. They also prevent us from feeling the texture and detail under our feet. If we wish to fully feel with our feet, we must remove our shoes. The voice told Moshe that if he hoped to understand the inner meaning of this vision, he must apply himself fully. He must open his mind and feel carefully for both the subtlety and depth of the message.[51]

Abravanel offers a different explanation of this command. Moshe understood the vision as a representation of the suffering of Bnai Yisrael. This people had been thrown into the fire of persecution. Yet, they were not consumed. The survival of this tormented nation was a mystery to Moshe. He recognized that somehow the answer was contained in the vision. He began to contemplate the meaning of the vision more deeply. The voice instructed Moshe that he stood upon holy ground. The explanation of Bnai Yisrael's survival could not be found in natural

---

[50] Rav Yosef Dov Soloveitchik, recorded lecture on Parshat Shemot. Rav Soloveitchik develops an original interpretation of the meaning of the parable of the bush and its flame. He interprets this parable as a preamble and necessary introduction to the balance of the prophecy. In order for Moshe to master the meaning of this parable, he was required to abandon specific views related to the message of the parable and to adopt a fresh perspective communicated through the vision. The specifics of Rav Soloveitchik's interpretation of the parable require a separate discussion.
[51] Rabbaynu Levi ben Gershon (Ralbag), *Commentary on Sefer Shemot*, (Mosad HaRav Kook, 1994), p 9.

causes. The continued existence of Bnai Yisrael was an expression of G-d's providence. Moshe must enter upon holy ground. He must contemplate the ways of the Almighty and His providence to find the answer. This requires that Moshe remove his material shoes. He must abandon the search for material explanations.

And Moshe said to the L-rd: Who and I that I will go to Paroh and that I will take forth Bnai Yisrael from Egypt? (Shemot 3:11)
Don't Drink the Kool-Aid
1. Moshe is assigned his mission

Parshat Shemot opens with the passing of the generation that initially descended to Egypt. The *parasha* describes the Egyptians' oppression of Bnai Yisrael and the development of this oppression into a program of genocide. The Torah introduces Moshe. It describes the circumstances of Moshe's birth and his upbringing as a member of the Egyptian royal family. The narrative continues with a description of Moshe's resistance to the persecution of his brethren and his flight from Egypt.

Moshe becomes a shepherd. While shepherding his flocks in the wilderness, he experiences his first encounter with Hashem. Moshe observes a bush that is aflame but, yet, not consumed. His observation of this wonder introduces a dialogue between Hashem and Moshe.

Hashem reveals to Moshe that He will redeem Bnai Yisrael from Egypt. He tells Moshe that he will be His emissary to Paroh and that he will lead the people out of bondage. Moshe's response is in the above passage. He resists the assignment.

2. Moshe presents his objections to Hashem

The substance of Moshe's opposition to the assignment is not completely clear from the above passage. However, he seems to articulate two objections. First, he does not believe himself fit to serve as an emissary to Paroh. He is not a person of stature. Why should Paroh deal seriously with him? Second, he is not suitable for the role of leader of the people. An effective leader is charismatic. He is an effective and inspiring speaker. He ignites the imagination of his followers. He inspires their commitment to a vision and their willingness to sacrifice for its achievement. Moshe did not believe that he possessed either the charisma or the oratorical skills to lead the nation.

And He said: For I will be with you. And this is the sign for you that I have sent you. When you bring forth the nation from Egypt, they shall serve the L-rd at this mountain. (Shemot 3:12)
3. Hashem will be with Moshe

Hashem responds to Moshe's objections. He tells Moshe that He will be with him. This assurance is clearly relevant to Moshe's first objection. Hashem explains to Moshe that he will not be acting as an agent who is directed to perform a task and expected to accomplish his assignment using his own resources and ingenuity. Instead, Hashem will be with Moshe. Moshe will speak to Paroh. However, his success will not be achieved through his skill as a negotiator or through clever diplomacy. Hashem will accompany Moshe and He will induce Paroh to acquiesce to Moshe's demands. Conceivably, this element of Hashem's response also relates to Moshe's concerns regarding his own leadership potential. Hashem is assuring Moshe that his success as a leader will not depend upon his own gifts and talents. Hashem will support him and compensate for Moshe's inadequacies.

4. Hashem tells Moshe that He will provide a sign

Hashem adds that He will provide Moshe with a sign that He is sending him. Upon achieving its freedom, the nation will come to this mountain and serve Hashem. This part of Hashem's response is not easily understood. The interpretation of this element of the response is debated widely among the commentators.

One of the difficulties with this element of Hashem's response is that it seems to suggest that Moshe was uncertain that he was acting as Hashem's agent. Hashem responded that the sign or the indication that he is acting on behalf of Hashem will be Revelation. The difficulty with this simple interpretation of Hashem's response is that it does not seem to relate to Moshe's objections. Moshe does not suggest that he is uncertain of his agency. He questions his suitability for the assignment.

Another problem is that Moshe could not have questioned that he was acting as Hashem's agent. This entire dialogue is a prophetic interaction. Moshe is communicating with Hashem and is being charged by Hashem with his responsibilities. How can he question whether he is Hashem's agent?

One of the interesting responses to these problems is presented by Sefer HaChinuch. He suggests that in this statement Hashem revealed to Moshe the objective of the redemption. Bnai Yisrael would be redeemed from Egypt in order to achieve a far greater outcome than political independence. Their redemption from Egypt would be the first step toward their participation in Revelation at Sinai.

According to Sefer HaChinuch, Hashem told Moshe that the redemption would be a sign or a harbinger of a far greater and more significant event that would follow – Revelation.[52]

5. Redemption is an indicator of the approach of Revelation

This resolves one of the problems with Hashem's response. According to Sefer HaChinuch, Moshe did not doubt that he was Hashem's agent. He was not seeking a further proof of his appointment. The message of the prophetic experience was understood by Moshe and he accepted its authenticity without question.[53] Hashem's message to Moshe was that his role in the redemption was preliminary to a far more significant role and event. Redemption would be the first step of the nation upon a journey towards this great end. Redemption would be a sign that this end would be achieved.

In other words, according to Sefer HaChinuch, Hashem explained to Moshe that redemption and freedom were not the goals of the events that would take place in Egypt. Hashem was not demonstrating His providence in order to save a suffering nation from oppression. Hashem was undertaking a program to create a nation that would experience a unique relationship with Him. This would be Revelation. Because the redemption would only serve as an essential preliminary step towards this greater ends, the redemption would be a sure indicator that Revelation would soon follow.

---

[52] Rav Aharon HaLeyve, *Sefer HaChinuch*, Mitzvah 306.
[53] Sefer HaCinuch would translate the passage somewhat differently than suggested above.

6. The relevance of Hashem's response

Sefer HaChinuch's interpretation of Hashem's response to Moshe does not seem to address one of the difficulties outlined above. How does this response relate to Moshe's objections? Moshe does not question the purpose of redemption. He does not suggest that redemption is not a worthy goal and should be followed by some greater and more significant event.

Rav Yosef Dov Soloveitchik *Zt"l* responds to this issue. He explains that by informing Moshe of Revelation, Hashem addressed Moshe's second objection. Moshe could not understand his qualifications for appointment as leader of the nation. Hashem responded by explaining that the purpose of redemption was Revelation.

7. Moshe was primarily a teacher not a political leader

How did this information respond to Moshe's objection? Moshe would assume a fundamental role in Revelation. He would ascend the mountain. He would receive the Torah. He would descend from the mountain with the tablets of the Decalogue. He would receive from Hashem the Written Law and he would record it. He would also receive the Oral Law. He would be charged with teaching this Oral Law of the entire nation. He would instruct the leaders and the judges. He would also teach the common person. He would be responsible for the education of a nation and he would serve as its chief pedagogue.

Rav Soloveitchik explains that Hashem agreed with Moshe that he was far from the ideal political leader. If Hashem were seeking a political leader, He would have selected someone other than Moshe. Other individuals within the nation were more suitable for this role. Moshe was selected to be the teacher of the nation and its chief pedagogue. For this role, he was the most suitable candidate. This was Moshe's primary role and it was for this role that he was chosen.

Now, Sefer HaChinuch's interpretation of Hashem's response is better understood. The response did address Moshe's second objection. His objection assumed that the political freedom and independence of the nation was the fundamental objective of the redemption. The nation would require a leader who would inspire them to leave Egypt and follow him to a new land. Moshe felt he was not suited to this task. Hashem responded that political freedom was not the goal of redemption. The escape from oppression and persecution would serve as an indicator of a more important event to come. Moshe was selected for his role in this event.[54]

8. Lessons in seeking inspiration

Rav Soloveitchik's comments provide a very important insight into the responsibilities of the Torah scholar and teacher. His comments also communicate an important message to the would-be student. We assume that the effectiveness of a scholar of teacher is measured by his capacity to inspire. We expect an effective speaker to be charismatic and to use the devices of an orator to move his audience.

Moshe lacked the qualities of a polished speaker. He was selected by Hashem despite – or perhaps, because of – these deficiencies. His responsibility was to teach. Inspiration was to emerge from the wisdom and understanding that he would communicate. He would not seek to inspire his listeners through the force of his personality, his wit, stories, or other oratorical skills.

---

[54] Rav Yosef Dov Soloveitchik, *MePenenai HaRav,* p 240.

The message in Rav Soloveitchik's comments is that we should seek teachers who inspire and motivate through imparting knowledge and wisdom. Their clarity and the lucitidy of their teaching should inspire us. We should look past the packaging of the presentation and the magnetism of the speaker and seek meaning and inspiration in the substance.

And Moshe answered: They will not believe me and they will not obey my voice. For they will say, "Hashem has not appeared to you." (Shemot 4:1)
Moshe was the first prophet to act as Hashem's spokesman

Hashem directs Moshe to address Bnai Yisrael. He is to reveal to them his mission. He is to tell them that Hashem will redeem them from Egypt. Through Moshe, Hashem will take Bnai Yisrael out of Egypt and lead them to the Land of Israel. Moshe protests. The people will not follow him. They will not believe that Hashem has spoken to him. Certainly, they will not follow him through the wilderness to the Land of Israel.

Moshe's objections are difficult to understand. Moshe was not the first prophet. Hashem had spoken to the forefathers and others. None of these prophets raised Moshe's objections. They did not contend that their prophecies would be denied or that they would be dismissed as madmen. Why did Moshe bring up these issues?

Maimonides deals with this question in his *Moreh Nevuchim*. He offers an amazing answer. Maimonides begins by explaining that Moshe's objections were completely appropriate. He was to represent himself as Hashem's emissary. The nation should require Moshe to provide credentials. They would be fools if they followed Moshe without proof of his authenticity. Moshe recognized the legitimacy of Bnai Yisrael's suspicions.

Therefore, he asked Hashem to provide him with the means to verify his authenticity.

Based on this analysis, Maimonides reformulates our question. We cannot criticize Moshe's concerns. However, we must ask a different question. Why did previous prophets not raise these issues? Why did Avraham not ask Hashem for some means to confirm his authenticity?

Maimonides explains that Moshe was different from previous prophets. Previous prophets received prophecies aimed at guiding them towards their own personal perfection. Alternatively, their prophecies provided knowledge of their destiny or the future of their progeny. The people did not require these prophets to prove their authenticity. They did not speak to the people in the name of Hashem. Maimonides further explains that Avraham did not speak to humanity as Hashem's spokesman. He addressed humankind as a teacher. He provided instruction based upon reason and argument. He presented rational proofs for his theology and philosophy. Therefore, Avraham did not need to prove his prophetic status to the people. He never insisted that he be followed and obeyed as Hashem's spokesman. Moshe was the first prophet instructed to address a nation on behalf of Hashem. Moshe was to reveal Hashem's will and act as His spokesman. Moshe needed proof. He was confronted with a different and new mission. This mission required that he prove his authenticity.[55]

---

[55] Rabbaynu Moshe ben Maimon (Rambam) *Moreh Nevuchim*, volume 1, chapter 63.

"And take this staff in your hand. You will perform with it the signs." (Shemot 4:17)

Hashem tells Moshe to return to Egypt. He is to take his staff with him. With the staff, he will perform wonders. What was the purpose of the staff? Moshe performed miracles through the Almighty's intervention into nature. Hashem does not need Moshe's staff! This staff did not have magical powers. Rav Naftali Tzvi Yehuda Berlin (Netziv) suggests a simple interpretation of the staff. He maintains that the staff is a symbol of authority. Moshe would turn water into blood, cover Egypt in darkness and even split the sea. Moshe, through Hashem, would alter the natural order. Hashem had accorded Moshe power and authority over nature. Moshe was to be nature's ruler. The staff symbolized this authority over natural law.

And the nation believed and they heard that Hashem had remembered Bnai Yisrael and that He had seen their suffering. They kneeled and they bowed. (Shemot 4:31)

The Fragility of our Convictions
The capacity of the Jewish people to believe in Moshe

Parshat Shemot describes Paroh's implementation of a strategy to oppress the Jewish people. This program eventually evolved into a campaign of genocide. Moshe is introduced and the initial stages of our redemption from bondage are recounted.

In his first prophecy, Moshe is directed by Hashem to convene the elders of the Bnai Yisrael. He is to tell them that Hashem will take them forth from Egypt and bring the nation into the land that He promised to their forefathers. Hashem provides Moshe with wonders that he is to perform for the elders. The performance of these miracles will assure the elders that Moshe is an authentic prophet and that Hashem has indeed determined that the moment of redemption has arrived.

Moshe is joined by his brother Aharon. Together, they address the elders. Aharon acts as Moshe's spokesman. They communicate to the elders Hashem's message and perform the wonders that Hashem empowered them to execute.

What was the reaction of the nation and its elders to this wonderful but unanticipated message? The above passage explains that they believed Moshe and Aharon. The Talmud comments that through their response to Moshe, the elders and the people demonstrated that they were "believers, descendant of believers".[56] The intent of this comment is that the people exhibited a capacity to embrace a vision of the future completely inconsistent with their current condition. They were oppressed slaves subjected to wonton cruelty by powerful masters. Moshe and Aharon told them that soon they will emerge from bondage and take possession of a land long-ago promised to their forefathers. Accepting the truth of a message so incongruent with their current miserable condition required enormous courage and trust.[57]

---

[56] Mesechet Shabbat 97a.

[57] Torah Temimah (Sefer Shemot 4:1, note 1) further develops the Talmud's comment. He explains that the people do not deserve to be described as "believers, descendant of believers" simply because they were impressed by the wonders performed by Moshe and Aharon. They earned this accolade because they accepted that the ancient promise of redemption was now coming to fruition. It is their belief in that promise made to Avraham in a long-ago age, that earned for them the distinction described by the Talmud.

And they said to them: Hashem should reveal Himself regarding you and execute judgment. For you have made our spirit disgusting in the eyes of Paroh and in the eyes of his servants – to the extent of placing a sword in their hands to kill us. (Shemot 5:21)

Bnai Yisrael's abandonment of their belief

Moshe, Aharon, and the elders present Paroh with their demands. Paroh dismisses them and orders new measures designed to further oppress and break the spirit of the Jews. Moshe and Aharon are confronted by the elders. The elders condemn them for failing them and for exacerbating their suffering. They have not brought closer the redemption of Bnai Yisrael. Instead, they have provoked Paroh to inflict further suffering upon his slaves.

How can this response be reconciled with the Torah's previous description of the people and the elders? The Torah tells us that they believed in Moshe and Aharon and in their message. The Talmud praises our ancestors for their response to the news of their coming redemption. How can the commendations of the Torah and Talmud be reconciled with the nation's immediate abandonment of Moshe and Aharon at the first disappointment and set-back?

And I know that the king of Egypt will not allow you to leave without a mighty hand. (Shemot 3:19)

Moshe forewarned the people of setbacks

The response of the elders and the people to this setback is even more disturbing when we consider the above passage. Hashem tells Moshe that Paroh will not easily or quickly accede to the demand to free the Jews. Hashem will reveal His might. Only in response to the overwhelming omnipotence of Hashem, will Paroh grant the Jews their liberation. Moshe was directed by Hashem to share with the elders his prophecy – including this forewarning that freedom would not be attained quickly or easily. The elders and the people knew from Moshe that there would be setbacks. Why did they abandon Moshe and Aharon when they encountered the first of these obstacles?

We envision our path and its challenges

Rav Yisrael Chait addresses this issue. The solution that he proposes has two components. The first is an important insight into how our beliefs and convictions function as personal motivators. He explains that we do not act upon abstract assurances or predictions. When a person embarks upon a challenging journey, the person also has a vision of the path and its challenges. He has considered these and is prepared to move forward and encounter these challenges. This vision of the path and its challenge defines the person's commitment. He is committed to travel the path and endure the challenges he has envisioned.

Let's consider an illustration. I decide that I need to get into better shape. I have started to diet and to exercise more regularly. The journey to which I have committed is not merely an abstract concept. I have a rather specific vision of the the path I will travel and the obstacles I may encounter. This vision is integral to my commitment and capacity to move forward. I am not committed to an abstract goal. It is to this vision that I am committed.

The impact of unanticipated setbacks

What happens when a person encounters a major setback? It depends on the nature of the setback. If the setback was envisioned and anticipated, or even similar to the type anticipated, then the person will accept the disappointment and move forward. But what happens when the setback is of a type completely unanticipated? Then, the person's commitment will be severely challenged.

Let's return to our illustration. I recognize when I embark on my crusade to become fit that I will encounter setbacks. There will be days that I will get onto the scale and it will tell me that I have not lost the pounds I had anticipated shedding. I know that on some days I will go to the gym and have no energy and feel completely exhausted at the end of my workout. I am prepared for these setbacks. When they are encountered my commitment will not waiver. But what happens if I diet diligently, get onto the scale, and discover that after all of my deprivation I have gained two pounds? What happens if on the way to the gym, I slip and fracture my ankle? These are not the setbacks that I anticipated and that I am prepared to endure. If I encounter these setbacks, then my commitment may be severely challenged.

Now, let us apply this analysis to the experience of the elders and the people of Bnai Yisrael. Moshe had warned them that Paroh would resist their demands. They understood that they would need to strive with Paroh, stand up to him, and act with courage. They were prepared for all of this. It was included in their vision of the path they must travel and the challenges that they must endure in order to secure their freedom. But they could not anticipate or be prepared for the actual outcome of their first encounter with Paroh. He ridiculed them, dismissed their demands, and instituted additional cruel measures to further oppress them. If Hashem has decided that the moment of their liberation has arisen, sent to them His messenger, and charged them to demand from Paroh their freedom, then how can He allow Paroh to respond in this manner? They could not reconcile their vision of the path they must travel and its challenges with the reality before them.

And the quota of bricks that they produced yesterday and the prior day place upon them. Do not diminish it. For they are lazy. This is why they cry out saying, "Let us go and offer sacrifices to our G-d." (Shemot 5:8)

The importance of personal dignity

A second factor contributed to the collapse of the determination of the elders and the people. Dignity and self-respect are important to every person. However, we cannot acquire and sustain our dignity and self-respect without reinforcement from our environment. It is very difficult to be proud of oneself if this pride is not confirmed by the people who are important to us. A child seeks the confirmation of parents. Students require the acknowledgment of their teachers. Employees need to hear from their superiors that they are valued members of the organization. And even a slave seeks the approval of his master. In fact, because of the slave's psychological over-estimation of his master, this approval or disapproval is very potent.

Paroh's response to the demands of Bnai Yisrael, demonstrate shrewd insight into human psychology. He did not respond to the demands of the Jews by simply denying them. He was completely dismissive. He declared that they were motivated by slothfulness. They were simply a collection of lazy servants seeking to shirk their responsibilities.

Paroh's assessment of the psychological susceptibilities of the Jews was completely accurate. The elders immediately complained to Moshe and Aharon saying, "You have made our spirit disgusting in the eyes of Paroh and in the eyes of his servants." They were completely unprepared to endure their shame and embarrassment.

Rav Chait concludes that there is no contradiction between the Torah's and our Sages' description of elders and the people as "believers" and their immediate deterioration in response to Paroh's rejection of their demands. They were "believers" but they were also human beings. They were confronted by an unanticipated setback for which they were completely unprepared. Furthermore, Paroh succeeded in completely undermining their dignity and self-respect. The combination of these factors undercut the strength of their convictions.[58]

> *And after this Moshe and Aharon came. And they said to Paroh: Thus says Hashem the G-d of Yisrael, "Send forth my nation and they will celebrate before Me in the wilderness." And Paroh said: Who is Hashem that I should obey His voice to send forth Yisrael? I do not know of Hashem. Furthermore, I will not send forth Yisrael. (Shemot 5:1-2)*

Moshe altered the relationship between Paroh and the people

Based upon the above discussion, another element of the dynamic within this encounter becomes evident. Moshe and Aharon came to the elders in order to enlist them as partners. They asked that the elders join them in placing their demands before Paroh. They were seeking in the elders great courage of confidence. The elders responded by accepting upon themselves this role.[59] How did Moshe and Aharon inspire this courage?

Moshe and Aharon offered the elders and the people an opportunity to address Paroh in a framework that was very appealing. They would be making their request in a framework that is inconsistent with the slave-master relationship. They would demand to be sent forth to serve their G-d. Consider how inconsistent this demand was with the creed of the Egyptians. A vanquished people was demanding to worship its own G-d! Moshe and Aharon offered the elders the opportunity to speak to Paroh as leaders of a people with its own powerful G-d – Who must be obeyed.

Let us consider the implications of this framework. Moshe and Aharon told the elders and the people that they would confront Parorh as a proud people, demanding the right to worship its own G-d. This is a confrontation in which one can engage with dignity and even gratification. It is not a conversation between a master and a slave begging for his freedom. It is demand made by a proud people, insisting on its right to serve its powerful G-d.

Now, let us review Paroh's response. Again, his shrewd psychological insight is evident. He does not simply reject their demand. He dismisses their god. He refuses to allow the discussion to rise above the pleadings of a slave before his master. He would not allow the Jews and their elders to imagine themselves other than as lowly slaves.

Recognizing the fragility of our convictions

A conclusion that emerges from this investigation is the fragility of our convictions. This discussion focuses on a few of the factors that undermine even firmly established and strongly embraced convictions. One factor is our estimation of the challenges we will face in living by our convictions. The other is the difficulty that every person encounters in remaining true to

---

[58] Rav Yisrael Chait, TTL C-200, *Aral Sefasayim*.
[59] It is not clear from the passages that they actually executed the responsibility that they accepted upon themselves. According to Rashi (5:1), after agreeing to accompany Moshe and Aharon, the elders lost their courage. As Moshe and Aharon proceeded to the palace of Paroh the elders slowly slipped away.

convictions and values when they evoke ridicule and derision. The Torah's account should be sobering for us. It should be a warning. The elders of Israel were incapable of maintaining their commitment when confronted with unanticipated setbacks and intense ridicule. We are foolish if we think that we can be more steadfast than these giants.

This discussion should inform our plans and how we live. Let's consider an example. Parents and their teenagers put significant time, effort, and thought into selecting their college. If the above discussion is taken seriously, then this selection process must include the following consideration:

The environment of the secular college campus is often very dangerous for our young people. Students encounter hostility toward traditional values, religion, and especially toward Judaism. This hostility takes the form of implied and even manifest ridicule. A day school education and even a year or two of study in Israel will not immunize our teens from the deleterious impact of this environment. Many of our young people succumb to the pressures of this environment and either abandon observance or loose the intensity of their commitment. It is important to take seriously the challenges teens encounter on campus. Our teens should not be expected to overcome the type of challenges that defeated our elders.

Young people and their parents must carefully consider the extent and quality of Jewish life on the campus. The institutions on campus that promote Jewish life and provide a Jewish environment will likely be the only consistent refuge for our teens from the challenges that surround them. Their future as committed members of the Jewish people will not be secured through the education that they received before moving on to the campus. It will depend on the degree of our teens' Jewish experience on campus.

And Moshe returned to Hashem and he said: G-d, why have you mistreated this nation? Why have you sent me? (Shemot 5:22)

Moshe's bewilderment with Hashem's silence

Moshe goes to Paroh. He tells Paroh that Hashem has commanded Bnai Yisrael to go out to the wilderness and worship Him. Paroh refuses to allow Bnai Yisrael to travel into the wilderness or worship Hashem. Furthermore, Paroh increases the burden of Bnai Yisrael. He demands more labor from them. Moshe is troubled by this outcome. In our *pasuk*, Moshe addresses Hashem. He recounts that Hashem told him that Bnai Yisrael would be redeemed. He sent him to Paroh to demand their freedom. Moshe had dutifully followed Hashem's directions. However, he had failed to achieve any positive result. Instead, Moshe's actions had increased the suffering of the nation! How can this outcome be reconciled with Hashem's promise to redeem His nation?

The commentaries are troubled by Moshe's question. Hashem had revealed to Moshe that Paroh would not acquiesce to his request. Paroh would only relent as a result of overpowering plagues.[60] Moshe should not have been surprised by Paroh's response. The required plagues had not yet begun!

Rabbaynu Avraham ibn Ezra offers an interesting response. The final redemption would be the exodus from Egypt. Moshe understood that this ultimate step would require overwhelming

---

[60] Sefer Shemot 3:20.

force. Moshe understood that this final stage of rescue had not yet arrived. However, Moshe expected some immediate improvement in the condition of Bnai Yisrael. In other words, he assumed that redemption would be a process. The final step would only be secured through the plagues. But the process would begin immediately. Therefore, Moshe was shocked by the deterioration in Bnai Yisrael's condition.[61]

Nachmanides explains Moshe's question differently. Moshe understood that Paroh would only respond to force. He was not surprised that Paroh increased his torment of the Jewish people. But he was shocked that Hashem did not respond and punish Paroh. Moshe expected the plagues to begin immediately. Instead, Hashem was silent. Moshe was puzzled. If the time had come for redemption, let the process begin. If the moment of redemption had not yet arrived, why had he been sent to Egypt? Moshe had spoken to the people of their salvation but not produced any positive results. This could only undermine Moshe's credibility.[62]

And Moshe returned to Hashem, and said: L-rd, why have You dealt ill with this people? Why is it that You have sent me? For since I came to Paroh to speak in Your name, he has dealt ill with this people; neither have You delivered Your people at all. (Shemot 5:22-23)

Building Observance Upon a Torah Foundation

1. **Moshe's failed mission and his protest to Hashem**

Parshat VaEyra continues a discussion between Hashem and Moshe that began at the end of Parshat Shemot. Moshe initiates the conversation. He expresses to Hashem his confusion over his mission. He was directed by Hashem to confront Paroh and to demand that he allow Bnai Yisrael to travel into the wilderness and serve Hashem. He did exactly as directed. However, the outcome has been disastrous. Rather than acquiescing to his demand, Paroh has refused to grant Bnai Yisrael leave from their labors. Instead, he has increased their burden. Moshe has performed his assigned task but the plight of his people has only been made more disparate through his efforts.

The initial element of Hashem's response is included in Parshat Shemot. Hashem tells Moshe that he will see that, in the end, Paroh will eagerly send forth Bnai Yisrael from Egypt. In Parshat VaEyra, Hashem's response continues. He explains to Moshe that the revelation that will occur in Egypt will exceed the revelation granted to the Patriarchs. The covenant that Hashem made with the Avot – the Patriarchs – will be fulfilled; their descendants will be redeemed from bondage in Egypt and they will be brought to the Land of Canaan.

The commentaries note that Hashem's response to Moshe seems incomplete. He tells Moshe that He will redeem Bnai Yisrael from Egypt. However, Moshe did not question whether Hashem would rescue the nation. His confusion was in regard to his personal role in this process. He asked Hashem why he had been sent to Paroh on a mission that Hashem had allowed to fail and also worsen the plight of the people.

The commentaries offer a number of interesting responses to this question. However, in order to better appreciate their responses, another issue must be considered.

---

[61] Rabbaynu Avraham ibn Ezra, *Commentary on Sefer Shemot*, 5:22-23.
[62] Rabbaynu Moshe ben Nachman (Ramban), *Commentary on Sefer Shemot* 5:22.

And Hashem said to Moshe: Behold, I come unto you in a thick cloud, that the people may hear when I speak with you, and may also believe you forever. And Moshe told the words of the people unto Hashem. (Shemot 19:9)

2. The proper foundation for a theology and religion

The narrative contained in the first portion of Sefer Shemot can be summarized in two sentences. Bnai Yisrael is placed in bondage in Egypt. Hashem rescues Bnai Yisrael from persecution through a series of miracles. This summary of the narrative suggests two questions. First, why did Hashem allow the Egyptians to subject the descendants of His faithful Patriarchs to severe persecution and even genocide? Second, why did Hashem rescue Bnai Yisrael through wonders and miracles? Why did He not redeem Bnai Yisrael through more natural or conventional means? Both of these questions are important. However, the second question is relevant to the above discussion.

Maimonides describes the method by which the first patriarch – Avraham – discovered Hashem. His comments are based upon the midrash. He explains that Avraham did not discover Hashem through a personal encounter. Instead, he concluded that there must be a creator based upon an assessment of the complexity of the universe. In other words, he studied the universe, recognized its complexity, and concluded that the universe, like all complex entities emerged through design. The design evident in the universe provides testimony to the existence of an intelligent creator.

Rabbaynu Yehudah HaLeyve explains that Avraham's method of discovering G-d cannot be the basis for the theology of a nation. Only the most advanced thinkers – individuals like Avraham – can discover Hashem through this method. A religion or theology intended to be embraced by an entire people must provide evidence of Hashem's existence that is accessible to even the unsophisticated common person. He explains that the Sinai Revelation provided this evidence. The people heard Hashem and they experienced His "presence". This event provided evidence of Hashem's existence that could be equally grasped by the scholar and the common person.

However, the Sinai Revelation also confirmed other basic principles of the Torah. Maimonides, identifies thirteen basic principles of the Torah. In addition to demonstrating the existence of Hashem, Revelation established the truth of other of these principles. It confirmed that Hashem communicates with human beings through prophecy. It proved that the Torah is from Hashem. It demonstrated the uncommon nature of Moshe's prophetic achievement. This is expressed in the above passage. The passage explains that the purpose of Revelation was to create a permanent foundation for the authenticity of Moshe's prophecy and the Torah.

Therefore say unto the children of Israel: I am Hashem. I will bring you out from under the burdens of the Egyptians, and I will deliver you from their bondage, and I will redeem you with an outstretched arm, and with great judgments. I will take you to Me for a people, and I will be to you a G-d. And you shall know that I am Hashem your G-d, who brought you out from under the burdens of the Egyptians. (Shemot 6:6-7)

3. The educational objectives of the redemption

The above passages explain that the redemption of Bnai Yisrael from Egypt was not intended to merely rectify the injustice of their suffering and punish their persecutors. It was intended to mold the people into a nation that woud serve Hashem. Hashem tells Moshe that He will take Bnai Yisrael to Himself as a nation and He will be their G-d. However, Hashem adds that through the process of their redemption they will know "I am Hashem your G-d who brought you out from under the burdens of Egypt". In other words, the redemption process was intended to be educational and to establish beyond doubt fundamental truths. Nachmanides explains that among these truths is that Hashem is omnipotent. He has a degree of control over all nature that can only be asserted by nature's creator. He also notes additional fundamental principles demonstrated by the redemption. For example the redemption demonstrated Hashem's involvement in events in the material world – an issue reconfirmed by Revelation.

4. Miracles and wonders were essential to the educational objectives

From this discussion, the issue raised above is resolved. Why did Hashem choose to redeem Bnai Yisrael through wonders and miracles? The redemption was not merely designed to rescue Bnai Yisrael from persecution. It was designed to serve as the firm foundation of a new religion and theology. In order to achieve this objective, Hashem repeatedly revealed himself through wonders and miracles. These demonstrations testified to His omnipotence and His involvement with humankind.

Now, the original question can be reconsidered. Moshe protested to Hashem that he had done exactly as He had commanded. Yet, rather than his efforts helping Bnai Yisrael, they had only led to greater persecution. Hashem seems to merely respond that He will redeem the people. How does this response relate to Moshe's objection?

And G-d spoke unto Moses, and said to him: I am Hashem. (Shemot 6:2)

5. Fear of G-d is reserved for Hashem

Chizkuni notes that Hashem continues His response to Moshe in the opening passages of Parshat VaEyrah with the declaration "I am Hashem". What is the message intended in this pronouncement? Chizkuni suggests that it is a reference to an earlier passage. When Hashem initially appointed Moshe and Aharon to their mission of leading the people forth from Egypt, He assigned each a specific role. Moshe was to be the "master" and Aharon was to speak on his behalf. In other words, Moshe would be the leader and the individual wielding the power and authority. Aharon would only act as his spokesperson. Chizkuni explains that Moshe's role as leader was limited by an important consideration. The ultimate objective of the redemption was for the people to accept and to fear Hashem. In this opening statement of the parasha, Hashem tells Moshe that yes, you have been appointed leader. But the objective is for the people to recognize that I am Hashem and to fear and serve only Me.

Through this insight, Chizkuni attributes to Hashem a response to Moshe's objection. Moshe asked Hashem why he had appointed him to a mission and then not secured its success. According to Chizkuni, Hashem answered that this was an essential step in the educational process imbedded in the redemption. The process was intended to demonstrate that only Hashem is the true G-d. Only He is fit to be awed and worshiped. No other power and certainly no other person is His rival – not even Moshe. Therefore, Moshe's initial failure to secure results was essential. It demonstrated to the people that even Moshe was powerless to rescue them. Moshe had no power of his own and could not command Hashem's response. Moshe's efforts only became meaningful and effective when Hashem began to act through him.

6. **Placing practice and observance upon a firm foundation**

The fundamental lesson that emerges from this discussion is that the redemption from Egypt in conjunction with Revelation was intended to demonstrate and teach to the people the fundamental principles of the Torah. Most of the thirteen principles identified by Maimonides are confirmed through these events. It is true that Torah Judaism places a premium upon practice and observance. However, it is also evident from the Torah's narrative regarding these events that practice and observance are to be built upon a foundation. This foundation is formed of these principles. This lesson suggests that attention should be given to knowing and understanding these principles. They are the foundation of all other aspects of our observance.

VaEyrah

And I appeared to Avraham, Yitzchak, and Yaakov as, Kel Shakai, and by my name Hashem I did not make myself known to them. (Shemot 6:3)

The Tetragrammaton and Hashem's other Names

The Torah uses various names in referring to G-d. Each name has a specific meaning. In general, each describes a unique aspect of G-d's behavior or a characteristic we descriptively ascribe to Him. Two of these names are discussed in this passage. One of these names is *Kel Shakai*. The other is the Tetragrammaton – the Name of Four Letters. This is the most sacred of G-d's names. Its sanctity is represented by the manner in which the name is pronounced. The actual letters of the name are not sounded. Instead, a form of the term Master is substituted. Why is this name more sacred than G-d's other names? It seems that whereas the other names describe some aspect of G-d's behavior, or a characteristic that we ascribe to Him; the Tetagrammaton seems to approach being a reference to G-d's nature. It is, therefore, fitting that the name is not pronounced as it is written. We cannot know G-d's true nature. We can only comprehend a descriptive approximation of His nature. Through not expressing the name as it is written, we symbolize the unattainable nature of true knowledge of G-d. The Tetragrammaton is often replaced by the term "Hashem".

In our *pasuk*, G-d explains to Moshe that He revealed Himself to the Forefathers. However, this revelation was limited. He revealed Himself only as *Kel Shakai*. He did not reveal Himself as the G-d "described" by the Tetagrammaton. The exact meaning of the name *Kel Shakai* is discussed by the commentaries. But regardless of the exact meaning of this name, the intent of the passage is clear. In Egypt, Hashem will reveal Himself more fully.

How will the revelation in Egypt be different from the previous revelations experienced by the Forefathers? Nachmanides explains that the *Avot* – the Forefathers –witnessed Hashem interfere with natural events. The interference was often subtle and barely detectable. However, these miracles were of a limited scale. In Egypt, Hashem will perform incredible miracles. These events will not be minor alterations in the natural order. The laws of nature will be abrogated in a manifest and fantastic manner.

It should be noted that Nachmanides maintains that there is a natural order. Physical laws govern this order. We release a ball and it falls. This is because the Creator instituted physical laws that govern mundane events. Gravity is one of these laws. Nachmanides also maintains that Hashem performs hidden miracles. He rewards us for merits and punishes evil. These rewards and punishments are concealed miracles. Physical law does not dictate that the righteous should prosper or the evil should perish. These outcomes involve interference with natural cause and effect. Therefore, Nachmanides regards these outcomes as minor miracles.[1]

Why does Hashem need laws of nature in order to govern the universe? Could not the Creator guide every single event, directly? This question is based upon a lack of appreciation of the beautiful wisdom expressed in these laws. The laws governing our universe are an awesome expression of the unfathomable wisdom of Hashem.

Minor miracles – even those experienced by the *Avot* – fail to express the extent of Hashem's authority over nature. The basic pattern of nature remains intact. Often these

---

[1] Rabbeinu Moshe ben Nachman (Ramban), *Commentary on Sefer Shemot* 6:3.

interventions are not even identifiable. In this sense, these miracles represent a limited revelation of Hashem. In Egypt, miracles were performed that shattered the very pattern of natural phenomena. The Reed Sea split. The firstborn died. Hashem was revealed as the G-d ruling the universe. He was recognized as the cause of all that exists and capable of altering the universe to suit His will.

And Hashem said to Moshe: Now you shall see what I will do to Paroh; for by a strong hand he shall send them forth, and by a strong hand he shall drive them out of his land. And the L-rd spoke to Moshe, and said to him: I am Hashem; and I appeared to Avraham, to Yitzchak and to Yaakov, as L-rd Almighty, but by My name Hashem I was not known to them. (Shemot 6:1-3)

The What and Why of Redemption

Moshe's failure and protest to Hashem

The above quote is composed of three passages. The first of these passages is the final passage of Parshat Shemot. In this passage Hashem responds to the question posed by Moshe in the preceding passages. In order to understand this dialogue between Hashem and Moshe, its context must be identified.

Hashem directed Moshe to demand of Paroh that he permit Bnai Yisrael to travel into the wilderness and serve Him. Moshe and Aharon followed Hashem's instructions. They came before Paroh and told him Hashem commanded that he release Bnai Yisrael so that they may worship Him in the wilderness. Paroh rejected this request. He also implemented measures that he believed would discourage any future requests for respite. He commanded those who oversaw the oppression of Bnai Yisrael to suspend supplies of straw – a necessary ingredient for producing bricks – but to continue to demand the production of the same quota of bricks.

Moshe was astounded by this outcome. Hashem had sent him back to Egypt in order to bring about the liberation of Bnai Yisrael. He followed Hashem's instructions completely. Instead of initiating a process leading to liberation, the implementation of Hashem's instructions led to an increase in the oppression of the people. Moshe protested to Hashem. He asked Hashem, "Why did You send me? Why have You not rescued Your nation?"

The first of the above passages communicates Hashem's response. He tells Moshe that Paroh will release the people. He will send forth Bnai Yisrael. Paroh will drive them out of Egypt!

Hashem's response is divided between two sections of the Torah

Hashem's response continues in the second and third passages above. These are the opening passages of Parshat VaEyra. In other words, the Torah divides Hashem's response to Moshe between Parshat Shemot and Parshat VaEyra. The first passage of the response concludes Parshat Shemot and then, the response continues in Parshat VaEyra. Why does the Torah interrupt the response, begin a new section, and in it complete the response?

This question suggests that Hashem's response is composed of two discrete elements. Apparently, the Torah divides the response between these two sections in order to communicate that it is composed of the two distinct elements. But what are these elements? Let us begin by considering more carefully the second element of the response – the element contained in Parshat VaEyra.

Hashem did not completely reveal Himself to the patriarchs

The precise meaning of these passages is discussed by the commentaries. Various interpretations are suggested. The general meaning is more easily identifiable. Hashem tells Moshe that He was not known to the patriarchs by His true name – the Tetragrammaton. What does this mean?

The apparent meaning of this statement is that Hashem did not fully reveal Himself to the patriarchs. In some respect He was hidden from them. Now, He was prepared to reveal Himself more fully. In what respect was Hashem concealed from the patriarchs and how would He now more fully reveal Himself?

Therefore, say to the children of Israel: I am Hashem, and I will bring you out from under the burdens of the Egyptians, and I will deliver you from their bondage, and I will redeem you with an outstretched arm, and with great judgments; and I will take you to Me for a people, and I will be to you a L-rd; and you will know that I am Hashem your L-rd, who brought you out from under the burdens of the Egyptians. And I will bring you into the land, that I swore to give to Avraham, to Yitzchak, and to Yaakov; and I will give it to you for a heritage. I am Hashem. (Shemot 6:6-8)

Hashem will reveal Himself in Egypt

In these passages Hashem concludes His response to Moshe. He tells Moshe that He is prepared to deliver Bnai Yisrael from their oppression in Egypt. He will do this with an outstretched arm and with great judgments. Malbim explains the meaning of these terms. Hashem will stretch forth His arm to perform great wonders. He will perform great judgments to exact from the Egyptians punishment for their wicked oppression of Bnai Yisrael. In other words, Hashem tells Moshe that He will reveal Himself to humanity as ruler over the material universe. He will bend its laws to His purposes. He will also reveal Himself as the judge of humanity. The oppressed will be redeemed and the oppressor will be severely punished.

But this is not the full extent of Hashem's response. Hashem tells Moshe that He will take Bnai Yisrael to Himself as a nation and He will be to Bnai Yisrael as their L-rd. What does this mean? Was not Hashem already the L-rd of Bnai Yisrael and the entire universe? Were not all people already His? Nachmanides and others respond that this is a reference to the Sinai revelation. Hashem will manifest His sovereignty through giving the Torah to Bnai Yisrael. He will forge a unique relationship with this nation. He will not be the remote ruler abiding in the heavens. He will forge with Bnai Yisrael a relationship of intimacy. He will command the people, and His presence will be palpable in the midst of the nation.

In short, Hashem told Moshe that he was now prepared to reveal Himself and to engage with Bnai Yisrael in a manner that would surpass even His relationship with the patriarchs. But how precisely did His relationship with the patriarchs differ from the forthcoming relationship? Was He not present at their side? Did he not perform wonders for them, protect them and save them from those who would harm them?

Also, I established My covenant with them to give to them the Land of Cana'an – the land of their wanderings, wherein they sojourned. (Shemot 6:4)

Hashem's relationship with the patriarchs focused on the future

In this passage, Hashem explains to Moshe that the wonders that He will soon perform and the relationship into which He will enter is the fulfillment of His covenant with the patriarchs. This passage also identifies the difference between Hashem's relationship with the patriarchs and the relationship that will now emerge. Hashem's relationship with the patriarchs was focused upon the future that He promised them. It is true that He protected them and performed wonders on their behalf. But these were not the focus of His relationship with our forefathers. They were necessities of the moment. These wonders were not intended as a revelation of Hashem's omnipotence. Hashem's relationship with our forefathers focused upon His promises regarding the destiny of their progeny – they would be the nation of Hashem and that they would possess the Land of Cana'an. He provided the patriarchs with a vision of a future that would be realized through their descendants. Bnai Yisrael would be the realization of that vision. Rashi summarizes this distinction. Hashem made promises to the patriarchs. But they did not experience the fulfillment of these promises. Now, those promises will be fulfilled.

Hashem's response deals with the what and why of redemption

We have focused on the portion of Hashem's response that opens Parshat VaEyra. With this understanding of that portion of the response, let's return to our opening question. Why is Hashem's response divided into two sections? Why is it divided between Parshat Shemot and Parshat VaEyra?

The first portion of the response is a direct and limited reply to Moshe. Moshe was astounded that obedient execution of Hashem's instructions had evoked further suffering for the people he had been sent to redeem. Hashem responds that this is part of the plan. Paroh has demonstrated his obstinacy, his animosity toward Bnai Yisrael, and his dismissal of Hashem. Yet, in the end, he will be compelled to put aside all of these attitudes and he will send forth Bnai Yisrael; he will drive them out of his land. In other words, Hashem provides Moshe a description of His strategy; He describes *what* He is doing.

In Parshat VaEyra Hashem is no longer describing what He is doing. He is not dealing with the details of His strategy. He is communicating to Moshe the reasons for His actions – their *why*. He is providing Moshe with insight into the meaning of the strategy, its importance, and its metaphysical purpose. This redemption is the fulfillment of the promise to the patriarchs and through it Hashem will reveal Himself to Bnai Yisrael and to humanity.

And Hashem spoke to Moshe and He said: I am Hashem. I appeared to Avraham, to Yitzchak, and to Yaakov as Kel Shakai, but [by] My name Hashem, I was not known to them. (Shemot 6:2-3)

The Moshe Innovation

1. A strange opening

The above passages open Parshat VaEyra. To recognize the problem they present, one must understand their meaning and context. What is the meaning of the passages? The passages refer to two of Hashem's names. One is Kel Shakai; the other is the Tetragrammaton – the four-letter name represented by "Hashem". Ramban – Nachmanides – explains that the two names describe different aspects of our understanding of Hashem. The name Kel Shekai refers to His sovereignty over nature. It communicates His capacity to manipulate nature for the benefit of the righteous and on their behalf. The Tetragrammaton describes Him as the cause of all existence. He is the creator, and He sustains the universe and its laws. He can overturn these laws and perform miracles that completely contravene the natural order.

In the above passages, Hashem tells Moshe that He revealed Himself to the Avot – the Patriarchs – as Kel Shakai. He performed wonders that were consistent with the general pattern of nature. He did not reveal Himself as Hashem. He did not perform wonders that overturned the natural order. Now, He is prepared to reveal Himself as Hashem.[2]

What is the context of these passages? In the passages that follow, Hashem tells Moshe that He has heard the cries of Bnai Yisrael and He is prepared to fulfill the covenant He made with the Patriarchs. He will redeem their descendants from bondage. He will take them as His people. He will bring them to the Land of Israel. Then, He appoints Moshe and Aharon to their roles in the redemption.

Now, we can identify the problem presented by these passages. They continue a conversation recorded at the end of Parshat Shemot. There, Moshe protests to Hashem that he confronted Paroh as directed by Him. This led only to intensifying the Jewish people's suffering. Paroh reacted to Moshe by increasing their burden. Hashem responds to Moshe. He tells him that he will soon see Him act against Paroh and that Paroh will chase the Jewish people from Egypt. Arguably, this is the strangest opening of any of the Torah's parshiyot. Why does Parshat VaEyra open in the middle of a conversation? Why does the Torah divide Hashem's conversation with Moshe between Shemot and VaEyra?

And Hashem said to Moshe: Behold I have appointed you as master of Paroh and Aharon, your brother, will be your spokesperson. (Shemot 7:1)

2. The meaning of navi

Let us begin by considering another issue. Hashem appoints Moshe and Aharon to their mission. They will confront and overcome Paroh. Moshe will become Paroh's master. Aharon will act as Moshe's spokesperson. He will address Paroh and communicate to him Moshe's messages. The above translation of the passage is provided by Unkelus. He translates the word navi in the passage as "spokesperson". However, in most instances the word navi means "prophet". Obviously, navi, in this passage, does not mean prophet. Aharon will not be Moshe's prophet. He will be his spokesperson. But why does Hashem use the word navi to describe Aharon's role? What does His use of this term reveal about its underlying meaning?

Rashi approves of Unkelus' translation. He adds that navi means one who speaks to the people providing guidance and rebuke.[3] Rabbaynu Avraham ibn Ezra objects to this translation and Rashi's support of it. He objection is revealing. He points out that Hashem refers to Avraham as a navi.[4] Avraham never spoke to humanity as Hashem's spokesperson. If navi means spokesperson, it cannot be applied to Avraham. Ibn Ezra suggests that navi means one's intimate associate. One reveals secrets to one's navi. Aharon was Moshe's navi. Moshe revealed

---

[2] Rabbaynu Moshe ben Nachman (Ramban), Commentary on Sefer Shemot 6:2-5.
[3] Rabbaynu Shlomo ben Yitzchak (Rashi), Commentary on Sefer Shemot 7:1.
[4] Sefer Beresheit 20:7.

to him his prophecies. Similarly, Avraham and Hashem shared a close relationship and Hashem granted Avraham prophecies.[5]

What does this dispute teach about the term navi and about the prophets it typically describes? Rashi and Ibn Ezra disagree over which aspect of the prophet the term navi describes. The navi has a mission. The navi speaks to the people and urges them to develop spiritually. The navi also has a special relationship with Hashem. According to Rashi, the term navi describes the role of the prophet. He guides and rebukes his community. According to Ibn Ezra, it describes the prophet's relationship with Hashem. They are intimates. Hashem reveals His "secrets" to His prophets.

And Hashem spoke to Moshe saying: Come to Paroh the king of Egypt and speak to him. And he will send Bnai Yisrael from his land. (Shemot 6:10-11)

3. Moshe's role

Let us consider more carefully one detail in the above discussion. Ibn Ezra observed that Avraham was not Hashem's spokesperson. Rambam – Maimonides – explains this more fully. Avraham was a prophet. However, Hashem did not communicate to him messages to be transmitted to humanity. Avraham's prophecies were more akin to private communications. In contrast, Moshe was appointed by Hashem to be His spokesperson. Moshe received communications from Hashem to transmit to others.[6]

This observation is relevant to the above passages. The first passage is "And Hashem spoke to Moshe saying." This is a recurring passage in the Torah. The above is the conventional translation and conforms with the opinion of Rabbaynu Avraham ibn Ezra.[7] The translation is difficult. What is the function of the term "saying"? The passage is complete without this word. Radak suggests an alternative translation – "And Hashem spoke to Moshe [directing him] to say". According to Radak, the term introduces a commandment or statement that Moshe is directed to repeat to others.[8] Ramban notes many instances in which this translation is untenable. Nonetheless, Radak's position reflects the special character of Moshe's prophecy. He was directed to communicate Hashem's commandments and messages to others. He was to act as Hashem's spokesperson.

A strange comment of the Sages is now understood. The Sages state that the Divine Presence spoke from the throat of Moshe.[9] What does this mean? Did Hashem act as a ventriloquist and use Moshe as His puppet? Based on the above discussion, the meaning of the

---

[5] Rabbaynu Avraham ibn Ezra, Extended Commentary on Sefer Shemot 7:1. Ibn Ezra's objection to Rashi is not conclusive. Rashi is not suggesting that the literal meaning of navi is "spokesperson". He is approving of Unkelus' rendering of navi as "spokesperson" in the context of this passage. Rashi then explains that the literal meaning of navi is one who addresses the people with guidance or rebuke. This was Avraham's role. When Hashem describes Avraham as a navi He is using the term in this literal sense. Avraham offered guidance to his generation and provided rebuke.

[6] Rabbaynu Moshe ben Maimon (Rambam) Moreh Nevuchim, volume 2, chapter 39.

[7] Rabbaynu Avraham ibn Ezra, Extended Commentary on Sefer Shemot 6:10.

[8] Rabbaynu David Kimchi (Radak), Commentary on Sefer Sherashim, שרש אמר.

[9] This statement is quoted widely among the commentators. However, its exact source is not clear. Bait HaLeyve, Derashot, Vol 3, Derush 4, cites the source as Zohar, Parshat Pinchas 232a.

statement emerges. Moshe differed from the prophets who preceded him. Those prophets were not Hashem's spokespersons. They were not directed to speak to humanity on Hashem's behalf. Moshe was directed to communicate Hashem's message to others. Hashem spoke to Bnai Yisrael, Paroh, and humanity through Moshe.

4. Moshe's appointment

Let us further consider the significance of Moshe's appointment to a new version of prophecy. Hashem's appointment of Moshe as His prophet was part of an enormous transition in His relationship with humanity. Previously, Hashem was the hidden force behind nature. He manipulated nature from behind His screen. He did not reveal Himself through manifest miracles that contravened nature. He spoke to His prophets, but their conversations were private and personal. They were not directed to humankind.

Now, Hashem is prepared to reveal Himself. He will perform wonders that demonstrate His complete control over nature. Hashem will reveal Himself as Creator. His will sustains the universe and its laws. His will can overturn those laws. Also, He will reveal His will through His prophet. He will address humanity through His spokesperson, Moshe.

5. The split conversation

Now, let us return to our original question. Why is the conversation between Moshe and Hashem divided between Parshat Shemot and Parshat VaEyra? Why does VaEyra open in the middle of this conversation?

The conversation between Moshe and Hashem has two distinct parts. In the first portion of the conversation, Hashem responds to Moshe's objection. Moshe asks Hashem why the redemption has not begun. Hashem responds that it will now begin. This portion of the conversation is placed in Parshat Shemot. Moshe raises his objection at the end of the parasha and the response belongs in that parasha.

In Parshat VaEyra, Hashem is revealing to Moshe the meaning and significance of the redemption. He tells Moshe that He will emerge from His concealment. He will reveal Himself as He is described by the Tetragrammaton. Nature will be overturned. Also, He will communicate, through Moshe, with humanity.

In short, Hashem's conversation to Moshe includes two components. The first is His response to Moshe. The time of redemption has arrived. This component concludes Parshat Shemot. In the second component Hashem tells Moshe that He is prepared to reveal Himself to humanity in action and in word. This component introduces Parshat VaEyra. It introduces Hashem's appointment of Moshe as His spokesperson and the initiation of the miracles of the redemption.[10]

"And Hashem spoke to Moshe and Aharon and He appointed them regarding Bnai Yisrael and regarding Paroh – the king of Egypt – to take Bnai Yisrael out of Egypt." (Shemot 6:13)

---

[10] In Parshat Shemot, Hashem instructed Moshe to speak to Bnai Yisrael and to lead the elders in confronting Paroh. In response to Moshe's questions, Hashem provides Moshe some specific directions. However, in Parshat VaEyra, He appoints Moshe as His prophet – His spokesperson.

I do not know why but at least a few times each year some individual or group of individuals will approach me in the street and proselytize me. Sometimes I just try to politely ignore the appeal. But occasionally, I will engage the would-be missionary in conversation. I am curious as to why this person feels that I should abandon my faith for another. I generally, find that the appeal is not based upon some objective argument that one religion is superior to the other. Instead, the would-be missionary assures me that his or her faith is so strong that on this basis I should abandon my false beliefs. I find it remarkable that the missionary feels that this argument should sway me. Certainly, this is not the Torah's outlook.

In this week's *parasha* Moshe goes into action and the redemption of Bnai Yisrael begins to unfold. In this process of redemption Moshe will perform wonders that surpass those of any other prophet. As we read the Torah's account of Moshe's actions we can appreciate the meaning of the Torah assessment of Moshe. The closing passages of the Torah tell us that there no other arose in Bnai Yisrael that was Moshe's equal. No other knew Hashem as intimately or performed wonders on the same scale as Moshe.[11]

However, Maimonides makes an astounding assertion regarding Moshe. Maimonides explains Moshe was the first true *navi* – prophet.[12] This is an amazing statement. The Torah tells us that others – who lived before Moshe – spoke with Hashem. Adam, Noach Avraham, Yitzchak, Yaakov and others received prophetic visions. How can Maimonides contend that Moshe was the first true *navi*?

> *"And Hashem said to Moshe, "Now, I have appointed you as a lord over Paroh and Aharon your brother will be your navi." (Shemot 7:1)*

Before we begin to explore Maimonides' position, it will be helpful to consider this passage. Hashem tells Moshe that he has been appointed as a lord over Paroh. Through Moshe, Hashem will punish Paroh and eventually Paroh will be forced to yield to Hashem's will. Hashem adds that Aharon – Moshe's older brother will act as his *navi*. The description of Aharon as Moshe's *navi* must be understood. The term *navi* is generally understood to mean prophet. It is clear that this interpretation of the term *navi* is not appropriate in this context. In no sense was Aharon Moshe's prophet. On the contrary – Moshe was Aharon's prophet. Hashem communicated with Moshe – not Aharon – and Moshe provided Aharon with instructions. Targum Unkelus responds to this problem. He translates the term *navi* – in this instance – to mean spokesperson. Hashem is telling Moshe that he will yield the power but Aharon will be the spokesperson. However, Unkelus' interpretation of the term *navi* requires further explanation. How can the term *navi* – which generally means prophet – have a different meaning in this instance?

Rashi responds to this difficulty. After quoting Unkelus' explanation of the term *navi*, Rashi explains the basis for Unkelus' novel interpretation. Rashi explains that the term *navi* actually has a consistent meaning. It describes a person that makes announcements to the people and provides public rebuke.[13] According to Rashi, a *navi* is not merely a prophet. A *navi* is a person that speaks on behalf of Hashem, and speaks to the people in Hashem's name. In other words, every *navi* is a spokesperson. Generally, the term *navi* is used to refer to a person who

---

[11] Sefer Devarim 34:10-11.
[12] Rabbaynu Moshe ben Maimon (Rambam) *Moreh Nevuchim*, volume 1, chapter 63.
[13] Rabbaynu Shlomo ben Yitzchak (Rashi), *Commentary on Sefer Shemot* 7:1.

speaks in the name of Hashem. In this instance the term is used to describe Aharon – who acted as a spokesperson for Moshe.

This is an important point. According to Rashi's interpretation of the term *navi*, not everyone who receives a prophecy deserved to be regarded as a *navi* in the fullest sense of the term. For example, if Hashem communicates with an individual but does not instruct the individual to share the communication, then the person is not a *navi* in the full sense. So, although Hashem spoke with Yitzchak, He did provide Yitzchak with commandments or instructions that he was to share with humanity. It follows that according to Rashi's reasoning, Yitzchak cannot be referred to as a *navi* in the same sense that the term is used in relationship to Moshe.

Now, we can return to Maimonides' comments. Maimonides explains that although there were individuals who communicated with Hashem prior to Moshe – for example, the forefathers – these prophets did not speak to humanity in the name of Hashem. Maimonides discusses the distinction between Avraham and Moshe. He explains that Avraham did not communicate commandments to humanity from Hashem. Instead, he provided instruction to humanity based upon rational argument and proof. In contrast, Moshe communicated commandments in the name of Hashem. Avraham was a prophet – in the sense that he communicated with Hashem. He was also a teacher to humanity. However, he was not a *navi* – a person who speaks in the name of Hashem.

Maimonides concludes that this is the reason that Moshe is the first person provided with wonders that he would perform. Moshe was required to establish his credibility as a *navi* – a spokesperson of Hashem. Avraham had no need for such miracles. He did not speak to humanity as Hashem's spokesperson. So, there was no need for him to provide proofs of his prophecy.[14]

Maimonides acknowledges that his position presents a number of problems. One problem is that it would seems that there were a number of people – before Moshe – that acted as spokespeople for Hashem provided direction to humanity. Did not Noach warn his generation of the impending Deluge and urge the people to repent?

Maimonides offers a bold answer. He suggests we carefully read the Torah and we will find that the text of the Torah does correspond with this popular impression. The Torah does not describe Noach speaking to the people in the name of Hashem. Furthermore, the Torah seems to tell us that Hashem did not send a messenger to forewarn humanity of His designs. The Torah describes Hashem as "grieved to His heart."[15] According to Maimonides, this phrase means that Hashem's decision to destroy humanity was not announced. It was held in His heart. Only Noach was told and he was not instructed to share this knowledge.[16]

Maimonides raises other questions. In some cases his answers are not clear. However, his main point is completely unambiguous. Moshe was the first prophet provided with wonders. This is because any person who speaks in the name of Hashem should expect to be required to establish his credibility. Hashem would not expect Bnai Yisrael to believe that Moshe was Hashem's spokesperson, without evidence that this was the case.

---

[14] Rabbaynu Moshe ben Maimon (Rambam) *Moreh Nevuchim*, volume 1, chapter 63.
[15] Sefer Beresheit 6:6.
[16] Rabbaynu Moshe ben Maimon (Rambam) *Moreh Nevuchim*, volume 1, chapter 29.

Furthermore, Maimonides' description of the work of Avraham is consistent with this outlook. Avraham did not perform wonders in order to establish himself. This was not necessary for a teacher that did not claim to speak on Hashem's behalf. However, Avraham did not merely urge the people of his time to change. He offered proofs and arguments. Again, Maimonides is asserting that it is not appropriate for us to expect a person or group to change religious beliefs without basis. Just as Moshe was required to provide proof of his status as Hashem's spokesperson, Avraham provide proofs of his religious teachings. This is very different from the attitude of the would-be missionaries described above who expect a person to radically reassess one's faith without any evidence.

"And Hashem spoke to Moshe and Ahron and He commanded them regarding Bnai Yisrael and Paroh the king of the Egyptians that they should take Bnai Yisrael out of Egypt." (Shemot 6:13)

This passage introduces a seemingly odd discussion. After this passage, the Chumash initiates a discussion of the families of Bnai Yisrael. The Torah enumerates the families of the tribe of Reuven. Then, the Torah lists the families of the tribe of Leyve. Once the Torah reaches Moshe and Ahron, this discussion ends.

In order to understand these passages, we must consider a related issue. Maimonides, in his Mishne Torah, describes the appropriate qualities for a judge of a major court. Among these qualities is lineage. There is a standard for the evaluation of this lineage. This standard is the ability to marry into a family of Kohanim. A candidate permitted to marry into a family of Kohanim, may be appointed as a judge of a major court. A person not permitted to marry into a family of Kohanim, is not appointed as a judge. What is the source for this requirement? Maimonides quotes a passage from Sefer BeMidbar.[17] There, seventy Elders are appointed to serve with Moshe. Hashem tells Moshe that these Elders, "will stand there with you." Maimonides explains that the phrase, "with you" implies that the Elders must be "with" Moshe in certain fundamental qualities.[18] Lineage is one of these qualities. Future judges of major courts are also required to meet this standard. Maimonides derives his comments directly from the Talmud in Tractate Sanhedrin. Nonetheless, this law and its derivation are difficult to understand. Moshe possessed various personal characteristics. These were physical qualities and spiritual perfections. The Torah tells us that all judges must posses some of Moshe's qualities. The Talmud concludes that one of the characteristics is lineage. However, the reason that lineage is chosen is unclear. Of all of Moshe's personal qualities, why is lineage so fundamental? Tosefot ask a similar question on the Talmud.[19] Another quality required in a judge of a major court is physical perfection. Certain physical blemishes render the judge unfit to serve. This requirement is derived from a specific passage. Tosefot note that according to the Talmud, Moshe was free of all blemishes. The Talmud maintains that there is an equation between Moshe and judges of major courts. This equation should be adequate to disqualify a person afflicted with a physical blemish. Why is a separate passage needed to disqualify candidates with such blemishes? Tosefot offer a rather enigmatic answer. They respond that the passage's equation is not adequate to disqualify a person with a blemish. Although it is difficult to understand Tosefot's answer, the

---

[17] Sefer BeMidbar 11:16.
[18] Rabbaynu Moshe ben Maimon (Rambam) Mishne Torah, Hilchot Sanhedrin 2:1.
[19] Tosefot, Mesechet Sanhedrin 36b.

general message is clear. The equation between Moshe and other judges is not total. The equation only extends to certain specific characteristics. Other characteristics of Moshe cannot be extended to all judges through this equation. Apparently, Tosefot maintain the physical perfection is one of the characteristics that cannot be implied through this equation. Therefore, this requirement must be established through a separate passage.

We must understand the limits of this equation. What characteristics are suggested by the equation? Rav Yitzchak Zev Soloveitchik suggests that the answer to this question is found in our passage. The Torah states the Hashem commanded Moshe regarding Bnai Yisrael. Sforno[20] explains that the passage is not telling us that Hashem provided Moshe and Ahron with specific instructions. The pasuk records the appointing of Moshe and Ahron, by Hashem, as the leaders of Bnai Yisrael. The following passages describe the families of Bnai Yisrael. However, the account suddenly stops once Moshe and Ahron are introduced. Rashi[21] comments that these passages are a description of Moshe and Ahron's lineage. In short, the Torah describes Moshe and Ahron's lineage in the context of their appointment as leaders. This answers all of our questions. All judges of major courts are equated to Moshe. They must share his perfect lineage. Why is lineage selected as a characteristic of Moshe that other judges must share? The answer is now obvious! This is the very quality the Torah immediately discusses following the appointment of Moshe and Ahron. Tosefot's comments are also easily understood. We cannot extend the equation between Moshe and other judges to include physical perfection. This quality is not discussed in reference to Moshe's appointment. Therefore, it is not included in the equation.[22]

These are the heads of their extended families. The sons of Reuven, the firstborn of Yisrael were Chanoch, Phalu, Chetzron, and Karmi. These were the families of Reuven. (Shemot 6:14)

The lineage of Moshe and Aharon and their Appointment as leaders

In our *parasha*, the Torah describes the lineage of Moshe and Aharon. This description begins with our *pasuk*. Why does the Torah provide with this narrative? Rabbaynu Ovadia Sforno explains that Moshe and Aharon were appointed as the leaders of Bnai Yisrael. The Torah provides us with the lineage of these individuals who were charged with the leadership of the Jewish people.[23]

This explanation is difficult to understand. Moshe was appointed as leader of Bnai Yisrael in Parshat Shemot. There, Moshe experienced his first prophecy. Hashem revealed that He would redeem Bnai Yisrael from bondage in Egypt and Moshe would lead the Jewish people out of Egypt and into the Land of Israel. At that time, Aharon was also appointed. He was assigned the task of speaking for Moshe before Bnai Yisrael and Paroh. Why is the Torah now describing the lineage of Moshe and Aharon? Their lineage should be recorded at the juncture of their initial appointment!

---

[20] Rabbaynu Ovadia Sforno, Commentary on Sefer Shemot 6:13.
[21] Rabbaynu Shlomo ben Yitzchak (Rashi), Commentary on Sefer Shemot 6:13.
[22] Rav Yitzchak Zev Soloveitchik, Chidushai MaRan RIZ HaLeyve on the Torah, Parshat VaEra.
[23] Rabbaynu Ovadia Sforno, *Commentary on Sefer Shemot*, 6:14.

In order to answer this question, we must deal with another issue. The end of Parshat Shemot describes Moshe and Aharon's initial conversation with Bnai Yisrael. The Torah explains that Aharon spoke to the people. He told the nation that Hashem would redeem the Jewish people from Egypt. Then, Moshe and Aharon addressed Paroh. They asked Paroh to allow Bnai Yisrael to enter the wilderness and serve Hashem. Apparently in this conversation, Aharon served as spokesman. Paroh was incensed with this request. In response, he increased the labor required of the Jewish people. The people confronted Moshe and Aharon and strongly criticized them for angering Paroh.

Moshe asked Hashem to explain these events. In the beginning of our *parasha*, relates the answer Hashem provided. Then, He told Moshe to speak with Bnai Yisrael and offer reassurance. Moshe obeyed. He spoke to the people. In this conversation, Aharon did not act as spokesman. Moshe addressed the nation directly. The question is obvious. Why did Moshe speak to the people? Aharon had been appointed as spokesman. Moshe was to provide the message Aharon was charged with responsibility for the delivery!

Hashem then instructed Moshe to again speak to Paroh and petition Paroh to release Bnai Yisrael. Moshe responded that he would not be effective. He was not an articulate speaker. He argued that he was unable to communicate with Bnai Yisrael. Certainly, there was little hope that he could motivate Paroh!

Clearly, Moshe's understanding was that he was to address Paroh. Aharon would not be his mouthpiece. Why did Moshe come to this conclusion? Aharon had already been appointed as spokesman!

Sforno offers an explanation for Moshe's actions. Moshe understood that Aharon was appointed to act as his spokesman. However, his understanding was that this appointment was limited. Aharon was appointed to present the initial messages to Bnai Yisrael and Paroh. Aharon did this. Moshe did not assume that an ongoing relationship had been created. Therefore, after the delivery of these first two messages, Moshe took-on the role of speaker. He understood Aharon's role to be over.[24]

Gershonides also explains Moshe's behavior. His explanation is similar to Sforno's. However, there is significant difference. He explains that Moshe was correct. His understanding of Aharon's appointment was completely accurate. Aharon's appointment as spokesperson was limited. He was assigned this role for the purpose of delivering the initial messages to Bnai Yisrael and Paroh. He did not have any ongoing authority. After the communication of these messages, Aharon could no longer speak for Moshe. Therefore, Moshe assumed the responsibility of communicating his prophesies. According to Gershonides, Moshe was completely correct!

Based on this insight, Gershonides answers our original question. Why is the lineage of Moshe and Aharon discussed in our *parasha*? He agrees that this lineage is recorded in the context of Moshe and Aharon's appointment as leaders. However, this leaves him with a problem. This appointment took place in Parshat Shemot!

Gershonides responds that the question is based upon a faulty premise. The leadership of Bnai Yisrael was not determined in Parshat Shemot. The relationship established there – that

---

[24] Rabbaynu Ovadia Sforno, *Commentary on Sefer Shemot*, 6:12.

Moshe would receive the message and transmit it to Aharon for communication – was not permanent or even ongoing. That relationship was created on a temporary basis. It would function during the initial communications with Bnai Yisrael and Paroh. It was not authorized beyond that point. In our *parasha,* an ongoing relationship is created. Moshe and Aharon would permanently assume the role of leaders.

This answers our question. The Torah records the lineage of Moshe and Aharon in our *parasha*. This is because only at this point is the leadership finalized. With this finalization, it is appropriate to record the lineage of the leaders.[25]

"And Egypt will know that I am Hashem when I stretch my hand over Egypt and I take out Bnai Yisrael from among them." (Shemot 7:5)

We have all been moved by the death and destruction brought about by the recent tsunami. I have received many emails from various Jewish organizations that are involved in raising funds for disaster relief. Each of these organizations has contacted our school and requested that we make every effort to support their efforts. However, at the same time, I have been following an interesting dialogue on the web critiquing this massive fundraising effort. One of the issues alluded to in this dialogue relates to our responsibility as Jews for non-Jews. Are we responsible to respond to a tragedy that primarily affects non-Jews?

This week's *parasha* speaks directly to this issue. In the above passage, Hashem tells Moshe that He will punish the Egyptians with terrible plagues. Through experiencing this punishment, the Egyptians will come to recognize Hashem. In the context of our redemptions from Egypt, this is a strange statement. We generally, assume that the events of the redemption were designed essentially or exclusively for the benefit of Bnai Yisrael. The Egyptians were punished in order to save the Jewish people. Yet, this passage seems to state that this popular view is not entirely accurate. According to the *pasuk*, the plagues Hashem brought upon the Egyptians were not solely designed to benefit Bnai Yisrael. The plagues had an additional purpose. Hashem's also intended – through the plagues – to educate the Egyptians.

Gershonides argues that there is no contradiction between our *pasuk* and the view that the plagues were designed exclusively for the benefit of Bnai Yisrael. According to Gershonides, Hashem was not interested in the perfection of the Egyptians. However, it was important to discourage the Egyptians from pursuing Bnai Yisrael. The plagues and the destruction of the Egyptian army at the Reed Sea would persuade the remnant of the Egyptian people that they could not overcome the will of Hashem. Hashem told Moshe that Egypt will be thoroughly defeated and through this defeat it will recognize that it cannot battle the will of the Almighty.[26]

However, Sforno has a completely different understanding of our passage. According to his view, Hashem was concerned with the perfection of the Egyptians. Hashem told Moshe that he would bring plagues upon the Egyptians and punish them for their treatment of the Jewish people, in order to provide a compelling moral lesson. The plagues and punishments were designed to save Bnai Yisrael

---

[25] Rabbaynu Levi ben Gershon (Ralbag / Gershonides), *Commentary on Sefer Shemot*, (Mosad HaRav Kook), pp. 28-29.
[26] Rabbaynu Levi ben Gershon (Ralbag / Gershonides), *Commentary on Sefer Shemot*, (Mosad HaRav Kook, 1994), p 30.

and to demonstrate to the Egyptians Hashem's awesome power over the universe and His justice. Hopefully, they would learn the lesson communicated by their experience and repent.[27]

It is clear from Sforno's comments that Hashem is not concerned with the welfare of only Bnai Yisrael. His attention is also directed towards the welfare of all peoples of the world. This outlook is reflected in many of the comments and observations of our Sages.

Rav Tzvi Hirsch Chajes discusses at length the Torah's attitude towards non-Jews and its expectations regarding our relationship with the non-Jewish community. His discussion begins with the investigation of an interesting paradox. Rav Chajes observes that the Sages instituted a number of restrictions regarding our interactions with non-Jews. For example, it is prohibited to travel or be alone with a non-Jew. It is prohibited to seek medical treatment from a non-Jew.[28] These and various other injunctions are indicative of a basic and intense distrust of non-Jews. But Rav Chajes observes that other statements of our Sages express a very different perspective. The Mishne teaches – according to Rav Chajes' interpretation – that we are not permitted to treat any person disgracefully.[29] Rav Chajes asserts that the requirement to treat others with respect applies to our interactions with all people – Jewish or non-Jewish. The Mishne also teaches that the human being must be regarded a precious creation; we are created in the image of G-d.[30] Rav Chajes quotes the comments of Tosefot Yom Tov on this Mishne. Tosefot Yom Tov observes that the Mishne is apparently referring to all human beings – Jews and non-Jews. We are all created in Hashem's image.[31]

How can we reconcile these two very different perspectives? We are instructed to conduct ourselves with extreme care and caution in our interaction with non-Jews. Yet, we are required to treat all human beings with the greatest respect! Rav Chajes observes that the answer lies in understanding the context of the injunctions limiting our interactions with non-Jews. He explains that these injunctions reflect the reality of the historical relationship between the Jewish and non-Jewish communities. Our Sages lived in an environment in which this relationship was predicated upon intense anti-Semitism. During much of our history – and even in modern times – the murder of a Jew has not been viewed as a crime or even worthy of casual condemnation. Our Sages were responding to this unpleasant and dangerous reality. Their injunctions were a response to this historical relationship and designed to protect the safety of the Jewish community.

This interpretation is supported by Maimonides' treatment of these injunctions. He includes his description of these injunctions in his discussion of the laws governing our obligation to care for our health and well-being. The inclusion of these injunctions in this discussion indicates that these prohibitions are not designed to foster segregation or inform our attitudes towards non-Jews. Instead, they are intended to protect and insure the safety of the community.

Based on this understanding of these injunctions, Rav Chajes explains that they do not at all contradict the imperative to respect and cherish all human beings. Every person is a reflection of the Creator and we must build our relationships upon that foundation. However, this does not mean that we can act without caution or disregard our personal safety.

---

[27] Rabbaynu Ovadia Sforno, *Commentary on Sefer Shemot*, 74.
[28] Rabbaynu Moshe ben Maimon (Rambam) *Mishne Torah*, Hilchot Rotzeach U'Shemirat HaNefesh 12:7-12.
[29] Mesechet Avot 4:3.
[30] Mesechet Avot 3:14.
[31] Rav Yom Tov Lippman, *Tosefot Yom Tov Commentary on Mesechet Avot* 3:14.

Perhaps, the most interesting part of Rav Chajes' discussion deals with the Torah's attitude towards other major religions – specifically Islam and Christianity. The level of religious tolerance expressed in these comments is remarkable. In order to appreciate his comments we must first acknowledge that conventional religions are not generally notable for their tolerant attitudes. Many of the most vicious wars and persecutions have been justified on religious grounds. In our own time this remains true. If we consider the various conflicts around the word, differences over religious doctrine remain a common element underlying many of these conflicts – or at least a basis used for their justification.

In general, each religion claims to be the absolute and incontrovertible truth. The corollary of this contention is that all other religions should be suppressed. Followers of other faiths are condemned to damnation and should be either converted or eliminated. Rav Chajes contrasts this general, prevalent outlook with the Torah's perspective. Rav Chajes must acknowledge that we contend that the Torah is a divinely revealed truth. However, this conviction does not generate the intolerance commonly associated with organized religion. The Torah does condemn – in the most unequivocal terms – idolatry. However, the Torah establishes specific perimeters for classifying idolatry. Religious faiths that do not fall within these perimeters are not condemned. The Torah does not endorse the details of these faiths, but neither does it suggest that we should persecute or mistreat the adherents of these religions. Rav Chajes – in a lengthy analysis – concludes that neither Christianity nor Islam come close to falling within the perimeters of idolatry. Therefore, we are required to demonstrate uncompromised tolerance towards these religions.

Rav Chajes closes his comments with another remarkable observation. Most religions contend that its adherents have the exclusive rights of entry into heaven. One who accepts the tenets of the faith is assured eternity and those who reject the religion are condemned to eternal damnation. Rav Chajes' observes that this is not the view of the Torah. According to the Torah, a non-Jew who accepts the seven Noahide laws as a revealed truth is worthy of eternity.[32] Furthermore, we are required to care for and sustain these individuals.[33] Rav Chajes observes that both Christianity and Islam accept these laws as a revealed truth and direct their adherents to observe these laws. On this basis, they are worthy of eternity and deserve our support.[34]

I realize that this brief summary is not a comprehensive treatment of these issues and certainly additional issues can be raised. But I hope that these thoughts will provide some insight and direction.

"When Paroh will say to you, "Provide for yourself a *mofait* (wonder)." And you will say to Ahron, "Take your staff and throw it before Paroh. It will become a *tanin* (serpent)." (Shemot 7:9)

The wonders that Moshe and Ahron performed in Egypt are referred to with two terms. These terms are *ote* and *mofait*. What is the difference between these terms?

Sforno explains that these terms have very different meanings. These meanings can be understood through better appreciating Moshe's situation. Moshe claimed to be the messenger of a G-d. This G-d was represented as the absolute ruler of the universe. Moshe's credibility

---

[32] Rabbaynu Moshe ben Maimon (Rambam) *Mishne Torah*, Hilchot Melachim 8:11.
[33] Rabbaynu Moshe ben Maimon (Rambam) *Mishne Torah*, Hilchot Esurai Biah 14:7-8.
[34] Rav Tzvi Hirsch Chajes, *Teferet LeYisrael(Collected Writings,* pp 483-491).

depended upon his response to two issues. He must prove that he was the messenger of Hashem. He must also prove that Hashem is omnipotent.

The term *mofait* is best translated as wonder. A *mofait* provides evidence of the Almighty's authority over the physical universe. Paroh denied that Hashem possessed this power. Paroh required a *mofait*. He could only be convinced by a wondrous act that would testify to the awesome power of the Almighty. The transformation of Ahron's inanimate staff into a living creature served this purpose.

The term *ote* means sign. Bnai Yisrael accepted the existence of a Creator. The Creator rules the universe He formed. However, Moshe was required to establish that he was the messenger of Hashem. They needed an *ote* or sign that Moshe was Hashem's servant. Moshe's ability to alter nature indicated that he had been empowered by Almighty.

Sforno notes that the same act can function both as an *ote* and *mofait*. The purpose of the act will determine the term by which it is described. Therefore, the transformation of the staff before Paroh was a *mofait*. The same act performed in front of Bnai Yisrael was an *ote*.[35]

And Paroh called to the wise men and to the magicians. And the sorcerers of Egypt also did so with their sorcery. (Shemot 7:11)

The transformation of Aharon's staff into a serpent

Moshe and Aharon perform their first wonder before Paroh. Moshe instructs Aharon to cast his staff in front of Paroh. The staff miraculously is transformed into a *tanin* – a serpent. Paroh summons his wise men and magicians. These are the masters of Egyptian sorcery. Paroh instructs his servants to duplicate Moshe and Aharon's miracle. The sorcerers are able to duplicate the transformation to Paroh's satisfaction. However, Moshe and Aharon prove that their miracle is superior. Aharon's serpent swallows the serpent produced by the Egyptians.

How were the Egyptians able to duplicate the miracle performed by Moshe and Aharon? The commentaries explain that the magicians had not really performed a transformation. These sorcerers were masters of illusion. They used their skills to create an illusion of a serpent. Rabbaynu Ovadia Sforno explains that the serpent created by the sorcerers was not a living creature. Their illusion of a serpent had no movement. This distinction was demonstrated when Aharon's serpent swallowed the sham serpent created by the Egyptians.[36]

Malbim offers a different explanation of the magician's illusion. The key to Malbim's explanation lies in the details of the episode. This was not the first time Moshe had performed the miracle of transforming the inanimate into a living creature. Hashem had instructed Moshe to transform his staff for Bnai Yisrael. However, in that incident, the staff had been converted into a snake. The transformation performed in Paroh's presence was much more impressive. The staff became a serpent. A snake has dimensions similar to the staff. A serpent is a large creature.

Malbim explains that the magicians used the serpent's size to their advantage. Their illusion required the coordinated efforts of two parties. One magician threw forth his staff. A second magician was hiding nearby. This accomplice was disguised as a serpent. As the staff

---

[35] Rabbaynu Ovadia Sforno, *Commentary on Sefer Shemot*, 7:9.
[36] Rabbaynu Ovadia Sforno, *Commentary on Sefer Shemot*, 7:12.

flew through the air, the second magician jumped forth from his hiding place. He grabbed the staff in mid-air, hid it within his disguise and landed on the ground. These magicians were experts in this type of deception. They carefully arranged the lighting and other factors. It appeared that the magician's staff had been transformed.[37]

What was this creature that the Chumash calls a serpent or *tanin*? How were the Egyptians able to create a convincing disguise to use in their illusion? In 1481 a Jewish traveler, Meshulam ben Rav Manahem, traveled from Italy to Rhodes. From Rhodes Meshulam traveled through much of the Middle East. His travels took him to the Land of Israel and also Egypt. He kept a diary of his travels. As Meshulam traveled along the Nile, he was astonished to encounter very large serpents. Many were larger than humans. He describes these serpents in detail. He also indicates the name given to these serpents in various languages. In English, they are called crocodiles.[38]

This account seems to support the explanation of Malbim. The serpent costume might well have been the complete skin of a crocodile. Unfortunately for the Egyptians, a man in a crocodile suit is no match for the real thing – Aharon's serpent.

"And Paroh's heart was strong and he did not listen to them, as Hashem had spoken. And Hashem said to Moshe, "Paroh's heart is heavy; he has refused to send forth the nation." (Shemot 7:13-14)

Parshat VaEyrah describes Moshe's efforts to persuade Paroh to release Bnai Yisrael. Most of the plagues are described in this parasha. Each of these plagues was miraculous. Each afflicted the Egyptians with suffering and misery. Each demonstrated that Moshe was Hashem's prophet. Nonetheless, Paroh withstood these plagues and remained steadfast in his refusal to release Bnai Yisrael.

Our passage describes Paroh's response to the first of the wonders that Moshe and Aharon performed before him. Moshe and Aharon appear before Paroh. Aharon throws his staff to the ground and it is transformed into a serpent. Paroh instructs his magicians to duplicate Aharon's feat. They throw their staffs to the ground and they also are transformed into serpents. But Aharon's serpent swallows the serpents of the magician.

Our pasuk tells us that Paroh was unmoved by this demonstration. The Torah uses two terms to describe Paroh's reaction. First, we are told that Paroh's heart was strong. Then, Hashem speaks to Moshe and describes Paroh's heart as heavy. Apparently, these two descriptions are intended to communicate two ideas regarding Paroh's obstinacy. However, the precise difference between these two ideas – that Paroh's heart was strong and it was heavy – is not completely clear.

In order to understand the meaning of these two terms it is useful to first consider a related issue: Until the sixth plague, each time that the Torah refers to Paroh's "strong heart," the Torah tells us that Paroh's heart was strong. However, with the advent of the plague of shechin – boils – the Torah introduces a different phraseology.

---

[37] Rav Meir Leibush ben Yechiel Michel (Malbim), *HaTorah VeHaMitzvah – Commentary on Sefer Shemot*, 7:11.
[38] Elkan Nathan Adler ed., *Jewish Travelers of the Middle Ages* (Dover,1987), p 164.

"But Hashem strengthened Paroh's heart, and he did not listen to them, as Hashem had spoken to Moshe." (Shemot 9:12)

After experiencing the plague of shechin, the Torah does not tell us that Paroh's heart was strong. Instead, we are told that Hashem made Paroh's heart strong. This seems to imply that until this plague Paroh's obstinacy was "self-induced." Now, Hashem is inducing Paroh's obstinacy. What had changed? Why was it now necessary for Hashem to influence Paroh's reaction and reinforce his obstinacy? Nachmanides discusses this issue: He contends that there was a basic difference between the initial wonders performed by Moshe and Aharon and the last five plagues. In order to understand this distinction, it is helpful to review these initial miracles.

Let us return to the first wonder performed by Moshe and Aharon. Both Aharon and Paroh's magicians performed wondrous transformations. However, there was a distinction between their feats. Aharon's serpent consumed the serpents created by the Egyptian magicians. Rashbam suggests that despite this distinction, Paroh concluded that there was no fundamental difference between the wonder performed by Moshe and Aharon and the transformation executed by his magicians. He assumed that both were achieved through magic or illusion.[39]

"And the magicians of Egypt did likewise with their secret rites, and Paroh's heart was strong, and he did not heed them, as Hashem had spoken." (Shemot 7:22)

The first plague brought about by Moshe and Aharon was the transformation of all uncovered water in Egypt into blood. Again, Paroh's magicians claimed that they too could perform this transformation. They filled a vessel with water and transformed it into blood. Rabbaynu Avraham ibn Ezra notes that there was a substantial difference between the wonder performed by Moshe and Aharon and the trick of the Egyptian magicians. The magicians did succeed in turning a small amount of water directly in front of them into blood. However, Moshe and Aharon transformed all the uncovered water in the land into blood. Furthermore, the phenomenon that they brought about was lasting. As new water flowed into the land, it too was transformed into blood.[40] Rashi explains that despite this obvious distinction, Paroh chose to view both transformations as essentially equal. He asserted that Moshe and Aharon's methods were no different from those of the magicians.[41]

"And the magicians did likewise with their secret rites to bring out the lice, but they could not, and the lice were upon man and beast. And the magicians said to Paroh, "It is the finger of God," but Paroh's heart remained strong, and he did not listen to them, as Hashem had spoken." (Shemot 8:14-15)

Aharon struck the dust and lice were brought forth. These lice infested the Egyptians and their animals. This was the third plague. Again, Paroh's magicians attempted to duplicate the wonder performed by Moshe and Aharon. However, this time they failed. They were forced to acknowledge that this plague was not a manipulation of the forces with which they were familiar. They admitted that this plague was an act of G-d. Again, Paroh's heart is strong and he remains obstinate.

---

[39] Rabbaynu Shemuel ben Meir (Rashbam) *Commentary on Sefer Shemot,* 7:13.
[40] Rabbaynu Avraham ibn Ezra, *Commentary on Sefer Shemot,* 7:22.
[41] Rabbaynu Shlomo ben Yitzchak (Rashi), *Commentary on Sefer Shemot,* 7:22.

However in this instance, Paroh's reaction is difficult to understand. How could he remain obstinate even after his own magicians admitted that this plague was an act of G-d? Furthermore, the passages juxtapose the admission of the magicians with Paroh's continued stubbornness! This seems to imply that their admission somehow encouraged Paroh's continued obstinacy.

There are various responses to this problem. Rabbaynu Avraham ibn Ezra contends that the magicians did acknowledge that this plague was different from those that preceded it. However, he notes that they did not advise Paroh that it had been brought about by Hashem – the deity introduced by Moshe and Aharon. Instead, they described the plague and an act of G-d. Their intention – in making this distinction – was that the plague was a natural phenomenon and did not represent an act of providence. Paroh accepted the magician's explanation and continued to refuse to release Bnai Yisrael.[42]

Nachmanides explains that in each of these instances Paroh did experience fear and anxiety. However, in each instance, he accepted the contention of his magicians that the wonder, or plague, could be explained or minimized. With the encouragement of his magicians he overcame and dismissed his fears. In other words, in each of these instances, Paroh engaged in a pseudo-intellectual analysis of the phenomenon he had witnessed and experienced. The fallacy of the magicians' claims was evident. But Paroh chose to dismiss his fears and doubts and accepted the questionable explanations offered by the magicians.[43] Now, let us consider the plague of shechin – boils.

"And the magicians could not stand before Moshe because of the boils, for the boils were upon the magicians and upon all Egypt. But Hashem strengthened Paroh's heart, and he did not listen to them, as Hashem spoke to Moshe." (Shemot 9:11-12)

Nachmanides explains that the plague of shechin completely undermined the influence of Paroh's magicians. They too experienced the misery of the plague. They could not duplicate the plague or even protect themselves from the affliction. They were embarrassed to appear before Paroh and offered no further explanations of Moshe's power. Paroh could no longer resort to his pseudo-intellectual rationalizations. His heart could no longer draw strength from the encouragements offered by the magicians. But now Hashem strengthened Paroh's heart. He gave Paroh the ability to dismiss the overwhelming evidence of Moshe's power and relationship with Hashem.

Based on this analysis, it seems that "strengthening of heart" describes Paroh's analysis of the wonders and plagues he observed and experienced. Paroh did not wish to accept Moshe's claims that he represented Hashem and acted as His agent. He was presented, time and again, with evidence supporting Moshe's claim. But in each instance, he dismissed the objective implications of the evidence in order to sustain his corrupt, biased world-view. Let us compare this to the reaction described by a "heavy heart."

"When Paroh saw that there was relief, he made his heart heavy, and he did not listen to them, as Hashem had spoken." (Shemot 8:10)

---

[42] Rabbaynu Avraham ibn Ezra, *Commentary on Sefer Shemot*, 8:15.
[43] Rabbaynu Moshe ben Nachman (Ramban), *Commentary on Sefer Shemot* 7:19.

The passage describes Paroh's response to the second plague – frogs. Aharon extended his staff over the waters of Egypt and a swarm of frogs emerged. The frogs overran the land. Paroh's magicians were also able to bring forth a few frogs. But their unimpressive imitation of Moshe and Aharon's plague did little to relieve Paroh and the Egyptians from the infestation. Paroh was reduced to begging Moshe to end the plague. Moshe complied and the frogs died – leaving the land covered with their carcasses. Here, there is no mention of Paroh strengthening his heart. He had been forced to submit to Moshe and beg for his assistance. No explanation offered by the magicians could relieve Paroh of his humiliation. Yet, Paroh remained obstinate. The Torah does not indicate that Paroh's stubbornness was founded upon any rationalization. Instead, the Torah tells us that Paroh saw that the plague had ended. With the removal of the pressure that the plague had exerted upon him, he returned to his former obstinacy.

"And Hashem did according to Moshe's word, and He removed the mixture of wild beasts from Paroh, from his servants, and from his people; not one was left. And Paroh made his heart heavy this time also, and he did not send forth the nation." (Shemot 8:27-28)

The forth plague was an invasion of wild beasts. In this instance, Paroh's magicians did not make an appearance. They did not offer Paroh council or attempt to minimize Moshe's actions. With Egypt overrun with wild beasts, it is unlikely Paroh would have had much interest in or patience for the magicians' explanations. Again, Paroh is forced to appeal to Moshe. Moshe prays to Hashem and the wild beasts retreat from the land. Paroh makes his heart heavy and refuses to release Bnai Yisrael.

As in the instance of the plague of frogs, Paroh's stubbornness is not founded upon any rationalization or minimization of Moshe's claims. Again, with the removal of the suffering and fear engendered by the plague, Paroh returns to his previous obstinacy.

We can now appreciate the difference between these two phrases: "strengthening of the heart" and "making the heart heavy." Paroh's "strong heart" describes his dismissal of any evidence that would threaten his world-view. It describes a complete retreat and embracement of a false and imagined view of reality. It is an intellectual failure. Paroh's "heavy heart" describes a different reaction. Heavy objects are difficult to move. If an object is extremely heavy, only a massive force cannot budge it. The moment that force is eliminated, the object will come to rest. The plagues were this massive force. They were powerful enough to move Paroh. But the moment a plague ended, Paroh's "heavy heart" came to rest. Paroh's "heavy heart" describes his total inability to alter his engrained patterns of behavior.

Perhaps, there is a little bit of Paroh in most people. We need to be careful not to become so attached to our views and perspectives that we are dismissive of evidence that challenges our world-view. We must also recognize that we too can become fixed in a pattern of behavior that is outmoded and unrealistic. We must take care that our decisions are not merely an attempt to preserve these habitual patterns.

And the sorcerers of Egypt also did so with their sorcery. And Paroh's heart became strong. And he did not listen to them, as Hashem had foretold. (Shemot 7:22)

Pharoh's Sorcerers' Imitations of Moshe's Wonders

Hashem instructed Moshe to perform the first plague. Aharon struck the river with his staff. All of the water in Egypt was transformed into blood. Paroh summoned his sorcerers. They were also able to change water into blood. Paroh concluded that the wonder performed by Moshe and Aharon had been duplicated by the magicians. He decided that Moshe had not proven himself to be Hashem's prophet, nor had he established Hashem's omnipotence. He refused to release Bnai Yisrael.

It seems odd that Hashem should command Moshe to perform a miracle that could be duplicated by these magicians! Why did Hashem not instruct Moshe to offer more convincing proof of his claims?

Rabbeinu Avraham ibn Ezra explains that the transformation performed by the Egyptians was a weak imitation of the miracle performed by Moshe and Aharon. He outlines three essential differences. First, Moshe and Aharon transformed all the water in Egypt. The magicians only changed a small quantity of water into blood. Second, the water altered by Moshe and Aharon was flowing. As new water entered Egypt, it was changed into blood. The sorcerers performed their illusion with stagnant water held in a utensil. Third, the miracle performed by Moshe and Aharon continued for a period of days. However, the water transformed by the Egyptians only retained the appearance of blood for a short period.[44]

The miracle performed by Moshe and Aharon provided adequate proof of their claims. This evidence was not truly challenged by the trick of the magicians. Paroh chose to equate the illusion of the sorcerers to the miracle of Moshe and Aharon. This choice provided him a rationalization for refusing to heed the message of Hashem.

"And the magicians said to Paroh. "It is the finger of the L-rd." And Paroh's heart became hard and he did not listen to them as Hashem had spoken." (Shemot 8:15)

Paroh's magicians could not duplicate the plague of Lice. They told Paroh that this plague was the "finger of the L-rd". Rashi seems to indicate that the magicians were attesting to the authenticity of Moshe's claims. This plague was caused by the G-d of the Jewish people. Moshe was His agent. Hashem was intervening in nature to save His people.[45]

Rabbaynu Avraham ibn Ezra disagrees with this interpretation. The magicians did not say that the plague was from *Hashem*. They counseled that the cause was the *L-rd*. Ibn Ezra explains that the Egyptians did not deny the existence of a Creator. They understood that this Creator ruled the universe through a system of natural law. The issue in dispute was the Torah concept of a Creator with a providential relationship to His people. This understanding of G-d is expressed by the Tetragrammaton – the name we pronounce as "Hashem". The Creator fashioned a universe in which natural disasters occur. Floods, earthquakes, terrible storms destroy cities and even civilizations. The magicians did not understand such phenomenon to be providential. The magicians acknowledged that this plague was not merely an illusion or impressive trick. It was the work of the Creator. But, they claimed, it did not support the concept of Hashem.[46]

Nachmanides offers a third interpretation. The magicians accepted Moshe's claim that the plague was from Hashem. They did not use this name. It was a foreign term to the Egyptians. Speaking among themselves, they would not refer to G-d with an unfamiliar name. However

---

[44] Rabbeinu Avraham ibn Ezra, *Commentary on Sefer Shemot*, 7:22.
[45] Rabbaynu Shlomo ben Yitzchak (Rashi), *Commentary on Sefer Shemot* 8:15.
[46] Rabbaynu Avraham ibn Ezra, *Commentary on Sefer Shemot*, 8:15.

they claimed it was only the "finger" of G-d. The plague caused discomfort and some suffering. However, it was not catastrophic. They advised Paroh to be calm – to recognize the limited effect of the plague and maintain his resolve.[47]

And I will set apart on that day the Land of Goshen in which My nation dwells so that there will not be wild beasts there. Through this, you will know that I, Hashem, am in the midst of the Land. (Shemot 8:18)
Bnai Yisrael's Exclusion from the Plague of Wild Beasts

Hashem announces the fourth plague to Moshe. He tells Moshe,that in this plague, will not affect the Land of Goshen. Wild beasts will overwhelm all of Egypt. However, the Land of Goshen – in which Bnai Yisrael live – will be protected from the infestation. This protection will provide another indication of the providential nature of the plagues.

This creates an interesting question. Did the first three plagues affect Bnai Yisrael? The simple implication of the passage is that Bnai Yisrael were not spared from the plagues of Blood, Frogs, and Lice. Only now would Hashem differentiate between the Jewish people and the Egyptians. Rabbaynu Avraham ibn Ezra explains that this indeed was the case. Bnai Yisrael experienced the first three plagues. During the plague of Blood, the Egyptians were forced to dig wells to secure potable water. The Jews were required to take the same measures. Bnai Yisrael also suffered through the Frogs and Lice. However, now Hashem differentiated between the two nations.

Why did Hashem only begin to differentiate now? Rabbaynu Avraham ibn Ezra explains that there is a basic difference between the plague of Wild Beasts and the previous punishments. The plagues were progressively more severe. The first three plagues caused discomfort and suffering. However, they did not endanger the people. Hashem does not perform miracles gratuitously. Bnai Yisrael was not mortally threatened by these first plagues. Therefore, they were not spared from them. The plague of Wild Beasts added a new dimension to the torment of the Egyptians. Now, their lives were threatened. It was necessary for the miracle of the plague to be accompanied by another miracle. The Jewish people would be protected from the infestation.[48]

Nachmanides disagrees. He maintains that Bnai Yisrael were protected from all of the plagues. The Jews did not experience the previous plagues of Blood, Frogs, and Lice. What, then, is the meaning of our passage? Nachmanides explains that Hashem is not saying that He will now first separate the Jews from the suffering of the Egyptians. Hashem is telling Moshe that this protection will have a new significance. This special protection will reinforce the providential nature of the plagues. The previous plagues could be interpreted as localized phenomena. The water of Goshen was not contaminated. Frogs and Lice did not fill the Land of Goshen. This could be explained through natural causes. However, no natural explanation could be offered for the rescue of Goshen from the wild beasts. These beasts roam at will. They should have infested Goshen. But somehow they were held back. This was a miracle. The influence of Hashem was clearly demonstrated.[49]

---

[47] Rabbaynu Moshe ben Nachman (Ramban), *Commentary on Sefer Shemot* 8:15.
[48] Rabbeinu Avraham ibn Ezra, *Commentary on Sefer Shemot*, 7:24.
[49] Rabbeinu Moshe ben Nachman (Ramban), *Commentary on Sefer Shemot* 8:18.

It seems that Ibn Ezra and Nachmanides have different views on the message the plagues were intended to communicate. According to Ibn Ezra, the plagues were designed as punishments for the Egyptians and as demonstrations of Hashem's omnipotence. The first three plagues also affected Bnai Yisrael. This was not their intended purpose. However, this incidental impact did not detract from the effectiveness of the plagues. The Egyptians suffered as intended and they witnessed Hashem's power over the elements of their environment. Bnai Yisrael was shielded from the plague of Wild Beasts only because of the physical devastation caused by the plague.

Nachmanides agrees that the plagues were intended as punishments and as demonstrations of Hashem's omnipotence. However, he maintains that the plagues were also intended to differentiate between the Egyptians and Bnai Yisrael. Each plague not only communicated Hashem's displeasure with the Egyptians and His power over the material world; it also communicated the cause of His anger and His ultimate objective. The exclusion of Bnai Yisrael from the affects of the plagues demonstrated that His anger was on their behalf and His objective was their liberation.

"And Moshe said to him, "When I leave the city, I will spread my hands to Hashem. The thunder will cease. There will not be any more hail. This is so you will know that the land is Hashem's." (Shemot 9:29)

Our *pasuk* describes the conclusion of the plague of hail. Paroh beseeches Moshe to pray to Hashem. He should appeal to the Almighty to end the plague. Moshe responds that he will comply. However, he adds an important phrase. He tells Paroh that first he will leave the city. Only then, will he spread his hands to Hashem in prayer. Why did Moshe stipulate that he must first leave the city?

Rashi quotes the Midrash Michilta in response to this question. The Midrash explains that the city was permeated with idols. Moshe would not pray in this abominable environment. First, he would remove himself from this city of idolatry. Only then, would he pray to Hashem.[50]

Moshe was waging a battle against idolatry. He was asserting that Hashem is the only true G-d. The deities of Egypt were false gods. He would not pray in a place dominated by these idols. Perhaps, he feared that his prayers might be misinterpreted as appeals to the abominations of the Egyptians. He would leave the city and its idols. He would pray to Hashem only in a place free of these false gods.

The commentaries are troubled by the Midrash's comments. This was not the first occasion on which Moshe prayed on behalf of Paroh and the Egyptians. On these other occasions, Moshe did not stipulate that he must first leave the city. Why, now, does Moshe add this requirement?

Rav Naftali Tzvi Yehuda Berlin *Zt"l* – the Netziv – offers an answer to this question. His answer is based upon a previous passage. Let us consider this *pasuk*.

As we have explained above, Moshe was not immediately successful in winning the support of Bnai Yisrael. His initial appeal to Paroh resulted in an intensification of the bondage. Bnai Yisrael sharply criticized Moshe for this outcome. Moshe sought an explanation from

---

[50] Rabbaynu Shlomo ben Yitzchak (Rashi), *Commentary on Sefer Shemot* 9:29.

Hashem. The Torah uses an interesting phrase in describing Moshe's communion with the Almighty. The Torah says that Moshe "returned to Hashem" and sought His counsel.[51]

Netziv asserts that this phrase should be understood somewhat literally. Moshe actually went somewhere. He went to a place that he had designated for prayer and prophecy. He had established a synagogue – a *Bait HaKenesset*. Moshe retreated to this sacred place to commune with the Almighty.[52]

Netziv explains that this provides a partial answer to our question. Actually, each time Moshe prayed to Hashem he carefully considered his environment. He was consistently concerned with the problem of praying to Hashem in place associated with idolatry. In order to address this issue, Moshe established a special place that was sacred and devoted to the worship of the Almighty. Each time Moshe prayed or sought prophecy, he retreated to his *Bait HaKenesset*.

Netziv acknowledges that this insight does not completely answer our question. Why did Moshe now insist on leaving the city? Why did Moshe not follow his established practice? He should have entered his synagogue and prayed to Hashem?

Netziv explains that the answer is provided by another stipulation made by Moshe. He told Parch that his prayers would be accompanied by a physical demonstration. Moshe would spread his hands to Hashem. Netziv explains that Moshe intended to spread his hands towards the heavens. This could not be done inside a building. Moshe intended to pray outside.

Moshe could not fulfill this requirement in his *Bait HaKenesset*. Therefore, he was confronted with a problem. He would not pray to Hashem in a place associated with idolatry. Yet, his accustomed refuge was indoors and consequently inappropriate for the prayer he planned. Moshe solved his dilemma by leaving the city. In this manner, he was able to pray outside in a proper environment.[53]

Netziv's insight provides an explanation for an amazing *halacha*. Tur explains that one should always pray in a *Bait HaKenesset*. He adds that the synagogue must have a *minyan* a quorum of ten males. Bait Yosef observes that there is an obvious implication in Tur's formulation of this *halacha*. If a synagogue does not have a *minyan*, one is not required to pray there. Bait Yosef questions this formulation. He explains that many Sages maintain that one should pray in a *Bait HaKenesset* regardless of the presence of a *minyan*. He explains the reason for this position. A synagogue is designated for prayer.[54]

Why is this designation important? According to the comments of Netziv, we can answer this question. Prayer involves making an exclusive commitment to the service of

Hashem. Like Moshe, we live in an environment that is dominated by the expressions of other religions. It is appropriate for us to remove ourselves from our ambient surroundings when demonstrating our exclusive devotion to Hashem. The synagogue provides this opportunity. It is our refuge. It is a place completed designated for the service of the Almighty.

---

[51] Sefer Shemot 5:22.
[52] Rav Naftali Tzvi Yehuda Berlin (Netziv), *Commentary Hamek Davar on Sefer Shemot* 5:22.
[53] Rav Naftali Tzvi Yehuda Berlin (Netziv), *Commentary Hamek Davar on Sefer Shemot* 9:29.
[54] Rabbaynu Yaakov ben HaRash, *Tur Shulchan Aruch, Orech Chayim* 90.

"When Paroh will say to you, "Provide for yourself a mofait (wonder)." And you will say to Ahron, "Take your staff and throw it before Paroh. It will become a tanin (serpent)." (Shemot 7:9)

The wonders that Moshe and Ahron performed in Egypt are referred to with two terms. These terms are ote and mofait. What is the difference between these terms? Sforno explains that these terms have very different meanings. These meanings can be understood through better appreciating Moshe's situation. Moshe claimed to be the messenger of a G-d. This G-d was represented as the absolute ruler of the universe. Moshe's credibility depended upon his response to two issues. He must prove that he was the messenger of Hashem. He must also prove that Hashem is omnipotent.

The term mofait is best translated as wonder. A mofait provides evidence of the Almighty's authority over the physical universe. Paroh denied that Hashem possessed this power. Paroh required a mofait. He could only be convinced by a wondrous act that would testify to the awesome power of the Almighty. The transformation of Ahron's inanimate staff into a living creature served this purpose.

The term ote means sign. Bnai Yisrael accepted the existence of a Creator. The Creator rules the universe He formed. However, Moshe was required to establish that he was the messenger of Hashem. They needed an ote or sign that Moshe was Hashem's servant. Moshe's ability to alter nature indicated that he had been empowered by Almighty.

Sforno notes that the same act can function both as an ote and mofait. The purpose of the act will determine the term by which it is described. Therefore, the transformation of the staff before Paroh was a mofait. The same act performed in front of Bnai Yisrael was an ote.[55]

"And the river will swarm with frogs. And they will emerge and go into your house and bedroom and bed. And they will enter the houses of your servants and people and into your ovens and kneading bowls." (Shemot 7:28)

Hashem instructs Moshe to threaten Paroh with the plague of frogs. Moshe is to describe the extent of the plague. The frogs will infest the entire land. They will overrun the homes of the Egyptians. They will even invade their beds and ovens. These instructions stress the impact of the plague upon the Egyptians. This raises a question. Would Bnai Yisrael also suffer from this plague? Would Bnai Yisrael somehow be spared from this affliction? Our Sages differ on this issue.

Maimonides[56] presents his view in his commentary on Tractate Avot. The mishne in Tractate Avot states[57] that our ancestors experienced ten miracles in Egypt. What were these ten miracles? Maimonides asserts that the plagues only affected the Egyptians. The frogs did not invade the homes of Bnai Yisrael. Why were Bnai Yisrael spared from these ten plagues? The most obvious answer is that this was an expression of Hashem's kindness to the Jewish people. This interpretation is implied by the mishne in Avot. The mishne states that Hashem performed ten miracles for Bnai Yisrael in Egypt. The exclusion of the Jewish people from the affliction of

---

[55] Rabbaynu Ovadia Sforno, Commentary on Sefer Shemot, 7:9.
[56] Rabbaynu Moshe ben Maimon (Rambam) Commentary on the Mishne, Mesechet Avot 5:4.
[57] Mesechet Avot 5:4.

the plagues is described as a miracle done on there behalf. This supports the thesis that the Almighty spared Bnai Yisrael as an expression of love.

Rav Yisrael Lipschitz in his commentary on the Mishne Teferet Yisrael[58] supports this interpretation of the Mishne. He adds that this kindness was an expression of the Almighty's love for the forefathers. Maimonides offers a different interpretation of Bnai Yisrael's exclusion from the plagues. He explains that there are two types of miracles. Some miracles are apparent aberrations from nature. The splitting of the Reed Sea is an example of this class of miracle. Other miracles are not inconsistent with the natural order of the universe. Nonetheless, these events qualify as wonders. Of course, this raises a question. Events that seemingly contradict natural law are obviously miraculous. However, the second class of miracles is not inconsistent with the natural order. Then, what is miraculous about these events? Maimonides explains that three characteristics can elevate an event from the commonplace to the wondrous. The first characteristic is timing. The event occurs at the exact moment predicted by the prophet. For example, a prophet predicts that the home of an evil person will be immediately struck by lightening. We would not normally view a destructive lightening bolt as an act of G-d. However, lighting striking immediately upon the pronouncement of the prophet deserves to be regarded as a wonder. The second quality is the extent of the phenomenon or the presence of an element of discrimination. Rain is not a miracle. However, the Deluge was a wondrous event by virtue of the magnitude of the phenomenon. According to Maimonides, the ten plagues were all wondrous events because they exclusively affected the Egyptians. The selective exclusion of Bnai Yisrael from the suffering endowed these events with a miraculous aspect. Third, the presence of a consistent pattern can render an event into a miracle. The blessings in the Torah are examples of this third characteristic. Abundant crops or famine are not miraculous occurrences. However, a consistent relationship between behavior and material well-being over an extended period is a wondrous phenomenon!

Maimonides' comments provide another perspective on Bnai Yisrael's exclusion from the plagues. Any of the above characteristics can render a commonplace event into a wonder. Certainly, the convergence of all three characteristics is convincing evidence of the wondrous nature of an event or series of events. It seems that every characteristic identified by Maimonides was present in the plagues. Generally, Moshe predicted the onset and termination of each plague. On one occasion, he even allowed Paroh to chose the moment of cessation. The plagues involved sudden massive catastrophes. At the same time, these calamities did not affect the Jewish people. Finally, the plagues corresponded with Paroh's behavior. His refusal to release Bnai Yisrael was followed by suffering. His repentance, inevitably lead to a cessation of the plague. This consistent pattern continued throughout the ten plagues.

In short, according to Maimonides the exclusion of Bnai Yisrael from the plagues was not necessarily a manifestation of Hashem's love. Instead, this discrimination was needed to endow these events with a wondrous aspect.

"And the magicians said to Paroh, "It is the finger of the L-rd." And Paroh's heart became hard and he did not listen to them as Hashem had spoken." (Shemot 8:15)

---

[58] Rav Yisrael Lipshitz, Teferet Yisrael Commentary on the Mishne, Mesechet Avot 5:4.

Paroh's magicians could not duplicate the plague of Lice. They told Paroh that this plague was the "finger of the L-rd." Rashi seems to indicate that the magicians were attesting to the authenticity of Moshe's claims. This plague was caused by the G-d of the Jewish people. Moshe was His agent. Hashem was intervening in nature to save His people.[59]

Rabbaynu Avraham ibn Ezra disagrees with this interpretation. The magicians did not say that the plague was from Hashem. They counseled that the cause was the L-rd. Ibn Ezra explains that the Egyptians did not deny the existence of a Creator. They understood that this Creator ruled the universe through a system of natural law. The issue in dispute was the Torah concept of a Creator with a providential relationship to His people. This understanding of G-d is expressed by the Tetragrammaton-the name we pronounce as "Hashem."

The Creator fashioned a universe in which natural disasters occur. Floods, earthquakes, terrible storms destroy cities and even civilizations. The magicians did not understand such phenomenon to be providential. The magicians acknowledged that this plague was not merely an illusion or impressive trick. It was the work of the Creator. But, they claimed, it did not support the concept of Hashem.[60]

Nachmanides offers a third interpretation. The magicians accepted Moshe's claim that the plague was from Hashem. They did not use this name. It was a foreign term to the Egyptians. Speaking among themselves, they would not refer to G-d with an unfamiliar name. However, they claimed it was only the "finger" of G-d. The plague caused discomfort and some suffering. However, it was not catastrophic. They advised Paroh to be calm-to recognize the limited effect of the plague and maintain his resolve.[61]

"And I will separate on that day the land of Goshen, that my nation stands upon, so that there will not be there wild beasts; so that you will know that I, Hashem, am in the midst of the land." (Shemot 8:18)

G-d tells Paroh, through Moshe, that the upcoming plague of Wild Beasts will affect only the Egyptians. Bnai Yisrael will be protected from the infestation. Nachmanides explains that Bnai Yisrael were also spared the suffering caused by the previous plagues. The waters of Goshen were not affected by Blood and Frogs. There was no outbreak of Lice in Goshen. However, this aspect of these plagues was not stressed. Moshe could not point to this localization as proof of the plagues' Divine origin. It was understandable that these plagues were localized phenomena. However, the infestation of Wild Beasts should not have been localized. There was no natural reason for the beasts to stop at the border of the Jewish province. Only providence could explain this behavior.[62]

Rabbaynu Avraham ibn Ezra disagrees. He maintains that the Jews were not exempt from the effects of the previous plagues. Bnai Yisrael also suffered from lack of water and infestations of frogs and lice. These plagues did not threaten lives. Hashem did not insulate His people. However, the wild beasts were an actual danger. This infestation would result in death, not mere

---

[59] Rabbaynu Ovadia Sforno, Commentary on Sefer Shemot, 7:9.
[60] Rabbaynu Avraham ibn Ezra, Commentary on Sefer Shemot, 8:15.
[61] Rabbaynu Moshe ben Nachman (Ramban), Commentary on Sefer Shemot 8:15.
[62] Rabbaynu Moshe ben Nachman (Ramban), Commentary on Sefer Shemot 8:18.

suffering. In order to protect the lives of His people, G-d shielded the Jewish people from this plague.[63]

"And the magicians could not stand before Moshe because of the boils, for the boils had attacked the magicians and all the Egyptians." (Shemot 9:11)

The Torah explains that the plague of Boils represented a turning point in the punishment of the Egyptians. The magicians of Egypt were rendered helpless. This is difficult to understand. The magicians had not been spared the previous plagues. They had not been exempt from the suffering of their countrymen. Why was this plague more devastating for the magicians? Rabbaynu Avraham ben HaRambam[64] addresses this question. The magicians had attempted to duplicate each of Moshe's miracles. They had some success. This allowed them to boast that their power was comparable to Moshe's. Perhaps, Moshe was a better magician and more knowledgeable. However, they claimed that the difference was quantitative. They and Moshe used similar means. This plague completely undermined their claim. Moshe overpowered the magicians. The boils debilitated them. They could not even appear before Moshe to challenge his miracles. They were humiliated. They could no longer compare their power to Moshe's. Moshe had demonstrated that he was not working through the same means as the Egyptians. He was acting as the agent of some greater power.

"And Moshe said to him, "When I leave the city, I will spread my hands to Hashem. The thunder will cease. There will not be any more hail. This is so you will know that the land is Hashem's." (Shemot 9:29)

Our pasuk describes the conclusion of the plague of hail. Paroh beseeches Moshe to pray to Hashem. He should appeal to the Almighty to end the plague. Moshe responds that he will comply. However, he adds an important phrase. He tells Paroh that, first, he will leave the city. Only then will he spread his hands to Hashem in prayer. Why did Moshe stipulate that he must first leave the city?

Rashi quotes the Midrash Michilta in response to this question. The Midrash explains that the city was permeated with idols. Moshe would not pray in this abominable environment. First, he would remove himself from this city of idolatry. Only then, would he pray to Hashem.[65]

Moshe was waging a battle against idolatry. He was asserting that Hashem is the only true G-d. The deities of Egypt were false gods. He would not pray in a place dominated by these idols. Perhaps he feared that his prayers might be misinterpreted as appeals to the abominations of the Egyptians. He would leave the city and its idols. He would pray to Hashem only in a place free of these false gods.

The commentaries are troubled by the Midrash's comments. This was not the first occasion on which Moshe prayed on behalf of Paroh and the Egyptians. On these other occasions, Moshe did not stipulate that he must first leave the city. Why, now, does Moshe add this requirement?

---

[63] Rabbaynu Avraham ibn Ezra, Commentary on Sefer Shemot, 8:18.
[64] Rabbaynu Avraham ben HaRambam, Commentary on Sefer Shemot 9:11
[65] Rabbaynu Shlomo ben Yitzchak (Rashi), Commentary on Sefer Shemot 9:29.

Rav Naftali Tzvi Yehuda Berlin Zt"l the Netziv offers an answer to this question. His answer is based upon a previous passage. Let us consider this pasuk. As we have explained above, Moshe was not immediately successful in winning the support of Bnai Yisrael. His initial appeal to Paroh resulted in an intensification of the bondage. Bnai Yisrael sharply criticized Moshe for this outcome. Moshe sought an explanation from Hashem. The Torah uses an interesting phrase in describing Moshe's communion with the Almighty. The Torah says that Moshe "returned to Hashem" and sought His counsel.[66] Netziv asserts that this phrase should be understood somewhat literally. Moshe actually went somewhere. He went to a place that he had designated for prayer and prophecy. He had established a synagogue a Bait HaKenesset. Moshe retreated to this sacred place to commune with the Almighty.[67]

Netziv explains that this provides a partial answer to our question. Actually, each time Moshe prayed to Hashem, he carefully considered his environment. He was consistently concerned with the problem of praying to Hashem in place associated with idolatry. In order to address this issue, Moshe established a special place that was sacred and devoted to the worship of the Almighty. Each time Moshe prayed or sought prophecy, he retreated to his Bait HaKenesset.

Netziv acknowledges that this insight does not completely answer our question. Why did Moshe now insist on leaving the city? Why did Moshe not follow his established practice? He should have entered his synagogue and prayed to Hashem?

Netziv explains that the answer is provided by another stipulation made by Moshe. He told Paroh that his prayers would be accompanied by a physical demonstration. Moshe would spread his hands to Hashem. Netziv explains that Moshe intended to spread his hands towards the heavens. This could not be done inside a building. Moshe intended to pray outside.

Moshe could not fulfill this requirement in his Bait HaKenesset. Therefore, he was confronted with a problem. He would not pray to Hashem in a place associated with idolatry. Yet, his accustomed refuge was indoors and, consequently, inappropriate for the prayer he planned. Moshe solved his dilemma by leaving the city. In this manner, he was able to pray outside in a proper environment.[68]

Netziv's insight provides an explanation for an amazing halacha. Tur explains that one should always pray in a Bait HaKenesset. He adds that the synagogue must have a minyan, a quorum of ten males. Bait Yosef observes that there is an obvious implication in Tur's formulation of this halacha. If a synagogue does not have a minyan, one is not required to pray there. Bait Yosef questions this formulation. He explains that many Sages maintain that one should pray in a Bait HaKenesset regardless of the presence of a minyan. He explains the reason for this position. A synagogue is designated for prayer.[69]

Why is this designation important? According to the comments of Netziv, we can answer this question. Prayer involves making an exclusive commitment to the service of Hashem. Like Moshe, we live in an environment that is dominated by the expressions of other religions. It is appropriate for us to remove ourselves from our ambient surroundings when demonstrating our

---

[66] Sefer Shemot 5:22.
[67] Rav Naftali Tzvi Yehuda Berlin (Netziv), Commentary Hamek Davar on Sefer Shemot 5:22.
[68] Rav Naftali Tzvi Yehuda Berlin (Netziv), Commentary Hamek Davar on Sefer Shemot 9:29.
[69] Rabbaynu Yaakov ben HaRash, Tur Shulchan Aruch, Orech Chayim 90.

exclusive devotion to Hashem. The synagogue provides this opportunity. It is our refuge. It is a place completely designated for the service of the Almighty.

Bo

And Hashem said to Moshe: Go to Paroh. For I will make his heart stubborn and the hearts of his advisors so that I may place these wonders of mine in his midst, and so that you will retell to your children and grandchildren that I played with Egypt and the wonders that I placed among them. And you will know that I am Hashem. (Shemot 10:1-2)

The Objective of the Plague of Locusts

This pasuk introduces the plague of Locusts. Hashem tells Moshe that with this plague He will "play" with the Paroh and his nation. The apparent meaning is that Hashem will humiliate Paroh and the Egyptians. Why was this plague more degrading than those that preceded it?

There is another interesting issue raised by the plague of Locusts. The essential affect of this plague was that locusts would consume all grain and produce that had survived the plague of Hail. Egypt would experience severe famine. In order for Paroh to rescue his people from this plague, he would need Moshe's immediate intercession. Once the crops were consumed, the devastation of the plague would be complete. As the damage of the plague was inflicted, Paroh resisted calling for Moshe and Aharon. Only after the crops had been totally destroyed, did he beseech Moshe and Aharon to pray on his behalf. Paroh had already persevered through the worst of the plague. Why break down at this point?

Rav Simcha Zissel Broida Zt"l offers an interesting approach to these problems. He posits that these two questions are interrelated. Paroh withstood the destruction of the plague without weakening. However once the locusts had ravaged the land, he was confronted with a scene of total destruction. This landscape of devastation overwhelmed Paroh. Paroh knew he could not reverse the damage of the plague. But he had to have relief from the sight of locusts. This was his reason for beseeching Moshe and Aharon to pray on his behalf. This is not the behavior of an individual who is in control. It is characteristic of an emotionally shattered person, unable to bear even a reminder of his misfortune. This approach identifies the unique element of degradation affected by the plague. The first seven plagues never broke Paroh emotionally. He was able to retain his self-respect. On occasion, the pressure of a plague forced him to promise Bnai Yisrael freedom. But with the cessation of each plague, Paroh quickly regained his confidence and sense of control. The plague of Locusts was different. The devastation of this plague shattered Paroh. He called for Moshe and Aharon even though he could no longer reverse or even suspend the damage. He needed Moshe and Aharon to relieve the pain of seeing the locusts – the reminder of his folly and demise. This is the degradation referred to in the opening pesukim.[1]

And Hashem said to Moshe: Come to Paroh for I have made his heart heavy and the heart of his servants. [This is] in order to place My signs in his midst. And [this is] in order that you will tell your son and grandson that I mocked [those] in Egypt and [tell of] My signs that I placed among them. And you will know that I am Hashem. (Shemot 10:1-2)

The Simple Meaning

---

[1] Rav Shimon Yosef Miller, Shai LaTorah (Jerusalem 5753), volume 2, pp. 213-215.

1. The purpose of the coming plagues

Hashem addresses Moshe. He tells him that the coming plagues are not intended to persuade Paroh to release the Jewish people. Hashem has made Paroh's heart heavy. Despite the suffering he and his people will experience, he will stubbornly refuse to free Bnai Yisrael. The coming plagues are intended to demonstrate Hashem's omnipotence. Future generations will recount these events – the wonders that Hashem will perform.

The translation of the above passages is based upon Rashi's comments. Hashem tells Moshe that in recounting the coming events, future generation will describe Hashem mocking the Egyptians.[2] However, Unkelus and many others provide an alternative translation of the second passage. In their translation, Hashem tells Moshe that He has hardened Paroh's heart in order that "you will tell your son and grandson the wonders that I performed in Egypt and the signs I placed among them."[3] These commentators remove from the passage reference to Hashem mocking Paroh.

These alternative translations describe differently the purpose of the coming plagues. According to Unkelus, their objective is solely to demonstrate Hashem's omnipotence – His complete sovereignty over nature. Rashi's interpretation of the passage suggests a second objective. The coming plagues are intended to humiliate Paroh. Hashem will demonstrate to His people that the mighty ruler of Egypt is powerless and even pathetic. He will come to Moshe and plead with him to immediately lead forth the Jewish people from his land. He will beseech Moshe to pray to Hashem on his behalf.[4] The mighty will be humbled before Hashem.

Why is this second objective important? According to Unkelus, the message of the plagues is educational or intellectual. The plagues provide objective and incontrovertible evidence of Hashem's omnipotence. This, in turn, demonstrates that Hashem is the creator.[5] The events are to be recounted in each generation. Conveying to our children and grandchildren the narrative of our redemption from Egypt will establish in each generation these fundamental convictions.

Rashi is suggesting that the coming events are also designed to produce a profound emotional impact. They will reshape Bnai Yisrael's perception of Paroh and of mortal masters. The Jewish people will observe the utter destruction of the king who was their master. The humiliation of Paroh will communicate to them that there is no sovereign greater than Hashem. Even the mighty Paroh will grovel before Him.

2. Arguing with Unkelus

It is notable that Rashi rejects Unkelus' Aramaic translation of the passages. Rashi comments in Mesechet Kiddushin that Unkelus' Aramaic translation was received by Moshe at Sinai.[6] Rashi notes that his comment is based upon the Talmud's discussion in Mesechet Megilah. There, the Talmud explains that the Torah was given to Moshe with its targum –

---

[2] Rabbaynu Shlomo ben Yitzchak (Rashi), Commentary on Sefer Shemot 10:2.
[3] The dispute over the proper translation of the passage focuses upon the literal meaning of the word "hitalalti/התעללתי".
[4] Sefer Shemot 12:31-32.
[5] Rabbaynu Moshe ben Nachman (Ramban), Commentary on Sefer Shemot 13:16.
[6] Rabbaynu Shlomo ben Yitzchak (Rashi), Commentary on the Talmud, Mese. Kiddushin 49a.

translation. With the passage of time, this translation was forgotten. Unkelus, the proselyte, studied under Ribbi Eliezer and Ribbi Yehoshua; based upon these studies, he reconstructed the targum. Despite Rashi's acknowledgment of the impressive origins of Unkelus's translation, in this and in many other instances, he takes issue with it.

Rashi's treatment of Unkelus' translation raises an interesting question. Given his acknowledgment of its origins, why does Rashi feel entitled to contest it and substitute his own interpretations of words and phrases in the Torah? Furthermore, why was the Torah given to Moshe with a translation? Why was this necessary?

He preserves kindness for thousands of generations. He forbears iniquities, rebellions, and sins. He forgives those who return to the Law and those who do not return He does not forgive...
(Devarim 34:7)

3. Valid and invalid translations

The first step to answering these questions is provided by a discussion in Tractate Kiddushin. The Talmud discusses a person who has presented himself as one able to read the Torah. Now, he is called upon to prove his assertion. He is understood to be claiming a level of literacy. To satisfy his claim, he must read and translate three passages.

The Talmud adds that he does not satisfy this requirement though providing his own translation. He must provide Unkelus' translation. Why is his own translation not adequate? The Talmud explains that one who translates passages literally promotes falsehood. One who adds interpretation is a blasphemer.[7] Rashi explains the meaning of these comments. Some passages are not intended to be understood literally. If one translates one of the passages literally, one attributes to it a false meaning. One who adds interpretation may pervert the meaning of the passage. This is blasphemy. Rashi continues and explains that Unkelus' translation is not subject to these concerns. It is authoritative.[8] It translates literally those passages that are to be so understood and it interprets properly those passages that are not to be understood literally.

The Talmud's discussion reveals the purpose of Unkelus' translation. The Torah can be understood at various levels. The Talmud explains that included among these levels is the simple meaning of its passages. Each passage has a simple or plain meaning. However, sometimes the simple meaning is not literal.

This is illustrated by the above passage. The translation is based upon Unkelus' Aramaic translation. Hashem reveals to Moshe the extent and limits of His kindness. He tells Moshe that "He forgives those who return to the Law and those who do not return He does not forgive". Rashi observes that this is not the literal translation of the phrase. Its literal meaning is "He does not entirely forgive". According to Unkelus, this literal meaning is not the simple meaning of the passage. He is providing the simple meaning.

4. The Sinai translation

Now, we can identify the reason Hashem gave Moshe the Torah with its translation. The significance of this translation is not that it expresses the content of the Torah in another language. Its importance is that it provides the simple meaning of the text.

---

[7] Mesechet Kiddushin 49a.
[8] Rabbaynu Shlomo ben Yitzchak (Rashi), Commentary on the Talmud, Mes. Kiddushin 49a.

In other words, Hashem gave to Moshe the Written Law – the Five Books of the Torah – and the Oral Law. This Oral Law interprets the Torah and finds meaning in every word and phrase. However, the Oral Law also includes the simple meaning of each passage. The translation given to Moshe conveyed this simple meaning. Unkelus' Aramaic translation is a reconstruction of this ancient translation.

Another question can now be answered. The Talmud in Kiddushin taught that one who claims he can read the Torah proves the truth of his assertion by reading three passages with Unkelus' translation. Why is his claim satisfied only if he provides Unkelus' translation? The answer is that this person has claimed literacy in the Torah. This means he can read the passages and that he knows their meaning. Unkelus' translation is the simple meaning of the passages. If he cannot provide this translation, he has merely demonstrated that he can read Hebrew. He has not demonstrated literacy in Torah.

5. Disputing Unkelus

Unkelus' Aramaic translation was not received by Moshe at Sinai. That translation was lost. Unkelus' translation is his reconstruction of the original translation. He based his translation upon the teachings of Ribbi Eliezer and Ribbi Yehoshua – masters of the Oral Law. Because he created his translation using this resource, his translation is authoritative. It does not mean that his work cannot be challenged or disputed. Rashi used his vast knowledge of the Oral Law to critique Unkelus' work. On occasion, he concludes that the simple meaning of the text is different from that proposed by Unkelus. In those instances, Rashi states his objections and offers his alternative.

6. Lessons from Rashi and Unkelus

In virtually every age, the conclusions of our Sages are challenged. Generally, the new generation suspects that the interpretations of the Sages reflect the attitudes and values of their era. Certainly, their ancient interpretations are not in-sync with our modern more enlightened perspectives! Yet, the Talmud asserts that one who composes his own "updated" translation promotes falsehood and engages in blasphemy. Sensitivity to contemporary values cannot take the place of thorough and penetrating scholarship. One must be a master of the Written and Oral Law if one proposes to compose a translation of the Torah.

The same is true of interpretation of its laws. To interpret the Torah and apply its laws to issues arising in the modern milieu, it is not adequate to understand the contemporary setting. One must have enormous erudition in the vast body of Torah law.

"And he said to them, "May Hashem only be with you. Just as I send you with your children. See that evil is before you". (Shemot 10:10)

Moshe tells Paroh of the plague of Locusts. This plague will consume all grain and vegetation that survived the preceding plagues. Paroh agrees to allow Bnai Yisrael to leave Egypt to serve Hashem. However, only the adults may leave. The children must remain. In our pasuk, Paroh tells Moshe that he acquiesces to the request to leave Egypt. However, he adds that evil awaits Bnai Yisrael. In other words, he predicts that Bnai Yisrael are destined to suffer. What was Paroh's basis for this prediction?

The commentaries offer various explanation of Paroh's prediction. One of the most interesting is provided by Gershonides.[9] He explains that Paroh could no longer deny the existence of a deity that caused these plagues. However, he claimed that this powerful god could only produce destruction. His proof was that all of the plagues were destructive. He warned Bnai Yisrael that if they chose to follow this god they would be doomed. Ultimately, they too would suffer the wrath of the god of destruction. Based on this interpretation of Paroh's prediction, Gershonides answers a number of other difficult questions. At Sinai, Hashem threatened to destroy Bnai Yisrael. Moshe pleads with Hashem to spare the nation. He tells Hashem that the annihilation of Bnai Yisrael will confirm the claims of the Egyptians. We can now understand Moshe's argument. According to the interpretation of Gershonides, Paroh had claimed that a deity only capable of destruction had redeemed the Jewish nation. The destruction of the nation would lend credibility to the Egyptian's claim.

This also explains another incident. Upon leaving Egypt, Bnai Yisrael came to Marah. The water in Marah was too bitter to drink. The nation came to Moshe. "What will we drink?" they asked. Hashem showed them a tree. This tree was placed in the water. The water became potable. Moshe then spoke to the nation. He told them that they must follow the laws of Hashem. If they are faithful, they will not suffer the afflictions experienced by the Egyptian. He concluded by referring to the Almighty as the healer of the nation. This is a very difficult incident to understand. First, why did Hashem lead the nation to a location that was without water? Certainly, He knew they would need water to survive. Why wait until the nation appealed to Moshe before providing potable water? Second, what is the meaning of Moshe's speech? He tells the nation that if they observe the mitzvot, they will not suffer. This would seem self-evident! Why did Moshe need to make this point? Finally, why does Moshe refer to Hashem as a healer? Of all the characteristics of Hashem, why mention this one?

According to the insight of Gershonides, all of these questions are answered. Hashem realized that some members of Bnai Yisrael would be concerned with Paroh's prediction. They had been rescued from Egypt but only through the destruction of the Egyptians. This reinforced Paroh's claim. Hashem wished to indicate that He also does good. Therefore, he brought them to Marah. Here, He performed a miracle that did not involve any element of destruction. Moshe's comments can now be understood. Moshe told the people that Paroh's concept of Hashem was wrong. True, Hashem had destroyed the Egyptians. But this was not because Hashem's only tools are suffering and destruction. The Egyptians were destroyed because they were evil. If Bnai Yisrael observed the mitzvot, they would not experience this suffering. Moshe then proves his point. Hashem had "healed" the water. This proved that far from being a god of destruction, the Almighty removed suffering and healed. A god that removes imperfection and heals cannot be the god envisioned by Paroh.

"And the locusts invaded all of the land of Egypt. And they settled within all of the boundaries of Egypt. It was a severe plague. Never before had there been a comparable infestation of locusts and never again would there be such an infestation." (Shemot 10:14)

---

[9] Rabbaynu Levi ben Gershon (Ralbag / Gershonides), Commentary on Sefer Shemot, (Mosad HaRav Kook, 1994), pp. 41-42.

The Plague of Locusts

This pasuk describes the plague of Locusts. The locusts covered the Land of Egypt. They consumed all of the grain and vegetation that had survived the previous plagues. The Torah asserts that an infestation of this magnitude had never previously occurred. Furthermore, an infestation of such magnitude would never occur again.

Rashi raises an interesting question. The Navi tells of an infestation of locusts in the Land of Israel, during the time of the prophet Yoel. The Navi describes it as greater than any previous infestation or any that would occur in the future.[10] This seems to clearly contradict our passage. Our passage asserts that the plague in Egypt was the greatest infestation.

Rashi answers his question with a simple distinction. The plague in Egypt involved the infestation of a single species of locust. The plague of Yoel involved a combination of species. Both statements are true. The plague in Egypt was the greatest infestation by a single species. The plague described in Yoel was the greatest infestation involving a combination of species.[11]

Rabbaynu Chananel offers a different solution to Rashi's question. Essentially, he argues that the passage is merely asserting that no equivalent plague ever occurred in Egypt. However, our pasuk does not claim that greater infestations would not occur elsewhere in the world. The plague of Yoel's time occurred in the Land of Israel. This resolves the contradiction. Rabbaynu Chananel adds that Egypt's climate does not favor locusts. They are rarely found in Egypt. Therefore, a major infestation is remarkably out of the ordinary.[12]

Nachmanides offers a third answer. His explanation is the simplest. He explains that our pasuk merely states that no natural infestation ever occurred that can be compared to this plague. The passage is not comparing this infestation to other miraculous plagues. The plague of Yoel's time was a punishment. By definition, a punishment is an act of divine intervention and therefore, it is a miracle. The Chumash is not comparing the Egyptian infestation to other miraculous infestations.[13]

What is the basis for this dispute between the commentaries? It seems that each answer suggests a different approach to understanding the intended message of our passage. In order to understand the dispute, we must identify these various interpretations of the pasuk.

As mentioned above, Nachmanides offers the simplest explanation of the Torah's claim. Also, he seems to adopt the most obvious understanding of the pasuk's intended message. According the Nachmanides, the pasuk is providing the evidence that the plague was a miracle. The infestation can be judged as miraculous if it exceeded the norm. In other words, if no natural explanation of the infestation is plausible, it is obviously a miracle. The pasuk asserts that this infestation was of tremendous magnitude. The magnitude could not have been the result of normal causes. Therefore, it could only be a miracle!

According to Rabbaynu Chananel, the pasuk has a deeper message. The infestation was far greater than any that had ever occurred in Egypt. It was beyond the experience of the Egyptians. The Torah is telling us that the plague was specifically designed to impress the

---

[10] Sefer Yoel 2:2.
[11] Rabbaynu Shlomo ben Yitzchak (Rashi), *Commentary on Sefer Shemot* 10:14.
[12] Rabbaynu Moshe ben Nachman (Ramban), *Commentary on Sefer Shemot* 10:14.
[13] Rabbaynu Moshe ben Nachman (Ramban), *Commentary on Sefer Shemot* 10:14.

Egyptians. In order to impress the Egyptians, their experience and their assessment were essential. It was important for the Egyptians to appreciate that a miracle was occurring. Rabbaynu Chananel's further comments confirm this interpretation. Locusts were uncommon in Egypt. Therefore, a plague of locusts had a special significance to the Egyptians.

Rashi sees a different message in the passage. The pasuk is stressing the degree of divine intervention implied by the plague. Beyond communicating that the plague was miraculous, the pasuk stresses the magnitude of the miracle. The plague in Egypt involved a single, specific species. Other similar species of locust did not participate in the plague. This demonstrates the high degree of providence involved in the event. An example will help illustrate this concept. Assume there are five locusts sitting in the grass. Suddenly, a strong wind blows. We can expect all five locusts to be snatched up by the wind and delivered to a new location. If the five locusts are members of different species, they will still share the single experience of being swept up by the wind. Imagine only one of the locusts is swept up by the wind. The other four are members of another species. They are unaffected by the wind. Such a phenomenon would clearly involve some sort of unusual intervention. This example exactly describes the plague experienced by the Egyptians. One species reacted to the stimulus and infested Egypt. Other similar species remained undisturbed. This demonstrated the high degree on providence involved in the plague.

And he said: I have sinned against Hashem and against you. Now, forgive my sin this one time and beseech Hashem, your G-d and He should remove form me (only) this death. (Shemot 10:17-18)

In this corner….

One of the most interesting elements of the Torah's account of our rescue from Egypt is its description of the evolution of the relationship between Moshe and Pharaoh. The relationship is enigmatic. As a young man, Moshe had killed an Egyptian taskmaster who he encountered abusing a Jew. When Moshe realized that he had been observed, he recognized that his life was in jeopardy. He fled Egypt and settled in Midyan.[14] He feared the Pharaoh of his youth and understood that he was eager to punish his defiance of Egyptian authority.

The Pharaoh of Moshe's youth died and Moshe returned to Egypt. Moshe and Aharon demanded that this new Pharaoh allow the Jews to travel into the wilderness and serve Hashem. Pharaoh's treatment of Moshe is fascinating. Rather than condemning Moshe as an agitator and punishing him, Pharaoh is dismissive of Moshe.[15]

---

[14] Ibn Ezra notes that even in Midyan Moshe did not feel that he was safe. Midyan was aligned with Egypt and paid tribute to its king. Moshe feared that if the Egyptian authorities became aware of his presence in Midyan, they would demand that he be returned to face judgement and punishment. Moshe became a shepherd and lived in unpopulated areas in order to avoid detection.

[15] He says to Moshe and Aharon, "Return to your burdens." Most commentators understand this statement as directed to the Jews. Pharaoh instructed the Jews through Moshe and Aharon – their representatives – to return to their tasks as slaves. Rashi suggest that the statement was directed to Moshe and Aharon. They and the rest of the tribe of Levi had succeeded in avoiding bondage. Pharaoh was not telling them to return to their tasks as slaves. He was telling them to go back to their business – whatever that might be.

Even as the conflict between Moshe and Pharaoh becomes more intense, Pharaoh does not seek to imprison or punish Moshe. He does not treat his as a treasonous insurgent. Instead, he consistently demonstrates deference toward Moshe and Aharon.

The above passage describes one of the strange exchanges between Pharaoh and Moshe. This exchange takes place after the onset of the plague of Locusts. Pharaoh summons Moshe and Aharon and pleads with them to end the plague. Pharaoh acknowledges that he has sinned against Hashem. Pharaoh had acknowledged sinning against Hashem also during the plague of Hail. However, this time Pharaoh adds, that he has sinned against Moshe and Aharon.

Rabbeinu Avraham ibn Ezra explains that Pharaoh is acknowledging that he has acted inappropriately toward Moshe and Aharon. In their previous encounter, Pharaoh has ejected them from his court. Now, he was apologizing for treating them disrespectfully.

And Hashem said to Moshe: I will bring one more plague upon Paroh and upon the Egyptians and afterward they will send you forth completely. They will chase you out from here. (Shemot 11:1)

The Purpose of the Ten Plagues

1. The Plague of the Firstborn was intended to secure Bnai Yisrael's freedom

The above passage introduces the last of the ten plagues – the Plague of the Firstborn. Hashem describes the plague to Moshe. Moshe then warns Paroh that this terrible plague will be brought upon him and Egypt if he does not allow Bnai Yisrael to leave the Land. Paroh refuses to heed Moshe's warning and the plague strikes Egypt. The impact of the plague is unbearable and Paroh is forced to release Bnai Yisrael.

In the above passage, Hashem tells Moshe that this plague will force Paroh to release Bnai Yisrael. This suggests that although Hashem was prepared to force Paroh and the Egyptians to liberate Bnai Yisrael, for some reason, He delayed this horrible plague until this point. In other words, Hashem's intent in bringing the plagues upon Egypt was not solely to secure the freedom of Bnai Yisrael. If this were His sole purpose, this outcome could have been secured much earlier.

For now, I could have sent out My hand and struck you and your nation with pestilence and you would have been removed from the land. But in truth, for this reason I have sustained you – in order to demonstrate to you My strength and in order that My name will be declared in all the land. (Shemot 9:15-16)

2. The first nine plagues were not designed to secure Bnai Yisrael's freedom

The above passages are part of the warning that Moshe delivered to Paroh after the Plague of Pestilence and before the Plague of Boils. The Plague of Pestilence decimated the Egyptians' livestock. However, this pestilence did not affect humans – only animals. Moshe tells Paroh that had Hashem wished, He could have extended the plague's affect. He could have directed the pestilence against the Egyptian people and not only against their livestock. However, He fashioned the plague in a manner that limited its damage and allowed the Egyptian people to survive. Hashem spared the Egyptians from eradication.

This passage provides additional confirmation of the message implicit in the first passage above. Hashem did not bring the plagues upon the Egyptians solely to coerce Paroh to release Bnai Yisrael. Some other objective was served through the plagues.

This means that the Plague of the Firstborn was fundamentally different from the other plagues. The Plague of the Firstborn was intended to secure the release of Bnai Yisrael. This plague was preceded by nine other plagues. These plagues were not designed to secure Bnai Yisrael's release. These plagues had some other objective.

> *And you should say to Paroh, "So says Hashem: Israel is My firstborn son. I say to you send out My son that he may serve Me. If you refuse to send him out, I will kill your firstborn son." (Shemot 4:22-23)*

3. Hashem revealed to Moshe the Plague of the Firstborn when He assigned him his mission

Rav Yitzchak Zev Soloveitchik *Zt"l* notes this distinction between the Plague of the Firstborn and the preceding plagues. He adds that this distinction explains an odd set of passages found earlier in Sefer Shemot. Hashem commands Moshe to return to Egypt and assigns him the mission of redeeming Bnai Yisrael. He tells Moshe to confront Paroh; demand the release of Bnai Yisrael, and warn him that if he resists, he will be subjected to the Plague of the Firstborn. It is odd that Hashem tells Moshe of the final plague before revealing to him the preceding nine plagues. Furthermore, Hashem describes the warning Moshe will deliver before the final plague is brought upon Egypt. However, Moshe is not instructed to deliver this warning until all of the preceding plagues have been brought upon the Egyptians. Why does Hashem describe to Moshe the plague and its warning at this point? It would have made more sense for Hashem to wait until the time had arrived for the final plague. At that moment, He should have revealed the plague to Moshe and instructed him to warn Paroh.

Rav Soloveitchik responds that in the context of the discussion described in the passages, these instructions are relevant and appropriate. Hashem is sending Moshe to Egypt with the mission of leading Bnai Yisrael forth from bondage. He assigns Moshe this mission and reveals to him the instrument through which the mission will be fulfilled. This instrument is the Plague of the Firstborn. It is this plague that will coerce Paroh to release the people. This is not the function of the other plagues. Therefore, in charging Moshe with his mission, he communicates to him the instructions regarding the final plague and does not mention those that will precede it.

What was the function of these preceding plagues?

> *And Hashem said to Moshe: Behold, I have appointed you as a judge over Paroh and Aharon your brother will be your spokesperson. (Shemot 7:1)*

4. Moshe was Paroh's judge

Hashem speaks to Moshe. He tells Moshe that he has been appointed as Paroh's judge. Rashi comments, that with this statement, Hashem transmitted to Moshe the authority to judge and punish Paroh. This means that the process that unfolded with Moshe's arrival in Egypt was not only one of redemption for Bnai Yisrael. Moshe was charged with a second mission. He was appointed as judge and executioner of Paroh and the Egyptians. Rav Soloveitchik explains that this appointment reveals the role of the first nine plagues. These plagues were not intended to secure the release of Bnai Yisrael. These plagues were intended to punish the Paroh and his people for their persecution of Bnai Yisrael.

And He said to Avram: You should know that your descendants will be aliens in a land that is not theirs. They (the inhabitants) will subjugate them and afflict them for four hundred years. But this nation that they will serve I will judge and afterward they will go forth with great wealth. (Beresheit 15:13-14)

5. Dual objective of the plagues was revealed to Avraham

These passages were part of a prophecy and a covenant entered into by Hashem and Avraham. Hashem foretold Avraham of the bondage of his descendants in Egypt. Also, He revealed to Avraham that his descendants' bondage will end with the judgment of their oppressors and their own redemption. Rav Soloveitchik explains that this covenant was the basis for the design of the plagues. The plagues fulfilled this ancient promise. They punished Bnai Yisrael's oppressors and they secured their release from bondage.

One of the greatest mysteries of the Torah's account of Bnai Yisrael's redemption is its description of Hashem suspending Paroh's freewill. The Torah explains that Hashem instructed Moshe to warn Paroh of the consequences of continuing to enslave Bnai Yisrael. Before many of the plagues, Moshe goes to Paroh and warns him. He tells Paroh that if he does not release the people, he will experience another plague. However, the Torah also reveals that Hashem hardened or strengthened Paroh's heart. He deprived Paroh of the volition to heed Moshe's warning. A bizarre routine evolved. Moshe warned Paroh; Paroh was prevented from acquiescing; the plague was brought upon Paroh and Egypt.

In itself, this suspension of volition implies that the first nine plagues were not designed to secure Bnai Yisrael's freedom. If that was their design, it would not make sense for Hashem to deprive Paroh of the capacity to surrender Bnai Yisrael. Rav Soloveitchik's conclusions provide a simple solution for this mystery.

It is possible that a person will commit a great sin or many sins and the judgment of the True Judge will be that the punishment for this willfully committed sin or sins will be that he is prevented from repenting. He (the sinner) is not provided the volition to repent from his wickedness. This is in order that he should die and be destroyed for the sin he has committed... Therefore, it is written in the Torah, "I will strengthen the heart of Paroh". Because he first sinned by his own volition and acted evilly to the people of Israel who dwelled in his land ... it was the judgment that repentance should be denied him so that he should be punished. Therefore, Hashem strengthened his heart... (Maimonides, Mishne Torah, Laws of Repentance 6:3)

6. Suspension of Paroh's freewill

Maimonides' comments respond to a difficult issue. One of the fundamental principles of the Torah is that human beings are endowed with freewill – the capacity to make their own moral decisions. Because we have freewill, Hashem revealed to us His commandments, rewards us for our observance of them, and holds us responsible for their violation. Maimonides asks: How can we reconcile the principle of free choice with various passages in the Torah that indicate instances in which specific individuals or people have been deprived of their freewill? Maimonides cites as an example the Torah's description of Hashem strengthening Paroh's heart and depriving him of the ability to respond to the plagues by releasing Bnai Yisrael. In other words, the Torah tells us that Paroh would have surrendered Bnai Yisrael in response to the plagues if he had freewill. However, he was deprived of the ability to choose freely. Therefore, despite the suffering that he and his nation experienced, he could not release Bnai Yisrael.

Maimonides responds, that in this instance, Paroh was only deprived of volition after he had acted with terrible wickedness. He made freewill choices to oppress, afflict, and murder Bnai Yisrael. As a consequence of these freewill choices, he was punished by losing the ability to repent. His freewill was suspended in order to assure that he would be punished for his wickedness.

With these comments, Maimonides reconciles the principle of freewill with the passages in the Torah that suggest that freewill can be suspended. He also provides an important insight into the mystery of Hashem's treatment of Paroh. Hashem deprived Paroh of freewill as punishment for his willful wickedness. He then brought the plagues upon him. Moshe's warnings demonstrated Paroh's helplessness. Even after being warned by Moshe, he could not repent. His volition was suspended.

In the course of answering his own question, Maimonides confirms Rav Soloveitchik's position that the plagues were intended as a punishment for Paroh and the Egyptians. Hashem gave Paroh the ability to withstand the plagues so that he would be punished with additional plagues. Clearly, Maimonides understands the plagues as an instrument of punishment and not merely as a coercive measure designed to force Paroh to release Bnai Yisrael.

To the One Who struck the Egyptians through their first born – for His kindness is eternal. (Tehilim 136:10)

7. Hallel HaGadol

It is customary to recite the 136th chapter of Psalms on Shabbat and festivals. This chapter is referred to as *Hallel HaGadol* – the Great Praise. The chapter begins with a number of more general praises. The tenth passage begins a series of praises that focus on the acts of kindnesses Hashem performed for Bnai Yisrael – beginning in Egypt. The first of these kindnesses is identified as the Plague of the Firstborn. The chapter does not mention the nine preceding plagues. This implies that these plagues were not performed as a kindness towards Bnai Yisrael. This characterization and the contrast between the first nine plagues and the final plague conforms to Rav Soloveitchik's conclusions. The first nine plagues were intended as punishment for the Egyptians. They were not designed as a kindness towards Bnai Yisrael. In contrast, the final plague – the Plague of the Firstborn – was intended to force Paroh and the Egyptians to release Bnai Yisrael. This plague was a kindness performed on behalf of Bnai Yisrael.

"Speak now into the ears of the nation. And they should borrow, every man from his neighbor and every woman from her neighbor, silver vessels and gold vessels." (Shemot 11:2)

Bnai Yisrael Left Egypt with the Wealth of Their Masters

Why did Hashem command Moshe to instruct the people to borrow from their Egyptian neighbors? Rashi explains that Hashem had promised Avraham that his descendants would experience four-hundred years of exile and affliction. At the end of this period they would be redeemed and leave the land of their exile with great wealth. The first portion of this promise had been fulfilled. Bnai Yisrael had experienced the bondage of Egypt. Now was the moment for the realization of the second portion of Avraham's prophecy. The gold and silver that Bnai Yisrael would take from the Egyptians would fulfill the promise of great wealth.[16]

Rashi's comments explain Hashem's command. However, these comments raise a related question. Why, in the first instance, did Hashem promise Avraham that his descendants would amass wealth?

Rashi, in commenting on the promise made to Avraham, notes that the promise was fulfilled with the despoiling of Egypt. Rashi stresses the loss of the Egyptians, not only the gain of the Jews. This perhaps implies that the plundering of Egypt was not only intended as a repayment to Bnai Yisrael. It was also a punishment of the Egyptians. The message in Hashem's promise was that Avraham's descendants would be tormented but ultimately the wicked would be judged. The tormentors would be deprived of the wealth they had gained through the exploitation of Bnai Yisrael.[17]

Gershonides seems to indicate another possibility. Hashem was communicating to Avraham the miraculous nature of the promised redemption. Slaves sometimes achieve emancipation through the gradual enlightenment of their masters or through upheaval or uprising. However, the masters do not suddenly transfer their wealth to their former servants. This sudden reversal in the relative economic conditions of the masters and slaves is an expression of providence. Hashem promised Avraham that His intervention would not be subtle or hidden. Providence would be clearly revealed. It would be demonstrated through a redemption that would be remarkable and profound.[18]

Rabbaynu David Kimchi suggests that these riches were payment to Bnai Yisrael for their labor on behalf of the Egyptians. Hashem promised Avraham that although his descendants would be afflicted, they would not escape slavery in destitution. They would acquire the wealth of their masters.[19] Based on this explanation, Rav Shlomo Ephraim Luntshitz – Klee Yakar – explains an enigmatic discussion in the Talmud.

Our Sages were concerned with a second aspect of Hashem's instruction to Moshe. Hashem tells Moshe that he should address Bnai Yisrael with this command "now." The actual word used in the pasuk is nah. Unkelus and others provide this translation for the term. However, the Talmud offers a different translation for the term nah. In Tractate Berachot, the Sages explain that the term means please. According to this translation, Hashem was asking Moshe to request that Bnai Yisrael loot Egypt.[20]

It is unusual for Hashem to express Himself in the context of a request. Instead, He commands and instructs. Why then is this strange mode of expression used here? The Talmud responds that Hashem did not want to be criticized by Avraham. If the nation did not leave with the Egyptian's wealth, Avraham could complain that Hashem had not completely fulfilled His covenant. He had subjected the nation to suffering. But He had not provided the promised reward.[21]

---

[16] Rabbaynu Shlomo ben Yitzchak (Rashi), *Commentary on Sefer Shemot* 11:2.
[17] Rabbaynu Shlomo ben Yitzchak (Rashi), *Commentary on Sefer Beresheit* 15:14.
[18] Rabbaynu Levi ben Gershon (Ralbag / Gershonides), *Commentary on Sefer Beresheit*, (Mosad HaRav Kook, 1994), p 116.
[19] Rabbaynu David Kimchi (Radak), *Commentary on Sefer Beresheit* 15:14.
[20] Mesechet Berachot 9b.
[21] Mesechet Berachot 9b.

This entire discussion is difficult to understand. The Talmud seems concerned with the implications of the omnipotent Hashem making a request rather than a demand. Yet, the response seems inadequate. If Hashem wanted to fulfill His promise to Avraham, let Him command Bnai Yisrael to loot Egypt. Furthermore, should Hashem be preoccupied by human perceptions? He should be true to His commitments regardless of human perceptions! In other words, the important issue in fulfilling His promise is not that He meet Avraham's expectations. The issue is that Hashem has made a promise and He must be true to His word!

The Talmud provides some assistance in answering this question. It explains that Bnai Yisrael were perfectly content to leave Egypt without these spoils. There are a number of reasons offered for their attitude. First, they were escaping bondage. A person rescued from such terrible suffering does not think about wealth; freedom is sufficient achievement. Second, the people knew that they were to travel to the Land of Israel and would be required to transport any possessions they took out of Egypt. Understandably, the people wished to minimize their burden.[22]

In order to appreciate the relevance of these comments to the above problem, these comments must be carefully analyzed. The people did not want the wealth of the Egyptians. Why was Hashem concerned with the fulfillment of His promise that Bnai Israel leave with all of Egypt's wealth? The people's disinterest in the wealth of their masters relieved Him of any obligation to provide them with this wealth. Klee Yakar responds that we must better understand the promise that Hashem made to Avraham. Hashem had promised that Bnai Yisrael would leave the land of their affliction with wealth. Why was this wealth necessary? Klee Yakar explains that this wealth was intended as compensation to Bnai Yisrael for their labor. This has two implications. First, it was important that Bnai Yisrael receive payment. Second, the compensation must come from those who owed the payment – the Egyptians. Both of these requirements must be met to avoid any perception of injustice.

Now our questions can be answered. The use of the term nah is designed to communicate an important message. Literally, the term means "now". However, it also can mean "please." Why did the Hashem use this term? He was acknowledging that the wealth of the Egyptians was intended as compensation. Therefore, the nation had the right to decline this payment. However, declining would create a perception of injustice.

Now Hashem's concern with perceptions is understood. Hashem promised Avraham that Bnai Yisrael would receive compensation. Because the spoils were intended as compensation, Avraham's descendants had the right to refuse them. However, a perception of injustice would result. Bnai Yisrael would have worked without payment. The Egyptians would have benefited from their evil actions. In order to avoid this perception of injustice, it was essential that Bnai Yisrael confiscate the wealth of the Egyptians.[23]

"And every firstborn in the land of Egypt will die, from the firstborn of Paroh who sits on his throne to the firstborn of the servant woman who is behind the millstones, and every firstborn animal." (Shemot 11:5)

---

[22] Mesechet Berachot 9b.
[23] Rav Shlomo Ephraim Luntshitz, *Commentary Klee Yakar on Sefer Shemot* 11:2.

Moshe warns Paroh that if he continues to refuse to release Bnai Yisrael, Hashem will bring upon him and his nation the plague of the firstborn. Moshe describes to Paroh the scope of the plague. All of the firstborn will be killed. The plague will extend from the most exalted households in the land – Paroh's own household – to the most humble households – the households of servants. Even the firstborn animals will not be spared.

Rashi comments on this passage: "…to the firstborn of the captive." Why were the captives smitten? So that they would not say, "Our deity has demanded [vengeance] for their [our] degradation, and brought retribution upon Egypt." Rashi is explaining the reason that the families of captives in Egypt were included in the plague. He explains that the captives were included in order to assure that the significance of the plague would not be misunderstood. Like Bnai Yisrael, these captives were also afflicted by the Egyptians. These captives might be tempted to attribute the plague to their own deities. Perhaps, they would assert that their deities had brought the plague upon the Egyptians in order to avenge their suffering. In order to negate this fallacious claim, even the firstborn of these captives were killed by the plague.

There is an obvious problem with these comments. The passage actually makes no mention of the inclusion of the firstborn of the captives in the plague! The Torah does indicate that these firstborn were included in the plague. However, the passage that describes their inclusion is in the next chapter.

"It came to pass at midnight, and Hashem struck every firstborn in the land of Egypt, from the firstborn of Paroh who sits on his throne to the firstborn of the captive who is in the dungeon, and every firstborn animal." (Shemot 12:29)

This passage describes the actual events of the plague of the firstborn. The passage confirms the scope of the plague. It extended from the household of Paroh to the households of captives in the land of Egypt. In this passage the captives, to whom Rashi referred, are mentioned.

In this passage, Rashi again discusses the inclusion of the households of the captives in the plague. Rashi makes two points: He explains that the servant woman mentioned in the earlier passage is not the same person as the captive described in this latter passage. In other words, "servant woman" and "captive" are not alternative descriptions of the same person. Rashi also returns to the issue of the inclusion of the captives' households in the plague. Why were these households included? Rashi recounts the explanation he offered earlier: The inclusion of these households in the plague assured that these captives could not attribute the plague to their own deities. However, in this instance, Rashi offers a second explanation for the inclusion of the captives' households. He explains that these captives rejoiced in the subjugation and affliction of Bnai Yisrael. In order to punish them for this mean-spirited, baseless hatred, their firstborn were included in the plague.

This raises a second problem: In Rashi's initial discussion of the inclusion of the captives in the plague, he offered a single explanation. They were included in order to preclude any attribution of the plague to their own deities. However, in Rashi's subsequent treatment of the issue, he offers a second explanation for their inclusion: They were included as a punishment for their baseless hatred of Bnai Yisrael. Why does Rashi not include this second explanation in his initial treatment of the issue? Why does Rashi introduce this second explanation only in his subsequent return to the issue? In order to answer these questions, we must consider a further comment by Rashi.

"Moshe said, "So said Hashem: Near midnight, I will go out into the midst of Egypt." (Shemot 11:4)

In this *pasuk,* Moshe reveals to Paroh the hour at which the plague of the firstborn will take place. The commentaries dispute the exact translation of the passage. Rashi suggests that the proper translation is that "near midnight" the plague will befall the Egyptians.[24]

Rashi recognizes that this translation presents a problem: It is odd that Moshe described the moment of the plague's onset as "near midnight." Certainly, Hashem would initiate the plague at the exact moment He desired! In fact, in the next chapter – in describing the actual events of the plague – the Torah tells us that the plague began at precisely midnight. Why did Moshe tell Paroh that the plague would begin "near midnight"?

Rashi responds that Moshe was reluctant to specify the precise moment of the plague's onset. Paroh's astronomers might attempt to calculate the exact moment of midnight. If their calculations were marginally imprecise, the plague would either precede or follow the moment they had calculated as the time for its foretold onset. These astronomers would not consider the possibility that their calculations were in error. Instead, they would claim that Moshe had not been correct in his pronouncement. In order to avoid this accusation, Moshe declined to indicate the precise moment of the plague's onset, and instead, provided an approximate time. So, if the astronomers incorrectly concluded that the plague began a few moments before or after midnight, this would not contradict Moshe's prophecy or undermine his credibility.[25]

Let us consider Rashi's comments more carefully. According to Rashi, Moshe introduced an approximation – near midnight. He did this in order to assure that there would be no mistake regarding the accuracy of his prophecy. But why was this important? Why did Moshe feel that it was imperative that Paroh and the Egyptians recognize that his prophecy was completely accurate?

Apparently, Moshe concluded that it was important that there be no confusion regarding the nature of the plague. Paroh and the Egyptians were to understand the plague as Divine retribution. Moshe insured that there would be no confusion regarding the providential nature of the plague by foretelling the event. However, Moshe recognized that his prophetic revelation of the plague would only be meaningful if it was completely accurate. If Moshe's prophecy was perceived as inaccurate or flawed, Paroh and the Egyptians would be tempted to deny the authenticity of Moshe's prophecy. They would argue that a flawed prediction could not be actual prophecy. If Moshe's prophecy was discredited, then the providential nature of the plague could also be denied.

Now, we can answer our first question. We noted above that Rashi initially discussed the captives on a passage 11:5. But, the passage does not mention these captives. The inclusion of these households is first noted by the Torah in the following chapter. In order to answer this question, it is important to appreciate that Rashi's initial comments regarding the captives directly follow his explanation of Moshe's use of the phrase "near midnight." This juxtaposition provides a context for Rashi's comments regarding the captives.

---

[24] Rabbaynu Shlomo ben Yitzchak (Rashi), *Commentary on Sefer Shemot* 11:4.
[25] Rabbaynu Shlomo ben Yitzchak (Rashi), *Commentary on Sefer Shemot* 11:4.

It appears that Rashi includes these comments at this point in order to respond to a question. Moshe provided an approximate time for the onset of the plague in order to assure that the plague would be recognized as Divine retribution. How did Moshe know that it was important to communicate to Paroh and the Egyptians that the plague was providential? Rashi is responding to this question. Moshe knew that the plague would extend to the households of the captives. He understood the reasons for their inclusion in the plague. They were included in order to preclude any misunderstanding regarding the origin of the plague. These captives would not be able to attribute the plague to their own deities. Only Bnai Yisrael would be protected from the devastation. Only Hashem – the G-d of Bnai Yisrael – could be the source of this punishment. Moshe concluded that a fundamental element of the plague was its manifest origin. Moshe understood that his prophecy was another means of demonstrating the Divine origin of the plague. Therefore, he constructed his prophecy in a manner that conformed to this objective. Through this adaptation of the prophecy, he assured that its credibility would not be undermined.

Now, let us consider our second question. In Rashi's second treatment of the inclusion of the captives in the plague, he offers two explanations. Only one of these explanations is included in his first treatment of the issue. The above analysis suggests a simple solution to this problem. In his initial comments, Rashi's intention is limited to providing an explanation for Moshe's actions. Rashi wishes to explain Moshe's basis for introducing an approximation into his prophecy. Rashi is not interested in enumerating all of the factors that dictated the inclusion of the captives in the plague. The captives were included in the plague for two reasons: First, Hashem wanted the origins of the plague to the manifest. Second, the captives deserved the punishment. Only the first of these reasons informed Moshe's decision to introduce an approximation into this prophecy. The second reason was not relevant to Moshe's decision. Therefore, Rashi does not include this second reason in his initial treatment of the issue.

"But among Bnai Yisrael a dog will not bark at a man or animal. This is so you will know that Hashem has distinguished between the Egyptians and the Israelites." (Shemot 11:7)

Moshe tells Paroh of the final plague. Hashem will strike the firstborn of the Egyptians. This terrible plague will fall upon Paroh's own son. It will even destroy the firstborn children of the Egyptians' servants. Only the firstborn of Bnai Yisrael will be spared.

Moshe adds that at the time of the plague, complete peace will prevail among Bnai Yisrael. He asserts that even the dogs will refrain from snapping at other animals or strangers. Moshe explains that the unusual behavior of the dogs will demonstrate that the Almighty distinguishes between the Egyptians and Bnai Yisrael.

Moshe's comments are difficult to understand. Moshe explains that Hashem will destroy the firstborn of the Egyptians. The plague will extend from the firstborn of Paroh to the firstborn of the Egyptians' servants. Only Bnai Yisrael will be spared. Clearly, the exclusion of Bnai Yisrael from this horrible plague will demonstrate Hashem's special treatment of Bnai Yisrael. However, Moshe adds that, among Bnai Yisrael, even an unfriendly dog will not disturb the peace. He then asserts that the unusual docile behavior of the dogs will demonstrate the Almighty's preferential treatment of Bnai Yisrael. True, this animal behavior is unusual. However, it is not nearly as remarkable as the pattern of the plague. The fact that this pervasive death would not touch Bnai Yisrael is far more remarkable than the silence of the dogs! Why does Moshe insist that the behavior of the canines is so impressive?

We will consider two approaches to answering this question. The first approach requires that we carefully consider the impact of this plague upon the Egyptians. What effect would the plague of the firstborn have upon the Egyptian people? Obviously, this plague would bring widespread death upon the Egyptians. However, Moshe stresses another impact. He explains that the Egyptian people will be thrown into a state of complete panic and despair. He tells Paroh that the cries of the people will exceed anything in the past or future. Total chaos will reign. In short, Moshe described two impacts. First, the firstborn will die. Second, the Egyptians will be thrown into a state of complete panic and despair.

Now, we can provide an explanation of Moshe's comments. Why did Moshe refer to canine behavior? Moshe wanted to contrast the experience of Bnai Yisrael during the plague of the firstborn to the experience of the Egyptians. As we have explained, the plague would impact upon the Egyptians in two ways. It would bring widespread death. It would create intense panic and despair. Moshe contrasted the experience of Bnai Yisrael to that of the Egyptians in both of these areas. He explained that while the firstborn of the Egyptians would die, the firstborn of the Jewish people would pass the night unharmed. Then, he explained that, whereas panic and despair would overrun the Egyptians, Bnai Yisrael would experience complete calm and peace. Moshe contented that this contrast would demonstrate the complete separation between Bnai Yisrael and the Egyptian people.

The second approach requires that we briefly discuss the concept of contrast. Contrast is the greatest between opposites. For example, we can contrast a brilliant person with an individual of normal intelligence. A certain degree of contrast does exist between these two individuals. However, greater contrast emerges when we compare opposites. In our example, if we compare the brilliant person, and an extremely dull-witted individual, a greater level of contrast emerges.

Hashem wished to create the greatest possible level of contrast between Bnai Yisrael and the Egyptians. Some level of contrast would emerge simply because Bnai Yisrael would be excluded from the plague. However, this is not the highest possible level of contrast. A greater degree of contrast emerges, when opposites are compared. Therefore, Hashem created an uncommon climate of peace among the people of Bnai Yisrael. This is the opposite of the state that would exist among the Egyptians. This would enhance the contrast between the experiences of the two nations.

"And all of these servants of yours will come down to me and they will bow to me and say, "Leave – you and all of the nation at your feet." And afterwards I will leave. And he left from Paroh in anger." (Shemot 11:8)

I work with teenagers. Many – maybe even most – have some ambivalence towards authority. This ambivalence can turn to outright antagonism when the student feels that he or she has been wronged by a figure of authority. I do not think that these feeling just go away as teenagers develop into adults. Instead, adults develop greater control over expressing these feelings. Nonetheless, each of us probably knows at least one adult who struggles with controlling resentment towards authority. And this struggle is always the most volatile when an actual wrong has occurred. So, this raises an interesting question. How far should we go in opposing wrongs done to us? Is there a point at which we are overreacting and just expressing an innate antipathy towards authority? What is that point? In order to gain some insight into the Torah's perspective on these issues, let us consider Moshe's relationship to Paroh.

Now, this relationship is a perfect paradigm for analyzing our question. Moshe was commanded by Hashem to vigorously oppose Paroh. This opposition to Paroh was not over imagined wrongs. Paroh was evil and deserved to be destroyed. Yet, did Moshe set limits upon himself? Did he feel that there was some level of restraint that must be retained even when dealing with an evil despot like Paroh?

Let us begin our investigation by considering our passage. Moshe tells Paroh about the plague of the firstborn. He tells Paroh that all of the firstborn in Egypt will die – except the firstborn of Bnai Yisrael. Then, he tells Paroh that his servant will come to him – Moshe. They will prostrate themselves before him and beg him to leave Egypt with Bnai Yisrael.

In the end, the scenario that Moshe described did not unfold precisely as he predicted. Actually, Paroh himself sought out Moshe and begged him to lead Bnai Yisrael out of Egypt. This discrepancy between Moshe's prediction and actual events concerned our Sages and they offered an interesting explanation. According to Rebbi Yannai, Moshe knew that Paroh would himself seek him out. However in deference to Paroh's position as ruler, Moshe did not reveal to Paroh that he would humiliate himself.[26] Rebbi Yannai's position reflects a sentiment expressed by Rebbi Channina. Rebbi Channina taught that a person should regularly pray for the welfare of the government. He explained that if it were not for the presence of government authority, there would be no order or safety in society.[27] Rebbi Yannai maintains that Moshe's behavior reflected his conflict was with Paroh as an individual. But he respected Paroh as the head of his government. Moshe did not wish to show disrespect or undermine this position.

> "Go to Paroh in the morning. He will go out to the water and you should stand opposite him on the bank of the river. And the staff that was transformed into a serpent you should take in your hand." (Shemot 7:15)

The Sages were not unanimous in their support of Rebbi Yannai's position. Their dispute focuses on the above passage from Parshat VaEra. Hashem tells Moshe to demand that Paroh release Bnai Yisrael. If Paroh refuses, Hashem will turn the water in Egypt into blood. Hashem tells Moshe to confront Paroh in the morning as Paroh goes out to the water. Resh Lakish and Rebbi Yochanan dispute the tone of Moshe's message. Rebbi Yochanan shares the perspective of Rebbi Yannai. He comments that Moshe was required to address Paroh with respect. But Resh Lakish disagrees. He asserts that Moshe was required to demonstrate disrespect to Paroh.[28] This raises an obvious question. We understand Rebbi Yannai and Rebbi Yochanan's reasoning. They maintain that Moshe was required to keep the dispute focused. His dispute with Paroh could not turn into a rebellion against authority. Moshe must make clear that his conflict is with Paroh the individual but he is not an anarchist. Why does Resh Lakish disagree with this reasonable approach?

But before we can begin to understand the dispute between these Sages we must recognize and deal with another difficulty in Resh Lakish's position. There is no question that in our *parasha* – as explained above – Moshe omitted telling Paroh that he himself would be required to humiliate himself and beg Moshe to lead Bnai Yisrael out of Egypt. Rebbi Yaanai and Rebbi Yochanan can easily explain this act of deference. But according to Resh Lakish,

---

[26] Mesechet Zevachim 102a.
[27] Mesechet Avot 3:2.
[28] Mesechet Zevachim 102a.

Moshe was required to humiliate Paroh. How can Resh Lakish account for Moshe's apparent deference to Paroh?

"And the servant of Paroh said to him, "Until when will this be a menace to us. Send the men and they will worship Hashem their G-d. Do you not yet know that Egypt is being destroyed?" (Shemot 10:7)

Moshe tells Paroh that Egypt will be overrun by locusts. The locusts will consume any foodstuffs that survived the plague of hail. Paroh refuses to relent. But Paroh's servants oppose him. They strongly advise him to release Bnai Yisrael and they question the soundness of his judgment.

It is interesting that the Chumash includes this dialogue between Paroh and his ministers in the account. We have to wonder why this element is included in the narrative.

Perhaps, the answer is that this dialogue reveals that in the battle between Moshe and Paroh, Paroh's own ministers had begun to believe that Paroh could not prevail. Paroh was a mighty king. Paroh's ministers are characterized as his servants. Yet, these ministers accepted that Moshe was more powerful than Paroh.

If this is the message of this incident, we have an insight into Resh Lakish's position. Paroh was a powerful ruler. His entire persona was dependant upon the manner in which he was viewed by his servants, ministers, and followers. Moshe told Paroh that his servant would seek him – Moshe – out and ask that he lead Bnai Yisrael from Egypt. According to Resh Lakish, Moshe was not sparing Paroh or showing him deference. He was adding to Paroh's humiliation. He was telling Paroh that his most trusted servants would abandon him. Forced to choose between their loyalty to their king and their fear of death, they would realize that Paroh could not protect them and they would abandon him. They would run to Moshe to seek salvation. Paroh would be revealed to be powerless and fragile.

In short, there are two possible reasons for Moshe telling Paroh that his servants – and not Paroh himself – would ultimately appeal to Moshe to lead the people from Egypt. According to Rebbi Yannai and Rebbi Yochnan, this was consistent with Moshe's policy focusing on his conflict with Paroh as an individual and avoiding turning this dispute into a campaign of anarchy. According to Resh Lakish, Moshe was heaping additional humiliation upon Paroh. He was telling Paroh that in the end his most faithful servants will abandon him.

This leaves us with one question. Why does Resh Lakish disagree with the reasonable approach and considerations of Rebbi Yanai and Rebbi Yochanan?

"And a new king arose over Egypt that did not know Yosef." (Shemot 1:8)

This passage is one of the opening passages of Sefer Shemot. Rashi's comments on this passage are very well-known. Rashi quotes a dispute between Rav and Shmuel. According to Rav, the passage is to be understood literally. A new king arose that did not know Yosef. But Shmuel disagrees. He contends that no new king assumed power. However, the existing king adopted a new outlook and set of policies. He disavowed any recognition of the guidance and counsel that Yosef had provided to Egypt's people and leadership. In other words, he chose to forget his debt to Yosef. [29]

---

[29] Rabbaynu Shlomo ben Yitzchak (Rashi), *Commentary on Sefer Shemot* 1:8.

As interesting as this dispute is, it is difficult to understand its importance. What difference does it make – in term of the overall account of the redemption from Egypt – whether the king was actually new to the throne or only new in his policies? In order to answer this question, we must analyze the dispute more carefully.

In its context, the passage above is providing an explanation for the oppression of Bnai Yisrael by the Egyptians. The Torah tells us that Yosef and his brother had died, Bnai Yisrael prospered in Egypt and then a new king arose who did not know Yosef. There are two ways to understand this last element – the new king. One possibility is that the new king simply was not a contemporary of Yosef. He did not have intimate knowledge of Yosef's contribution to Egypt. To him Yosef was an historical figure without relevance to the current age. What was real was the prosperity of Bnai Yisrael. Faced with the phenomenon of this astounding prosperity and lacking any sense of debt to Yosef, the king exhibited the same xenophobia that has surfaced over and again in our own times. However, according to Shmuel, this king knew Yosef. He chose to ignore his contribution to Egypt. Why was he compelled to engage in this fanciful denial? He must have felt threatened by Yosef or by something that Yosef represented.

There is a fascinating comment made by our Sages regarding Yosef's power and influence. Our Sages assert for forty years Yosef served as the minister of Paroh. In the following forty years, Yosef's power eclipsed that of Paroh and his influence extended over the entire civilized world.[30] With this comment as a backdrop, it is not difficult to identify the probable roots of Paroh's attitude towards Yosef. After Yosef's death, Paroh began to see Yosef as a usurper whose power and influence had surpassed that of the throne of Egypt. Paroh's battle was not an expression of xenophobic paranoia. It was an attempt to reestablish the position of the Parohs to its former – pre-Yosef – zenith. In other words, the destruction of Bnai Yisrael was an attempt to erase the memory of an embarrassing episode in the history of the Paroh's. It was an attempt to rewrite that history.

Viewed in this manner, Rav and Shmuel's provide two opposing perspectives on the conflict between Moshe and Paroh. According to Rav, Moshe's conflict was with Paroh as an individual. As an individual, Paroh was an evil, paranoid racist. But according to Shmuel, Moshe's conflict was not a personal battle. Paroh was attempting to reassert the supremacy of the authority of the Parohs through the oppression and destruction of Bnai Yisrael. Moshe was battling this corrupted expression of political authority.

Perhaps, these two perspectives are also reflected in the dispute between Rebbi Yannai, Rebbi Yochanan and Resh Lakish. Rebbi Yochanan and Rebbi Yanai's position corresponds very well with Rav's postion. Paroh's hatred of Bnai Yisrael was an expression of his own personal wickedness. Accordingly, Moshe opposed Paroh on a personal level. But he did not allow the dispute to turn into a battle with authority. But according to Shmuel, Paroh's entire campaign against Bnai Yisrael stemmed from an attempt to reassert the power of the Parohs and to destroy a people – Bnai Yisrael – that were a reminder of the former weakness of the Parohs. From this perspective, Resh Lakish's position makes sense. Moshe needed to prove that Paroh's reinterpretation of kingship was corrupt. No king can be the omnipotent ruler that Paroh would have the world accept. For Moshe to win this battle, he was required to publicly humiliate Paroh. And according to Resh Lakish this was accomplished when Paroh's own servants abandoned him to beg for Moshe's mercy.

---

[30] Pirkai De'Rebbi Eliezer, chapter 10.

And all of these servants of yours will come down to me. And they will bow to me saying, "Go forth – you and all of the nation at your feet." And afterwards I will depart. And he left Paroh in a show of anger. (Shemot 11:8)

Moshe's treatment of Paroh and the obligation to respect monarchs and rulers

After nine plagues, Paroh refuses to release Bnai Yisrael. Moshe tells Paroh of the final plague. In the tenth plague, Hashem will destroy the firstborn of the Egyptians. Moshe reveals to Paroh that this punishment will break the will of the Egyptians to resist. Paroh's closest ministers will plead with Moshe to take Bnai Yisrael out of bondage. The plague had the effect foretold by Moshe. The Egyptians entreated the Jewish people to leave the Land. Paroh himself beseeched Moshe to lead Bnai Yisrael out of the Land.

Rashi explains that Moshe knew that Paroh himself would seek him out and plead with him to spare Egypt. Moshe did not reveal this detail to Paroh. This omission was intentional. Moshe was showing respect for the dignity of the king. He, therefore, indicated that the ministers would petition him.[31]

Paroh was a rasha – an evil person. He had persecuted the Jewish people and refused to heed to the command of Hashem. He remained obstinate even after his own people had suffered terribly. It seems odd that Moshe would feel compelled to respect the honor of this corrupt monarch!

In order to answer this question, let us consider a related issue. Shulchan Aruch explains that we are required to recite a blessing upon seeing a king or ruler. This applies even to a non-Jewish ruler. The blessing recited is Blessed are You Hashem, our G-d, the King of the universe, who gave from His glory to creatures of flesh and blood.[32] This blessing is required regardless of the moral standing of the king. There is an important lesson to be learned from this requirement. We must recognize the importance of governmental authority within society. This concept is succinctly expressed in another teaching of our Sages. The Talmud instructs us to pray regularly for the welfare of the government. The Sages explain that without government, people would cruelly destroy one another.[33] A specific ruler may be evil and abuse his or her power. However, the institution of governmental authority is essential to the survival of society. This concept provides insight into the blessing. The blessing is not designed to praise the ruler. The blessing is an acknowledgment of the institution represented by the monarch or leader. Therefore, the blessing is required, regardless of the moral integrity of the specific king.

Paroh did not deserve respect as an individual. He was an evil, despicable despot. Despite these personal qualities, he still represented an important institution. He was ruler of Egypt. Moshe recognized the importance of governmental authority. He showed respect to that institution not to Paroh.

This understanding of the obligation to respect the king – even a despot – suggests a solution to another problem. Maimonides explains in his Mishne Torah – his code of law – that we are required to treat a King of Israel with deep respect. We are obligated to behave towards

---

[31] Rabbaynu Shlomo ben Yitzchak (Rashi), Commentary on Sefer Shemot 11:8.
[32] Rav Yosef Karo, Shulchan Aruch, Orech Chayim 224:8.
[33] Mesechet Avodah Zarah 4a.

the King with deference and awe. Among the laws that are designed to instill a proper sense of respect for the king are a prohibition against sitting upon the throne or even the chair of the King, or riding upon his horse. Personal elements of his property may not be used by others. His widow may only remarry another King of Israel. In addition to the many laws that govern the behavior of the people towards their King, there are also a number of laws designed to assure that the King conduct himself in a dignified manner. Among these laws is even a requirement for meticulous personal grooming.[34] This requirement upon the King seems intuitively reasonable. The people are required to respect the King. He is required to act in a manner that encourages this respect and to avoid behaviors that will undermine the people's deference towards him.

We are also required to act respectfully to Torah scholars. Maimonides explains that the level of deference due a Torah scholar even supersedes that due a parent. However, in describing the requirement to respect the Torah scholar, Maimonides does not mention any requirement upon the scholar to conduct himself in a dignified manner.[35] In other words, Maimonides does not describe a set of requirements upon the Torah scholar parallel to the King's requirement to conduct himself with dignity.[36]

Rav Chaim Soloveitchik suggested that Maimonides' divergent treatments of the King and the Torah scholar reflects that we are required to act with deference to both. However, whereas the King is required to act in a manner that encourages other to treat him with esteem, the Torah scholar is not subject to a similar requirement.[37] Of course, this raises an obvious question: Why does the Torah not require the scholar to conduct himself with dignity – as it requires of the King?

The above discussion provides a plausible explanation for Maimonides' distinction between the King and a Torah scholar. The respect due to the King is not directed to him personally. We are required to respect and act with deference to the institution represented by the monarch. This obligation applies to the people of Israel and extends to the King as well. The people must respect the institution and the King must conduct himself in a manner that dignifies the institution. In contrast, the respect and deference due to the Torah scholar are not directed to

---

[34] Rabbaynu Moshe ben Maimon (Rambam) Mishne Torah, Hilchot Melachim 2:1-5.
[35] Rabbaynu Moshe ben Maimon (Rambam) Mishne Torah, Hilchot Talmud Torah 5-6.
[36] It should be noted that in his discussion of the requirement to act with respect towards Torah scholars, Maimonides omits mention of a requirement of the scholar to conduct himself with dignity. However, he does describe a detailed set of requirements that govern the personal conduct of the Torah scholar in an earlier section of his Mishne Torah. This section deals with development of proper personal character and the importance of moderation in one's personal behavior. His inclusion of these laws in that section suggests that they are not an expression of a requirement upon the scholar to conduct himself with dignity. Instead, these laws are intended as a standard of personal behavior consistent with the Torah scholar's pursuit of personal excellence. For example, this section includes laws governing proper dress for a Torah scholar. The scholar must dress in clean, modest, and moderate clothing. However, this is not an expression of personal dignity associated with his status as a scholar. Instead, Maimonides posits that it is a personal virtue for a person to dress with reasonable care and moderation. A Torah scholar should seek personal excellence even in this area of life and therefore, dress in an appropriate manner.
[37] Kol Brisk, Introduction p 20a.

the scholar on a personal level. Neither is there an institution of "Torah scholar" that these requirements are intended to uphold. Instead, we are required to honor the Torah. The Torah scholar represents Torah. It is for this reason alone that we are required to act towards him with respect and deference.

The intent and design of the obligation to honor the Torah scholar is reflected in Maimonides' formulation of the obligation. In his introduction to the Laws of Torah Study, he explains that this section of his Mishne Torah discusses the laws included in two commandments:

- The study of Torah.
- Honoring those who teach Torah and know Torah.

At first glance, this wording seems needlessly cumbersome. Why did Maimonides not define the second mitzvah as "to honor Torah scholars"? Why did he adopt a more complex and wordy description for the commandment? The above discussion suggests that Maimonides carefully selected his words. His intention is to communicate that the Torah scholar is not honored because he has achieved a station or status that demands respect. In other words, he is not honored because of who he is. Instead, he is treated with reverence because of his association with the Torah. He is a teacher of the Torah or one who knows the Torah.

Now, the distinction between the King and the Torah scholar can be understood. The King shares with the people the obligation to promote respect of the institution of governmental authority. The people must act with deference to the King and the King must conduct himself with appropriate dignity. In contrast, the respect we are required to demonstrate to a Torah scholar is an expression of reverence for the Torah. The scholar and the people must demonstrate this reverence through their conduct towards those who are associated with Torah – its teachers and scholars. However, there is no institution of "the Torah scholar" that the Torah scholar is required to promote.

This discussion provides a possible explanation for another apparent inconsistency in Maimonides' treatment of these two instances of mandated reverence. In his discussion of the obligation to respect the Torah scholar, Maimonides asserts that this obligation is engendered by a specific commandment. However, in his discussion of the respect due to the King, Maimonides does not identify a commandment that specifically legislates this attitude and behavior of deference. The inescapable conclusion is that the obligation to behave with respect towards the monarch is not engendered by its own specific commandment. Instead, this obligation is included in the commandment that authorizes the institution of the King of Israel. In other words, in creating this institution, the Torah implicitly created an obligation to honor the institution. The institution is meaningless unless it is associated with an obligation of obedience to the King and respect towards the monarch.

However, the obligation to honor the Torah scholar must be legislated by a specific commandment. This is because the scholar's status and station do not intrinsically produce an obligation to revere the scholar. Instead, this obligation expresses the relationship between the scholar and the Torah. A specific mitzvah is required in order to legislate this association or to establish that the Torah is honored through the reverence we demonstrate towards the scholar.[38]

---

[38] Maimonides explains in Mishne Torah, Hilchot Klai Mikdash that the Kohen Gadol – the High Priest – must conduct himself with dignity. Maimonides does not cite a mitzvah specifically

This month is to you the beginning of months. It is the first to you of the months of the year. (Shemot 12:2)

The Selection of Nisan as the First Month of the Calendar

This pasuk refers to the month of Nisan. Bnai Yisrael will leave Egypt during Nisan, and Hashem tells Moshe that this month should be regarded as the first month. This creates a paradox. Nisan is the first month. It follows that the first day of the year should be the first day of Nisan. However, the year begins on the first day of Tishrai. Tishrai is the seventh month from Nisan!

Nachmanides explains that the Hebrew names now used to identify the months are of Babylonian origin. They originate from the time of Ezra and Nechemyah. Prior to this period, the months were numerically identified. In the Torah, Nisan is referred to as Chodesh HaRishon — the First Month. Similarly, Iyar is Chodesh HaSheni — the Second Month. These numerical designations were the exclusive means used to identify the months until the time of Ezra and Nechemyah. In other words, before the time of Ezra and Nechemya, the months did not have names. Therefore, dates were not assigned to events by identifying the name of the month and the day of the month associated with the event. Instead, an event could only be assigned date relative to the first month of the calendar.

An example will help illustrate this distinction. What is the date of Sucot? We are accustomed to referring to its date as the 15th of Tishrai. However, this simple system of dating did not exist before Ezra and Nechemya. Before their time, the date of Sucot was identified relative to the first month of the calendar. Its date was identified as the 15th day of the Seventh Month.

Nachmanides explains that this numerical system used to identify dates has an obvious objective. It relates every date of the anniversary of the redemption. For example: Through referring to the date of Sucot as the 15th day of the Seventh Month, we are really saying that the festival is observed on the 15th day of the seventh month from the anniversary-month of our redemption from Egypt and bondage. This system mimics in its structure and its objective the Torah's system for identifying the days of the week. The days of the week do not have names. Instead, they are identified relative to Shabbat. The first day of the week is identified as one day from Shabbat, the second as two days from Shabbat, and so on. The obvious objective is to relate every event associated with a day of the week to Shabbat or to the completion of the creation of the universe. In this manner, the Torah uses a common every-day practice as an opportunity to remind us of important events. When we refer to a day of the week, we recall creation. When we refer to a date in the year, we recall our redemption.

Based upon this analysis, Nachmanides resolves the paradox. How can the year begin on the first day of the Seventh Month? The year should begin on the first day of the First Month! He explains that the above pasuk does not say that the month we now call Nisan is the first month of

---

legislating this requirement. This suggests that this obligation stems from the mitzvah that establishes the institution of the priesthood. In creating this institution, the Torah demanded that the person heading this institution – the Kohen Gadol – conduct himself in a manner that dignifies the institution.

the year. Instead, the Torah states that it is the first of the months. This does not mean that the year begins in Nisan. It means that all events should be dated by and associated with the anniversary-month of the redemption. The various months should not receive distinct names. Instead, each should be identified relative to the anniversary-month of the redemption from Egypt. The paradox is resolved. The first day of the year, is indeed, the first day of the Seventh Month. In other words, the first day of the year occurs on the month that is the seventh month from the anniversary-month of the redemption. This is the first day of the month that we now refer to as Tishrai.

This leaves one issue to be resolved. Why was the Torah's system of dating that associates every date and event with the redemption replaced by a system that gives each month an individual name? This innovation severs the identification of the month and dates with the redemption from Egypt! Nachmanides responds by referring to a passage in Yermiyahu. The Navi tells the nation that they will be redeemed from their exile. When they return to the Land of Israel from the lands of their exile, they will no longer praise Hashem as their redeemer from Egypt. Instead, they will praise Hashem for restoring them to the Land from their more immediate exile.

Nachmanides explains that when the prophecy of their redemption was fulfilled, they adopted the names for the months that were used in the land of their exile. They replaced the dating system outlined in the Torah with these adopted names. These names would remind them of their recent exile and redemption. This was a fulfillment of Yermiyahu's prophecy. The Torah system of dating was designed to recall the redemption from Egypt. The new system recalled the more recent exile and redemption of the nation.[39]

"This month shall be for you the head of the months. It shall be for you the first of the months of the year." (Shemot 12:2)
Declaring the New Moon with the Appearance of Its Crescent

There is an interesting midrash on the above pasuk. An introduction is needed to understand the midrash's comments. The Torah calendar is lunar. The new months are declared on the basis of the appearance of the new moon. Ideally, the new month is declared on the basis of the testimony of two witnesses. These witnesses appear before the high court in Yerushalayim and declare that they have seen the crescent. It is true that the appearance of the new moon can also be calculated mathematically. However, in the ideal situation, the mathematical calculations play only a secondary role. The primary means for declaring the new month is through eyewitness testimony.

Today we do not have a high court. Therefore, we cannot determine the advent of a new month on the basis of testimony. Instead, we rely on mathematical calculations. The Jewish calendar is the product of these calculations.

Now, the midrash's comments can be introduced. The midrash explains that Moshe had difficulty understanding this mitzvah. In order to solve Moshe's problem, Hashem showed Moshe the exact crescent shape that must be seen by the witnesses. He explained to Moshe that when this specific shape is seen, the new moon is declared.[40]

---

[39] Rabbaynu Moshe ben Nachman (Ramban), *Commentary on Sefer Shemot* 12:2.

The apparent meaning of the midrash is that Moshe could not visualize the amount of a crescent that the witnesses must see. He wanted to know how much of a crescent must be seen in order for the new month to be declared.

This interpretation of the midrash and Moshe's question presents a problem. It seems from this interpretation that the new month cannot be declared on the basis of the appearance of any crescent of minimal size. Hashem instructed Moshe that the crescent must reach a required size before a new month can be declared. However, this interpretation of the midrash cannot be reconciled with actual halachah. According to halachah, any visible crescent – regardless of its size – is adequate. When the witnesses report that they have observed the crescent, the new month is declared. The court does not require the witnesses to report the dimensions of the observed crescent.[41]

In order to understand the meaning of this midrash, another question must be considered. Because there is now no court in Yerushalayim, the new month is determined through mathematical calculations. What event or phenomenon is calculated to determine the new month? In other words, mathematical calculation is used to determine the time that an event occurs and the new month is initiated by this event. What is this crucial event?

The obvious answer is that the new month is defined by the appearance of the new moon. Therefore, the new month begins on the first evening that the new moon appears. The calculations need only determine this date. However, this answer ignores an important problem. In order to understand this problem, some background information is needed.

The moon does not generate its own light. The light of the moon is actually the reflected light of the sun. When the moon and sun are in exact alignment, the illuminated side of the moon faces away from the Earth. As the moon begins to stray from its alignment with the sun and Earth, the crescent of the new moon appears. However, the crescent does not appear immediately. After the disjunction of the alignment of the Earth, sun, and moon, some amount of time is required for the crescent of the new moon to be visible. The amount of time depends on the location of the observer on Earth. In Yerushalayim, six hours are required. Therefore, if the disjunction occurs before midday, the crescent will appear immediately with nightfall. If it occurs after midday, the crescent will not appear directly after nightfall.[42]

Now we can appreciate the problem posed by mathematically calculating the date of the new month. When does the new month begin? This requires an exact definition. Is the new month initiated by the disjunction of the moon and sun's alignment with Earth or is it determined by the actual appearance of the new crescent in the skies above Yerushalayim?

Maimonides deals with this issue. He explains that the calendar calculations determine the moment that the crescent appears. This answers our question. The new month is not defined by the disjunction of Earth's alignment with sun and moon. It is defined by the appearance of the crescent.[43]

---

[40] Michilta, Parshat Bo, Chapter 1.
[41] Rav Yechiel Michal HaLeyve Epstein, *Aruch HaShulchan HaAtede*, Hilchot Kidush HaChodesh 88:12.
[42] Mesechet Rosh HaShannah 20b.
[43] Rabbaynu Moshe ben Maimon (Rambam) *Mishne Torah*, Hilchot Kiddush HaChodesh 7:2. See also Rav Yechiel Michal HaLeyve Epstein, *Aruch HaShulchan HaAtede*, Hilchot Kidush

Rav Yitzchak Zev Soloveitchik Zt"l explains that this was Moshe's question: How would the precise definition of the new month be determined? Hashem showed Moshe the crescent of the new moon. He told Moshe this crescent must be seen in order to sanctify the new month. Hashem explained that the disjunction of the Earth's alignment with the sun and moon does not create a new month. The actual appearance of the new crescent creates the new month. In other words, He was not telling Moshe that a specific size or dimension was required. He was communicating to Moshe that a visible crescent is required.[44]

Why is a visible crescent required? In order to answer this question, a well-known principle of halachah must be considered. This principle is that the Torah was not given to "the ministering angels." Loosely explained, the principle dictates that halachic standards correspond with realistic expectations, and that an unrealistic level of exactitude is not appropriate. The following example will illustrate this principle and its application.

It is prohibited to derive personal benefit from hekdesh – the property of the Bait HaMikdash. This law applies to the garments worn by the kohen. However, there is an important exception regarding these garments. The prohibition only applies once the garments are no longer fit for use in the Bait HaMikdash. As long as the garments are fit for use, the prohibition against deriving personal benefit from them does not apply.[45] This is an odd exception. We would expect to be required to treat the serviceable garments with greater deference than those no longer serviceable. Retired garments should have less sanctity than those in use!

The Talmud deals with this issue in Tractate Kiddushin. The Talmud offers an amazing explanation for this law by evoking the principle, "The Torah is not given to the ministering angels".[46] How does the application of this principle explain why the kohens' garments require greater deference when they are rendered unserviceable?

Rashi explains the Talmud's comments. The garments of the kohen are initially sanctified with a qualification. This qualification is that their sanctity is not violated through inadvertent personal use. Why does this qualification accompany the initial sanctification? This is because inadvertent personal use is inevitable. The kohen cannot be expected to immediately remove his garments upon the completion of his sacred tasks. In the intervening time required to remove the garments, it is quite likely that some personal benefit may occur. In order to avoid a violation of the garments' sanctity through such use, the initial sanctification is qualified. Inadvertent personal benefit does not violate the garments' sanctity. Of course, once the garments are retired, this qualification does not apply. Once retired, the sanctity of the garments is violated through any personal use. This is the meaning of the Talmud's comment that the Torah was not created for angels. The Torah was given to human beings. It must conform to reasonable standards of human behavior. The Torah does not legislate laws that are inconsistent with reasonable expectations for human behavior.[47]

This principle – that the Torah was not given to the ministering angels – seems to be a common sense notion. However, the requirement for declaring a new moon provides an

---

HaChodesh 88:12.
[44] Rav Yitzchak Zev Soloveitchik, *Chidushai MaRan RIZ HaLeyve on the Torah*, Parshat Bo.
[45] Rabbaynu Moshe ben Maimon (Rambam) *Mishne Torah*, Hilchot Me'eilah 6:14.
[46] Mesechet Kiddushin 54a.
[47] Rabbaynu Shlomo ben Yitzchak (Rashi), *Comm. on the Talmud,* Mesechet Kiddushin 54a.

important insight into this concept. As explained, the new month does not begin with the actual disjunction. The month begins with the appearance of the crescent. Why is the appearance of the crescent required?

Gershonides offers many reasons for this law, yet we will only consider one. He explains that the Torah was given to be observed at all times. The calculation of the moment of disjunction is difficult to perform. It is not reasonable for a mitzvah to depend upon such a calculation. Gershonides argues that such a dependency on complicated mathematical calculations would create an obligation that many less-educated generations would not be able to perform. Simply expressed, the term mitzvah, or commandment, implies an expectation. The directive will be observed. This expectation implies that the commandment is formulated in a manner that is realistic.[48]

We can now better understand the principle discussed by the Talmud in Tractate Kiddushin. The Torah was not given to the ministering angels. The Torah was given to people. The recipients are expected to observe the commandment of the Torah. Therefore, its mitzvot must be formulated in accordance with reasonable expectations.

"This month shall be for you the head of the months. It shall be for you the first of the months of the year." (Shemot 12:2)

This pasuk introduces the first mitzvah that Hashem revealed to Moshe. We are commanded to establish a calendar. The calendar is to be based on the cycles of the moon. The emergence of the new moon will determine the beginning of each month. The courts are charged with the responsibility of accepting testimony regarding the appearance of the new moon and declaring the new month. Today's Rabbinic courts do not have the authority to accept this testimony and cannot declare a new month. We determine the date of the new month based upon a calendar developed our Sages.

The first day of the month has some special observances. One of these observances is that the Hallel prayer is recited in the morning service. The Talmud explains that the recitation of the Hallel on Rosh Chodesh – the new month – is not a Rabbinic decree. It is custom – a minhag.[49]

In order to appreciate this observation some background is required. The Sages enacted the practice of reciting the full Hallel on festivals. The Sages established an obligation to recite the complete Hallel on eighteen days of the year. These are, the eight days of Chanuka, the seven days of Sukkot, Shemini Atzeret, the first day of Pesach and on Shavuot. Outside of Israel, the complete Hallel is recited twenty-one days. In addition to the days it is recited in Israel, it is recited on Simchat Torah, the second day of Pesach and the second day of Shavuot.[50]

Although the complete Hallel is recited only on the first day of Pesach – or the first two days, outside of Israel – an abbreviated version of Hallel is recited on the remaining days of the festival. This abbreviated Hallel is also recited on Rosh Chodesh.

---

[48] Rabbaynu Levi ben Gershon (Ralbag / Gershonides), *Commentary on Sefer Shemot*, (Mosad HaRav Kook), p 45.
[49] Mesechet Ta'anit 28b.
[50] Mesechet Ta'anit 28b.

Why do we sometimes recite the complete Hallel and on other occasions an abbreviated form? The Talmud explains that the Sages established a Rabbinic obligation to recite the complete Hallel on the eighteen days outlined above. However, the custom developed to recite Hallel on additional occasions. This custom is not part of the original decree of the Sages. In order to identify the occasions on which the recitation of Hallel is customary but not part of the original decree, an abridged Hallel is recited on those occasions that are established through custom. In other words, when Hallel is recited in response to the original decree of the Sages, the complete Hallel is read. When Hallel is recited in response to custom, an abbreviated Hallel is read.[51]

What is the reason for the custom to recite an abridged Hallel on these additional occasions? Tosefot explain that Hallel is recited to recognize a miracle or to celebrate a festival.[52] Based on this criterion, we can easily explain the custom to recite Hallel on all of the days of Pesach. Although the original decree of the Sages only requires that the complete Hallel be recited on the first day of the festival, the custom extends the requirement to the entire festival. The custom is consistent with the original decree and is an extension of this decree. However, the custom to recite an abridged Hallel on Rosh Chodesh is more difficult to understand. Rosh Chodesh is not a festival. What is the basis for this custom?

Aruch HaShulchan offers an interesting explanation of this custom. Before we can review his explanation, an introduction is required. The Sages established a blessing that is recited each month at the appearance of the new moon. This blessing – Birkat HeLevanah – is composed of two themes. The blessing begins with recognition that the renewal of the moon reflects the system of natural laws that Hashem created to govern the universe. We acknowledge the wonders of this system and that the natural laws are an expression of Hashem's majesty. The blessing then take up a second theme. They compare the cyclical renewal of the moon to the inevitable redemption and renewal of the Jewish people. We declare that the renewal of the moon is symbolic of the eventual salvation of our people.

The blessing can be understood on a deeper level. Most people take for granted the regularity of the physical laws. We go to sleep at night certain that the sun will rise in the morning. We are sure that just as the moon renewed itself this month, so too it will renew itself next month. Yet, it is more difficult to affirm with absolute conviction that we will be redeemed from exile. We are aware of the promises of the Torah that the Jewish people will be redeemed. But our exile has extended over a period of centuries. It seems far less certain than the renewal of the moon and the rising of the sun.

The blessing responds to this confusion and insecurity. It declares that the physical laws operate in conformity with the will of the Creator. Their regularity and consistency is a reflection of His will. So too, our eventual redemption is promised by the Creator. Therefore, the certainty of our redemption is as absolute as the regularity of the physical laws.

Aruch HaShulchan suggests that this blessing identifies a basic theme of Rosh Chodesh. He suggests that Rosh Chodesh is associated with the theme of the redemption of Bnai Yisrael. As we explained above, Hallel is recited on the occasion of a festival or in response to a miracle. The miracle of our redemption has not yet occurred. However, on Rosh Chodesh we

---

[51] Mesechet Ta'anit 28b.
[52] Tosefot, Mesechet Ta'anit 28b.

acknowledge the inevitability of the miracle of redemption. The recitation of the abbreviated Hallel on Rosh Chodesh is an affirmation of our conviction in the certainty of this future redemption.[53]

Our parasha suggests an alternative explanation of the custom to recite an abridged Hallel on Rosh Chodesh. In order to develop this explanation, we must consider our pasuk more carefully. As we have explained, the courts are charged with the responsibility of accepting testimony regarding the new moon and declaring the new month. This obligation is a positive mitzvah. The declaration of the new moon is fundamental to establishing the dates of the festivals and – the annual Torah calendar. However, the annual calendar cannot be put in place simply by declaring each new month. The courts must consider another issue. Another passage in our parasha identifies this issue.

"Today you go forth in the month of the springtime." (Shemot 13:4)

Hashem identifies the month of the redemption from Egypt as the month of the springtime. From this passage, the Sages understood that Pesach must be celebrated in the springtime. However, this requirement creates a dilemma. The seasons are determined by the solar year. In other words, each season occurs at a specific point in the solar year. The lunar year – composed of twelve lunar months – is shorter than the solar year. Pesach occurs on the fifteenth day of the first lunar month. If every year of the Torah calendar were composed of twelve lunar months, it would be impossible for date of Pesach to consistently occur in the springtime. Because a lunar year of twelve lunar months is shorter than a solar year, each year Pesach would occur at an earlier date on the solar calendar. The first Pesach – that was observed in Egypt and the wilderness – occurred in the springtime. However, without some adjustment, in a few years, Pesach would have occurred in the winter! Therefore, the Torah authorized the Sages to occasionally add a thirteenth month to the lunar year. This thirteenth month was used to reconcile the lunar and solar calendars. This reconciliation assures that Pesach always occurs in the springtime.[54] In short, in order to set the annual calendar, the courts must take two steps. First, they must declare the new months. Second, they must occasionally add a thirteenth month to the lunar year – creating a leap year. This additional month reconciles the lunar and solar calendars.

The responsibility of declaring the new month is a positive command. According to Maimonides, the responsibility of the courts to declare an occasional leap year is also included in this commandment. Nachmanides and others disagree. They argue that these two functions are authorized by two separate mitzvot. One mitzvah authorizes the courts to declare the new month and the other authorizes the courts to reconcile the lunar and solar calendars through creating an occasional leap year.[55]

Superficially, Nachmanides position seems to be compelling. The declaring of the new month and the considerations involved in declaring a leap year are two separate functions. How does Maimonides include these two separate functions in one commandment?

It seems that according to Maimonides both of these functions – declaring the new month and creating an occasional leap year – are aspects of one single function. This function is the

---

[53] Rav Aharon HaLeyve Epstein, *Aruch HaShulchan*, Orech Chayim 422:6
[54] Rabbaynu Moshe ben Maimon (Rambam) *Mishne Torah*, Hilchot Kiddush HaChodesh 4:1.
[55] Rav Aharon HaLeyve, *Sefer HaChinuch, Mitzvah* 4.

establishment of the annual calendar. According to Maimonides, there is a single mitzvah. This mitzvah is for the courts to establish the calendar. This single mitzvah includes two elements – declaring new months and creating an occasional leap year.

This explanation of Maimonides' position has an important implication. According to his position, the courts are charged with the responsibility of establishing the annual calendar. The Torah calendar is lunar. So, the courts must declare each month. But part of the courts obligation in establishing the calendar is to declare an occasional leap year. This implies that the placement of the festivals in their proper season – for example, Pesach in the springtime – is an integral element of the task of establishing the annual calendar. Therefore, the mitzvah of creating the annual calendar requires that the courts consider the seasonal timing of the festivals and evaluate the need for a leap year. Let us express this in simpler terms. The single mitzvah that Maimonides describes can best be defined as an obligation upon the courts to establish the times of observance of the festivals.

Let us now return to the custom of reciting an abridged Hallel on Rosh Chodesh. As Tosefot explain, the Sages enacted a requirement to recite a complete Hallel on festivals. The recitation of this Hallel is part of the observance of the festival. This is directly relevant to the custom of reciting an abridged Hallel on Rosh Chodesh. According to Maimonides, the declaration of Rosh Chodesh is part of a more general mitzvah of establishing the times for observance of the festivals. It is reasonable to assume that in our observance of Rosh Chodesh, we are fulfilling the same mitzvah. By observing each Rosh Chodesh, we acknowledge the new month and participate in the establishment of the annual calendar and the times for the observance of the festivals. This fundamental element of our observance of Rosh Chodesh is expressed through the recitation of an abridged Hallel on these days. The recitation of the abridged Hallel expresses the relationship between our observance of Rosh Chodesh and the observance of the festivals. Through reciting the abridged Hallel we are acknowledging that this observance is directly related to our observance of the festivals.

And Hashem spoke to Moshe and Aharon in the Land of Egypt, saying: This month shall be to you the beginning of months. It shall be the first month of the year to you. (Shemot 12:1-2)

Time on Your Side

1. **Elements of the commandment to establish a calendar**

The Torah includes 613 commandments. Each of the commandments is given for all generations. They cannot be annulled; neither can new commandments be added to those of the Torah. The first of the commandments that was given to the Jewish people is recorded in Parshat Bo. This is the commandment creating the Torah calendar. There are various elements to this commandment. These elements include the following:

- The establishment of a modified lunar calendar. The Torah's calendar is composed of twelve lunar months. However, the Torah requires that the lunar calendar correspond with the longer solar calendar. In order to align our lunar calendar with the solar calendar, an occasional 13th month must be added to the year.

- Assignment to the courts of authority to administer the calendar. The Torah assigns to the courts the authority to declare the onset of each month and to decide when it is necessary to add an additional lunar month.
- The identification of the first month of the calendar cycle. The Torah selects Nisan as the first month of the annual calendar cycle. Bnai Yisrael was redeemed from Egypt in the month of Nisan and the Torah gives it the distinction of being selected as the first month of the calendar cycle.

And G-d said: Let there be lights in the firmament of the heavens to divide the day from the night; and let them be for signs, and for seasons, and for days and years. (Beresheit 1:14)

2. Authority over the calendar expresses control over one's time

The creation of a Torah calendar deserves consideration. The Torah did not invent the concept of a calendar. Measuring the passage of time through observation of the heavens predates this *mitzvah*. In fact, in its account of creation, the Torah notes that the bodies in the heavens serve the purpose of marking the passage of time and the seasons. Calendars were in place before the Torah created its calendar. But, as Rashbam notes, this *mitzvah* creates for the Jewish people its own calendar. It directs the Jewish people to measure time by a calendar that is uniquely their own and to not avail themselves of the calendars used by other people and nations.[56] Why must the Jewish people have their own calendar?

Rabbaynu Ovadia Sforno addresses this issue. He explains that a slave is not in control of his own time. His time is managed by his master. This master tells him when he should rise in the morning. He assigns to the servant the activities that will dominate his day. He tells the servant when he may eat and when he may rest at night. The slave does not control his time and neither is time meaningful to him. Time passes and he merely flows helplessly within its current.

In creating a calendar, the Torah returned to the Jewish people the management of their own time. Now, they would decide how to spend their time. Furthermore, even the ordering of time and the measurement of its passage would be in their hands.[57]

According to Sforno's reasoning, it is fitting that creation of the calendar should be the first *mitzvah* given to the Jewish people. There are other commandments that recall our redemption. Shabbat and Pesach both remind us of our deliverance by Hashem from slavery to freedom. However, these commandments are reminders only. The commandment to administer the calendar and to seize control of the very measurement of time is more than a reminder of our redemption. It is an exercise of the freedom gained through that redemption.

This day you go forth in the month of the spring. (Shemot 13:4)

3. The selection of Nisan as the first month of the calendar cycle

Many of the commentators take note of the selection of Nisan as the first month of the calendar cycle. Nachmanides gives much attention to this issue. He and many other commentators explain that the selection of Nisan as the first month and the counting of all other months from Nisan engender an ongoing reminder of the redemption from Egypt. Nachmanides notes that the names that we use in referring to the months are not found in the Torah or most of

---

[56] Rabbaynu Shemuel ben Meir (Rashbam) *Commentary on Sefer Shemot*, 12:2.
[57] Rabbaynu Ovadia Sforno, *Commentary on Sefer Shemot*, 12:2.

NaCh. Instead, months are identified by ordinal numbers. The months are simply identified as the first, second, third month and so on. The names currently in use originate from the time of the return to the Land of Israel after the Babylonian exile.

Nachmanides explains that the identification of months by their ordinal number designations established a virtually constant reminder of the redemption. Every mention of a date identified the month relative to the month of the redemption from Egypt. For example, the 5th of Tishre was identified as the 5th day of the seventh month – the seventh month from the month of the redemption.[58]

The ideas developed by Sforno and by Nachmanides and his fellow commentators are closely related. As Sforno explains, administration of the calendar is an exercise of freedom. The designation of Nisan as the first month of the calendar cycle reminds us of from whence our freedom is derived. It is the outcome of Hashem's redemption of his people from Egyptian bondage.[59]

Rav Yosef Dov Soloveitchik *Zt"l* suggests a beautiful addition to these ideas. Before considering his comments, we will review a related discussion in the Talmud.

And Hashem spoke unto Moses, saying: Speak to the children of Israel, and say to them, "The appointed seasons of Hashem, which you shall proclaim to be sacred assemblies, even these are My appointed seasons. (VaYikra 23:1-2)

4. Bnai Yisrael sanctifies the festivals

The central blessing to the *Amidah* on each festival ends with praising Hashem, who "sanctifies Israel and the appointed times". The Talmud explains the meaning of this phrase. Hashem gave us the festivals. These are very special times and are endowed with sanctity. However, Hashem gave us the authority to administer the calendar. Through our administration of that calendar we bring about the occurrence of each festival. For example, by our determination that the first day of Nisan has arrived, we establish that Pesach will occur in 15 days. By declaring that Tishre has arrived, we determine that it is Rosh HaShannah, that Yom Kippur will be in 10 days and that Succot arrives in 15 days. In other words, we declare the arrival of the month and in doing so, we endow the appropriate days of the month with their sanctity as festivals.

Based on this elucidation of the role of the Jewish people in creating the festivals' sanctity, the Talmud explains the ending phrase of the festival *Amidah's* central blessing. The phrase means that Hashem sanctified the Jewish people with His commandments. Because of this sanctity, the Jewish people has attained the authority to endow time with sanctity through determining the occurrence of the festivals.[60]

As noted above, Sforno explains that through the calendar commandment, Bnai Yisrael was assigned control over time. Rav Soloveitchik adds that the calendar *mitzvah* also assigns to us the capacity to sanctify time – to endow time with special meaning and sacredness.[61]

5. Sanctifying time – a *halachic* and personal concept

---

[58] Rabbaynu Moshe ben Nachman (Ramban), *Commentary on Sefer Shemot,* 12:2.
[59] Rabbaynu Ovadia Sforno, *Commentary on Sefer Shemot*, 12:2.
[60] Mesechet Berachot 49a.
[61] Rav Hershel Schachter, *Divrai HaRav* (Mesorah, Yerushalayim, 5770), p 308.

Rav Soloveitchik's comments are closely related to those of Sforno. The calendar *mitzvah* expresses a free person's empowerment to be the master of one's own time. However, freedom creates only the potential to grow and thrive. The choices that the empowered individual makes – how the person uses the time he now controls – determines whether the person will achieve his potential.

As Rav Soloveitchik explains, we are not only the masters of our own time; we also have the capacity to sanctify that time. This is both a *halachic* capacity and a personal existential capacity. Rav Soloveitchik's comments focus upon the *halachic* expression of the capacity to sanctify time. We declare the advent of the new month. Thereby, we endow the designated days of the month with the sanctity of a festival. However, in the way we choose to use our time, we also are challenged to sanctify our personal use of our time.

6. Making choices in how we use our time

We cannot view this challenge as an abstract quest or a religious platitude. We make choices about how we will prioritize use of our time. We balance family and profession, recreation and household chores. And, somewhere in the mix, we try to find time for spiritual and Torah growth. To sanctify one's time means to examine priorities. It requires translating religious and spiritual values into an action plan for personal growth. We can make the choice to devote our time to the exclusive pursuit of material ends. If this is the choice that we make, then we use our freedom to choose a new master who enslaves our souls. But we have the capacity to make a different choice. We can order our priorities and the time devoted to them in a manner that promotes our growth and sanctifies our time. If we make this choice, then we choose to use our freedom to grow and to thrive as complete human beings and Jews.

Speak to the congregation of Yisrael saying: On the tenth of this month each man should take a lamb for the family – a lamb for the household. (Shemot 12:3)

And it will be guarded by you until the fourteenth of this month. And the entire assembly of the congregation of Yisrael will slaughter it in the evening. (Shemot 12:6)

Deserving Redemption

1. A special requirement of the first Pascal Lamb

Parshat Bo describes the conclusion of the ten plagues and the exodus of Bnai Yisrael from Egypt. The parasha also describes the first commandments that Moshe communicates to the people. Moshe establishes the Torah's calendar. The month of the redemption is identified as the first month. Other months are identified as the second month from the redemption, the third month from the redemption, and so on, through the twelfth month from the redemption. Moshe also communicates the laws governing the Pesach – the Pascal Lamb. This sacrifice is to be slaughtered on the eve the fifteenth of the month. The blood of the sacrifice is to be placed upon the inside of the doorposts of the homes of Bnai Yisrael.

This sacrifice is linked to the final and most terrible plague. Makot BeChorot – the striking down of the firstborn of Egypt. This plague will break the will of Paroh and the Egyptian people. Finally, Bnai Yisrael will be liberated. The blood of the sacrifice – placed upon the doorposts of the homes of Bnai Yisrael will save them from terrible death and destruction of the plague.

The two passages above deal with one of the requirements of this sacrifice. The lamb for the Pesach is to be secured on the tenth of the month – four days before its slaughter on the afternoon of the fourteenth of the month. During these four days the lamb is to be inspected in order to establish that it is free of any blemish that disqualifies it from use as a sacrifice.

The Talmud explains that this requirement was unique to the Pesach that was sacrificed in Egypt. Each year the Pesach will be offered in celebration of the redemption. However, future Pascal Lambs need not be secured four days in-advance.[62,63] Why did the Pesach sacrificed in Egypt have this special requirement?

2. Bnai Yisrael did not merit redemption

Rashi responds to this question by quoting the Midrash. Rashi explains that when the time of redemption approached, Bnai Yisrael was bereft of commandments. Rashi continues and explains that the nation's imminent redemption required that the people involve themselves in the observance and performance of mitzvot. In response to this crisis, Hashem communicated – through Moshe – two commandments to the people. He instructed the people to secure their lambs. He also explained to the people that a prerequisite for participation in the sacrifice is milah – the circumcision of the male members of the household. All uncircumcised males must be immediately circumcised. Through the nation's involvement in these two commandments, the redemption would be secured.[64,65]

And Moshe said to Hashem, "Who am I to go to Paroh and will I bring forth Bnai Yisrael from Egypt?" And He said, "For I will be with you. And this is the sign that I have sent you. When you bring forth the nation from Egypt, you will worship G-d at this mountain." (Shemot 3:11-12)

3. Bnai Yisrael's redemption as a prelude to the Sinai Revelation

In Moshe's initial encounter with prophecy, an angel presents himself as a flame burning in the midst of a bush. Amazingly, the fire burns intensely within the bush but the bush is not

---

[62] Mesechet Pesachim 96a.
[63] There is some discussion among the commentators regarding whether future Pascal Lambs require four days of inspection. Many authorities understand the Talmud to exclude future Pascal Lambs from the requirement of being secured and designated four days in advance. However, the Lamb must be inspected for four days. According to this interpretation of the Talmud, a person may charge the seller with the responsibility of inspecting the lamb for four days and purchase the lamb from the seller immediately prior to its slaughter. Others understand the Talmud to exclude future Pascal Lambs from the entire four day inspection requirement.
[64] Rabbaynu Shlomo ben Yitzchak (Rashi), Commentary on Sefer Shemot 12:6.
[65] Rashi also notes that by securing the lamb for sacrifice the people rejected the idolatry of Egypt. The lamb was regarded by the Egyptians as sacred. Therefore, the four day "grooming" of the lamb for its sacrifice was an act of defiance and a renunciation of the Egyptian idolatry. In the standard text of Rashi, this explanation for the commandment and the explanation above – that their redemption required the people's involvement in mitzvot – are intertwined. However, in the Midrash Rashi is quoting, these two explanations are clearly presented as alternatives. One authority quoted by the Midrash suggests that the commandment to secure the lamb addressed the imperative that the people involve themselves in commandments. A second authority rejects this explanation for the commandment and suggests that the mitzvah forced the people to renounce the Egyptian idolatry.

consumed. Hashem speaks to Moshe and charges him with the mission of leading Bnai Yisrael out of oppression and bondage and into the Land of Cana'an. The two passages above relate the initial dialogue between Hashem and Moshe. Moshe protests that he is unfit for this impossible mission. Hashem responds that He will accompany Moshe. He makes reference to the wonder of the bush that is not consumed by the fire in its midst as a sign of His relationship to Moshe. However, Hashem then adds that redemption from Egypt will be followed by the nation's arrival at this place – Mount Sinai – and at this mountain the people will serve Hashem. This last element of Hashem's response is apparently a reference to the Sinai Revelation that will follow redemption. Why is Hashem – at this moment – telling Moshe that the people will come to this place and experience the Revelation? How is this information relevant to Moshe's objection?

Rashi explains that Moshe's objection was actually composed of two elements. First, he questioned his own qualifications for the mission that Hashem was assigning to him. Second, he questioned whether Bnai Yisrael merited redemption. Moshe had observed the behaviors of Bnai Yisrael in Egypt. He saw little in their behaviors or values that suggested that they deserved to be redeemed. According to Rashi, Moshe had initially been troubled by the injustice of the suffering endured by his brothers. But after carefully observing their behaviors and attitudes, he had concluded that their terrible oppression was a deserved and fair punishment.[66]

Based on his interpretation of Moshe's protest, Rashi explains Hashem's response. Hashem agreed with Moshe that he was not qualified to speak to Paroh. However, Hashem would be with Moshe and He would secure the success of Moshe's mission. He also acknowledged that the people were not deserving of redemption. However, He explained to Moshe that their redemption was not a response to their righteousness or the injustice of their suffering. Instead, Hashem would redeem an undeserving and a meritless people because of the people's destiny. The people were bereft of merits. However, because of their destiny – the experience of Revelation – they would be redeemed.[67,68]

4. A contradiction in Rashi's comments

Rashi's comments seem to contradict one another. According to his interpretation of the dialogue between Moshe and Hashem, Bnai Yisrael would not be redeemed through its merits. However, despite the absence of merits, the people would be redeemed in order to achieve their destiny. They were to be the witnesses of Revelation and they would receive Hashem's Torah. In other words, the lack of merit in the present was irrelevant. Bnai Yisrael's destiny dictated that redemption was imperative.

---

[66] Rabbaynu Shlomo ben Yitzchak (Rashi), Commentary on Sefer Shemot 2:14.

[67] Rabbaynu Shlomo ben Yitzchak (Rashi), Commentary on Sefer Shemot 3:11-12.

[68] As explained, Rashi is suggesting that the people's destiny is of such enormous importance as to engender the imperative of its redemption. This is the generally accepted interpretation of Rashi's comments. Rabbi Reuven Mann suggests an alternative interpretation. Moshe could not understand the basis for the people's rescue. They seemed undeserving and beyond salvation. Moshe could not, at this point, appreciate the transformative potential of the Torah. Hashem responded to Moshe that although the people were meritless and incapable of bringing about their own spiritual revival, Torah would transform the people into a nation worthy of its relationship with Hashem.

In his comments on Parshat Bo, Rashi suggests the opposite view. Hashem gave Bnai Yisrael commandments to observe prior to redemption. The people's involvement in these commandments was a pre-requisite to redemption. This means that without the merit of their involvement in these mitzvot, the people could not have been redeemed![69]

He performs the will of those who fear Him and He hears their cries and saves them. (Tehilim 145:19)

5. The "why" and the "how" of redemption

It seems that Rashi is distinguishing between two issues. These are the "why" and the "how" of redemption. First, Rashi asks – in the name of Moshe – why were Bnai Yisrael redeemed. What merit earned them Hashem's attention? Rashi explains that the people had no merit; they had a destiny. Their redemption was Hashem's response to this destiny and not to the people's merits. However, according to Rashi, this response leaves an important issue unresolved. How could the people be redeemed? Redemption would express and be predicated upon a relationship between Hashem and Bnai Yisrael. In order for that relationship to be forged, the people must acquire a spiritual identity.

An example will help illustrate these two issues. Imagine that a benevolent person creates a generous scholarship for a young man or woman to study at any yeshiva, college, or school he or she chooses. Interested young people are invited to submit applications. The benefactor selects one of the applicants. The applicant selected has not shown enormous promise, neither has he accomplished much to date. Nonetheless, after careful consideration, the benefactor concludes that this specific young person is destined for greatness. Despite his selection of this fortunate young person as the scholarship recipient, the benefactor cannot unilaterally secure the recipient's success. The recipient must now respond and demonstrate initiative. He must set goals for himself and strive to meet these goals. He must apply himself and take advantage of his opportunity.

Bnai Yisrael was selected by Hashem to fulfill a destiny of enormous importance – witnessing Revelation and receiving His Torah. However, this selection was only the reason for the people's redemption. It was the "why" of their redemption. Still required of the people was their emergence as a spiritual nation capable of participating in a relationship with Hashem. Redemption would take place in the framework of this relationship and this relationship was the "how" of redemption. The mitzvot that Bnai Yisrael embraced and practiced in the waning days of their exile in Egypt were the foundation of this relationship.

Rashi's thinking is reflected in King David's words. David declares that Hashem hears the cries of those who fear Him and saves them from affliction. His response to our prayers is an expression of the relationship between Hashem and the petitioner. The petitioner must fear Him; he must engage in this mutual relationship. Hashem's response is an expression of the relationship between Hashem and the one who fears Him and turns to Him for salvation.

And they shall take of the blood, and put it on the two doorposts and on the lintel, upon the houses wherein they shall eat it. (Shemot 12:7)

Walking the Walk

---

[69] Rabbi Reuven Mann, Recorded lecture, C-0-40 Korban Pesach.

1. **An unusual aspect of the Pesach sacrifice in Egypt**

Parshat Bo is notable for a number of its characteristics. It is the penultimate parasha dealing with the redemption from Egypt. The plague of the firstborns is described. This plague brought Egypt to its knees. The Torah describes a broken and humiliated Paroh beseeching Moshe to lead forth Bnai Yisrael from Egypt and to end the devastation of the plague. The parasha also includes the first commandments that were given to Bnai Yisrael as a nation.

Among the commandments described in the parasha are those related to the Pesach sacrifice. This sacrifice was first offered in Egypt. However, it is to be offered annually as an integral element of the festival of Pesach. The initial version of the Pesach sacrifice differed somewhat from the version that was incorporated into normative observance. In general, animal sacrifices include an element of service involving the slaughtered animal's blood. This element includes sprinkling the blood on the altar. However, the Pesach sacrifice of Egypt was offered without an altar. So, the typical service with the blood could not be performed. Instead, the people were commanded to place the blood upon their doorposts and lintel.

And the blood shall be to you a sign upon the houses where you are. When I see the blood, I will pass over you, and there shall no plague upon you to destroy you, when I smite the Land of Egypt. (Shemot 12:13)

2. **The placement of the blood of the Pesach sacrifice**

Rashi, quoting the Midrash Michilta, explains that the blood was to be placed on the inside surface of the doorposts and lintel. It was to be visible to those inside the home but not visible from the outside of the home.[70] Michilta offers two explanations for the requirement that the blood be visible from the inside of the home and not from outside. Ribbi Shimon suggests that the requirement is expressed in the above passage. Hashem tells Bnai Yisrael that He will see the blood and He will spare the household from the plague of the firstborn. In other words, the members of the household will be safe from the devastation of the plague. Ribbi Natan also suggests that the requirement is expressed in the passage. He notes that the passage states that the blood should be a sign "for you". He understands this to mean that the blood should be a sign and visible to those within the home but not to those outside.[71]

In summary, these Sages agree that the blood was placed on the inside surfaces. However, they disagree on the source for this requirement – each suggesting a different biblical reference. What is the basis of their dispute? What insight might be reflected in their references to different elements within the above passage?

In addition to these two positions that agree that the blood was placed on the inside surfaces of the doorposts and lintel, Michilta quotes a third opinion. Ribbi Yitzchak suggests that the blood was placed on the outside surfaces of the doorposts and lintel. He does not provide a passage to support his position. Instead, as an explanation for his position he offers an enigmatic comment. He explains that by placing the blood on the outside of the homes the Egyptians would see the blood and their "bowels would be severed."[72] What does Ribbi Yitzchak intend to communicate by this comment?

---

[70] Rabbaynu Shlomo ben Yitzchak (Rashi), *Commentary on Sefer Shemot* 12:13.
[71] Michilta, Parshat Bo 12:7.
[72] Michilta, Parshat Bo 12:7.

And Moshe said: It is not fitting to do so; for we shall sacrifice the abomination of the Egyptians to Hashem our G-d. If we sacrifice the abomination of the Egyptians before their eyes, will they not stone us? (Shemot 8:22)

3. The Pesach sacrifice was a rejection of Egyptian idolatry

Before addressing these two questions, it will be helpful to review the objective or function of the Pesach sacrifice offered in Egypt. Moshe provided an illusion to the function in an earlier conversation with Paroh. After the fourth plague – an infestation of wild beasts – Paroh summoned Moshe. He agreed to release Bnai Yisrael from their labors for a period suitable to serve Hashem. However, he was not willing to meet all of Moshe's demands. Moshe had told Paroh that they would travel into the wilderness and there offer sacrifices to Hashem. Paroh insisted that the service to Hashem should take place in Egypt. Moshe responded that the Egyptians worshiped the animals that Bnai Yisrael would offer to Hashem. The Egyptians would never tolerate the sacrifice to Hashem of these deified animals.

In his response to Paroh, Moshe omitted mention of an important aspect of the planned sacrifices. From his comments to Paroh, one could conclude that the conflict between these sacrifices and the Egyptians' religious beliefs was merely coincidental. However, the Sages explain that the contradiction was intentional. Hashem required Bnai Yisrael to renounce the pagan beliefs and practices of Egypt. Toward this end, He directed them to sacrifice the very animals that their Egyptian masters regarded as sacred. Their participation in this service would announce their rejection of Egyptian idolatry and their initiation into service of Hashem.[73]

4. Bnai Yisrael's redemption was linked to the nation's spiritual awakening

In Parshat Bo, Bnai Yisrael is directed to offer the Pesach sacrifice. Through this sacrifice the objectives described above were achieved. The sacrifice of the Pesach lamb served as the beginning of Bnai Yisrael's spiritual redemption from the paganism of Egypt. Their participation proclaimed their spiritual awakening and their emergence from the darkness of Egypt. However, the sacrifice had another dimension. The blood on the doorposts and lintel protected Bnai Yisrael's homes from the devastation of the plague of the firstborns. The material safety of the people was linked to their spiritual renaissance.

However, the awakening that would save Bnai Yisrael from the plague raging outside their homes and lead to their redemption was to be an intense and meaningful spiritual transformation. A superficial adoption of behaviors would not be adequate. Such a total metamorphosis is complex. It involves a capacity to and willingness to wholeheartedly embrace a new and alien perspective. Also, if this change is to be meaningful, the new perspective that is embraced cannot be vague or poorly grasped. It is only meaningful if its content is a clearly defined and understood value or perspective. Finally, the full embrace of a new and alien perspective requires tremendous intellectual and spiritual courage. This is not achievable by those who are faint-hearted or easily intimidated.

The Sages quoted by the Michilta all agree that the redemption required an authentic spiritual awakening. Also, they agree that this awakening was expressed through the Pesach

---

[73] See, for example, Rabbaynu Shlomo ben Yitzchak (Rashi), *Commentary on Sefer Shemot* 12:6.

sacrifice offered in Egypt. However, they differ on the role played by the placement of the animal's blood in the emergence of the new spiritual personality.

6. Bnai Yisrael were expected to internalize the lessons of the redemption

Ribbi Shimon and Ribbi Natan agree that that blood of the sacrifice was to be placed upon the inside of the homes. Ribbi Natan explains that this requirement is expressed in the passage cited above. The blood was to serve as a sign to those in the home. Therefore, its proper place was inside the home. According to Ribbi Natan the placement of the blood communicated a moving and profound message. It communicated the definition of authentic spiritual change. The salvation of the household depended upon an intimate and personal transformation within its members. They must completely reinvent their world-view and their understanding of reality. They must abandon the familiar pagan perspective in which they had been raised and replace this primitive outlook with a strange new vision of the world. They must embrace Hashem as the only true G-d, as the Creator, and the source of all reality. No purely external, superficial, declaration can suffice for such a transformation. Their salvation depended upon achieving a real and meaningful change. Such a change must be an internal and personal realization.

7. Hashem's omniscience and the source of true security

Ribbi Shimon explains that this requirement is expressed in the passage previously cited. Hashem must see the blood and then He will spare the members of the household from the plague. Malbim notes that Ribbi Shimon's position is explained in a later comment of Michilta. Ribbi Yishmael notes that in the passage cited by Ribbi Shimon Hashem states that He will see the blood and spare those inside from the plague. Ribbi Yismael asks, "Does Hashem need to see the actual blood in order to ascertain whether the members of the household should be spared?" He responds that Hashem does not need to see the actual blood. The passage is not to be understood in a rigorously literal manner. Hashem is stating that as a consequence of their participation in the Pesach sacrifice, the household will be spared.[74,75]

Apparently, according to Malbim, the blood was placed inside to communicate the message that Hashem is omniscient. He is aware of everything – the external and the internal, our outward behaviors and our personal thoughts. The placement of the blood on the inside of their homes challenged people to seek security through a device only meaningful to an omniscient G-d. The forces of destruction outside of their homes would not be kept in abeyance by any manifest characteristic of the home but by the devotion of those inside the house to a service that was invisible from without. According to Ribbi Natan, the blood's placement communicated a specific message regarding Hashem and the true source of human security. A true spiritual metamorphosis can only be founded upon embrasure of specific values and perspectives. The blood's placement provided this specific lesson.

In summary, Ribbi Natan and Ribbi Shimon agree that the blood was placed within the homes. However, the sources they cite to support their positions reflect different interpretations of the requirement. According to Ribbi Natan, the blood was placed inside the home to communicate the nature of an authentic transformation. Adoption of external behaviors would not suffice. An intensely personal and intimate reorientation of the household members'

---

[74] Michilta, Parshat Bo 12:13.
[75] Rav Meir Leibush ben Yechiel Michel (Malbim), *HaTorah VeHaMitzvah – Commentary on Sefer Shemot*, 12:7.

worldview was required. Ribbi Shimon suggests that the placement of the blood was not intended to suggest the nature of the required transformation. Instead, it created the opportunity for meaningful change by providing the content of the new perspective. The fundamental content of this metamorphosis was acceptance of an omniscient G-d, the realization that our safety and security rests with Him alone, and that security is achieved through the fulfillment of His will.

8. Achieving physical and psychological freedom

Ribbi Yitzchak maintains that the blood was placed on the outside of the homes. His only explanatory comment is that by placing the blood on the outside of their homes they would "sever the bowels" of the Egyptians.

Ribbi Yitzchak's position seems to reflect the comments of another Sage, Rav Chiya the son of Rav Acha, quoted in another Midrash. He explains that the intention of the Pesach sacrifice was to engineer a confrontation between Bnai Yisrael and their Egyptian masters.[76] Akaydat Yitzchak expands upon this idea and explains that the redemption of Bnai Yisrael could not be complete if it only achieved release from bondage. The redemption required that they also break free from the psychological shackles imposed by slavery. They must reinvent themselves as a free people. They must replace the obsequious character of the slave with the confident outlook of the free person. This transformation could only be achieved through the emergent free individual confronting and humbling his former master.[77] This is Ribbi Yitzchak's message. The one-time slaves were required to stand up to those who fashioned themselves their superiors and "sever their bowels."

According to Ribbi Yitzchak the placement of the blood provided the people with the opportunity to reinvent themselves as a confident and courageous nation. Only through attaining this new healthy self-image would they be able to fully throw off the false beliefs of their former masters – the beliefs that they themselves had adopted – and embrace a new and revolutionary perspective.

9. Walking the Walk – the elements of meaningful change

These Sages disagree over the proper place for the blood and the message or lesson communicated by the blood's placement. However, the underlying message regarding meaningful change emerges from their collective views. Each sees in the blood's placement a different element of authentic change. Ribbi Natan sees in the blood's placement a lesson regarding the definition of meaningful change. The redemption from Egypt required Bnai Yisrael to progress beyond mere external expressions of change. They were expected to affect a fundamental internal change. Ribbi Yitzchak teaches us through the blood's placement that values are only meaningful when they are clearly focused and have substance and content. It is not enough to say, "I believe". We must understand what we believe. Finally, Ribbi Yitzchak reminds us that in order to serve Hashem wholeheartedly, we must free ourselves of subservience to other masters.

---

[76] Rav Menachem Mendel Kasher, *Torah Shelymah on Sefer Shemot* 12:21, note 427.
[77] Cited by Rav Yisachar Jacobson, *Binah BaMikre*, p 73.

BeShalach

And it was when Paroh sent forth the nation that the L-rd did not lead the nation by the way of the Pelishtim – for it was close. For the L-rd said: Perchance, the nation will reconsider when it encounters battle and return to Egypt. (Shemot 13:17)

The Downside of Parting in Peace

1. The problem with the short route to Cana'an

Bnai Yisrael has left Egypt. Hashem is leading the nation to the promised Land of Cana'an. He does not direct the nation along the shortest route to the Land of Cana'an, but instead selects a longer route. The passage relates this decision to the people's emotional state. They were not yet prepared to face a fierce enemy in battle. If they too quickly arrived at the Land of Cana'an, and were challenged by the nations inhabiting the land, they would not have the confidence and courage to face their enemies. They would flee from before them and return to Egypt.

The above translation of the passage is suggested by Unkelus and many other commentators. However, Rabbaynu Avraham ibn Ezra acknowledges an alternative translation. In this translation the passage states: And it was when Paroh sent forth the nation that the L-rd did not lead the nation by the way of the Pelishtim – *even though* it was close.

Both of these translations agree that the shortest route to the Land of Cana'an is by way of the Land of the Pelishtim. According to Unkelus, this route's directness was its shortcoming. Using this route to travel to Cana'an would provide the people with a direct path that they could travel back to Egypt. According to the alternative translation noted by Ibn Ezra, the route's directness was not a shortcoming. It was, in fact, the preferable route. But it was rejected by Hashem. The people needed to be prepared to face battle. This would take time and the longer route would provide this opportunity. Over the course of their travels along this longer route, the people would mature and prepare for the challenges that they would encounter.

These two translations suggest very different understandings of the message of the passage. In order to appreciate these alternative interpretations, the opening of the passage needs to be more carefully considered.

2. Paroh's farewell to Bnai Yisrael

The *pasuk* begins: And it was when Paroh sent forth the nation. This seems a strange description of Bnai Yisrael's redemption. Hashem redeemed His nation. Paroh was forced to release the nation and was only responding to the plagues that Hashem brought upon Egypt. Why does the passage attribute the liberation of Bnai Yisrael to Paroh?

The midrash addresses this issue. It explains that Paroh actually accompanied Bnai Yisrael as the nation left his land. He conducted himself as a host bidding farewell to an honored guest. Apparently, the passage's point is that Bnai Yisrael did not leave Egypt in defiance of Paroh. They did not engage in a rebellion, arm themselves, and wage battle to achieve freedom. They left with Paroh's blessing – at his behest.

3. The impact on Bnai Yisrael of leaving Egypt without conflict

The manner in which Bnai Yisrael departed from Egypt impacted their preparedness to face the nations of Cana'an. First, they did not fight for their freedom. They were passive actors in their redemption. This left them unprepared to confront the warriors of the Land of Cana'an. This adversary would not welcome them and give-up to them their land and their homes. They could be expected to wage a determined and even desperate fight to protect their land.

Second, they did not leave Egypt as escaping slaves rebelling and defying their rulers. They left Egypt in peace and with the blessings of their former masters. They could easily imagine returning to Egypt and being welcomed.

Now, let us reconsider the two interpretations of the passage. According to Unkelus, the passage explains that Hashem did not lead Bnai Yisrael along the shorter route. He recognized that when faced with war the people might retreat from the threat and return to Egypt along this easy road. The overall message of the passage is that Bnai Yisrael left Egypt accompanied by Paroh. They parted in peace. The manner in which they parted suggested to the people that if necessary, they could return to Egypt. Therefore, Hashem avoided the shorter route – the route that would have facilitated their return to Egypt.

Ibn Ezra's alternative interpretation is that Hashem lead them along the longer route in order to provide the nation with the time needed to mature and develop courage and confidence. The overall message of the passage is that Bnai Yisrael left Egypt without a fight. They were not required to test their courage and overcome adversity. A period of nation building was needed before these freed slaves would be prepared to face a fierce enemy. Hahsem led the nation along the longer road to Cana'an in order to provide the time needed for this maturation process.

Both interpretations recognize the inevitability of adversity and the necessity of building the confidence and courage to face it. If we are to face adversity, we must not delude ourselves into believing that it can be avoided by seizing false alternatives. We cannot imagine that we have the opportunity to return to our own Egypts. In other words, the easier alternative to facing adversity is tempting, but often illusionary. Furthermore, we must develop our confidence and courage. If we constantly avoid adversity, then we cannot grow and mature. We remain uncertain of our abilities and timid. But when we take on challenges and test ourselves we grow in confidence and self-assuredness.

"It came to pass when Paroh sent forth the people, that G-d did not lead them [by] way of the land of the Philistines for it was near, because G-d said, "Lest the people reconsider when they see war and return to Egypt." (Shemot 13:17)

Hashem leads Bnai Yisrael from Egypt. He will now guide the people to the Land of Israel. Our passage explains that Hashem did not lead the people to the land of Israel by the shortest, most direct route. The most direct route would have brought the people to the Land of the Pelishtim – the Philistines. In our passage, the Torah explains Hashem's reasoning for foregoing this more direct route and selecting a circuitous path. However, the exact meaning of this passage is disputed among the commentaries.

The above translation of the passage is based upon Rashi's commentary. He explains that the passage indicates two considerations that influenced Hashem's decision to select the more circuitous route. First, the route leading through the territory of the Pelishtim was more direct. Second, Hashem reasoned that when faced with war, the people might panic and attempt to return to Egypt. This second element is easily understood. However, the first factor – the directness of the route leading through the territory of the Pelishtim – does not seem to be a liability. On the contrary, the directness of the route would seem to favor its selection. Rashi explains that a direct route is more easily retraced. In contrast, a more circuitous route cannot be easily retraced. According to Rashi, these two elements are related. If Bnai Yisrael panicked when confronted with battle, the people would consider retreat back to Egypt. A direct route could easily be retraced. This option would encourage the people to surrender to their panic and return to Egypt. A more circuitous route cannot be easily retraced. Faced with war, the option to return to Egypt would be closed. Bnai Yisrael would be forced to confront their fears and go to battle; they simply would not have the option of retreat.[1]

Nachmanides rejects Rashi's interpretation of the passage. He raises an obvious objection: According to Rashi's interpretation, the passage is disjointed. Hashem's decision was based upon two related factors – the ease of retreat along the more direct route and the possibility of panic. If this is the intention of the passage, then it should group these two factors together and present both as Hashem's considerations. The passage should read: G-d did not lead them [by] way of the land of the Philistines because G-d said, "It was near. Lest the people reconsider when they see war and return to Egypt." Instead, the passage tells us that the route through the territory of the Pelishtim was more direct, and then the passage introduces Hashem's reasoning with the phrase "because G-d said."

Nachmanides offers an alternative translation for the passage: According to Nachmanides, the proper translation is: G-d did not lead them [by] way of the land of the Philistines, although it was near, because G-d said, "Lest the people reconsider when they see war and return to Egypt." The passage provides a single reason for forsaking the direct route: The people might panic when confronted by war and attempt to return to Egypt.

According to Nachmanides' interpretation, the more direct route was not abandoned because it would facilitate retreat. The route was forsaken because it would more quickly bring the nation into conflict with the inhabitants of the Land of Canaan – the land Bnai Yisrael must conquer. Hashem wished to delay this inevitable battle. Bnai Yisrael were not prepared to face the terror of an armed conflict. Therefore, a circuitous route that would delay this inevitable conflict was preferable.

Nachmanides recognizes that his interpretation of the passage presents a problem: Bnai Yisrael did enter into battle soon after leaving Egypt. The nation was attacked by Amalek. According to Nachmanides' interpretation of the passage, it seems that Hashem's plan was not completely successful! Although the route selected by Hashem delayed the inevitable battle with the inhabitants of Canaan, the Land of Israel, Bnai Yisrael was not shielded from an immediate confrontation with Amalek.

Nachmanides offers an interesting response to this problem: He explains that Hashem was not concerned with the response of Bnai Yisrael to this confrontation with Amalek. Nachmanides notes a fundamental difference between Amalek and the nations of Canaan: The nations of Canaan fought Bnai Yisrael in order to protect themselves from conquest and to retain possession of their land. They responded to a threat posed by Bnai Yisrael. Their war was defensive. Amalek was not motivated by these considerations -- it waged a war of aggression. Although Bnai Yisrael did not pose a threat to its security, Amalek attacked Bnai Yisrael out of hatred.

---

[1] Rabbaynu Shlomo ben Yitzchak (Rashi), *Commentary on Sefer Shemot* 13:17.

Based on this distinction, Nachmanides resolves the difficulty in his position. Hashem knew that Bnai Yisrael would fight Amalek. But, in this battle, retreat would not be a reasonable option. Bnai Yisrael would recognize the character of Amalek's attack. They would understand that Amalek was waging a war of aggression. Retreat would not save Bnai Yisrael. Amalek would continue to pursue the nation even as it retreated.

In contrast, Bnai Yisrael might be tempted to consider retreat when confronted with the battle over the Land of Israel. In this instance, retreat would be an option. The nations of Canaan would be fighting a defensive battle. They would be unlikely to pursue Bnai Yisrael once they felt they were no longer threatened.[2]

Of course, Rashi disagrees with this distinction. He explains that the circuitous route selected by Hashem was designed to discourage retreat when attacked by Amalek. According to Rashi, Hashem was concerned that Bnai Yisrael might panic when attacked by Amalek. In their panic, they might make the foolish decision to attempt a retreat. The circuitous route discouraged this choice.[3]

How might Rashi respond to Nachmanides' objection to his interpretation of the passage? According to Rashi's interpretation, the wording of the passage is somewhat disjointed. One of the most interesting responses to this objection is offered by Gur Aryeh. He suggests that Rashi was aware of the objection posed by Nachmanides and provided a response. Gur Aryeh notes that Rashi adds to his interpretation of the passage an enigmatic statement. Rashi comments that there are numerous interpretations of the phrase "for it was near" in the midrash.[4] Rashi does not quote any of the interpretations. Why does Rashi alert us to the existence of these interpretations?

Gur Aryeh suggests that Rashi's reference to the midrash is a response to Nachmanides' objection. Rashi is acknowledging that the passage's wording is not completely consistent with his interpretation. However, Rashi is explaining that the wording is designed to accommodate an allusion to the various insights provided by the midrash.

Gur Aryeh offers an illustration that clarifies his comments. Avraham made a covenant of peace with the Pelishtim. This covenant was to extend a number of generations. According to the midrash, the phrase "for it was near" refers to this covenant. Bnai Yisrael could not enter into battle with the Pelishtim because of Avraham's covenant. It was "too near" – too recent. The period of the covenant had not yet passed. [5],[6] The passage's odd construction provides an allusion to this and similar interpretations. The passage describes Hashem attributing his decision to two factors: One is clearly related to the insecurities of Bnai Yisrael – they may retreat when confronted by battle. According to Rashi, the other factor, "for it was near," is an amplification of this concern. A direct route would facilitate retreat. Rashi maintains that this is the simple meaning of the passage. However, the disjointed phrasing in the passage alludes to an additional interpretation. The wording implies that an additional factor – separate and independent of Bnai

---

[2] Rabbaynu Moshe ben Nachman (Ramban), *Commentary on Sefer Shemot* 13:17.
[3] Rabbaynu Shlomo ben Yitzchak (Rashi), *Commentary on Sefer Shemot* 13:17.
[4] Rabbaynu Shlomo ben Yitzchak (Rashi), *Commentary on Sefer Shemot* 13:17.
[5] Rav Yehuda Loew of Prague (Maharal), *Gur Aryeh Commentary on Sefer Shemot* 13:17.
[6] Michilta, Parshat BeShalach, Chapter 1.

Yisrael's insecurities – influenced the selection of this route. In short, the passage is constructed so as to communicate an overt message and to allude to the additional messages suggested by the midrash.

It is important to note that there are two fundamental differences between Rashi and Nachmanides' interpretations. First, according to Rashi, Hashem was concerned that Bnai Yisrael's response to an attack by Amalek. He was concerned that Bnai Yisrael would panic and attempt a foolish retreat. This would be a foolish response. Amalek would not break off its attack. Even as Bnai Yisrael fled, Amalek would press the attack. Hashem selected a circuitous route in order to discourage this panicked reaction. According to Nachmanides, Hashem's decision was not directed towards addressing the challenge posed by Amalek. It was designed to prepare the nation for its inevitable confrontation with the nations of Canaan. In this confrontation, retreat would be a practical option. Bnai Yisrael could avoid war through retreat. Hashem's plan was designed to create an interlude between the escape from Egypt and the conquest of the land. During the interlude, the nation would mature and develop the confidence to face battle. Rashi and Nachmanides do not necessarily differ on Bnai Yisrael's likely response to Amalek's attack. But, they do differ on whether Hashem's plan was designed to address this issue.

Second, according to Rashi, Hashem's decision was an extension of the redemption from Egypt. It was designed to assure that the redemption would not falter. Hashem wished to prevent a negation of the redemption. He had redeemed Bnai Yisrael from Egypt. They were not to return. However, according to Nachmanides, Hashem's decision was designed to prepare the nation for the conquest of the Land of Israel. In other words, the travels in the wilderness provided an interlude between the redemption from Egypt and the conquest of the Land of Israel. This interlude had a purpose. It was designed to prepare the nation for the conquest of the land. Also, it was essential that during this interlude the redemption remain intact. It was essential that the redemption not be negated by the return to Egypt. Rashi and Nachmanides differ on which aspect of this interlude dictated the selection of a circuitous route. According to Rashi, the selection of this route was designed to assure the preservation of the redemption. According to Nachmanides, the route was selected in order to facilitate the conquest of the Land of Israel.

And it was when Paroh had sent forth the people that G-d did not lead them by the way of the Land of the Philistines, because it was near; for G-d said: Lest the people reassess when they see war, and they return to Egypt. And G-d led the people about, by the way of the wilderness, by the Reed Sea. And Bnai Yisrael went up armed out of the Land of Egypt. (Shemot 13:17-18)

Time for a Road Trip

1. Hashem led Bnai Yisrael on a detour

The passages above describe the initial travel plan of Bnai Yisrael in its exodus from the Land of Egypt. The Torah explains that the most direct route to the promised Land of Cana'an was the northern route. This route would have brought the Jewish people to the western border of the land in less than ten days.[7] However, Hashem did not lead them along this route. Instead, He led the Jewish people along a southerly route. This route would bring the people to the Reed Sea that separated Egypt from most of the Sinai Peninsula and its harsh desert. After crossing the

---

[7] Rabbaynu Avraham ibn Ezra, *Extended Commentary on Sefer Shemot*, 13:17.

Reed Sea, Bnai Yisrael would be able to approach the Land of Israel from the south or even enter the land from the east.

Why did Hashem lead the people along this detour? The passages seem to say that the Pelishtim blocked the western approach to the Land of Israel. They would oppose Bnai Yisrael's passage. Within a few days from escaping the Land of Egypt, the Jewish people would be confronted by a very capable and intimidating adversary. Rather than confront the Pelishtim, Bnai Yisrael would panic and seek to return to Egypt. Therefore, Hashem led the nation along a more southerly course. Immediate confrontation with an imposing enemy was avoided.

> *And Hashem spoke unto Moshe, saying: Speak to Bnai Yisrael, that they should turn back and encamp before Pi-Hahachirot, between Migdol and the sea, before Baal-Tz'fon, over against it shall you encamp by the sea. And Paroh will say of Bnai Yisrael, "They are entangled in the land, the wilderness has shut them in." And I will harden Paroh's heart, and he shall follow after them. And I will glorify Myself through Paroh, and through all his host. And the Egyptians shall know that I am Hashem. And they did so. (Shemot 14:1-4)*

2. The objective of the miracle of the Reed Sea was the destruction of Paroh

There are a number of difficulties with the Torah's explanation of this detour. This first difficulty is found in an interesting comment of Maimonides. Maimonides discusses the various wonders Moshe performed. He explains that each of these was done in order to address a need of the moment. He then details these wonders and their purposes. Among these is the splitting of the Reed Sea. He explains that this wonder was performed by Moshe in order to destroy the Egyptians.

Avodat HaMelech notes that this is an odd characterization of this wonder's purpose. We would expect Maimonides to describe its purpose as the salvation of the Jewish people from their pursuers. In other words, why does Maimonides focus upon the death and destruction of the Egyptians and not upon the rescue and salvation of Bnai Yisrael?

Avodat HaMelech responds that a careful reading of the relevant passages confirms Maimonides's characterization of the splitting of the Reed Sea. In the above passages, Hashem tells Moshe that he should lead the nation back toward Egypt and encamp the people opposite Ba'al Tz'fon. Paroh will believe that the people are lost and wandering. This will induce him to reconsider his decision to free Bnai Yisrael. He will quickly assemble a force to recapture his escaped slaves. In other words, Hashem describes to Moshe a plan to entrap Paroh.

Of course, this elaborate scheme leads to Paroh chasing Bnai Yisrsael into the Reed Sea. Paroh and his mighty army are crushed by the collapsing waters of the Reed sea and destroyed. Avodat HaMelech explains that these passages clearly state that the purpose of the splitting of the Reed Sea was not to save the Jewish people. The purpose was to destroy Paroh and his legions.[8]

This analysis presents the first problem with the opening passages to the *parasha*. Those passages seem to explain that Bnai Yisrael was led along the more southerly route in order to avoid confrontation with the Pelishtim. However, the above analysis demonstrates that there was

---

[8] Rav Menachem Krakavski, *Avodat HaMelech, Commentary of Mishne Torah*, Hilchot Yesodai HaTorah 8:1.

another more immediate reason for selecting the more southerly route. This route would lead to the shore of the Reed Sea and to the destruction of the Egyptians.

And Moshe said to G-d: Who am I, that I should go to Paroh, and that I should bring forth Bnai Yisrael out of Egypt? And He said: Certainly I will be with you. And this shall be the sign for you that I have sent you: when you have brought forth the people out of Egypt, you shall serve G-d upon this mountain. (Shemot 3:11-12)

3. Before entering the Land of Israel the nation must receive the Torah

The second problem with these opening passages is more obvious. The Torah describes Moshe's first prophecy. He experienced a vision while shepherding flocks. He took the flocks to the Sinai wilderness and at Mount Sinai he experienced a vision. In that prophecy, Hashem told Moshe that he will lead Bnai Yisrael out of Egypt. He will bring them to this mountain and there they will experience the Revelation.

In order for this prophecy to be fulfilled, Moshe would need to lead the nation out of Egypt and deep into the Sinai wilderness. A southerly route was required to arrive at the mountain of the Revelation. In other words, the most fundamental reason for not taking the northern route is that the nation's first destination was not the Land of Israel. Their first destination was a lonely mountain deep in the Sinai wilderness.

4. Hashem selected for Bnai Yisrael the less traveled road

Rabbaynu Ovadia Sforno answers these questions through reinterpreting the opening passages of the *parasha*. He understands these opening passages as communicating an enormous amount of information in a very abridged form.

According to Sforno, the most-traveled and developed route from Egypt to the Land of Cana'an was the "Land of the Pelishtim Road". Hashem's plan was to lead the nation to Sinai and to Revelation. Along the way, he would bring Bnai Yisrael to the Reed Sea. He would induce Paroh and his army to chase after the Jewish nation and He would destroy these enemies. Only after Revelation would the nation turn north and proceed to the Land of Can'an. In other words, the Pelishtim Road could not bring the people to their initial destinations – the Sinai wilderness and to the site of Revelation. However, it would have been efficient to use this well maintained route for the initial stages of the journey and then to divert from the road and turn south. Instead, Hashem immediately led the nation into the wilderness.

The initial passages provide the reason for avoiding the well-traveled route. This is because it was the most efficient route between Egypt and the Land of Cana'an. The Torah continues to explain why this made the route unacceptable. Hashem will induce the Paroh to launch a campaign to recapture his escaped slaves. If Bnai Yisrael travels along the Pelishtim Road, they will quickly learn of Paroh's plans from the many travelers leaving Egypt. Bnai Yisrael will be overcome with fear and surrender their freedom.[9]

In other words, according to Sforno, the passage is not suggesting that Hashem's plan was to immediately take Bnai Yisrael to the Land of Cana'an. The plan was for the nation to proceed to the Reed Sea. There, their enemies will be destroyed. From the sea, they will travel into the Sinai wilderness and to Revelation. The passage is explaining why Hashem did not lead the nation along the most developed route for even the shortest portion of their journey. It is

---

[9] Rabbaynu Ovadia Sforno, *Commentary on Sefer Shemot*, 13:17.

communicating the fragile state of the nation. Because of the nation's timidity, Hashem did not allow them to become aware of Paroh's pursuit until the very last moment.

> *Speak to Bnai Yisrael, and say to them: When you pass over the Jordan into the Land of Cana'an, then you shall drive out all the inhabitants of the land from before you, and destroy all their figured stones, and destroy all their molten images, and demolish all their high places.*
> *(BeMidbar 33:51-52)*

5. Hashem delayed Bnai Yisrael's entry into the Land of Israel

Rav Naftali Tzvi Berlin – Netziv – provides a simpler but more remarkable explanation of the *parasha's* opening passages. He explains that Hashem did not lead the people along the shorter northern route because this route would quickly bring the people to the Land of Cana'an. The people were not spiritually prepared for the challenge of entering a land occupied by idolaters. Rather than conquering these nations, these liberated slaves would try to settle among the land's population. Quickly, they would assimilate and lose their identity. Before they could face the inhabitants of the Land of Cana'an, Bnai Yisael needed to develop and mature into a confident and thoughtful people. This required Revelation and the other experiences they encountered – including the destruction of their former masters.

However, Hashem did not reveal to Bnai Yisrael His full motives for not leading them directly into the land He had promised to them. He did not reveal to them the extent of their deficits and the extensive process of education and maturation that they must undertake. Instead, He only told the people that they were not prepared to face war.[10]

6. The search for freedom during life

Both of these approaches to explaining the *parasha's* opening passages share a common theme. Freedom is not achieved through removal or restraint. It is only achieved when the liberated individual develops the capacity to boldly and confidently make choices. Sforno explains that Bnai Yisrael were so fragile when they left Egypt, that they would have quickly abandoned their newly won freedom rather than face their masters. Netziv explains that without an extensive process of education, Bnai Yisrael would have squandered its freedom and quickly assimilated.

In many ways, our lives are an ongoing search for freedom. As teenagers, we seek freedom from our parents and the liberation of living away from home. As we enter the professional world, we strive to achieve financial freedom for ourselves and our families. As we become older, we contemplate retirement and freedom from the schedules and demands of our professional lives. We imagine at each stage the anticipated freedom that will change our lives and secure our happiness.

The story of our ancestors tells us that freedom is not easily achieved. Removing the restraints imposed by parents, financial responsibilities, or professional obligation does not result in personal freedom. Personal freedom is achieved when we understand ourselves, and when we seize the courage and confidence to pursue goals and objectives that are truly meaningful and transformative.

---

[10] Rav Naftali Tzvi Yehudah Berlin (Netziv), *Commentary Hamek Davar on Sefer Shemot* 13:17.

"And Hashem hardened the heart of Paroh the king of Egypt and he pursued Bnai Yisrael. And Bnai Yisrael left in triumph." (Shemot 14:8)

The Egyptians are struck with the plague of the firstborn. Paroh agrees to allow the Jewish people to leave Egypt. Bnai Yisrael leaves Egypt and travels towards the wilderness. Hashem hardens Paroh's heart. He decides to pursue the Jewish people. This ultimately leads to the miracle of the splitting of the Reed Sea. The sea miraculously separates before Bnai Yisrael. The nation crosses the sea. The Egyptians follow and the sea closes upon them. Paroh and his army are destroyed. Bnai Yisrael are redeemed. It is clear from our pasuk that the Almighty led Paroh and his nation to their destruction at the Reed Sea.

Paroh's heart was hardened by Hashem. This caused him to chase Bnai Yisrael into the sea. Rashi comments that Hashem carefully planed the route of Bnai Yisrael's escape.[11] His objective was to encourage Paroh's pursuit of Bnai Yisrael. After escaping from Egypt, Hashem told Moshe to lead the nation back in the direction of Egypt. He then commanded Moshe to instruct the people to camp near Baal Tzafon an Egyptian deity. Rashi explains that these instructions were explicitly designed to mislead Paroh and his people. The backtracking implied that the nation was lost. The proximity of this confused wandering to Baal Tzafon implied that this deity was somehow acting against Bnai Yisrael. The deity was foiling the nation's attempt to escape. Rashi's interpretation raises an immediate question. According to Rashi, the Almighty was enticing Paroh to pursue Bnai Yisrael. Why was this complicated plan needed? Hashem had harden Paroh's heart. Paroh was forced to chase after the nation! Why was any inducement needed? It seems clear from Rashi's interpretation of the pesukim that Hashem hardened Paroh's heart through these inducements. Hashem did not just turn-off Paroh's ability to chose his course of action. Instead, Hashem maneuvered Paroh into a situation in which he would not be able to resist the urge to pursue Bnai Yisrael. The Almighty knows the inner workings of every person's heart. He knew that given the proper inducements, Paroh simply would not be able to resist the urge to chase after Bnai Yisrael.

This interpretation resolves an apparent contradiction in the writings of Maimonides. Maimonides explains in the fifth chapter of Laws of Repentance that every person has the ability to choose the path of the good or the path of evil.[12] Hashem does not decree that any person should be evil or righteous. It seems that this is an unqualified statement. Every person has this ability to choose. Oddly, in the very next chapter Maimonides explains that sometimes the Almighty withholds from an evil person the opportunity to repent from sin.[13] This is a punishment. This person performed willful evil. Hashem prevents the person from repenting. This assures that this evil individual will suffer for his or her wickedness. These comments seem to contradict Maimonides earlier assertion that every person has the freewill to choose between good and evil! How can these two statements be reconciled? Rashi's approach to explaining Paroh's experience provides a resolution.

Humans are created with the ability to choose between right and wrong. However, this does not mean that we can exercise this ability in every area of our lives. We are all subject to strong, overpowering feelings. Confronted with these powerful emotions, we may be helpless to choose freely between options. On balance, we have enough freedom to constantly choose to

---

[11] Rabbaynu Shlomo ben Yitzchak (Rashi), Commentary on Sefer Shemot, 14:2.
[12] Rabbaynu Moshe ben Maimon (Rambam) Mishne Torah, Hilchot Teshuvah 5:1-2.
[13] Rabbaynu Moshe ben Maimon (Rambam) Mishne Torah, Hilchot Teshuvah 6:3.

improve ourselves. We are responsible to make the proper choices in those areas in which we are empowered. If we make the proper choices, we become better individuals. We become more empowered. With time, we can even overcome desires that once were irresistible. In short, we have freewill. But this does not mean that we have volition in every area of our lives. It is completely consistent for Maimonides to state that every person has freewill. Yet, in a specific situation one may be bereft of the ability to choose. This is clearly illustrated by the experiences of Paroh. Hashem did not disable any faculty in Paroh. He did not suddenly hit a switch and turn-off Paroh's volition. Instead, he placed Paroh under the control of an irresistible urge. Paroh found himself outside of the area in which he could make choices. He had no option. He had to chase Bnai Yisrael.

And Paroh approached. Bnai Yisrael lifted its eyes and the Egyptians were traveling after them. They were very fearful and Bnai Yisrael cried out to Hashem. Bnai Yisrael said to Moshe: Are there not enough graves in Egypt – that you took us to die in the wilderness? What have you done to us in bringing us out of Egypt? (Shemot 14:10-11)

Perceptions and Reality

1. Bnai Yisrael's panic at the Reed Sea

Bnai Yisrael leaves Egypt. However, Hashem again strengthens Paroh's heart. Paroh amasses an army and pursues Bnai Yisrael into the wilderness. Bnai Yisrael see that Paroh and his army are approaching. They call out to Hashem. Then, they begin to sharply criticize Moshe. They confront and challenge him. They ask, "Why did you lead us out of Egypt if the sole outcome of our liberation will be our death in the wilderness?"

The commentaries note that the wording used by the nation in its criticism of Moshe is odd. They described their expected fate as "death in the wilderness". This seems to be a rather vague description of the fate that they feared. Paroh and his army were closing in pursuit. They should have described their expected fate as "death at the hands of Paroh and his army"!

Rabbaynu Ovadia Sforno offers an explanation for the people's phrasing of their fear. He suggests that the people were uncertain of Paroh's plan. They did not know whether he planned to attack or to merely block their path. They reasoned that Paroh did not need to enter into a battle with them in order to vanquish them. He could use his army to block their path and isolate them in the wilderness. Without a path of escape from the wilderness, Bnai Yisrael would not be able to secure water and provision and would die.[14]

Rashbam offers a simpler explanation for Bnai Yisrael's phrasing. He explains that Bnai Yisrael were protesting to Moshe that they were doomed regardless of the outcome of their confrontation with Paroh. Even if somehow they survived this impending conflict, they were destined to die in the wilderness from thirst and starvation.[15] According to Rashbam, the impending attack completely undermined any confidence that the people had achieved and it initiated an overwhelming panic. In their panic, the people foresaw inevitable doom. If Paroh and his army do not destroy them, then they will be annihilated by the harsh wilderness.

---

[14] Sforno 14:11.
[15] Rashbam 14.11.

And Yisrael saw the great hand of Hashem at work in Egypt. And the nation feared Hashem. They believed in Hashem and Moshe His servant. (Shemot 14:31)

2. Bnai Yisrael regains it confidence

Hashem rescues Bnai Yisrael. He separates the waters of the Reed Sea before them. They descend into the dry seabed, cross the sea, and ascend onto its shore. The Egyptians follow Bnai Yisrael into the sea. The waters come crashing down upon them and they are destroyed. Bnai Yisrael see their adversary's destruction. They are awed by the might of Hashem and they believe in Hashem and Moshe His servant.

Moshe then leads the nation in the Shirat HaYam – the Song of the Sea. In this song of praise, the nation acknowledges Hashem and gives thanks to Him for their salvation. They extol His praises. They express their confidence in the fulfillment of His promise that they will return to Cana'an and take possession of it.

Rashbam comments that with the destruction of the Egyptians, Bnai Yisrael not only recognized that they had been rescued from their adversary. Their confidence was also restored. Now, they were certain that they would survive their sojourn in the wilderness and enter the Land of Cana'an and take possession of it.[16] In other words, the intense panic that had overwhelmed the people subsided. In its place emerged a restored sense of confidence.

In summary, Rashbam's position is that within a few hours time the people experienced a series of intense and ever-changing feeling. The impending attack of Paroh and his arm unleashed a sense of complete panic. The people lost all confidence and were certain of their impending death – either at the hands of their adversaries or through exposure to the harsh environment of the wilderness. With the destruction of the Egyptians, the nation embraced a renewed sense of confidence. They had been saved from their enemies. They would safely transverse the wilderness. They would conquer the mighty kings of Cana'an and take possession of the Promised Land.

This extreme swing in attitude and perception is not easily understood. In fact, it continues to characterize Bnai Yisrael's conduct throughout the balance of the parasha. At times, the nation again questions whether it can survive the wilderness experience. However, with the passing and resolution of each challenge, their confidence is restored – but only until the next threat or challenge arises.

Hashem is the strength and the song of Bnai Yisrael. He was my salvation. This is my G-d and I beautify Him. He is the G-d of my forefathers and I will exalt Him. (Shemot 15:2)

3. The encounter with Hashem at the Reed Sea

The above passage is from the Song of the Sea. It is translated according to Rashbam's understanding of its message. In his comments on the passage, Rashi quotes a famous teaching of the Sages. The people said, "This is my G-d!" Rashi comments that Hashem revealed Himself in His glory at the Reed Sea. The people pointed to Him with their finger and said, "This is our G-d." Rashi continues and explains that the most humble and simple person at the Reed Sea encountered Hashem at a level not achieved even by some of the greatest prophets.[17]

---

[16] Rashbam 14:31.
[17] Rashi 15:2

Rashi's comments are difficult on a number of levels. Hashem does not have a material form. He cannot be seen nor can one point at Him. Furthermore, the assertion that the most humble person at the Sea achieved some level of encounter with Hashem that exceeded the experiences of the greatest prophets seems remarkable. What is the basis for this contention?

Rashbam comments that the people did not actually see Hashem.[18] Apparently, Rashbam means that Hashem revealed Himself through His actions. He does not have a material form that can actually be observed. These comments reveal the meaning of the passage and Rashi's insight. It is human nature to accept the perception of the senses as being real. We have a saying: Seeing is believing. We are most convinced of that which we can see. Other information – facts or knowledge that is not observable – has less of an impact upon us. Rashi's understanding of the passage is that the revelation of Hashem at the Reed Sea was so powerful that those present felt that they had seen Hashem. That is not to say that they believed they had observed a form or figure that they identified as Hashem. But the experience was equal in impact to a sensual encounter. The comparison of this encounter to the prophetic experience of the greatest prophets is intended to convey this understanding of the passage. This encounter with Hashem was similar in its intensity to the prophet's encounter with Hashem in the prophetic experience.

In this manner the righteous and the prophets appealed in their prayers to Hashem to help them in their pursuit of the truth. As David said, "Teach me Your way." He meant to say, "My sins should not prevent me from finding the path of truth. I wish to know Your way and (understand) the unity of Your name".... (Maimonides, Mishne Torah, Laws of Repentance 6:4)

4. The forces that shape human perception

Based upon Rashi's comments, Rashbam's understanding of Bnai Yisrael's shifting attitudes and beliefs can be understood. However, it will be helpful to first consider an interesting comment by Maimonides. In the above quotation, Maimonides explains that the righteous and Hashem's prophets appealed to Hashem for His assistance in their search for truth. They believed that their shortcomings and sins could easily pervert their efforts and conceal the truth from them. This is an amazing statement. However, it reflects a remarkable humility. Essentially, Maimonides asserts that the success or failure of our quest for truth is not merely a consequence of our intelligence and commitment to the pursuit. We can easily be mislead or led down the wrong path by our own shortcomings and sins. These cloud our mind, obscure the truth, and pervert our intellectual vision. Even the most wise and righteous realized that their inevitable shortcomings created an imposing barrier between them and the truth they sought. They prayed to Hashem for His help in overcoming this barrier.

The fundamental premise of Maimonides' comments is that our intellectual perceptions, our convictions, and our beliefs are as much a consequence of our moral and emotional state as our intellectual prowess. Our sins and wrongdoings influence and contribute to who we are. They help shape our personality and our moral state. These, in turn, strongly influence our intellectual perceptions and our conclusions regarding the truth.

Rashbam's comments illustrate Maimonides' contention. Bnai Yisrael was liberated from Egypt. They left with confidence and exultation. They did not flee bondage. They marched out of Egypt as free people. However, their confidence was a consequence of their understanding of

---

[18] Rashbam, Chorev edition, 15:2.

their recent experiences and the emotionally liberating impact of observing their masters' humiliation. These factors combined to engender their sense of buoyancy and confidence. They were not threatened by the prospect of crossing the wilderness and they were confident in their ability to conquer the Land of Cana'an.

Their mood changed when they saw their former masters in pursuit. Their confidence was shattered and their exaltation was replaced by fear and apprehension. Without their former confidence, their perceptions regarding their prospects changed radically. Now, they wondered how they had ever agreed to enter the wilderness. Why had they believed that they were freed of their oppressors or that they could cross the barren and hostile wilderness? Their understanding to reality changed – reshaped by fear and trepidation.

Then, they observed their adversary's destruction. Hashem was revealed to them! They experienced an intense encounter with Hashem. At that moment, doubt and hesitation became impossible. The people joined Moshe in the Song of the Sea. They declared their confidence in their conquest of the Promised Land. Doubt had been completely replaced by assurance in achievement of their destiny.

Of course, as the parasha continues, the impact of the encounter at the Reed Sea fades. With the weakening of its impact, old doubts reassert themselves. The balance of the parasha describes these recurring doubts and the people's internal battle to recapture the confidence they experienced as they marched forth from Egypt and encountered Hashem's revelation at the Reed Sea.

"And Moshe said to the nation: Do not be afraid. Stand firm and see the salvation of Hashem that He will do for you today. For although you will see the Egyptians today, you will not ever again see them." (Shemot 14:13)

The Weak Self-confidence of the Generation Liberated from Egypt

Bnai Yisrael arrive at the Reed Sea pursued by the Egyptians. They fear that they will be destroyed. Moshe urges the nation to have courage. Hashem will save His people.

Bnai Yisrael had left Egypt armed. The nation included six-hundred thousand adult males. The Egyptians had been ravaged by ten debilitating plagues. Why did Bnai Yisrael confront their pursuers and fight?

Rabbaynu Avraham ibn Ezra explains that Bnai Yisrael could have fielded a formidable army against the Egyptians. However, two-hundred and ten years of slavery had undermined the confidence of the people. Newly gained freedom could not immediately erase the effects of their prolonged subjugation. The liberated slaves could not envision themselves opposing and overcoming their former masters.

Ibn Ezra explains that this same shortcoming prevented the generation that was liberated from slavery from entering the Land of Israel. It lacked the confidence to battle the fierce nations inhabiting Canaan. A new generation reared in the desert would be better prepared for this challenge. This new generation would not know slavery. It would be nurtured in an environment of freedom. Self-doubt would be replaced with self-assurance.[19]

---

[19] Rabbaynu Avraham ibn Ezra, *Commentary on Sefer Shemot*, 14:13.

Ibn Ezra does not intend to imply that the forty years of wandering in the desert were predetermined from the moment of the exodus. As the Chumash relates, spies were sent to survey the land and plan its conquest. Instead, the spies emphasized the unassailable obstacles that awaited them. The nation accepted this report and the spies' conclusion that the conquest was unachievable. The people lost hope in regaining the homeland of the forefathers and questioned Moshe's leadership. It was in response to this failing of the people that Hashem decreed forty years of wandering in the desert.

Ibn Ezra is explaining the cause of this debacle. The crisis created by the report of the spies was a result of the nation's low level of self-confidence. The challenge posed by the conquest was more imagined than real. Hashem had assured the nation that He would defeat the nations of Canaan as He had destroyed mighty Egypt. But this generation of liberated spies that could not confront its former masters also lacked the self-assurance to wage a campaign against the inhabitants of Cannan. In short, heeding the counsel of the spies condemned Bnai Yisrael to wandering. But the self-doubt that underplayed this failing was exhibited first at the Reed Sea.

And Hashem said to Moshe: Why do you cry-out to me? Speak to Bnai Yisrael and they should travel. (Shemot 14:15)

Too Much Prayer

1. Crisis at the Reed Sea

In the above passage, Hashem tells Moshe to stop praying to Him. It is odd that Hashem directs His prophet to not petition Him on behalf of His nation. To understand Hashem's objection, we must understand the context of the passage.

The Jewish people have left Egypt. They are traveling to Sinai and from there they will continue to the Land of Israel. Hashem tells Moshe that He will induce Paroh to reconsider his decision to release Bnai Yisrael. Paroh will amass an army and pursue Bnai Yisrael. Hashem will demonstrate His glory through the final destruction of Paroh and his mighty legions.

Bnai Yisrael arrive at the shore of the Reed Sea. They see Paroh and his army in pursuit. Their path forward is blocked by the sea. They turn to Hashem, petitioning Him for their rescue. Also, they challenge Moshe, "Why bring us into the wilderness to be slaughtered by the sword?"

Moshe responds to the people. He tells them that they should not be afraid. Hashem will wage war on their behalf. He will completely destroy the Egyptians. Moshe joins the people in prayer to Hashem.

This is the context of the passage. Hashem tells Moshe to not petition Him. He should simply lead the people forward. He then explains to Moshe that He will split the waters of sea. The Jewish people will pass between walls of water. Hashem will induce Paroh to lead his army into the parted waters and they will be destroyed.

Moshe should not pray

Why was Moshe told to stop praying? The nation faced a crisis. They were trapped between the sea and the Egyptians. Is it not appropriate to turn to Hashem when confronted with catastrophe? The commentators provide many responses. We will focus on two that are offered by Rashi.

"We learn [from the passage] that Moshe stood and prayed. The Holy One Blessed be He said to him, "This is not the time for protracted prayer. Israel is in distress!" Another opinion [states] "Why do you cry-out to Me? This matter depends upon Me, not upon you."" (Rashi, Shemot 14:15)

Both explanations present problems. Rashi's first explanation is that Hashem criticized Moshe for engaging in protracted prayer, while the people are in danger. Did not Moshe intercede on behalf of the nation for forty days and nights after the sin of the Golden Calf? As in this instance, they were in great danger. Moshe feared Hashem might destroy them for their sin. Why was the intercession at Sinai appropriate but lengthy prayer at the Reed Sea not fitting?

Rashi's second explanation is also troubling. Hashem told Moshe there is nothing for him to do. It is Hashem's place to take action. Moshe certainly realized that Bnai Yisrael required Hashem's intercession to be saved. He prayed for that intercession. Why did Hashem criticize him for such prayers?

2. The stakes at the Reed Sea

It is apparent that Moshe was not entirely confident that Bnai Yisrael would be rescued. He believed that their fate had not been completely determined. Hashem might allow them to be destroyed or harmed by the Egyptians. Hashem had assured him that He would destroy Paroh and his army. But Moshe had doubts. Since Hashem gave His assurance, the people had been overtaken by panic. They had accused him of bringing them into the wilderness to be destroyed. Moshe asked, "Were his people still worthy of the miracles Hashem had foretold?" Moshe prayed to Hashem to rescue His people and overlook their shortcomings.[20]

With this background, let us first consider Rashi's second answer. Hashem responded to Moshe that He will provide salvation. There is nothing for Moshe to do. He explained to Moshe that he was misinterpreting the situation. The people will be saved. Their rescue is not in doubt. Moshe does not need to pray on their behalf. Hashem's plan is materializing. Moshe must allow it to reveal itself. In other words, there is no real crisis. The plan is unfolding according to Hashem's design.

3. Types of prayer

Rashi's first answer is that Hashem criticized Moshe for engaging in protracted prayer while the nation is in distress. Why was this wrong? Should not Moshe pray for them until they

---

[20] See comments of Sforno. Sforno attempts to resolve a difficult problem. Moshe seems to be in doubt of Bnai Yisrael's rescue. However, Moshe had assured Bnai Yisrael that Hashem would rescue them from Paroh and the Egyptians. The authenticity of a prophet is determined by the accuracy of his prophecies. If positive prophecies do not come true, then the claimant is deemed to be a false prophet (Rambam, Hilchot Yesodai HaTorah 10:1-2). How could Moshe be uncertain of Bnai Yisrael's rescue? He had shared with them his prophecy that Hashem would save them? Sforno responds that Moshe was confident they would be saved. However, he feared that they would not follow him into the parted waters of the sea. His turned to Hashem asking for His assistance in motivating the people to enter the sea. Hashem responded, "Why do you cry-out to me? You misunderstand the people. They will follow you." According to Rashi, it seems Moshe was not confident that the people would be saved. Rashi does not explain how he would resolve the difficulty addressed by Sforno.

are rescued? The hint or key to understanding Rashi's position is recognizing that Hashem did not criticize Moshe for praying. He reproved him for engaging lengthy prayer. Prayer was appropriate; extended prayer was not.

Rashi's position reflects an idea developed more fully by Rambam – Maimonides. Rambam explains that when the Jewish people are in distress they must turn to Hashem in prayer.

"This is part of the process of repentance. When an affliction occurs and they cry-out and sound the trumpets,[21] they all know that the misfortune came upon them because of their actions… This causes the affliction to be removed from them. But if they do not cry-out and sound the trumpets; rather, they say, "This is a natural event that has occurred to us. This affliction is happenstance", this is cruelty. It causes them to cleave to their wicked actions. It adds afflictions upon the affliction…" (Rambam, Mishne Torah, Hilchot Taaniyot 1:2-3)

Rambam explains that when confronted with a crisis, we respond with prayer. He explains that our prayers are part of the process of repentance. We are recognizing that our afflictions express Hashem's will and are a result of our faults and sins. This recognition hopefully leads to repentance.

Rav Yisroel Chait observed that it is interesting that Rambam does not say that the affliction is removed through repentance. He says we earn reprieve by recognition that our suffering is the consequence of our behaviors. Apparently, Rambam's position is that repentance is not required to cancel the punishment. Only the first step on the path of repentance is necessary. We must recognize that we have brought our suffering upon ourselves through our sins.[22]

Rambam is explaining that prayer is not only petitioning of Hashem. It is an acknowledgment of His role in our lives and our dependency upon Him. Typically, when suffering we petition Hashem for His intervention. Rambam is asserting that the fundamental element of these prayers is not our fervent plea for rescue. It is our recognition that our suffering is a consequence of our sins. To summarize, prayer is not just petition. It is also acknowledgment of Hashem's role in our lives.

4. The message of Moshe's prayer

According to Rashi, Hashem told Moshe, "You have prayed enough." He told Moshe that he does not need to plead for the rescue of the people. He needs only to ask Hashem – to demonstrate to the people that their approaching rescue is His response to their plight. Prayer is necessary. Without it the people may make the same error as the Egyptians. They may conclude that the winds parting the waters are an unusual but natural event. Moshe prayed before the people and then the water parted. The people recognized that they were being saved through Hashem's miracle.

5. Lessons from Rashi, #1

---

[21] These trumpets were sounded in the Tabernacle and in the Temple at times of affliction. They are an expression of prayer.
[22] Rav Yisroel Chait, author's personal notes.

Bnai Yisrael believed they faced destruction. They were trapped between the sea and their enemies. Moshe was concerned. Hashem responded, "This is part of My plan. Yes, the Egyptians are directly behind you. But this will encourage them to follow you into the sea. They will be at your heels when the walls of the sea collapse upon them."

The lesson is familiar but important. Crisis does mean we are abandoned. We do not know Hashem's plan. Sometimes a crisis is the prelude to salvation. This does not mean that real tragedies do not occur. It means we should not lose hope when we experience a period of distress. Our distress may be the darkness before the dawning of a bright day.

6. Lessons from Rashi, #2

Rashi's second lesson is less obvious and more profound. Moshe was required to pray before the sea parted. His prayer was important because through it he demonstrated that Hashem parted the water. We are required to pray repeatedly. We may wonder why these persistent entreaties are required. Rashi's comments provide an important insight. In prayer, we petition Hashem. But this is not the only function of prayer. Rashi teaches us that prayer is also a statement. We acknowledge our dependence upon Hashem and that our blessings are bestowed by Him.

Our ancestors at the Reed Sea needed prayer to recognize that Hashem was parting the sea. We also need prayer to recognize that our blessings come from Hashem. We easily forget Hashem's role in our lives. We need to constantly remind ourselves of our dependence upon Hashem and that He grants us the blessings we enjoy. We need constant prayer.

"And Moshe said to the nation: Do not be afraid. Stand firm and see the salvation of Hashem that He will do for you today. For although you will see the Egyptians today, you will not ever again see them." (Shemot 14:13)

"And the Egyptians will know that I am Hashem when I triumph over Paroh, his chariots and his calvary." (Shemot 14:18)

The Importance of Convincing the Egyptians of Hashem's Omnipotence

Both of the above passages deal with the miracle of the parting of the Reed Sea. In the first pasuk, Moshe tells Bnai Yisrael that miracle Hashem will presently perform complete the salvation of Bnai Yisrael and the destruction of the Egyptians.

Hashem tells Moshe to proceed into the sea. The water will be parted and the nation will transverse the uncovered dry seabed. Hashem tells Moshe that He has hardened Paroh's heart. He will cause Paroh to pursue Bnai Yisrael into the sea. Hashem will destroy the Egyptian army.

In the second pasuk, Hashem explains to Moshe that through the destruction of Paroh and his legions, the remnant of the Egyptian people will come to recognize the omnipotence of Hashem.

The two passages seem to communicate different messages regarding the parting of the sea and its collapsing upon the Egyptians. The first pasuk indicates that the objective of this miracle was the salvation of Bnai Yisrael. The destruction of the Egyptians was required to complete this salvation. The destruction of Paroh and his army will assure that the Egyptians will not longer pursue Bnai Yisrael. The second pasuk suggests that the destruction of Paroh and his army served another purpose. Hashem was concerned with the impressions of the Egyptians. He told Moshe that the destruction of Paroh and his army was designed to convince the surviving Egyptians of the greatness of Hashem.

Rabbaynu Ovadia Sforno confirms this interpretation of the second pasuk. He explains that the destruction of Paroh and his army would provide the remaining Egyptians with compelling evidence of Hashem's greatness. Hopefully, this demonstration will inspire them to repent. Sforno concludes by observing that Hashem does not seek the death of the wicked; rather, He seeks their repentance.[23]

Gershonides disagrees. He argues that the second pasuk does not intend to suggest that Hashem was concerned with the Egyptians appreciation of His omnipotence. They had already been provided with the opportunity to discover Hashem. Why did Hashem wish to impress upon the Egyptians His omnipotence? Gershonides explains that this was not for the purpose of perfecting the Egyptians. Instead, Hashem wanted to deter the Egyptians from any other attempts to recapture Bnai Yisrael. Hashem presented the Egyptians with undeniable proof of His omnipotence. This convinced the survivors that they could not hope to overcome Hashem and recapture His nation. With this realization, they were discouraged from any further efforts to recapture Bnai Yisrael.[24]

"And Moshe extended his hand over the sea. And Hashem drove back the waters with a powerful east wind the entire night. And it made the seabed into dry land. And the waters were divided." (Shemot 14:27)

The Miracle of the Parting of the Reed Sea

Bnai Yisrael flee from Egypt. The people arrive at the shores of the Reed Sea. The sea stands before the nation. The Egyptians are directly behind them. Bnai Yisrael is trapped. Hashem performs one the greatest wonders recorded in the Torah. He parts the Reed Sea. Bnai Yisrael enter the sea. They travel across the sea over its dry seabed. The Egyptians enter the sea in pursuit of their escaped slaves. The sea closes upon the Egyptians and they are drowned.

The Torah provides some interesting details regarding this miracle. Generally, we imagine that Moshe extended his hand over the water and suddenly they separated and dry land was revealed. However, this is not the description of these events provided by the Torah.

According to our pasuk, the sea did not immediately split in response to Moshe's command. Moshe extended his hand over the water and a mighty wind arose. The wind blew the entire night. What was the function of this wind? Why did Hashem require this wind? Why did He not immediately part the waters?

Nachmanides explains that the wind was part of an elaborate deception. Hashem had brought the Egyptians to the Reed Sea. Here, they were to be destroyed. However, what was to induce the Egyptians to enter the sea? After all, if Hashem had parted the sea in order to save Bnai Yisrael, it was not likely He would allow the Egyptians to follow them! What would the point be of a miracle that failed to save Bnai Yisrael? Certainly, the Egyptians would realize that Hashem would not prolong His miracle for the benefit of his nation's adversaries!

---

[23] Rabbaynu Ovadia Sforno, *Commentary on Sefer Shemot*, 14:18.
[24] Rabbaynu Levi ben Gershon (Ralbag / Gershonides), *Commentary on Sefer Shemot*, p 102.

Nachmanides suggests that the wind was part of a ruse. The Egyptians believed that the wind had split the sea. Bnai Yisrael were escaping into the sea as the result of remarkable good fortune. They just happened to reach the sea at the onset of a tremendous storm. The storm cleaved apart the waters. The Egyptians felt that they too could take advantage of this opportunity. The wind would continue to drive the waters apart. They could enter the sea and overtake Bnai Yisrael. The deception worked. The Egyptians were lured into the trap!

Of course, the Egyptians were mistaken in their interpretations of the phenomenon. They were not witnessing an unusual meteorological occurrence. They were seeing a miracle. They entered the sea and Hashem brought the waters crashing down upon them.[25]

Rashbam adopts a completely opposite approach to explaining this wind. He contends that the wind actually parted the water. The Creator performed His miracle through the vehicle of natural forces. Rashbam adds some detail. He explains that the wind had two functions. First, it caused the water to back up. Once the water backed up, the seafloor was revealed. Second, it dried the seafloor and created a passable path across the seabed.[26] Ibn Ezra adds that the wind continued to blow as Bnai Yisrael crossed the sea. Only the power of the wind prevented the water from rushing in on Bnai Yisrael.[27]

In short, we are faced with two approaches for explaining this wind. Nachmanides maintains that the wind was not a factor in splitting the sea. The wind was merely part of a ruse designed to lure the Egyptians into the sea. Rashbam and others disagree. They insist that the miracle of the sea parting was brought about through this wind. Hashem used the wind to split the sea, dry the seabed, and hold the waters apart for Bnai Yisrael.

This raises an interesting question. We can understand the position of Nachmanides. Hashem is the Creator of the universe. He formed the seas and established the boundaries between the oceans and the continents. Obviously, He can alter these boundaries. If He wishes to create dry land in the midst of the sea, He can. He is omnipotent. He does not need any wind to assist Him. The position of Rashbam is more difficult to understand. It seems as if the Rashbam is limiting Hashem. He seems to deny his omnipotence. Why does Hashem need a strong wind to do His bidding?

The answer to this question is very important. It provides an insight into the Torah's understanding of the natural world. The answer also indicates the Torah's attitude toward scientific knowledge.

We all realize that we are required to observe the Torah. Observant Jews might dicker over the specifics of observance. However, we would agree that Hashem revealed the Torah with the intention that we observe its commandments. The reason for observance is obvious. The commandments are an expression of the will of Hashem. As His servants, we must submit to His will.

However, it must be noted that the mitzvot of the Torah are not the only laws that Hashem created. In addition to the mitzvot, He created the laws of nature. These are the laws that govern the movement of the galaxies and the behavior of the smallest subatomic particle. Just as

---

[25] Rabbaynu Moshe ben Nachman (Ramban), *Commentary on Sefer Shemot* 14:21.
[26] Rabbaynu Shemuel ben Meir (Rashbam) *Commentary on Sefer Shemot* 14:21.
[27] Rabbaynu Avraham ibn Ezra, *Commentary on Sefer Shemot*, 14:21.

the Torah's mitzvot are an expression of His will, so too the laws of nature are a manifestation of the Divine. It is reasonable for the Creator to expect that these natural laws should be observed.

Now, we can understand Rashbam's position. Rashbam does not deny Hashem's omnipotence. He is not positing that the Creator needs a wind to split the sea. He is asserting that a perfect Creator would not disregard His own laws. He would not capriciously suspend or violate the laws He had established.

Rashbam is also providing us with an important perspective on scientific knowledge. In order to understand this perspective, let us ask a question: What is religion's attitude towards science? The answer is that science and religion have often contended with one another. Many religions have resisted science. What is the reason for this conflict?

There are many factors that have contributed to this contentious relationship. We will consider two of these. First, religion is often steeped in the mystical. For some, religion provides an explanation for the inexplicable. According to this perspective, religion begins where science ends and provides answers to the questions science cannot address. In such a relationship, the advancement of science must reduce the significance of religion. As science expands our knowledge of the universe, the realm of religion is reduced. Mysteries that were once explained through some mystical truth are interpreted by a set of scientific principles. The realm of the mystical is reduced, and the danger arises that religion will become trivial.

There is a second issue. In some religions, doctrine may seem to contradict science. Religious doctrine is regarded as a revealed or, at least, inspired truth. It is not subject to challenge. Therefore, any conflict with science must be eliminated.

When these conflicts arise, these religions must respond. There are a number of responses. At the extreme, the response can take the form of outright suppression of science. More commonly, these challenges lead to the disparagement of science and a marginalizing of its importance.

It is noteworthy that many of our greatest Torah Sages possessed extensive knowledge of science. Apparently, these Sages did not perceive any conflict between their religious outlook and scientific knowledge. The attitude of these Sages suggests that science and Torah can peacefully coexist. What is the basis for this coexistence?

Rashbam's explanation of our pasuk provides a response. It is clear that Rashbam regarded the laws of the universe as a manifestation the Creator's will. They are an expression of His infinite wisdom. Even Hashem will not flippantly disregard these laws. This implies that these laws deserve our respect.

This attitude eliminates the conflict between science and religion. The discoveries of science are not viewed as a threat to religion. On the contrary, these insights are an inspiration to the Torah scholar. They provide awesome testimony to the infinite wisdom of the Creator. The expansion of scientific knowledge does not diminish the significance of the Torah. This newfound knowledge gives us a greater appreciation of Hashem. These insights are a source of inspiration in our service to Hashem through the performance of His mitzvot.

It is important to note that we are not suggesting that the study of science is a substitute for the study of Torah. This is a completely different issue. Even within a single science, there is a proper order for its study. For example, in mathematics the study of algebra precedes that of calculus. In addition, some sciences are more easily understood and more suitable for general study. And of course, practical considerations can suggest that one science be given priority over another. All of these issues and others must be discussed in order to determine the relative merit of Torah study as compared to the study of science. Nonetheless, it is clear from the comments of Rashbam that scientific knowledge deserves our respect.

Thus Hashem saved Israel that day out of the hand of the Egyptians. And Israel saw the Egyptians dead upon the sea-shore. (Shemot 14:30)

Unity of Heart and Mind

1. The destruction of the Egyptians at the Reed Sea and the song of Bnai Yisrael

Parshat Beshalach continues the Torah's discussion of Bnai Yisrael's exodus from Egypt. The Torah relates that Paroh realized that Bnai Yisrael did not intend to return to Egypt. He regretted granting Bnai Yisrael permission to leave Egypt. He gathered his armies and set off in pursuit of his former slaves. Paroh overtook Bnai Yisrael as the nation was camped on the shores of the Reed Sea.

The Torah describes the reaction of Bnai Yisrael to the appearance of Paroh and his legions. They were trapped between the impassable sea and the Egyptian camp which was prepared to pounce upon them and destroy them. They initially responded to their perilous plight by praying to Hashem. Then, they began to criticize Moshe. They complained that they should have remained Paroh's servants in Egypt rather than die in the wilderness. Moshe responded that the people would soon witness their salvation and the utter destruction of their enemies. Hashem will fight for them.

Hashem then split the Reed Sea and Bnai Yisrael crossed upon the dry seabed. Paroh led his armies in pursuit. The sea closed upon them. The walls of the parted water came down upon them, crushing and drowning them within the depths of the sea. Bnai Yisrael observed the complete destruction of their enemies and, led by Moshe, they sang His praises.

Then Moshe and the children of Israel sang this song unto Hashem, and spoke, saying: I will sing unto Hashem, for He is highly exalted. The horse and his rider He has thrown into the sea. (Shemot 15:1)

2. Song is appropriate when the salvation is complete

The above passage introduces the Shirat HaYam – the Song of the Sea. This is the praise that was composed by Moshe and recited by Bnai Yisrael in response to the destruction of their enemies. The passage begins by explaining that "then Moshe and Bnai Yisrael sang this song" of praise. The passage places emphasis on the moment selected for the recitation of the Shirat HaYam. It was recited when the nation observed the complete destruction of its enemies.

Rav Naftali Tzvi Yehudah Berlin – Netziv – explains that only at this moment was it appropriate for this praise to be recited. Only when their salvation was complete could this praise be sung to Hashem. Netziv's intention in this comment can be better understood in the context of earlier comments. Netziv notes that on two prior occasions Bnai Yisrael gave thanks to Hashem for their salvation. The first time was when Moshe initially came to them and told them that Hashem would redeem them from Egypt. The Torah states that the nation believed Moshe and responded by bowing to Hashem. Netziv explains that this act of bowing or prostration was an expression of thanks. Later, Moshe told Bnai Yisrael that the Egyptians would be smitten with the plague of the firstborn. Bnai Yisrael would be spared from the devastation of the plague through their participation in the Pesach offering. The nation responded by bowing to Hashem. Again, Netziv notes that the bowing or prostrating of the nation was an act of acknowledgment and a giving of thanks to Hashem.

In other words, the nation twice before expressed its confidence in Moshe's message that Hashem would redeem them from Egypt. On both occasions they responded with prostration and thanks to Hashem. However, on neither of these occasions did Moshe lead the people in song.

Apparently, Netziv is explaining why a song of praise was only recited after the destruction of Bnai Yisrael's enemies at the Reed Sea. He explains that such praise is only appropriate when the salvation is complete and not before that point. Although at these previous moments the nation responded to Moshe's message with appreciation and gratitude, these could only be expressed though bowing and could not find expression in a song of praise. Netziv does not provide a reason for this rule. Why can a song of praise – like the Shirat HaYam – only be recited when the salvation is complete?

Hashem is my strength and song, and He has become my salvation. This is my G-d, and I will glorify Him; my father's G-d, and I will exalt Him. (Shemot 15:2)

3. Awareness of Hashem

The above passage is from the Shirat HaYam. The people declare, "This is my G-d and I will glorify Him." The Sages are troubled by the use of the term "this". The term "this" is used to make reference to a specific object or person. In the passage it seems to be superfluous and misleading. The passage could have stated: Hashem is my G-d and I will glorify Him. What is added by the term "this"? Furthermore, the term indicates that there was some image or material presence to which the people referred. This is not possible! One of the Torah's fundamental principles is that Hashem is not material.

Rashi responds that Hashem revealed Himslef to the people at the Reed Sea and the people pointed to Him with their fingers and declared, "This is our G-d". He adds that even a former maidservant at the Reed Sea achieved a vision and experienced an encounter that was unsurpassed by the great prophets.

Rashi's comments are not only difficult to understand but also seem to contribute little to resolving the problems in the passage. He seems to suggest that the term "this" is used because there was an actual presence or image to which the people referred. This assertion only confirms the difficulties presented by the passage. How can Hashem be described as a material entity or presence to which the people referred?

Thus Hashem saved Israel that day out of the hand of the Egyptians. And Israel saw the Egyptians dead upon the sea-shore. And Israel saw the great work which Hashem did upon the Egyptians, and the people feared Hashem; and they believed in Hashem, and in His servant Moshe. (Shemot 14:30-31)

4. Complete and compromised conviction

Rashi's comments can be better understood viewed in the context provided by the above passages. These passages are problematic. They explain that after Bnai Yisrael observed the destruction of their enemies at the Reed Sea they believed in Hashem and Moshe. These passages imply that prior to this point their conviction in Hashem and in Moshe was less than certain. Why were their convictions not complete until this point and how did their experience at the Reed Sea complete their convictions?

And when Paroh drew nigh, the children of Israel lifted up their eyes, and, behold, the Egyptians were marching after them. And they were sore afraid. And the children of Israel cried out unto Hashem. And they said unto Moshe: Because there were no graves in Egypt, have you taken us away to die in the wilderness? Why have you dealt thus with us, to bring us forth out of Egypt? Is not this the word that we spoke unto you in Egypt, saying: Let us alone, that we may serve the Egyptians? For it was better for us to serve the Egyptians, than that we should die in the wilderness. And Moshe said unto the people: Fear not, stand still, and see the salvation of Hashem, which He will work for you today; for whereas you have seen the Egyptians today, you shall never again see them. (Shemot 14:10-13)

5. Psychological perception and conflicting reality

In order to answer this question, it is important to consider a comment made by Rabbaynu Avraham ibn Ezra. Ibn Ezra poses a simple question on the above passages. The passages describe the response of Bnai Yisrael to the approach of Paroh and his armies. The passages communicate an image of panic and despair. Ibn Ezra notes that Bnai Yisrael included 600,000 able-bodied men. Their approaching adversaries had suffered through ten debilitating plagues. Certainly, both the health and numbers of Paroh's legions were severely depleted by these plagues. Why did Bnai Yisrael not face their adversaries and battle them?

Ibn Ezra responds that Bnai Yisrael were psychologically incapable of considering this option. They still viewed themselves as slaves and the Egyptians as their masters. They had witnessed the humiliation of the Egyptians through the plagues. Yet, as the Egyptians appeared on the horizon, Bnai Yisrael did not realize that their planned attack was the desperate final gasp of a dying kingdom. They saw them as the unvanquished and all-powerful masters to whom they were subservient. They could not imagine opposing or rising up against this invincible adversary.

Now, the passages introducing the Shirat HaYam are easily understood. Even before arriving at the Reed Sea, Bnai Yisrael had witnessed the plagues and seen the wonders performed by Hashem through Moshe. They intellectually understood that these wonders revealed the omnipotence of Hashem. They comprehended that Hashem had sent Moshe to rescue them from Egypt. However, their hearts and minds were not united. In their hearts, their awe of Hashem's omnipotence competed with their awe of their Egyptian masters. Their sense of freedom and deliverance from suffering could not be complete as long as they remained intimidated because of their subservience to Paroh and Egypt. Then, Bnai Yisrael witnessed the total destruction of Paroh at the Reed Sea. With ease and rapidity Hashem disposed of the invincible Paroh. Now, the people accepted Hashem in their minds and hearts. They could fully believe in Hashem and His servant Moshe.

Rashi's comments make the same point. Hashem revealed Himself to Bnai Yisrael at the Reed Sea. His existence, providence, and omnipotence emerged fully. With the total destruction of Paroh and his legions, the hearts and minds of the people became united in belief in Hashem. He became real; ambivalence was replaced by absolute certainty, and intellectual understanding was united with heartfelt wonder. Rashi is not suggesting that the people saw Hashem in the material sense. He is explaining that He became real and the people became certain in their conviction. The people expressed their new clarity of conviction by using the phrase "this is my

G-d". They were giving expression to the overwhelming awareness of Hashem that they experienced at the Reed Sea.

6. A song of praise is an expression of uncompromised convicton

A careful reading of the first passage of the Shirat HaYam reveals why it could only be recited at this time. The passage explains that the nation is singing Hashem's praises because of its awareness of His exalted greatness. He has thrown rider and chariot into the sea. Only after the victory at the Reed Sea did the people feel truly delivered from their oppressors. Only when they saw Paroh's complete destruction did they feel truly free. Now, their salvation was complete. Their hearts rejoiced in their deliverance. Before, when they had expressed their thanks to Hashem for their deliverance their sense of gratitude was compromised by their unresolved fear of their Egyptian masters. They could not recite Hashem's full praises because heart and mind were not united in their acceptance of Hashem as the only true ruler in their lives. Heart and mind were in conflict; ambiguity prevailed. At the Reed Sea, Hashem was revealed as the only G-d and as an absolute omnipotent ruler. Now, they were prepared and fit to sing Shirat HaYam.

Who is like unto You, Hashem, among the mighty? Who is like unto You, glorious in holiness, fearful in praises, doing wonders? (Shemot 15:11)

7. Seeking unity of heart and mind

We are obligated to serve Hashem with our entire being. We must draw close to Him through the effort of our intellect. However, intellect unaccompanied by heartfelt devotion does not produce true commitment and acceptance of Hashem. We must work to achieve unity of heart and mind. The work of the mind is not complete until the devotion of the heart is secured.

And Israel saw the mighty hand that Hashem had performed in Egypt. The nation feared Hashem. And they believed in Hashem and in Moshe, His servant. (Shemot 14:31)

Overcoming Doubts

The Jewish people responded to the drowning of the Egyptians with praise and thanksgiving

The first portion of Parshat BeShalach discusses the miracle of the Reed Sea. Bnai Yisrael emerged from Egypt. The nation began its journey to the Land of Israel. However, Paroh and the Egyptians reconsidered their decision to release the Jews from bondage. Paroh rallied his armies and they pursued Bnai Yisrael. The Jews were soon trapped on the shore of the Reed Sea. The waters of the sea were before them; Pharaoh and his armies were approaching. Bnai Yisrael entered the sea and Hashem parted its waters. They traveled along a path in the midst of the sea. The Egyptians entered the sea in pursuit of their prey. The waters of the sea collapsed upon them. Pharaoh and his mighty armies were instantly destroyed by the onrushing waters of the sea.

Moshe and Bnai Yisrael observed the destruction of their nemesis and recited a song of praise to Hashem. This song – *Az Yashir* – extolls Hashem's omnipotence and His destruction of Pharaoh and his mighty armies.

Only at this point did the Jews recite these praises acknowledging Hashem's omnipotence. They had observed His terrible plagues and the submission of Pharaoh and the Egyptians to the will of Hashem. They had departed from Egypt without opposition and left behind a defeated and completely vanquished nation. Why did they not extoll Hashem's greatness when they departed as a free people from Egypt?

The above passage introduces *Az Yashir*. It addresses this issue. The passage explains that only now – after observing the death of Pharaoh and his armies – did the people believe in Hashem and Moshe.

This explanation is difficult to understand. Apparently, until they observed the drowning of the Egyptians, the people were plagued by lingering doubts. They had doubts regarding Hashem and they were uncertain of Moshe's authenticity as His prophet. Now, these doubts were resolved and replaced by certainties. How did the miracle of the Reed Sea bring about this transformation? Why was this event able to resolve uncertainties that persisted even after they had observed all of the wonders that took place in Egypt?

There are a number of factors that contributed to the impact of the miracle of the Reed Sea. We will discuss one of these. This factor is identified and discussed by Rav Aharon Soloveitchik *Zt"l*.[28]

Therefore, say to Bnai Yisrael: I am Hashem. I will take you forth from under the burdens of Egypt. I will save (hatzalah) you from their servitude. I will redeem you with an outstretch arm and with great works. (Shemot 6:6)

And Hashem saved (yeshuah), on that day, Israel from the hand of the Egypt. And Israel saw Egypt die upon the shore of the sea. (Shemot 14:30)

My strength and my praise derive from G-d and He has been my salvation (yeshuah). (Shemot 15:2)

Two Hebrew terms describe salvation

Rav Soloveitchik suggests that the path to understanding this issue begins with an analysis of the terms used by the Torah to describe salvation. The Hebrew language includes a number of words for salvation or rescue. Two of those used in the narrative of the redemption from Egypt are *hatzalah* and *yeshuah*. In the opening portion of Parshat VaEyra, Hashem tells Moshe that He will soon redeem the Jewish people from Egypt. In the first passage above, Hashem describes various aspects of the redemption. In this description Hashem uses the term *hatzalah*. In our *parasha*, the Torah describes the rescue of the Jewish people at the Reed Sea. Here, the term *yeshuah* is used.

Rav Soloveitchik explains that the Torah's choice of terms is revealing. *Hatzalah* is used to describe the rescue of a passive individual. In speaking to Moshe, Hashem was describing the rescue of Bnai Yisrael from Egypt through the plagues. In this process, the Jewish people would be completely passive. They would not be required to participate in their redemption. In fact, the Torah describes Paroh and the Egyptians chasing Bnai Yisrael from Egypt.[29]

---

[28] Rav Soloveitchik discusses this issue in *The Warmth and the Light*, volume 1, pp. 127-131. His position is also discussed by his son Rav Chaim Soloveitchik in a recorded lecture. The following is based on both sources.
[29] Sefer Shemot 12:33.

The term *yeshuah* is used to describe the rescuer acting in unison with the rescued to bring about the rescue. This is the term used in the second two passages above. These passages describe the rescue of the Jewish people at the Reed Sea. The use of this term indicates that Bnai Yisrael were not passive participants in the events at the Reed Sea. How did Bnai Yisrael participate in their own rescue?

And Bnai Yisrael came into the sea upon dry land. The water was for them a wall to their right and their left. (Shemot 14:23)

The Jewish people were required to act on their own initiative

The Tosefta describes the events immediately preceding the parting of the sea's waters. The Egyptians were to the back of Bnai Yisrael and the sea barred their path forward. Moshe told them to proceed into the waters. The tribes began to debate who should lead the nation into the sea. The tribe of Yehudah detached itself from this deliberation and proceeded into the waters.[30] The midrash adds that the sea parted only after the people waded into it and its waters had reached their noses.[31]

These comments suggest an obvious question. Where was Moshe? Why was Moshe not leading his people into the sea just as he led them out of Egypt? Apparently, the miracle of the Reed Sea were to occur in response to the initiative of the Jewish people. This miracle was intended to be a *yeshuah* and not a *hatzalah*. Moshe could not lead them into the sea. They were required to move forward on their own.[32]

Let us now return to our initial question. Why only at this point did the people completely believe in Hashem and Moshe? Why did the plagues and miracles they observed in Egypt leave them with unresolved doubts?

Doubts derive from various sources

The answer is that doubt and ambivalence does not always derive from a deficiency in the evidence supporting a belief. In other words, even when the evidence of a truth is

---

[30] Tosefta Berachot 4:16.
[31] Midrah Rabbah, Shemot 29:9.
[32] Meshech Chuchmah (Sefer Shemot 14:15) suggests that this expectation is explicitly expressed in the passages. When Bnai Yisrael set forth from Egypt, they followed a *malach* – an angel – of Hashem and a pillar of cloud. In Shemot 14:19, the Torah describes the *malach* and pillar moving from the front of the camp of Bnai Yisrael to its rear. The Torah explains that the *malach* and cloud took a new position separating and protecting the Jews from the approaching Egyptians. However, Meshech Chachmah explains that this repositioning of the *malach* and cloud had a second impact. The *malach* and cloud would not lead the people into the sea. The people would not be permitted to follow these leaders into the sea's midst. Instead, the people must lead themselves.
Meshech Chachmah further proposes that this *malach* was not a heavenly emissary. It was Moshe. This position is supported by the comments of Rashi on BeMidbar 20:16. In this passage, Moshe refers to a *malach* sent to rescue the Jewish people. Rashi explains that this *malach* is Moshe, himself. According to Meshech Chachmah's understanding of 14:19, Moshe was directed by Hashem to retreat from the front of the nation and to allow the people to act on their own initiative.

overwhelming, doubt can persist. In order to overcome this ambivalence, one must make the decision to embrace the truth proven by the evidence and to move forward on that basis.

Rav Aharon explains that this dynamic is demonstrated by this account. The plagues and wonders the nation observed in Egypt conclusively demonstrated Hashem's omnipotence and Moshe's authenticity as His prophet. The residual doubts were not the result of an insufficiency of evidence. The doubts reflected an internal conflict; a hesitancy to move forward and embrace the new truths that had been firmly established in Egypt. These doubts were not resolved by new overpowering evidence that emerged at the Reed Sea. Doubt was replaced by conviction because the people discovered within themselves the courage to embrace and act on these beliefs. Once they acted, doubt and uncertainly were brushed aside.

Developing conviction through action

Rav Aharon's insight has important practical implications. First, we must acknowledge that his perspective is novel. We assume that action proceeds from and follows belief and conviction. In other words, we assume that when we are completely convinced of a truth we will act upon it. If we are struggling to move forward, we assume that our motivation is undermined by doubt. Rav Aharon is arguing that sometimes conviction proceeds from action. Our doubts are not the result of a deficiency in the evidence; they are based upon our resistance to embracing a challenging truth.

Let's consider an example. An acquaintance who became observant relatively late in life shared his story with me. He explained that many years ago, he and a friend sought out a rabbi in their community to study with them. They entered into their relationship with this rabbi only after establishing an understanding. The rabbi would study with them but not promote observance or any change in their lifestyles. The rabbi accepted the unusual arrangement. The rabbi and two friends studied together for many years. Occasionally, the rabbi would test whether there was any flexibility in the initial understanding. On each of these occasions, his study-partners assured him that they remained determined to not adopt observance or alter their lifestyles.

One day the rabbi asked his partners a question. "If you could observe a *mitzvah* without significantly altering your lifestyle, would you adopt that observance?" My acquaintance responded that he would consider it. The rabbi asked him whether he would consider shaving in the morning with an electric shaver. My acquaintance responded that he believed he could adopt that practice. He began to shave with an electric shaver. That little change was the first step in gradually implementing other changes.

No new evidence was provided to my acquaintance that finally won him over to the wisdom of the Torah. The barrier between him and observance was not authentic doubt reflecting a deficiency in the evidence of the Torah's wisdom. His internal resistances were undermining his advancement. Once he discovered – with the help of his rabbi/mentor – a path of action, his ambivalence was conquered.

We each should take a few moments to consider Rav Aharon's insight and this example. How often has this dynamic hindered us and prevented us from advancing and growing?

In short, once we have evaluated an issue and made a determination of the truth, we sometimes need to force ourselves to act on this determination. Only through moving forward will we overcome our resistances and the ambivalence they produce.

"Then Moshe and Bnai Yisrael sang this song to Hashem. And they said, "I will sing to Hashem for he is beyond all praise. The horse and its rider He threw into the sea." (Shemot 15:1)

Bnai Yisrael emerge from the Reed Sea. They have safely emerged and the Egyptians have drowned. Moshe leads Bnai Yisrael in a song of praise. Our pasuk is the opening passage of Shirat HaYam – the Song of the Sea. The translation above is based on the comments of Rashi.[33] According to this interpretation, Moshe begins with the pronouncement that Hashem is beyond all praise. This is a rather amazing introduction to his shira – his praise of Hashem. Essentially, Moshe is announcing that his praise is inadequate. But yet, this does not discourage Moshe from engaging in the praise!

"Then Moshe and Bnai Yisrael sang this song to Hashem. And they said: I sing to Hashem for He is the most exalted. The horse and its rider He threw into the sea." (Shemot 15:1)

The Angels Were Forbidden from Singing Praise at the Reed Sea

The Egyptians pursued Bnai Yisrael into the sea. The walls of water collapsed and the Egyptians were drowned. Moshe composed a song of praise to Hashem. This pasuk introduces Shirat HaYaam – the Song of the Sea. Moshe and Bnai Yisrael recited the song.

The Talmud comments, in Tractate Megilah, that the angels observed the destruction of the Egyptians and the salvation of Bnai Yisrael. The angels were moved to praise Hashem with song. Hashem protested. He explained that song was inappropriate. Bnai Yisrael had been saved – but only through the destruction of others. The Egyptians were creations of Hashem. The tragedy of their death was commingled with the salvation of Bnai Yisrael.[34]

This teaching gives rise to an obvious question. It was inappropriate for the angels to utter song to Hashem on this occasion. Why, then, was it fitting for Moshe and the Bnai Yisrael to compose and recite the Song of the Sea?

Rav Chaim Volozin Zt"l offers a brilliant answer to this question. He explains that a miracle can be evaluated in an objective and subjective manner. The angels do not personally benefit from the salvation of the righteous or the destruction of the wicked. Therefore, they are incapable of a subjective reaction. They can only analyze and react to the objective aspects of a miracle. The angles' reaction to the miracle of the Reed Sea must be understood from this perspective.

The angels were moved by the awesome significance of the moment. Hashem had revealed His mastery over nature. The wicked had been destroyed. The promise made to the Avot – the forefathers – was now closer to fulfillment. Indeed, the very purpose of creation was closer to being realized. Bnai Yisrael had been freed and were on the path to Sinai and Revelation. The angels reasoned that this objective analysis dictated that the moment be celebrated through song to Hashem.

---

[33] Rabbaynu Shlomo ben Yitzchak (Rashi), *Commentary on Sefer Shemot* 15:1.
[34] Mesechet Megilah 10b.

Hashem responded that this objective analysis was incomplete. The Egyptians were also creations of Hashem. None of His creatures is created to be destroyed. Therefore, from an objective perspective, the miracle of the Reed Sea included an element of tragedy.

People, unlike angels, can benefit personally from miracles. We can evaluate a miracle on a subjective level. Bnai Yisrael had been saved. For the Bnai Yisrael, this was a great moment. The beneficiaries of Hashem's benevolence were obligated to recognize this kindness.

In an objective sense this miracle was not perfect. The angels could not offer praise. However, in a subjective sense, the event demanded recognition of Hashem. Therefore, Bnai Yisrael offered their praise to Hashem for their salvation.

"My strength and song is G-d. And this will be my deliverance. This is my G-d and I will glorify Him. He is the G-d of my father and I will exalt Him." (Shemot 15:2)

Many of the passages in the shira – this song of praise – are difficult to translate. The exact meaning of numerous phrases is debated by the commentaries. The above translation of the later the part of the passage is based upon the commentary of Rashbam.[35] Gershonides expands on this translation. He explains that this passage is a continuation of Moshe's introduction. In the previous passage, Moshe acknowledges that Hashem is above all praise. In this passage Moshe is acknowledging that in his praises he will resort to material characterizations of Hashem.[36]

If the first passage of Moshe's introduction seems odd, this passage is amazing. One of the fundamental principles of the Torah is that Hashem is not material and that no material characteristics can be ascribed to Him.[37] Nonetheless, Moshe acknowledges that he will employ material imagery in his praise of Hashem. After this introduction Moshe uses various material images to describe Hashem. He refers to Hashem as a "man of war." He discusses the "right hand" of Hashem. In fact virtually every praise that Moshe formulates ascribes some material characteristic to Hashem.

The combined message of these two first passages is completely confusing. Moshe first acknowledges that no praise of Hashem is accurate; it cannot begin to capture Hashem's greatness. In the second passage Moshe excuses himself for ignoring one of our most fundamental convictions regarding Hashem – that He is not material. Instead of providing an appropriate introduction to the shira, these two passages seem to argue that the entire endeavor is not only futile but is an act of blasphemy!

> *"I shall relate Your glory, though I do not see You. I shall allegorize You, I shall describe You though I do not know You. Through the hand of Your prophets, through the counsel of Your servants, You allegorized the splendorous glory of Your power. Your greatness and Your strength, they described the might of Your works. They allegorized You but not according to*

---

[35] Rabbaynu Shemuel ben Meir (Rashbam) *Commentary on Sefer Shemot* 15:2.
[36] Rabbaynu Levi ben Gershon (Ralbag / Gershonides), *Commentary on Sefer Shemot*, (Mosad HaRav Kook, 1994), pp. 111-112.
[37] Rabbaynu Moshe ben Maimon (Rambam) *Commentary on the Mishne*, Mesechet Sanhedrin 10:1.

Your reality. And they portrayed You according to Your actions. The symbolized You in many visions. You are a unity in all of these allegories."

(Shir HaKavod)

Our liturgy contains many profound insights. Unfortunately, sometimes, we do not carefully consider the meaning of the words. In many synagogues the Shir HaKavod – composed by Rav Yehuda HaChassid – is recited every Shabbat at the closing of services. The Shir HaKavod deals with the same issues that Moshe is discussing in his introduction to the Shirat HaYam. Let us carefully consider these lines.

We begin by acknowledging that we cannot see Hashem. In fact, we cannot truly know Hashem. Human understanding is limited. We cannot begin to conceptualize the nature of Hashem. This creates a paradox. How can we praise of even relate to Hashem? How can we relate to a G-d that is beyond the boundaries of human understanding? We respond that we will employ allegories.

But the use of allegories creates its own problems. If we do not know or understand Hashem's nature, then on what basis will be form these allegories? What allegory can we formulate for a G-d so completely beyond the ken of human understanding? We respond that we will rely on the allegories provided by the prophets. We do not trust ourselves to create our own allegories. Instead, we must employ the allegories that are provided to us by Moshe and the other prophets.

Of course, this does not completely answer the question. Even Moshe was unable to achieve an understanding of the fundamental nature of Hashem. So, how can he help us? What allegory can Moshe provide for that which even he could not comprehend? The answer is that we never attempt to describe Hashem's nature. No allegory can be adequate. All of our allegories are designed to describe Hashem's actions and deeds. In other words, our allegories do not describe what Hashem is, only what He does.

Yet, at the same time that we employ the allegories of the prophets, we are required to acknowledge the limitation of these descriptions. We cannot – even for a moment – delude ourselves as to the accuracy of the terms we use when referring to Hashem. The allegorical terms are not in any way a description of Hashem's reality. This means these terms are not a true description of Hashem's real nature.

Finally, we acknowledge Hashem's unity. Hashem is a perfect unity. This means He has no parts or characteristics. The multitude of allegories that we employ cannot lead us to err on this issue of unity. All of the various allegories that we employ relate back to a G-d that in fact is one. He does not have various characteristics or any characteristics. He is the perfect unity. Even when we refer to Hashem as kind or omniscient, we must recognize the limitation of this reference. Hashem does not truly have the characteristic of being kind or the quality of omniscience. These are allegorical characterizations.

The Shir HaKavod provides a fundamental insight. It attempts to resolve an important paradox. We need to relate to Hashem. Yet, we cannot truly comprehend His exalted nature. How can we form a relationship with that which we cannot know? In response to our human need, the Torah allows us to employ allegorical terms in reference to Hashem. But we must recognize that this is an accommodation. We are permitted to use allegorical terms and phrases. We are not permitted to accept these allegories as being accurate depictions of Hashem's nature.

We can now understand Moshe's introduction to Shirat HaYam. At the Reed Sea Bnai Yisrael experienced salvation. The people needed to respond. They needed to express their outpouring of thanks to Hashem. Moshe formulated Shirat HaYam in response to this need. But Moshe's shira – like all praise of Hashem – is a not an accurate portrayal of Hashem. Instead, it is an accommodation to the human need to relate to Hashem. We are permitted this accommodation. But there is a precondition. We must first recognize that it is an accommodation. Our praise cannot capture the true greatness of Hashem – who is above all praise. And we must recognize that all of our praises rely on allegories but that are not true depictions of Hashem. This is Moshe's introduction. Before he led Bnai Yisrael in song, he explains the limitations of our praises. They are incomplete and are merely allegories and not accurate descriptions of Hashem.

And he cried unto Hashem; and Hashem showed him a tree, and he cast it into the waters, and the waters were made sweet. There He made for them a statute and an ordinance, and there He proved them. (Shemot 15:25)

Marah: A Textual Anomaly and its Message of Liberation

1. Arriving at Marah and the wonder of the waters

Parshat Beshalach describes the exodus from Egypt and the events that followed that exodus. Included in the *parasha* is a description of the Reed Sea splitting and Bnai Yisrael passing through its suspended waters. This is followed by the collapse of the sea upon Paroh and his legions. After these events, the people travel three days in the wilderness and find no water. They arrive at Marah. There, they discover water. However, the water was so bitter that it is not potable. The people cannot understand or endure their predicament. They complain to Moshe. Moshe petitions Hashem. Hashem indicates a tree to Moshe and directs him to cast it into the water. Moshe follows Hashem's directions. The water is sweetened and rendered potable.

The Torah tells us that after these events – while the people were still encamped at Marah – Hashem gives to them laws and statutes.

2. The mystery of Marah

The Torah provides no indication of which laws and statutes were communicated to the people at Marah. However, commenting on this passage, Rashi provides additional detail. He explains that, according to our Sages, at Marah the people received the *mitzvah* of Shabbat and various elements of the civil law.[38]

Rashi's contribution only partially addresses the difficulty in these passages. He indentifies the commandments and laws that were communicated at Marah. However, the message and meaning of the above passage remains a mystery. Why does the Torah tell us that laws and statutes were communicated to the people but conceal the identity of the specific material? Furthermore, what was the purpose of this prelude to Revelation? Why were these unidentified laws and statutes communicated to the people at this time? Before considering these issues another problem must be discussed.

3. Pre-Sinai commandments

---

[38] Rabbaynu Shlomo ben Yitzchak (Rashi), *Commentary on Sefer Shemot* 15:25.

Maimonides explains that although some of the commandments of the Torah were communicated before the Revelation at Sinai, we do not observe these commandments on the basis of this pre-Sinai communication. The commandments we observe are derived from the Sinai Revelation. Those commandments that were previously communicated are observed only because they were renewed at Sinai.

Maimonides provides as an example, the commandment of *milah* – circumcision. This commandment was given to Avraham. Avraham was instructed in the observance of the commandment and told that the commandment must be observed also by his descendants. Maimonides explains that with revelation the commandment given to Avraham was replaced by the Sinai commandment. Today, we do not perform circumcision because of the commandment given to Avraham. We observe it because it was renewed at Sinai.[39]

It can be presumed that this principle applies to those commandments that were communicated to the nation when it was still in Egypt. Hashem communicated to Moshe the commandment establishing and regulating the Torah's lunar calendar. This commandment includes the designation of Nisan as the first month. Also, commandments regarding the observance of the Pesach festival were given in Egypt. The commandments regarding *tefilin* where first communicated to the nation at the time of the exodus. In all of these instances, it can be presumed that although these commandments were revealed to the people before Sinai, we observe these commandments only because they were renewed at Sinai.

And he that is eight days old shall be circumcised among you, every male throughout your generations, he that is born in the house, or bought with money of any foreigner, that is not of your descendants. (Beresheit 17:12)

4. Deriving laws from pre-Sinai narratives

In all of these instances the Torah includes a relatively detailed account of the initial instructions regarding the commandment. Many of the laws regarding *milah* are derived from the passages describing Hashem's instructions to Avraham regarding the commandment. The same applies to the commandments given to Bnai Yisrael at the time of the exodus. The Torah provides a detailed account of Hashem's instructions to Moshe regarding these commandments and of Moshe's instruction to the people. Many of the laws regarding these commandments are derived from these passages.

Superficially, this seems to contradict Maimonides' principle. If the commandments are binding upon us only because of their renewal at Sinai, how can we derive many of the specific laws governing these commandments from the instruction given before Sinai?

5. The role of the Sinai Revelation in authenticating pre-Sinai commandments

Answering this question requires a better understanding of the reason that pre-Sinai communications are not binding. Let us consider the commandment of *milah*. Hashem gave this commandment to Avraham. He instructed him to observe the commandment and He directed Avraham to instruct his descendants to observe the commandment.

How do we know that Avraham had this prophecy and that he and his descendants were commanded to perform the *mitzvah* of *milah*? We know this is true only because the prophecy is recorded in the Torah. We accept the authenticity of the Sinai Revelation, the Torah, and its contents.

---

[39] Rabbaynu Moshe ben Maimon (Rambam) *Commentary on the Mishne*, Mesechet Chullin 7:6.

The same reasoning applies to the commandments given to Bnai Yisrael at the time of the exodus. We do not observe these commandments because of some tradition we have received from our ancestors. We observe these commandments because we accept the authenticity of the Sinai Revelation and the Torah. These commandments are recorded in the Torah and therefore, we observe them.

In other words, the Sinai Revelation is the source of all commandments. Only because a commandment is recorded in the Torah do we accept it as being authentic.

6. The legislative character of pre-Sinai texts

Now, our problem is resolved. Let us review the problem. Maimonides explains that we only observe the Torah's commandments based upon their inclusion in the Sinai revelation. Yet, *milah* and other commandments were communicated to us before Sinai. The Torah records this initial communication of the *mitzvah* and laws governing their observance. These laws are incorporated into halachah even though they are derived from these pre-Sinai communications. How can laws be derived from these pre-Sinai communications?

The answer is that we do not accept these laws because of, or based upon their *initial* communication. We do not observe *milah* because of some tradition that Hashem commanded Avraham to perform circumcision and to instruct his descendants in the commandment. We observe *milah* because the Torah of the Sinai Revelation records this ancient prophecy. The inclusion of the account in the Torah given at Revelation authenticates the pre-Sinai prophecy and endows it with halachic validity.

7. Rashi's enigmatic comments regarding the Marah anomaly

Let us return to Marah. As already noted above, it is odd that the Torah conceals the identity of the commandments communicated at Marah. However, this omission is not only odd. It is an anomaly. Many commandments are primarily presented in the context of their pre-Sinai origins. For example, many of the laws governing *milah* are derived from the Torah's account of Avraham's prophecy. In fact, virtually every *mitzvah* that was communicated before Sinai is introduced by the Torah in the context of the original pre-Sinai communication. However, there is one substantial exception. The commandments given at Marah are not described in the narrative. The Torah tells us laws were given at Marah. Our Sages identify the commandments that were revealed. However, the actual narrative does not include any description of the commandments! In other words, according to our Sages, the people were instructed in the commandment of Shabbat at Marah. However, the Torah itself does not present the *mitzvah* of Shabbat in the context of its initial communication to the people. Why are the commandments communicated at Marah not discussed in the context of their initial presentation to the people?

Rashi makes an additional comment that suggests an explanation. As noted above, Rashi provides a brief summary of the commandments that were communicated at Marah. Then, Rashi addresses another issue. Why were these commandments given at this time? Rashi explains that these commandments were give at this time because Hashem wanted the people to become involved in them.[40]

Rashi's meaning is not obvious. His phrasing is unusual. He does not say that these commandments were communicated in order to initiate their observance. He says that they were

---

[40] Rabbaynu Shlomo ben Yitzchak (Rashi), *Commentary on Sefer Shemot* 15:25.

communicated in order that they should become a focus of the community's "involvement". What does Rashi mean? Beyond observance, what other "involvement" were the people to have with these commandments?

The apparent answer emerges from recognizing that every commandment has two aspects. A commandment is a directive that must be obeyed. A commandment is also the subject of study, analysis and contemplation. Rashi explains that the people were not expected to merely observe these commandments. They were expected to become involved in them. This suggests that they were required to study them carefully and contemplate them.

8. The unique purpose of the Marah commandments

According to Rashi, the Marah commandments were different from all other commandments communicated before Sinai. These other commandments were communicated at their respective times because the moment was uniquely appropriate. Avraham was communicated the commandment of *milah* when the moment arrived for its observance. Hashem communicated through Moshe the laws governing the calendar because the moment had arrived for the establishment of that calendar. The laws of the Pesach festival were discussed at the time of the exodus because of the appropriateness of the moment. In each of these instances the Torah discusses the commandment in the context of its initial pre-Sinai origin. This is because the origin is relevant to the content of the commandment.

This suggests that the commandments of Marah were not communicated at that time because of the relevancy of the moment. Shabbat is not uniquely linked to the events that took place at Marah. Civil law is not intimately connected to the Marah episode. Instead, these commandments were communicated at that time for another reason. Hashem wished for the people to immerse themselves in the study and contemplation of *mitzvot*. For that purpose, he selected these commandments.

This explains the Torah's concealment of the specific commandments communicated at Marah. These commandments were not selected on the basis of a specific relevance. Also, the anomalous treatment of the Marah commandments is understood. The Torah elaborates on commandments in the context of their pre-Sinai origins only when that origin is specifically relevant to the *mitzvah*.

Why were commandments communicated at this time? Why was it important for the people to immerse themselves in Torah *mitzvot*? Apparently, although the people had been physically liberated, their intellectual and emotional liberation was far from complete. This next step toward freedom could only be achieved through Torah study.

9. Lessons from Marah

Our ancestors were provided with commandments at Marah in order to facilitate their liberation from the bondage they had escaped. We also are subject to the many demands placed upon us by the necessities of our livelihoods and the support our families. If we are honest, we will acknowledge that we are also driven by the demands of personal desire. These masters are our contemporary Paroh. Like our ancestors, we must strive to liberate ourselves and our minds from our many masters. Like our ancestors the study and contemplation of the Torah provides this opportunity.

"And Hashem said to Moshe: I will rain down to you bread from the heavens. And the nation will go forth and they will collect a daily portion. This is in order that I may test them to determine if they will go in the way of my laws or not." (Shemot 16:4)

The Test of the Mun

Bnai Yisrael had no food in the desert. Hashem told Moshe that he would provide them with mun – manna. This miraculous food would rain down from the sky every day. The people were instructed to collect enough for a single day's use. They were not to gather extra. They also were required to entirely consume the day's ration. They were not to horde for the future. On Friday – Erev Shabbat – they were to collect a double ration. This amount was to suffice for Friday and Shabbat. On Shabbat the mun did not fall. The people were instructed not to go out to the fields and seek the mun on Shabbat.

Our pasuk explains that the mun represented a test. The commentaries differ on the nature of the test. Rashi explains that the test lay in the observance of the mitzvot related to the mun. Specifically, the people must resist the urge to create a reserve of mun through saving a portion of the daily ration. Also, they must accept the command not go into the fields on Shabbat to seek the mun.[41]

Rashi seems to imply that these mitzvot regarding the mun were designed to impact and revise the nation's attitude towards personal security. By nature, we seek security. We tend to delude ourselves and assume that we can attain this security through our personal efforts. In reality, we cannot completely secure our future through our own practical provisions. We are dependent upon the benevolence of Hashem. Only through fulfilling His will can we attain true security. The mun helped the people understand that Hashem is the real source of security. The nation was forced to be dependent upon the grace of Hashem. They could not take any action to provide for the next day. They could only follow the will of Hashem and depend upon His daily support.

This was an important lesson to learn before entering the Land of Israel. This would be a fertile, rich land. It would be easy for the people to delude themselves and conclude that their own efforts secured their future. They might forget that they are dependent upon Hashem. The mun reinforced the concept that Hashem, and not our own material efforts, sustain us.

This, of course, does not mean that we are not responsible to work towards securing our own future. The message of the mun is that of our efforts, alone, are ineffective. We need the benevolence of the Creator.

Malbim provides another explanation of the test. The pasuk explains that the mun tested whether the nation would follow the way of the Torah. Malbim explains that the way of the Torah is not merely the observance of the few mitzvot related to the mun. Instead, it is full devotion to the observance and study of all the mitzvot. How did the mun test this commitment?

The sojourn in the desert provided the people with the opportunity to totally devote themselves to the Torah. All material needs were met with minimal effort. The clothing of the people did not wear out. They had a convenient supply of water. Their food fell from the heavens each day. There were no distractions. This environment was perfect for complete dedication to

---

[41] Rabbaynu Shlomo ben Yitzchak (Rashi), *Commentary on Sefer Shemot* 16:4.

the study and observance of the Torah. This was the test of the mun. Given this wonderful opportunity, would Bnai Yisrael commit themselves to the way of Torah?[42]

And Hashem said to Moshe: Now, I will rain for you bread upon the camp from the heavens. The nation will go forth each day and collect (it). In this manner, I will try them as to whether or not they will go in the way of my laws. (Shemot 16:4)

The Reciprocal Relationship between Thought and Action

The introduction of the mun and its laws

Parshat BeShalach provides the Torah's first mention and a description of the mun – the manna – that sustained Bnai Yisrael in the wilderness. One month after the nation's departure from Egypt, the people arrived at the Wilderness of Sin. In this wilderness, there was no obvious source of food. The people bemoaned their plight and grumbled that death in Egypt would have been preferable to their impending starvation in this wilderness; in Egypt, at least they had food to eat – even meat. In response to the complaints of the nation, Hashem gave them mun in the morning. Also, in response to their longing for meat, Hashem brought the people quail in the evening.

Hashem established a number of laws related to the daily collection of the mun. The people were only permitted to collect enough for the day. They were required to completely consume the daily portion and they were not permitted to save any for the next day. If any was hoarded, it spoiled that day and was unusable the next day. On Friday, they were to collect a double-portion that would suffice for that day and for the entire Shabbat. It would not spoil. On Shabbat, the mun did not fall and the people were enjoined against leaving the camp to search for the mun.

In the above passage, Hashem explains His reason for providing the nation with mun. Through the mun, He will try the nation and determine whether the people will follow the laws He has established. This is a strange statement. The mun was granted in order to sustain the people. Testing the people's obedience seems to be a secondary objective. Yet, in Hashem's explanation of His reason for granting the gift of mun, He does not mention the people's legitimate need for sustenance and identifies as His primary objective the testing of the nation.

Greed and its origins

A comment of Rashi can help explain this passage. Rashi comments that the nation's request for sustenance was appropriate. However, the longing for meat was not warranted. This is for two reasons: First, the people should have realized that meat is a luxury and not a necessity. Second, the nation left Egypt with all of their cattle. If they truly desired meat, then they could have slaughtered their own cattle and satisfied their perceived need.[43]

Of course this raises an interesting question: why did the people not slaughter their own cattle? If their need for meat was so intense, they could have easily satisfied it! Rav Yisroel Chait suggests that apparently the nation was motivated by greed. They were unwilling to slaughter their own animals in order to satisfy their desire for meat. He further explained that generally,

---

[42] Rabbaynu Meir Libush (Malbim), *Commentary on Sefer Shemot* 16:4.
[43] Rabbaynu Shlomo ben Yitzchak (Rashi), *Commentary on Sefer Shemot* 16:8.

greed stems from one of two sources. For some people, greed is an expression of haughtiness. These individuals are driven to amass more and more wealth because they believe that their possessions and resources reflect upon their own greatness and accomplishments. They are unwilling or unable to share with others lest they diminish their wealth and thereby, its representation of their own greatness. However, for others, greed is an expression of an almost opposite attitude. It stems from a deep sense of insecurity. Such individuals are dominated by fear of impending disaster and they cannot overcome their anxiety. In response, they devote themselves to preparing for the potential catastrophe that may come with the new day. They cannot arrest their need to amass resources because this is their response to their anxiety and they cannot share their resources because they believe that this may jeopardize their own survival when the doom they fear does arrive.

Rav Chait explained that it is unlikely that the greed of recently liberated slaves was driven by a fantasy of greatness. However, we can easily imagine the fears and anxieties of a generation that had barely survived its generation's Holocaust – the bondage and persecution of Egypt. They were now in the wilderness. They had no source of sustenance. Yes, they longed for meat; but they were unwilling to draw upon the one finite source of nourishment that was available to them – their cattle.

Mun as a response to the nation's anxiety

Based upon this insight, Rav Chait explains that the mun was intended to address the nation's sense of anxiety and insecurity. The mun fell each and every day – except Shabbat. It was a miracle granted by Hashem. Hashem demonstrated to the people that He is the only real source of security. The message of the mun was that through their relationship with Hashem they can achieve the only true security.[44]

It is now possible to re-approach the above passage. The objective of the mun was not merely to provide sustenance. Other means could have accomplished the same end. Instead, the mun was designed to address the nation's anxieties and insecurities. It was intended to instill within the people a confidence based upon reliance upon and trust in Hashem. The message of the passage seems to be that this objective could not be accomplished merely through the consistent appearance of the mun on a daily basis. In other words, even though the people would see the mun spread upon the ground day-after-day, they would continue to struggle with their anxiety. Only through observance of the laws related to the mun would they overcome their insecurities. Why would they not be able to overcome their fears through observing Hashem's constant care for them and His commitment to their welfare? Why were the laws needed?

Action and Thought

Sefer HaChinuch notes that there is a reciprocal relationship between our thoughts and our actions or behaviors. We all realize that our thoughts inform and guide our actions. For example, when we feel threatened, we may respond through either engaging in action to defend ourselves or to attack and eliminate our adversary. But our actions also inform and influence our thoughts and attitudes. For example, if we force ourselves to engage in positive behaviors, we eventually influence and improve our self-image. Often actions have a more powerful impact upon our ideational reality – our thoughts and attitudes – than can be achieved though reflection and contemplation.[45] This can be illustrated. Consider a person who suffers from agoraphobia –

---

[44] Rav Yisroel Chait, *Shir al HaYam*, YBT TTL #C-059.

fear of open spaces. No doubt this person has been told by countless friends and colleagues that his fear is irrational. He probably, at some level, realizes that this is true. But despite all of the assurances he has received that his fear is baseless, he cannot shake his sense of foreboding when challenged to travel outside of his home. However, if this person can be persuaded to take a first small step towards confronting his fear – perhaps, just standing in the doorway of his home and gazing upon the world outside – he may begin to overcome his anxieties.

Now, the function of the mitzvot regarding the mun is more clearly grasped. These laws demanded that the people act in a manner that expressed security in Hashem. They were commanded to collect only enough mun for the day. They were forbidden from hoarding the mun. They were commanded to collect a double portion on Friday and trust that it would not spoil over the course of the following day. Each and every one of these laws reinforced through action the ideas and attitudes the mun was designed to communicate. The people not only observed Hashem's constant attention to their well-being. They also, acted in a manner that reinforced their acceptance of Hashem as their trusted provider. Through this process, the nation was provided the opportunity to gradually overcome its anxieties.[46]

"As Hashem commanded Moshe, Ahron placed it before the Ark as a keepsake." (Shemot 16:34)

During the travels of Bnai Yisrael in the desert the nation ate manna mun. Hashem commanded Moshe to instruct Ahron to create a reminder of this miracle. Ahron was to fill a container with the mun. This container would be placed before the Ark in the Mishcan. The miracle of the mun has an interesting expression in halacha. Shulchan Aruch explains that on Shabbat we are obligated to recite the blessing of HaMotzee on two loafs of bread.[47] The Talmud explains that this recalls the mun of the desert.[48] How do these double loaves represent the mun? The Talmud in Tractate Shabbat discusses this issue. A short introduction is required.

Generally, the mun fell in the desert each day. The people would collect enough mun for the day's consumption. They were not permitted to collect extra. They were prohibited from

---

[45] Rav Aharon HaLeyve, *Sefer HaChinuch*, Mitzvah 16.
[46] Rav Chait suggests an alternative explanation for the function of these laws. He explains that in order to cultivate within the nation a sense of security based upon its relationship with Hashem, it was necessary for Hashem to become a reality for them; the people must enter into a relationship with Hashem. This relationship is created through the observance of *mitzvot* and the study of their laws. The *mitzvot* and their laws reflect the wisdom of Hashem. Through Torah observance and study, we draw closer to Hashem and He becomes more real to us. He points out that in a preceding similar incident in Marah, Hashem responded to the nation's fears through providing *mitzvot* and requiring their regular study. The Sages identify the *mitzvot* given at that time and they are not specifically related to the incident or related to issues of insecurity. This implies that the study and observance of *mitzvot* – any *mitzvot* – is helpful in nurturing a person's sense of reliance upon Hashem and security. This is because through study and observance of *mitzvot*, Hashem becomes more real and a relationship is forged between Hashem and the person.
[47] Rav Yosef Karo, Shulchan Aruch, Orech Chayim 274:1.
[48] Mesechet Shabbat 117b.

saving a portion for the next day. Any portion, which was left at the end of the day, would quickly spoil. On Shabbat the mun did not fall. What did the people eat on Shabbat? On Friday the people were permitted to deviate from their regular practice. They were to collect a double portion. One portion would be eaten on Friday. The second portion would be saved and consumed on Shabbat. Miraculously, this mun would not spoil. The Talmud explains that the dual loaves recall the double portion of mun that provided for Shabbat.[49]

There is another requirement of the Shabbat meal that recalls the mun. When the kiddush is recited the loaves are covered with a cloth.[50] A number of explanations are offered for this requirement. One explanation offered by the Tur is that the covering recalls a characteristic of the miracle of the mun.[51] Each day before the mun fell a layer of dew formed on the ground. The mun fell upon this dew. A second layer of dew then covered it. The covering over the loaves duplicates the dew that covered the mun. Tur explains that according to this explanation one cloth should be placed under the loaves and a second over the loaves. It is somewhat difficult to understand these laws. The mun did not fall on Shabbat. The double portion fell on Erev Shabbat on Friday. In other words, the double portion did not fall on Shabbat. On Shabbat the people ate a single portion that remained from Friday! How do the double loaves on Shabbat recall a miracle that occurred on Erev Shabbat? In order to answer this question, we must more clearly understand the message of the double loaves.

Our Sages created, through these loaves, a reminder of the miracle of the mun. What aspect of the miracle is recalled through the loaves? The Sages did not attempt to duplicate, through the loaves, the Shabbat portion. On Shabbat the people ate a single portion, not a double portion. Instead, the Sages created a reminder of the origins of the Shabbat portion. The Shabbat portion was derived from the double portion of Erev Shabbat. The dual loaves recall this origin.

Bnai Yisrael experienced many miracles in the desert. They were provided with water and shelter. All of the needs of the nation were miraculously met in this desolate wilderness. Why did the Sages choose the miracle of the mun for special treatment? Why must this miracle be recalled each week? At a basic level, our pasuk provides a response. Hashem commanded Moshe to create a permanent reminder of the mun. This was accomplished through placing a container of the mun by the Ark. This command implies that the mun has a unique significance. Hashem singled out this miracle for constant remembrance. The Sages created an additional symbol designed to recall the mun. They reinforced the message of our pasuk. However, this does not completely answer the question. First, why did Hashem single out the mun? Why did this miracle require a constant reminder? Second, why did the Sages specifically relate their reminder of the mun to Shabbat? The mun was an ongoing miracle. We need to understand the implications of this miracle.

The miracle required a manipulation of nature. Nature was altered in order to conform to the needs of Bnai Yisrael. This is an important lesson. The Torah promises us that we will be rewarded for following the Torah. All of our material needs will be satisfied. This means that if we observe the Torah, nature will be altered. Nature is influenced by our virtue. The mun proves the veracity of this promise. It represents nature conforming to our needs. Through recalling the mun, we confirm the reality of the blessings in the Torah. The mun contained a second message.

---

[49] Mesechet Shabbat 117b.
[50] Rav Yosef Karo, Shulchan Aruch, Orech Chayim 271:9.
[51] Rabbaynu Yaakov ben HaRash, Tur Shulchan Aruch, Orech Chayim 271.

The laws of Shabbat forbade collecting mun on Shabbat. In order to provide for the needs of Bnai Yisrael, a double portion fell on Erev Shabbat. Nature conformed to the requirements of halacha! This provides an important message about halacha. We all recognize the reality of the physical world and the laws that govern it. However, the laws of halacha often seem less important or less real. The miracle of the mun taught that the halacha has a greater reality than the physical world! Nature conformed to the requirements of halacha! We can now better appreciate the lesson of the double loaves. The Sages chose to create a symbol recalling the double portion of mun that fell on Erev Shabbat. This double portion captures the concept of nature conforming to halacha.

And Hashem Said to Moshe: Write this as a record in a book and place it in the ears of Yehoshua, that I will destroy the memory of Amalek from under the heavens. (Shemot 17:14)

And it will be when Hashem gives you rest from all of your enemies that surround you in the land that Hashem your G-d gives to you to possess, you should destroy the memory of Amalek from under the heavens. Do not forget. (Devarim 25:19)

Bnai Yisrael's Responsibility to Destroy Amalek

1. Two versions of Amalek's destruction

Bnai Yisrael were saved from the Egyptians through wonderful miracles. They traveled from the Reed Sea toward Mount Sinai. At Sinai, they would receive the Torah. As they traveled, they were attacked by the nation of Amalek. Moshe instructs Yehoshua to assemble an army and to battle Amalek. Moshe ascends to the top of a hill and raises his hands in prayer. Through the combination of Moshe's prayer and the valor of Yehoshua's army Amalek is defeated.

Following the victory, Hashem commands Moshe to record the events and to enjoin Yeshoshua to preserve the record. He further tells Moshe that He will do battle with Amalek throughout the generations until even the memory of this wicked nation is eradicated.

Moshe reviews this incident in his final message to Bnai Yisrael. However, Moshe's address includes an additional element. He tells Bnai Yisrael that it is their responsibility to destroy Amalek. It seems that Moshe's message is somewhat different from the message communicated in Parshat BeShalach. In the passages in Parshat BeShalach, the only charge given to Bnai Yisrael is to remember the wickedness of Amalek. Hashem declares that He will wage war with Amalek throughout the generations. Moshe's address shifts the responsibility for retribution to Bnai Yisrael. Bnai Yisrael is to destroy Amalek.

And he said: For the hand is upon the throne of Hashem. Hashem is at war with Amalek from generation to generation. (Shemot 17:16)

2. Hashem's oath to destroy Amalek

Moshe elaborates on Hashem's commitment to destroy Amalek. He declares that Hashem has placed His hand upon His throne and He has sworn that He will do battle with Amalek throughout the generations.

It is clear from Moshe's declaration that the imperative to destroy Amalek is somehow unique. In this instance Hashem – so to speak – takes an oath that He will destroy the nation.

Hashem had previously told Moshe that He would punish Egypt for its persecution of Bnai Yisrael and its denial of His kingship. However, Hashem did not accompany this assurance with an oath. Hashem tells Bnai Yisrael that they will be His agent for destroying the pagan nations of the Land of Cana'an. These nations are both religiously and morally degenerate. They deserve to be eradicated. Nonetheless, Hashem does not take an oath regarding their destruction. What distinguished Amalek and evoked Hashem's solemn oath that He would destroy them?

Remember that which Amalek did to you on the road when you went forth from Egypt. They came upon you on the road. They struck from behind all those who were weak. You were tired and weary and they did not fear Hashem. (Devarim 25:17-18)

And Amalek came and waged war with Bnai Yisrael at Refidim. (Shemot 17:8)

3. Amalek's objective in attacking Bnai Yisrael

In his account of Bnai Yisrael's encounter with Amalek that Moshe includes in his final address, he adds details that are not part of the account in Parshat BeShalach. He explains that Amalek attacked Bnai Yisrael from behind and focused the attack upon the weakest members of the nation – those who were struggling to keep pace with the march and had fallen back toward the rear of the camp. Moshe also says that Amalek happened upon Bnai Yisrael. This seems to mean that Amalek was not seeking this battle but instead came upon Bnai Yisrael. Amalek assessed the condition of their potential target. They discerned that the people were weary from their travels and undisciplined. They concluded that Bnai Yisrael was a target of opportunity and decided to launch an attack.

The account of the encounter in Parshat BeShalach begins with the statement "Amalek came and waged war with Bnai Yisrael." This phrasing suggests that Amalek did not merely come upon Bnai Yisrael by accident. The phrasing implies that Amalek came – seemingly with an intent and design – to attack Bnai Yisrael.

Rashi suggests a homiletic solution to this problem. He reinterprets the phrasing of Moshe's account. According to Rashi, Moshe did not say Amalek "came upon" Bnai Yisrael. He said that Amalek came to "cool off" Bnai Yisrael. Rashi explains that after the nations of the region learned of Bnai Yisrael's rescue from Egypt and the destruction of the Egyptians at the Reed Sea, they were overcome by fear and awe. Amalek sought out Bnai Yisrael for the purpose of demonstrating that this nation was not invincible. Amalek was determined to "cool off" or moderate the nations' perception of Bnai Yisrael as unassailable.[1]

Nations heard and they trembled. Terror took hold of the people of Pelashet. Then, the chiefs of Edom were confused and the leaders of Moav were seized with trembling. All of the people of Cana'an melted. (Shemot 15:14-16)

4. The impact of Egypt's destruction

Parshat BeShalach describes the destruction of the Egyptians at the Reed Sea. The Egyptians pursued Bnai Yisrael and overtook them at the Reed Sea. Bnai Yisrael was trapped between the sea and the approaching enemy. Moshe stretched forth his arm toward the sea and its waters parted. Bnai Yisrael entered the sea and crossed on a dry sea-bed. The Egyptians pursued Bnai Yisrael into the sea. Suddenly, the water came crashing down upon the Egyptians and they were destroyed. Bnai Yisrael emerged from the sea and saw that their enemies were

---

[1] Rabbaynu Shlomo ben Yitzchak (Rashi), Commentary on Sefer Devarim 25:18.

annihilated. Moshe and the people sang a song of praise to Hashem. This is the Shirat HaYam – the Song of the Sea.

The song describes the destruction of the Egyptians and the might of Hashem. The closing lines describe the impact of Egypt's utter destruction upon the surrounding nations. It describes their paralyzing terror and uncontrollable dread.

The implication of the Shira is that this impact was one of the objectives of the miracles of the Reed Sea. These miracles were intended as a demonstration for Bnai Yisrael and all of the nations of Hashem's omnipotence. The demonstration had its impact. The events of the Reed Sea communicated to much of humanity an awe of Hashem and an appreciation of His glory. For a moment in history an unprecedented degree of recognition of Hashem was achieved.

5. The reason Hashem takes an oath to destroy Amalek

Now, Hashem's oath can be understood. Amalek came with the intent of undoing the events of the Reed Sea. Amalek's objective was not to protect its territory, secure wealth through spoils, or avenge the Egyptians. Amalek's purpose was to undermine the objective achieved at the Reed Sea. They sought to demonstrate that Bnai Yisrael could be successfully attacked and that Hashem's apparent omnipotence was not real. Amalek's initial success in its attack did have an impact and it produced some diminution in Hashem's glory.

Amalek's purpose distinguishes it from the other nations that Hashem has condemned to destruction. Its purpose was to moderate the awe of Hashem that was inspired by the destruction of Egypt and to diminish His glory. It is because of this purpose that Hashem took an oath to destroy Amalek.

And all the assembly of Bnai Yisrael traveled from the Wilderness of Tzin according to their travels by the word of Hashem. And they camped at Refidim and there was no water for the nation to drink. And the nation argued with Moshe and they said, "Give us water and we will drink." And Moshe said to them, "Why do you argue with me? Why do you test Hashem?"
(Shemot 17:1-2)

6. The rebellion at Refidim and its impact

The Torah notes that Amalek attacked Bnai Yisrael at a place named Refidim. Amalek's attack is not the only event that the Torah records as taking place at Refidim. The description of this other event directly precedes the Torah's description of the Amalek's attack.

Bnai Yisrael arrive at Refidim and discover that there is no water in this place. The people complain to Moshe. He criticizes the people for arguing with him and for testing Hashem. Moshe's rebuke has no effect. The nation continues to complain with growing intensity. Ultimately, the people question whether Hashem is really in their midst. Moshe prays to Hashem and He provides the nation with water.

This event and the attack of Amalek are juxtaposed in the text. Furthermore, the Torah notes that Amalek attacked Bnai Yisrael at Refidim – the site of the unruly protest just described. The implication is that Amalek's attack and Bnai Yisrael's behavior at Refidim are related.

Rashi confirms this interpretation and adds that Bnai Yisrael had reacted to not having water by questioning Hashem's presence. In other words, they demanded that Hashem provide ongoing proof of His presence through providing for their needs. In response to this attitude, Hashem exposed Bnai Yisrael to the wickedness of Amalek. In this manner He demonstrated that His providence is constant. It is sometimes evident and at other times it is less easily observed. However, even a brief interruption in Hashem's providence exposes Bnai Yisrael to dangers and threats.[2]

Amalek's attack did compromise Hashem's glory. The attack was occasioned and made necessary by Bnai Yisrael's failings at Refidim. Hashem diminished His glory in order to communicate an important lesson to His people.

7. Bnai Yisrael's responsibility to destroy Amalek

Now, the account in Parshat BeShalach and Moshe's address can be reconciled. The restoration of Hashem's full glory demands that Amalek be destroyed. Hashem takes an oath that Amalek will be destroyed. However, it is Bnai Yisrael's responsibility to act as Hashem's agent in His battle with Amalek. This is because Bnai Yisrael is directly responsible for Amalek's success in its attack and the consequent compromise of Hashem's glory. Bnai Yisrael's attitudes at Refidim required a response from Hashem. If Bnai Yisrael was to advance in its relationship with Hashem, the people needed to learn and understand that Hashem's providence is constant – even when it might not be completely obvious. Each day and each moment Bnai Yisrael is threatened by dangers and enemies of which it is not aware. The failure of these threats to harm Bnai Yisrael is an expression of Hashem's providence. Hashem demonstrated this principle through Amalek. He allowed Amalek to execute its wicked plan against Bnai Yisrael.

Because Bnai Yisrael's deficiencies created the necessity for this attack and the consequential diminishment of Hashem's glory, it is Bnai Yisrael's responsibility to restore Hashem's glory. Bnai Yisrael must exact Hashem's punishment from Amalek.

"And Moshe said, "Eat it today (ha'yom) for today (ha'yom) is Shabbat to Hashem. Today (ha'yom), you will not find it in the field." (Shemot 17:25)

During their travels in the desert, Bnai Yisrael was sustained by mun – manna. The mun fell in the morning. A portion suitable for the day's consumption was collected. However, on the eve of the Shabbat – Erev Shabbat – a double portion of mun fell. This double portion sufficed for Friday and Shabbat. In our pasuk, Moshe explains that on Shabbat the mun will not descend and the people are to eat the mun collected the previous day.

On Shabbat day we are required to eat three meals. One is eaten on the night of Shabbat and two are eaten on the day of Shabbat. The Talmud explains that the obligation to eat three meals on Shabbat is reflected in our pasuk. In his instructions to the people, Moshe uses the term "today" – ha'yom – three times. Each use of the term ha'yom is a reference to one of the Shabbat meals.[3]

What is the nature of this obligation to consume three meals on Shabbat? Shabbat is essentially a day on which we refrain from creative labor – melachah. Through abstaining from melachah we acknowledge that Hashem created the universe in six days and "rested" on the seventh. How is the obligation to consume three meals related to the theme of Shabbat?

---

[2] Rabbaynu Shlomo ben Yitzchak (Rashi), Commentary on Sefer Shemot 17:8.
[3] Mesechet Shabbat 117b.

Maimonides includes his discussion of the obligation to partake of three Shabbat meals in his discussion of Oneg Shabbat – indulging oneself on Shabbat. Indulging ourselves on Shabbat, is an extension of our obligation to honor Shabbat. Through fulfilling the obligation of Oneg, we demonstrate that Shabbat is a special day. It is evident from Maimonides' treatment of the three Shabbat meals that they are an expression of the obligation of Oneg Shabbat.[4]

Maimonides explains that the obligation of Oneg Shabbat was established by the Sages.[5] This does not seem to be consistent with the Talmud's assertion that the requirement of the meals is reflected in our pasuk. According to the Talmud, it seems that at least this element of Oneg – partaking of three meals – is actually contained in the Torah! Based on this consideration, some authorities argue with Maimonides and assert that the obligation of three Shabbat meals is a Torah level requirement.[6]

There is an obvious reconciliation between the position of Maimonides and the Talmud's treatment of the obligation of the Shabbat meals. Often, the Sages relate laws that they create to passages in the Torah. This is not intended to imply that the law is actually derived from the passage. Instead, the Sages are attaching their decree to a theme or message contained in the passage.

Aruch HaShulchan is not completely satisfied with this response. He observes that the Talmud provides numerous admonitions regarding the importance of the three Shabbat meals. Maimonides himself admonishes us to be careful to not in any way detract from these meals. Aruch HaShulchan argues that the Talmud's stress on the importance of the three Shabbat meals is not consistent with the thesis that these meals are a requirement established by the Sages.

It should be noted that one can argue that this question is not completely compelling. It is not uncommon for the Sages to provide extensive admonitions regarding their decrees. This is intended to reinforce decrees that we might be tempted to treat lightly – precisely because they were established by the Sages. However, Aruch HaShulchan does not suggest this explanation for the Sages' admonitions in this instance. Instead, he provides an interesting alternative.

Aruch HaShulchan suggests a novel resolution of the apparent contradiction between Maimonides and the Talmud. As noted above, the Talmud explains that the three-time use of the term ha'yom in our pasuk reflects the obligation to eat three meals on Shabbat. Aruch HaShulchan notes that according to Tur, Hashem actually caused each person to be supplied with three portions of mun for Shabbat. By providing these three portions, Hashem communicated that it is appropriate to consume three meals on Shabbat.

Based on Tur's comments, Aruch HaShulchan offers a simple resolution of the apparent contradiction between the Talmud and Maimonides' assertion that Oneg Shabbat and the obligation of three Shabbat meals is a decree of the Sages. He explains that the requirement of three meals may have been established by Moshe. Moshe based his decree on the pattern of the mun. A triple portion of mun was provided for Shabbat. Moshe made the obvious deduction that through providing this triple portion Hashem communicated that it is appropriate to partake of

---

[4] Rabbaynu Moshe ben Maimon (Rambam) *Mishne Torah*, Hilchot Shabbat 30:9.
[5] Rabbaynu Moshe ben Maimon (Rambam) *Mishne Torah*, Hilchot Shabbat 30:1.
[6] Rav Yechiel Michal HaLeyve Epstein, *Aruch HaShulchan, Orech Chayim* 291:1.

three meals on Shabbat. Therefore, although the obligation of three Shabbat meals is a decree of the Sages – perhaps from Moshe – it is reflected in the Torah.

This explains the Talmud's admonitions regarding the importance of these three Shabbat meals. Although the meals are required by a decree of the Sages, they are reflected in the Torah – in the pattern of the mun. This decree is qualitatively different than most other decrees of the Sages. Other decrees are designed to reinforce laws of the Torah. Because these more common decrees are safeguards for and reinforcement of Torah laws they are treated less stringently than the Torah laws they reinforce. In contrast, the requirement of three Shabbat meals is not merely a reinforcement of the Torah law. It is a reflection of a theme in the Torah itself.[7]

> *"And Moshe and Aharon said to all of Bani Yisrael, "In the evening you will know that Hashem took you out of Egypt." (Shemot 17:8)*

How are the three Shabbat meals an expression of Oneg Shabbat? In order to answer this question we must consider this pasuk. Bnai Yisrael complained to Moshe that they did not have adequate food. Moshe responded that Hashem would provide them with food in the evening and in the morning. In the evening, quail would descend upon the camp of Bnai Yisrael. The quail would provide the people with meat. In the morning the mun would appear. They would collect the mun and have food for the day. However in introducing this solution, Moshe and Aharon began with the pasuk above. They explained that in the evening – with the descent of the quail upon the camp – the people would recognize that Hashem had redeemed them from Egypt.

The commentaries are concerned with an obvious problem. How did the descent of the mun reinforce the message that Hashem had taken Bnai Yisrael out of Egypt? Certainly, the sudden descent of the quail was a miracle. But it was not nearly as great as the wonders that the people had already observed during the exodus from Egypt. It cannot be compared to the plaques or the splitting of the Reed Sea!

Sforno explains that Bani Yisrael experienced both physical and spiritual bondage in Egypt. They were slaves. Their labor and their very bodies were not their own. But their spiritual and emotional bondage was as great – perhaps greater – than their physical bondage. In Egypt, they had developed the habits, attitudes, and outlook of slaves. Their complete redemption required their liberation from their servitude to the Egyptians and also their development of attitudes and habits fitting a free people.

Sforno notes that according to the Talmud, Bnai Yisrael did not have set times for eating. They were dependant upon their masters to provide them with food and the opportunity to eat. After the exodus from Egypt, Moshe established fixed meal times for Bnai Yisrael.[8]

Why were these fixed meal times important? The constant anxiety and preoccupation of Bnai Yisrael over food was a remnant of their emotional bondage. In order for Bnai Yisrael to continue to develop into a free people, it was important that they shed this anxiety and preoccupation and replace it with a sense of security essential to a free person.

Sforno explains that the quail and the mun addressed this problem. The quail descended in the evening and the mun appeared in the morning. Set and regular evening and morning meals

---

[7] Rav Yechiel Michal HaLeyve Epstein, *Aruch HaShulchan, Orech Chayim* 291:1
[8] Mesechet Yoma 75b.

were instituted through the pattern of the mun and quail. Moshe suggested that this constancy and regularity would free the people of their anxiety and preoccupation with food.

According to Sforno, this is the meaning of the above pasuk. Moshe and Aharon prayed that through the descent of the quail and the appearance of the mun in the morning, the people would be further liberated from their emotional and spiritual bondage. They were not asserting the descent of the quail was a greater miracle than the wonders that the people had already observed. They prayed for this miracle to help the Bnai Yisrael continue on their path of liberation from the bondage of Egypt. Moshe and Aharon prayed that through this miracle the people would realize that Hashem was not only redeeming them from their physical bondage but also from their emotional and spiritual bondage.[9]

This insight provides a simple answer to our question. How are the three meals Shabbat meals an expression of Oneg Shabbat? According to the Talmud – as understood by Sforno – the pattern of the mun and quail established a fixed pattern of meals for Bnai Yisrael. This pattern consisted of two daily meals – one in the morning and one in the evening. The triple portion of mun for Shabbat was an exception to this weekday pattern. The triple portion indicated that it is appropriate to have a third meal on Shabbat. Because this third Shabbat meal is an addition to the daily weekday pattern, it is an expression of the special character of the day.[10]

"Through the window she looks forth and cries. The mother of Sisera peers through the lattice. "Why is his chariot delayed in coming? Why are the wheels of his chariot late?" *(Shoftim 5:28 - Haftarat Beshalach)*

Devorah the prophetess describes the pain of Sisera's mother. She awaits the return of her son from battle with Bnai Yisrael. He is late. She senses he will not come home. Her ministers comfort her. They assure her that Sisera has defeated the Jews. He is delayed collecting spoils. But Sisera will never return. The army of Bnai Yisrael, inspired by Devorah, has defeated Sisera. Yael has killed him.

Why does Devorah describe the anguish of the mother of Sisera? Should we feel pity for the mother of this wicked man? Does Sisera's mother deserve our sympathy?

Sisera's army was not merely defeated. These enemies of Bnai Yisrael were devastated. Sisera's mother and her nation awaited the outcome of the battle. But no news came. There were no refugees from the war. No one escaped to bring news of the outcome.

---

[9] Rabbaynu Ovadia Sforno, *Commentary on Sefer Shemot*, 17:8.
[10] There is well-known custom to refer to the third meal as *Shalos Seudos* – three meals. This appellation seems to be inaccurate. The third meal is a single meal, not three meals! I recall that Mr. Meyer Twersky A"H once explained this custom. He explained – based on sources I do not recall – that it is this third meal that gives all of the meals their unique Shabbat character. The Torah recognizes a set of two meals as appropriate for weekdays and a set of three meals as appropriate for Shabbat. The Shabbat set of three meals only emerges and becomes fully evident with our participation in the third meal. This third meal gives all of the Shabbat meals their special character as the set of three Shabbat meals. Therefore, it is appropriate to refer to this third meal as *Shalos Seudos* – all three meals derive their special Shabbat character from this third meal.

The tears of Sisera's mother represent the totality of the defeat of Bnai Yisrael's enemies. Devorah, for this reason, included this image in her praise to Hashem.

Yitro

And Yitro – a leader in Midyan (and) the father-in-law of Moshe – heard all that G-d had done for Moshe and His nation Yisrael. That Hashem had taken forth Yisrael from Egypt (Shemot 18:1)

The Conversion of Yitro

1. Yitro and Moshe's reunion

Parshat Yitro begins with a description of Yitro's reunion with his son-in-law Moshe. During the many years that Moshe was a fugitive from Egyptian authority, he was sheltered in Midyan by Yitro. Moshe married Tzipora – Yitro's daughter – and together they had two sons. When Moshe retuned to Egypt – at Hashem's command –Tzipora remained in Midyan with their sons.

Yitro hears of the redemption of Bnai Yisrael from Egypt and travels from Midyan into the wilderness of Sinai to reunite with Moshe and to bring to him his family. From the Torah's description of this encounter, it is clear that Moshe and Yitro were very close friends. Upon meeting they warmly embrace. Moshe treats Yitro with care and respect.

Moshe carefully describes to Yitro the wonders that Bnai Yisrael had experienced and witnessed. Yitro rejoices, praises Hashem and declares his recognition of Hashem as the true G-d. In order to fully appreciate the significance of this encounter between Moshe and Yitro and to fully understand the impact of Moshe's message upon Yitro, it is important to review an earlier conversation between these two friends.

And Moshe went and returned to Yeter his father-in-law. And he said to him, "I will go now and return to my brothers in Egypt. I will see whether they yet live." And Yitro said to Moshe, "Go in peace." (Shemot 4:18)

2. Moshe's deception of Yitro

Moshe received his first prophecy during the period that he was living in Midyan in his father-in law's home. This prophecy came to Moshe while he was shepherding his father-in-law's flocks in the wilderness of Sinai. Moshe's prophecy began with a vision of a burning bush. An intense fire burned in the midst of the bush but the bush was not consumed by the flame. This vision initiated a dialogue with Hashem in which Moshe learned that Bnai Yisrael would be redeemed from bondage in Egypt and led to the Land of Cana'an. He learned that Hashem had selected him to serve as His messenger. He would address Paroh and his ministers and he would lead Bnai Yisrael to the land promised to their forefathers.

Moshe returned to his father-in-law and asked his leave to return to Egypt. However, Moshe did not reveal to his father-in-law the true purpose of his journey. The above passage describes the conversation between Moshe and his father-in-law – referred to by both the name Yeter and the name Yitro. Moshe tells Yitro that he wishes to return to Egypt in order to assess the welfare of his people. He does not indicate to Yitro that he has received a prophecy or that his mission is to redeem Bnai Yisrael. Why did Moshe conceal from his beloved friend his true motives and the purpose of his journey?

I am Hashem your G-d, your G-d, who took you forth from the Land of Egypt, from the house of bondage. You should have no other gods than I. (Shemot 20:2)

3. The intent of the first statement of the *Asseret HaDibrot*

This passage is the first statement of the Decalogue – the *Asseret HaDibrot*. Although the statement is brief, its ideational content is remarkably dense. The statement begins with a declaration – I am Hashem your G-d. This declaration does not contain an explicit directive. Nonetheless, it is understood by the Sages to be a commandment. We are enjoined by this declaration to accept Hashem as our G-d.[1]

The declaration presents an obvious problem. It seems that the same declaration could have been formulated more succinctly as "I am G-d." Why does the declaration include the identification of G-d with the name "Hashem"?

Rabbaynu Ovadia Sforno responds that the appellation "Hashem" communicates the idea of a creator of the universe who sustains its existence. According to Sforno, the actual meaning of the declaration is that Hashem – the Creator and the One Who Sustains all existence – is to be accepted by us as our G-d.

Sforno also notes that the term used in the passage for "I" is *anochi*. In Biblical Hebrew the word "I" can be represented by either of two terms – *ani* or *anochi*. *Ani* is the more common term and *anochi* is used only occasionally. Why is *anochi* used in this instance? Sforno explains that the term *anochi* means "I and no other". The meaning of the passage is that Hashem – the Creator and Sustainer of the universe – and He alone is our G-d. The passage enjoins us to serve the Creator and the Source of all existence. It is the positive formulation of the admonition that completes the statement – Have no other G-d than I.[2]

However, the passage includes another element. G-d identifies Himself as the One Who delivered us from Egypt. In other words, the passage identifies our G-d in two ways. He is identified as the Creator and Sustainer of all existence and as our Redeemer from bondage in Egypt. Why is it necessary for G-d to identify Himself in both ways?

Rav Naftali Tzvi Yehudah Berlin – Netziv – explains that as Hashem – Creator and Sustainer of the universe – G-d's relationship extends equally to all of His creations. He created all organic and inorganic matter. The brute animal and the human being are all the product of His act of creation and His constant sustaining will. As Redeemer, G-d gave expression to a special covenantal relationship with Bnai Yisrael. In our redemption from Egypt, Hashem revealed a unique providential relationship with Bnai Yisrael.[3]

From Netziv's perspective the passage commands us to accept as our only G-d, Hashem – Creator and Sustainer of all existence. It also enjoins us to recognize that this Sovereign of the universe revealed, through our redemption, His special relationship to and involvement with Bnai Yisrael. In other words, we are commanded to affirm a paradoxical truth. This Sovereign, who rules the entire vast universe, has entered into a covenantal relationship with a nation of human beings. This nation is a minute and seemingly insignificant element in the vast universe. Yet, Hashem has selected this nation as a special object of His attention!

I know now that Hashem is greater than all gods. For in the way that they planned (to execute Yisrael, they were executed). (Shemot 18:11)

---

[1] Rabbaynu Moshe ben Maimon (Rambam) *Mishne Torah*, Hilchot Yesodai HaTorah 1:1.
[2] Rabbaynu Ovadia Sforno, *Commentary on Shemot* 20:2.
[3] Rav Naftali Tzvi Yehuda Berlin (Netziv), *Commentary Hamek Davar on Sefer Shemot* 20:2.

4. Yitro's explanation of his transformation

After Yitro hears Moshe's description of the rescue of the Bnai Yisrael and the destruction of the Egyptians, Yitro declares his acceptance of Hashem as the only true G-d. This declaration clearly implies that, up to this moment, Yitro's commitment to Hashem was less than complete. Rashi confirms this interpretation of the passage. According to Rashi, Yitro was acknowledging that to this point his acceptance was incomplete.[4] In what respect was this acceptance deficient and what specifically brought about the transformation in Yitro's attitude?

In his commentary on Parshat Bo, Nachmanides outlines the false beliefs that were prevalent at the time of the exodus from Egypt. He explains that acceptance of a G-d Who is Creator and Sustainer of the all existence was not universal. Among those who did accept the existence of such a G-d, there was doubt regarding His relationship with His creation. Many rejected the notion that His knowledge extends to the mundane particulars of the material universe. Others assumed that His knowledge encompasses all. Yet, they regarded as preposterous the view that He should care about or involve Himself in the trivial affairs of humankind.

Nachmanides explains that the wonders of the exodus addressed all of these false beliefs. The miracles demonstrated Hashem's omnipotence. The sovereignty over the natural order that was demonstrated by these wonders left no doubt that Hashem is the Creator and the Sustainer of the universe and therefore, He has complete authority and control over its every aspect and element. Furthermore, the rescue of Bnai Yisrael from among the Egyptians demonstrated that this omnipotent sovereign is aware of and interacts with humankind. He has selected Bnai Yisrael as His people and the shield of His providence extends over them.[5]

In the context of Nachmanides' comments, the meaning of the first statement of the Decalogue is even richer. This declaration enjoins us to acknowledge and accept as our sole G-d the Creator and Sustainer. It also instructs us to acknowledge that He relates to humanity and to Bnai Yisrael. Implicit in the declaration is the message that He alone is our salvation.

Ultimately, all that befalls us is an expression of His will. We should place our trust and hope in no other – neither a false god nor a powerful person. In other words, this first statement of the Decalogue can be viewed as a statement and acknowledgment of the lessons of the redemption from Egypt.

Yitro's transformation can now be more thoroughly understood. Yitro attributed his transformation to the realization that Hashem had destroyed the Egyptians by the very means they had employed in their genocidal campaign against Bnai Yisrael. The Egyptians had condemned the male newborns of Bnai Yisrael to death by drowning. Paroh and his armies were drowned when the waters of the Reed Sea crashed down upon them.[6] In other words, the events of the redemption demonstrated to Yitro that Hashem's knowledge and involvement extends to the affairs of humanity and His justice reigns in the material world.

Apparently, this was the area of deficiency in his acceptance of Hashem that Yitro acknowledged. Until these events, he had readily accepted the existence of a Creator Who sustains all existence. However, he was unwilling to embrace the concept of a Sovereign of the

---

[4] Rabbaynu Shlomo ben Yitzchak (Rashi), *Commentary on Sefer Shemot* 18:11.
[5] Rabbaynu Moshe ben Nachman (Ramban), *Commentary on Sefer Shemot* 13:16.
[6] Targum Unkelus, Sefer Shemot 18:11.

universe who is also involved in the affairs of humankind. The events of the redemption transformed his perceptions. These events provided uncontestable evidence of Hashem's involvement with humanity in general and Bnai Yisrael in particular.

5. Moshe's reason for deceiving Yitro

Finally, Moshe's reason for concealing from Yitro his true reason for returning to Egypt can be identified. Moshe understood his father-in-law's theology. He realized that although his father-in-law fully accepted the reality of a Creator and Sustainer of the universe, he was not yet prepared to acknowledge the involvement of this G-d with humanity. The miracles and wonders through which Hashem would reveal Himself to all of humanity as the G-d of Providence had not yet occurred. Moshe was wary of asking Yitro to accept more than could be demonstrated. Therefore, Moshe asked his father-in-law's leave by providing a reason that he knew his friend could appreciate and accept and he bid his time waiting for the opportunity to lead Yitro to a higher level of knowledge and understanding.

"And Moshe's father in law, Yitro, the minister of Midyan, heard all that G-d had done for Moshe and for Yisrael, His people, that Hashem had taken Yisrael out of Egypt." (Shemot 18:1)

Moshe and Bnai Yisrael are joined in the wilderness by Moshe's father-in-law, Yitro. Yitro brings with him Moshe's wife and their two children. However, Yitro did not embark on this journey only to reunite Moshe and his family. Yitro had received news of the events in Egypt and the redemption of Bnai Yisrael. According to our Sages, Yitro was so impressed by these events that he converted to Judaism.[7]

There is a substantial dispute among the commentaries regarding the timing of these events. Nachmanides observes that events in the Torah are not always presented in chronological order. However, we should assume that the events are narrated chronologically in instances in which there is no concrete evidence to the contrary. In this instance, there is no reason to assume that the events presented are not chronologically arranged. Therefore, Nachmanides asserts that Yitro came to the encampment of Bnai Yisrael immediately after the confrontation with Amalek.[8]

Rabbaynu Avraham ibn Ezra disagrees with Nachmanides' position. He argues that there is significant evidence that Yitro came to Bnai Yisrael's encampment after the giving of the Torah. According to Ibn Ezra, the events related in our *parasha* are not presented chronologically. Our *parasha* first relates Yitro's arrival at the encampment and later describes the events of revelation. This order is opposite the order in which the events actually occurred.

Of course, this raises an obvious question: Why does the Torah depart from a chronological presentation of events? Ibn Ezra suggests that the Torah abandons a chronological presentation in order to juxtapose Yitro's support of Bnai Yisrael with Amalek's hatred. In response to Amalek's aggression and hatred, we are obligated to destroy it. In contrast, we are obligated to recognize the support of Yitro. We express this recognition by acting with kindness towards his descendants. Ibn Ezra observes that this lesson has a practical application: Yitro's descendants lived in proximity to Amalek. Bnai Yisrael is commanded to destroy Amalek.

---

[7] Rabbaynu Shlomo ben Yitzchak (Rashi), *Commentary on Sefer Shemot* 18:1.
[8] Rabbaynu Moshe ben Nachman (Ramban), *Commentary on Sefer Shemot* 18:1.

However, we must take care to not wage our war against Amalek in an indiscriminate manner. We must be careful to provide for the safety of Yitro's descendants even when battling Amalek.[9]

The roots of this dispute between Ibn Ezra and Nachminides are found in the Talmud. The Talmud describes a dispute between three Sages on the meaning of our passage. Our passage tells us that Yitro heard of all that Hashem had done for Bnai Yisrael and of their redemption from Egypt. These Sages ask: What specifically did Yitro hear? What was the specific news, or report, that encouraged him to join the Jewish people? One Sage suggests that Yitro heard of the war with Amalek. The second opinion is that he heard of the giving of the Torah. The final opinion is that he heard of the splitting of the Reed Sea.[10]

Two of these positions are easily understood. The parting of the Reed Sea revealed Hashem's omnipotence. His omnipotence is evidence that He is the Creator. We can understand Yitro's decision – based on this awesome demonstration – that he must devote himself to the service of Hashem. We can also appreciate the opinion that Yitro was inspired by the giving of the Torah. In the revelation, Hashem revealed Himself to Bnai Yisrael and gave to them the Torah. Hashem – the Creator – provided humanity with His guide to life. We can understand Yitro's decision as a response to revelation. However, it is difficult to understand the third opinion. According to this opinion, Yitro joined Bnai Yisrael in response to the war with Amalek. What aspect of this war motivated Yitro's decision? Bnai Yisrael's defeat of Amalek was miraculous. However, this was not the greatest miracle that the nation had witnessed to that point. It certainly did not compare with the plagues in Egypt or the splitting of the sea. Why would this event motivate Yitro to join the Jewish people?

In order to answer this question, it is important to consider the context of this dispute. All three opinions are expressed in response to a single question: What news did Yitro hear and convert? In other words, what specific information of events motivated Yitro's decision to convert? We can assume that the Sages regarded Yitro as a righteous convert. Yitro made his decision based upon proper and laudable motives. If we accept this assumption, then we can rephrase the Talmud's initial question: What was Yitro's – the ideal convert – motive for conversion?

Again, two of the responses are easily understood. However, with our reformulation of the Talmud's question, we can understand these two responses more clearly. One Sage suggests that Yitro's conversion was a response to the splitting of the Reed Sea. This miracle revealed Hashem as the omnipotent Creator. Yitro recognized that he must abandon all other worship and devote himself to the service of the one true G-d. Another Sage suggests that Yitro's conversion was a response to the revelation at Sinai. We can easily understand this motivation. Hashem gave His people a way of life. Yitro recognized that Hashem's instructions for living provided the ideal model for human existence. He wished to adopt the Torah life. It remains difficult to immediately grasp the third opinion. Why was the war with Amalek a proper motivation for conversion?

However, now that we understand that these Sages are discussing proper motivations for conversion, we can understand this third position. But first, we must review key elements of Amalek's attack on Bnai Yisrael.

---

[9] Rabbaynu Avraham ibn Ezra, *Extended Commentary on Sefer Shemot*, 18:1.
[10] Mesechdet Zevachim 116a.

Why did Amalek attack Bnai Yisrael? Amalek was not threatened by Bnai Yisrael. Bnai Yisrael had not been given their land and would not attempt to conquer Amalek. Obviously, Amalek's attack was not motivated by practical, territorial considerations. What was Amalek's motivation? Apparently, Amalek was unable to tolerate the existence of Bnai Yisrael and the message communicated by their redemption from Egypt. In other words, Bnai Yisrael's experiences in Egypt demonstrated Hashem's providence, His omnipotence, and His special relationship with the Jewish people. Amalek's attack on Bnai Yisrael was an attempt to silence these messages.

Amalek's attack on Bnai Yisrael marked the emergence of a great divide. Bnai Yisrael was not just another nation among the family of nations. Instead, Bnai Yisrael and the messages that their existence communicated evoked antipathy, hatred and opposition. With Amalek's attack, two opposing forces emerged. Bnai Yisrael's existence and experiences communicate a new world-view and perspective. Amalek represents those nations that are opposed to this view and seek to destroy Bnai Yisrael and their message.

We can now understand the third opinion. Yitro was motivated to convert by the war of Amalek. Yitro recognized that the nations of the world were choosing sides. He did not feel he could remain a passive observer of this battle. He, too, had to choose between two opposing world-views and he chose to align himself with Bnai Yisrael.

Now I know that Hashem is greater than all of the gods. For it is in the manner that they acted wickedly He punished them. (Shemot 18:11)
Yitro's Amazement with Hashem's Providence

Yitro, Moshe's father-in-law, comes to meet Bnai Yisrael in the desert. Moshe tells Yitro of the miracles of the redemption. Yitro reacts with joy to the account. He sees the work an all-powerful creator. In the above *pasuk*, Yitro notes the appropriateness of the punishment applied to the Egyptians. His comments seem to refer to the drowning of the Egyptians in the Reed Sea. The Egyptians had attempted to destroy Bnai Yisrael through drowning the male children. The Egyptians had met their end when the sea crashed down upon them.

Targum Unkelous offers an alternative translation to the *pasuk*. Unkelous explains that Yitro was impressed by a different aspect of the Egyptians' fate. Their punishment corresponded with and reflected the evil they had conspired to do to the Jews. Unkelous stresses a relationship between the punishment of the Egyptians and their plans—not their actual actions.

Rav Yitzchak Zev Soloveitchik *Zt"l* explained the meaning of Unkelous' translation through a story. Rav Yitzchak of Volozin *Zt"l* was approached by a minister of the Czar. The minister asked Rav Yitzchak to explain the meaning of a *pasuk* from *Tehillim*. The *pasuk* states, "Glorify Hashem all peoples. Praise Him all nations. For His kindness to us is overwhelming." The Minster asked, "Why should the nations of the world praise G-d because of the kindness He shows to the Jewish people?"

Rav Yitzchak explained that the Jews have no knowledge of the ministries' various plots developed to undermine and persecute them. Therefore, the ministers who design these devious plans have the best opportunity to assess G-d's intervention on behalf of the Jews. The *pasuk* instructs those who seek to destroy the Jewish people to consider the outcome of their plans. This reflection should inspire the plotters to repent and recognize the greatness of the Creator.

This explains the meaning of Unkelous' translation The Talmud in Tractate Sanhedrin teaches that Yitro was not always a friend of Bnai Yisrael. Before meeting Moshe, he had actually been one of Paroh's three principal advisors.[11] He was involved in designing the campaign against Bnai Yisrael. He had an intimate knowledge of Paroh's plans to harass and destroy the Bnai Yisrael. He recognized the thoroughness of Hashem's justice. Hashem's judgment was not limited to punishing the evil actions of the Egyptians. The punishment extended to even the wicked conspiracies that were not successfully executed. This established, for Yitro, Hashem's omniscience and omnipotence.[12]

And it was on the following day and Moshe sat to judge the nation. And the nation stood before Moshe from the morning until the evening. (Shemot 18:13)
The Torah's Preference for Mediation of Disputes Rather than Judgment

One of Moshe's responsibilities was to judge Bnai Yisrael. Legal disputes and questions regarding the law were brought to Moshe for resolution according to the principles of the Torah. Moshe executed this responsibility without assistance. Yitro, Moshe's father-in-law, concluded that Moshe's method of judging the nation was not efficient. He suggested that Moshe establish a system of judges. These judges would resolve simpler issues. Only the most difficult problems would be brought to Moshe. This suggestion was accepted and Yitro's system was instituted.

Our *pasuk* describes the scene Yitro encountered and that led him to recommend this system. Before Yitro's intervention, Moshe would begin his task of listening to people's cases and then judging them every morning. The various petitioners would wait to consult with Moshe. The process would continue throughout the day and into the evening.

Rashi quotes the comments of the Talmud in Tractate Shabbat. The Talmud explains that our passage should not be understood literally. Moshe did not actually spend the *entire* day executing his responsibilities as judge. Instead, the *pasuk* is alluding to the importance of justice. The message of the passage is that a judge may only require an hour to decide a case. However, if he decides a case in accordance with the truth, the *mitzvah* he fulfills is equal to studying the Torah the entire day. Furthermore, this judge is acting as Hashem's partner in Creation.[13] The Talmud's comments need some interpretation. Why does this specific *mitzvah* – judging according to the truth – elevate the judge into partnership with Hashem?

The Torah tells us that Hashem commanded Adam to conquer the earth.[14] In other words, Hashem did not create the earth as a finished product. Instead, He charged humanity with the responsibility of creating civilization. The establishment of civilization completes Hashem's creation of the earth. In order for humanity to discharge this task, its members must live together in peace. Peace only exists in a society governed by justice. Therefore, the judge's efforts are crucial to the survival of society and the realization of Hashem's plan in Creation.

---

[11] Mesechet Sanhedrin 106a.
[12] Rav Yitzchak Zev Soloveitchik, *Chidushai HaGRIZ on T'NaCH and Aggadah*, Parshat Yitro.
[13] Rabbaynu Shlomo ben Yitzchak (Rashi), *Commentary on Sefer Shemot* 18:13.
[14] Sefer Beresheit 1:28.

The Talmud, in Tractate Baba Metziah, makes an amazing statement. The Talmud explains that Yershalayim was destroyed because its judges decided the law according to a strict interpretation of the Torah law and did not attempt to go beyond the letter of the law.[15]

These comments are difficult to understand. In Tractate Shabbat, the Talmud praises the judge who decides the law according to the truth. Presumably, this requires the judge to make his decisions according to the laws of the Torah. Yet, the statement of the Talmud in Tractate Baba Metziah clearly indicates that merely deciding the law according to the precepts of the Torah is insufficient. The judge must seek a solution that goes beyond the letter of the law. He must search for a solution that is consistent with some greater truth. What is this greater truth – beyond the requirements of the law – that the judge must seek?

There is a related question that we must consider. According to the Torah, a dispute between two litigants can be resolved in two ways: The judge can decide the case on the basis of *din* (law). Alternatively, the judge can offer *p'sharah* – a mediated resolution. Which method is preferable? Our Sages teach us that a judge should always encourage the litigants to seek a *p'sharah*.[16] However, this raises a question: What is the basis upon which the judge constructs the *p'sharah*? If the *din* indicates a specific outcome, how can *p'sharah* produce a decision different than the law? Certainly, the law is perfectly just. How can *p'sharah* produce an outcome superior to *din*?

Rav Yitzchak Arama *Zt"l*, in his commentary Akeydat Yitzchak, explores this issue. Akeydat Yitzchak explains that a system of laws is designed to deal with general issues. Laws indicate the response that is generally appropriate. However, because laws deal with basic realities, they cannot assure an appropriate outcome in every circumstance. This is not because of a flaw in the legal system. This outcome is a consequence of the very nature of any system of rules. Consider the Torah's prohibition against stealing. It punishes all stealing equally. It must be admitted that some theft is motivated by simple greed and other thefts are the result of extreme desperation. The person violating the law out of greed is more evil than the unfortunate person compelled to steal because of unbearable poverty. Yet, the law treats both of the violators in the same manner. Both receive the same punishment. The unfortunate, desperate thief does not receive any leniency from the law. This is not because the law is unjust. The law is a system of general rules; it does not recognize the specific details and facets of every case.

Based on this concept, Akeydat Yitzchak explains the comments of the Talmud. A judge can seek *tzedek* – justice – or *chesed* – righteousness. A judge seeking *tzedek* decides each case according to the laws of the Torah. If he applies the laws accurately, he can be assured of producing a just outcome. However, the judge's strict adherence to Torah law cannot assure that good and evil will receive their appropriate recompense. This is because the laws of the Torah are created to apply to offenses without regard to unusual circumstances, motivations or intentions. They do not take into account every possible circumstance relevant to the case. The judge cannot be sure that his decision is consistent with *chesed*. *Chesed* is achieved when the decision corresponds to the specific circumstances of the case. This requires going beyond the law.[17]

---

[15] Mesechet Baba Metziah 30b.
[16] Rabbaynu Moshe ben Maimon (Rambam) *Mishne Torah*, Hilchot Sanhedrin 22:4.
[17] Rav Yitzchak Arama, *Akeydat Yitzchak on Sefer Shemot*, Parshat Yitro.

We can now understand the role of *p'sharah*. *P'sharah* does not ignore the law. *P'sharah* recognizes the limits of any legal system. Through *p'sharah*, the judge attempts to adapt the general principles of law to the specific circumstances of the case. In short, *p'sharah* goes beyond the letter of the law. Its goal is to secure an outcome that is both just and appropriate to the specific case. The objective of *p'sharah* is *chesed*.

This principle is not limited to monetary disputes between two litigants. When a judge is determining if a practice is permissible or prohibited – *issur ve'heter* – this principle applies. In other words, in resolving questions concerning *kashrut, Shabbat*, or any *mitzvah*, a rabbi (*rav*) can approach the issue from two perspectives. He can seek *tzedek* or *chesed*.

How do these two approaches differ? When applying *tzedek*, a *rav*, after hearing the question, can respond to the petitioner that the practice is either prohibited or permitted according to the law. His decision will embody *tzedek*. However, it may not represent *chesed*. A *chesed* decision requires more of the *rav*. He must consider the specifics of the case. After considering these specifics, it may be appropriate to seek a solution rather than simply render a decision. A solution does not ignore the law. A solution seeks to resolve the issue strictly within the framework of *halacha*. However, a solution suggests a means by which the action can be performed in a permissible manner In other words, *chesed* sometimes requires to the *rav* to respond, "What you want to do is prohibited. But here is a permissible way you can achieve your objective."

We can now understand the comments of the Talmud in Baba Metziah. Moshe did not simply decide cases on the basis of *tzedek*. In every case, he stove to achieve truth. This is the solution of *chesed*. The Talmud condemns judges who do not seek *chesed* but merely *tzedek*. According to the Talmud, this behavior contributed to the destruction of Yerushalayim.[18]

And it was on the following day and Moshe sat to judge the nation. And the nation stood by Moshe from the morning until the evening. (Shemot 18:13)

The Importance of a Just Societyx

Moshe was the leader of Bnai Yisrael. He cared for the people's material and spiritual well-being. Among his various tasks, he served as judge. Each day, he devoted time to resolving the various disputes that inevitably arose among individuals. The *pasuk* indicates that, at least on occasion, this required the entire day. Rashi comments, that according to the Talmud in Tractate Megilah, the *pasuk* alludes to an important lesson. The Talmud interprets the *pasuk* homiletically. Moshe did not actually devote the entire day to judging the people. The intent of the *pasuk* is to communicate the importance of this function. One who judges justly – even for an hour – is equated to a scholar absorbed the entire day in the study of Torah. Furthermore, the righteous judge is considered a partner with Hashem in the creation of the universe.[19] One can easily appreciate that a judge plays an essential role in sustaining a just society. However, describing a judge as Hashem's partner in creation seems exaggerated.

The meaning of this lesson can be understood through an insightful comment of Rabbaynu Yonah. Rabbaynu Yonah begins by noting an apparent contradiction in Pirke Avot.

---

[18] Rav Yitzchak Arama, *Akeydat Yitzchak on Sefer Shemot*, Parshat Yitro.
[19] Rabbaynu Shlomo ben Yitzchak (Rashi), *Commentary on Sefer Shemot* 18:13.

Shimon HaTzadik teaches that the world is supported upon three pillars. These are Torah study, service to Hashem and acts of kindness.[20] Raban Shimon ben Gamliel asserts that the world exists by virtue of justice, truth, and peace.[21] It seems that these two scholars are involved in a dispute regarding which practices and behaviors are most important. Rabbaynu Yonah explains that, in reality, these scholars are not contradicting one another and do not disagree. They are addressing two different issues. Humanity was created with a purpose and mission. What is this mission? This is the issue that Shimon HaTzadik is addressing. He explains that we are charged with the responsibility to seek the truth, serve the Creator, and act with kindness towards His other creations. However, in order for humanity to achieve its goals, a social infrastructure is essential. The advancement of humanity requires a coordinated effort; our goals are unattainable unless we can work together. If this social infrastructure does not exist and humanity cannot pursue its mission, then the creation of humanity loses its meaning. Raban Shimon ben Gamliel is identifying those elements that are essential to creating this social infrastructure. A cohesive, functioning society requires must uphold justice; its members must act truthfully towards each other and goodwill must exist among its members. A society lacking any one of these elements is doomed.

In short, these two Sages do not argue. Shimon HaTzadik is defining the purpose of humanity and its mission. The achievement of this purpose requires a functioning society. Raban Shimon ben Gamliel is outlining the fundamental elements of a healthy society.[22]

Rabbaynu Yonah's insight explains the teaching of our Sages quoted by Rashi. An equitable judge establishes justice within society. He helps create the society necessary for humanity to pursue its mission. The judge works towards assuring that creation has meaning and purpose. In this sense, the judge is a partner in creation.

"And you should seek from all of the nation men of valor, who fear Hashem, men of the truth, those who hate improper gain. And you should appoint them over the people as leaders of thousands, leaders of hundreds, leaders of fifties and leaders of tens." (Shemot 18:21)

Sometimes it is just wonderful to take a single passage of the Torah and consider the wonderful and exacting manner in which our Sages analyze its content. Every passage must make sense in all of its details. It must be internally coherent. It must be contextually consistent. It must correspond with established *halachic* principles. Let us consider one passage from our *parasha* and the manner in which our Sages analyze it.

Moshe and Bnai Yisrael are joined in the wilderness by Yitro – Moshe's father-in-law. Yitro observes Moshe judging and teaching the people. Moshe is fulfilling the role of judge and teacher without assistance. Yitro concludes that no single person can fulfill the role of serving as sole judge and teacher. He advises Moshe to recruit other leaders who will share his burden. Yitro describes the characteristics that Moshe should seek in these leaders. He also advises Moshe to appoint these leaders as leaders of thousands, hundreds, fifties, and tens. Moshe will

---

[20] Mesechet Avot 1:2.
[21] Mesechet Avot 1:18.
[22] Rabbaynu Yona ben Avraham of Gerona, *Commentary on Mesechet Avot* 1:2.

continue to serve as the highest judicial and governmental authority. Moshe accepts Yito's counsel and creates the system he has proposed.

Our Sages disagree as to the meaning of this last instruction. What is a leader of thousands, hundreds, fifties or tens? Rashi's explanation is well-know. His explanation is based upon the comments of the Talmud in Mesechet Sanhedrin. According to Rashi, Moshe was to create a multileveled judiciary. Each of the lowest judges would be responsible for a group of ten people. Above these judges would be appointed a second level of judges. Each judge would be charged with the responsibility of leading fifty people. The leaders of the hundreds would each care for the affairs of one hundred people. Those appointed over the thousands would each have one thousand people assigned to his care. Rashi continues to explain that the nation numbered six hundred thousand men. This means there were six hundred judges appointed at the highest level. At the next level, there were six thousand judges. The next level required twelve thousand judges. The lowest level required sixty thousand appointments.[23] The table below represents Rashi's explanation of the system Moshe was to create. As the table indicates, Moshe was to appoint a total of 78,600 leaders – representing slightly more than 13% of the total adult male population.

Judges of Thousands	600
Judges of Hundreds	6,000
Judges of Fifties	12,000
Judges of Tens	60,000
Total Appointments	78,600
Total Adult Male Population	**600,000**
Percentage of Population Serving in Leadership	13%

Ibn Ezra questions Rashi's explanation. He argues that Yitro and Moshe set very high standards for the leaders Moshe would appoint. The qualities that each and every leader was required to posses are not common, easily acquired traits. These leaders were to be morally and spiritually beyond reproach. It is difficult to imagine that Moshe would find close to 79,000 people possessing this unusual combination of traits. Ibn Ezra also questions the need for appointing close to one eighth of the nation as leaders. This seems to be the beginnings of the greatest bureaucracy in recorded history!

Based on these objections, Ibn Ezra suggests and alternative explanation of our passage. According to Ibn Ezra, a judge of thousands was not charged with judging one thousand people. Instead, the meaning of the passage is that the highest judges were to be selected from most powerful and influential elite. In order to qualify for this position, the candidate was required to be master of a household of at least one thousand individuals. In other words, he must have at least one thousand servants and assistants and others under his control. Leaders for each of the subsequent levels were chosen from a group of candidates who led proportionately smaller

---

[23] Rabbaynu Shlomo ben Yitzchak (Rashi), *Commentary on Sefer Shemot* 18:21.

households. At the lowest level, a candidate was required to be master over a household of ten people. According to this explanation, the *pasuk* is not indicating the number of leaders appointed or the number of people each was required to lead. Instead, the passage describes the number of servants and assistants a candidate must command to qualify for each level of leadership.[24]

Abravanel objects to Ibn Ezra's interpretation on both practical and philosophical grounds. From a practical perspective, he argues that Bnai Yisrael had just escaped from slavery in Egypt. It is hard to imagine that any of these former slaves were masters over the large households that Ibn Ezra describes as a requirement. From a philosophical perspective, he objects to the idea that wealth and power should be a criterion for selection.[25]

In addition to these objections, Ralbag points out that Ibn Ezra's interpretation of the passage is textually difficult to accept. Returning to the passage, it is clear that the passage is composed of two elements. The first portion of the passage describes the qualifications required of each judge. The second half of the passage describes the appointment of the judges. In other words, first Yitro suggests who should be selected and then how these leaders should be appointed. According to Ibn Ezra's interpretation, the passage looses its coherency. The second portion of the passage first describes the appointment of the leaders and then returns to the theme of the first potion of the passage; an additional qualification is described. If Ibn Ezra's interpretation were correct, the passage should read "And you should seek from all of the nation men of valor, who fear Hashem, men of the truth, those who hate improper gain. They should be leaders of thousands, leaders of hundreds, leaders of fifties and leaders of tens. And you should appoint them over the people."

This analysis leaves Ralbag with a perplexing problem. On the one hand he agrees with Ibn Ezra's critique of Rashi's explanation of the passage. However on the other hand, he does not feel that Ibn Ezra's explanation is much better.

In order to resolve this dilemma, Ralbag develops a third interpretation of the passage. Now, Ralbag must offer an explanation that responds to all of the questions that he has asked on Rashi and Ibn Ezra. And ideally, it should also respond to Abravanel's objections. This is quite a task! In order to avoid the questions on Rashi, Ralbag takes an approach similar to Ibn Ezra's. The passage is not describing the number of people placed under the authority of each leader. Neither does the *pasuk* indicate the number of judges to be appointed. But unlike Ibn Ezra, Ralbag maintains that the *pasuk* is divided into two clear portions and the second portion of the passage does not deal with selection criteria; it deals with the process of appointment. According to Ralbag, Moshe was to assign to each judge the resources he would need to enforce his decisions. The highest judges were to be assigned one thousand subordinates; each judge at the lowest level was to be assigned ten subordinates. Each judge was to be given the authority and the resources he would need to carry out his decisions. With this explanation Ralbag, responds to all of the objections he has raised against Rashi and Ibn Ezra.[26]

"And these are the laws that you should place before them." (Shemot 21:1)

---

[24] Rabbaynu Avraham ibn Ezra, *Commentary on Sefer Shemot*, 18:21.
[25] Don Yitzchak Abravanel, *Commentary on Sefer Sehmot*, p 156.
[26] Rabbaynu Levi ben Gershon (Ralbag / Gershonides), *Commentary on Sefer Shemot*, (Mosad HaRav Kook, 1994), p 134.

One of the most interesting elements of Ralbag's explanation is that it is reflected in normative *halacha*. This above *pasuk* is the opening passage of Parshat Mishpatim. In Mesechet Sanhedrin, the Talmud asks why the passage does not read, "These are the laws you should teach them?" What is the meaning of placing the laws before them? The Talmud suggests that the meaning of the passage is that before judging a case a judge must have placed before him the "tools of the judge." What are these tools? The Talmud explains that they include a staff with which to lead, a strap with which to administer lashes, and a shofar with which to announce excommunication.[27] This text from the Talmud is quoted by Tur and based on the authority of Rav Hai Gaon, he codifies this requirement into law.[28]

It is interesting the Tur places this law in the first chapter of Choshen Mishpat. The chapter deals primarily with the appointment of judges and their authority. Why does Tur include a detail regarding the physical organization of the courtroom?

According to Ralbag, Tur's organizational scheme makes perfect sense. Yitro and Moshe agreed that in appointing judges, each judge must be assigned the means for carrying out his decisions. This assignment of resources is part of the process of appointment. The appointment is meaningless if it is only ceremonial and does not include authority and the resources to carry out justice. Tur's organization of this first chapter of Choshen Mishpat reflects this same consideration. As part of his discussion of the appointment of judges and the extent of their authority, Tur includes the requirement that the judge have before him his tools – the tools used to carry out his decisions. Why must these tools be present? Consistent with Ralbag's reasoning, Tur is suggesting that the placement of these tools before the judge is part of the process of appointment. Without these resources at his disposal, his appointment and status as a judge is incomplete.

And you should select from the entire nation men of valor, who fear Hashem, men of truth, who despise profit, and place them upon the nation as ministers of the thousands, ministers of the hundreds, ministers of the fifties, and ministers of the tens. And they will judge the nation at all times. Any great matter they will bring to you. All minor matters they will judge. Your burden will be lightened and they will bear it with you. (Shemot 18:21-22)

1. Yitro's advice and Moshe's response

Bnai Yisrael came to Mt. Sinai. There, Yitro, Moshe's father-in-law, joins the nation. Yitro observes that Moshe was overwhelmed by his leadership responsibilities. Yitro asks Moshe to explain his various responsibilities. Moshe replies that he has three basic tasks. First, the people come to him to seek Hashem. Second, he judges between the people. Third, he reveals to the nation the laws of Hashem. The first set of passages above describes Yitro's concern and Moshe's response.

The second set of passages above describes the solution to which Moshe and Yitro agreed. It is immediately evident from these passages that the solution adopted by Moshe and Yitro was not consistent with the dilemma that Yitro described. Moshe outlined to Yitro three areas of leadership responsibility in which he was engaged. The ministers were to be assigned

---

[27] Mesechet Sanhedrin 7a.
[28] Rabbaynu Yaakov ben HaRash, *Tur Shulchan Aruch, Choshen Mishpat* 1.

only one of these areas. They would share with Moshe the responsibility for judging the people. Why were they excluded from the other two roles described by Moshe?

2. Moshe's leadership responsibilities

We need to better understand these three areas in order to answer this question. Rav Yitzchak Zev Soloveitchik Zt"l explains each of Moshe's responsibilities. Moshe explained that the people came to Moshe to seek Hashem. What function was Moshe describing? Moshe was the greatest of the prophets. The people came to Moshe to ask for guidance from Hashem. Moshe also prayed to Hashem for the nation.

The second function described by Moshe was that he judged the people. Moshe resolved legal disputes. In any society there are inevitable disagreements. The courts provide a peaceful means of resolution. Moshe was the judge and arbitrator of all legal disputes.

Third, Moshe revealed the law of the people. Moshe received the Torah from Hashem. He then delivered and taught this revealed truth to Bnai Yisrael.

3. Only one of Moshe's responsibilities could be shared

We can now understand Yitro's advice. He understood that Moshe was unique. He was Hashem's prophet. Moshe had two functions as a prophet. First, Moshe had a unique degree of prophetic access to Hashem. No other person could fulfill Moshe's role of petitioning Hashem on behalf of the people. Second, Moshe, as the greatest prophet, was charged with the responsibility of transmitting the Torah and teaching it to the nation. The leadership responsibilities associated with Moshe's role as prophet could not be transferred to ministers. In these areas the ministers could not assist Moshe.

However, Moshe was also a judge and arbitrator. This is not a function related to prophesy. Here, the ministers could offer assistance. They could share the responsibility of judging the nation.

4. Moshe sat and the nation stood before him

Rav Soloveitchik offers a simple proof to his explanation. The proof is based on our pasuk. Yitro noted that Moshe sat and the nation stood before him. This was the situation Yitro sought to end. Which function or functions was Moshe performing while he sat and the nation stood before him?

Yitro could not have been describing Moshe in the process of seeking prophecy. The prophet would not sit while he appealed to the creator! Also, Yitro was not describing Moshe engaged in instructing the nation. While instructing the nation Moshe did not sit with the nation standing before him. This is evident from Rashi's comments on Tractate Eruvin. Rashi explains that when Moshe expounded the Torah, the listeners sat before him.[29]

However, in the court the judge sits. The litigants stand before the judge.[30] This indicates that Yitro observed Moshe judging the people. He understood that Moshe's functions, as a prophet could not be transferred. It was the function of judging that he suggested Moshe share with others.[31]

---

[29] Rabbaynu Shlomo ben Yitzchak (Rashi), Commentary on the Talmud, Mesechet Eruvin 54b.
[30] Rabbaynu Moshe ben Maimon (Rambam) Mishne Torah, Hilchot Sanhedrin 21:3.
[31] Rav Yitzchak Zev Soloveitchik, Chidushai MaRan RIZ HaLeyve on the Torah, Parshat Yitro.

And Moshe went forth from the nation to greet the L-rd from the encampment. And they stood at the foot of the mountain. (Shemot 19:17)

The Mission of the Jewish People

The *pasuk* describes Bnai Yisrael as standing at the foot of Sinai. However, the Talmud comments that the nation stood under the mountain. Hashem uprooted Sinai and held it above Bnai Yisrael. He told the people that if they would not accept the Torah, they would be buried under the mountain.[32] If the comments of the Sages are intended to be understood literally, then it is strange that the Torah only makes reference to such a wonder through an allusion. Had this event actually occurred, the revelation at Sinai was very different from the description provided by the explicit meaning of the passages.

It seems that the Talmud is communicating to us two ideas. First, the development and existence of Bnai Yisrael is not a chance historical event. Bnai Yisrael was created and fashioned by Hashem. The nation was carefully nurtured in order to prepare it for revelation at Sinai and its acceptance of the Torah. This was Bnai Yisrael's destiny and its mission. Second, the exodus from Egypt and the awesome events of Sinai were essential elements of this process of preparation. These wonders were designed to provide overpowering evidence of the omnipotence of Hashem and revelation. They were designed to assure that Bnai Yisrael accept its mission. In short, Bnai Yisrael was created and formed for the moment of revelation; acceptance of the Torah was virtually predetermined or compelled. It was as if the mountain was raised over the heads of the people.

"And Hashem said to him, "Descend and then ascend – you and Ahron with you. And the Kohanim and the nation should not violate the boundary lest He send destruction among them." (Shemot 19:24)

Hashem's influence descends upon Sinai. Boundaries are set surrounding the mountain. The people are not permitted to approach the mountain beyond these boundaries. Hashem commands Moshe to remind the people that these boundaries cannot be violated. If this injunction is ignored, they will be severely punished.

Rashi explains that Moshe was permitted to ascend to the highest point on the mountain. Ahron could accompany him during most of his ascent. The *Kohanim* were allowed to ascend to a lower point. The rest of the nation was forbidden from approaching Sinai.[33]

What was the meaning of the boundaries? Why were these various individuals and groups permitted to ascend to different levels of the mountain?

Maimonides, explains that we cannot achieve complete understanding of the Almighty. Our material nature limits our ability. We can never completely overcome this limit. However, we can attain some understanding of Hashem. The level of comprehension we can acquire varies. This comprehension varies directly with one's spiritual level. Moshe reached the highest possible

---

[32] Mesechet Shabbat 88a.
[33] Rabbaynu Shlomo ben Yitzchak (Rashi), *Commentary on Sefer Shemot* 19:24.

spiritual plane. He achieved a correspondingly profound level of understanding of the Divine nature.

Maimonides seems to suggest that this concept is represented by the various boundaries. Ascending the mountain represents attaining understanding of the Almighty. Moshe could climb to the highest point on the mountain. This symbolizes the unique understanding he achieved of the Almighty. Ahron was not as spiritually perfected as Moshe. He could not attain the same profound comprehension. This is represented by the prohibition against accompanying Moshe to his destination. The *Kohanim* and the nation were less spiritually developed. They were assigned boundaries corresponding with their levels. Their boundaries represent the levels of understanding attainable.

Hashem warns each group against trespassing beyond its assigned border. A person must recognize personal limitation. Passing beyond one's boundary represents striving for a level of understanding beyond one's ability. This will result in disaster. The individual who overreaches will not properly understand the Divine essence. Instead, this individual will develop a flawed conception. In order to avoid false conclusion regarding Hashem, each person must respect personal limitations.[34]

And Hashem spoke all of these things saying: (Shemot 20:1)
Illusions of Freedom
1. The purpose of the universe

This passage introduces the Asseret HaDibrot – the Decalogue. Hashem's pronouncement of the Decalogue introduced His transmission of the Torah to Moshe and the Jewish people. The Sinai Revelation and the communication of the Torah fulfilled Moshe's original prophecy. Hashem told Moshe in that prophecy that following their redemption from Egypt, Bnai Yisrael would serve Hashem at Sinai. Rashi adds that the nation was redeemed to receive the Torah.[35]

The Sinai Revelation also fulfilled the objective of creation. Our Sages comment that Hashem gave the universe existence on the condition that the Jewish people accept the Torah.[36] The meaning of this comment is that the universe has a purpose. Its existence is dependent upon the realization of its purpose. The Revelation and communication of the Torah to humanity – represented by the Jewish people – is fundamental to the universe's purpose. Without the events of Sinai, the universe would be devoid of meaning and purpose. Hashem would have no reason to sustain its existence. Therefore, its existence was dependent upon Bnai Yisrael's acceptance of the Torah. In short, Revelation and the conveyance of the Torah were fundamental to the development of the Jewish people. Also, these events were fundamental to the existence of the universe.

2. Torah is liberating

---

[34] Rabbaynu Moshe ben Maimon (Rambam) *Moreh Nevuchim*, volume 1, chapter 5.
[35] Rabbaynu Shlomo ben Yitzchak (Rashi), Commentary on Sefer Shemot 3:12.
[36] Rabbaynu Shlomo ben Yitzchak (Rashi), Commentary on Sefer Beresheit 1:31.

The above discussion outlines the role of the Torah in the development of our people and in the universe's purpose. However, our Sages emphasize that the Torah is also essential to the development of the individual. They comment that the only free person is one involved in the study of Torah.[37] This comment is more than an empty platitude. It expresses their profound understanding of the make-up of human beings.

To understand the meaning of our Sages' comments, let's begin with a simple question. I have encountered many people who take issue with this comment. They argue that the Torah is restrictive. Torah study and observance of the mitzvot does not liberate them; it inhibits their freedom. This criticism of our Sages' comment seems legitimate. The Torah includes 613 commandments. Some commandments create obligations – like praying daily. Other commandments are prohibitions – such as to not work on Shabbat. How can observance and study of a set of obligations and restrictions the path to liberation?

3. Defining freedom

This objection is based upon two underlying assumptions. First, it assumes that freedom means the capacity to pursue one's will. This is a reasonable working definition, but it acknowledges that freedom has inherent limitation. To appreciate this definition and identify freedom's inherent limitation, let's apply it.

Consider an animal – perhaps, a lion – that has been captured from the wild. After its capture, it is placed in a cage. The lion tests its cage and seeks to regain its freedom. Eventually, the lion discovers a weakness in its containment and regains its freedom. Let us compare the lion's degree of freedom when in captivity and when not in captivity. In captivity, the lion is not capable of pursuing its will. It is not free. When the lion escapes its containment, it may pursue its will. It is free of external restraints. However, it must be noted that when the lion achieves its freedom it remains driven by its will – its irresistible instincts.

This illustration demonstrates an important aspect of our definition of freedom. Freedom is not synonymous with choice. Freedom has limitation. Its freedom empowers the lion to pursue its will, but its will is irresistible. The lion is free but cannot make choices.

4. A second assumption

For our lion, freedom was achieved though removing externally imposed restraints. This did not provide the lion with the capacity to make choices, but it became capable of pursuing its will. Our Sages propose that true freedom is achieved only though the study of Torah. The objection to this assertion is that the Torah imposes restrictions and obligations. This is antithetical to freedom. The objection insists that we are like the lion. Our freedom is attainted by eliminating any imposed restrictions upon behavior. Let's consider this more carefully.

Freedom is the capacity to pursue one's will. It was simple to identify the will of our lion. The lion is a relatively simple creature. Its will is its instinctual drives. The objection to our Sages assumes that we are simple creatures and our will is easily identified. Human will is the desires and urges one senses and experiences. Remove external restraint and one is empowered to pursue these desires. One is free.

And the L-rd created the human being in His image. In the image of the L-rd He created him – [as] male and female He created them. (Beresheit 1:27)

---

[37] Mesechet Avot 6:2.

5. Composition of the human being

Is human will so easily identified? To identify human will, we must discuss the composition or nature of a human being. What is the fundamental identity of the human being?

The message of the above passage is that human beings are unique. We are endowed with the "image of the L-rd". We need not delve into the exact meaning of this phrase; we need only to recognize that includes our spiritual and intellectual identity. The Torah reveals that our true fundamental identity is our Divine image – not our material instincts.

6. Human will

This perspective on human identity impacts our understanding of human will. Human will is not as easily established as our lion's. The lion is a purely instinctual creature. Its will is the drive of its instincts. A human being possesses instincts, but the Divine image is our more fundamental element. Human will is not the desires emerging from instinct; it is the spiritual drives of the Divine image. How does one attain the capacity to pursue these spiritual desires? The answer requires that we consider the factors that interfere with this pursuit.

External restraints sometimes prevent our pursuit of spiritual objectives. More often our freedom is restricted by our competing agendas. Our other desires – expressions of our instincts – insistently demand our attention and distract or deter us from spiritual development. We are not like our lion. Its freedom was restricted by external constraints; ours is restricted by internal forces – our material nature.

7. Torah and freedom

We noted above that freedom and choice are not synonymous. The liberated lion has freedom but not choice. The removal of external restraints provides the lion freedom but not choice. It will is its immutable instincts. Choice is impossible. For a human being to achieve freedom, one must first attain the capacity to choose the path of spiritual existence. If one succeeds in eliminating external restraints, one must yet overcome the internal forces. Only through subduing these internal drives can one attain the capacity to choose the spiritual life.

The meaning of our Sages' comment now emerges. Hashem gave us the means to overcome our internal limits and attain the capacity to choose our path. The Torah and its mitzvot are designed to cultivate a moderate personality. Through moderating our material drives, we secure the capacity to make choices. We can select a path. Our spiritual self – our true self – is empowered to pursue its will. The study of Torah is the ultimate spiritual experience.[38] This engagement in spiritual experience is the greatest act of freedom.

And the L-rd spoke all of these things saying: (Shemot 20:1)

The Challenge of Loving One's Neighbor

1. Serving Hashem through how we treat one another

---

[38] This may seem a strange assertion. Isn't prayer as spiritually meaningful as study? The Talmud in Mesechet Shabbat 10a discusses this issue. It recounts that Rava encountered Rav Hamnuna engaged in extensive prayer. Rava reprimanded him for neglecting Torah study for the sake of extended prayer.

The central element of the *parsha* is the Decalogue – the *Aseret HaDibrot*. The Decalogue is composed of ten statements which include a number of commandments. Why were these commandments selected by Hashem to be presented to the assembled nation and to be engraved on two tablets of stone? Rabbeinu Sa'adia and others suggest that all of the Torah's 613 commandments can be subsumed within the ten statements of the Decalogue.

The Decalogue reflects the diversity of the Torah's commandments and gives expression to one of the most remarkable aspects of our religious perspective. Our service and commitment to Hashem is inseparable from our responsibility to one another. The Decalogue commands us to serve Hashem exclusively and also admonishes us to not steal from one another or covet our neighbor's possessions. We can only serve Hashem if we honor and love one another.

Do not covet you neighbor's wife, his servant, his maid-servant, his ox, his donkey, and anything that is your neighbor's. (Shemot 20:13)

2. How does one escape jealousy?

The Decalogue orders us to not covet our neighbor's spouse or possessions. Many of the commentators ask how the Torah can require that we regulate our feelings. How can we suppress the involuntary reaction of coveting? One of the interesting responses to this question is formulated by Rav Yoel Frumkin.[39] His comments deal with both coveting and other forms of jealousy. He explains that jealousy is a consequence of twisted thinking. He enumerates a number of perverse ideas that underlie jealousy. Among these notions is one that we would not naturally associate with jealousy. He points out that we are all brothers and sisters. We should rejoice in each other's success and exhilarate in each other's accomplishments. If instead our happiness is overwhelmed by our jealousy, then we demonstrate a complete lack of fraternal love.[40]

Let us consider this insight. The members of a family will inevitably have their rivalries. But in a healthy family these rivalries are tempered by the identification that the members have with one another. If one receives an honor or is appointed to a position of esteem the other siblings might feel an instinctual pang of jealousy but these siblings will recognize that they should rejoice in the success of their brother or sister. So, any jealousy would be tempered by their sense of fraternity. Bnai Yisrael is a family. We are a nation of brothers and sisters. Perhaps, a passing pang of jealousy is natural. But the harboring of this jealousy and its persistence indicates a sad lack of fraternal love.

And they said to one another: We are certainly guilty for our brother – that we saw the sorrow of his soul when he pleaded to us and we did not listen. Therefore, this affliction has come upon us. (Beresheit 42:21)

3. Compassion for those we must scorn

How far does the obligation to love one another extend? One of the most remarkable implications of our duty to love one another emerges from considering the sin of Yosef's brothers. The brothers considered killing Yosef. They reconsidered and instead, sold him into

---

[39] Rav Yoel Frumkin was a student to Rav Chaim Volozhin. He is best known for his commentary on mishnah.

[40] Rav Yoel Frumkin, Final testament. Included in *Asher Yitzaveh*, Editor: Anonymous, pp. 16-17.

servitude. Eventually, the brothers recognized that they had sinned in their behavior toward Yosef. They articulated this realization. But the brothers' description of their sin is bewildering. We would expect them to confess that they had sinned in selling their brother into servitude. They do not focus on selling Yosef. Instead, the brothers declare that they sinned in disregarding Yosef's pleas. Why did the brothers focus on this aspect of their behavior?

Rabbeinu Ovadia Sforno explains that the brothers clearly remembered the deliberations that led to taking action against Yosef. To them, it was apparent that Yosef was self-absorbed and determined to dominate them. They understood that the sons of Yaakov had a destiny and they feared that Yosef would attempt to pervert that destiny for his own purposes. It was obvious to them that their father did not understand Yosef or the threat that he posed to their nascent nation. They felt that they were ethically compelled to remove Yosef from the family before he destroyed it.

The brothers did not condemn themselves for the action that they took against Yosef. They acted according to their understanding of the threat posed by Yosef and out of their commitment to the highest values. But, they did recognize that they had sinned in their callousness toward their brother. They declared, "How were we not moved by the cries of our brother? Why did we not recognize the tragedy of selling our own brother? Why were we not horrified by the prospect of cutting off our own flesh and blood?" They did not reproach themselves for the actions they took against Yosef; they condemned their cruelty, their insensitivity, their callousness.[41]

This is a profound message. When they sold Yosef the brothers believed that they had no other choice. They concluded that it was imperative to sever him from the family. They believed that their extreme measures were not only justified but demanded. Yet, they sinned in their callousness. They failed to recognize the tragedy in a brother acting against a brother.

How great is our obligation to love one another! Even when we must condemn or even eliminate from our community one its members, we must be aware of our brotherhood and mourn the tragedy of our loss.

If we must feel this fraternal bond even with one who deserves to be excised from our community, how great is our obligation to treat every Jew with love and compassion! Brothers and sisters do not always agree. Sometimes their differences are irreconcilable. Only the most extreme circumstances justify turning our backs toward another Jew. And if, G-d forbid, that circumstance should befall us, we should feel heart-broken as we turn away from one of our own.

"I am Hashem your G-d that took you out from the land of Egypt, from the house of bondage." (Shemot 20:2)

This passage is the first statement of the Decalogue. Maimonides understands this statement as a mitzvah. We are commanded to accept the existence of Hashem. Rav Elchanan Wasserman Ztl explains that this conviction is easily achieved. The complexity of the universe gives witness to the existence of a Creator. Nonetheless, many deny the existence of Hashem. Rav Elchanan explains it is not the inadequacy of the evidence that causes these denials. Instead,

---

[41] Rabbaynu Ovadia Sforno, *Commentary on Sefer Beresheit*, 42:21. See also ibid. 37:25.

there is a basic human bias that interferes with recognizing Hashem. Once a person accepts that there is a Creator, one is longer one's own master. This Creator has the right to mandate action and demand obedience. Conversely, if one denies the existence of the Creator, one is free to act as one pleases. We do not need to answer to a higher authority. An interesting incident illustrates this point. There was a student of the Volozin Yeshiva that abandoned the Torah. Instead, he devoted himself to the study of philosophy and joined the Haskala movement. The student had occasion to visit his former yeshiva. There, he met with Rav Chaim Soloveitchik Ztl who was serving as Rosh HaYeshiva. Rav Chaim asked the young to explain his reasons for abandoning the life of Torah and pursuing worthless endeavors. The young man was shocked by Rav Chaim's confrontational tone. After recovering, the young man responded. He explained that he was troubled by various doubts and questions regarding the Torah. He could not find answers for his questions. So, he abandoned the Torah. Rav Chaim told the young man that he was willing to answer every one of his questions. However, the young man must first agree to answer a single question. Rav Chaim's asked, "When did these various questions occur to you? Was it before you experienced the taste of sin of afterwards?" The young man was embarrassed. He responded that only after committing a serious sin had he begun to be bothered by questions. Rav Chaim responded, "If that is the case, these are not questions. Rather, they are answers you sought to excuse your evil actions." Rav Chaim continued, "I am sure that if you merit to achieve old age, your desires and yetzer harah will diminish. Then you will realize that you do not really have any questions. So, why not repent now?"

I am Hashem your G-d who brought you forth from the Land of Egypt. (Shemot 20:2)
Revelation: Parts I and II

1. **The first statement of the Decalogue is a commandment**

The above passage is the first of the statements of the Decalogue. The balance of the Decalogue is composed of commandments. This first statement seems to be an introduction of the rest of the Decalogue. The speaker and author of the Decalogue identifies Himself as the deity who redeemed the nation from Egypt.

This is not the view generally accepted among our Sages. Our Sages maintain that this statement is a commandment. The Talmud explains that 613 commandments are included in the text of the Torah that Moshe received at Sinai. The Talmud explains that although the number of commandments is not specifically stated in the text of the Torah, there is an allusion to the number in the text. Where is this allusion?

The Torah states, *"The Torah was commanded to us by Moshe. It is a legacy for the assembly of Yaakov."* (Devarim 33:4) Each letter of the Hebrew alphabet has a numerical value. The numerical values of the letters composing the word Torah is 611. The Talmud explains that this corresponds with the number of commandments the people received from Hashem, through the agency of Moshe. Hashem taught Moshe 611 of the Torah's commandments. Moshe taught them to the people. The Talmud adds that two other commandments were not received through Moshe. These the people heard directly from Hashem. They heard Hashem say, "I am Hashem your G-d, etc." They also heard Him say "You shall have on other gods before Me." The addition of these commandments to the 611 that were received through Moshe, provides a total of 613 *mitzvot*.

The discussion in the Talmud clearly treats the first statement of the Decalogue – "I am Hashem you G-d" as one of the 613 commandments. Based on this discussion, most of our Sages concluded that the Decalogue's opening statement is indeed a commandment.

What does this statement command? According to Maimonides, this statement commands that we know or accept that Hashem is the cause of all that exists and that all existence is sustained by His will.[42]

This first commandment of the Decalogue includes an interesting nuance of expression. The Hebrew language has two words for the first person singular pronoun – "I". One is *ani* and the other is *anochi*. The two words are near synonyms. However, they are not completely interchangeable.

And Yaakov said to his father: I (anochi) am Esav your first born. I have done as you commanded me. Please arise and eat from my game so that you will bless me. (Beresheit 27:19)

And Yaakov said to Shimon and Leyve: You have disturbed me by evoking hatred against me among the dwellers of the land – the Canaanites and that Prezites. I (ve'ani) am few in number. They will gather against me, strike me, and destroy me and my household. (Beresheit 34:30)

2. The difference between *ani* and *anochi*

Rav Yosef Dov Soloveitchik *Zt"l* suggests that the word *ani* is a simple first person singular pronoun. It does not, in itself, communicate anything beyond the identity of the speaker. *Anochi* is a more expressive term. It communicates the uniqueness of the speaker. *Anochi*'s the message is often "it is I and no other."[43]

The two passages above illustrate the contrast between *ani* and *anochi*. In the first passage Yaakov disguises himself as Esav in order to secure the blessings intended for his older brother. He approaches his father. Yitzchak's eyesight is failing and he asks his visitor to identify himself. Yaakov responds, "I am Esav your first born." Yaakov is responding to his father's uncertainty regarding the identity of his visitor. He responds: It is I, Esav, your first born. The term *anochi* is used because Yaakov is telling Yitzchak: It is I and no other.

In the second passage above Yaakov chastises his sons for destroying the city of Shechem. He tells them that they have incited the land's inhabitants against him. He says to them: I am a leader of a small group. He does not intend to emphasis the "I". Therefore, he employs the pronoun *ani*.[44]

---

[42] This position engenders a number of problems. First, we assume that commandments are volitional. In other words, one who chooses to perform the commandment has it within his power to do so. Issues of conviction do not seem to meet this criterion. One cannot will oneself to believe in something of which he is not convinced. Second, specifically Maimonides' formulation of the commandment is confusing. In his Mishne Torah he states that one is obligated to know the existence of Hashem. In his Sefer HaMitzvot – as the text is typically translated – he states that one must believe in Hashem's existence. Both of these issues have received extensive attention elsewhere.

[43] Rav Yosef Dov Soloveitchick, recorded lecture on aseret HaDibrot.

[44] The above examples support Rav Soloveitchik's interpretation of the words *ani* and *anochi*. However, it must be acknowledged that there are instances in which the use of these two words does not seem to conform to Rav Soloveitchik's view.

Based on this analysis, can any message be derived from the use of the word *anochi* in the first statement of the Decalogue? Let us begin by considering another instance in which the word *anochi* is used.

And Moshe said to G-d: Who am I (anochi) that I should go to Paroh and will I bring forth Bnai Yisrael from Egypt? And He said: For I will be with you. And this is the sign that I (anochi) have sent you – when you bring forth the nation from Egypt you will serve G-d upon this mountain. (Shemot 3:11-12).

3. Moshe's objection to his mission

In his first prophecy, Hashem spoke to Moshe and informed him that he had been selected to lead forth Bnai Yisrael from Egypt. Moshe questioned his suitability for this mission. He said to Hashem, "Who am I to challenge Paroh and demand that he release his slaves?" Moshe identifies himself with the word *anochi*. Based on the discussion above, this is to be expected. Moshe seems to be asking Hashem why he has been selected. Why he and not someone more appropriate?

Hashem responds, "For I will be with you." Here too the word *anochi* is used. However, the reason for the use of this word and not the word *ani* is less obvious.

In order to understand Hashem's use of *anochi*, Moshe's objection must be reconsidered. Moshe could not understand how he could influence or coerce Paroh into releasing Bnai Yisrael. He protested that he had neither the eloquence to persuade nor the power to force Paroh. Hashem responded, "I will be with you." He was not contesting Moshe's analysis. He was not suggesting that Moshe could accomplish the task he was assigned. Hashem responded that He – Hashem – would be the agent of Bnai Yisrael's liberation. Moshe would not secure his people's freedom. Without revealing to Moshe the specific events that would soon occur, Hashem responded that He would be involved in the forthcoming events in an unprecedented manner.[45]

4. Hashem tells Moshe that He will be with him

Now, Hashem's use of the word *anochi* is explained. He responded to Moshe that He would be with Moshe. The emphasis was upon His uniqueness. Because He will be Moshe's companion on this mission and He is omnipotent, the otherwise unachievable is possible.

Hashem explained to Moshe that the Egypt redemption would be brought about through a manifest expression of divine intervention without precedent. Hashem had performed miracles for the *Avot* – the patriarchs – but these were subtle or minor compared to those that would be performed in Egypt. In Egypt, Hashem would reveal Himself as ruler over all creation. He would demonstrate His omnipotence to the Egyptians, Bnai Yisrael, and humanity.

From the passages in the Torah one cannot determine the level of detail that Hashem shared with Moshe at this point. However, it is clear that Hashem communicated to him that something unique and unprecedented was about to take place.

5. The sign offered to Moshe that Hashem will be his companion

Hashem then provided Moshe with a sign that confirmed His message. After emerging from their bondage, the nation would serve Hashem at Sinai. The commentators note that this is

---

[45] Many commentators make this point. Some express themselves more clearly than others. See Rashi, Rabbaynu Yosef Bechor Shur, Emek Davar.

a difficult sign to understand. Hashem understood that Moshe required some assurance that He would be with him. He provided, as a sign, news of an event that will occur many months in the future. How would this sign reassure Moshe?

As explained above, Hashem had told Moshe that an unprecedented event was to take place in Egypt. Hashem would reveal and involve himself in the redemption of Bnai Yisrael to a degree that was never before experienced by humanity. He anticipated Moshe would receive this news with some degree of confusion. Moshe would not understand why Hashem would take such extraordinary measures on behalf of Bnai Yisrael.

Hashem responded that the explanation lay in the events that would take place at Sinai. At Sinai, the nation would serve Hashem. This Sinai experience would be a unique event in the experience of humanity. Hashem would reveal Himself to humanity and speak to Moshe and the nation. The nation would experience Divine Revelation. Sinai would represent the initiation of a new stage in Hashem's relationship with humanity.

The *Avot* and other special individuals had sought out Hashem and discovered Him. They experienced their own personal revelations. However, Hashem had never before revealed Himself though manifestly interacting and demonstrating His presence to a nation. At Sinai, He would speak to Moshe and to Bnai Yisrael. Sinai would not be a private and personal revelation like those experienced by the *Avot*. It would be a public and manifest revelation. In other words, the Sinai Revelation would be the beginning of a new relationship between Hashem and humanity. No longer would Hashem be revealed only to those who relentlessly pursued Him. Now, each and every person would have manifest evidence of Hashem and His omnipotence.

This explained to Moshe Hashem's extraordinarily overt involvement in the Egypt redemption. The goal of the redemption was not only to liberate an oppressed people. The redemption was the opening act of a very pubic manifestation of Hashem's existence, His omnipotence, and His providence.

Hashem was not telling Moshe that the events of Sinai – once they occurred – would be a sign or provide evidence of His partnership with Moshe in Egypt. He told Moshe that the explanation for everything He had told him about Egypt lay in understanding the destined future of the nation – in appreciating the meaning of the Sinai experience.

6. The phases of Revelation

Now, let us return to the Decalogue. In its first statement Hashem says, "I am Hashem your G-d who brought you forth from the Land of Egypt." Hashem identifies Himself as *anochi*. Why does He use this form of the first person singular pronoun? Hashem is introducing Himself – He who now addresses the nation – as the G-d who revealed Himself in Egypt. He is explaining that the events of Egypt were the precursor to this wondrous moment. That omnipotent G-d who had triumphed over Paroh and over nature itself now spoke to the nation and gave His commandments to the people. In Egypt, He revealed Himself to the nation as the omnipotent creator and ruler of the universe. At Sinai, He introduced Himself as the G-d who was encountered in Egypt and who would now speak to the people as teacher and lawgiver.

He identifies Himself as *anochi*. He declares, "It is I – the G-d who redeemed you with wonders and miracles. I am the one who now speaks to you as teacher and lawgiver." In this introduction Hashem provided to the people a meaning for their experiences. Suddenly, they understood all that had occurred to them and its purpose. They had encountered the omnipotent creator in Egypt so that now they would understand and appreciate the G-d who addresses them.

I am Hashem your G-d Who took you out from the Land of Egypt, from the house of slaves. (Shemot 20:2)

Notes on the first statement of the Decalogue

1. The description of Hashem as Redeemer.

Parshat Yitro describes the communication of the *Aseret HaDibrot* – the Decalogue – to Bnai Yisrael. The first statement of Decalogue is contained in the above passage. In this statement, Hashem introduces Himself as the G-d Who redeemed the Bnai Yisrael from Egypt. Our Sages note that Hashem does not introduce Himself as Creator. Instead, He describes Himself as the redeemer of Bnai Yisrael. Why does He choose to refer to Himself in this manner? Rashi quotes the Midrash as explaining that Hashem was communicating that the redemption of the nation from Egypt was in-itself an adequate event to bind the nation in service to Hashem.[46] In other words, the message of the Hashem's statement is that because He redeemed the nation from Egypt, the nation owes its service to Him.

Rav Yosef Dov Soloveitchik *Zt"l* explains that this first statement establishes the unique relationship between Hashem and Bnai Yisrael. This relationship was established or demonstrated through His rescue of the nation from oppression and the annihilation by the Egyptians. In this context – as a basis for the unique bond between Hashem and His nation – His role as Creator is not relevant. Acknowledgement and service to Hashem as Creator are responsibilities shared by all of humanity. He is the Creator of all humankind. Redemption from Egypt provides a basis for service to Hashem that is unique to Bnai Yisrael.

2. The purpose of the first statement of the Decalogue.

Rav Soloveitchik's interpretation of the Midrash's comments provides an important insight into the purpose and objective of this first statement of the Decalogue. The objective of this statement is not to educate the nation regarding Hashem's nature or His relationship with the universe and reality. If this were the intention of the statement, then it would have indeed been appropriate for Hashem to introduce Himself as the Creator and Sovereign of the universe. This description provides a more fundamental understanding to Hashem's relationship to all that exists than reference to His redemption of Bnai Yisrael. Instead, the objective of this introduction is to establish a basis or to serve as a preamble to the commandments that will follow. Bnai Yisrael are poised to enter into an exclusive relationship with Hashem. This introduction explains the foundation, rational, and the ethical imperative that underlie this relationship. We are compelled to serve the One who redeemed us from certain annihilation in Egypt.[47]

---

[46] Rabbaynu Shlomo ben Yitzchak (Rashi), *Commentary on Sefer Shemot* 20:2.

[47] Maimonides explains in his Sefer HaMitzvot that this passage is one of the 613 commandments of the Torah. He describes the commandment as recognition of Hashem as Cause of all existence. Others disagree and do not regard this statement as a commandment. Nachmanides, in his glosses to Sefer HaMitzvot, explains that those who dispute Maimonides' position, regard the statement as introductory to the commandments. Hashem introduces Himself to the nation. Once the nation accepts Him as Sovereign, then He will legislate the

3. Conflicting perceptions of Hashem.

Rashi continues his comments on the above passage. Again, drawing from the Midrash, he explains that there is an alternative explanation of the passage. The nation had observed Hashem at the Reed Sea as a young warrior vanquishing His enemies. Now, at Sinai, they see Him as a compassionate elder. These vastly different perceptions seem irreconcilable and suggest that the nation has witnessed the acts of two different deities – that the deity that had ruthlessly destroyed the Egyptians could not possibly be the same as the deity of Sinai. Hashem addressed this notion by responding, "I am Hashem your G-d that took you out to Egypt…" One deity destroyed Egypt and now, presents Himself at Sinai.

Rashi's comments from the Midrash present two challenges. First, it is clear from the Midrash that Bnai Yisrael believed that one god could not be responsible for both the destruction of Egypt and the Revelation at Sinai. Wherein lies the contradiction in these two perceptions of Hashem? Second, the Midrash seems to attribute a message to the statement that is not readily evident from the statement. What evidence does the Midrash find in the passage to support its interpretation?

Rav Soloveitchik explains that the Midrash is noting that the perception of Hashem's nature that emerged from the destruction of the Egyptians at the Reed Sea was that He is a G-d of vengeance. He destroyed the idolatrous Egyptians who had persecuted His nation. He showed no compassion for His enemies and granted them no mercy. The G-d revealed in the Decalogue was very different from this vengeful deity. He instructed His servant to treat each other with justice. He tought them to control their passions and not needlessly harm others. Hashem's servants must control their passions. They may not even covet another's possessions. These two perceptions seemed contradictory to Bnai Yisrael. It seemed that two different deities had

---

commandments. This dispute between Maimonides and his opponents can be readily understood based upon the above discussion. Maimonides opponents regard the statement as a rational or the basis for a moral imperative to serve Hashem. We must serve Him because He saved us. Maimonides disagrees. He regards the statement as an intellectual lesson. Hashem is providing the nation with the most profound understanding of the universe that humanity can achieve. Hashem is its Cause. He gives the universe its existence every moment. Maimonides regards the acknowledgement of Hashem's relationship with the universe and His centrality to its existence as a commandment. It is not a preamble to commandments or a rational for them. Instead, the statement is a profound and fundamental teaching that shapes the Jew's perceptions of the universe that surrounds him.

Of course, Maimonides' position seems suspect. Why did Hashem not describe Himself as Creator? Why did He refer to Himself as the Redeemer of the nation if His intent was to impart the profound understanding of Hashem and the universe that Maimonides attributes to this statement? Nachamanides actually addresses this issue in his commentary on the Torah at the end of Parshat Bo. He explains that the redemption of Bnai Yisrael from Egypt through unprecedented miracles that contravened the laws of nature and the natural order demonstrated Hashem's omnipotence and sovereignty over the universe. This omnipotence can only be attributed to the Creator. In other words, it was impossible for the generation that stood at Sinai to have first-hand knowledge of creation – an event in antiquity. However, the miracles of Egypt provided first-hand proof – proof the generation witnessed – that Hashem was Creator. (Shemot 13:16).

revealed themselves – one a mighty god of wrath and vengeance, the other a god of love and compassion. At Sinai, Hashem responded: I am One. The G-d revealed at Sinai is the self-same G-d Who revealed Himself at the Reed Sea.

What evidence of this message did the Midrash find in the passage? Rav Soloveitchik explain that the Midrash is based upon the very first word of the passage. In the Hebrew language there are two words that can be used to communicate "I" – the first person. Most commonly the word *ani* is used. Occasionally, the word *anochi* is employed. What is the difference between these two words? Generally, the term *anochi* is used when the speaker wishes to emphasis himself as the subject. Often, he is identifying himself in distinction from others. *Anochi* means "I" in a specific sense and in distinction from anyone else. A few examples will illustrate one manner in which the Torah employs the word *anochi*:

- Hashem asked Kayin where his brother Hevel was. Kayin responded "Am I my brother's guardian?" Kayin was responding that Hevel's welfare was not his responsibility. He was saying, "Why ask me?" In this context the Torah uses the word *anochi*. Kayin was protesting his appointment as Hevel's guardian. He was protesting, "Why me more than someone else?"
- Sarah gave her servant Hagar to Avraham as a wife. Hagar conceived and began to act towards Sarah with condescension. Sarah protested to Avraham. She said, "I placed my servant at your chest. She saw that she had conceived and I became inconsequential in her eyes." Sarah was emphasizing the unjust irony of her situation. She was the one – no one else – who gave Hagar to Avraham and now, she was suffering from Hagar's attitude of superiority. Again, in this context the term *anochi* is appropriate.
- Yaakov appeared before his father Yitzcahak disguised as his brother Esav. Yitzchak asked him to identify himself. He responded "I am Esav your first born." His was telling his father that he is the real Esav. In other words he was saying, "I – and I alone – am Esav. Again, the appropriate term is employed – *anochi*.

In the first statement of the Decalogue, Hashem says, "I –*Anochi* – am Hashem your G-d Who brought you out of Egypt. The use of the word *anochi* indicates that Hashem is saying, "I Who speaks to you now at Sinai am the same G-d that appeared to you at the Reed Sea." Hashem is telling the nation that the G-d of Sinai is the self-same G-d that annihilated the Egyptians. Now, the Midrash's understanding of the passage is easily grasped. Hashem is telling the people that one G-d redeemed them from Egypt and now is delivering to them the gift of Torah. This statement must have been necessitated by the nation's confusion stemming from their varied perceptions of Hashem. Hashem responds that He is One even though He is perceived differently in different situations.[48]

I am, Hashem, your Lord that brought you out from the land of Egypt, the house of bondage. (Shemot 20:2)

Inclusion of Conviction in the Existence of Hashem within Taryag

This is the first statement of the *Aseret HaDibrot* – the Decalogue. It presents the most fundamental premise of the Torah. There is a G-d. Maimonides understands this statement to be

---

[48] Rav Yosef Dov Soloveitchik, Recorded Lecture on Aseret HaDibrot, part 1, 1969.

a commandment; we are commanded to accept the existence of a G-d who is the source of all reality.[49]

The Halachot Gedolot differs with Maimonides. The author maintains that although acceptance of G-d's existence is fundamental to Judaism, it is not appropriate to classify this conviction as a commandment. Nachmanides explains the reasoning of the Halachot Gedolot. The six hundred thirteen commandments – the *Taryag Mitzvot* – can be compared to the decrees of a king. These decrees presuppose the acceptance of the king as sovereign. The act of acceptance is clearly not one of the decrees, but instead must precede them. Based on this reasoning, acceptance of the existence of Hashem logically precedes the *mitzvot* and cannot properly be viewed as one of these commandments.[50]

Rabbaynu Chasdia Kreskas also differs with Maimonides. He presents a very powerful argument against defining acceptance of Hashem's existence as a *mitzvah*. He argues that every *mitzvah*, by definition, must engender some obligation or result. A command to accept G-d's existence could not meet this criterion. Why? To whom is the command directed? If it is directed to a person who is already convinced, then the command engenders no new outcome. This person is already convinced! The alternative is even more absurd. This would require that the command be directed to the non-believer. But the non-believer could not take such a command seriously! Through this argument, Rabbaynu Chasdai is illustrating the impossibility of legislating belief in G-d. Based on this argument, Rabbaynu Chasdia sides with the Halachot Gedolot. He concludes that conviction in the existence of Hashem precedes *mitzvot* and cannot be counted among *Taryag*.[51]

Another criticism of Maimonides' position questions the logic of a commandment that legislates any belief. A person can be commanded or compelled to act or behave in a specific manner. However, a person cannot be commanded to adopt a belief. I person either accepts or rejects a specific. Acceptance of a belief is not accomplished through an act of will.

How can Maimonides' position be explained? This issue provides a fundamental insight into Maimonides' understanding of *Taryag Mitzvot*. Apparently, Maimonides disagrees with a basic premise of the Halachot Gedolot. This premise is that the *mitzvot* can be equated to decrees. Maimonides seems to maintain that *Taryag* must be defined in a more inclusive manner. He includes among the *mitzvot*, commandments that legislate actions and behaviors and others that describe beliefs. Obviously, this second group of commandments cannot be regarded as legislative for the reason explained above. However, they are included because combined with the other commandments they describe a model or a representation of human excellence. Not all aspects of this model can be emulated through sheer willpower and determination. Convictions cannot be attained through an act of will. Nonetheless, these fundamental convictions are essential components to the Torah's model of human excellence. Without adoption to these beliefs, excellence has not been achieved.

In other words, according to Maimonides, *Taryag* can best be described as the basic blueprint for excellence in a person and nation. This blueprint includes the guide to achieving this excellence as well as the basic description of the behaviors and convictions of the individual

---

[49] Rabbaynu Moshe ben Maimon (Rambam) *Sefer HaMitzvot, Mitzvat Aseh* 1
[50] R' Moshe ben Nachman (Ramban), *Critique on Maimonides' Sefer HaMitzvot, Mitzvat Aseh* 1.
[51] Rabbaynu Chasdai Kreskas, *Ohr Hashem*, Introduction (*HaTza'ah*).

who embodies this excellence. Based on this definition of *Taryag*, Maimonides' position can be appreciated. The most basic ingredient to human perfection is acceptance of Hashem who is the source of all other reality. No description of the *shalem* – the perfected individual – can be construed which does not include this fundamental conviction.

I am Hashem, your God, Who took you out of the land of Egypt, out of the house of bondage. (Shemot 20:2)

Conviction in the Existence of Hashem – the Creator

This week's *parasha* includes the Decalogue. The above passage is the first *pasuk* of the Decalogue. According to Sefer HaChinuch, this passage is the source of the commandment to accept that Hashem exists. He explains that this commandment requires that we respond to any inquiry regarding our convictions with the reply that we wholeheartedly accept the existence of Hashem. He adds that we are required to relinquish our lives for the sake of this conviction. In other words, we must affirm our conviction in the existence of Hashem and that there is no other is G-d. We are even required to sacrifice our lives in affirmation of this conviction.

Sefer HaChinuch adds that we should strive to establish clear proof of Hashem's existence. If we succeed in establishing such proof, then we have fulfilled the *mitzvah* at its highest level.[52] This is a troubling statement. It is understandable that complete fulfillment of the commandment requires basing our conviction on objective evidence. However, the implication of this statement is that even if we do not base our conviction on any evidence, the commandment has been fulfilled at least at to a minimal standard.

This implication presents two problems: First, Sefer HaChinuch acknowledges that one's conviction in the existence of G-d is the most fundamental element of Torah Judaism. All other elements of the Torah are based on this conviction.[53] If this conviction is not based upon evidence, then one's entire adherence to the Torah and observance of the commandments is based upon solely subjective belief. Among the Torah's commandments are various *mitzvot* that presume that the Torah is true and that other faiths are not valid. For example, the Torah includes many commandments directed against idolatry. These commandments include directives to execute idolaters. If our conviction in the Torah is based upon a completely subjective set of beliefs, then these beliefs are no more credible than those of the idolater. The Torah describes Hashem as a just G-d. How can a just G-d command us to execute those whose subjective beliefs – although different from our subjective beliefs – are every bit as credible?

Second, the implication that conviction in Hashem's existence based on subjective belief is adequate contradicts the position outlined by Sefer HaChinuch in his introduction to his work. There, the author explains that one of the unique elements of the Torah is the Sinai revelation described in this week's *parasha*. The Torah was revealed by Hashem to the entire nation. All of the people heard Hashem address the nation. The objective of mass revelation was to establish a firm basis for future generations' acceptance of the authenticity of the Torah as a G-d-given creed.

---

[52] Rav Aharon HaLeyve, *Sefer HaChinuch*, Mitzvah 25.
[53] Rav Aharon HaLeyve, *Sefer HaChinuch*, Mitzvah 25.

The details of Sefer HaChinuch's argument are beyond the scope of this discussion, but it is sufficient for our purposes to summarize his thinking. Mass revelation endows the giving of the Torah with the standing of an objective historical event. In other words, the Torah's account of revelation as a mass-witnessed event is so fantastic that the very acceptance of this claim indicates that it cannot be reasonably assumed to be a fabrication. No generation would have agreed to be the first to accept this fantastic claim were it not part of its established historical record.

According to Sefer HaChinuch, the objective of the Sinai revelation was to create a firm, objective basis for the authenticity of the Torah as a G-d-given truth. It is odd that, according to Sefer HaChinuch, Hashem gave the Torah through the Sinai revelation to provide an *objective* basis for our conviction in its authenticity – yet a *subjective* belief in Hashem's existence is acceptable!

Let us consider another issue. Conviction in the existence of G-d is, in itself, a meaningless requirement. Such a requirement lacks any description of the specifics of the required conviction. In other words, what is meant by "G-d"? Without a response to this question, the requirement is too vague to be meaningful. Sefer HaChinuch delineates three elements to the *mitzvah*: 1) We are required to accept the existence of a G-d Who is the source of all that exists; 2) This G-d is eternal; 3) This G-d redeemed us from Egypt and gave us the Torah.[54] These elements provide the specific details that give meaning to the requirement to accept the existence of Hashem.

Generally, Sefer HaChinuch adopts the position of Maimonides. However, there seems to be a disagreement between these authorities regarding the specifics of the *meaning* of acceptance of Hashem. In his Sefer HaMitzvot, Maimonides defines the commandment to accept the existence of G-d as a requirement to acknowledge there is a G-d Who is the cause of all that exists.[55] He does *not* include within the *mitzvah* a requirement to acknowledge Hashem as the G-d Who redeemed us from Egypt and gave us the Torah.[56]

Rabbaynu Yehudah HaLeyve also deals with the requirement to accept that Hashem exists. His position is very different from that of Maimonides. He explains that we are required to accept the existence of a G-d Who redeemed us from Egypt and gave us the Torah. He does *not* include within this basic requirement that we accept Hashem as the creator. He explains that while the Torah requires that we accept the existence of Hashem, this requirement does not include acknowledgement that He is the creator. There is a compelling reason for the requirement's exclusion of this element. Proof of a G-d Who is creator of the universe can only be attained through philosophical and scientific investigation and speculation. These investigations – and any proofs they provide of a creator – are subject to debate and criticism.

---

[54] Rav Aharon HaLeyve, *Sefer HaChinuch*, Mitzvah 25.
[55] Rabbaynu Moshe ben Maimon (Rambam) *Sefer HaMitzvot, Mitzvat Aseh* 1
[56] Maimonides also does not include in this description of the *mitzvah* acceptance of Hashem as eternal. However, in the first chapter of his Mishne Torah, Maimonides elaborates on this *mitzvah*. There he explains that we are required to accept that Hashem is the cause of all that exists and that His existence is unique. His existence is more "absolute". This is apparently a reference to the eternity of His existence. In other words, it appears that according to Maimonides, this commandment requires us to accept that only Hashem's existence is "absolute" or necessary existence. All other things exist as a consequence of His existence and will.

According to Rabbaynu Yehudah HaLeyve, the Torah does not wish to base acceptance of Hashem upon speculations and investigations that can be debated and are not accessible to the average person. Instead, the Torah instructs us to base our acceptance of Hashem upon historically credible, public events such as the revelation at Sinai.[57]

It is important to note that Rabbaynu Yehudah HaLeyve does not intend to imply that acceptance of Hashem as creator is not a fundamental element of the Torah. This would be a rejection of the opening chapters of the Torah. The position of Rabbaynu Yehudah HaLeyve is explained by Rabbaynu Nissim Gerondi in his commentary on the Torah. He explains that acceptance of Hashem as the creator of the universe is an essential element of the Torah. However, this is a truth we know through revelation. The requirement to accept Hashem focuses on accepting Him as our redeemer from Egypt and the giver of the Torah. Once we accept the Torah as a revealed truth, it follows that we must accept the contents of this revealed truth. An essential element of this revealed doctrine is that Hashem is creator.[58]

Rabbaynu Yehudah HaLeyve seems to present a compelling argument for his position. Why does Maimonides insist that the essential element of the *mitzvah* to accept Hashem is the recognition that He is creator? In order to answer this question, we must address an astounding oddity in Maimonides' Mishne Torah. Maimonides' Mishne Torah is a codification of Torah law. However, the third and fourth chapters of this work can be described as a brief summary of physics and astrophysics. Why is this material included in this work of Torah law? Furthermore, as an introduction to each section of this work, Maimonides provides a list of the commandments that will be described and explained in the section. Presumably, the material in the section that follows is an elaboration of these listed commandments. The first section of the Mishne Torah is preceded by such an introduction explaining that the section will deal with ten *mitzvot*. The list of these *mitzvot* includes acceptance of His existence and His unity. None of the *mitzvot* in this list seem to provide an imperative for instruction in and knowledge of physics or astrophysics. Under which of these commandments does Maimonides subsume his discussion of physics and astrophysics?

Maimonides deals with this issue in the final passages of the fourth chapter. He explains that this discussion is relevant to those *mitzvot* that require we accept Hashem's existence and unity, and that we adore and hold Him in awe. How is Maimonides' discussion of scientific matters relevant to these *mitzvot*?

According to Maimonides, acceptance of the existence of Hashem, His unity, and our adoration and awe of Him must be predicated upon an understanding of our universe and His centrality to all existence. We must understand the universe and His role as the source of all existence. It is not adequate to merely accept this assertion as true. We are required to understand the nature of the relationship between Hashem and the universe.

An analogy will help us understand Maimonides' position. As I record these thoughts I am using my computer. I know that my computer is composed of a motherboard and various other circuitries. I have no idea how all these elements operate and work together. Yet, I know that these elements exist. I do not understand them nor do I have any appreciation of their operations. My acceptance of their existence is absolute; yet, my understanding of their nature

---

[57] Rabbaynu Yehudah HaLeyve, Kuzari, part I, sections 11-25.
[58] Rabbaynu Nissim ben Reuven Gerondi (Ran), *Commentary on Sefer Beresheit* 1:1.

and operation is negligible. Maimonides maintains that the requirement that we accept Hashem's existence cannot be fulfilled simply through acknowledging the fact He exists. This acceptance cannot be akin to my acceptance of the existence of a motherboard and circuitries in my computer. Instead, my acceptance of Hashem must be akin to the engineer's more fundamental comprehension of the computer. It must include an understanding and an appreciation of the nature of the universe and Hashem's role and relationship with reality.

This is the essential difference in the perspectives of Maimonides and Rabbaynu Yehudah HaLeyve. According to Rabbaynu Yehudah HaLeyve, we are required to accept as a revealed truth that Hashem is creator and that He sustains the universe. We are *not* required to understand or appreciate the full meaning of this assertion. Maimonides rejects this perspective. According to Maimonides, the *mitzvah* to accept Hashem requires our appreciation of His relationship to the universe and an understanding of His centrality to its existence. In other words, this commandment addresses our overall understanding of reality. We are required to unmask the nature of the universe and the reality in which we exist.

We are now prepared to understand Sefer HaChinuch's position. Sefer HaChinuch adopts a position that is a compromise between these two perspectives. He agrees with Rabbaynu Yehudah HaLeyve that the *mitzvah* to accept Hashem requires that we accept Him as our redeemer from Egypt and the giver of the Torah. He adopts this position for the reasons that he outlines in the introduction to his work. The Torah must be based on objective evidence. It cannot be reduced to a set of subjective beliefs. Mass revelation and public miracles experienced by our ancestors provide us with the objective basis for our conviction in Hashem's existence. We do not need to resort of scientific proof and philosophical speculation in order to fulfill this most basic commandment.

However, Sefer HaChinuch is not willing to reject Maimonides' perspective. Our acceptance of Hashem is not complete without acknowledgement of His role as creator and sustainer of the universe. Our acceptance of Hashem must include this element to be meaningful. Nonetheless, Sefer HaChinuch does not completely agree with Maimonides' position. He asserts that although we should strive to achieve the level of understanding described by Maimonides, it is not essential to the minimal fulfillment of the *mitzvah*. However, an understanding of G-d in the manner explained by Maimonides is the highest fulfillment of the *mitzvah*.[59]

"I am Hashem your Lord that brought you out from the land of Egypt, the house of bondage." (Shemot 20:2)

This is the first statement of the *Aseret HaDibrot* – the Decalogue. It presents the most fundamental premise of the Torah. There is a G-d. Maimonides understands this statement to be

---

[59] It should be noted that none of these authorities ascribe to the position that acceptance of Hashem and the Torah can be founded upon blind faith. To my knowledge, this popular position has no basis or antecedents in the writings of the classical authorities. These authorities were unwilling to equate the Torah to other religions that are based upon personal belief and subjective conviction. Instead, the introduction of blind faith as a basis for acceptance of the Torah seems to be a relatively modern development. Perhaps, this more modern perspective is influenced by modern, conventional theology and existential philosophy.

a commandment. We are commanded to accept the existence of a G-d who is the source of all reality.[60]

In Maimonides' introduction to his *Mishne Torah*, he provides a list of the 613 commandments. In this list, Maimonides places the commandments in the same order that they appear in his *Sefer HaMitzvot*. The placement of the individual *mitzvot* on this list does not correspond with the placement of these commandments in the Torah. Instead, Maimonides constructed a hierarchical order. Maimonides' order reflects the relationship between the various commandments. The very first commandment in Maimonides' list is the *mitzvah* to accept the existence of Hashem. Apparently, Maimonides regards this *mitzvah* as fundamental to the system of *Taryag* – the 613 commandments.

In contrast to Maimonides, Rabbaynu Chasdia Kreskas argues that acceptance of Hashem cannot even be defined as a *mitzvah*. He presents a very powerful argument. He argues that every *mitzvah*, by definition, must engender some obligation or result. A command to accept G-d's existence could not meet this criterion. Why? To whom is the command directed? If it is directed to a person who is already convinced, then the command engenders no new outcome. This person is already convinced! The alternative is even more absurd. This would require that the command be directed to the non-believer. But the non-believer could not take such a command seriously! Based on this argument, Rabbaynu Chasdia concludes that conviction in the existence of Hashem precedes *mitzvot* and cannot be counted among *Taryag*.[61]

How can Maimonides' position be explained? This issue provides a fundamental insight into Maimonides' understanding of *Taryag Mitzvot*. Apparently, Maimonides disagrees with the Rabbaynu Chasdia's basic premise. This premise is that the *mitzvot* can be equated to decrees. Maimonides seems to maintain *Taryag* must be defined in a more inclusive manner. He posits that the *mitzvot* are the basic blueprint for the complete person and nation. This blueprint includes the guide to achieving personal and national fulfillment as well as the basic description of the behaviors and convictions of the *shalem* – the complete individual.

Based on this definition of *Taryag*, Maimonides' position can be appreciated. The most basic ingredient to human perfection is acceptance of the Almighty, Who is the source of all other reality. No description of the *shalem* can be construed which does not include this fundamental conviction.

If we consider Maimonides' position carefully, an important premise emerges. The most basic and fundamental *mitzvah* of *Taryag* is not a command to perform any act. It is the description of a conviction that is fundamental to the perfection of the human being. In other words, the most fundamental element of human perfection is our conviction in the existence of Hashem.

Maimonides discusses this issue more thoroughly in his *Commentary on the Mishne*. He explains that in order to be regarded as adhering to the Torah, we must accept the basic convictions outlined by the Torah. Maimonides outlines thirteen principles – *ikkarim* – that are the fundamental convictions contained in the Torah. He explains that in order to be regarded as adhering to the Torah, one must accept all of these principles. If a person accepts these *ikkarim*, he is regarded as adhering to the Torah even if he is not perfect in his observance. In contrast, a

---

[60] Rabbaynu Moshe ben Maimon (Rambam) *Sefer HaMitzvot, Mitzvat Aseh* 1
[61] Rabbaynu Chasdai Kreskas, *Ohr Hashem*, Introduction (*HaTza'ah*).

person who is scrupulous in observance, but unconvinced of the truth of these thirteen principles, cannot be regarded as a Torah Jew. [62] It is clear from Maimonides' discussion of this issue that our convictions are essential to our identity as Torah Jews. Without these convictions our actions are hollow and loose their meaning and significance.

Maimonides' position differs markedly from the view that is popular today. Even many Jews who unequivocally identify themselves as Torah observant give little or none of their attention to clearly understanding these thirteen *ikkarim* of the Torah. Many Jews – observant and non-observant – do give some attention to the study of Torah *machshava* – philosophy. But this attention is generally directed to the study of *mussar* – ethical thought and philosophy. Maimonides' thirteen principles – which are remarkably devoid of any extensive discussion of ethical philosophy – are almost completely neglected. At most, the thirteen *ikkarim* are quickly recited at the close of morning prayers with little thought or understanding. The popular view is that actions are more fundamental than convictions. We can hold ourselves responsible for acting properly but we cannot be expected to establish a clear system of convictions. Nonetheless, it behooves us to occasionally break from popular practice and give some serious thought to the thirteen *ikkarim* that Maimonides identifies as the underpinning of Judaism.

As explained above, Maimonides lists as the first *mitzvah* of the Torah acceptance of the existence of Hashem. Maimonides also lists this conviction as the first of the thirteen fundamental principles of the Torah. Of course, we need to define what we mean by Hashem. Maimonides explains that when we use the term Hashem or G-d we are required to understand that He is the cause of all that exists. In other words, all that exists is sustained by His will. In contrast, His existence is self-sustained and does not require any external cause.[63]

This principle is often confused with the Torah's assertion that Hashem created the universe. However, these two concepts are not interchangeable. Maimonides' first principle does not deal with the origins of the universe. It deals with the dependence of the universe upon Hashem's ongoing will. This is an important issue. The ancient philosophers – for example, Aristotle – were willing to acknowledge that the universe's existence is dependant upon G-d. However, they denied that He created the universe. They posited that the universe and

G-d share eternity. These philosophers maintained that although the existence of the universe is dependent on G-d, it is not created. Instead it is an emanation. It can be compared to the shadow of a wall. The existence of the wall causes the shadow. But the wall does not perform an act of creation in order to bring the shadow into existence. Instead, the shadow is a result of the existence of the wall. Similarly, these philosophers asserted that the universe is a result of G-d's existence but it not a creation of G-d.

It appears that Maimonides first principle does not contradict this perspective. It does not deal with the issue of creation. It merely asserts that the universe's ongoing existence is dependent upon Hashem.

"For in six days Hashem created the heavens, the earth, the seas and all that are contained in them. And He rested on the seventh day. Therefore, Hashem blessed the Shabbat and sanctified it." (Shemot 20:11)

---

[62] R' Moshe ben Maimon (Rambam) *Commentary on the Mishne*, Mesechet Sanhedrin 10:1.
[63] R' Moshe ben Maimon (Rambam) *Commentary on the Mishne*, Mesechet Sanhedrin 10:1.

Rav Yosef Albo criticizes Maimonides on this issue. He contends that Maimonides neglected to include within his thirteen principles the Torah principle that Hashem created the universe.[64]

We observe Shabbat every week. The above *pasuk* explains that Shabbat is designed to commemorate creation. It seems obvious that the attention the Torah gives to creation indicates that this is a fundamental element of the Torah. The Torah's emphasis on creation seems to support Rav Albo's criticism of Maimonides.

However, a careful study of Maimonides' thirteen principles indicates that they do include the assertion that Hashem created the universe. Maimonides' fourth principle is that Hashem is eternal and that no other existence is eternal. Maimonides elaborates on this principle and explicitly states that this principle includes a negation of the Aristotelian position. In other words, according to Maimonides' formulation of this principle, it includes the assertion that Hashem created the universe and it is not eternal.

It is amazing that Rav Albo criticizes Maimonides for neglecting to include within his thirteen *ikkarim* the Torah's assertion that Hashem created the universe. This is simply not accurate. As we have explained, Maimonides explicitly includes this assertion within his fourth principle! How can we explain Rav Albo's apparent error?

Appreciating Rav Albo's criticism requires a more thorough understanding of Maimonides' formulation of his thirteen principles. In order to reach this understanding, it is helpful to begin with a related question.

Maimonides' second principle is that Hashem is a unity. What is the meaning of the term "unity?" Maimonides explains that Hashem is not subject to division in any sense. This means that we can not view Hashem has having parts or even characteristics. We cannot view Hashem as possessing compassion or mercy. Such a view means that Hashem has attributes. The assignment of attributes to Hashem is inconsistent with the Torah's assertion that Hashem is one. It is true that the Torah does refer to Divine attributes. However, Maimonides explains that when the Torah refers to Hashem's mercy or other attributes it is resorting to an allegory and is not to be understood in a literal sense.[65]

Maimonides' third principle is that Hashem is not material and cannot be described as possessing any of the qualities or characteristics associated with material objects. It would seem that this third principle is superfluous. It is an obvious extension of the second principle. Hashem is a unity. This precludes conceiving of Him as material. All material objects have characteristics – for example dimension and size. It is quite impossible to conceive of a material object devoid of all characteristics. Similarly, Maimonides' fourth principle is that Hashem is eternal. This principle also seems to be an extension of the second principle. The reasoning behind this argument is somewhat abstract and is beyond the scope of this discussion. But the observation is nonetheless noteworthy. It indicates that the thirteen *ikkarim* are not independent of one another. They are interrelated and in some cases latter principles are easily derived from earlier principles.

---

[64] Rav Yosef Albo, *Sefer HaIkkarim*, volume 1, chapter 1.
[65] Rabbaynu Moshe ben Maimon (Rambam) *Mishne Torah*, Hilchot Yesodai HaTorah 1:9.

This suggests a question. What are these principles? We would have assumed that they are similar to a postulate system. In a postulate system, each element is independent of the others. Postulates are basic building blocks. One cannot be derived from another. It is easy to understand the role of postulates in a postulate system. They are the fundamental principles. All other elements of the system are derived from the postulates but the postulates cannot be derived from one another. The postulates are the foundation. The remaining elements of the system are derived and built upon this foundation. But Maimonides' thirteen principles are not independent of one another. In fact, they are interrelated. If one principle can be derived from another, on what basis is a principle defined as fundamental?

The implication of this question is that Maimonides' thirteen *ikkarim* are not a system of postulates. Instead, they are Maimonides' outline of the basic theological framework of the Torah. They describe a structure of concepts. These concepts are interrelated. But in their totality they depict the basic outline of the Torah's theology. They are a basic sketch of the Torah's outlook. They are an abstract of the elements that compose the Torah's perspective. They can be compared to an architect's preliminary drawing of a structure. The architect begins with an outline that includes the basic elements of the structure. These elements give the structure its form and function. Later the architect adds additional detail to his drawing. But the basic form emerges from the preliminary drawing. It contains all of the elements that give the structure its basic form and function. Similarly, Maimonides' principles are such an outline. The basic form and structure of the Torah's outlook is contained in this outline. The Torah adds much more detail. But the fundamental structure is contained in these thirteen principles.

Now, Rav Albo's question can be appreciated. As Maimonides notes, the Torah's assertion that the universe is created can be derived from the fourth principle. But this does not mean that this assertion should not be treated as a separate principle. Rav Albo argues that certainly creation is a fundamental element of the Torah's outlook. It deserves to be treated as such and enumerated as a separate principle. It is not adequate to include creation within another principle!

What is the basis of this dispute between Maimonides and Rav Albo? This is a difficult question to answer. However, it is possible to present an approach or hypothesis. Rav Albo maintains that creation is a fundamental proposition of the Torah. According to Rav Albo, the Torah directs us to regard the word as a creation of Hashem and not as coexistent with Him. We must recognize that the universe that we know is not eternal and is a result of an act of creation. Our relationship with and understanding of the universe must be predicated on this acknowledgement.

In contrast, a survey of Maimonides' thirteen principles reveals that they deal primarily with our relationship with and understanding of Hashem. It seems that according to Maimonides, the essence of the Torah is the perspective it provides on Hashem and our relationship with Him. A fundamental element of this understanding and relationship is that we are required to appreciate Hashem's uniqueness. He is eternal. In His eternity, He is unique. Nothing else partakes of eternity.

Maimonides' understanding of the role of creation in Torah thought is predicated on his contention that our understanding of and relationship with Hashem is the most fundamental element of the Torah. The Torah's assertion that the universe is created is important because this assertion confirms Hashem's uniqueness. If we fail to accept creation, we do not appreciate the uniqueness of Hashem's existence and His central role in all other existence. Without creation, we cannot regard Hashem as the most fundamental reality and the most central element of all reality.

Based on this perspective, Maimonides does not enumerate creation as an independent principle. Instead, he includes it in his fourth principle. We are required to acknowledge that Hashem is eternal. Hashem's eternal existence is unique. Nothing else partakes of this eternity. Therefore, we must accept that the universe is created and not eternal.

"I am Hashem your G-d that brought you out from the land of Egypt, from the house of bondage." (Shemot 20:2)

This is the first statement of the Decalogue. Hashem identifies Himself as the G-d that redeemed Bnai Yisrael from Egypt. Most authorities regard this statement as a commandment. This presents a problem. A commandment engenders some obligation. It requires us to perform some action or accept some conviction. However, this statement is merely the presentation of a fact. What does this commandment require of us?

The Sefer Mitzvot Gadol offers an interesting interpretation of this *mitzvah*. His explanation is based upon a careful interpretation of the passage. The *pasuk* is the Almighty's introduction to the revelation of the Torah. He identifies Himself. He says that He is the G-d that redeemed the nation from Egypt. The Sefer Mitzvot Gadol concludes that the *mitzvah* requires that we acknowledge that the G-d that revealed the Torah is the same Deity that redeemed us from Egypt.[66]

Most other authorities maintain that this *mitzvah* obligates us to acknowledge the existence of G-d. This interpretation of the *mitzvah* presents an obvious problem. What is meant by the term "G-d"? This term has different meanings to different people. In itself, it is rather vague. The term needs some clarification. Precisely, in what must we believe?

Maimonides contends that the term "G-d" refers to a Deity that is the cause of all that exists. He explains that we are obligated to acknowledge that there exists a Deity that is the cause of all other existence. This means that all that exist is a consequence of His will. Without this will nothing would exist. However, if nothing else existed, He would still exist.[67]

Rabbaynu Yehuda HaLeyve, in his Kuzari, seems to object to this definition. In order to understand his objection, some initial clarification is needed. Rav Yehuda HaLeyve does not disagree with Maimonides' assertion that the Hashem is the cause of all existence. This is one of the lessons of the Torah. However, he points out that the commandment requires that we acknowledge the existence of G-d. His objection relates to defining the term "G-d" as the cause of all existence. What is the basis of this objection?

Rabbaynu Yehuda HaLeyve contends that the commandment does not obligate us in abstract philosophical speculation. In other words, the commandment cannot obligate us to prove through philosophical analysis the existence of G-d. Rabbaynu Yehuda HaLeyve assumes a skeptical attitude towards such speculations. The great philosophers have different understandings of G-d. Some acknowledge that He is the Creator. Others reject this conclusion.

---

[66] Rabbaynu Moshe of Kotzi, *Sefer Mitzvot Gadol*, Mitzvat Aseh 1.
[67] Rabbaynu Moshe ben Maimon (Rambam) *Mishne Torah*, Hilchot Yesodai HaTorah 1:1-3.

Even if the speculations were conclusive, they might exceed the ability of the common person. The "G-d" identified by the commandment must be a Deity that everyone can acknowledge, not just the great scholars.

On this basis, it seems that Rabbaynu Yehuda HaLeyve would reject Maimonides' description of the commandment. It is likely that he would argue that Maimonides defines the commandment in a manner that requires philosophical speculation. How would one prove that Hashem is the cause of all existence? This would require an analysis that may exceed the ability of the common person!

What is Rabbaynu Yehuda HaLeyve's understanding of the *mitzvah*? He explains that we are obligated to believe in the G-d of the forefathers that led Bnai Yisrael out of Egypt and gave the Torah. He contends that anyone can make such an affirmation. This is a G-d that was encountered through personal experience and is known to subsequent generations though an unassailable chain of tradition. In other words, this G-d is revealed in history. Anyone can accept an historical fact![68]

In order to better understand the dispute between Maimonides and Rabbaynu Yehuda HaLeyve, it is helpful to consider a few scenarios. First, imagine a person that believes in G-d that delivered Bnai Yisrael from Egypt and gave the Torah. However, this person does not understand that this G-d is the cause of all existence. According to Rabbaynu Yehuda HaLeyve, this person's convictions do not conform to the Torah. However, it cannot be said that this person does not acknowledge the existence of G-d. Maimonides would clearly disagree. He would contend that this person does not fulfill the most basic of *mitzvot*. He does not acknowledge the existence of G-d.

Second, consider a person that accepts the existence of a Deity that is the cause of all existence. However, this person does not know that this G-d redeemed us from Egypt and gave us the Torah. Maimonides would contend that this person's belief system is not in conformity with the Torah. However, the primary command of acknowledging G-d has been fulfilled. Rabbaynu Yehuda HaLeyve seems to adopt the position that this person has not complied with the basic *mitzvah* of acknowledging G-d.

It is important to clearly understand the basis of the three positions we have described. Each position reflects a fundamentally different understanding of this commandment.

The position of the Sefer Mitzvot Gadol is the most astounding of the three positions. According to this interpretation, the commandment does not directly require an affirmation of the existence of G-d. Instead, the *mitzvah* requires that we acknowledge that the Deity that gave the Torah is the same G-d that redeemed us from Egypt. The commandment requires that we affirm the origins of the Torah. We must place the Torah in its proper context. We must appreciate that the Torah is a divinely revealed truth. Of course, this does imply acknowledgement of the existence of G-d. However, the commandment is formulated as an acknowledgement of the nature of the Torah. It is not inherently fashioned as an acknowledgement of G-d's existence.

Rabbaynu Yehuda HaLeyve and Maimonides disagree with this position. They argue that we are directly commanded to acknowledge the existence of G-d. However, they differ in the specifics of this obligation. Now, let us consider this dispute.

---

[68] Rabbaynu Yehuda HaLeyve, Kuzari, part I, sections 11-25.

Rabbaynu Yehuda HaLeyve's position is more easily understood. We have already explained his reasons for rejecting Maimonides' approach to this *mitzvah*. However, it is important to appreciate the outcome of Rabbaynu Yehuda HaLeyve's formulation. Essentially, he contends that we are obligated to acknowledge G-d as He has overtly and manifestly revealed Himself. He made Himself known through the forefathers – the *Avot*, through the wonders He performs and through revelation at Sinai. We are obligated to acknowledge the G-d that is manifested through personal experience and known through tradition.

Maimonides requires that we acknowledge the existence of a Deity that is the cause of all that exists. What is Maimonides' reason for insisting on this somewhat abstract formulation of the *mitzvah*?

Maimonides provides an important insight into his position in his Moreh Nevuchim. He begins with the premise that the perfection of a person's soul is determined by the degree to which the person perceives actual reality. Therefore, various mistakes have differing degrees of impact on human perfection. A misconception regarding an insignificant issue does not have a substantial impact upon human perfection. However, an error regarding a basic reality has a serious impact upon the soul's perfection.

Let us consider a simple example. Assume a person thinks that Reuven is sitting. However, really Reuven is standing. How serious is this person's misconception of reality? It is not very serious. Consequently, this error has little impact on the person's soul. Let us contrast this with a person that believes that the earth is flat or a person that sees ghosts and demons around every corner. This person's perception of reality is seriously flawed. A more basic aspect of reality is denied. The impact of such a misconception is far more serious. As a result, these misconceptions have a significant impact on the person's perfection.[69]

Let us proceed one step further in this analysis. What is the most basic aspect of reality? The answer is that all that exists is a result of G-d. He is the most fundamental aspect of the universe and all that exists. Denial of the existence of a Deity that is the cause of all reality is the greatest possible misconception! No other single error can have the same degree of negative impact upon the soul.

We can now understand Maimonides interpretation of the *mitzvah* to acknowledge G-d. The Torah is a blueprint. It describes the convictions and behaviors of the perfected individual. Maimonides contends that this perfection requires more than mere acknowledgement of G-d. Human perfection is achieved through acknowledging the fundamental nature of reality. We must understand that the entire reality that surrounds us is based upon the existence of G-d. He is the basis and source of all reality.

For in six days Hashem made the heavens and the earth and all that is within them and He rested on the seventh. Therefore, Hashem blessed the Shabbat day and He sanctified it. (Shemot 20:10)

And you should recall that you were a slave in the Land of Egypt and Hashem, your L-rd, took you forth from there with a mighty hand and outstretched arm. Therefore, Hashem, your L-rd, commanded you to observe the Shabbat. (Devarim 5:14)

Mo' Money

---

[69] Rabbaynu Moshe ben Maimon (Rambam / Maimonides) *Moreh Nevuchim*, volume 1, chp. 36.

Differences in the two texts of the Decalogue

The *Aseret HaDibrot* – the Decalogue – is presented twice in the Torah. It is presented first in our *parasha* and a second time in Parshat VaEtchanan. There are various differences in the texts of the Decalogue in these two presentations. Rabbaynu Avraham ibn Ezra dismisses many of these as inconsequential. He explains that in Parshat VaEtchanan, Moshe is reviewing the content of the Decalogue for the nation. His intention is to communicate its content, not to repeat it verbatim. Therefore, he chooses the words and phrases that he feels best communicate the material without regard to inconsequential deviations in the wording.[70]

However, some of the differences between the two presentation are not minor. Some are fundamental differences in content. One of these major differences is in the two presentations of Shabbat. The first quotation above is from our *parasha*. We are commanded to observe the Shabbat in order to reinforce a fundamental tenet of the Torah – the universe is the creation of Hashem.

The second quotation above is from Parshat VaEtchanan. This is Moshe's presentation or review of the imperative to observe Shabbat. He explains that we observe Shabbat in order to recall our redemption from slavery in Egypt. Moshe makes no mention of Shabbat memorializing creation. In other words, each version presents its own explanation for the observance of Shabbat. This is not a minor discrepancy. How can it be reconciled?

Among the commentators there are a number of responses to this problem. We will focus upon the solution and insight suggested by Maimonides. This solution resolves the apparent contradiction between the texts, it addresses additional issues, and it suggests an important message regarding our values and priorities.

Moshe's objective was to motivate

Maimonides' solution is based upon an implicit premise. What was Moshe's objective in reviewing with the nation the *Aseret HaDibrot* before his death? Maimonides seems to assume that his objective was not limited to recapitulating the content. Moshe was also focused upon encouraging the people to observe the commandments. This objective impacted his presentation. It determined the elements of the Decalogue that he addressed and how he presented them. In other words, the original presentation of the Decalogue in our *parasha* is focused solely upon the fundamental content of the commandments. Moshe's review has a broader or different perspective. It is designed to encourage and even admonish the people to carefully observe the commandments.

Let's consider an analogy. It's Friday afternoon and a parent wants his son to straighten up his room before Shabbat. As soon as his son arrives home, the dad instructs his son of the expectation. These instructions are detailed. Of course, the son has other things to do before he gets to this task. Shabbat is approaching and the father realizes that if the room is to be straightened-up, the chore requires immediate attention. He speaks to his son again and reviews the expectation. This review of the expectation is different than the original presentation. There is no need for the father to review the details. He wants to make sure the chore is completed. In this presentation, the dad focuses upon the importance of preparing for Shabbat and explains that this is the son's opportunity to participate in honoring the Shabbat. In both presentations the

---

[70] Rabbeinu Avraham ibn Ezra, *Commentary of Sefer Shemot*, 20:1.

father is discussing the same task. However, in the first the focus is upon the substance of the task. In the second, the substance of the task requires less attention. Now, the father focuses on motivating.

This illustration demonstrates how the same task will be presented differently as required by the situation. Maimonides employs this principle to explain the discrepancy between the presentations of Shabbat in the two iterations of the Decalogue.

The meaning of Shabbat

He explains that in the first presentation – found in our *parsha* – the Torah is presenting the basic concept of Shabbat. In this context, the Torah's focus is upon the innate meaning of Shabbat. It communicates the significance of the day. It is in this context that the Torah explains that Shabbat recalls the creation. Hashem created the universe. He fashioned it in six days and then rested on the seventh. The observance of Shabbat recalls and memorializes the universe's origin.

Shabbat was given to the Jewish people

Moshe's review focuses on *our* obligation to observe Shabbat. It explains Bnai Yisrael's selection for the role of observing this commandment.[71] We were selected because we were redeemed from Egypt. Our redemption endows this commandment – which is a day of rest – with a special significance. In other words, because of our redemption from slavery we are uniquely fit to observe this commandment. How does our experience of bondage and liberation endow us with this unique suitability?

Maimonides explains that in Egypt there was no day of rest. Our activities and our lives were controlled and fashioned by our masters. If on some occasion we did have a respite from our heavy burden, it was granted to us at the sole volition of a master. Such a hiatus in a slave's labor is not truly a respite; it is a reprieve that will soon be terminated at the whim of the master. Only a free person – one who is empowered to act upon is own volition – can experience authentic rest from labor and toil. According to Maimonides, our emergence from bondage into freedom uniquely prepared us to experience a day of rest. Any person can select a day of the week and decide to not labor on that day. But for us the designation of a day as a period for respite and contemplation has unique meaning.

---

[71] Maimonides' interpretation of the message of the second Decalogue is not completely clear. One could argue that we were selected to receive the Torah; Shabbat is one of its *mitzvot*. No special explanation is required for our selection to receive a specific commandment. Abravanel, in his commentary on Maimonides' comments, suggests that we would expect Shabbat to be included in the laws given to the descendants of Noach. Its message that Hashem is creator is universal. It is relevant to Jew and non-Jew. Maimonides understands the second text of the Decalogue to address this issue.
Possibly, Maimonides' position can be understood in the context of his comments in Hilchot Melachim 10:9-10. There, he explains that generally, a non-Jew may adopt observance of any of the Torah's *mitzvot*. For example, a non-Jew may adopt observance of the *mitzvot* of *kashrut*. However, a non-Jew may not adopt observance of Shabbat. From these comments, it is clear that the relationship between the Jewish people and Shabbat is different than the relationship with most other *mitzvot*. We enjoy an exclusive relationship with Shabbat; a non-Jew may not join us in its observance.

Again, let's employ an analogy to understand this insight. A baseball team fields nine players. The coach must decide who will play shortstop. He considers his options and he selects a player who his very agile, has an accurate throwing arm, and is focused and alert. The position of shortstop has its own unique objectives. The shortstop covers the gap in the infield between second and third bases. He fields most of the infield grounders or one-hoppers hit in his direction and often has to handle line-drives. It is his job to throw out runners to first base and sometimes make a play to second, third or even home. This is the position. In selecting the player to play the position, the coach needs to consider the requisite skills, gifts, and talents. These are agility, accuracy in throwing, focus, and alertness. Returning to our discussion, Shabbat commemorates creation. Bnai Yisrael were selected to observe Shabbat because background and history rendered us uniquely suited for the role.

Let's summarize before continuing. The first iteration of the *Aseret HaDibrot* focuses upon the objective of Shabbat. Its objective is to recall that Hashem is the creator of the universe. The second iteration focuses upon the selection of the Jewish people for the role of observing Shabbat. In order to understand our selection, we must recognize how Shabbat communicates its message. The means is through observing a day of rest, every week. The character of the day as respite from labor and dedication to contemplation is most intensely experienced by a people who has emerged from slavery to freedom. Therefore, we were selected to receive the Shabbat.

Shabbat summarizes Hashem's love for us

Maimonides adds that these two presentations of Shabbat combine to create an integrated and comprehensive message. The observance of Shabbat recalls Hashem's creation. Our selection as the nation who observes Shabbat reminds us of our redemption from bondage. These two messages merge into a comprehensive expression of Hashem's lovingkindness toward the Jewish people. He has provided us with a spiritual legacy – a Torah that teaches us the most fundamental truths. He has provided us with the foundation for material advancement – our liberation from slavery.[72]

The Shabbat liturgy reflects the two version of the Decalogue

Maimonides' insight resolves a number of additional problems. The Friday night *Amidah* for Shabbat focuses upon Shabbat as commemorating creation. Its central blessing includes the passages from the creation narrative that discuss Shabbat. The *Amidah* of Shabbat morning does mention the meaning of Shabbat but its focus is overwhelmingly upon the selection of Jewish people to observe Shabbat. Based upon Maimonides' insight, we can easily understand these two treatments.

The central benediction of Shabbat *Amidah* of Friday night begins with the statement:

You sanctified the seventh day for Your name. It is the completion of the creation of heavens and earth. You blessed it from among all of the days and sanctified it from among all periods of time.

This introduction sets the tone for the benediction. It mirrors the first iteration of the Decalogue. Its focus is upon the meaning of Shabbat. Therefore, the blessing discusses Shabbat as the memorial of creation and does not make mention of our redemption.

The Shabbat morning *Amidah* is not focused upon the objective of Shabbat. Instead, its focus is almost entirely upon our selection to observe it. This focus is derived directly from the

---

[72] Rabbaynu Moshe ben Maimon (Rambam) *Moreh Nevuchim*, volume 2, chapter 31.

second iteration of the *Aseret HaDibrot*. The theme of this second iteration was adopted by the Sages in this *Amidah*. Therefore, rather than focusing upon the meaning of Shabbat, the central benediction discusses our selection for the role of observing Shabbat.

Wealth and its meaning and purpose

Finally, Maimonides' insight provides us with an important message regarding priorities. As he explains, Hashem's lovingkindness is expressed in the spiritual and material gifts that he bestowed upon us. Shabbat is one of these spiritual gifts. It focuses upon one of the great and fundamental truths of the Torah – Hashem's creation of the universe. It also reminds us of our rescue from Egypt. This is a material gift. Our freedom is the foundation of every material achievement that has followed and been built upon it. Shabbat is designed to remind us of both of these expressions of Hashem's lovingkindness. The integration of both messages within Shabbat suggests their intimate relationship with one another. Let us further explore and delineate this relationship.

The experience of liberation gives the Jewish people the capacity to more fully appreciate a day of rest. In other words, material achievements create the foundation for a spiritual encounter. Also, the observance of Shabbat gives meaning and purpose to our liberation. The two acts of kindness complement one another. Liberation makes us more intensely appreciate Shabbat; observance of Shabbat endows freedom with meaning and purpose. This is an excellent model for the optimal interaction and relationship between our material and spiritual endeavors.

Our material achievements provide us with the opportunity to advance our spiritual development. Conversely, our spiritual endeavors provide meaning to our material achievements. Ultimately, Maimonides' message reminds us to devote ourselves to spiritual development. Focus on material achievement as an end in itself cannot really provide fulfillment and satisfaction. Once a person has provided for oneself and one's family, the pursuit quickly resolves into an exercise in greed or psychological insecurity. Greed can never be satisfied and deep insecurities do not yield to reason. Consequently, the single-minded pursuit of the accumulation of wealth does not end in fulfillment. However, the person who utilizes one's material wellbeing to support pursuit of spiritual development will endow these material accomplishments with real meaning. Furthermore, one who nurtures a strong spiritual life, will discover meaning and fulfillment.

Mishpatim

And these are the laws that you should place before them. (Shemot 21:1)

A Spiritual Experience

1. The Sanhedrin's location

The passage introduces Parshat Mishpatim. The parasha provides a detailed account of laws that Moshe received at Sinai. Most of the laws in the parasha concern civil matters. Areas covered in the parasha include the treatment of servants, the responsibilities of one who borrows or rents an object for its damage or loss, the punishment for theft, and responsibility for causing personal injury or property damage.

Commenting on the above passage, the midrash notes an interesting juxtaposition. The previous parasha ended with a discussion of the design for an altar. The midrash asks, "why do the laws of Parshat Mishpatim follow laws regarding an altar?" The midrash responds that this juxtaposition is intended to teach that the Sanhedrin – the highest court of the nation – must be located adjacent to the Bait HaMikdash – the Sacred Temple.[1]

These comments raise a question. Why is it necessary for the Sanhedrin to be situated adjacent to the Bait HaMikdash? Our Sages and commentators offer various explanations. Let's consider some of these.

2. The Sanhedrin's role in the Bait HaMikdash

Shelah suggests, based upon a comment of Rambam – Maimonides, that the requirement responds to practical necessity. Rambam explains that the Sanhedrin occupying the Granite Chamber adjacent to the Bait HaMikdash decided all issues regarding the suitability of a kohen to serve. This court resolved questions related to the lineage of a kohen and judged whether a physical blemish disqualified the kohen from service.[2] Shelah explains that because the Sanhedrin was charged with resolving issues directly related to service in the Bait HaMikdash, the Granite Chamber was the appropriate location for it.[3]

3. The role of justice

Rashal explains that the altar and the courts have similar functions. The sacrifices offered on the altar promote peace between the Jewish people and Hashem. The laws of Parshat Mishpatim promote peace among the members of the nation. The placement of the Sanhedrin within the compound of the Bait HaMikdash demonstrates that perfect peace requires service to Hashem and justice within society. Alone, neither is sufficient to produce harmony.[4]

Rashal suggests an alternative explanation. The Talmud comments that Hashem's presence within the Jewish people will not be restored until all corrupt judges are eliminated.[5] Rashal explains that the Bait HaMikdash is the place in which the Divine Presence is most intensely expressed. The Sanhedrin represents the courts of the nation and justice. The placement

---

[1] Michilta, Parshat Mishpatim, Introduction.
[2] R' Moshe ben Maimon (Rambam) Mishne Torah, Hil. Biyat HaMikdash Melachim 6:11.
[3] Rav Yishayahu Horowitz (Shelah), Shenei Luchot HaBerit, Vavei HaAmudim, Chapter 17.
[4] Rav Shlomo Luria, Gur Aryeh on Sefer Shemot, 21:1.
[5] Mesechet Shabbat 139a.

of the Sanhedrin in the compound of the Bait HaMikdash communicates that social justice is a prerequisite for the expression of the Divine Presence in the Bait HaMikdash.[6]

4. Practical issues and messages

In summary, these explanations adopt two approaches to explaining the placement of the Sanhedrin adjacent to the altar – in the compound of the Bait HaMikdash. Shelah contends this placement serves a practical end. It facilitates prompt resolution of issues relevant to the service – specifically, questions regarding the suitability of a kohen to participate in service. Rashal maintains that the location of the court is intended to communicate an important message. The basic message is the justice and devotion are interrelated. Alone, neither, is sufficient to produce harmony within a society or to secure the Divine Presence within the Jewish people.

5. Torah study and Hashem's presence

A novel explanation for the location of the Sanhedrin is offered by Rav Yitzchok Isaac Chaver.

> "It is written 'For from Tzion goes forth the Torah and the word of Hashem from Yerushalayim' (Yishayahu 2:3). This is because the Great Sanhedrin sits there in the Granite Chamber and from there goes forth teaching to all Yisrael. This is the essence of Torah – to determine the true [message] of the Torah and to teach [its observance] in accordance with the law.
>
> And the essence of the Divine Presence is there [in the Granite Chamber]. Therefore, it was required that the place of the Sanhedrin must be adjacent to the altar… This is because through it the Divine Presence resided in the Bait HaMikdash.
>
> Similarly, we find that in the wilderness the essence of the Divine Presence resided in the Mishcan (the Tabernacle) because from there The Blessed One communicated the entire Torah – its general principles and details…." (Ohr Torah pp 231-2)

Rav Chaver's contention is that the Divine Presence did not express itself in the Bait HaMikdash because of the ritual service performed there. The Divine Presence was expressed there because it was the place from which the Sanhedrin taught the nation the laws of the Torah. In other words, the Bait HaMikdash was made suitable as a place of worship by the Torah teaching that took place there. He further explains that the relationship of the Divine Presence to the Bait HaMikdash was consistent with the Divine Presence in the Mishcan – the Tabernacle of the wilderness. Hashem spoke to Moshe from the Mishcan. He taught Moshe the mitzvot of the Torah and their laws. This teaching and study of Torah endowed the Mishcan with the Divine Presence – not the sacrifices offered there.

In short, Rav Chaver's position is that the presence of Hashem is secured through Torah teaching and study. Ritual service is a response to the Presence; it is not the cause of the Presence.

6. Rethinking the meaning of spiritual experience

Rav Chaver's perspective on spiritual experience is very different than the popular view. Most assume that prayer is a more meaningful or direct means of connecting with Hashem and relating to Him. Rav Chaver insists that this not true. The most meaningful relationship with

---

[6] Rav Shlomo Luria, Chidushai Agadot, Mesechet Shabbat 139a.

Hashem is founded upon the study of His Torah. According to Rav Chaver's perspective, we can easily understand why our Sages incorporated the Torah reading into the weekly service. Our study of Hashem's Torah invites His presence and renders our prayers more meaningful.

And these are the laws that you should place before them. (Shemot 21:1)
The Importance of Civil Law in the Torah

This *pasuk* introduces Parshat Mishpatim. The laws, outlined in this *parasha*, regulate civil matters. These ordinances include regulations that govern responsibility and payment for damages, usury, and the rights of servants.

In the *pasuk* quoted above, Rashi comments that the word "and" indicates a connection between these laws, ordinances and regulations and those described in the previous *parasha*. The legal material in the earlier section governs issues of theology and ritual. The "and" indicates that just as the previous material was revealed at Sinai, so too is civil law derived from this same source. Rashi adds that the final section of the previous *parasha* – Parshat Yitro – discusses the design of the altar. The civil laws of Parshat Mishpatim are intentionally juxtaposed to this section. This relationship is the basis for housing the High Court adjacent to the Temple.[7]

Rashi's comments are intended to emphasize one of the unique aspects of the Torah. Religion, by definition, includes a theology and a set of rituals that embody the religion's concept of worship. However, it is often assumed that religion does not have a role in regulating behavior to one's fellow human-beings. Although it may be granted that religion should include some broad principles that urge moral conduct, it is not assumed that religion should include a specific legal framework that regulates commerce and interpersonal relationships. In this common conception of religion, service to G-d is divorced from an emphasis on the duty to behave ethically. In contrast, the Torah, teaches that moral conduct is integral to religious life. Devotion to Hashem must guide our interactions and conduct in every aspect of our lives.

This concept is explicitly taught in the Talmud. In Tractate Baba Kamma, our Sages teach that one who wishes to be righteous should be conscientious in the observance of these civil laws.[8] Torah observance cannot be limited to the synagogue—or even the home. It must guide all facets of our lives.

To remind us of the Divine obligation to live morally, the civil laws are connected to the ritual laws of the previous *parasha* with the word "and." Both are from Sinai. Both share the same origin and importance. As a visual reminder of this concept, the High Court – representing civil law – is placed next to the Temple, the site of worship.

"And these are the laws that you should place before them." (Shemot 21:1)

One of the debates that regularly emerge in education concerns the proper role of the teacher in the educational experience. Should the teacher impart knowledge to the student? Should the teacher assume a more passive role and merely act as a facilitator in the student's personal learning experience? The technological breakthroughs of the last few decades have

---

[7] Rabbaynu Shlomo ben Yitzchak (Rashi), *Commentary on Sefer Shemot* 21:1.
[8] Mesechet Baba Kamma 30a.

caused this debate to resurface. With the use of computers, the internet and other technological devices that have been introduced into the classroom, the option of creating a classroom in which the teacher is more a facilitator and less an instructor has become very real. But it is important to remember that we should not use technology simply because it is available. We always need to ask, "What is the best model for the student?" The first passage of this week's *parasha* offers some insight into this debate.

In the first passage of our *parasha*, Moshe is commanded to teach the laws of the Torah to Bnai Yisrael. However, Hashem does not merely instruct Moshe to teach the laws to the people. Instead, He tells Moshe to place the laws before the people. The Sages ask why Hashem refers to placing the laws in front of the people rather than using the more obvious formulation – to teach the people. Various responses are offered. Rashi quotes one of these responses. Hashem's instructions contain an injunction. Moshe cannot fulfill his mission simply by reviewing the laws repeatedly until the people are fluent in them. He is required to teach the laws in depth so that the people understand the underlying principles.[9]

The precise meaning of Rashi's comments is not clear. We would imagine that a thorough knowledge of the law – the achievement of fluency – is quite an accomplishment. What additional element is Moshe required to provide in his transmission of the law? Rabbaynu David, author of the Turai Zahav, explains that Hashem is commanding Moshe to not limit his teaching to the Written Law. In addition, he must transmit to the people the Oral Law. In other words, the Written Law represents only a portion of the corpus of the law. The Oral Law provides explanation and interpretation of the Written Law. Moshe's instruction must include the Oral Law.[10]

There is an interesting insight provided by this interpretation of Rashi. This interpretation of Rashi posits a specific relationship between the Written and Oral Law. The Written Law is the basic corpus of the entire Torah. However, it is very brief and concise. In order to fully understand its meaning a commentary or explanation is needed. This commentary is the Oral Law. This formulation of the relationship between the Written and Oral Laws is expressed in some interesting *halachot*.

One of the most fundamental differences between the Written and Oral Laws is contained in their names. The Written Law is recorded in written form in the Chumash. The Oral Law cannot be recorded. Our Sages only allowed the Oral Torah to be recorded in written form because they feared that a strictly oral transmission had become impractical. And if the Oral Law would not be recorded, large portions would be lost.

But let us consider the original requirement – that the Written Law should be recorded and the Oral Torah should not be recorded. Why was it initially prohibited to record the Oral Law in written form? Torah Temimah explains that this is an outcome of the relationship between the Written and Oral Law. As explained above, the Oral Law is a commentary and elaborate explanation of the Written Law. As a result, it can only be properly transmitted through the efforts of a scholar with his students. Because the Written Law is concise and relatively simple, it can be mastered from the text. In contrast, the Oral Law is far more detailed and

---

[9] Rabbaynu Shlomo ben Yitzchak (Rashi), *Commentary on Sefer Shemot* 21:1.
[10] Rabbaynu David ben HaRav Shemuel HaLeyve *Divrei David Torai Zahav*, (Mosad HaRav Kook, 1978), p 253.

intricate. It cannot be mastered simply through the reading of a text. It must be transmitted through the more intimate and personal forum of the teacher and student. In order to preserve the student – teacher relationship as the means of transmitting the Oral Law, it was not initially committed to written form.[11]

Following the lead of Torah Temimah, we can also understand the history of the recording of the Oral Law. At first the Mishna was redacted. This was followed by the compilation and recording of the Gemara. Later the commentaries on the Talmud were recorded. In other words, the Oral Torah was recorded in discrete stages. Why was this necessary? Once it was decided by the Sages that necessity dictated that the Oral be recorded, why was it not immediately recorded in its entirety? According to the Torah Temimah, this incremental approach is quite understandable. The Sages struggled with two conflicting considerations. First, it was necessary to commit the Oral Law to a written form. But they also recognized that the Oral Law could only be effectively transmitted through the teacher – student relationship. Recording the Oral Torah undermines this relationship. Once recorded, the Oral Torah can be accessed by any student. The role of the teacher is undermined. In order to resolve these conflicting considerations, the Sages recorded the Oral Law incrementally. At each stage the Sages balanced their concern with the preservation of the Oral Law with their determination to maintain the traditional and essential relationship between teacher and student. Enough of the Oral Law was recorded to assure its preservation. But as much as possible of the Oral Law was left in its original oral form to be transmitted by teacher to student.

Let us consider another interesting *halacha*. Maimonides explains that it is permitted for a teacher to accept payment for instructing students in the Written Law. However, it is not permitted to accept payment for providing instruction in the Oral Law.[12] It should be noted the common practice to compensate teachers of Oral Law is based on the position of Shulchan Aruch.[13] But let us consider the position of Maimonides. What is the basis of the prohibition against providing compensation for teaching the Oral Law? Why does this prohibition not apply to teaching the Written Law?

Maimonides provides an interesting response to the first question. He explains that just as the Almighty taught Moshe the Torah without receiving compensation, so too we are required to provide instruction without compensation.[14] This provides an explanation for the prohibition. But now our second question seems even more justified! Hashem did not just instruct Moshe in the Oral Law without compensation. He also provided Moshe with instruction in the Written Law. Based on Maimonides explanation of origins of the prohibition, we would think it should also extend to the Written Law.

Perhaps, based on the above analysis of the relationship between the Written and Oral Laws, we can answer this question. As we have explained, the written and oral formats of these elements of the Torah reflect two different instructional models. The Written Torah is recorded in order to make it readily accessible to every student. However, the Oral Law is not written in order to foster transmission by teacher to student. If this is the case, let us consider the role of the teacher in the instruction of each Law. In the case of the Written Law, the recorded format is

---

[11] Rav Baruch HaLeyve Epstein, *Torah Temimah*, Introduction.
[12] Rabbaynu Moshe ben Maimon (Rambam) *Mishne Torah*, Hilchot Talmud Torah 1:7.
[13] Rav Yosef Karo, *Shulchan Aruch, Yoreh De'ah* 246:5.
[14] Rabbaynu Moshe ben Maimon (Rambam) *Mishne Torah*, Hilchot Talmud Torah 1:7.

designed to make the Written Law accessible even without the aid of an instructor. Therefore, the instructor is not an inherent element in the transmission of the Written Law. The student learns from the text. The teacher provides assistance and facilitates learning. But he is not the source of the knowledge. The teacher has a completely different role in the transmission of the Oral Law. In this case, the Law is designed to be transmitted from teacher to student. The teacher is not merely a facilitator and aid to the student. The teacher is charged with the responsibility of acting as the agent for the transmission of the Law.

This distinction suggests an answer to our question on Maimonides. A teacher can be compensated for providing assistance to the student in mastering the Written Law. This is because the teacher is not truly acting as an instructor. The student learns from the text with the aid of the teacher. However, we cannot provide compensation for actually providing Torah instruction. In the case of the Oral Law the teacher is actually assuming an instructional role. Maimonides maintains that for such a role, the instructor cannot be compensated.

So is it best for a teacher to facilitate the student's own learning? Is it the role of the teacher to assume a more active role as an instructor? If we use the Torah as a model, there is no one answer. It depends on the material the student is studying. There are some cases in which the teacher can best serve the student by acting as a facilitator. However, in some areas this is not the appropriate role. Some areas knowledge cannot be transmitted without the teacher – student interaction and dialogue. In such cases, the teacher is an essential element of the learning process.

And these are the laws that you should place before them. (Shemot 21:1)
Deciding Disputes in Civil Court

Parshat Mishpatim describes many of the civil laws of the Torah. The Talmud explains in Tractate Gitten that we are required to resolve disputes regarding civil law in *bait din* – a Jewish court convened in accordance to Torah standards. We are not permitted to submit such disputes before non-Jewish civil courts.[15] Rashi elaborates on this requirement. He explains that there are areas of civil law in which secular law may closely follow Torah law. In these cases, submitting a dispute to a secular court will likely produce a decision that is consistent with Torah law. Nonetheless, one may not take the dispute to a secular court.[16] Rashi does not explain the reason for this restriction. Why is it prohibited to submit any civil issue to a secular court? Assume that one is certain that the laws enforced by this court are consistent with the Torah. What is wrong with availing oneself of this secular authority?

Maimonides discusses this issue in his Mishne Torah. He explains that one who submits a dispute to a secular court is considered wicked. He is a blasphemer and has raised his hand against the Torah of Moshe, our master.[17] This is a very serious condemnation. It seems extreme. The term, blasphemy, implies a denial of a central principle of the Torah! How has this person blasphemed? Furthermore, how does one who utilizes a secular court "raise his hand against the Torah"?

---

[15] Mesechet Gitten 88b.
[16] Rabbaynu Shlomo ben Yitzchak (Rashi), *Commentary on Sefer Shemot* 21:1.
[17] Rabbaynu Moshe ben Maimon (Rambam) *Mishne Torah*, Hilchot *Sanhedrin* 26:7.

In order to understand Maimonides' comments, a brief introduction is required. In his commentary on the mishne, Maimonides identifies and defines the fundamental principles of the Torah. One of these principles is that the entire Torah was revealed to Moshe. Every law of the Torah was given to us by Hashem.[18] We are required to uphold this conviction. This requirement is not fulfilled simply through an intellectual commitment to the principle; the principle must also guide and be confirmed by our behaviors. We must act in a manner consistent with the conviction that the Torah is a revealed truth. Any behavior that implies otherwise is prohibited and is regarded as a rejection of revelation.

We can now understand Maimonides' comments regarding secular courts. We received the Torah from Sinai. It is a revealed truth. Therefore, it is a perfect system of law. This status applies to the laws governing ritual and it also applies to the civil law of the Torah. A person cognizant of the divine origins of the Torah's laws would not willingly submit oneself to the jurisdiction of another system. This person would only wish to be judged by Torah law. Abandonment of Torah law – even in a civil matter – implies denial of the Torah's status as a revealed truth. It follows that submission of a civil dispute to a secular court is prohibited. One who does seek justice in a secular court has raised his hand against the Torah of Moshe. This is regarded as blasphemy against the Divine origins of the Torah.

And these are the laws that you should place before them. (Shemot 21:1)

Good People, Bad People, and Those in Between

Our tendency to classify people as good or evil

We tend to classify people as either good people or as bad people. The good people conduct themselves according to standards that we establish. If these good people deviate from these standards, it is in minor or excusable ways. The bad people have violated these standards in a way that we cannot overlook or forgive. This classification helps us navigate our social lives. We have goodwill toward the good people. We want them to be our friends. We avoid or shun the bad people. After all, they deserve our disdain. They are the bad people.

The reality of human behavior is more complicated. No one is completely evil or thoroughly righteous. Each of us is a combination of traits. Some of these traits are meritorious and others are less so. Even those who have serious character flaws and sometimes act despicably, often possess some wonderful distinctive traits. Recognizing the complexity of human beings makes our social interactions and attitudes far more challenging.

When we recognize the complexity of human character, we realize that most of our animosities are not truly justified and that many of our friendships include an element of self-imposed blindness. We are blind to the good in the objects of our animosity and to the failings of those we admire.

Problems with the classification system

One of the results of this classification system is that we struggle to treat people fairly. We speak poorly of the people we have classified as evil. We do not feel any responsibility to

---

[18] R' Moshe ben Maimon (Rambam) *Commentary on the Mishne*, Mesechet *Sanhedrin* 10:1.

treat such a person with compassion in his or her time of need. And if our animosity toward a person involves money, we may not be objective in weighing our respective claims.

If we want to be just and fair individuals, we need to overcome this tendency. We need to act fairly toward everyone – even toward those we dislike and whom we feel deserve any evil that befalls them. But how do overcome our innate prejudices and resentments?

Might is to the king Who loves judgment. You have established equity. Judgment and justice You made for Yaakov. (Tehilim 99:4)

The laws of the Torah "create" conflicts

Parshat Mishpatim deals primarily with the laws that govern the relationship between an individual and his or her fellow individual. Included are regulations regarding loans and admonitions to treat the less fortunate with compassion and sensitivity. Many of these laws concern financial obligations between individuals and liabilities for theft and damages.

In its opening comments of the *parasha*, Midrash Rabbah quotes the above passage and makes the following observation: *You, Hashem, established just behaviors for Your beloved. Through the laws that You gave to them they create conflicts with one another. They come for judgment and they make peace.*

The comment of the midrash is difficult to understand. It seems to say that we create conflicts through the laws that Hashem gave to us in the Torah. This sounds like a very critical description of our behavior. Is the midrash suggesting that we take advantage of the laws of the Torah in order to harass others? Is the message of the midrash that we use the laws of the Torah to concoct trivial or specious claims against one another? If this is the message, then the closing statement of the midrash contradicts this assessment. The closing statement is that we subject our conflicts to judgment and then reunite in peace. People who present invented or exaggerated accusations do not place their conflict before a judge, and then after his ruling, come together in peace. How can we understand the comments of the midrash?

The Torah and the Noahide court systems

Before addressing this issue, let us consider another question. Hashem gave the Jewish people His Torah. He also gave a set of laws to humanity. These are seven general commandments that He gave to the descendants of Noach. These two sets of laws have many shared features but they also differ in some respects. One of their shared features is that both require the establishment of a court system. However, the systems differ. The court system required by the Torah is extensive. In the Land of Israel, we are required to establish courts in every district and in every city. The commandment given to the descendants of Noach requires that courts be established only in every district but not in every city.

Why are the Jewish people commanded to create a more extensive court system than required of other nations? Is this because we are more quarrelsome and litigious? Are we more unethical than the rest of humanity and therefore, more prone to conflicts?

The court system reflects the Torah's focus on implementing justice

The answer is that we are expected to care deeply about justice. When we come into a conflict with another person, we are expected to seek a fair and just resolution and not merely prevail by wearing down or overpowering one's opponent.

In order to understand this, let's compare the ideal promoted by the Torah with everyday experience in our contemporary society. If I feel my mobile provider has overcharged me, what is my recourse? I can call the provider and seek resolution. I will need to be prepared to confront endless automated menus, none of which include the option I am seeking. If I somehow defeat this system and manage to speak with an actual human being, it will not be the person who can help me. Probably, the second person to whom I am passed on will also not be able to help me. He will offer to place me on hold and then connect me with the person who can be helpful. After waiting on hold for ten minutes, I will be cut off. Now, I can decide whether I want to start over. In the end, I may decide to drop the entire issue. First of all, maybe I am wrong and there is a reason for the unexplained higher charge. And even if I have been overcharged, is correcting the overcharge worth the time it will take?

Consider this story. How was my conflict with my carrier resolved? The resolution did not reflect justice. I was merely subdued by the obstacles I encountered. This is a trivial example, but it illustrates how so many conflicts are resolved in our society. Justice is replaced by surrender of one's claim.

The Torah intends to communicate that winning is not as important as acting justly. Conflicts should be resolved ethically and not through one party imposing a resolution on the other. The greater the drive for justice, the more courts needed by society. The Torah requires an extensive court system because it expects us to resolve conflicts justly rather than through the stronger party imposing his position upon the weaker party.

Acting with justice even in confronting perceived enemies

Now, we can return to the comments of the midrash. The midrash states that the laws that Hashem gave us create conflicts. This is absolutely true. The Torah provided us with an extensive set of laws that regulates our interpersonal and business interactions. It gave us these laws because we are to be committed to justice. These laws are to be the basis for our conflicts. This means that we look to the laws to inform our behaviors toward one another, to define our respective rights, and to regulate our interactions. Our conflicts are to be the product of our desire to realize the justice embodied in these laws and not by the desire to vanquish those we oppose. If our conflicts are the result of our desire to adhere to the justice to which these laws give expression, then we will place our views before the court of judgment; we will accept the decision, and we will depart friends. In other words, the midrash does not mean that the laws of the Torah create conflicts. It means that these laws are to be the basis of our conflicts. If our conflicts are based upon and guided by these laws then justice will prevail and peace will be restored.

Learning to treat everyone fairly and to judge others equitably

Let us now return to our original question. How do we overcome the prejudices that we have toward one another and treat each other fairly? The preceding discussion provides the Torah's response. We must be strict with ourselves in our observance of the laws regulating our social and commercial interactions. We must impose these laws upon ourselves equally, whether dealing with a friend or a perceived adversary. We must be as scrupulous in paying a stranger for his services as in paying a friend. And even if we have a falling-out with an individual, we must be scrupulous in our treatment of that person.

There is a personal reward that the individual accrues by imposing upon oneself this expectation. In time, it becomes much more difficult to classify people as good or evil. Our actions impact our thinking and feelings. We treat people fairly and our perspective on people begins to mature. We force ourselves to treat others with objectivity and, hopefully, we begin to assess other objectively. The categorization of people into good and bad is replaced by an appreciation of the complexity of the human character and recognition of the good in every person.

And these are the ordinances that you should place before them. (Shemot 21:1)
It's Not Just about Hashem
Two classes of commandments

A large portion of Parshat Mishpatim is devoted to laws. Most of the laws in the *parasha* can be apportioned between the following groups:

- Laws governing the treatment of servants and of the less fortunate and underprivileged.
- Laws regarding personal injury and property damage.
- Laws of jurisprudence.

As a class, these laws establish the rights of the individual and standards of behavior. These standards regulate our interactions as individuals and groups within the community. Within the scope of these laws is the regulation of both commercial and personal interactions.[19] This class of *mitzvot* is commonly referred to as *mitzvot ben adam le'chavero* – interpersonal commandments. The balance of the *mitzvot* of the Torah are described as *ben adam la'makom* – commandments defining one's relationship with Hashem.[20]

What is the significance of this classification? Is there a fundamental difference between these two classes of *mitzvot*? On the surface, it seems that the distinction is superficial rather than fundamental. Let's consider this assertion more carefully.

> *And when you spread out your hands, I will hide My eyes from you, even when you pray at length, I do not hear; your hands are full of blood. Wash, cleanse yourselves, remove the evil of your deeds from before My eyes, cease to do evil. Learn to do good, seek justice, strengthen the robbed, perform justice for the orphan, plead the case of the widow. (Book of Yeshayahu 1:15-17)*

The importance of the interpersonal commandments

The Torah repeatedly equates those *mitzvot* that are *ben adam le'chavero* to those that are *ben adam la'makom*. For example, the *Aseret HaDibrot* – the Decalogue – gives similar attention to both classes of commandments. In the above passages, the prophet Yeshayahu chastises the people for their treatment of those who are less fortunate. He emphasizes that

---

[19] According to Maimonides, there are 44 commandments in Parshat Mishpatim. Among the first 33 commandments, 29 are *ben adam le'chavero*.

[20] Sometimes a third category is identified. These are *mitzvot ben adam le'atzmo* – commandments regarding one's internal life or personality. However, many or all of these can be apportioned between the categories of *ben adam le'chavero* and *ben adam la'makom*.

Hashem will not respond to the prayers of a nation that disregards the affliction of its oppressed. It is clear from his admonition that the *ben adam le'chavero* commandments are on equal footing with those that address our relationship with Hashem. If the Torah repeatedly equates these two classes and the prophet admonishes us to not distinguish in the attention we give to them, then is there any fundamental distinction between the classes?

Sins against others should be openly confessed

Maimonides makes a remarkable comment in his discussion of repentance that suggests a fundamental distinction between these two classes of commandments. Repentance is an obligation and privilege. One who sins is required to repent and therefore, it is an obligation. However, it is also a privilege. Through repentance a person may atone for one's sins.[21] Part of the process of repentance is the verbal declaration of one's specific sin and one's commitment to repentance. Maimonides explains that it is appropriate for this declaration – *vidui* – to be made publicly. In other words, one should willingly and publicly acknowledge one's failings. Maimonides adds that this applies only to sins committed against one's fellow. However, one should not publicly declare sins committed against Hashem. A public declaration of one's sins against Hashem is regarded as arrogant. These sins, a person should privately acknowledge and declare.[22]

The difficulty with these comments is obvious. All commandments – those that address our relationship with Hashem and those dealing with our interpersonal relationships – are derived from a single source. All are included in the Torah's 613 *mitzvot*. All are commandments of Hashem. When one sins against another human being, one concurrently sins against Hashem. How can Maimonides distinguish between these two classes and require that those committed against Hashem should be privately confessed and sins committed against our fellow should be publicly declared? The sin committed against our fellow is also a sin against Hashem!

We are directly responsible to one another

Maimonides is communicating a profound message. He is explaining to us that although Hashem is the source and legislator of all commandments, there is a difference between those *mitzvot* that are *ben adam le'chavero* and those that are *ben adam la'makom*. In legislating commandments that are *ben adam le'chavro,* Hashem made us directly responsible for our actions to our fellow. Therefore, when we violate one of these *mitzvot*, the Torah treats the sin as directly against another human being and only indirectly against Hashem.

Let's use an illustration to clarify this distinction. The CEO of a corporation appoints an executive who will oversee marketing. This director of marketing heads a department with many employees. To whom are these employees responsible? It is true that the authority of the department head is derived from his appointment by the CEO. However, these employees are not directly responsible to the CEO. They are directly responsible to their department head and only indirectly responsible to the CEO.

---

[21] Repentance alone atones for some sins. For other sins, repentance atones when combined with other measures. However, in all cases repentance is an essential component of the atonement process. See Maimonides, *Mishne Torah*, Hilchot Teshuvah 1:4.
[22] Rabbaynu Moshe ben Maimon (Rambam) *Mishne Torah*, Hilchot Teshuvah 2:5.

This illustration demonstrates the principle Maimonides is applying. One who is in authority can endow another with authority over others. Once this is done, these others will become directly responsible to the endowed person and only indirectly to the higher authority. Hashem endowed every human being with rights, responsibilities toward others, and privileges. When we violate the rights of another, act irresponsibly toward another, or deprive another of one's privileges, then we have violated our obligations toward this individual. Hashem made us directly responsible to our fellow human being.

When we sin against Hashem, we do not publicly advertise our wrongdoing. When we sin against an individual, we have sinned against Hashem as well but not directly. Directly, we have sinned against an individual whom Hashem has endowed with rights and privileges and in regard to whom we have been negligent. Therefore, when we repent we give precedence to the wrong directly committed. We publicly confess and declare our sin.[23]

The requirement to actively seek the forgiveness of one whom we wrong

This comment of Maimonides explains another interesting law of repentance. When a person sins against another, one must secure the wronged party's pardon. This applies even if there are other penalties. In other words, even if one must make payment to the injured party, this payment does not suffice to atone for the wrongdoing. The sinner must make the required payment and also secure the pardon of the wronged individual.

This requirement is completely reasonable. However, there is a further requirement. The sinner must appease the injured party. He must ask for his pardon. In other words, it seems that if the injured party spontaneously forgives the one who wronged him, the sin is not atoned. Atonement requires that the sinner reach out to the injured party and seek forgiveness.[24]

This requirement seems strange. If the injured party freely and fully forgives the person who has wronged him, why is this not adequate? Why must the sinner sue for forgiveness? The explanation emerges from Maimonides' understanding of *ben adam le'chavero* commandments. These commandments make us directly responsible to one another. When one sins against another, one neglects this responsibility. Atonement is achieved only when the sinner acknowledges and renews one's acceptance of this responsibility. When the injured party spontaneously forgives his antagonist, this requirement has not been met. The sinner has not restored his commitment to his responsibilities toward others. Only when the sinner seeks the pardon of the wronged person, does he redress his neglect of his responsibilities toward others.[25]

In summary, the classification of commandments as *ben adam le'chavero* is not superficial. It expresses a profound message. We are not only responsible to Hashem. Hashem

---

[23] This has long been my understanding of Maimonides' comments. However, I am pleased to have recently heard a similar interpretation of these comments from Rav Yisrael Chait in a recorded lecture.

[24] Rabbaynu Moshe ben Maimon (Rambam) *Mishne Torah*, Hilchot Teshuvah 2:9.

[25] Maimonides begins his discussion of this issue by commenting that when one sins against another, repentance and observance of Yom Kippur do not secure atonement. This comment is consistent with and indicative of his understanding of *ben adam le'chavero* commandments. He is explaining that although every sin is a violation of Hashem's will and requires reconciliation with Hashem, a sin that is *ben adam le'chavero*, directly violates our relationship to another individual. Therefore, reconciling oneself with Hashem cannot, alone, atone for such a sin.

endows human beings with rights, privileges, and responsibilities to one another. When we violate one of the *ben adam le'chavero* commandments, we have sinned against Hashem; He legislates all commandments. However, we have also sinned against a person endowed by Hashem with rights and privileges, and we have disregarded our responsibilities toward this person. We can only redress this wrong through restoring our relationship with this person and renewing our acceptance of our duties toward others. This requires our active pursuit of reconciliation.

And these are the laws that you should place before them. (Shemot 21:1)
Thou Shall Not Steal and Other Vague Platitudes

1. The laws of the *parasha* are derived from Sinai

The commandments of the Torah can be divided into two groups – commandments that speak to our relationship with Hashem and those that regulate our relationships with other people. The major portion of Parashat Mishpatim is devoted predominately to laws that are from this second group.

The above passage introduces the laws of the *parasha*. This introductory passage is atypical. Generally, in introducing Hashem's communication of laws to Moshe, a different introductory phrase is employed. The more common introduction is "And Hashem spoke to Moshe saying: Speak to Bnai Yisrael" followed by the specific commandments communicated to Moshe. Our Sages note our *parasha's* departure from this formula and analyze it in detail.

Rashi begins his analysis of the passage by noting it states "*And* these are the laws." He quotes the midrash's comment that the conjunction "and" suggests a common characteristic shared by the laws presented in the *parasha* and those previously discussed. What is this common characteristic? The midrash responds that the laws in the last *parasha* – presumably the laws in the Decalogue – are derived from Sinai. The conjunction informs us that the laws being introduced are also derived from Sinai.[26]

This is a remarkable interpretation of the intent of the conjunction! Rashi points out elsewhere in his commentary that all of the *mitzvot* of the Torah are derived from Sinai.[27] In quoting the midrash's interpretation of the conjunction, he is suggesting that in this instance we would not apply this generality. Because we would not naturally assume that the laws in the *parasha* are derived from Sinai, the conjunction is required. The conjunction informs us that these laws are to be included in the general assumption. These laws are also derived from Sinai.

What is special about these laws? Why would we assume that they are not derived from Sinai? Why does the Torah specifically alert us that these laws are derived from Sinai? Divrei David offers an interesting response to this question. His response requires a more careful analysis of the type of laws discussed in our *parasha*.

When you acquire a Hebrew manservant he shall serve for six years and in the seventh year he shall go free without making payment. (Shemot 21:2)

2. The laws of the *parasha* regulate civil and commercial interactions

---

[26] Rabbaynu Shlomo ben Yitzchak (Rashi), *Commentary on Sefer Shemot* 21:1.
[27] Rabbaynu Shlomo ben Yitzchak (Rashi), *Commentary on Sefer BeMidbar* 25:1.

The above passage initiates the first section of laws in the *parasha*. This section regulates the treatment of male and female bond servants. The section discusses the rights of these servants, the length of period of their servitude, and responsibilities of the master. Divrei David points out that an individual may never put to practice the laws discussed in this section. If one never acquires a bond servant, then one does not become involved in the laws regulating the master-servant relationship. Divrei David notes that most of the laws in the portion introduced by the *parasha's* first passage are of this type. They discuss laws related to situations that a person may or may not encounter in practice. For example, the section includes laws that define the responsibilities of a borrower for the borrowed object. The payments for various types of damages to another's property or person are enumerated.

Rav Yosef Dov Soloveitchik *Zt"l* makes a related and similar observation regarding the content of the portion. He explains that in this section, the Torah does not focus primarily on moral imperatives. Instead, its focus is the laws that regulate interpersonal and commercial relationships. Few, if any, statements of moral and ethical expectations or admonitions to conduct ourselves ethically are included.[28]

Divrei David suggests that this is the reason one might assume that this content was not derived from Sinai. One might assume that Revelation was devoted to imperatives. We might assume that at Sinai, Hashem outlined for us standards that encompass our religious behavior and interpersonal relations. We would assume that the mundane details contained in Parshat Mishpatim are not part of Revelation.[29]

And Moshe came into the cloud. He ascended the mountain. And Moshe was upon the mountain forty days and forty nights. (Shemot 24:18)

3. The sequence of Revelation

Rabbaynu Ovadia Bertinoro offers an alternative explanation of Rashi's comment. Before considering his explanation the sequence of events that took place at the Sinai Revelation must be reviewed.

Prior to the pronouncement of the statements of the Decalogue, Moshe ascended Sinai. When Hashem communicated the contents of the Decalogue, the people were assembled at the base of the mountain and Moshe was upon the mountain. After the contents of the Decalogue were revealed to the people and to Moshe, he descended the mountain. The closing portion of Parshat Mishpatim explains that upon his descent Moshe told the people that they were invited to enter into a covenant with Hashem. The people declared their desire to bind themselves to Hashem in this covenant. Moshe completed the execution of the covenant.

As explained in the above passage, after execution of the covenant, Moshe was again summoned to the mountain. He ascended and remained on the mountain for forty days and nights. During this period Hashem communicated to Moshe the commandments and laws of the Torah.

Rashi quotes the midrash. The midrash explains that the conjunction "and" communicates that the laws in the opening section of the *parasha* are like the laws of the Decalogue. Both are

---

[28] Rav Yosef Dov Soloveitchik, Recorded lecture on the *parasha*.
[29] Rabbaynu David ben HaRav Shemuel HaLeyve *Divrei David Torai Zahav*, (Mosad HaRav Kook, 1978), p 452.

derived from Sinai. Bertinoro explains that the midrash does not mean that the laws of Parshat Mishpatim were communicated to Moshe during the forty days and nights that were initiated after execution of the covenant. The midrash means that these laws were communicated along with the Decalogue. In other words, after Hashem pronounced the contents of the Decalogue, Moshe did not immediately descend from the mountain. Instead, he remained upon the mountain. At that time Hashem communicated to him these laws.[30]

> And Moshe came and he told to the nation all of the words of Hashem and all of the laws. And the entire nation responded in a single voice and they said: All of the things that Hashem has spoken we will do. (Shemot 24:3)

4. The laws of the *parasha* accompanied the Decalogue

The comments of Bertinoro are consistent with the narrative of the Torah. In the above passage, Moshe communicates to the people the laws described in the opening portion of the *parasha*. The people accept the responsibility to observe these laws and all of the words of Hashem. Moshe then executes the covenant and ascends the mountain for forty days and nights. It is clear from the narrative that the laws described earlier in the *parasha* were communicated to Moshe before he returned to the mountain for forty days and nights. When were these laws communicated? According to Bertinoro, the answer is simple. They were given to Moshe immediately after the Decalogue.[31] This is the message intended by the midrash. These laws are not like all of the other laws derived from Sinai. These laws were communicated in conjunction with the Decalogue.

Why are these laws so important? As Divrei David observes, this section of laws does not focus on ethical imperatives. Its focus is regulation of civil and commercial relationships. Why was Moshe not permitted to return to the people and initiate them into the covenant with Hashem until he had received these laws and taught them to the people?

5. Transforming platitudes into meaningful directives

A comment of Nachmanides is relevant to this issue. He explains that the laws of the *parasha* are directly related to the Decalogue. The Decalogue commands us to not covet that which is our neighbor's. This imperative presumes that one has a clear understanding of the laws that regulate ownership of property. If I am not to covet my neighbor's property, I must know the laws that determine the extent and limits of his property.[32]

Nachmanides seems to suggest that the admonitions of the Decalogue are not meaningful in themselves. Ethical admonitions are not meaningful unless they are supported by laws that regulate relationships. Without these laws the ethical admonitions are reduced to platitudes. A few examples will illustrate this point.

---

[30] Rabbaynu Ovadia Bertinoro, *Commentary Amar Neke on Rashi*, Sefer Shemot 21:1.

[31] These passages are consistent with Bertinoro's opinion but do not prove his contention that these laws were given in conjunction with the Decalogue. Torah Shelymah notes that according to a number of Sages the laws outlined in the *parasha* and communicated to the people before Moshe returned to the mountain were not yet derived from Sinai. Instead, these laws predated Sinai. They had been communicated to Moshe and taught to the people soon after their departure from Egypt. These laws were among the body of laws communicated to Moshe at Marah.

[32] Rabbaynu Moshe ben Nachman (Ramban), *Commentary on Sefer Shemot* 21:1.

We are commanded to not steal. Virtually every reasonable person accepts this commandment as an essential ethical expectation. Yet, this does not mean that we do not steal. Some individuals cheat on their taxes. Many of us would acknowledge taking a sheaf of paper from the office for personal use. We do not engage in these activities because we reject the ethical expectation to not steal. We simply have trouble with "gray areas" and we persuade ourselves that these activities are not contrary to the ethical imperative.

We all accept the commandment to not murder. This is a universal ethic accepted even by those who are completely secular. Yet, society debates the morality of abortion and euthanasia. This is not because those favoring liberal attitudes toward abortion and euthanasia reject the immorality of murder. They do not believe that these actions are murder.

6. The character of the Torah was communicated to the nation

Moshe descended from Sinai after the Decalogue was declared with the laws of our *parasha*. These laws are not statements of ethical imperatives. They regulate human interaction. These laws provide meaning and give substance to the moral imperatives of the Decalogue. These laws transform the Decalogue from a statement of platitudes into a meaningful code of ethics.

It was essential that Moshe communicate these laws to the people before they entered into a covenant with Hashem. This covenant was a commitment to observe the laws of the Torah. The Decalogue, in itself, did not communicate to the people the character of Torah. Much of the Decalogue is composed of laws that are universally accepted standards of behavior. Hashem gave to Moshe the laws of our *parasha*. He directed Moshe to teach these laws to the people before inviting them into the covenant. These laws gave meaning and substance to the imperatives of the Decalogue. After Moshe taught these laws to the people, they understood that the Torah is not composed of platitudes but that it is a meaningful code of ethical, moral and religious behavior.

"If he came alone, he will leave alone. If he is married, his wife leaves with him." (Shemot 21:3)

This pasuk discusses the eved ivri the Jewish slave. This law applies to a person who steals and cannot make restitution. The court has the authority to sell the person into slavery in order to pay his debt. The master of the slave the eved is permitted to give the servant a non-Jewish maidservant as a wife. Any children resulting from this union are the property of the master and are born into servitude. Our pasuk restricts the rights of the master to provide the Jewish eved with a non-Jewish maidservant. If he is already married, at the time that he enters into servitude, the master may provide the eved with a maidservant. However, if he is not married, the master may not give the servant a maidservant wife. This lesson is communicated through the phrase, "if he came alone, he will leave alone". The meaning of this phrase is that if the entered servitude unmarried, he must remain unmarried. The master may not provide the eved with a maidservant. The usual term for "alone" is levad. Our pasuk does not use this term. Instead, it uses the term begapo. The commentaries differ on the exact meaning of this term. Rashi maintains that it means, "with his garment, alone". In other words, if he entered servitude with his garment, alone without a wife, he may not be given a maidservant wife. Rabbaynu Avraham ibn Ezra disagrees with this interpretation of begapo. He asserts that the term means with his body. In other words, if he entered slavery with only his body without a wife, the master may not provide him with a maidservant.

We can more fully understand the dispute between Rashi and ibn Ezra through analyzing this prohibition. Let us first consider Rashi's interpretation. Rashi maintains that begapo means with only his clothing. It seems that the term alludes to poverty. What is the relationship between poverty and the restriction against providing the eved with a maidservant? The Torah regards servitude as an undesirable state. It is permitted under specific circumstances. However, it is not encouraged. The Torah provides a deterrent through eliminating any positive elements from servitude. Consider a person entering servitude without a wife. His life is incomplete. In this sense, he is impoverished. The master cannot provide this eved with a wife. This would improve the servant's life. He now would have a wife. The servant would benefit from his servitude. This cannot be permitted. Ibn Ezra seems to understand the issue differently. According to him, begapo is a direct reference to the servant entering servitude without a wife. Basically, the pasuk is stating that the master may not provide the eved with a maidservant as a sole wife. We must consider the difference between a maidservant who is a sole wife and one who is a second wife.

If the slave enters servitude with a wife, he already has a companion. He is already bound by obligations to his existing wife and family. The master may provide this eved with a maidservant. In contrast, an eved without a family, lacks this foundation. He is unconnected to any existing family structure. If he is permitted to live with a maidservant, this union will become his family. The Torah allows the eved to live with a maidservant. However, apparently the Torah does not wish to encourage a strong bond between these partners. This is because she lacks the complete sanctity of a Jew. If the eved has an appropriate wife, we can hope that a strong bond will not develop with the maidservant. However, without a pre-existing family, the eved cannot live with a maidservant. This is because he can easily develop a permanent relationship with her.

If you buy a Hebrew servant, six years he shall serve; and in the seventh he shall go out free for nothing. If he comes in by himself, he shall go out by himself; if he is married, then his wife shall go out with him. If his master gives him a wife, and she bears him sons or daughters; the wife and her children shall be her master's, and he shall go out by himself. (Shemot 21:2-4)

Contemplations of the Life of a Slave

1. The basic laws of a Jewish servant

Parshat Mishpatim opens by outlining the laws governing the treatment of Jewish servants. There are two ways in which a Jewish person can enter into servitude. First, a person who steals and is unable to make restitution may be sold by the court. Second, a person may sell himself into servitude. This is permitted only if the person is completely destitute and has no other alternative. In either instance, the person must enter into the service of a fellow Jew and not a non-Jew.

Three basic laws are derived from the above passages. First, whether the person is sold by the court or sells himself, the period of service is for no longer than six years. With the onset of the seventh year, the servant is liberated.[33]

Second, the master of the servant may assign to him a non-Jewish servant with whom to procreate. The offspring of this union will be regarded as the children of their mother and share her status as non-Jewish servants.[34] There is an important qualification to this law. The servant may be given a servant- mate only if he enters into servitude with a wife and child. However, if he is unattached when he enters servitude, the master may not assign a servant-mate to the servant.[35]

Third, at the end of his period of servitude, the servant leaves behind his servant-mate and any biological children that were produced by their union.

The Torah's legitimization of the institution of servitude presents many questions. Perhaps, the most troubling aspect of the institution is the union between the servant and a non-Jewish woman servant. The Torah requires that we marry within our nation and not take a spouse from without. It is remarkable that in this instance, the master may ignore this restriction and that the Jewish servant is required to obey his master's directive. Furthermore, it is strange that this law applies only to the man entering servitude with a wife and child. Why is having an existing family a prerequisite for being assigned a non-Jewish servant-mate? Moreover, as will be shown, the Torah's attitude to this strange union is ambiguous and confusing.

But if the servant shall plainly say: I love my master, my wife, and my children; I will not go out free;then his master shall bring him unto the judges, and shall bring him to the door, or unto the door-post; and his master shall bore his ear through with an awl; and he shall serve him forever.
(Shemot 21:5-6)

2. The servant who wishes to extend his period of servitude

The above passages explain that the period of servitude can be extended beyond six years. A servant who wishes to extend his servitude beyond six years is taken to court. There, his ear is pierced. With the taking of this measure, his servitude is extended to the Jubilee year – the *Yovel*. With the arrival of the *Yovel*, the servant's freedom is restored whether or not he wishes so.

Why would a person wish to extend his servitude beyond the required period? The passages address this issue. As explained above, when one leaves servitude, he is required to abandon his servant-mate and the children of that union. This may be a heart-rending expectation that the servant is unwilling to accept upon himself. Second, he may have developed a very close relationship with his master and not wish to be separated from him. The Torah is very solicitous of the rights of the servant. A considerable set of laws regulate the master's treatment of his

---

[33] Rashi, Shemot 21:2 explains that the above passages are dealing with the laws governing a person sold into servitude by the court. However, he maintains that the six-year limit on the period of servitude applies also to a person who sells himself into servitude. The Sages actually dispute this issue. Maimonides adopts the position that a person who sells himself into servitude may bind himself to his master for a longer period (Hilchot Avadim 2:3).

[34] This law applies to a person sold into servitude by the court. Some Sages extend it to a person who sold himself. Maimonides rules that a non-Jewish servant is forbidden to a person who sells himself into servitude (Hilchot Avadim 3:3).

[35] Rabbaynu Moshe ben Maimon (Rambam) *Mishne Torah*, Hilchot Avadim 3:4. Rashi, Shemot 21:3 notes that the servant must enter servitude with a wife but does not mention that he must also have children.

servant. These laws are designed to assure that the master cares for his servant's welfare. Also, he is forbidden to oppress the servant or to subject him to unreasonable labors. This combination of care and reasonable labor may be an improvement over the servant's previous condition. He may not be eager to return to the challenges that previously overwhelmed him.

The passages do not provide much insight into the significance of piercing the servant's ear. However, Rashi explains that the pierced ear is intended to be a sign of disgrace.[36] In other words, although the servant is permitted to extend his period of servitude, he is discouraged from doing so.

The Torah's negative attitude toward servitude becomes even more pronounced with the arrival of the *Yovel*. As explained, at the arrival of the *Yovel*, the servant must leave his master. His freedom is restored whether or not he seeks it. The Talmud explains that the master is even permitted to use force in ejecting his former servant from his home. If in the course of using necessary force the servant is harmed, the master is not held responsible. The Talmud explains that the reason the master is permitted to resort to force is that the servant is now forbidden to continue his relationship with his servant-mate. The master is acting properly using force to separate these parties.[37] It is amazing that the strange relationship between the servant and the non-Jewish mate was initially permitted and with the arrival of the *Yovel* is regarded with such extreme disfavor that the master may use force to terminate it!

For unto Me the children of Israel are servants; they are My servants whom I brought forth out of the land of Egypt: I am Hashem your G-d. (VaYikra 25:55)

3. The problem with servitude

Let us put aside our questions regarding the Torah's strange attitude toward the servant's union with a non-Jewish mate, and more carefully consider its attitude toward the basic institution of servitude. It is clear from the above discussion that the Torah's attitude is measured and nuanced. Servitude is permitted and even utilized by the courts. However, its nature and duration are carefully restricted. The welfare of the servant is protected by a body of regulations. The duration is restricted to six years. It may be extended at the insistence of the servant, but he is discouraged with the threat of stigmatization. In no event, may he enter into a permanent state of servitude. With the Yovel, he is liberated – even against his will.

These various aspects of the institution suggest that the Torah viewed servitude as an innately destructive state – dangerous for both the master and servant. Yet, in some instances the state is justified or even required. Servitude is treated like a form of chemotherapy. It is terribly toxic. But it may save the life of a cancer patient.

Rashi identifies the reason for the Torah's cautious attitude toward servitude. Every person should respond to a single master – Hashem. A servant has a second master.[38] Both from a practical and from the psychological perspective, his devotion to Hashem as his sole master are compromised. Psychologically, his master assumes the role of a powerful authority in his life. Practically, he cannot devote himself to the development of his relationship with Hashem. He has given up control over his own life and placed in the hands of another.[39]

---

[36] Rabbaynu Shlomo ben Yitzchak (Rashi), *Commentary on Sefer Shemot* 21:6.
[37] Mesechet Baba Kamma 28a.
[38] Rabbaynu Shlomo ben Yitzchak (Rashi), *Commentary on Sefer Shemot* 21:6.

Why did the Torah allow servitude? Apparently, it is only permitted as a rehabilitative measure. Because it is intended as a rehabilitative measure, it must be temporary. Its goal is to address the behaviors and attitudes, the personal chaos, and desperation that led to either abject poverty or crime. The goal is to return the servant to the normative state – personal freedom. When the servant seeks to extend his servitude, he is defeating its very purpose.

In short, a healthy person devotes oneself to a personal mission and journey of ongoing spiritual development – a journey to come closer to G-d. Freedom provides the opportunity to pursue this mission and travel on this journey. Servitude diverts a person from this mission and journey.

> ... that you may remember and do all My commandments, and be sacred unto your G-d. I am Hashem your G-d, who brought you out of the Land of Egypt, to be your G-d: I am Hashem your G-d. (BeMidbar 15:40-41)

4. The servant's relationship with his servant-mate is biological

Understanding the phenomenon of the servant's non-Jewish mate requires that we refocus on two essential details. First, this relationship is only permitted when the servant enters servitude with a family to whom he is attached and bound. He will remain the father and husband in that family during his period of servitude and beyond. Second, the servant who is assigned a non-Jewish servant-mate will procreate with that partner but he will never succeed in creating a family. He cannot marry this non-Jewish partner. The children will be his biological offspring but *halachah* will not recognize a familial relationship between them. They will be servants, like their mother. They will not be his true children or he their father.

What is the nature of the relationship between the servant and this servant-mate? What is its tenor and meaning? It is not a family. It is more a biological relationship than a spiritual union. It is pitted against the family life that the servant enjoys with his true wife and family. It is a comparison that is intended to demonstrate its shallowness when compared to his life in his real family. The intent is to frame the relationship with the servant-mate as reflecting a loss of dignity and a commentary on the servant's humanity.

This relationship communicates a very powerful message. The servant is a diminished individual. He cannot devote himself to the mission and journey that is the foundation of our humanity. His sacredness as a member of the nation of Israel is compromised by his servitude. Because of the compromise of his sanctity, this relationship with the servant-mate becomes permitted. This biological relationship is permitted and appropriate because the loss of personal freedom must be understood and recognized as a terrible defect in one's humanity. On the continuum of lifestyles between human and beast this person has moved closer toward the lifestyle of the beast.

5. Choosing freedom in our own lives

We are not servants. However, we do make decisions that impact our personal freedom. The lesson of this Torah section is that we must set priorities. We need to ask ourselves difficult questions and answer them honestly. What are our lives about? What do we expect to accomplish? Do we have the freedom to achieve our goals or have we accepted upon ourselves

---

[39] For more thorough discussion of this issue see Rav Reuven Mann, *Eved Ivri*, TTL C-056.

masters who divert us from our missions and journeys? Do we have the courage to reject those masters?

And his master shall bring him close to the judges. And he shall bring him close to the door or to the doorpost. And he shall pierce his ear with an awl. And he will be his slave forever. (Shemot 21:6)

The Piercing of the Indentured Servant's Ear

The Jewish indentured servant slave serves his master for six years. At the end of this period the master must free the servant. If the servant refuses to leave his master, servitude may be extended until the *Yoval* – the Jubilee Year. A specific ceremony must be followed to extend the period of indenture. The servant is taken to the court by his master. The master then pierces the ear of the servant at the doorpost.

Rashi explains the meaning of this ceremony. There are two circumstances that can initially lead to bondage. A man steals and cannot make restitution. He is sold into bondage. The proceeds are delivered, by the court, to the victim of the theft. Alternatively, extreme destitution can lead to bondage. In such desperate circumstances a person may sell himself. If, after the initial term, the servant chooses to renew his status as an indentured servant, his ear is pierced. This applies to both situations.

Rashi explains that the piercing of the servant's ear communicates a symbolic message. The basic message is that the servant was inattentive to the commandments revealed at Sinai. However, the message's specific details differ according to the circumstances that led to the servant's descent into bondage. In the case of the person who sold himself in response to poverty, the piercing recalls that at Sinai, he heard Hashem state that we are His servants. This person elected to enter into bondage. His duty to exclusively serve Hashem was disregarded. He placed himself under the authority of a human master. The indentured servant who entered bondage as a consequence of stealing was inattentive to a different commandment. At Sinai we were commanded not to steal. He disregarded this command.

The doorpost is also a symbol. In Egypt the Jews placed the blood of the *Pesach* sacrifice upon their doorposts. Hashem passed over these homes and did not afflict them with the plague of the firstborn. Through this act of compassion, Hashem earned the devotion of His people. The individual who sells himself into bondage compromises his devotion to G-d. As a slave, he must split his devotion between Hashem and a human master.[40]

Rashi's moving explanation is appropriate in the instance of a person who willingly sells himself. A person who sells himself out of desperation does not immediately deserve to be punished; desperation drove him to this choice. However, the decision to extend his bondage indicates a moral failing. At this point, his servitude must be stigmatized. The servant must be discouraged from electing to extend his period of service to a human master. At the moment he is prepared to enter into this extended service, his ear is pierced.

However, Rashi's explanation is difficult to understand in the case of the thief. In this instance, the piercing of the servant's ear is a reference to his disregard of the prohibition against stealing. This crime was committed long ago—before he entered bondage. If we wish to remind

---

[40] Rabbaynu Shlomo ben Yitzchak (Rashi), *Commentary on Sefer Shemot* 21:6.

the servant of his crime, the piercing should be done when the servitude is initiated. Why wait until the slave renews his bondage to teach this lesson?

It seems that Rashi is providing an important insight. The thief is sold into slavery in order to pay his debt to the victim. But bondage is not only a practical means to provide restitution to the victim, it is also intended as a punishment for the criminal. The decision of the slave to renew his status indicates that this purpose was not fulfilled. The thief was comfortable with bondage. Servitude had been a positive experience. The status can be continued, but only after a stronger stigma has been attached to the servitude. The ear is pierced to place a mark upon him that signifies he has disregarded the law of the Torah. Hopefully, with this added stigma, servitude will not be as pleasant. The criminal will experience a consequence.

Rashi's comments are now clear. The piercing of the ear of the thief is a reference to the moral failing in the past. However, this punishment was not originally deemed necessary. The servitude alone should have served as adequate punishment. But the thief did not perceive his status as an indentured servant as a negative consequence. The servant must be punished anew for his crime. This is done by further stigmatizing the status he seeks to perpetuate.

And regarding he that did not hunt his victim and the L-rd caused it to happen, I will assign to you a place to which he may flee. (Shemot 21:13)

Punishing the Guilty while Protecting the Innocent

The punishment for murder is death. If a life is taken by accident, the punishment is exile. Specific cities for exiles are designated throughout the land of Israel. The killer must flee to one of these refuges.

Rashi, in explaining this *pasuk*, quotes an enigmatic teaching of the Sages. The *pasuk* refers to accidental killing as an event caused by G-d. Why does Hashem cause such a tragedy? Our Sages responded by constructing a scenario in which the accident is an expression of divine justice. In this scenario, one person murders another, and a second kills another person by accident. In both cases there were no witnesses. Neither crime is punished by the courts. Hashem arranges for the individual responsible for the accidental death to climb a ladder. The murderer is maneuvered by Hashem into a position under the ladder. A rung breaks. The climber falls and lands upon the hapless fellow below. The murdered is killed in the accident. There are witnesses present. The climber will now be required to flee to a city of refuge. Justice has been served. The murderer has been executed. The accidental killer is exiled.[41] What is the message of the teaching? What is the lesson our Sages are delivering through this story?

Any legal system is faced with a conflict. There must be law and order. Criminals must be punished. If there is no consequence for evil, crime is encouraged. Yet, the rights of the individual must be protected. Care must be taken not to wrongfully punish the innocent. It often seems impossible to protect the citizens of society from harm and, simultaneously, respect the rights of the defendant.

The Torah gives priority to protecting the innocent. The laws of evidence are very strict. Two witnesses are required to determine the guilt of a defendant. These witnesses are carefully

---

[41] Rabbaynu Shlomo ben Yitzchak (Rashi), *Commentary on Sefer Shemot* 21:13.

and completely cross-examined. As a result of these strict requirements, executions were uncommon. It is very likely that this extreme caution resulted in many criminals eluding the justice of the courts. How are the citizens of society protected from these freed criminals?

This is the issue our Sages are addressing. The conflict between the safety of society and the rights of the defendant cannot be resolved. A court system, alone, cannot simultaneously accomplish both goals. A choice must be made. The Torah teaches that the rights of the individual take precedence. The defendant cannot be punished if a possible doubt exits concerning guilt. Yet, we are assured that the guilty will not avoid punishment. Hashem will punish those who are beyond the reach of the courts. We are required to carry out justice to the best of our ability. If we execute this responsibility, Hashem will punish those who escape human justice.

If he gets up and goes outside under his own power, the one who struck him is absolved. He shall only pay for his lost time and he shall provide for his healing. (Shemot 21:19)

The Boundaries of Our Reliance on Hashem

Parshat Mishpatim outlines many of the laws regulating liability for causing harm to a person or his property. If a person harms another individual he must make restitution to the injured party. Our pasuk indicates two forms of restitution. The injured party is entitled to be reimbursed for his lost wages. The person causing the injury is also responsible for all medical expenses.

The Talmud comments that from this passage we learn that it is permitted for a medical professional to provide medical care.[42] The commentaries are concerned with an obvious problem with this comment. According to the Talmud, it is not self-evident that a physician is permitted to provide treatment to those who are ill. In other words, the Talmud implies that without the express instructions included in this passage, we are to assume that it is not permitted to provide medical treatment! Why would we assume that medical treatment would not be appropriate?

Rashi explains that the comments of the Talmud are not limited to a physician who provides care for an injury inflicted by another individual. Instead, the comments of the Talmud must be understood in a more general sense. The Talmud is telling us that a physician is permitted to provide treatment even in a case in which the patient has become spontaneously ill. Based on this understanding of the Talmud's comments, Rashi identifies the issue with which the Sages are grappling. Some may assume that a spontaneous illness is an expression of Hashem's will; Hashem wishes the person to be stricken with this illness. Consequently, the person's recovery should also be left to Hashem. By providing medical treatment, the physician is usurping Hashem's role and interfering with His plan. In order to avoid having people make these dangerous assumptions, the Talmud tells us that we are not to make this argument. Instead, the physician is permitted to provide treatment to those whose illness is not caused by the hands of another.[43]

---

[42] Meschet Baba Kamma 85a.
[43] R' Shlomo ben Yitzchak (Rashi), *Commentary on the Talmud,* Mesechet Baba Kamma 85a.

According to Rashi, the Talmud is telling us that we are not to assume that we should leave to Hashem the recovery of a person who is ailing. Instead, it is appropriate to provide medical treatment. However, Rashi's comments raise an additional question. Rashi is asserting that without the direct instructions of the Torah permitting medical treatment, we would reason that the recovery of the person should be left to Hashem. The Torah tells us that this reasoning is somehow incorrect. But Rashi does not provide any indication of *why* the Torah does permit the physician to provide treatment. In other words, Rashi identifies the prima-facie reasoning for denying treatment, yet he does not identify the flaw in this reasoning. Rashi only tells us that the Torah rejects this reasoning.

Nachmanides discusses this issue. According to Nachmanides, this discussion in the Talmud provides an insight into the Torah's understanding of the role of providence. Nachmanides explains that the Torah expects us to conduct ourselves in accordance with the natural laws. The laws of the Torah are constructed to be observed within the framework of the natural law that Hashem created to govern His universe. Torah law does not contradict or ignore the laws of nature. Therefore, it is appropriate to respond to illness through a physician's medical treatment. We are to live our lives in a manner that is consistent with the natural laws that govern the universe. We are to care for our health properly and medical treatment is appropriate when we are ill.[44]

Kitzur Shulchan Aruch further develops Nachmanides' comments. He explains that based on Nachmanides' reasoning, it is incumbent upon a person who is ill to seek the treatment of a physician and it is prohibited to not seek this treatment. He explains that there is a well-known principle that we are not permitted to rely on miracles. A person who does not seek medical treatment violates this principle.

Kitzur Shulchan Aruch explains that there is another reason for requiring a person who is ill to seek medical treatment. This second reason is also based on a comment of Nachmanides. Nachmandies points out the Torah does promise that Hashem will care for those who are righteous. Nachmanides explains that Hashem does perform miracles for the righteous.[45] Kitzur Shulchan Aruch explains that a person who refrains from consulting a physician and instead relies on Hashem's intervention is making the implicit assumption that he is a righteous person deserving of a miracle. Kitzur Shulchan Aruch points out that this is a shockingly haughty attitude. The Torah distains haughtiness and requires that we conduct ourselves with humility. Humility demands that we do not regard ourselves as *tzadikim* – as righteous people deserving of a miracle from Hashem.[46]

This discussion suggests an important question. According to these authorities it is appropriate – even required – for a person who is ill to seek medical treatment. What, then, is the role of prayer? If we are expected to conduct ourselves within the laws of nature and we are prohibited from relying on Hashem's intervention, why pray? When we pray, are we not asking Hashem to intervene – on our behalf – in His natural order? Are we not asking for a miracle?

Rabbaynu Ovadia Sforno discusses this issue in his commentary on Parshat VaYetzai. The Torah explains that Rachel – Yaakov's wife – was unable to conceive. However, in response to her

---

[44] Rabbaynu Moshe ben Nachman (Ramban), *Commentary on Sefer VaYikra* 26:11.
[45] Rabbaynu Moshe ben Nachman (Ramban), *Commentary on Sefer VaYikra* 26:11.
[46] Rav Shlomo Ganzfried, *Kitzur Shulchan Aruch* 192:3.

prayer, she conceived and gave birth to Yosef.⁴⁷ Sforno observes that Hashem only responded to Rachel's prayers after she had endeavored to do everything in her own power to conceive.⁴⁸ In other words, Hashem responded to prayers that were accompanied by personal endeavor and initiative – not to prayer alone.

Sforno's analysis suggests an explanation of the role of prayer. We do not replace with prayer our own efforts to assure our well-being. Instead, prayer accompanies our efforts. We do not pray in place of our own endeavors; we pray for the success of these endeavors.

Rabbaynu David Kimchi's, RaDaK, comments on a related issue used to further develop this theme. He indicates that although in seeking Hashem's aid we are asking for His intervention into the natural law, we should seek to minimize this intervention. He explains that when Hashem deems it necessary to perform a miracle, He does so minimally. He also prefers to hide His work. Hashem regards hidden miracles as preferable to astounding wonders. RaDaK cites various examples to prove his point. Hashem commanded Shemuel the prophet to anoint David as the new king of Bnai Yisrael. Shemuel realized that Shaul – the current king – would feel threatened and would make every effort to stop Shemuel from fulfilling his mission. Hashem instructed Shemuel to conceal his intent from Shaul. Hashem would make sure that Shaul did not stop Shemuel from fulfilling his mission. But Hashem preferred to do so by quietly working behind the scenes. He wished to avoid an open confrontation that would require an explicit miracle. RaDaK summarizes his thesis. Hashem prefers to clothe His miracles within the pattern of natural events rather than overtly overturn natural patterns.⁴⁹

Similarly, when we pray, we acknowledge that all of our efforts cannot assure the recovery of the person who is ill. Only Hashem can assure this recovery. But even in seeking Hashem's intervention, we are required to minimize the necessary intervention. We must make every possible effort to seek the appropriate treatment for the person who is ill and then we pray to Hashem for the success of these efforts. Through combining our personal endeavors with prayer, we are seeking to minimize any necessary intervention.

Why are minimal interventions into the laws of nature preferable to overt miracles? Gershonides deals with this issue and explains that we are troubled by this question because we are impressed by miracles. However, miracles are not nearly as impressive as the laws that govern the universe. We take for granted the majesty of the universe. For example, here I am typing out this article. My fingers move across the keys of my keyboard. I take this function for granted. But let us consider this phenomenon for a moment: Is a finger and its function so simple? Can an MIT engineer create a manipulative machine that is as efficient as a finger? What about duplicating the movements of a simple spider? How many brilliant engineers does it take to make a mechanical spider? And these are just a few of G-d's most simple inventions. His universe full of wonderful inventions and the laws He created to govern their functions.

Any miracle – at some level – interrupts the operations of the natural universe. Gershonides explains that Hashem did not create the most possibly perfect universe just so He could turn around and interrupt its perfect functioning. Hashem seeks to avoid miracles – which

---

[47] Sefer Beresheit 30:22.
[48] Rabbaynu Ovadia Sforno, *Commentary on Sefer Beresheit*, 30:22.
[49] Rabbaynu David Kimchi (RaDaK), *Commentary on Sefer Shemuel I*, 16:2.

are interruptions of nature. When He must interfere with nature, He does so minimally. And He preserves as much of the existing patterns of nature as possible.[50]

Similarly, in seeking medical treatment, we emulate Hashem. Just as Hashem seeks to minimize His miracles, we are required to minimize our dependency on His interruption into His natural laws on our behalf. We are required to do all in our power to help ourselves. We only seek Hashem's assistance in assuring the success of these efforts.

"If the stolen article is found in his possession whether a bull, a donkey, or a lamb [and it is] alive, he shall pay twofold." (Shemot 22:3)

Everyone acknowledges that it is wrong to steal. However, what is stealing? Where should the line be drawn between borrowing and stealing? If a person takes something from someone else as a harmless prank, is this stealing?

Parshat Mishpatim outlines many of the laws regulating liability for causing harm to a person or his property. Our passage describes the punishment for theft. In general, a person who steals must pay back to the victim twofold the value of the stolen object. In other words, in addition to making restitution, the thief must make a further payment equal to the value of the stolen object.

In his Mishne Torah, Maimonides explains that the Torah prohibits stealing any amount. Even if the stolen object is of minimal value, the commandment prohibiting stealing has been violated. Maimonides adds that it is prohibited to steal something as a prank. It is also prohibited to steal with the intent of later returning the object or making restitution. Maimonides explains that these latter activities are prohibited in order to assure that such behaviors do not become accepted.[51]

Maimonides seems to distinguish between the prototypical instance of stealing and stealing as a joke, or with the intent to return the object. By commenting that these latter activities are prohibited in order that a person should not habituate these behaviors, Maimonides seems to imply that these activities are not the primary subject of the commandment against stealing. However, they are nonetheless prohibited because they can develop into negative behaviors.

This is Lechem Mishne's understanding of Maimonides' position. He maintains that, according to Maimonides, the Torah does not prohibit a theft that is performed as a prank or with the intention of returning the object. These activities are prohibited by the Sages. In other words, the Sages extended the definition of theft to include these behaviors.[52]

Sefer HaChinuch disagrees with this ruling. He argues that the Torah does in fact prohibit a theft performed in jest or with the intention of returning the object.[53] Sefer HaChinuch generally follows Maimonides' position. Therefore, it is reasonable to assume that Sefer HaChinuch maintains that Maimonides would concur with this ruling. Maimonides' comments in his Sefer HaMitzvot seem to support this interpretation of his position.[54]

---

[50] Rabbaynu Levi ben Gershom (Gershonides), *Commentary on Sefer Beresheit*, p 91.
[51] Rabbaynu Moshe ben Maimon (Rambam) *Mishne Torah*, Hilchot Genayvah 2:2.
[52] Rav Avraham di Boton, *Lechem Mishne*, Hilchot Genayvah 2:1.
[53] Rav Aharon HaLeyve, *Sefer HaChinuch*, Mitzvah 224.

Sefer HaChinuch's interpretation of Maimonides' position presents two problems: First, in his Mishne Torah, Maimonides clearly seems to distinguish between the prototypical case of theft and a theft performed as a prank or with the intention to return the object. Second, Maimonides does state that these latter activities are prohibited because they may develop into habitual behaviors. According to Sefer HaChinuch, this statement seems – at best – superfluous. The activities are prohibited because they meet the Torah definition of stealing! Even if they would not lead to any further evil, they are completely prohibited!

In order to answer these questions, it will be helpful to consider the unusual ruling of the Sheetah Mekubetzet. Sheetah Mekubetzet argues that any theft performed with the intent of returning the object – unauthorized borrowing – is not included in the prohibition against theft. However, if a person does not intend to return the object, the commandment against stealing has been violated. The person's motives for stealing are irrelevant. In other words, the Torah prohibits stealing as a prank or in order to annoy someone. In any instance in which the intention is to keep the object, the mitzvah is violated.[55] On the surface, this ruling is quite amazing. Stealing with the intention of returning is not even prohibited by the commandment against stealing! How is this possible? We might be tempted to explain this odd ruling by proposing that the thief does not really intend to steal the object. He is just borrowing without permission. But, Sheetah Mekubetzet goes on to explain that a thief's intentions are irrelevant. One who steals as a prank or to create an annoyance does violate the commandment.

In order to understand Sheetah Mekubetzet's position, it is essential to distinguish between two ideas: the innate objective of an action and its purpose. The objective of an action is defined by the end result for which it is performed – the fundamental product of the activity. The purpose of an action is the reason for which this product is desired. Let us consider a simple example: The object of sewing is to create stitches. The stitches are the product of the activity. One may have various reasons for desiring these stitches. One's purpose may be to create embroidery. An alternative purpose may be to sew to pieces of cloth together. In both instances, the objective of the action is determined by its product. The objective is to create the stitches. However, the motive, or purpose, for creating these stitches differs.

It seems that according to Sheetah Mekubetzet, the mitzvah prohibiting stealing legislates against an activity whose objective is absolute seizure. Seizure is defined as an unqualified transfer of an object from the owner to the thief. But, if the thief intends to return the object to its rightful owner, the requirement of absolute seizure has not been meet. Without absolute seizure, the commandment is not violated. However, once the objective of the theft is absolute seizure, the purpose, or motive, of the seizure is irrelevant. The thief may have no real interest in the object he has stolen. His intent may be to carry out a prank or to annoy the victim. Nonetheless, once absolute seizure has taken place, the mitzvah prohibiting theft has been violated.

This provides an important insight into Maimonides' position. As noted above, Maimonides seems to distinguish between the prototypical act of theft and theft performed as a prank or with the intention to return the object. How does a theft performed as a prank, or with the intention to return the object, differ from the prototypical case? Apparently, according to Maimonides, the prototypical case of theft has two fundamental qualities: First, the objective of the theft is absolute seizure of the object. Therefore, if the thief intends to return the object, the

---

[54] Rabbaynu Moshe ben Maimon (Rambam) *Sefer HaMitzvot, Mitzvat Lo Ta'aseh* 244.
[55] Rav Betzalel Ashkenazi, *Sheetah Mekubetzet*, Commentary on Mesechet Baba Metzia 61b.

case is atypical. But, Maimonides adds a second quality: In the prototypical model the purpose of the theft must also be the absolute seizure of the object. Therefore, a theft performed as a jest is atypical. The thief may intend to keep the object. The purpose of this theft is not seizure. In other words, the prototypical case of theft exists when the objective of the activity is absolute seizure and this seizure is also the purpose for which the act is performed.

We can now easily understand and appreciate Lechem Mishne's interpretation of Maimonides. According to Lechem Mishne, the Torah's definition of theft extends only to the prototypical case. The Torah commandment is violated only when the objective of the theft is absolute seizure and this seizure is also the purpose of the activity. The Sages extended the Torah's prohibition to the atypical cases in which either this objective or purpose is missing.

However, Sefer HaChinuch's interpretation of Maimonides' position remains difficult to understand. Sefer HaChinuch must acknowledge that Maimonides identifies two levels of theft. He clearly states that theft performed with the intent to return the object, or in jest, is prohibited in order to discourage habituation of such behaviors. Yet, Maimonides indicates that even in these atypical cases the theft is prohibited on a Torah level.

It seems that Maimonides maintains that there are two elements included in the mitzvah prohibiting stealing: First, the mitzvah prohibits a specific action. The specific action prohibited by the mitzvah is the prototypical model of theft. In this model, the objective and purpose of the action is the absolute seizure of the object. A theft performed in jest, or with the intent or returning the object, does not meet the requirements of this model. However, there is a second element of the mitzvah: The mitzvah has an objective. Its objective is to establish clear perimeters of ownership. Any theft – even if it is not the prototypical case – demonstrates disregard of the perimeters of ownership. Therefore, although the activity is not the action explicitly prohibited by the action, it is included in the prohibition of commandment. It contradicts the objective of the commandment.

An illustration will help clarify this formulation. We are all familiar with illegal file sharing. If a person purchases a music CD, copies it, and resells the copies, he has clearly violated the copyright on the CD. This is the specific action that the copyright law prohibits. But, assume that the person does not resell the copies. Instead, he lends his CD to various individuals and invites them to copy the music onto their hard-drives. This may not be the activity specifically prohibited by the copyright law, but there is no question that this activity undermines the objective of the law. The law is designed to protect the investment of the CD producer. Widespread distribution of the music files on the single purchased CD undermines the objective of the law. Now, in this case, we might debate whether the CD purchaser should be responsible to respect the objective of the copyright law. But, we cannot deny that the purchaser's activities contradict this objective.

Sefer HaChinuch is suggesting that in the case of the mitzvah prohibiting theft, the objective of the mitzvah is definitely legally binding. Therefore, in addition to the specific act of theft prohibited by the mitzvah, atypical forms of theft that undermine or contradict the rights of the owner are also prohibited.

Let us close with a short review of the laws. According to most opinions, it is prohibited to take or steal an object with the intent to return it. There is some debate as to whether this behavior is prohibited by the Torah or by the Sages. But, the bottom line is that ownership rights must be respected. Taking an object without the authorization of the owner directly undermines and contradicts the rights of the owner. Therefore, the fact that the thief does not intend to keep the object is irrelevant.

Stealing in jest, or in order to annoy someone, is clearly prohibited. Again, there is some debate as to whether this activity is prohibited by the Torah or the Sages. But, this activity is an obvious denial of the owner's rights and is therefore prohibited.

Do not curse judges. Do not curse a leader of your people. (Shemot 22:27)

Do Not Curse Judges – Recognizing the Limits of Personal Objectivity

On the simplest level, the above passage prohibits us from cursing judges. What is the reason for this prohibition? A study of Maimonides' treatment of this *mitzvah* provides an obvious and straightforward response. Maimonides discusses this prohibition in his codification of the laws governing the courts.[56] He does not explicitly state a reason for this restriction. However, his general treatment of the law indicates his position. In the prior chapter of his code, Maimonides states that we are obligated to respect judges and others appointed to positions of authority within the community.[57] He then outlines some of the specific behaviors engendered by this obligation. Maimonides juxtaposes this discussion with the restriction against cursing a judge. It seems from Maimonides' presentation of these laws, he regards cursing a judge as an extreme form of disrespect. In other words, the restriction against cursing a judge is engendered by the obligation to respect judges. This is a reasonable position and the most obvious explanation for the restriction.

Rabbaynu Ovadia Sforno takes a completely different—and quite novel—approach to explaining the prohibition against cursing judges. He begins by asserting the commandment includes the special case in which the court has ruled against a litigant. The prohibition admonishes the disappointed litigant to not express anger through cursing the judge. Sforno continues and explains that it is natural for a person to believe in the justice of one's own cause. Therefore, the disappointed litigant may feel deeply wronged. The litigant will feel that the judges decided the case unfairly. They deserve to be cursed! These judges have miscarried justice! The Torah admonishes the irate litigant to exercise restraint. One must recognize the influence of one's own personal bias. True, in the litigant's view, a miscarriage of justice has occurred. However, one must recognize that the court is in a position to be more objective concerning the validity of one's own claim.[58]

Sforno's interpretation of the passage requires further consideration. Why does Sforno insist on focusing on a specific case – the disappointed litigant? We are obligated to respect judges. Of course, this duty applies even when we do not agree with the judges' conclusion!

It seems that according to Sforno, this commandment is not merely an admonishment against acting disrespectfully towards the court. This *mitzvah* should not be viewed as one of the many commandments regulating the conduct and reinforcing the authority of the courts. Instead, the *mitzvah* regulates our personal character – *midot*. It admonishes us against compromising our objectivity. We are not permitted to assume that we are completely objective about ourselves.

---

[56] Rabbaynu Moshe ben Maimon (Rambam) *Mishne Torah*, Hilchot Sanhedrin 26:1.
[57] Rabbaynu Moshe ben Maimon (Rambam) *Mishne Torah*, Hilchot Sanhedrin 25.
[58] Rabbaynu Ovadia Sforno, *Commentary on Sefer* Shemot 22:27.

We must recognize that the court's position is every bit as legitimate as our own. In abstract, it is easy to agree with this assertion. The challenge is to recognize this truth even at the moment of anger and frustration. Even at that moment, we must recognize our own personal bias and not overreact. In short, the passage commands us to accept the validity of an objective analysis of our own position – even when the conclusions of this analysis differ sharply from our own.

Do not follow the majority to do evil. Do not speak up in a trial to pervert justice. A case must be decided on the basis of the majority. (Shemot 23:2)

Following the Conclusion of the Majority in Issues Other Than Halachah

The above passage includes three injunctions. The meaning and rationale of last of these is easily understood. In deciding a legal issue, the court must follow the opinion of the majority of its members. For example: A person brings a question of *halachah* before the court. The court discusses the issue and the judges differ on the resolution of the issue. The members of the court vote. The issue is decided according to the majority opinion. The law also applies to civil disputes. For example: Two litigants bring a case before a court. After hearing from both parties to the dispute, the court votes. The decision of the court is determined by the majority's position.

The first injunction in the passage is more difficult to interpret. The *pasuk* tells us not to follow the majority to do evil. This is an odd statement. Obviously, we should never intentionally act wickedly. A court cannot knowingly issue an inappropriate decision based on the opinion of the majority! What is the case to which the injunction in the passage applies? The *Torah She'Be'Al Peh* – the Oral Law answers this question. Our Sages explain that the opening portion of the passage deals with capital cases. In these cases, if the defendant is found to be guilty, he or she will be executed. Our Sages also explain that the term "evil" in the passage should not be interpreted literally. Instead, it refers to a guilty verdict. In other words, the passage tells that a simple majority is not sufficient to execute a defendant. What is the criterion that must be met in order to execute a defendant? A majority of at least two judges is required.[59]

In short, two messages are communicated by these two injunctions. The final portion of the *pasuk* instructs us that court's decisions should generally follow the majority's opinion. The first portion of the passage establishes an exception. The execution of a defendant requires a majority of at least two judges.

Baal HaTumim – an outstanding scholar – was once asked to defend his commitment to the Torah. The question posed to him was based upon our passage. Our *pasuk* tells us to follow the majority opinion. It seems reasonable to apply this principle beyond the confines of court cases. In fact, the Talmud does apply this principle to other areas of *halachah*. This means that heeding the opinion of the majority is a rational rule and should be applied wherever appropriate. Baal HaTurim's opponent observed that the Jewish people are a minority within civilized humankind. Furthermore, even among the Jewish people, the Torah is not universally accepted and observed. Other religions can rightfully claim larger followings. Therefore, should we not abandon the Torah based on the principle in our passage? We should follow the majority opinion and embrace most widely accepted religion!

---

[59] Rabbaynu Moshe ben Maimon (Rambam) *Mishne Torah*, Hilchot *Sanhedrin* 8:1.

Baal HaTumim responded that this question is based upon a basic misunderstanding of the principle in the passage. The *pasuk* does not suggest that we follow the majority in areas in which we have definite knowledge. The *pasuk* deals with a court case in which an issue is in doubt. The issue may be how a *halachah* is applied in a novel situation; it may involve the resolution of a civil dispute between two litigants; in may concern whether a defendant committed a crime over which the court has jurisdiction. In all of these instances, the court must consider the matter, review the evidence, examine the testimony of relevant witnesses, and after assessing the data provided from all sources, come to a conclusion. In all of these instances, there is a legitimate question and the answer is in doubt. In the resolution of the doubt, we follow the majority opinion. However, we are not swayed by the majority in areas in which we are certain. For example, assume a person knew that a certain food was not *kasher* – permitted. A group approaches this individual and claims the food is permitted. The person cannot eat something that one knows with certainty is not *kasher*. It is irrelevant that a large group claims the food is permitted. A person cannot ignore his personal knowledge simply because a number of ignorant people hold a different view. Baal HaTurim explained that we know that the Torah is true. We received it through a public revelation to the entire Jewish people and its content and design also reflect its Divine source. The truth of Torah is not an issue that is in doubt and must be resolved through resorting to the judgment of the majority. Therefore, regardless of the number of people who deny its authenticity, we cannot abandon the truth.

Rav Elchanan Wasserman *Zt"l* suggests an alternative response to the question posed to Baal HaTurim. He argues that the question is based upon a different error in the meaning of the passage. The passage requires us to follow the majority opinion of a group of judges. This does not mean that the principle in the passage is limited to decisions of jurisprudence. However, the principle in the passage does require that the issue in balance be decided by individuals qualified to render a decision. In matters of *halachah*, the judge's knowledge and wisdom endows his opinion with credibility. The opinion of a simpleton is not given credence. Rav Elchanan argues that religious issues cannot be evaluated on the basis of popular appeal. The masses of humanity do not make religious decisions as a result of thorough analysis. Only scholars of religion are credible judges. Rav Elchanan points out that the Torah has been scrutinized by countless scholars. The Sages of the Talmud and of subsequent generations have subjected every detail of the Torah to painstaking critical analysis. No religion has been subjected to more thorough scrutiny over a period of centuries. Therefore, application of the principle in the passage only confirms the authenticity of the Torah.[60]

"Do not take a bribe. For the bribe blinds those with sight and perverts the words of the righteous." (Shemot 23:8)

The Torah prohibits the judge from accepting a gift from a litigant. Even the legitimate compensation received by the judge is influenced by this consideration. In general, both litigants must contribute equally to the compensation.

Rashi explains that the Torah, through other commandments, prohibits the judge from favoring a litigant or perverting justice. This prohibition against accepting bribes is not a repetition of these injunctions. This commandment adds a new element to the laws governing

---

[60] Rav Elchanan Wasserman, *Kobetz Ma'amarim*, Essay on Conviction.

jurisprudence. The judge may not even accept an unconditional payment from a litigant. In other words, consider a litigant offering to compensate a judge for his efforts. The litigant asks for no special treatment. He instructs the judge to decide the case fairly and without favoritism. The judge must not accept this payment.[61]

It is clear that the Torah assumes that, in this case, the impartiality of the judge has been impugned. He can no longer trust his own objectivity. He may unconsciously favor the litigant making the payment. Alternatively, he may feel a need to overcompensate for possible favoritism and unfairly favor the other litigant. It is not feasible for the judge to insulate himself from these motives.

Rav Elchanan Wasserman *ztl* explained that this lesson is not limited to judges. In everyday life we make judgments and must be aware of "bribes" which may influence us. One of the areas in which we are easily bribed is in our relationship with the Almighty. Rav Wasserman explained that the evidence of the Creator's existence is not hidden. We live in a universe that contains many testimonies to the existence of an omnipotent designer. Why do so many reject this sublime evidence of the Creator?

Rav Wasserman responds that we are all bribed. The human is an instinctual creature. We resist restrictions. The acceptance of a Creator and a design implies that life has meaning and that humanity has a mission. We are not free to pursue instinctual pleasure without restraint. We must inquire into the meaning of creation and the mission of humanity.

These considerations bias our judgment and act as a bribe. Therefore, we cannot be influenced by the attitude of many intelligent individuals towards the evidence of a Creator. The negative reaction of many of these individuals can be understood as the expression of an innate prejudice.[62]

In many areas in life it is impossible to be completely objective. How do we ever know that our decisions are not the outcome of some innate bias? There is no absolute guarantee of objectivity. However, there is a means by which we can somewhat limit the influence of our prejudices. A prejudice is most harmful when it is not recognized. A prejudice of which we are unaware influences us without our knowledge. Once we identify our biases we can protect ourselves, to some extent, from their influence. In reviewing the decision process, we now know where to look for the effect of the prejudice and can hope to identify its influence.

And Moshe came and told the people all the words of Hashem, and all the ordinances; and all the people answered with one voice, and said: All the words which the L-rd has spoken will we do. (Shemot 24:3)

The Covenant of Sinai

1. The prototypical conversion

Conversion to Judaism requires that a candidate for conversion commit oneself to the observance of the Torah's commandments. This is the most fundamental element of conversion. However, three other steps are potentially required. All conversions require immersion in a

---

[61] Rabbaynu Shlomo ben Yitzchak (Rashi), *Commentary on Sefer Shemot* 23:8.
[62] Rav Elchanan Wasserman, *Kobetz Ma'amarim*, Essay on Conviction.

mikveh – a body of water that meets specific standards. During the Temple periods, a specified sacrifice was required. Males must undergo circumcision. The Talmud explains that the elements of the conversion process are derived from the Torah. All of these elements were included in the prototype for all conversions. This prototypical conversion was the transformation of the descendants of the patriarchs into the Nation of Israel.[63] Much of the Torah's description of this process is included in Parshat Mishpatim.

The conversion or transformation of the descendants of the people redeemed from Egypt into the Nation of Israel is referred to in the parasha as the creation of a covenant. Through the creation of this covenant between the people and Hashem, the transformation occurred. Subsequent converts enter into the nation through accepting upon themselves the terms of the covenant.

2. When did the people enter into the Sinai covenant?

The commentators disagree over when the events described in the parasha occurred. Rashi asserts that the people entered into the covenant prior to Revelation. Only after the execution of the covenant did the newly emerged Nation of Israel experience Revelation and hear the pronouncement of the Decalogue.[64]

Nachmanides disagrees with Rashi. He contends that the covenant was enacted after the initial stage of Revelation – after the pronouncement of the Decalogue. According to his opinion, after the nation heard Hashem pronounce the Decalogue, Hashem instructed Moshe to invite the nation into the covenant and thereby, become the Nation of Israel.[65]

Each of these opinions presents a difficulty. According to Nachmanides, the process of Revelation was initiated with Hashem's pronouncement of the Decalogue. Then, it was interrupted and did not proceed until the people entered into the covenant. Why was the execution of the covenant inserted into the midst of Revelation?

Rashi contends that the covenant was executed prior to Revelation. Superficially, this seems to be a more reasonable position. According to Rashi, the acceptance of the terms of the covenant was a prerequisite for receiving the Torah. Revelation could not begin until the people entered into the covenant with Hashem. However, on more technical grounds Rashi's position is troublesome.

As explained above, the very essence of the conversion process is the candidate's commitment to observance of the Torah's mitzvot. Presumably, this was also the fundamental element of this prototype conversion of the people into the Nation of Israel. However, the Torah came into existence through Revelation. Prior to Revelation the Torah did not exist as a halachic entity. How could the people commit themselves to observance of the Torah's mitzvot before these even existed in a halachic sense?

I am Hashem your G-d, who brought you out of the land of Egypt, out of the house of bondage.
(Shemot 20:2)

3. Acceptance of Hashem is a prerequisite for acceptance of His commandments

---

[63] Mesechet Keritot 9a.
[64] Rabbaynu Shlomo ben Yitzchak (Rashi), Commentary on Sefer Shemot 24:1.
[65] Rabbaynu Moshe ben Nachman (Ramban), Commentary on Sefer Shemot 24:1.

Although Nachmanides disagrees with Rashi over the sequence of events at Revelation, he does provide an important insight that helps explain Rashi's position.

The passage above is the first statement of the Decalogue. According to Maimonides, this statement is the source of one of the Torah's 613 commandments. The mitzvah in this passage is acceptance of the existence of the Creator – One who created and who at every moment sustains the universe. Others disagree with Maimonides. They acknowledge that acceptance of Hashem's existence is fundamental to the Torah. However, they argue that this acceptance does not qualify to be counted as one of the Torah's commandments.

Nachmanides explains the reasoning of Maimonides' opponents. He explains that before a ruler can effectively legislate laws for his subjects, he must be accepted by his subjects as their ruler. This submission to the authority of the ruler is a prerequisite to his legislation of laws. Therefore, this acceptance of the ruler's authority should not, itself, be regarded as a commandment. Instead, it is introductory to the legislation of commandments. Similarly, Hashem first required the people to accept Him as their ruler and to submit to His authority to legislate mitzvot. Once this was accomplished, He then revealed His mitzvot. In short, acceptance of Hashem is a necessary prerequisite to commandments but not itself a mitzvah.[66]

Rashi seems to maintain that before the people could receive the Torah through Revelation they were required to enter into a covenant. The fundamental element of this covenant was acceptance of Hashem and submission to His authority. Once this covenant was enacted and the people submitted themselves to Hashem's authority revelation of the commandments proceeded. In other words, in this prototypical conversion, the people were not required to accept the commandments. These did not yet exist. They were required to acknowledge Hashem's authority to legislate for the nation. This was accomplished through the covenant.

The contemporary candidate for conversion is also required to accept Hashem and acknowledge His authority to legislate commandments. However, this contemporary conversion is taking place post-Revelation. Therefore, the candidate for conversion expresses his acceptance of Hashem and his submission to His authority through his commitment to observe His commandments.

And Hashem said unto Moshe: Behold, I come unto you in a thick cloud, that the people may hear when I speak with you, and may also believe you forever. And Moshe told the words of the people to Hashem. (Shemot 19:9)

4. Moshe's unique prophetic achievement

According to Nachmanides, the covenant was enacted after Hashem spoke to the people and revealed the Decalogue. Revelation was interrupted in order to enact the covenant. Why was the covenant inserted into the midst of Revelation? In order to understand Nachmanides' position, the above passage must be considered.

This passage precedes Revelation. In the passage Hashem tells Moshe that He will speak to him in front of the entire nation so that the nation will believe in Moshe forever. Rabbaynu Ovadia Sforno explains the meaning of the passage. Before considering his explanation some background regarding prophecy is required.

---

[66] R' Moshe ben Nachman (Ramban), Critique on Maimonides' Sefer HaMitzvot, M.A. 1.

Moshe was not the first or the last of the prophets. However, Maimonides explains that Moshe's prophecy was superior to that of all other prophets. In his prophetic experience he encountered Hashem and communicated with Him in a more intimate manner than any other prophet. Because of the unique character of Moshe's prophetic experience, he was able to receive the Written Torah from Hashem word by word as well as the Oral Law. No other prophet achieved a level of prophecy necessary for such an elaborate and detailed communication.[67]

The validity of the Torah depends upon not only accepting the authenticity of prophecy but accepting also, that a material creature can achieve the degree of prophecy unique to Moshe.

Now, Sforno's comments can be considered. Hashem tells Moshe that He will come to him in a thick cloud. He will experience a prophecy. Hashem will reveal to him the Decalogue. However, this prophecy will not be revealed to Moshe alone. The entire nation will participate and share the prophetic experience. All will hear the voice of Hashem declare the contents of the Decalogue word by word. This experience will prove that the degree of prophecy required for communication of the Torah is achievable by a mortal being. After this experience, the rest of the Torah will be revealed to Moshe. He will deliver it to the people and they will believe that it is the authentic word of Hashem. They will believe this because they themselves, for a few special moments, shared in that unique prophetic experience. They too heard the words of Hashem.[68]

Now these are the ordinances which you shall set before them. (Shemot 21:1)

5. The laws of Parshat Mishpatim

Before Nachmanides' opinion can be fully understood, two other aspects of his position must be noted. First, according to Nachmanides, the covenant was not enacted immediately after the revelation of the Decalogue. Moshe received the prophecy of the Decalogue. The people shared in all or a portion of this prophecy. The people's prophetic experience then ended but Moshe's continued. He received additional commandments and laws. These are recorded at the end of Parshat Yitro and compose the first portion of Parshat Mishpatim. After receiving this material and before receiving the balance of the Torah's mitzvot and laws, Moshe was instructed to enact the covenant.

And he took the book of the covenant, and read in the hearing of the people; and they said: All that Hashem has spoken will we do, and obey. (Shemot 24:7)

7. Acknowledgment of the authenticity of the Torah as Hashem's word

Second, the Torah explains that Moshe created a Sefer HaBrit – a Book of the Covenant. In enacting the covenant, he read the contents of the Sefer HaBrit to the people and they committed to obey its contents. What was recorded in the Sefer HaBrit? According to Nachmanides, the Sefer HaBrit was a record of the laws contained in the end of Parshat Yitro and the first portion Parshat Mishpatim. Why were these specific laws recorded in the Sefer HaBrit and selected as the laws over which the covenant should be executed?

According to Nachmanides, these laws were among the first revealed to Moshe alone.[69] At least a portion of the Decalogue was revealed in a prophecy in which the entire nation shared. The authenticity of the Decalogue as the word of Hashem was beyond question. However, they

---

[67] Rabbaynu Moshe ben Maimon (Rambam) Mishne Torah, Hilchot Yesodai HaTorah, chp. 7-8.
[68] Rabbaynu Ovadia Sforno, Commentary on Sefer Shemot, 19:9.
[69] Rabbaynu Moshe ben Nachman (Ramban), Commentary on Sefer Shemot 24:1.

would not participate in the balance of Revelation. They would not hear the words of Hashem dictated to Moshe. Therefore, the people were required to affirm their unqualified acceptance of the authenticity of Moshe's prophecy. They were required to acknowledge that the laws that would be communicated by Moshe are the words of Hashem – even though they would not themselves participate in this prophecy. This affirmation took place through the execution of a covenant over the Sefer HaBrit.

As explained above, Nachmanides maintains that the Sefer HaBrit was composed of the laws at the end of Parshat Yitro and the first portion of Parshat Mishpatim. These were revealed to Moshe alone. The people did not hear these laws directly from Hashem. In the covenant they accepted upon themselves the responsibility of observing these laws as the word of Hashem. In so doing, they affirmed the authenticity of Moshe's unique level of prophecy and the legitimacy of the rest of the Torah that Moshe would communicate to them as the words of Hashem.

Therefore, Revelation was interrupted. Before Hashem would dictate the balance of the Torah to Moshe, He required the people to affirm the authenticity of Moshe's unique prophetic level and the authenticity of the Torah he would communicate as the words of Hashem.

And Hashem said to Moshe: Ascend the mountain to Me and be there. And I will give to you the tablets of stone, the Torah, and the commandments that I have written to teach them. (Shemot 24:12)

The Significance of the Ten Statements of the Decalogue

1. The ten statements of the Decalogue encompass all 613 mitzvot

Hashem directs Moshe to ascend Mount Sinai. He tells Moshe that He will give to him the tablets of the Decalogue, and the entire Torah and its commandments. In his comments on this passage, Rashi explains that all of the Torah's six hundred and thirteen – taryag – mitzvot can be subsumed within the ten statements of Decalogue. Rashi notes the Saadia Goan composed a liturgical poem – Azharot – that organizes the 613 mitzvot in ten groups corresponding with the ten statements of the Decalogue.[70]

According to Rashi, apparently there is some allusion in the above passage to his contention that all of the commandments may be subsumed within the ten statements of the Decalogue. What is this allusion? Gur Aryeh suggests that the allusion is found in the words "that I have written." The passage seems to attribute to Hashem the writing of the tablets and also the Torah with its mitzvot. This presents a problem. Hashem did carve the statements of the Decalogue into the tablets. However, He did not record the Torah and its commandments. This responsibility was given to and executed by Moshe. Rashi's comments resolve this difficulty. Hashem carved the statements of the Decalogue onto the tablets. These ten statements encompassed within their messages the entire Torah and its taryag mitzvot. Therefore, in carving the statements of the Decalogue onto the tablets, Hashem indirectly recorded all of the Torah and its mitzvot.[71]

Rashi's comments resolve a troubling problem. What is the significance of the Decalogue? Why did Hashem initiate Revelation and the transmission of the Torah with the

---

[70] Rabbaynu Shlomo ben Yitzchak (Rashi), Commentary on Sefer Shemot, 24:12.
[71] Rav Yehuda Loew of Prague (Maharal), Gur Aryeh Commentary on Sefer Shemot, 24:12.

pronouncement of these ten statements? Rav Yosef Dov Soloveitchik Zt"l explains that according to Rashi this question is easily answered. These ten statements are inclusive of the entire Torah. All of the Torah's mitzvot are encompassed within the themes of these statements. Therefore, in pronouncing these ten statements, Hashem outlined the thematic content of the entire Torah. The remainder of the Torah and its commandments are the detailed implementation of the themes enunciated in the Decalogue. Furthermore, the people's commitment to conform to the contents of these statements was an affirmation of all the commandments subsumed within their themes.[72]

The assignment of the 613 mitzvot to ten categories or themes seems to imply an important message. If the Torah's commandments can be divided into ten broad categories, then presumably they can also be divided into a larger number of more precise or specific categories. Is there a reason that Hashem decided upon ten themes or groups and not twenty or fifty?

Rabbaynu Avraham ibn Ezra notes that the number ten has an important meaning and function in our number system. The numbers one through ten each represents either a singularity or plurality. However, the number ten represents a group.[73] Thus, the number 26 is composed of two units of ten and six individual elements. This raises an interesting question. Does the division of the taryag mitzvot into ten categories or themes suggest that all of the mitzvot are interrelated and form a single group? The answer to this question seems to be contained in a mysterious remark of our Sages.

And Hashem spoke all of these things saying: (Shemot 20:1)

2. The ten statements of the Decalogue were simultaneously pronounced

The above pasuk introduces the Decalogue. The passage states that Hashem spoke all of the statements of the Decalogue to the people. In his comments on this passage, Rashi quotes the Midrash. According to the Midrash, Hashem pronounced all ten statements of the Decalogue twice. First, all were stated simultaneously. Then, each was individually repeated.[74] Of course, the question on the Midrash is obvious. Why were the statements first stated simultaneously, if they were to be immediately individually repeated? In other words, what purpose was served or message communicated by merging the ten statements into a single simultaneous pronouncement?

Gur Aryeh responds that the simultaneous presentation of the ten statements communicated the important message that they are a single integrated system. The ten statements should not be regarded as ten independent themes. Instead, they should be understood as ten components of a single system of law. Gur Aryeh adds that these ten statements are inclusive of all of the Torah's commandments. Therefore, through the simultaneous presentation of these statements, all of the commandments that are subsumed within them are combined into a single system.[75]

According to Gur Aryeh's comments, the division of the Torah's 613 commandments into ten categories or themes is very significant. As Ibn Ezra notes, the number ten represents a

---

[72] Rav Yosef Dov Soloveitchik, Recorded Lecture on the Aseret HaDibrot.
[73] Rabbaynu Avraham ibn Ezra, Commentary on Sefer Shemot, 3:15.
[74] Rabbaynu Shlomo ben Yitzchak (Rashi), Commentary on Sefer Shemot, 20:1.
[75] Rav Yehuda Loew of Prague (Maharal), Gur Aryeh Commentary on Sefer Shemot, 20:1.

group and the themes that compose the Decalogue and the mitzvot that are included in these themes are a single integrated group and system of law.

3. Some mitzvot were not revealed at Sinai

This analysis is relevant to a disturbing question posed by Nachmanides. The Talmud states that six hundred and thirteen commandments were given to Moshe at Sinai.[76] This statement does not seem to accord to the Torah's account of the origins of the mitzvot. The Torah describes Hashem revealing various commandments after Moshe descended from Mount Sinai. For example, before entering the Land of Israel, Moshe was approached by the daughters of Tzlafchad. They posed a question to him regarding the laws determining the apportionment of the Land of Israel. In response to their inquiry, Moshe received a prophecy in which Hashem revealed the laws of inheritance. Clearly, some of the Torah's commandments were not given to Moshe at Sinai. What, then, is the meaning of the Talmud's declaration that the 613 mitzvot were revealed to Moshe at Sinai?[77]

Based on the above analysis, Nachmanides' question can be answered. The taryag mitzvot comprise a single system of law. The Talmud's comments that taryag mitzvot were given to Moshe at Sinai is a reference to the system. Although a few of the commandments were revealed to Moshe after Sinai, it is still proper to characterize the system, on a whole, as derived from Sinai.

A simple example will illustrate this point. If I invite a group of guests to my home and prepare a sumptuous meal, I can fairly take credit for the meal even if I purchased a single element from the grocery. When I boast that I prepared the meal, I refer to the meal on a whole and the characterization is fair and honest. The inclusion of a single element purchased from the grocery does not undermine the honesty of my claim. Nachmanides' own response to his question is similar to this solution.

And Moshe presented their legal inquiry before Hashem. (BeMidbar 27:5)

4. Some mitzvot were withheld from Moshe at Sinai

A slightly different response to Nachmanides' question is suggested by a comment of Rashi. Rashi is bothered by an interesting question regarding the incident involving the daughters of Tzlafchad. These women came to Moshe with a question. He presented their question to Hashem. Hashem responded by teaching Moshe the laws of inheritance. Why did Hashem not teach Moshe these laws at Mount Sinai? Why did Hashem wait until this point in time to reveal these laws?

One of Rashi's responses is that the laws could have been revealed earlier but Hashem delayed the revelation. He wished to reward the daughters of Tzlafchad for their desire to possess a portion of the Land of Israel. Their reward was that a portion of the Torah was withheld from Moshe, for a time, and only revealed to him in response to their inquiry. In other words, they were rewarded by serving as the catalyst for the revelation of these laws.[78]

---

[76] Mesechet Makkot 23b.
[77] Rabbaynu Moshe ben Nachman (Ramban), Critique on Maimonides' Sefer HaMitzvot, First Principle.
[78] Rabbaynu Shlomo ben Yitzchak (Rashi), Commentary on Sefer BeMidbar, 27:5.

According to Rashi, these laws were not formulated or created in response to the inquiry of the daughters of Tzlafchad. They already existed as part of the Torah. The inquiry of the daughters served only as the catalyst for the revelation or communication of the laws. In other words, these laws were always part of the system of 613 commandments. They were not added in response to the daughters' inquiry. Instead, this part of the system was initially withheld from Moshe and only revealed in response to the question posed by the daughters.

The same analysis can be applied to all of the mitzvot that were communicated to Moshe after he descended from Sinai. These mitzvot were not new commandments that were added to the Torah in response to evolving events. They were always elements of the system of taryag mitzvot. However, the communication of these elements was initially withheld from Moshe. Only after he descended from Sinai were these elements revealed. Therefore, the statement of the Sages is correct. However, it requires interpretation. The Sages said that the 613 commandments were reveled to Moshe at Sinai. The reference to the 613 commandments is not intended as a reference to each individual commandment. It is a reference to the system of 613 commandments. All of the mitzvot – regardless of when they were revealed to Moshe – are part of a single system. The system was given to Moshe at Sinai.

And Hashem said to Moshe: Ascend the mountain to Me and be there. And I will give you the stone Tablets and the torah and mitzvah that I have written for you to teach to them. (Shemot 24:12)
Reconciling the Written and Oral Laws
1. The Torah is comprised of a Written and Oral Law

Parshat Mishpatim continues the enumeration and explanation of the Torah's commandments and laws that began at the end of Parshat Yitro. The end of Parshat Mishpatim returns to the events at Sinai. In these passages, Moshe is instructed to ascend the mountain and there he will receive the Luchot – the Tablets of the Decalogue, the "torah and the mitzvah". The term "torah" generally is used to refer to the entire body of law that includes the individual mitzvot. However, in this passage it is clear that the terms "torah" and "mitzvah" refer to two mutually exclusive entities. In this context to what do these terms refer?

Rabbaynu Avraham ibn Ezra and others respond that the term "torah" refers here to the Written Law. The term mitzvah refers here to the Oral Law.[79] This interpretation is drawn from the comments of midrash.[80] Maimonides expands on these comments. In his very first remarks introducing his code of law – Mishne Torah – he interprets the above passage. He explains that, in the above passage, the term "torah" refers to the Written Law and that the term "mitzvah" refers to its explanation.

2. The relationship between the Written and Oral Laws

Maimonides' comments add to the interpretation of Ibn Ezra. Maimonides comments include a description of the relationship between the Written and the Oral Laws. The Oral Law provides the interpretation of the Written Law. In itself, the Written Law is often vague or

---

[79] Rabbaynu Avraham ibn Ezra, Abbreviated Commentary on Sefer Shemot, 24:12.
[80] Rav Menachem Mendel Kasher, Torah Shelymah, volume 5, p 278.

confusing. The Oral Law provides the interpretation and commentary required to understand and properly observe the Written Law.

Six days you shall perform your tasks and on the seventh you shall rest. (This is) so that your oxen, and donkeys will rest and the son of your maidservant and your convert. (Shemot 23:12)

Shabbat is one of the commandments included in the Decalogue. Parshat Mishpatim returns to the discussion of Shabbat. Shabbat is a day of rest. Nowhere does the Torah actually describe in precise terms the meaning of the admonition to rest on Shabbat. However, the Oral Law provides directions for fulfilling the commandment. It is the Oral Law that identifies the thirty-nine major categories of prohibited activities and their many derivatives. This is an example of the relationship between the Written and Oral Laws. The Written Law provides a brief and basic description of the commandment. In the instance of Shabbat, the Written Law commands that we rest on Shabbat. The Oral Law provides the additional detail that is essential for observance of the commandment. In the example of Shabbat, it provides a description of those activities from which we are required to rest.

And his master shall bring him close to the judges. And he shall bring him close to the door or to the doorpost. And he shall pierce his ear with an awl. And he will be his slave forever. (Shemot 21:6)

3. The freeing of the Jewish servant with the arrival of the Jubilee year

The above passage provides another fascinating example of the relationship between the Written and Oral Laws. The parasha describes the laws governing a Jewish slave or servant. The Torah allows for a Jewish male to be sold into servitude in two circumstances. A Jewish man can be sold by the court. This occurs if the individual is convicted of stealing and cannot repay the victim. The court sells the thief into servitude to another Jew. The proceeds of the sale are used to reimburse the victim of the theft. There is a second circumstance in which servitude is permitted. If an individual is in debt and cannot repay his creditors, he may sell himself. The proceeds are used to repay the creditors.

In both of these cases the sale is for a six-year period. If the Jewish servant wishes to remain with his master, then the master and servant must consult bait din – the court. The above pasuk describes the procedure for extending the term of the servitude. The pasuk explains that the ear of the servant is pierced against the doorpost of the court. The pasuk states that as a result of this procedure the term of servitude is extended "forever". Targum Unkelus interprets the passage in a very literal sense. According to this interpretation, the passage indeed requires that the servant remain in bondage indefinitely. Rashbam suggests a very similar interpretation. He explains the passage as meaning that the servant remains in servitude for the duration of his life.[81] However, both of these interpretations seem to contradict the interpretation of the passage provided by the Oral Law. The Oral Law teaches that the servitude is extended only to the Yovel – the Jubilee. At the Jubilee the servant must be freed. The Talmud explains that the term "forever" is not to be understood literally. It should be interpreted to mean until Yovel.[82]

4. A reconciliation of the Written and Oral Laws

---

[81] Rabbaynu Shemuel ben Meir (Rashbam) Commentary on Sefer Shemot 21:6.
[82] Mesechet Kiddushin 21b.

How can the message of the Written Law as confirmed by Unkelus and Rashbam be harmonized with the Oral Law's interpretation of the passage? A possible answer is provided by an interesting comment of Nachmanides. Nachmanides explains that the above passage is not the source for the requirement of freeing the slave at the Jubilee. Instead, the source is found in Sefer VaYikra. There, the Torah explains the restoration law. This law states that at the time of the Jubilee every man returns and is restored to his portion of land in the Land of Israel.[83] In other words, each person is restored his ancestral legacy in the Land. According to Nachmanides, the Talmud concludes from this requirement that the servant too is released and restored to his legacy. Nachmanides acknowledges that the Talmud interprets the term "forever" in the above passage to mean until Yovel. However, he suggests that this interpretation is only intended to reconcile the passage with the restoration law in Sefer VaYikra.[84]

Nachmanides' assertion that – the servant's emergence into freedom with the Jubilee is derived from the restoration law in Sefer VaYikra – has an important implication. It suggests that the servant is not freed because his period of servitude has reached its natural termination with the arrival of the Jubilee. Instead, it seems that the servitude has no natural termination – as suggested by the literal interpretation of "forever". Servitude ends because the Jubilee arrives and the restoration law takes effect. Every person – even the slave – must be restored to his legacy.

An analogy will help clarify this distinction. Marriage creates a relationship between man and woman. This relationship continues indefinitely. These two individuals may terminate the marriage, after any period, through divorce. Nonetheless, it is proper to say that, by nature, a marriage represents an agreement to enter into a relationship for an indefinite period.

The piercing procedure, like marriage, creates a relationship that is indefinite in length. However, as in the case of marriage, this relationship is subject to termination through an outside force. In marriage this outside force is divorce. For the servant, this agent is the Jubilee.

Apparently, Unkelus and Rashbam share Nachmanides' view. These commentators maintain that the Jubilee does not represent a limitation of the period of the servitude. Indeed, the period of servitude does extend indefinitely or throughout the life of the slave. This is the message of the term "forever" in the passage. However, the Jubilee interrupts the servitude and ends it.

5. An alternative reconciliation of the Written and Oral Laws

Rabbaynu Avraham ibn Ezra offers another approach to reconciling the Written Law to the Oral Law. He suggests that term forever – leolam – in the pasuk means until the Yovel. How is this possible? He explains that the term leolam can best be translated as "for an age". Adopting this translation transforms the meaning of the passage. It is telling us that as a result of the ear piercing procedure the servitude is extended "for an age". Now, the period represented by the term "age" must be identified. According to Ibn Ezra, an age must be the longest calendar unit recognized by halachah.

Halachah recognizes various calendar units. These units include day, week and month. Halachah also has created two calendar units that are composed of groups of years. Six years

---

[83] Sefer VaYikra 25:10.
[84] Rabbaynu Moshe ben Nachman (Ramban), Commentary on the Talmud, Mesechet Kiddushin 21b.

followed by a seventh Sabbatical year is recognized as a unit. Seven of these units contain forty-nine years. The fiftieth year is the Yovel. This fifty-year period is the largest calendar unit used by halachah. Ibn Ezra explains that this is the "age" specified in the pasuk.[85]

6. Two distinct approaches to reconciliation

These two interpretations suggest different approaches to reconciling the Written and Oral Laws. Nachmanides seems to suggest that the Written Law and Oral Law do actually suggest different messages. Our passage suggests that the servant's period of servitude extends indefinitely. This does not conform to the actual law derived from the Oral Law. However, the Written Law presented by Parshat Mishpatim is composed in a manner that seems to contradict the Oral Law in order to communicate a deeper and more meaningful understanding of the law. The contrast between the Written and Oral Laws alert the student that the servant's servitude is not naturally limited to a fifty year period. Instead, it ends at Jubilee because it is interrupted and canceled by the restoration law. Unkelus and Rashbam seem to accept this perspective.

Ibn Ezra's interpretation suggests an alternative approach to reconciling the Written and Oral Law. His approach resolves the perceived conflict. The Oral Law provides interpretation and meaning. The Oral Law forewarns the reader to replace "forever" with "for an age" and then provides a meaningful interpretation of the term "age".

"And the appearance of the glory of Hashem was as a burning fire at the summit of the mountain to the eyes of Bnai Yisrael." (Shemot 24:17)

Most of the *parasha* is devoted to describing a number of the laws given at Sinai. The end of the *parasha* continues the discussion of the events of Revelation. The Torah explains that Mount Sinai was covered in a thick cloud. The influence of the Divine Presence was expressed through an intense flame at the summit of the mountain.

Rabbaynu Avraham ben HaRambam explains that this imagery can be understood in both a literal and figurative sense. From a literal perspective, these *pesukim* describe the visual impressions of the people. What is the figurative meaning?

Sinai was a revelation. The commandments of the Torah were revealed to humanity. There was a second aspect to Revelation. The Almighty, in some sense, revealed Himself to humankind. The figure in these passages tells us something of the nature of this second aspect of Revelation. We must carefully consider the image, in the Chumash, in order to understand this second aspect of Revelation.

The Almighty cannot be perceived by the material senses. Only through our spiritual soul can we approach an understanding of Hashem. This understanding is not easily attained. Our material nature prevents us from clearly comprehending Hashem's exalted essence. As Hashem later explained to Moshe, no living creature can achieve absolute knowledge of Hashem. However, we can achieve some lower level of understanding. The degree to which we can attain this knowledge depends upon our own spiritual perfection. There is a direct relationship between the spiritual perfection of the individual and the ability to approach an understanding of the Almighty.

---

[85] Rabbaynu Avraham ibn Ezra, Commentary on Sefer Shemot – Unabridged, 21:6.

The image in the *pesukim* describes our material nature as a dense cloud that blocks our vision of the Creator. Contemplation of Hashem requires that we look through this cloud and gaze upon the intense flame in its midst.

A very bright light can damage the eyes. Consider a person looking directly at the sun. Such a person might damage his or her sight. Once such damage occurs the eyes may never again see properly. Instead, even the familiar will be distorted.

In a similar sense, there are dangers in considering the Almighty's nature. The student who wishes to enter into this area must be carefully and fully prepared. Without this preparation, the student will fail to comprehend. Rather than finding truth, the unprepared student will become confused. Truth will be replaced by distortion and falsehood. The Talmud explains that even great scholars were harmed as a result of their consideration of this area.

Nonetheless, the sun can be observed. Careful preparation is needed. The observer will not be able to see the sun clearly and in detail. The light is too bright. Yet, some image is obtained by the observer. So too, with proper spiritual preparation the Almighty's nature can be considered. Moshe was properly prepared. He was able to enter into the cloud and penetrate it. He gazed upon the flame. Even for Moshe the light was too bright for a perfect view. However, Moshe did achieve the highest level of understanding possible for a material being.[86]

---

[86] Rabbaynu Avraham ben HaRambam, *Commentary on Sefer Shemot* 24.

Terumah

And let them make Me a sanctuary, that I may dwell among them. (Shemot 25:1)

The Challenge of Meaningful Prayer

1. The Tabernacle as a place of prayer

Parshat Terumah initiates the Torah's account of the creation of the *Mishcan* – the Tabernacle. This portable structure accompanied the Jewish people during their travels in the wilderness. The presence of Hashem was expressed most intensely in the *Mishcan*. The ark containing the tablets of the Decalogue was housed in the *Mishcan*. In the courtyard of the *Mishcan* was the altar upon which the nation offered its sacrifices to Hashem. Hashem addressed Moshe from between the cherubs of the ark cover.

After Bnai Yisrael conquered and settled the Land of Israel, the *Mishcan* continued to serve as the spiritual center of the nation. Eventually, the *Mishcan* was destroyed. King Shlomo replaced the *Mishcan* with the *Bait HaMikdash* – the Sacred Temple. The *Bait HaMikdash* became the permanent sanctuary of Bnai Yisrael and the center of national spiritual life.

With the destruction of the *Bait HaMikdash*, animal sacrifice was suspended and replaced by daily prayer. However, prayer did not first become a form of spiritual expression with the Temple's destruction. The *Mishcan* and the *Bait HaMikdash* were places for prayer. Chanah prayed for a son in the *Mishcan*.[1] Her prayers were answered with the birth of a son who became the prophet Shemuel. When King Shlomo dedicated the *Bait HaMikdash* he described it as a place of prayer.[2]

2. Negative attitudes toward prayer

Prayer and sacrificial service have much in common. Both are forms of service to Hashem or expressions of devotion. Also, both are highly structured by an extensive body of *halachah*. *Halachah* regulates the times for prayer; it orders its components; and even dictates much of the text of our prayers.

Prayer is one of the most basic and pervasive of Jewish practices. We are required to pray three times each day. Prayer and especially Shabbat prayers are the focal point of synagogue life. Yet, despite its ubiquitous nature, prayer is one of the least appreciated elements of Jewish practice. Many contemporary Jews are alienated from prayer. They do not find meaning in it. They regard it as a burden, and many individuals have abandoned seeking meaningful prayer experiences.

The characteristic of prayer that is perhaps most responsible for alienating the contemporary Jew is its highly structured and formalized design. There are at least two reasons that this design is responsible for so much estrangement.

And Moshe said unto G-d: Who am I, that I should go unto Paroh, and that I should bring forth the children of Israel out of Egypt? (Shemot 3:11)

3. Jewish attitudes toward and responses to authority

---

[1] Sefer Shemuel I 1:9-12.
[2] Sefer Melachim I 8:28-50.

First, our generation has developed a healthy skepticism toward authority that sometimes transmutes into a general discomfort and suspicion. In other words, the Torah expects us to question authority. In the above passages, we observe the most remarkable example of this proposition. Moshe is commanded by Hashem to return to Egypt and to lead the Jewish people out of bondage. Moshe questions Hashem. Our Sages explain that he questioned both his own fitness for this assignment and the worthiness of the Jewish people to be rescued.[3] The Torah expects us to seek understanding and knowledge. This imperative gives legitimacy even to questions like Moshe's.

However, in contemporary times, questioning and scrutiny is often transformed into a fundamental distrust and suspicion of many or most expressions of authority. Jewish prayer imposes upon its performer structure and rules. These laws and the resulting structure are associated with authority. The individual's experience is that the prayer activity is one of submission to authority. The very fact we perceive prayer as an attempt to impose upon us structure and regulation evokes the response of distrust and suspicion.

A simple example will help illustrate this phenomenon. As a high school student I resisted reading many of the literature assignments that were in the school's curriculum. Not many years after completing high school, natural curiosity and a developing interest in literature lead me to read many of the same works that I had resisted reading just a few years earlier. When I allowed myself to discover these works, I found inspiration, intellectual stimulation, unanticipated beauty.

Obviously, my disparate experiences with the same works of literature were not evoked by the works themselves, but rather by the circumstances. Works of literature that I came to deeply value when read at my own initiative, I had resisted reading when they were imposed upon me by authority.

Similarly, for many of us, our attitude toward prayer is shaped not by its content but in response to our perception that prayer is imposed upon us, rather than willingly embraced.

A second factor that contributes to the negativity toward prayer is our contemporary emphasis on individuality. We champion the value of individual expression. The importance of individual expression and fulfillment is perhaps the most universal Western value. The structured format of Jewish prayer seems to us to suppress our prerogative to give expression to our personal feelings and yearnings. We must squeeze our thoughts and feelings into the highly structured format of Jewish prayer and the outcome seems impersonal and even cold.

And you shall serve Hashem your G-d, and He will bless your bread, and your water; and I will take sickness away from your midst. (Shemot 23:25)

4. Confusion over the nature of prayer

To an extent, our negativity to prayer is an attempt to make it into something that it is not. We approach prayer as a means of personal expression. We want to address G-d and give expression to our own thoughts and feelings. However, fundamentally, prayer is an act of humble submission to Hashem. Maimonides derives the commandment of daily prayer from the above passage. The passage does not mention prayer. Instead, it directs us to serve Hashem with

---

[3] Rabbaynu Shlomo ben Yitzchak (Rashi), *Commentary on Sefer Shemot* 3:11.

our hearts. Maimonides explains that prayer is the means through which we offer our heart's service to G-d.

5. Prayer as a reflective experience

This does not mean that we do not express our longings and petition Hashem in prayer. However, prayer is intended to be reflective as well as expressive. The *amidah* is the centerpiece of our daily prayers. It is composed primarily of petitions. In the blessings of the *amidah* we petition Hashem for health, wisdom, sustenance, justice, forgiveness, redemption and virtually every other human need. Our Sages recommend that we personalize these blessings. We do this by personalizing the *amidah*'s various blessings with our own petitions.[4] Why are we directed to incorporate our petitions into the blessings of the *amidah*? Why can we not simply focus on our own needs instead of reciting the *amidah*?

By integrating petition for our needs into the *amidah* two outcomes are hopefully achieved. First, the petitions of the *amidah* are all formulated as prayers for the Jewish people. We are encouraged to personalize the blessings with our own needs. But when we do this, we integrate our personal needs into a blessing that petitions Hashem on behalf of our entire people. Through this process, we recognize that others share our plight and may be experiencing the same even more terrible suffering. We pray for a dear friend or relative who is ill. We do this in the context of a blessing that is constructed as a petition for all those who are ill. In this process we are moved to see ourselves as part of a greater community that includes people who we may not know but who are also suffering and need our prayers.

Second, as noted, the *amidah* is composed of a set of blessings that encompass the breadth of human needs. Through reciting and meditating upon these blessings we place our personal needs in perspective. We may have a friend who is ill. We may be struggling to support our family. Perhaps, we are praying for a friend who needs wise guidance in choosing between the paths that stretch forth before him. But when we integrate these petitions into the blessings of the *amidah*, we include within our prayers our requests for Hashem's forgiveness and mercy. We ask that Hashem help us find the courage and strength to repent and become better people. We also ask Him to redeem His people and restore us to our sacred homeland. If we consider our words, we recognize the enormous extent of our dependence upon Hashem. We realize that we need Him not only when we are desperate for the restoration of a friend's health or feel oppressed by financial stresses. Every day and in every aspect of our lives we rely upon and we are blessed by His benevolence.

The incorporation of our individual prayers into the *amidah* transforms a personal, often selfish and shallow expression into a reflective and thoughtful encounter with G-d.

6. The study of prayer enriches the activity of prayer

The "take away" from this exploration is that perhaps the greatest obstacle standing in the way of our appreciation of prayer is that we do not take the time or invest the energy into considering the beautiful contents of the our prayers. We are quick to reject or look askance at any imposed activity. But if we are willing to study and reflect upon the texts of our prayers, we can discover their eloquent expression of a passionate relationship with Hashem.

---

[4] Rav Yosef Karo, *Shulchan Aruch, Orech Chayim* 119.

Speak to Bnai Yisrael and take for Me an offering. From every person as his heart moves him, take My offering. (Shemot 25:2)

Secular Humanism and Torah Ethics

The challenge of treating one another properly

Last week's *parasha* primarily dealt with *mitzvot* that regulate our interpersonal behaviors. These laws establish standards for social and commercial interactions. Included in the *parasha* are laws protecting those who might easily be oppressed, laws establishing civil liability for damage caused to another or to one's property, and laws that regulate loans. Overall, the message of the *parasha* is that we are expected to treat one another fairly, to act toward one another with compassion, and give special attention to those who are less fortunate than ourselves.

Every one of us can embrace the message of the *parasha*. But we also recognize that we sometimes do not conduct ourselves according to the standard exemplified by its *mitzvot*. In other words, we can envision how we should treat one another, but we struggle to transform that vision into a standard of behavior to which we consistently adhere. In contemporary terminology – it is easier to talk the talk, than to walk the walk. Does the Torah have some insight for us that can help us achieve the level of sensitivity and fairness toward others to which we aspire?

In order to address this issue, we will embark on a short journey.

1. We will discuss the significance of the creation of the *Mishcan*.
2. This will lead us to consider Hashem's relationship with humanity.
3. Better understanding this relationship will help us appreciate the uniqueness of humanity in the creation drama.
4. With this understanding, we will uncover an underlying connection between the *Mishcan* and the interpersonal laws in Parshat Mishpatim.
5. Finally, we will arrive at our destination; we will identify a fundamental attitude that, when embraced, will support us in treating others fairly and with compassion.
6. As a bonus, once we have completed this journey, we will briefly discuss the enormous gulf that separates the Torah perspective from secular humanism.

It is notable that last week's *parasha* is followed by Parshat Terumah. This week's *parasha* deals with the commandment to build the *Mishcan* – the Tabernacle. This Tabernacle was the transportable temple of the wilderness. During the sojourn in the wilderness, it was erected in the center of the encampment and the tribes positioned their individual camps around it in a prescribed order. Parshat Terumah seems to represent an abrupt and unexplained change of topic. The Torah has suddenly transitioned from dealing with the interpersonal to a discussion of the Tabernacle. Is there some specific relevance that Parshat Terumah has to the standards of interpersonal conduct described in the previous *parasha*?

And He said: For I will be with you. And this is the sign that I have sent you. When you take forth the nation from Egypt, you will serve the L-rd at this mountain. (Shemot 3:12)

The objective of the redemption: Forging a relationship between Hashem and Bnai Yisrael.

In order to address these questions, let us return to Moshe's first encounter with Hashem. This occurred when Moshe beheld the burning bush that was not consumed by the flames that burned within it. That prophecy took place in the wilderness surrounding Mount Sinai. Hashem told Moshe that after leading Bnai Yisrael out of Egypt he would return to this mountain with the nation. At this mountain, the nation would be initiated into service of Hashem.

What was the specific form of the initiation into service of Hashem? Commenting on this *pasuk*, Rashi explains that the reference is to Revelation. Hashem told Moshe that the nation will receive the Torah and the observance of its *mitzvot* will be the basis of the nation's service to Hashem. However, the midrash explains that the creation of the *Mishcan* and the service performed in it are also included in this initiation. In other words, Bnai Yisrael's initiation into the service of Hashem was only completed with the creation of the *Mishcan* and through the service performed in it.

Why did Hashem reveal to Moshe that Bnai Yisrael was destined to receive the Torah? Rashi explains, in his comments on the passage, that the redemption of the nation from Egypt was not only intended to redress the injustice of their oppression. Also, it was not only the fulfillment of an ancient promise made to Avraham. The redemption's most fundamental objective was to bring the nation to Sinai so that it should receive the Torah. In other words, the nation was redeemed so that it would enter into a relationship with Hashem.

However, as noted above, the midrash adds that Hashem was also communicating to Moshe that the nation would create the *Mishcan*. Why did Hashem reveal this to Moshe as he charged him to lead his people out of Egypt?

And make for Me a sanctuary and I will dwell in their midst. (Shemot 25:8)

The *Mishcan* embodied the objective of the redemption

The above *pasuk* does not describe the *Mishcan* as a place of worship. It describes it as embodying or representing the presence of Hashem within the nation. Through the *Mishcan*, the presence of Hashem would be actualized within the midst of the people. The *Mishcan* would represent and communicate the ongoing providence of Hashem. His cloud would hover over it; His flame would descend from the heavens and consume its sacrifices; His voice would be heard by Moshe emanating from its inner-sanctuary.

Now, we can understand Hashem's message to Moshe. He told Moshe that the nation would not only receive the Torah and through its commandments serve Hashem, but in response to their service, Hashem would dwell in the midst of the nation. The nation would exist in virtual communion with Hashem. The creation of the *Mishcan* fulfilled the destiny for which the nation was redeemed

And they heard the sound of Hashem, the L-rd, traveling westward in the garden. And Adam and his wife hid from before Hashem, the L-rd, among the trees of the garden. (Beresheit 3:8)

The *Mishcan* restored the relationship between Hashem and humanity

Rav Yosef Dov Soloveitchik *Zt"l* explains that another destiny was fulfilled through the creation of the *Mishcan* – the destiny of humanity. Midrash Lekach Tov explains that before their sin Adam and Chavah dwelled in Gan Eden – the Garden of Eden – and they experienced an intimate personal relationship with Hashem. They sinned by disobeying Hashem's commandment. After their sin, the Torah describes them hearing the steps of Hashem. Lekach

Tov comments that they heard the sound of Hashem's retreating steps as He departed from Adam and Chavah. From that moment onward, Hashem maintained His aloofness. He remained distant from humanity. The *Mishcan* reestablished the intimacy between Hashem and Bnai Yisrael as representative of humanity. In other words, the *Mishcan* restored the relationship that was intended in the creation of humankind.

We can now identify the close connection between the interpersonal laws of Parshat Mishpatim and the commandment to create the *Mishcan*. Humankind has a special relationship with Hashem. The Torah tells us that we are created in the likeness of our Creator. This endows every human being with a sacredness that distinguishes the human race from every other element of the created universe. It is because of this unique sacredness, that Hashem dwelled within the Gan – the Garden of Eden – and then reestablished His presence within humanity with the creation of the *Mishcan*. We have an intimate relationship with the Creator. As described in the Shlomo's Shir HaShirim – Song of Songs – we are each other's beloved. In other words, the creation of the *Mishcan* and the presence of Hashem in our midst expresses the unique sacredness of the human being.

Parshat Mishapatim describes a community in which individuals treat each other with compassion and justice. This compassion extends to the most humble member and every person, regardless of position is required to act and be treated with justice. These laws are the concrete expression of the understanding of the human being expressed by the *Mishcan*. Every human being is sacred. Humanity is the beloved of Hashem among whom He has elected to dwell. The Torah expects our treatment of one another to reflect the sacredness of the human being and his or her likeness to the Creator.

Secular humanism and the Torah's perspective

In order to more fully appreciate the significance and impact of this perspective, it is useful to compare it to secular humanism. Secular humanism divorces our responsibility to act ethically from any religion foundation. It argues that human beings have the capacity to create a system of ethics that is founded upon reason and science without recourse to religious dogma or faith.

From the Humanistic perspective, the imperative to treat one another ethically is based upon utilitarian considerations. Our ethical behavior promotes the interests of the human race. However, Humanism, because of its complete rejection of religious faith, cannot escape the conclusion that the human being is no more than an evolutionary accident. The human being is the product of a blind, mindless, evolutionary process. This process has no objective or goal. No product of the process is more significant than any other. The flea and human being are of equal significance. Any perception we have of the superiority of the human race over the beast is purely subjective and without scientific basis. Therefore, the imperative for ethical treatment of animals is as compelling as the imperative to treat one another properly.

In contrast, the Torah teaches that the human being is unique and that our treatment of one another is founded upon and recognizes the sacredness of the individual. Does this distinction make a difference? Is there reason to believe that the Torah or Humanistic doctrine better promotes human welfare? History in replete with persecutions conducted in the name of religion and at the hands of those embracing Humanism. For example, The repressions of the Soviet system and the ruthlesspunishments meted out by its leaders – from Lenin onward – rival the worst persecutions carried out in response to religious intolerance.

Nonetheless, there is a fundamental difference between these two perspectives. Although, history provides many examples of religious intolerance, these are very often the result of the perversion or political manipulation of religious doctrine. In other words, the persecution represents a contradiction to the religion's authentic doctrine. In contrast, the Humanist recognizes only the utilitarian considerations of the human race. The individual is not significant nor is the individual endowed with unique rights and privileges. In other words, the sacrifice of the individual or a dissident group for the sake of the larger community is consistent with the Humanist ethic.

In closing, an important message for us to take from this week's *parasha* is that Hashem chose humanity to be the object of His love and attention. This expresses the sacredness of each and every human being. The Torah is communicating to us that we are to treat one another as sacred. We achieve this through acting toward every person fairly and with compassion

And they should create for Me a sanctuary and I will dwell among them. (Shemot 25:8)

Our parasha discusses the construction of the Mishcan. The Mishcan was the portable sanctuary that accompanied Bnai Yisrael in the wilderness. Once Bnai Yisrael entered and conquered the Land of Israel, this Mishcan—Tabernacle—was replaced by a permanent structure. This structure was the Bait HaMikdash—the Sacred Temple—constructed by King Shlomo.

Our passage contains the specific command to construct the Mishcan. However, Maimonides indicates in his Sefer HaMitzvot that this passage is also the source for the commandment to build the Bait HaMikdash. This suggests an obvious problem. The passage is not discussing the Bait HaMikdash. It is specifically commanding the construction of the Mishcan. How can Maimonides contend that this passage is the source for the obligation to build the Bait HaMikdash?[5]

Minchat Chinuch offers an answer to this question. He suggests that our pasuk legislates the requirement to establish a sanctuary. This institution does not have a specific form. Instead, the structure of the sanctuary is flexible. This commandment includes the Mishcan constructed in the wilderness and the Bait HaMikdash constructed by Shlomo.[6] How are these different structures included in one mitzvah? Minchat Chinuch maintains that sometimes it is appropriate for this sanctuary to be a portable structure. At other times, a permanent structure is more fitting. The environment in which the sanctuary will be placed determines its specific form. When Bnai Yisrael were traveling in the wilderness, the nation was not permanently situated, and so it was appropriate for the sanctuary to travel with the camp. Once Bnai Yisrael settled in the Land of Israel, the nation was permanently situated. At this point, a permanent structure became appropriate.

This answers our question on Maimonides. In fact, our pasuk is not legislating the construction of the Mishcan or the Bait HaMikdash. It is commanding Bnai Yisrael to create an institution of "sanctuary." The surrounding "camp" will determine the exact form to be assumed by this sanctuary. In the wilderness, this camp was mobile because the nation was traveling to

---

[5] Rabbaynu Moshe ben Maimon (Rambam) Sefer HaMitzvot, Mitzvat Aseh 2.
[6] Rav Yosef Babad, Minchat Chinuch, Mitzvah 95, note 1.

the Land of Israel. Therefore, the sanctuary described in our parasha was a portable Mishcan. When the surrounding camp is the nation that settled in the Land of Israel, the sanctuary must be a permanent structure—the Bait HaMikdash. Our pasuk requires a sanctuary. The Bait HaMikdash is a variation of this sanctuary.

This is a reasonable explanation for the derivation of the requirement to build the Bait HaMikdash from our passage. However, it does present one difficulty. Maimonides seems to indicate that the commandment to construct a sanctuary does not include the creation of the Mishcan. In describing the commandment to create a sanctuary, Maimonides quotes the Midrash Sifri. The midrash enumerates three commandments that came into effect when Bnai Yisrael entered the Land of Israel: to appoint a king, to build a Mikdash, and to destroy Amalek. It seems that Maimonides is asserting that the commandment to construct the Mikdash—a sanctuary—is comparable to the other two commandments mentioned by the Sifri. These other two commandments did not apply in the wilderness. Similarly, it appears that the commandment to build a Mikdash did not apply in the wilderness. Instead, the commandment first became operative with Bnai Yisrael's conquest of the Land of Israel.

According to this analysis of Maimonides' comments, the creation of a Mishcan is not included in the commandment to create a Mikdash. However, this is problematical. The commandment to create a Mikdash is derived from our passage. Our pasuk is clearly referring to the Mishcan. How is it possible that the pasuk commanding us to create a Mikdash is a passage referring to the Mishcan – yet the Mishcan is not included in this mitzvah?

It must be noted that Maimonides' position on the status of the Mishcan is not completely clear. As we have indicated in Sefer HaMitzvot, Maimonides seems to exclude the Mishcan from the commandment to create a sanctuary. However, his comments in the Mishne Torah are somewhat ambiguous. There, after describing the commandment to create a sanctuary, he immediately describes the Mishcan. Rabbaynu Moshe ben Maimon (Rambam / Maimonides) Mishne Torah, Hilchot Bait HaBeChirah 1:1. Maimonides does not explicitly state that the construction of the Mishcan is included in the commandment. However, his discussion of the mitzvah to build a sanctuary is immediately followed by his a description of the mishcan. This suggests that it is somehow included in this commandment. In short, the two treatments seem to be contradictory. No mention of the Mishcan is made in the Sefer HaMitzvot. But in his Mishne Torah, Maimonides seems to include the Mishcan within the mitzvah to build a sanctuary.

Gershonides offers an interesting but enigmatic explanation of the relationship between the Mishcan and the Bait HaMikdah. He suggests that the Mishcan was a preparatory institution. The nation was to create a sanctuary in the Land of Israel. They would serve Hashem in this Bait HaMikdash. The Mishcan provided an opportunity to prepare for this duty. The Mishcan was a practice facility for the activities to be performed in the Mikdash.

Gershonides explains that our passage refers to both the Mishcan and the Bait HaMikdash. However, the fundamental aspect of the commandment is to build the Bait HaMikdash. The Mishcan was merely a preparatory step towards this ultimate goal.[7] Perhaps, this is also Maimonides' position as well.

---

[7] Rabbaynu Levi ben Gershon (Ralbag / Gershonides), Commentary on Sefer Shemot, (Mosad HaRav Kook), pp. 339-340.

There are a number of problems with Geshonides' contention that the Mishcan was merely a preparatory institution. First, the Torah strictly regulates the services performed in the Bait HaMikdash. Each sacrifice and service must be performed precisely as described by the Torah. Deviations result in serious consequences and punishments. Of course, the same requirements apply to the performance of these services in the Mishcan. The objective of this practice is to perform a specified activity exactly as will ultimately be required. If the objective of the Mishcan is to create an opportunity to practice these services, the practice services should emulate the actual service that will be performed in the Bait HaMikdash. However, it is remarkable that deviations that occurred in the Mishcan were treated as seriously as those occurring in the Bait HaMikdash. They resulted in the same consequences and punishments as those occurring in the Bait HaMikdash! We would expect deviations in a practice service to result in lesser consequences and punishments.

Second, the completion of the Mishcan was followed by an initiation period. The purpose of this initiation was to train the Kohanim and Leveyim in the services they would perform in the Mishcan. It seems strange that the Torah required a practice, or training process, for service in the Mishcan. The Mishcan was only a preparatory institution. It seems the Torah required training for a practice activity. This seems somewhat redundant!

The first step required to address these problems is to recognize that they suggest Gershonides does not completely disagree with Minchat Chinuch. He agrees with the fundamental premise that the Torah commanded the creation of a sanctuary. This sanctuary takes different forms. In the wilderness, the concept of sanctuary was expressed in the Mishcan. In the Land of Israel, the Bait HaMikdash embodied the concept of sanctuary. Therefore, service in the Mishcan was treated as seriously as service in the Bait HaMikdash.

If this is the case, what is Gershonides' meaning in his contention that the Mishcan was a practice facility? Gershonides is providing an insight regarding the reason for including the Mishcan in the commandment to create a sanctuary. On this issue, he differs dramatically from Minchat Chinuch. In order to identify their disagreement, let us focus on a specific aspect of Minchat Chinuch's position.

Minchat Chinuch assumes that the Mishcan and the Bait HaMikdash are of equal significance. They are two equally valid expressions of a single institution—a sanctuary. Gershonides disagrees, maintaining that the Bait HaMikdash is the ultimate expression of the institution of sanctuary. However, this does not mean that the Mishcan's sanctity was inferior to that of the Bait HaMikdash. Instead, Gershonides is asserting that the Mishcan is modeled after, and is a prelude to, the Bait HaMikdash. In other words, were there no requirement to create a Bait HaMikdash, there could not be a Mishcan. Gershonides does not intend to imply that the service performed in the Mishcan was merely "practice." Instead, he is explaining the relationship between the two versions of a sanctuary. The Mishcan was modeled after the Bait HaMikdash and was its prelude.

We can now fully understand Maimonides' position. Maimonides maintains that the essential definition of the mitzvah described in our pasuk is to create a Bait HaMikdash. This is the fundamental aspect of the mitzvah. However, this commandment engenders an additional obligation. This is the obligation to create a Mishcan in the wilderness. In Sefer HaMitzvot, Maimonides defines the fundamental aspect of the mitzvah. He explains that the essential element of the commandment only applies once the Land of Israel is conquered. Maimonides appreciates that our passage includes the Mishcan. However, he maintains that the obligation to create the Mishcan was engendered by the requirement of Bait HaMikdash.

We can now also resolve the apparent contradiction between Sefer HaMitzvot and the Mishne Torah. In Sefer HaMitzvot, Maimonides defines the essential component of the commandment. This is to build a Bait HaMikdash. However, in Mishne Torah, Maimonides acknowledges that this fundamental requirement engendered the obligation to create the Mishcan in the wilderness.

"And they should create for me a sanctuary and I will dwell among them." (Shemot 25:8)

In this *pasuk* Hashem instructs Moshe to command Bnai Yisrael to construct the *Mishcan*. Hashem tells Bnai Yisrael that through this *Mishcan*, He will dwell among the people.

This passage cannot be understood literally. In order to understand the difficulty presented by a literal interpretation of the *pasuk,* an introduction is needed. Maimonides, in his commentary on the Mishne enumerates the basic foundations of the Torah. The third of these basic principles is that the Almighty is not, in any sense, material.[8]

Maimonides discusses this principle in further detail in his Mishne Torah. He again explains that the Almighty is not material. He adds that it is also inappropriate to attribute to Hashem any of the characteristics associated with physical bodies. For example, Hashem does not have a front of back. One cannot ascribe physical actions to the Almighty. Also, one cannot ascribe a place to Hashem.[9]

This principle, identified by Maimonides, is a logical extension of the proposition that Hashem is a unity. The Torah clearly states that "Hashem is one".[10] This statement tells us that there is only one G-d. However, our Sages understand the passage to also mean that the Almighty is a perfect unity. This means that He has no parts or aspects. He is not subject to division. He is an absolute representation of "oneness".[11] The principle of Hashem's unity precludes attribution of a material existence to Him. Any material entity is has parts or aspects. It has a front and back or dimensions. These characteristics contradict the concept of absolute unity.

Furthermore the Torah clearly states that Hashem is not material. This principle is communicated in Moshe's review of the event of Revelation. He reminds the nation that they had experienced Revelation at Sinai. In this experience the Almighty was not represented by any material image.[12]

We can now understand the difficulty presented by our passage. If our passage is interpreted literally, it contradicts this principle. Literally understood, our passage attributes location to the Almighty. The passage states that Hashem will dwell among Bnai Yisrael! This is impossible. Hashem is not material. Therefore, it is not correct to say He dwells in any place.

---

[8] Rabbaynu Moshe ben Maimon (Rambam) *Commentary on the Mishne*, Mes. Sanhedrin 10:1.
[9] Rabbaynu Moshe ben Maimon (Rambam) *Mishne Torah*, Hilchot Yesodai HaTorah, 1:11.
[10] Sefer Devarim 6:4.
[11] Rabbaynu Moshe ben Maimon (Rambam) *Mishne Torah*, Hilchot Yesodai HaTorah, 1:7.
[12] Sefer Devarim 4:15. See (Rambam) *Commentary on the Mishne*, Mesechet Sanhedrin 10:1.

Unkelus is sensitive to this anthropomorphism. In his translation of our passage, he alters the problematic phrase. In his rendering the phrase reads, "and I will cause the Divine presence to dwell among them". Unkelus' intention is to remove any attribution of place to the Almighty. According to Unkelus, the passage's refers to Hashem's Divine presence or influence. In other words, the passage describes a providential relationship. The Almighty will exercise His providence over the *Mishcan* and the people.

Rav Yosef Albo, in his Sefer HaIkkrim, uses the same approach to explain various anthropomorphic expressions found in the Torah. A few examples will illustrate this approach. Hashem tells us, in reference to the Temple, "Mine eyes and Mine heart shall be there perpetually".[13] Hashem does not have eyes or a heart. The intent of the passage is to communicate that a special providential influence exists over the *Mikdash*.[14] The Torah states that at Revelation, "the appearance of the glory of the Lord was like a devouring fire on the top of the mountain".[15] This passage does not intend to communicate that Hashem was present at Revelation. This would attribute a place to the Almighty. Instead, the passage is stating that the influence of the Almighty was evidenced through a physical manifestation. In this case, the manifestation was the conflagration that appeared at the top of Sinai.[16] It should be noted that the *pasuk* refers to the "glory" of the Almighty. This supports this interpretation. The Almighty was not present. However, His "glory" or influence was indicated by the fire.

One anthropomorphic expression has occasioned considerable discussion among the Sages. One of the names used for the Almighty is *HaMakom* – the Place.[17] This is popularly understood to mean that the Divine presence extends everywhere. However, our Sages provide a different explanation of the term. They explain that the term means that Hashem is the *makom* – the place – of the universe.[18]

This explanation is very difficult to understand. How can the Sages refer to Hashem as the place of the universe? Hashem is not material. He is not a place! Rav Yitzchak Arama offers a novel interpretation of the Sages' comments. He explains that the term place can be understood as the base upon which something rests or is supported. As an example, he cites the second mishne of Tractate Avot. The mishne explains that the world stand on three pillars – Torah study, Divine service and acts of kindness. The intent of the mishne is that these three activities are essential to the existence of the world. The mishne expresses this idea by representing the world as standing on these activities. In other words, standing in a place – upon the pillars of Torah study, Divine service and acts of kindness – represents dependency. Rav Arama explains that the name *HaMakom* communicates the universe's dependency upon the Almighty. He is the "place" upon which the universe stands. This means the universe only exists as a result of His continuing will. His will supports the universe's existence. Without His will, the universe would cease to exist.[19]

---

[13] Melachim I 9:3.
[14] Rav Yosef Albo, *Sefer HaIkkarim*, volume2, chapter 14.
[15] Sefer Shemot 24:17.
[16] Rav Yosef Albo, *Sefer HaIkkarim*, volume2, chapter 17.
[17] See, for example, Mesechet Avot 2:9.
[18] Midrash Rabba, Sefer Beresheit 68:9.
[19] Rav Yitzchak Arama, *Akeydat Yitzchak on Sefer Shemot*, Parshat Terumah.

And they shall make for Me a sanctuary and I will dwell among them. (Shemot 25:8)

The Relationship between the Bait HaMikdash and the Synagogue

1. The source of the commandment to build the Bait HaMikdash

Our parasha discusses the construction of the Mishcan. The Mishcan was the portable sanctuary that accompanied Bnai Yisrael in the wilderness. Once Bnai Yisrael entered and conquered the Land of Israel, this Mishcan – Tabernacle – was replaced by a permanent structure. This permanent structure – the Bait HaMikdash – was constructed by King Shlomo. Its construction was completed in approximately 950 BCE. Shlomo's Bait HaMikdash was destroyed by Nebuchadrezzar's armies in approximately 587 BCE. Shortly thereafter, much of the Jewish population of the Land of Israel was exiled to Babylonia. Eventually, the exiled Jewish people return to the Land of Israel and rebuild the Bait HaMikdash. The second Bait HaMikdash was dedicated in approximately 515 BCE and stood until 70 CE when it was destroyed by Titus.

The above passage contains the specific command to construct the Mishcan. Maimonides indicates in his Sefer HaMitzvot that this passage is also the source for the commandment to build the Bait HaMikdash.[20]

And My Shabbats you should observe and My Mikdash you should fear. I am Hashem. (VaYikra 19:30)

2. The sanctity of the Bait HaMikdash and the synagogue

The Bait HaMikdash's sanctity is derived from the Torah commandment that enjoins Bnai Yisrael in its construction. This sanctity expresses itself in many ways. One expression is in the commandment found in the above passage. Bnai Yisrael are commanded to treat the Bait HaMikdash with awe. This commandment requires that a person enter with respect the area of the Bait HaMikdash and conduct oneself appropriately while in the Bait HaMikdash. Jewish Law – halachah specifies various behaviors that are inappropriate in the Bait HaMikdash.

A synagogue is also endowed with sanctity. Awareness of the sanctity is expressed through acting respectfully inside of a synagogue. However, the requirement of a community to create a synagogue does not seem to be expressed anywhere in the Torah. This raises an interesting question. The institution of synagogue does not seem to be the subject of a Torah mitzvah. What then is the source of the synagogue's sanctity?

Rabbaynu Nissim suggests that the synagogue's sanctity is not based upon a Torah commandment and is not conferred by the Torah. Instead, the Sages endowed the synagogue with its sanctity. He explains that the synagogue is designated as the place in which the most solemn prayers are offered. Therefore, the Sages conferred upon it a degree of sanctity consistent with its function as a house of prayer.[21]

Others disagree with Rabbaynu Nissim and suggest that the synagogue's sanctity is conferred by the Torah itself. Rav Yosef Dov Soloveitchik Zt"l included Maimonides among Rabbaynu Nissim's opponents. This conclusion is based upon Maimonides' summary of the 613

---

[20] Rabbaynu Moshe ben Maimon (Rambam) Sefer HaMitzvot, Mitzvat Aseh 20.
[21] Rabbaynu Nissim ben Reuven, (Ran) Notes to Commentary of Rabbaynu Yitzchak Alfasi, Mesechet Megilah 8a.

mitzvot included in his introduction to his code of Torah Law – Mishne Torah. Maimonides explains that the 65th negative commandment includes a prohibition against destruction of the Bait HaMikdash, a synagogue, and house of Torah study. Maimonides is outlining the Torah level prohibitions included in the commandment. This implies that the synagogue and house of Torah study are endowed by the Torah with sanctity. Therefore, it is prohibited to destroy them. In short, Maimonides seems to regard the synagogue's sanctity as conferred by the Torah. However, he does not provide any indication of his basis for this conclusion.

> *Therefore say to them, "So says Hashem, G-d: Although I have removed them far away among the nations and although I have dispersed them to many lands, I will be with them a minor sanctuary in the lands to which they shall come." (Sefer Yechezkiel 11:16)*

3. The synagogue is a minor sanctuary

The prophet Yechezkiel shared the above message with Bnai Yisrael. He assured the people that although they would be scattered among the lands of their exile, Hashem would remain in their midst. In the Diaspora, they would not be able to serve Hashem in His Bait HaMikdash. However, they would have access to a "minor sanctuary". The Talmud suggests that the synagogue is the "minor sanctuary" to which the prophet refers. The Sages of the Talmud understand the passage as a reassurance. Even when the major or primary sanctuary – the Bait HaMikdash – has been destroyed, Hashem will continue to be found in the minor sanctuary – the synagogue.

According to Rav Soloveitchik, the Talmud is positing an analogy between the Bait HaMikdash and the synagogue. This analogy is in regard to the basis of their sanctity. In other words, the Bait HaMikdash and the synagogue derive their sanctity from similar – if not identical – sources.

> *And you shall make an Ark of acacia wood. Its length shall be two and a half cubits. Its width shall be one and a half cubits. Its height shall be one and a half cubits. (Sefer Shemot 25:10)*

> *And you shall place in the Ark the Testimony that I will give to you. (Sefer Shemot 25:16)*

> *This is the accounting of the Mishcan – the Mishcan of Testimony – that was determined by the command of Moshe (and was) the responsibility of the Leviyim under the authority of Etamar the son of AhAhron the Kohen (Shemot 38:21)*

4. The centrality of the Tablets of Testimony to the Mishcan

In Hashem's commandment to Moshe regarding the construction of the Mishcan, the first component that is described is the Ark – the Ahron. The Ahron was to contain the Luchot – the Tablets of the Decalogue. According to Rashbam, because the Luchot were to be placed within it, the Ahron is referred to as the Ahron of Ark of Testimony.[22] Nachmanides adds that the Mishcan is referred to as the Mishcan of Testimony because it was to house the Luchot.[23]

Rav Soloveitchik suggests that the very identity of the Mishcan as the Mishcan of Testimony communicates that the Luchot are the fundamental component of the Mishcan. The primacy assigned to the Ahron in the instructions for the creation of the Mishcan also supports this

---

[22] Rabbaynu Shemuel ben Meir (Rashbam) Commentary on Sefer Shemot 25:16.
[23] Rabbaynu Moshe ben Nachman (Ramban), Commentary on Sefer Shemot 38:21.

conclusion. Based upon this insight, Rav Soloveitchik suggests a solution to a troubling problem in Maimonides' code – Mishne Torah.

> And he said to the Leviyim who taught all of Yisrael, who were sacred to Hashem: Place the sacred Ark in the house that Shlomo the son of David, the King of Israel built. It will no longer be a burden for you to be carried upon the shoulders. Now, go and serve Hashem your G-d and Yisrael His nation. (Sefer Devrai HaYamim II 35:3)

5. King Yoshivahu's actions to preserve the Bait HaMikdash

King Yoshiyahu foresaw the destruction of the first Bait HaMikdash. He understood that he was responsible to preserve the Ahron, its contents, and other critical components of the Bait HaMikdash. Shlomo had included in the construction of the Bait HaMikdash hidden underground chambers. Yoshiyahu commanded the Leveyim to remove the Ahron, with its contents to these chambers to assure their preservation.

As a result of Yoshiyahu's actions the Ahron, its contents, and other fundamental elements of the Bait HaMikdash were saved from destruction. However, when the Bait HaMikdash was rebuilt, these items were not restored to their proper places and they remained hidden in Shlomo's underground vaults.

Maimonides' Mishne Torah is a work of halachah. Maimonides rarely discusses philosophical issues in this work. There is almost a complete absence of descriptions of historical events. Maimonides includes philosophical or historical material in order to explain halachic issues. Therefore, it is surprising that Maimonides includes in his discussion of the laws of the Bait HaMikdash a complete description of Yoshiyahu's actions.[24]

6. The sanctity of the second Bait HaMikdash

Rav Soloveitchik suggests that Maimonides includes a description of the precautions taken by King Yoshiyahu in order to solve a perplexing problem. As demonstrated above, the central component of the Mishcan and the Bait HaMikdash is the Luchot. However, the Ahron and its Luchot were not restored to their place in the second Bait HaMikdash. How could the second Bait HaMikdash be endowed with sanctity if it was bereft of its most fundamental component?

Rav Soloveitchik responds that Maimonides is addressing this question in his description of King Yoshiyahu's actions. King Shlomo included in his Bait HaMikdash hidden underground chambers. Shlomo's vaults were an integral part of the design and structure of the Bait HaMikdash. Yoshiyahu removed the Ahron from its usual place and hid it in Shlomo's vaults. By taking this precaution, he not only preserved the Ahron and its contents. He also secured them within the structure of the Bait HaMikdash. Therefore, the second Bait HaMikdash was not deprived of the Ahron and Luchot. They were not restored to their former location. However, they remained within the structure. The second Bait HaMikdash included within its structure the Ahron and its Luchot!

7. The Torah source of the synagogue's sanctity

Based upon this analysis, Rav Soloveitchik concludes that the sanctity of the Bait HaMikdash is derived from the Ahron and its Luchot. Now, the source of the synagogue's

---

[24] Rabbaynu Moshe ben Maimon (Rambam) Mishne Torah, Hilchot Bait HaBechirah 4:1.

sanctity can be identified. As explained by the Talmud, the synagogue is a minor sanctuary. It is a version of the Bait HaMikdash. In order for the synagogue to be analogous to the Bait HaMikdash, must derive its sanctity from a similar or identical source. This means that, like the Bait HaMikdash, the synagogue derives its sanctity from its Ahron and its contents – the Sefer Torah. Because the synagogue derives its sanctity from fundamentally the same source as the Bait HaMikdash, it is endowed by the Torah itself with its sanctity.[25]

And let them make Me a sanctuary, that I may dwell among them. (Shemot 25:8)

The Trouble with Greatness

1. The commandment to create a Bait HaMikdash and its fulfillment

Parshat Terumah is devoted to describing the design of the Mishcan – the Tabernacle. Included in the parasha is also a detailed description of the design of the fundamental components of the Mishcan. These components include the aron, kaporet, shulchan, and menorah – the ark, the ark-cover, the table upon which the shew-bread was placed, and the candelabra.

In the above passage, Hashem commands Bnai Yisrael to create the Mishcan and its components as they are described in the parasha. This Mishcan was the focal point of Bnai Yisrael's encampments during their travels through the wilderness. At each encampment, the people arranged their tents around the Mishcan. The Mishcan was the center of worship in the wilderness. All sacrificial worship took place there. The cloud communicating the presence of Hashem hovered over the Mishcan. When Hashem spoke with Moshe His voice was perceived as emerging from between the cherubs of the kaporet – the ark-cover.

According to Maimonides, the above passage is not only the directive to create the Mishcan. It is also the source for the commandment to build the Bait HaMikdash – the Holy Temple.[26] The first Bait HaMikdash was constructed by King Shlomo upon the Temple Mount in Yerushalayim. This Temple was destroyed. It was replaced by the second Temple created by those who returned from the Babylonian exile. The second Temple was constructed upon the site of its predecessor. This second Bait HaMikdash was also destroyed. It will be replaced by the third Bait HaMikdash. It too will be constructed upon the same site. It will be the final Temple – never to be destroyed or replaced.

This first Bait HaMikdash was constructed many generations after Bnai Yisrael's entry into the Land of Israel. This delay was in accordance with the stipulations of the Torah. Maimonides explains that the Bait HaMikdash was only to be constructed after appointment of a king and the destruction of Amalek.[27]

And it came to pass, when the king dwelt in his house, and Hashem had given him rest from all his enemies round about, that the king said unto Natan the prophet: See now, I dwell in a house of cedar, but the ark of G-d dwells within curtains. (Sefer Shemuel II 7:1-2)

2. King David's request and Hashem's reponse

---

[25] Rav Hershel Schachter, Eretz HaTzvi (Genesis Jerusalem Press) pp. 88-92. The above is a much condensed version of Rav Shachter's presentation of Rav Soloveitchik's analysis.
[26] Rabbaynu Moshe ben Maimon (Rambam) Mishne Torah, Hilchot Bait HaBechirah 1:1.
[27] Rabbaynu Moshe ben Maimon (Rambam) Mishne Torah, Hilchot Melachim 1:1-2.

During the reign of King David all of the prerequisites were apparently in place for the construction of the Bait HaMikdash. David ruled as king over the nation. Amalek had been vanquished and Bnai Yisrael lived in security. David concluded that the time had arrived for fulfillment of the mitzvah to build the Bait HaMikdash. He consulted with the prophet Natan. Natan agreed that the time had arrived for building the Temple and advised David to proceed with the project.

Immediately after speaking with David, Natan received a prophecy from Hashem. Hashem told Natan that David will not build the Bait HaMikdash. Instead, this privilege will be given to his son who will succeed him on the throne. In that same prophecy, Hashem instructed Natan to reveal to David that his descendants will rule Bnai Yisrael. The kingship of Bnai Yisrael will never be removed from the House of David.

There are two interesting elements to Natan's prophecy. First, no reason is provided by Hashem for His refusal to allow David to build the Bait HaMikdash. Second, Hashem's rejection of David's request is accompanied with the promise of permanent sovereignty. Each of these elements must be more thoroughly considered. Why was David denied the privilege of fulfilling his vision of building the Bait HaMikdash? Why was this refusal accompanied by an assurance of permanent sovereignty?

> *And David said to Shlomo: My son, as for me, it was in my heart to build a house unto the name of Hashem my G-d. But the word of Hashem came to me, saying: You have shed blood abundantly, and have made great wars. You shall not build a house unto My name, because you have shed much blood upon the earth in My sight. (Sefer Devrai HaYamim I 22:7-8)*

3. Shedding blood disqualified David from building the Temple

The Navi's account to Natan's prophecy does not provide an explanation for Hashem's rejection of David. However, Devrai HaYamim includes a description of David's instructions to his son Shlomo to build the Bait HaMikdash. In David's instructions he explains that Hashem denied him the privilege of building the Bait HaMikdash because of the enormous amount of blood that he had spilled and the wars he had waged.

The commentators discuss the meaning of David's explanation. The passages seem to say that David was disqualified from the role of building the Bait HaMikdash because of his role as a conqueror and warrior king. David consolidated Bnai Yisrael's conquest of the Land of Israel and he brought the people security from attack by their enemies. These accomplishments were a great legacy that he left the nation. However, this legacy also rendered him unfit to build the Bait HaMikdash.

This is difficult to understand. The wars waged by David were just and ordained by the Torah. Why then did his role of obedient servant to Hashem and protector of his people disqualify him from building the Bait HaMikdash?

4. Preserving David's legacy as protector of the nation

The commentators offer a number of responses. One of the most interesting is provided by Gershonides. He argues that the Bait HaMikdash would be permanently associated with the king who would build it. David was a controversial ruler. He was loved and revered by Bnai Yisrael. However, among the surrounding nations, he was at best feared and at worst reviled. They regarded him as a dangerous enemy and ruthless conqueror.

The first Bait HaMikdash was destined to be destroyed by Bnai Yisrael's enemies. Its destruction was a terrible tragedy. If this Temple had been associated with David, the tragedy would have been even greater. It would have provided Bnai Yisrael's enemies the opportunity to claim that its destruction was a final verdict and condemnation of David's conquests. They would claim that the Temple was David's most significant legacy. Its destruction indicated that his violence rendered him unworthy of this precious legacy. The legitimacy and justice of the many wars fought by David would have been undermined. Therefore, Hashem refused David permission to build the Bait HaMikdash. Only the universally respected and loved Shlomo was permitted to build the Bait HaMikdash.[28]

5. The preconditions required for building the Temple were not met in David's time

Malbim offers a simpler explanation. He explains that the Bait HaMikdash was to be built in a time of peace. Malbim argues that during David's lifetime the requisite level of peace was not secured. David did defeat Bnai Yisrael's enemies. However, they remained subdued out of fear and intimidation. Shlomo ushered in a period of true peace and harmony. Therefore, he was a more appropriate choice than his father for the role of building the Bait HaMikdash.[29]

And if you make Me an altar of stone, you shall not build it of hewn stones; for if you lift up your tool upon it, you have profaned it. (Shemot 20:22)

6. Violence is antithetical to the message of the Bait HaMikdash

One of the most well known explanations is provided by RaDak. He explains that the Bait HaMikdash must be associated with peace. Therefore, regardless of the justice of his campaigns, David's very association with violence and bloodshed disqualified him from building the Bait HaMikdash.

RaDak supports his explanation with the above passage. The Torah explains that the altar used to offer sacrifices to Hashem should not be constructed of hewn stones. These stones have been manufactured using stone-cutting tools. RaDak and others explain that these tools are made of metal – a material used to create weapons. The use of stone-cutting tools creates an association between the finished stones and violence represented by these tools. The altar is to be associated with peace. Therefore, it cannot be constructed of these hewn stones. RaDak argues that the same consideration disqualified David from building the Bait HaMikdash. Like its altar, the Temple is associated with peace. David, like stone-cutting tools, was associated with violence. Therefore, he was not the appropriate person to build the Bait HaMikdash.[30]

Even them will I bring to My holy mountain, and make them joyful in My house of prayer. Their burnt-offerings and their sacrifices shall be acceptable upon My altar; for My house shall be called a house of prayer for all peoples. (Sefer Yeshayahu 56:7)

7. The Bait HaMikdash is for all nations

The above passage suggests a simple explanation for Hashem's rejection of David and His selection of Shlomo for the role of the Bait HaMikdash's builder. The prophet Yeshayahu describes a future time in which all of the nations will perceive the Temple as a house of prayer

---

[28] Rabbaynu Levi ben Gershon (Ralbag), Commentary on Sefer Devrai HaYamim I 22:8.
[29] Rabbaynu Meir Libush (Malbim), Commentary on Sefer Shemuel I 7:5.
[30] Rabbaynu David Kimchi (Radak), Commentary on Devrai HaYamim 22:8.

for all people. In this vision, the prophet declares that the mission of the Bait HaMikdash is universal and applies to all humanity.

King David was loved by his own people. However, he was a conqueror of other nations. He was not the best ambassador for the message that Yishayahu is communicating. To the people, of other nations David was feared and perhaps resented. He could not effectively invite the nations of the world to pray at his Temple. Furthermore, if associated with his name, the Bait HaMikdash would continue to evoke resentment among the nations.

Moreover, concerning the stranger that is not of Your people Israel, when he shall come out of a far country for Your name's sake – for they shall hear of Your great name, and of Your mighty hand, and of Your outstretched arm; when he shall come and pray toward this house, hear in heaven Your dwelling-place, and do according to all that the stranger calls to You; that all the peoples of the earth may know Your name, to fear You, as does Your people Israel, and that they may know that Your name is called upon this house which I have built.
(Sefer Melachim I 8:41-43)

8. Shlomo's message to the nations of the world

Shlomo was an appropriate choice to build the Bait HaMikdash. Unlike David, he was beloved by his own people and respected and revered by the people of other nations. His association with the Bait HaMikdash provided an opportunity to reach out to all people and to invite them to accept this sacred temple as their house of prayer. In the above passages, Shlomo communicates this message of inclusiveness. These passages are taken from Shlomo's prayers offered at the completion of the building of the Bait HaMikdash. He envisions people from all of the nations coming to the Temple to offer their prayers to Hashem.

9. The promise of the House of David

All of these explanations address the question of why David was disqualified from building the Bait HaMikdash. They also provide a possible explanation for the other element of Natan's prophecy. In the same prophecy in which Hashem rejected David's request to build the Bait HaMikdash, Hashem promised David his family's permanent sovereignty. Why was this promise made in conjunction with Hashem's rejection of David's request to build the Temple?

All of the above explanations for Hashem's denial to David of the privilege of building the Bait HaMikdash have a common theme. Hashem was not punishing David or suggesting a criticism in this denial. David's life – led righteously – nonetheless, rendered him less than ideal for this task. Perhaps, Hashem was communicating to David that rejection of his request did not reflect a failing in David. David was the appropriate king for his time. He created a great legacy that would continue to impact Bnai Yisrsael for all generations. However, he was not the appropriate king for this specific task – the building the Bait HaMikdash. His very greatness as the protector of Bnai Yisrael disqualified him from this role.

10. The trouble with greatness

There is an important message in this lesson. We tend to judge others harshly for their deficiencies. However, sometimes a deficiency is the unfortunate but inevitable consequence of a person's greatness. David was not associated with peace. In this sense, he was inferior to his son Shlomo. Shlomo earned the respect of leaders of near and distant nations. They came to meet this remarkable ruler and learn from his wisdom.

David never succeeded in communicating a message of inclusion or universality. However, this was a direct result of his greatness as a warrior and as the protector of the Jewish people. To criticize David for his shortcomings, when compared to Shlomo, is to fail to recognize and appreciate his greatness.

And they shall make for Me a sanctuary and I will dwell among them. (Shemot 25:8)

Our *parasha* discusses the construction of the *Mishcan*. The *Mishcan* was the portable sanctuary that accompanied Bnai Yisrael in the wilderness. Once Bnai Yisrael entered and conquered the Land of Israel, this *Mishcan* – Tabernacle – was replaced by a permanent structure. This structure was the *Bait HaMikdash* – the Sacred Temple – constructed by King Shlomo.

Our passage contains the specific command to construct the *Mishcan*. However, Maimonides indicates in his Sefer HaMitzvot that this passage is also the source for the commandment to build the *Bait HaMikdash*.[31] Sefer Mitzvot Gadol – SeMaG – agrees that there is a commandment to build the *Bait HaMikdash*. However, he objects to Maimonides' contention that the *mitzvah* is derived from our *pasuk*. He suggests that the proper source for the commandment to build the *Bait HaMikdash* is a set of *pasukim* in Sefer Devarim. In these pesukim, Moshe tells Bnai Yisrael that they will cross over the Jordan and inhabit the Land of Israel. Moshe then tells the people that Hashem will choose a place for His *Mikdash*, and it is to that place that all sacrifices will be brought.[32,33]

Rav Yosef Karo suggests that there is an obvious reason for SeMaG's rejection of Maimonides' position. Our passage is not discussing the *Bait HaMikdash*. It is specifically commanding the construction of the *Mishcan*. How can Maimonides contend that this passage is the source for the obligation to build the *Bait HaMikdash*?[34]

It seems that SeMaG's objection to Maimonides' position is reasonable. Why does Maimonides insist on citing our passage as the source for the commandment to build the *Bait HaMikdash*? Rav Yosef Karo suggests that Maimonides' position is based upon a problem within the wording of our passage. What is this problem?

In our *pasuk*, Bnai Yisrael are commanded to build a sanctuary for Hashem. There are two terms used in the Torah for "sanctuary." These terms are *Mishcan* and *Mikdash*. The term *Mishcan* is generally used to refer to the Tabernacle of the wilderness. In our passage, Hashem directed Bnai Yisrael to build this Tabernacle of the wilderness. Therefore, it seems that the passage should have used the term, *Mishcan*. However, in our passage, Hashem does not tell Bnai Yisrael to build a *Mishcan* – a Tabernacle. He tells Bnai Yisrael to build a *Mikdash*. Why does the passage use the term *Mikdash* and not the seemingly more appropriate term *Mishcan*?

Rav Yosef Karo suggests that Maimonides is answering this question. According to Maimonides, the term *Mikdash* is a more general term than *Mishcan*. It includes both the Tabernacle and the *Bait HaMikdash*. The passage specifically uses the term *Mikdash* in order to

---

[31] Rabbaynu Moshe ben Maimon (Rambam) *Sefer HaMitzvot, Mitzvat Aseh* 2.
[32] Sefer Devarim 11:10-11.
[33] Rabbaynu Moshe ben Yaakov of Coucy (SeMaG), *Sefer Mitzvot Gadol, Mitzvat Aseh* 163.
[34] Rav Yosef Karo, *Rav Yosef Karo*, Hilchot Bait HaBechirah 1:1.

include both forms of sanctuary – the portable Tabernacle, and the permanent *Bait HaMikdash*.[35] It seems that according to Rav Yosef Karo, Maimonides maintains that our *pasuk* legislates the requirement to establish a sanctuary. This institution does not have a specific form. Instead, the structure of the sanctuary is flexible. This commandment includes the *Mishcan* constructed in the wilderness, and the *Bait HaMikdash* constructed by Shlomo.

How are these different structures included in one *mitzvah*? Sometimes it is appropriate for this sanctuary to be a portable structure. At other times, a permanent structure is more fitting. The environment in which the sanctuary will be placed determines its form. When Bnai Yisrael were traveling in the wilderness, the nation was not permanently situated. It was appropriate for the sanctuary to travel with the camp. Once Bnai Yisrael settled in the Land of Israel, the nation was permanently situated. At this point, a permanent structure became appropriate.

This is a reasonable explanation of Maimonides' position. However, SeMaG raises an important objection to this position. The Midrash Sifri enumerates three commandments that came into effect when Bnai Yisrael entered the Land of Israel. These *mitzvot* are to appoint a king, to build a *Mikdash,* and to destroy Amalek. It seems that Sifri is asserting that the commandment to construct the *Mikdash* – a sanctuary – is comparable to the other two commandments mentioned by the Sifri. These other two commandments did not apply in the wilderness. Similarly, it appears that the commandment to build a *Mikdash* did not apply in the wilderness. Instead, the commandment first became operative with Bnai Yisrael's conquest of the Land of Israel.[36] It is interesting that Maimonides also quotes this midrash in his Sefer HaMitzvot.[37] How can Maimonides' position be reconciled with this Midrash?

Maimonides explains that there is a fundamental difference between the *Mishcan* and the *Bait HaMikdash*. He explains that the *Mishcan* was originally constructed in the wilderness and was intended to serve as a temporary structure. When the nation entered the Land of Israel, the *Mishcan* was established in Gilgal. It was then moved to Shiloh. The *Mishcan* was subsequently replaced by a sanctuary constructed in Nov. The Nov sanctuary was also eventually replaced by a sanctuary build in Givon. In turn, the sanctuary of Givon was replaced by the *Bait HaMikdash*. Once the *Bait HaMikdash* was constructed, its site became the permanent location for any subsequent sanctuary. The second *Bait HaMikdash* was constructed upon this location, and the third will also be built on this site. In short, all of the sanctuaries built before the *Bait HaMikdash* were temporary. These sanctuaries were erected at a site for a period of time and then moved to a new location and, sometimes, even replaced by a new structure. However, once the *Bait HaMikdash* was built upon the Temple Mount in Yesushalayim, this site became the permanent location of the structure.[38]

This distinction reflects a fundamental difference between the sanctuaries that preceded the *Bait HaMikdash* and the *Bait HaMikdash* itself. As explained above, the institution of the sanctuary is expressed in different forms. In the wilderness, the sanctuary took the form of the *Mishcan* – a portable structure. The sanctuary took other forms once the nation entered the Land of Israel. However, all of the iterations of the sanctuary were innately temporary and precursors to the *Bait HaMikdash*. The *Bait HaMikdash* represents the ultimate and final form of the

---

[35] Rav Yosef Karo, *Kesef Mishne*, Hilchot Bait HaBechirah 1:1.
[36] Rabbaynu Moshe ben Yaakov of Coucy (SeMaG), *Sefer Mitzvot Gadol, Mitzvat Aseh* 163.
[37] Rabbaynu Moshe ben Maimon (Rambam) *Sefer HaMitzvot, Mitzvat Aseh* 20.
[38] Rabbaynu Moshe ben Maimon (Rambam) *Mishne Torah*, Hilchot Bait HaBeChirah 1:1-3.

sanctuary. Once the *Bait HaMikdash* was built, it was the final form and site for the sanctuary. All subsequent sanctuaries are reconstructions of this King Shlomo's *Bait HaMikdash* and built on its site.

This distinction between the *Bait HaMikdash* and its precursors resolves the contradiction between Maimonides' position and the Sifri. Although versions of the sanctuary existed before the nation entered the Land of Israel, the final and ultimate fulfillment of the commandment to build a sanctuary could not be achieved until the Land of Israel was completely secured and the *Bait HaMikdash* was constructed.

Let us now reconsider the dispute between Maimonides and SeMaG. According to Maimonides, the *mitzvah* to build a sanctuary includes the *Bait HaMikdash* and all of its precursors. According to SeMaG, the commandment specifically instructs us to build the *Bait HaMikdash*. It does not include the precursor of the *Bait HaMikdash*. Why does SeMaG exclude the *Mishcan* from the commandment?

It seems that according to SeMaG, the *Bait HaMikdash* is a fundamental element of the sanctity of the Land of Israel. In other words, the sanctity of the Land of Israel has a specific structure. This sanctity requires that the Land of Israel include as a central element the *Bait HaMikdash*. The *Mishcan* and the other sanctuaries that preceded the *Bait HaMikdash* were places for the offering of sacrifices and the worship of Hashem. But, these structures were not expressions of the sanctity of the Land of Israel.

Maimonides disagrees. He argues that the commandment to build a sanctuary was given in the wilderness. It was first fulfilled through the construction of the *Mishcan*. According to Maimonides, the sanctuary is a central element within the national community of Bnai Yisrael. This community first emerged in the wilderness. With its emergence came the requirement to build this community around a sanctuary. The appropriate sanctuary for the nation as it traveled through the wilderness was the *Mishcan*. The structure of the national community evolved, and did not achieve its final form until the people possessed the Land of Israel. In other words, Bnai Yisrael evolved from a nomadic nation into a people with a land. As the national community evolved, the institution of the sanctuary evolved. Once the people achieved possession of the land, the nation became complete. The complete community required a permanent *Bait HaMikdash*. In short, Maimonides and SeMaG disagree on the framework of the sanctuary. According to SeMaG, the sanctuary is an expression of the sanctity of the Land of Israel. Therefore, the *Mishcan* and the *Bait HaMikdash* are fundamentally different institutions. According to Maimonides, the sanctuary is a fundamental element of the national community of Bnai Yisrael. Therefore, at different times in the history of Bnai Yisrael, the *Mishcan* and the *Bait HaMikdash* have served as appropriate expressions of this institution. Of course, Maimonides acknowledges that the *Bait HaMikdash* is the ultimate form of the institution of the sanctuary. However, this is because the nation of Bnai Yisrael is only complete once it is in possession of the Land of Israel.

"And they will make a sanctuary for Me and I will dwell among them." (Shemot 25:8)

The Torah contains thousands of laws. However, there are only 613 mitzvot. The various laws are subsumed within the commandments. For example, there are thirty-nine melachot – forms of creative labor – that may not be performed on Shabbat. There are many laws regarding each of these melachot. But all of these melachot and the laws that govern them are subsumed under two mitzvot – the prohibition against performing melacha on Shabbat and the positive command to rest or refrain from melacha on Shabbat.

Although there is general agreement on the number of mitzvot in the Torah, neither the Written Torah nor the Talmud clearly identifies the specific commandments. Therefore, there is considerable debate on the specific identities of the commandments. Various authorities have proposed lists of the 613 mitzvot. The most famous list was composed by Maimonides. Maimonides presented his list and his criteria for delineating the commandments in his Sefer HaMitzvot. Others disagreed with Maimonides' list. Nachmanides authored a critique of Maimonides Sefer HaMitzvot and suggested an alternative list.

This raises a question. Why is the specific list important? What difference does it make if a law is included in one commandment or another or if a specific injunction is counted as a mitzvah or included within some other mitzvah? There are various answers to this question. This week's parasha provides one insight into the importance of identifying the specific mitzvot.

In this week's parasha, the Torah begins a thorough description of the Mishcan – the Tabernacle – and its components. The Mishcan was a portable structure that accompanied Bnai Yisrael in the wilderness. After Bnai Yisrael conquered the land of Israel the Mishcan was eventually replaced by the Bait HaMikdash – the Holy Temple – in Yerushalayim. According to Maimonides and most other authorities, the passage above is the source for the mitzvah to construct not only the Mishcan but also the Bait HaMikdash.[39] In addition to this commandment, our parasha includes specific directions for the fabrication of most of the fundamental objects – such as the Aron, Menorah, and Shulchan – that are situated in the Mishcan.

And make Me a sanctuary and I will dwell among them. (Shemot 25:8)

Why Do We Pray?

1. The *Mishcan* was a precursor to the *Bait HaMikdash*

Parshat Terumah is devoted to the commandment to create the *Mishcan* – the Tabernacle. The *Mishcan* was a portable sanctuary. Its central component was the *aron* – the ark – in which the tablets of the Decalogue were placed. At each of the nation's encampments along the journey to the Land of Israel, the *Mishcan* was assembled. When the nation was directed to leave the encampment and resume its journey, the *Mishcan* was disassembled to be erected again at the site of the next encampment.

The *Mishcan* was not a permanent institution. Instead, it was a precursor to the *Bait HaMikdash* – the Sacred Temple. King Shlomo built the *Bait HaMikdash* on the Temple Mount in Yerushalayim. There are a number of differences between the *Mishcan* and the *Bait HaMikdash*. The most fundamental of these is that the *Mishcan* of the wilderness was not associated with any specific location. It was a portable structure designed to be moved from site to site. The *Bait HaMikdash's* location is permanent. Shlomo's *Bait HaMikdash* was destroyed and then replaced by a new structure. The new Sacred Temple was constructed upon the ruins of Shlomo's structure. This second *Bait HaMikdash* was also destroyed. We await the building of

---

[39] Rabbaynu Moshe ben Maimon (Rambam) *Sefer HaMitzvot, Mitzvat Aseh* 20.

the third and final *Bait HaMikdash*. The final temple will be build upon the same location as its predecessors.

And you should make the altar of acacia wood. Its length should be five cubits and its width should be five cubits. The altar should be square. And its height should be three cubits. (Shemot 27:1)

2. The purpose or function of the *Bait HaMikdash*

What is the function of the *Bait HaMikdash*? As indicated in the above passage, an important component of the *Mishcan* and the *Bait HaMikdash* is its altar. Maimonides explains that the *Bait HaMikdash* has two functions. It is a place designated for the offering of sacrifices. Second, it is the destination-site for the three annual pilgrimages.[40] These pilgrimages are associated with the *Regalim* – the three Pilgrimage Festivals. The people are obligated to appear at the *Bait HaMikdash* during these three festivals. These festivals are Pesach, Shavuot, and Succot.

Maimonides does not describe the *Bait HaMikdash* as a place of prayer. Nonetheless, there is no doubt that it is a place of prayer. The childless Chanah went to the *Mishcan* to pray to Hashem. Hashem responded to her fervent entreaties and provided her with a son. This son, Shemuel, grew up to become one of our greatest prophets and leaders. When King Shlomo built the *Bait HaMikdash*, he initiated it with a prayer to Hashem. In his prayer, King Shlomo does not describe his temple as a place for sacrifices. Instead, he describes the *Bait HaMikdash* as a place in which the individual and nation should seek Hashem in prayer. Why does Maimonides ignore these associations between the *Bait HaMikdash* and prayer? Why does he not identify the temple as a place for sacrifices and for prayer?

3. The relationship between prayer and the *Bait HaMikdash*

Both prayer and sacrifices are associated with the *Bait HaMikdash*. However, they are associated in different ways. In his discussion of the *Bait HaMikdash* and sacrifices, Maimonides is defining the purpose of the temple. The *Bait HaMikdash* is an institution created for the purpose of sacrifice. He does not mention prayer in this context because the *Bait HaMikdash* is not a place *dedicated* to prayer. However, the sanctity of the *Bait HaMikdash* is a reflection of its association with the Divine Presence. Prayer is essentially an encounter with Hashem. Because the Divine Presence is so closely related to the *Bait HaMikdash,* it is an appropriate place for the prayerful encounter with Hashem.

4. Two conceptions of the function of prayer

What is the role and function of prayer according to the Torah? Maimonides rules that daily prayer is a Torah commandment.[41] Nachmanides disagrees. He argues that the institution of regular prayer is a rabbinic innovation. The Torah does not include a commandment to pray daily or according to any set schedule. However, although Nachmanides dismisses the notion that the Torah requires daily or regular prayer, he acknowledges that when the community suffers an affliction or is endangered, there is a Torah level obligation to turn to Hashem in prayer.[42]

---

[40] Rabbaynu Moshe ben Maimon (Rambam) *Mishne Torah*, Hilchot Bait HaBechirah 1:1.
[41] Rabbaynu Moshe ben Maimon (Rambam) *Mishne Torah*, Hilchot Tefilah 1:1.
[42] R' Moshe ben Nachman (Ramban), *Critique on Maimonides' Sefer HaMitzvot, M. A. 5.*

This dispute is uncharacteristic of the disagreements between our Sages. In this dispute, the two sides are at opposite extremes. Maimonides regards prayer as a fundamental activity. It is a Torah level obligation that is performed daily. Nachmonides' position is at the opposite extreme. He rejects prayer as a daily or regular Torah obligation. Prayer is an occasional obligation that the community performs when it is confronted with danger or catastrophe.

In order to understand the basis for this dispute, we must more carefully consider Maimonides' description of prayer. Maimonides explains that the prayer process begins with praise. Then, one petitions Hashem for his needs. This is followed by praise and thanksgiving for all of Hashem's kindness. Praise, petition and thanksgiving are all elements of prayer. However, his comments indicate the fundamental element of prayer is petition and supplication.[43]

5. Two views on prayer and their common ground

It emerges from Maimonides' comments that he and Nachmanides do share a conception of the fundamental construction of prayer. Both maintain that the fundamental element of prayer is petition and supplication. They differ only on the circumstances that compel a person to appeal to Hashem for His support. According to Maimonides, the individual's daily and common needs compel a person to pray and are the text of prayer. According to Nachmanides, only the community confronted with serious danger or threat is compelled to appeal to Hashem in prayer.[44]

Actually, the positions of Maimonides and Nachmanides are very similar. They share a concept of the basic substance of prayer. It is a petition to Hashem in response to need. They differ only on the type of need that occasions prayer. According to Nachmanides, it is communal and serious affliction. As a result, prayer is occasional and irregular. When the community is confronted with serious danger or affliction it is required to turn to Hashem and appeal to Him for salvation. According to Maimonides, the individual's needs are the subject of prayer's petitions. We are constantly in need. In other words, the human condition obligates us in prayer. Each day we recognize our needs and turn to Hashem in petition and supplication.

6. Prayer as a response to personal need or communal affliction

A question arises. Maimonides and Nachmanides agree that prayer is a response to need. However, the type and degree of need that each associates with prayer are very different. According to Nachmanides, serious affliction demands a response of prayer. Prayer is a response to impending communal tragedy or disaster. According to Maimonides, the simple challenges that we face each day and our personal needs are worthy of expression in prayer. Nachmanides' position is more easily understood. Of course, we should appeal to Hashem for salvation from impending disaster. It is more difficult to regard the common needs of every human being as worthy subjects for prayer.

---

[43] Rabbaynu Moshe ben Maimon (Rambam) *Mishne Torah*, Hilchot Tefilah 1:2.
[44] Rav Yosef Dov Soloveitchik *Zt"l* (Recorded lecture on Parshat Terumah) suggests that Maimonides and Nachmanides agree that prayer is a response to a time of affliction. They differ on the character of the affliction that demands a prayerful response. According to Nachmanides, the affliction must be serious and impact the community. According to Maimonides, even the personal struggles and needs of the individual are treated by the Torah as afflictions that should compel the individual to petition Hashem.

In order to understand Maimonides position, we must proceed a step further in our analysis. As noted above, both Maimonides and Nachmanides regard prayer as fundamentally composed of petition. Both agree that it is a response to need or affliction. However, we must also consider the objective or goal of prayer. Of course, we engage in prayer to enlist Hashem's help. We hope that our prayers will be answered. However, this is not the sole purpose of prayer.

7. Prayer in the process of repentance

Let us reconsider the purpose of prayer. Nachmanides maintains that prayer is the community's response to impending disaster. Actually, Maimonides agrees with Nachmanides that when Bnai Yisrael is faced with an impending danger or disaster, it is required to turn to Hashem in prayer. In his discussion of this requirement, Maimonides explains that we must recognize that any tragedy befalling our nation is a Divine consequence of our behaviors. We turn to Hashem in prayer. Through prayer, we recognize that we are not experiencing random misfortune. We are experiencing consequences for our behaviors. Prayer is the initiation of a process of repentance. In this context, the purpose of prayer is to recognize and acknowledge national culpability for the afflictions that we are experiencing.

8. Prayer as an expression of humility

Clearly, our daily prayers do not share this objective. We pray for sustenance, health, and every and any other need. These needs are reflections of our own finite power. They demonstrate the limited influence of the human being upon one's own destiny. We are weak and relatively helpless creatures. We are threatened by illness we cannot cure. Unexpected financial developments can undermine our hard-earned financial security. We cannot protect ourselves from the extremes of weather. In this context, prayer is not an acknowledgment of wrongdoing or culpability. It is a humble acknowledgment of our limitations and our dependence upon Hashem.

This is a fundamental difference in the views of Maimonides and Nachmanides. According to Nachmanides, prayer is a response to impending disaster or affliction. It is an act of recognition and the beginning of a process of repentance. Maimonides maintains that prayer is a daily activity. It is a response to the relatively minor frustration or challenges that we each experience. In this conception of prayer, it is not an acknowledgment of wrongdoing. It is a humble declaration of our humanity.

As all I show you concerning the structure of the Mishcan and the structure of all of its utensils so you should do. (Shemot 25:9)

The Significance of the Laws Governing the Design of the Mishcan

Rabbaynu Ovadia Sforno explains that the command to build a Mishcan was not given until after the worship of the Egel HaZahav – the Golden Calf. Prior to this sin there was no institution for centralized worship.[45] It is for this reason that the incident of the Egel is inserted in the middle of the account of the construction of the Tabernacle.[46] Rashi agrees with this opinion. He explains that the Torah's account of the commandment to construct the Mishcan and the

---

[45] Rabbaynu Ovadia Sforno, Commentary on Sefer Shemot, 25:9.
[46] Rabbaynu Ovadia Sforno, Commentary on Sefer Shemot, 31:18.

section describing the incident of the Egel are not a chronological presentation of events. The command of the Tabernacle was given only after the sin of the Egel.[47]

Many commentators disagree with Sforno and Rashi. Nachmanides is among this group. Rabbaynu Moshe ben Nachman (Ramban / Nachmanides), Commentary on Sefer Shemot 25:1. They maintain that these sections of the Torah are in chronological order. They argue that the commandment to build the Mishcan was given at Sinai prior to the incident of the Egel HaZahav. The commentators agree that the Torah is not a chronological history. However, they contend that there is a specific reason for every departure from the chronological presentation. In other words, the Torah does present events in chronological order unless there is some specific reason to deviate from this order.[48] On this basis, the position of Nachmanides is understandable. The command to construct the Mishcan is presented prior to the event of the Egel. He argues that there is no reason to assume that this order is not chronologically correct.

In addition to Nachmanides' objection, Sforno and Rashi's position presents a problem. According to Rashi and Sforno, the command of the Mishcan followed the sin of the Egel. This implies that the sin somehow occasioned the command to build the Tabernacle. This is difficult to understand. Was not the Tabernacle a blessing? Why should the people be rewarded for the sin of the Egel with the command to build a Tabernacle?

There are two important aspects of the Tabernacle. First, it is part of a detailed system of law. These laws define the exact manner in which we serve Hashem. Halacha dictates every aspect of the sacrifices. The appearance and clothing of the kohanim offering the sacrifices are described by the laws. Every element of the construction of the Mishcan is determined by halacha. Halacha leaves little opportunity for the intrusion of personal interpretation into divine worship. Why does the Torah impose this detailed system of law upon the worshipper?

Maimonides indicates that the Torah is concerned with the possible intrusion of pagan worship into divine service. In order to prevent such perversions, the individual is prohibited from devising the mode of worship. We must follow the prescription of the Torah. Adherence to the sacred laws of divine service assures that no pagan influences enter into our worship.[49]

The second aspect of the Tabernacle is that its construction and structure reflected a profound system of wisdom. The Mishcan was not only physically beautiful—it also possessed an intellectual grandeur. The laws combined into a system of awesome wisdom. The halachah not only dictates every aspect of the Tabernacle's design and construction, but its structure also symbolically expresses various theological, scientific and philosophical ideas.[50] The worshipper, in contemplating the structure of the Tabernacle, was inspired by its wisdom. The desire to serve Hashem resulted in a profound transformation in the worshipper. The worshipper was transported from the mundane to a spiritual universe of ideas.

Nachmanides maintains that the essential element of the Mishcan is the abstract system of wisdom represented through the structure. In the Torah, divine worship is not merely a subjective expression of the need to appeal to and form a relationship with a higher power. Instead, through worship, the Torah seeks to foster an objective relationship with Hashem. This

---

[47] Rabbaynu Shlomo ben Yitzchak (Rashi), Commentary on Sefer Shemot 31:18.
[48] Rabbaynu Moshe ben Nachman (Ramban), Commentary on Sefer VaYikra 7:2.
[49] Rabbaynu Moshe ben Maimon (Rambam) Moreh Nevuchim, Volume 3, Chapter 32.
[50] Don Yitzchak Abravanel, Commentary on Sefer Sehmot, pp. 243-254.

relationship is based upon wisdom and truth. The objective of elevating our relationship with Hashem is fundamental to the Torah. Therefore, Nachmanides maintains that the command to build a Mishcan was part of the Torah revealed to Moshe at Sinai. It was not a reaction to the Egel.

Sforno and Rashi recognize that the laws of worship are a profound system of wisdom. This is true for the laws regulating every mitzvah. However, they maintain that the essential element of the Mishcan is the super-determination of every aspect of worship. The halachah is designed to prevent the intrusion of any pagan element. This objective became essential only after the Egel HaZahav. Therefore, Sforno and Rashi argue that the command to build the Tabernacle was given after the sin.

As all I show you concerning the structure of the Mishcan and the structure of all of its utensils so you should do. (Shemot 25:9)

The Sanctity of the Mishcan and its Component Utensils

Parshat Terumah discusses the design of the Mishcan – the Tabernacle – that traveled with Bnai Yisrael through the wilderness. After the people entered the Land of Israel the Mishcan, in derivative forms, continued to function as the most sacred place of worship in the Land. Ultimately King Shlomo constructed the Bait HaMikdash – the Temple. The Bait HaMikdash replaced the Mishcan and became the focal point of sacrificial worship. In our parasha Hashem directs Moshe in the construction of the Mishcan – the Tabernacle, its components and utensils. Rashi explains that these instructions were to serve as the design for all generations.[51] If any utensil should require replacement, these design specifications must be followed. For this reason, in the construction of the Bait HaMikdash, these basic design outlines were followed.

The Chumash explains that in order to be initiated into service, each utensil of the original Mishcan was anointed with a specially formulated oil. The Talmud explains that this requirement did not extend beyond the initial Mishcan.[52] A utensil constructed to replace an original component did not require anointing. For example, one of the component utensils of the Mishcan was the Shulchan – a golden table positioned directly outside of the compartment of the Mishcan that housed the Aron – the sacred Ark. The Shulchan that was fabricated in the wilderness as a component of the Mishcan was anointed with the special oil. However, if it becomes necessary to construct a new Shulchan as a replacement for the original table, the new Shulchan does not require anointing. This suggests an interesting question. If the original components required anointing, why are replacements not subject to this requirement?

This question indicates an important concept. The initial anointing was performed upon specific objects. However, the process did not merely sanctify that object. Instead, the process sanctified the abstract element represented by the specific object. Let us consider an example. The original Shulchan – table – was anointed. This was not merely a sanctification of that specific object. With the anointing of the specific Shulchan in the Mishcan, the abstract element – the institution of Shulchan – was sanctified and incorporated into the Mishcan.

---

[51] Rabbaynu Shlomo ben Yitzchak (Rashi), Commentary on Sefer Shemot 25:9.
[52] Mesechet Shavuot 15a.

Now, it is possible to understand the Torah's treatment of the replacement Shulchan. From where does this replacement derive its sanctity? It acquires its sanctity because it is a replacement or a new expression of an abstract element or institution already sanctified by the special oil. In other words, the anointing sanctified the abstract Shulchan. The new Shulchan is sanctified because it adheres to the specifications of this object. It is an expression of the element already sanctified.

This formulation reflects an important idea. The Mishcan and the Temple are permanent components of the Torah. This institution was created and sanctified in the wilderness. Each new Temple or component represents a new expression of a continuing institution. The third Bait HaMikdash will be a renewal of this permanent institution.

"As all I have shown you regarding the form of the Mishcan and the form of its utensils. And so you should do." (Shemot 25:9)

In this passage, Hashem tells Moshe that the Mishcan and its components must be constructed according to the instructions that He has provided. Hashem then adds the phrase, "And so you should do." This phrase seems redundant. However, the Sages offer an explanation for this apparently superfluous phrase. They explain that this phrase refers to future generations. If one of the components – the Menorah, Shulchan or other element – is lost and must be replaced, the replacement must be constructed in a manner consistent with the specifications in our parasha.[53]

It appears that Maimonides maintains that although this requirement applies to the most of the components of the Mikdash, it does not apply to the Aron. Maimonides explains that when Shlomo constructed the Bait HaMikdash, he realized that it would ultimately be destroyed. Therefore, he created a system of hidden storage areas. These secret storage areas would be used to hide the Aron and its contents before the Bait HaMikdash's destruction. When King Yoshiyahu realized that the destruction of the Temple was approaching. He commanded that the Aron and its contents be removed and hidden in the facilities that Shlomo had constructed.

When the Bait HaMikdash was rebuilt, the Aron and its contents were not recovered. Neither were they replaced. Instead, the Bait HaMikdash was rebuilt without restoring the Aron and its contents to their proper place.

Meggilat Esther posits that Shlomo's treatment of the Aron and its contents reflects a fundamental difference between them and the other components of the Mishcan. If any of the other components become damaged or lost they can be replaced. But the Aron was constructed one time. It can never be replaced by a new Aron.

Based on this distinction, Meggilat Esther answers our questions on Maimonides. He explains that the commandment to build the Aron was not given to all generations. Instead, the commandment was given at a specific time for execution at that time. The only Aron is the one that was constructed under Moshe's supervision. No other can replace it. This explains Maimonides' decision not to count the building of the Aron as a mitzvah.[54] This explanation also explains Maimonides' omission of the design of the Aron from his discussion of the laws of

---

[53] Rabbaynu Shlomo ben Yitzchak (Rashi), *Commentary on Sefer Shemot* 25:9.
[54] Rav Yitzchak DeLeon, *Meggilat Esther, Comm. on Maimonides' Sefer HaMitzvot*, M.A. 33.

the Bait HaMikdash. Maimonides' code is limited to those laws that apply – in some manner – throughout the generations. However, since the Aron will not and cannot be built again, the laws of its construction are omitted.

It is clear from this discussion that Maimonides' decision to not count the construction of the Aron as a mitzvah has significant implications. According to Kinat Sofrim, Maimonides' position implies that the Aron is a component of the Mishcan and can be compared to the Menorah and Shulchan. Meggilat Esther rejects this interpretation of Maimonides. He contends that the Aron is unique and, unlike the other components, cannot be replaced.

However, Meggilat Esther's explanation leaves us with a problem. It seems odd that the Aron – which was the central fixture of the Bait HaMikdash is not essential. The Aron was not recovered and returned to its proper place in the second Temple. Nonetheless, the second Temple had the sanctity of the Bait HaMikdash. Furthermore, the Mishcan is referred to in the Torah as the Mishcan HaEydut – the Tabernacle of the Testimony.[55] This name is apparently derived from the Aron which is referred to as the Aron HaEydut.[56]

The obvious implication of the name Mishcan HaEydut is that the Aron is central and essential to the Mishcan and Bait HaMikdash. If this is the case, how did the second Temple acquire its sanctity without the Aron in its proper place?

Rav Yosef Dov Soleveitchik Z"tl offers an answer to this question. He explains that although the Aron was not returned to its proper place, it was nonetheless regarded as present in the second Temple. Even though its place was unknown and it was not recovered, it was not considered lost or destroyed. It remained – in its hiding place – a fundamental element of the second Temple.[57]

By applying Rav Soloveitchik's reasoning to Meggilat Esther, the contrast between his understanding of the Aron and the position of Kinat Sofrim becomes even clearer. According to Kinat Sofrim, the Aron is an element of the Mishcan akin to the other elements. However, according to Meggilat Esther, the Aron is far more central. The Mishcan derives its identity and sanctity from the Aron. Furthermore, the Aron created under Moshe's supervision is completely unique. It is the only Aron and it cannot be replaced. It is this unique Aron that is central to the sanctity of the Mishcan.

"And they should make an Aron of acacia wood. Its length should be two and a half cubits, its width a cubit and a half, and its height a cubit and a half." (Shemot 25:10)

This passage begins the description of the Aron – Ark. The Aron held the tablets of the Decalogue. The Aron was covered by the Kaporet – the Ark cover – described later in the parasha. According to Maimonides, the instructions to fabricate the Aron and Kaporet are not among the 613 commandments. Why does Maimonides not regard the requirement to create the Aron and Kaporet as a mitzvah? There are various answers proposed to this question. First, we will consider the most obvious answer.

---

[55] *Sefer BeMidbar* 1:53.
[56] *Sefer Shemot* 40:21.
[57] Rav Yosef Dov Soloveitchik, *M'Peninai HaRav* (Jerusalem, 5761), p 335.

"And you should overlay it with pure gold. On the inside and outside you should overlay it. And you should make a gold crown surrounding it." (Shemot 25:11)

The Torah describes the construction of the Aron – the Ark. The Aron was made of acacia wood. It was overlaid with gold. The gold covered the inner and outer surfaces of the Ark.

Rashi explains that the Ark was composed of three separate boxes. The smallest box was made of gold. A slightly larger box was constructed from acacia wood. The largest box was made of gold. The acacia box was placed within the largest gold box. The smallest gold box was placed within the acacia box. This fulfilled the requirement of the passage. The inner and outer surfaces of the wood box were covered with gold.[58]

The Chumash refers to the gold as an "overlay." The term overlay implies that the gold was an adornment of the Ark. The essential material was apparently the wood. This is difficult to reconcile with Rashi's description of the Aron's construction. According to Rashi, the Aron was constructed of three boxes. Each had its own structural integrity. In fact, it would seem more correct to define the gold as the essential component. The wood box was hidden within the two gold boxes!

Rabbaynu Avraham ibn Ezra disagrees with Rashi. He maintains that the gold overlay was not created through constructing a series of boxes. Instead, he interprets this requirement literally. The overlay was a coating over the wood of the Aron.[59] We can easily appreciate the reason for Ibn Ezra's position. The Torah refers to the gold as an overlay. According to Ibn Ezra, this description is completely accurate. However, according to Rashi, this does not seem to be an appropriate description.

Rabbaynu Avraham ben HaRambam offers a brilliant explanation of Rashi's position. An introduction is necessary to understand his insight.

The Chumash describes the dimension of the Aron. It was two cubits long, one and a half cubits wide and a cubit and a half high.[60] This requirement presents an interesting problem. The Aron was composed of three boxes. Each had different dimensions. Obviously only one box could conform to the dimensions required by the Torah! To which box did the required dimensions apply?

Rabbaynu Avraham ben HaRambam responds that the measurements were applied to the acacia box. This box was required to conform to the dimensions dictated by the Torah. The inner and outer gold boxes were designed to accommodate the measurements of the middle acacia box.[61]

This answers our question. The application of the measurements to the acacia box indicates that this was the essential box. In this manner, the Torah acknowledges the fundamental nature of this middle box. Accordingly, it refers to the gold boxes as an overlay. It is true that these boxes had independent structural integrity. However, in function, they were an overlay.

"The poles should be in the rings of the Ark. They should not be removed." (Shemot 25:15)

---

[58] Rabbaynu Shlomo ben Yitzchak (Rashi), *Commentary on Sefer Shemot* 25:11.
[59] Rabbaynu Avraham ibn Ezra, *Commentary on Sefer Shemot*, 25:10.
[60] Sefer Shemot 25:10.
[61] Rabbaynu Avraham ben HaRambam Commentary on Sefer Shemot 25:11.

A ring was attached to each corner of the Ark. Poles were passed through these rings. These poles were used to carry the *Aron* – the Ark. The Torah commands us that the poles must remain in the rings at all times. Even when the *Mishcan* is erected and the *Aron* is at rest the poles are to remain attached.

The poles were designed for the transport of the Ark. When the *Aron* was moved the poles were needed. But when the Ark was at rest the poles did not have any apparent function. Why should they not be removed at such times?

Gershonides discusses this issue. He explains that the Ark represented the Torah. The Torah is perfect. Therefore, the Ark must always be perfect. With the removal of the poles, the Ark would no longer be complete. An incomplete *Aron* is unfit to represent the Torah.[62][1]

Gershonides explanation seems difficult to understand. In order for an object to be perfect it must be complete. However, perfection also requires that the object have no extra or meaningless components. Imagine the perfect machine. Every part would serve a purpose. No needed component would be absent. No component would lack purpose.

When the Ark was at rest the poles had no purpose. They were extra. It seems the *Aron* would have better represented the perfection of the Torah without this superfluous component!

Gershonides is providing us with an important insight into the nature of the *Aron*. The Ark constructed in the wilderness was transported as the nation traveled. Therefore, the *Aron* was constructed so that it could be carried. However, this design was not merely a practical necessity. The portability of the Ark was essential to its very definition. In other words, the Ark was defined as a portable item. The *Aron* could only be considered perfect when it expressed this definition. Even at rest the Ark was required to conform to this definition. It must remain completely portable. For this reason the *Aron* of the permanent *Bait HaMikdash* remained unchanged in design. The poles were part of the design and could not be removed.

Perhaps, this provides a message regarding the perfection of the Torah. This perfection, in part, lies in the portability of Torah. Torah is a way of life that applies to all times and places. Even when Bnai Yisrael are dispersed throughout the world, Torah is still to be the guide.

And make two Keruvim (Cherubs) of gold. Make them as beaten work from the ends of the Kaporet (Ark cover). (Shemot 25:18)

Cherubs and Baseball

The *Keruvim* should not be confused with idolatry

This week's *parsha* is devoted exclusively to the commandment to create the *Mishkan* – the Tabernacle. The *Mishkan* was the precursor to the Sacred Temple – the *Bait HaMikdash*. It was the place in which Bnai Yisrael offered their sacrifices during their travels in the wilderness. They continued to worship in the *Mishkan* even after settling the Land of Israel. The *Mishkan* was destroyed by the Plishtim at the end of the period of the *Shoftim* – the Judges. Eventually, it was replaced by the *Bait HaMikdash* that was constructed by King Shlomo.

---

[62] Rabbaynu Levi ben Gershon (Ralbag), *Commentary on Sefer Shemot*, (Mosad HaRav Kook, 1994), p 342.

In last week's *parsha* an allusion was made to the *Bait HaMikdash*. We are commanded to observe the three *Regalim* – pilgrimage festivals. We fulfill this commandment by traveling to the *Bait HaMikdash* on these festivals – Pesach, Shavuot, and Sukkot. It is interesting that immediately prior to discussing these *Regalim*, the Torah admonishes us to take care and not associate ourselves with idolatry.[63] Meshech Chochmah suggests the discussion of the festivals is preceded by this warning because the festivals may themselves promote idolatrous attitudes. This is because during the period of the first *Bait HaMikdash*, it was customary to part the curtains that normally hid the inside of the *Kodesh HaKodashim* – the Holy of Holies. The pilgrims could gaze into the inner sanctuary and observe the *Keruvim* – the Cherubs. The Cherubs were integrated into the *Kaporet* – the Ark-cover. Seeing these forms occupying the most sacred place in the *Bait HaMikdash* might be misinterpreted. It might be construed as a license to employ similar images or idols in the service of Hashem. In order to dismiss this conclusion, the Torah reiterates its rejection of idolatry directly before its discussion of the *Regalim*.[64]

The confusing message of the *Mishkan*

Meshech Chochmah's comments provide an explanation for the placement of an admonition against idolatry before the commandment to observe these festivals. However, his interpretation of the passages suggests an even more fundamental question. What is the meaning of these *Keruvim*? Why were they incorporated into the *Kaporet*? One of the main themes of the Torah is its opposition to idolatry. Why are these golden images required in the space that *halachah* regards as most sacred?

There are other explanations for the Torah's placement of an admonition against idolatry immediately before its discussion of the *Regalim*. However, the concern raised by Meshech Chochmah is real. Let us consider another aspect of the *Mishkan* that seems to invite a conclusion that is strongly discouraged by the Torah.

The organization of the commandment to create the *Mishkan*

The commandment to create the *Mishkan* includes a precise description of its components. The Torah first provides a description of the *Aron* – the Ark – and *Kaporet*. These are placed within the *Kodesh HaKodashim* – the Holy of Holies. This is followed by a precise description of the *Shulchan* and *Menorah*. The *Shulchan* is the table upon which the Shew Bread are placed. The *Menorah* is the candelabra. Both are stationed directly outside of the *Kodesh HaKodashim*. The function of the *Aron* and *Kaporet* is clear. They contain the *Luchot* – the Tablets of the Covenant. What are the functions of the *Shulchan* and *Menorah*?

---

[63] Sefer Shemot 23:13-17.
[64] Rav Meir Simcha of Devinsk, *Meshech Chochmah on Sefer Shemot* 23:13-14. Meshech Chochamah points out that according to Talmud in Mesechet Yoma 54b, when the Babylonians entered the *Bait HaMikdash* they observed the *Keruvim*. They were shocked to find figures in the *Kodesh HaKodashim*. They brought them forth into the thoroughfare and declared that the Jews also engage in idolatry. It should be noted that these *Keruvim* were not those of the *Kaporet*. The *Aron, Kaporet*, and their contents were placed in hiding before the conquest of the Babylonians and the destruction of the *Mikdash*. The *Keruvim* discovered by the Babylonians were those installed by King Shlomo (See: Melachim I 6:23-28).

Rabbeinu Avraham ibn Ezra discusses this issue. His comments are made in the context of addressing a related issue. The *Mishkan* features two altars. One is a large altar situated in the courtyard of the *Mishkan*.[65] This altar is used for animal sacrifices and other offerings. The second altar is used solely for offering incense. This altar – the *Mizbe'ach HaKetoret* is placed inside the *Mishkan*. In the commandment to create the *Mishkan*, the *Shulchan* and *Menorah* are described immediately after the *Aron* and *Kaporet*. The *Mizbe'ach HaKetoret* which is situated with them in the *Kodesh* – the sanctuary – is not mentioned at this point. It is described at a much later point in the instructions. Ibn Ezra asks why this altar's description is postponed. One would expect it to be described along with the other components situated within the *Kodesh* – the sanctuary. Rather than paraphrase, let's consider his position as expressed in his own words.

"The Glory does not cease (from the Mishkan). Therefore, the Aron is in the form of (i.e. similar to) a chair. And there is a candelabra and a set table. Therefore, the Mizbe'ach HaKetoret is mentioned after the sacrificial altar. This is in order to admonish, 'You should not offer upon it an Olah sacrifice, a Mincha offering, or libation.'"[66]

Rav Yosef Dov Soloveitchik *Zt"l* explains the meaning of Ibn Ezra's comments. The Torah describes the *Mishkan* as the place in which the presence of Hashem – His Glory – resides. In Ibn Ezra's view this is the fundamental function of the *Mishkan* – to create a place in which this Glory will reside. This fundamental function is given full expression in the design of the *Mishkan*. Its most essential components are the *Aron* and *Kaporet*, the *Shulchan*, and *Menorah*. The *Aron* and *Kaporet* are the chair – the specific place in which the Glory resides. The *Shulchan* with its Shewbread is the table set before Him. The *Menorah* is the candelabra that illuminates His residence. In other words, these are the components that bestow upon *Mishkan* its basic character as the residence of the Glory. The altars are of secondary significance. Although the *Mizbe'ach HaKetoret* is stationed in the sanctuary along with the *Shulchan* and *Menorah*, its secondary significance is given expression through the postponement of its description to a latter point in the presentation of the commandment.[67]

And make for Me a sanctuary and I will dwell among them. (Shemot 25:8)

Guard yourselves carefully. For you did not see any image on the day that Hashem spoke to you at Chorev from within the fire. (Devarim 4:15)

Hashem's Glory is present in the *Mishkan*

When we consider these comments carefully, we notice that Ibn Ezra does not describe the *Mishkan* as the residence of Hashem. He refers to it as the residence of His Glory. Why does Ibn Ezra make this distinction?

---

[65] The *Mishkan* is a tent. Its structure is composed of a panel of curtains supported by upright planks. This structure is surrounded by a series of curtains that creat a courtyard. The altar upon which sacrifices are offered is placed in this courtyard before the entrance to the *Mishkan*.
[66] Rabbaynu Avraham ibn Ezra, *Commentary of Sefer Shemot* 25:22.
[67] Rav Herschel Schachter, recorded lecture. Rav Soloveitchik notes the description of the room that the Shunamit woman prepared for the prophet Elisha (Melachim II 4:10). The room included a chair and sleeping couch, a table and candelabra. He explains that the hostess prepared the space with these items because they are the essential components of a residence. In the *Mishkan*, the *Aron* and *Kaporet* function as the chair and couch. The *Shulchan* and *Menorah* complete the furnishings.

Ibn Ezra is concerned with an issue that he later discusses in his commentary. In the first passage above, we are instructed to create a *Mishkan* and Hashem will dwell in our midst. Ibn Ezra is asserting that this passage requires interpretation. It cannot be understood as associating Hashem's presence with a space. Let us understand the reason for this conclusion.

In the second passage above Moshe is delivering his final address to Bnai Yisrael. He reviews with them the events of Revelation. Then, he reminds them that they saw no image at Revelation. They perceived Hashem only through the voice that emerged from within the conflagration at the top of the mountain. Moshe is emphasizing that Hashem is not material. He does not have a body or physical form. This understanding of Hashem is one of the Torah's fundamental principles.[68]

The characteristic of occupying space applies to material bodies. It is not possible to associate this characteristic with that which is not material. In asserting that Hashem will reside among the people or between the *Keruvim* upon the *Aron*, He is assigned the characteristic of occupying space – a characteristic of material bodies. This contradicts Moshe's stern admonition against attributing to Hashem a material existence.

Now, Ibn Ezra's intentions are more clearly evident. He refers to Hashem's Glory as residing in the *Mishkan*. He wants to avoid any expression that assigns a position in space to Hashem. However, this carefully constructed phrasing results in a troubling paradox. Ibn Ezra is very sensitive to the problem of ascribing a position in space to Hashem. He scrupulously avoids this error. But the Torah does describe Hasham as dwelling among the people. What is the meaning of the Torah's description? How can it be explained without violating the fundamental principle of Hashem's non-material existence?

The meaning of Hashem's presence

Ibn Ezra addresses this issue in latter comments. He is intentionally vague in his comments but he provides an analogy to help us understand the meaning of the Torah's description of Hashem dwelling in the *Mishkan*.

---

[68] Rabbaynu Moshe ben Maimon (Rambam) *Mishne Torah*, Hilchot Yesodai HaTorah 1:8. See also Hilchot Teshuva 3:7 and the comments of Ra'avad. A careful reading of these comments indicates that he agrees with Maimonides' basic position regarding Hashem's non-material existence. However, he is critical of Maimonides' unqualified condemnation of anyone rejecting this principle. Ra'avad argues that a person who is misled by passages in the Torah and confusing sections of the Aggadah to the erroneous conclusion that Hashem has material form should not be included within Maimonides' condemnation. These individuals wish to carefully observe all aspects of the Torah but err in their understanding of these expectations. Such a well-intentioned error should moderate the seriousness of the person's sin.
It is often noted that Ra'avad speaks in very laudatory terms of those who have made such an unfortunate error. See comments of Kesef Mishna who is astounded by this aspect of Ra'avad's comments. He suggests that Ra'avad is misquoted in the standard text and supports this assertion by noting other texts in which Ra'avad's position is cited that do not include this laudatory description. See also the Frankel edition of *Mishne Torah* which notes divergent texts of Ra'avad's comments. These texts differ from the standard version only in a single word. However, the divergence completely alters the meaning of the comments and, to a great extent, eliminates the difficulty in Ra'avad's comments.

The moon does not generate its light. When we observe the shining moon, we are observing the reflected light of the sun. When an eclipse occurs, Earth intervenes between the sun and the moon. We do not see a shining moon because the sun's light is obstructed; it does not reach the moon and cannot be reflected by it. The sun does not change. It is sending forth its light at all times. However, whether we will observe the light reflected by the moon depends upon the changing circumstances of the moon's orbit and the orbit of Earth.

Ibn Ezra explains that Hashem's influence or "presence" should be understood in the same manner. Like the sun, Hashem is unchanging. However, the capacity of a person or place to experience that influence is dependent upon his or its nature and circumstances.[69] Moshe had a unique relationship with Hashem because Moshe was a unique individual. Similarly, Hashem commanded that we create a *Mishkan* whose nature and circumstances – that it is the sanctuary of the people of the covenant – render it fit to experience the influence of Hashem.

The take-away from these comments is that Hashem was not present in the *Mishkan* in the sense of occupying space. His influence was uniquely expressed. Only in this sense, was He "present" between the *Keruvim*.

> *And the Keruvim – they will extend their wings upward. They will cover with their wings the Kaporet. They will face one another. They will face toward the Kaporet. (Shemot 25:20)*

The message of the *Keruvim*

Ibn Ezra adds that when we understand this idea we will also comprehend the meaning of the *Keruvim*. He does not elaborate on this meaning. He only comments that *Keruvim* are figures who wings are extended. Presumably, he is referring to the above passage in which the wings are described as extending upward. In other words, the *Keruvim* are stationed upon the *Aron* reaching upward toward the heavens. It seems that the *Keruvim* are designed to represent the nature of Hashem's presence in the *Mishkan*. Hashem's nature is constant and unchanging. He is not "present" in one place more than in another place. However, the suitability of a person or place to experience His influence is variable and dependent upon the nature and circumstances of the place or person. The *Keruvim* stretch forth their wings toward the heavens. They give expression to the special nature of the *Mishkan*. The influence of Hashem is present because of the *Mishkan*'s nature and circumstances. It is designed precisely as required by the Torah and it is the *Mishkan* of the people of the Sinai covenant. The *Mishkan* "reaches up" to bring down upon itself this Divine influence.

An analogy will help us understand the message of the *Keruvim*. The baseball season is quickly approaching. So, let's consider a pitching machine that is constantly throwing fastballs toward the plate. Imagine that the machine continues to pitch whether a batter is in the batter's box or whether the box is empty. A batter steps up to plate, swings, and hits the ball over the fences. The machine was pitching continually. What caused this one pitch among the many hurled toward the plate to fly over the fences? The actions of the batter who came to the plate.

The *Keruvim* who reach out toward the heavens communicate that the *Mishkan* is like the batter who swings his bat at the ball. Like the batter, who changes the projection of the ball through his actions, the nature of the *Mishkan* and its circumstances bring forth the influence of Hashem.

Considering the impact of one's actions

---

[69] R' Avraham ibn Ezra, *Commentary of Sefer Shemot,* short essay between 25:40 and 26:1.

Let us now return to the comments of Meshech Chochmah. The *Keruvim* are designed to communicate a message regarding the relationship between Hashem and the *Mishkan*. They are designed to dispel the idea that Hashem is more present in one place than in another or that His nature changes as it influenced by circumstances. However, their impact can be contrary to their intended message. Their message is intended to dispel misconceptions regarding Hashem. However, contrary to this intention they can lead to idolatry. The Torah is wary of this potential outcome and introduces the *Regalim* with an admonition against idolatry.

Meshech Chochmah's comments should give us pause. How often do we not consider how our words or actions – however well-intentioned – may be perceived and interpreted by others. We excuse our behavior by emphasizing that our actual words and actions were not inappropriate; perhaps they were praiseworthy. We argue that we bear no responsibility for the manner in which others have interpreted our completely well-intentioned words and actions. However, according to Meshech Chochmah, the Torah is demonstrating for us a higher standard of behavior. Despite the intended purpose of the *Keruvim*, the Torah recognizes that their presence may be misinterpreted. It accepts responsibility for this outcome and acts to prevent it by inserting a warning against this misinterpretation immediately prior to introducing the occasion upon which the *Keruvim* would be observed by the people – the *Regalim*. The Torah treatment of the *Keruvim* and *Regalim* urges us to give our attention to not only the content of our words and actions but also to the manner in which others may perceive them.

And the cherubs shall spread their wings upward, their wings covering the Ark-cover. And they shall face one another. They should face the center of the Ark cover. (Shemot 25:20)

The Torah Promotes Peace among the Members of a Society

The Aron – Ark – in the Mishcan held the tablets of the Decalogue. The opening of the Ark was sealed by the Kaporet – the Ark cover. Mounted on this golden cover were two cherubs. The golden cherubs were positioned at the ends of the cover. The cherubs faced one another. Their wings were spread forward and upward.

There are various opinions regarding the meaning of these cherubim. Don Yitzchak Abravanel explains that the cherubim symbolize two relationships.[70] Their up-stretched wings represent the relationship between the individual and Hashem. The cherubim faced one another. This represents the relationship between a person and his or her friend. The cherubim were placed upon the Ark that contained the tablets. This communicates the message that both of these relationships must be based upon the commandments of the Torah.

The importance of the Torah in regulating relations between individuals is reflected in a well-known teaching of the Sages. "Torah scholars increase peace in the world."[71] This concise dictum communicates the lesson that the Torah is a guide for the treatment of one's neighbor. Through following the principles of the Torah, a healthy community is formed.

It is interesting that our Sages taught that Torah scholars increase peace. Why did the Sages not say that the scholars create peace? Rav Zalman Soroskin zt"l offers an insightful response to this question. He explains that two issues must be addressed in order for peace to be

---

[70] Don Yitzchak Abravanel, Commentary on Sefer Shemot, p 252.
[71] Mesechet Berachot 64a.

achieved. First, there must exist, among the members of the society, a desire to establish peace. Second, wisdom is required to translate this goodwill into concrete rules for relationships. The scholar, through the Torah, can provide the framework in which peace can develop and flourish. However, in order for these efforts to be successful, there must first exist a sincere desire to pursue peace.

Based in this insight, the meaning of the Sages emerges. The Torah scholar cannot create peace. First, the desire must exist. However, given this desire, the scholar can help society achieve its goal.

"And you should make a Shulchan of acacia wood. Its length should be two cubits, and its width one cubit, and its height one and a half cubits." (Shemot 25:23)

This passage begins the description of the construction of the Shulchan – the Table – of the Mishcan. This table held the Show Bread. Like the instructions for the fabrication of the Aron, the instructions for the creation of the Shulchan are not regarded by Maimonides as one of the 613 commandments. However, in the instance of the Shulchan, Maimonides provides an explanation for his reasoning.

Maimonides' reasoning is based upon a fundamental principle. In his introduction to his Sefer HaMitzvot, Maimonides outlines fourteen criteria he used in developing his list of mitzvot. His twelfth shoresh – principle – is that it is not appropriate to count the parts of a mitzvah as separate mitzvot. Maimonides continues to explain that many mitzvot are composed of various components. All of the components are subsumed within the general mitzvah. Maimonides then cites various examples of this principle. His first example concerns the Mishcan and the Shulchan. He explains that the Mishcan is composed of various components. The Shulchan and the Menorah – the Candelabra – are two of these components. Maimonides argues the instructions to fabricate the Shulchan, the Menorah and the other components of the Mishcan should not be counted as mitzvot. Instead, these instructions are included within the more encompassing mitzvah of creating the Mishcan.

Kinat Sofrim applies this same reasoning to the Aron. Maimonides does not count the instructions to create the Aron as a mitzvah. Kinat Sofrim argues that this follows from Maimonides reasoning in regard to the Shulchan and Menorah. Like the Shulchan and Menorah, the Aron is a component of the Mishcan. Therefore, the instructions to create the Aron are subsumed within the mitzvah to create the Mishcan.[72]

Although the basic logic of this explanation is sound, it is subject to two criticisms. The first criticism is based on the language used by Maimonides in describing the commandment to construct the Mishcan and Bait HaMikdash. In his description of this commandment, Maimonides again explains his reason for not counting the instructions in regards to the components of the Mishcan as separate commandments. Maimonides states, "We have already explained that this general commandment includes various parts and that the Menorah, Shulchan, the altar, and the other components are parts of the Mikdash and are referred to as Mikdash."[73] Although Maimonides clearly includes the Menorah, Shulchan and altar among the components

---

[72] Rav Chananya Kazim, *Kinat Sofrim, Commentary on Maimonides' Sefer HaMitzvot, M.A.* 33.
[73] Rabbaynu Moshe ben Maimon (Rambam) *Sefer HaMitzvot, Mitzvat Aseh* 20.

of the Mishcan, he makes no mention of the Aron. Now, one may argue that reference to the Aron is made in the phrase "other components." However, this is unlikely. The Aron was a very essential component of the Mishcan. It is unlikely that Maimonides would not mention the Aron specifically and include this very important component in a general phrase.

The second criticism of Kinat Sofrim's position presents a more fundamental problem. In his Mishne Torah, Maimonides explains in detail the laws included in the commandment to create a Mikdash. His discussion includes a discussion of the fabrication of the Menorah, the Shulchan and the other components of the Temple. However, Maimonides does not provide a description of the construction of the Aron. The absence of this description from the laws regarding the mitzvah of creating the Mikdash clearly indicates that the construction of the Aron is not part of this mitzvah.

However, this omission is not merely a basis for objecting to the thesis of Kinat Sofrim. It is the basis for a fundamental question on Maimonides. Not only does Maimonides omit any description of the Aron from the laws regarding the Mikdash. Nowhere in his entire Mishne Torah – his comprehensive codification of halacha – does he describe the construction of the Aron! In other words, not only does Maimonides not consider the construction of the Aron to be a mitzvah, he completely ignores this fundamental element of the Mikdash!

Based on these objections to Kinat Sofrim's explanation of Maimonides and the fundamental problem posed by Maimonides' complete omission of any discussion of the Aron's construction in his Mishne Torah, Meggilat Esther offers an alternative explanation of Maimonides' position.

"Speak to Bnai Yisrael and they should take for Me an offering. From each person whose heart moves him you should take My offering." (Shemot 25:2)

In this passage, Hashem instructs Moshe to collect contributions for the construction of the Mishcan. Maimonides does not count this instruction as one of the 613 mitzvot. The reason for this omission is explained by anther of Maimonides criteria for counting mitzvot. Maimonides third principle is that it is not appropriate to count as one of the 613 mitzvot a commandment that does not apply to all generations. Maimonides explains that in order to a commandment to be included in the list of 613 mitzvot, it must be relevant to all generations. Any commandment that is given and executed at a specific point in time and thereafter has no relevance, is not included within the 613 mitzvot. The instruction to Moshe to collect contributions for the Mishcan was given in the wilderness and executed immediately. It has no further application to future generations. Therefore, this commandment cannot be counted among the 613 mitzvot.

Meggilat Esther contends that the same reasoning can be applied to the instructions for creating the Aron. But before we can understand this application, we must consider one basic difference between the Aron and the other components of the Mikdash.

And you shall make the Menorah of pure gold. The Menorah, its base, its trunk, shall be a beaten work. Its decorative cones, its spheres, and its flowers shall be made from it. (Shemot 25:31)

The Golden Role

1. **So many details!**

Parshat Terumah describes the design of the Mishcan – the Tabernacle – and its contents. The Mishcan was the precursor of the Bait HaMikdash – the Sacred Temple. It was created after the Sinai Revelation and was the focal point of the encampment in the wilderness. It served two purposes. First, all sacrifices were offered there. Second, the Divine Presence was manifested there and Hashem addressed Moshe from within the Mishcan.

The Torah describes the design of the Mishcan with unusual detail. Why is this detail required? Why does the Torah dictate the specific design of the Mishcan and its components? Hashem could have provided a general description of the Mishcan and its essential contents, leaving the specific design to the artisans who fabricated them.

2. **The Menorah is a beaten work**

Let's explore this issue though considering some of the details provided for the design of the Menorah – the Mishcan's candelabra. The Torah describes the basic structure of the Menorah and its decorative details. Among the decorative details are cones, flowers and spheres. The Temple Institute in Jerusalem fabricated a model of the Menorah. A picture of the model is below.

The cones are the lowest decorative elements at the top of each branch. The cones on each branch are topped by a sphere. A flower interrupts between the branch and the actual receptacle into which the wick and oil are placed.

The above passage explains that the Menorah is fashioned from a single block of gold that is beaten and trimmed into the shape of the Menorah. Rashi explains that the Menorah cannot be made by forming its components separately and then combining them. For example, the arms cannot be separately fabricated and then joined to the trunk.[74]

3. **The fabrication of the decorative elements**

Rashi extends this requirement to the decorative details. These too must be created from the single block through beating and trimming the metal.[75] This position reflects the ruling of the Talmud.[76] Ramban – Nachmanides – observes that this position is not universally accepted. He cites another Talmudic authority who rules that the decorative elements of the Menorah need

---

[74] Rabbaynu Shlomo ben Yitzchak (Rashi), Commentary on Sefer Shemot 25:31.
[75] Rabbaynu Shlomo ben Yitzchak (Rashi), Commentary on Sefer Shemot 25:31.
[76] Mesechet Menachot 88b.

not be formed from the block. The cones, spheres, and flowers can be formed separately and added onto the Menorah.

Ramban explains the reasoning supporting this position. The Torah describes the Menorah as formed from a block of gold. However, the Talmud explains that the Menorah may be made from other metals.[77] If it is made from another metal, the decorative details are not required. In other words, if the Menorah is made from gold then the decorative elements are mandatory; their absence renders the Menorah unsuitable for use. However, a silver Menorah is acceptable and it need not include the decorative elements enumerated in the passage.[78]

Ramban explains that this law demonstrates that the decorative elements are not essential components of the Menorah's design. The authority he cites maintains that the Torah requires that the essential elements of the Menorah are formed from the single gold block. Elements that are not essential to the Menorah need not be formed from the block. Since the decorative elements are not essential to the design, they need not be formed from the single block.[79]

There is a problem with Ramban's argument. It is correct that a Menorah made of some metal other than gold does not require the decorative elements. However, a gold Menorah must have these elements. If the gold Menorah does not include its cones, spheres, and flowers, it is unacceptable. These elements are essential to the gold Menorah. Ramban's argument is that only the essential elements of the Menorah must be formed from the single block of gold. The decorative elements are essential to the gold Menorah. Why according to the opinion cited by Ramban are they permitted to be added rather than formed from the single block?

4. The fundamental Menorah

To answer this question, Ramban's argument requires further clarification. Let us begin by considering an analogy. There are many types of fixed-wing aircraft. Obviously, wings are an essential element of these aircraft. A helicopter is not a fixed-wing aircraft because it does not have this essential element – wings. Among fixed-wing aircraft some are powered by jet engines. Others are powered by propellers. Within the subcategory of jet aircraft, jet engines are essential. Aircraft powered by propellers cannot be classified within the subcategory of jet aircraft. The aircraft powered by propellers is within the more basic category of fixed-wing aircraft, but not included in the subcategory of jet aircraft.

Now, consider a specific jet aircraft – perhaps, a Boing 737 sitting at the tarmac at your local airport. Is it correct to posit that its jet engine is one of its essential components? The answer is that it depends upon the framework of the question. If the question is whether the jet engine is essential to the aircraft as a fixed-wing aircraft, then the answer is "no". If the question is whether the jet engine is essential to the aircraft as a jet aircraft, the answer is "yes".

Ramban's argument is that the Torah established a definition of the basic Menorah. Let's call this the definition of the "fundamental Menorah". Every Menorah, regardless of the material from which it is formed, must conform to this definition. The components of the fundamental Menorah include its trunk and six branches. The fundamental Menorah does not include any decorative elements. The Menorah made from gold or any other metal must include all the

---

[77] Mesechet Menachot 28b.
[78] See Rabbaynu Moshe ben Maimon (Rambam) Mishne Torah, Hilchot Bait HaBechirah 3:3-4.
[79] Rabbaynu Moshe ben Nachman (Ramban) Commentary on Sefer Shemot 25:31.

components of the fundamental Menorah. If it is made of a metal other than gold, these are the only elements required. It must include only the components of the fundamental Menorah. Therefore, decorative elements are not necessary. In fact, it also need not be formed from a single block.[80] This requirement is not included in the design of the fundamental Menorah

5. The Gold Menorah

The gold Menorah is a subcategory of Menorah. Let's understand the meaning of this statement. A silver, a copper, or an iron Menorah is not a subcategory of Menorah. These are just executions of the fundamental Menorah. No new requirements are added to the fundamental Menorah when it is executed in silver.

In contrast, the gold Menorah is a true subcategory of Menorah. It is not just the fundamental Menorah rendered in gold. "Gold" is not just an adjective modifying Menorah. It is the Gold Menorah. Gold alters the identity of the Menorah and transforms it into a subcategory of Menorah. This subcategory of Gold Menorah includes all the requirements of the fundamental Menorah and its own specific requirements. These include decorative elements.

6. "A beaten work": the fundamental Menorah

The requirement to form the Gold Menorah from a single block distinguishes between requirements imposed by the fundamental Menorah and requirements specific to the Gold Menorah. Those elements required to meet the definition of the fundamental Menorah must be formed from the single block. The decorative elements are required only because a Gold Menorah is being formed. These need not be formed from the single block.

Let us now return to the picture of the Menorah, above. How many Menorah's are depicted in the picture? This seems like a silly question – one, of course! But let's reconsider the issue from Ramban's perspective. The picture features a model of a Menorah fashioned in gold. This Menorah embodies the fundamental Menorah. This Menorah is expressed in its trunk and its branches. The picture embodies the Gold Menorah. This identity is expressed through its cones, spheres, and flowers. Two Menorahs are represented in the picture – the fundamental Menorah and the Gold Menorah. The elements of the fundamental Menorah are distinguished from the Gold Menorah by the requirement that they be formed though beating and trimming the block of gold.[81]

7. Meaning in details

We opened our discussion asking why the Torah provides detailed directions for the fabrication of the Mishcan and its components. Why were the details not left to the artisans? If an artisan is charged with the task, he or she will complete the design based upon efficient fabrication and artistic considerations. The Torah's detailed instructions provide insight into the halachic structure of the Mishcan and its components.

---

[80] See Rabbaynu Moshe ben Maimon (Rambam) Mishne Torah, Hilchot Bait HaBechirah 3:4.
[81] The Gold Menorah requires a higher level of perfection or workmanship. There are two ways in which this requirement is expressed. a) It includes mandatory decorative elements and b) It must be a formed from a single block of gold. Each of these perfections are imposed upon the fundamental Menorah. To require that the decorative elements be formed from the single block of gold would be to impose a perfection upon a perfection.

Through the above analysis of a few of its halachot – laws – we discovered that creating the Menorah from gold transforms the fundamental Menorah into the Gold Menorah. We uncovered the elements of the fundamental Menorah and the elements unique to the Gold Menorah. Finally, we identified the role of "beaten work" in distinguishing between the elements of the fundamental Menorah and the Gold Menorah.

Six branches should extend from to its sides – three branches from one side and three branches from its second side. (Shemot 25:32)

Two Opinions Regarding the Design of the Menorah

The Mishcan included a candelabrum – the Menorah. The Menorah consisted of a central trunk and six branches. Three branches extended from the right to the trunk. Exactly opposite these branches – on the left side of the Menorah – extended another three branches. The central trunk and each branch were capped with a flame.

The Chumash provides this general description of the Menorah. However, there is an interesting dispute regarding the specific design of the Menorah. According to Rashi, the branches of the Menorah were completely straight.[82] They extended from the sides on a diagonal. Rabbaynu Avraham ibn Ezra disagrees. He maintains that the branches were curved. Each curved outward and then up from the trunk. What is the basis for this argument?

We can gain some insight into Rashi's position through a careful analysis of his comments. He begins by asserting that the branches were straight and angled upward. He then explains that the branches differed in length. Those branches lower on the trunk were longer. Those higher were shorter. This design assured that all the lights, located at the top of the branches, were at the same height.

It is clear from Rashi that a fundamental element of the Menorah's design was the height of the lights. The Torah required all the lights to be at the same height. Perhaps, this consideration determined the design of the branches. The branches were designed to serve a single purpose. They connected and related the lights to the trunk of the Menorah. If we assume that this is the sole function of the branches, we can understand their design. A straight diagonal branch describes the simplest path from the light to the body of the Menorah. In short, according to Rashi the fundamental design components of the Menorah were the trunk and the lights. The branches were required solely to relate the lights to the trunk.

Ibn Ezra seems to understand the design differently.[83] According to him, the branches curved out from the trunk of the Menorah. They then rose in a path parallel to the trunk. These branches have their own design requirement and are not merely appendages joining the lights to the body. They seem to be an essential component of the Menorah. The Menorah was fundamentally a many-branched candelabrum.

In short, Rashi and Ibn Ezra differ on the function of the branches. According to Rashi, they are a functional element of the Menorah. They are required to relate and connect the lights to the trunk. Their form is dictated by this simple function. According to Ibn Ezra, the branches

---

[82] Rabbaynu Shlomo ben Yitzchak (Rashi), Commentary on Sefer Shemot 25:32.
[83] Rabbaynu Avraham ibn Ezra, Commentary on Sefer Shemot, 25:32.

are a fundamental element of the form of the Menorah – a many-branched candelabra. Therefore, they are assigned their own unique design.

Tetzaveh

"And you shall make sacred garments for Ahron your brother for dignity and glory." (Shemot 27:2)

    The garments of the Kohen Gadol the High Priest were designed to create an impressive visual appearance. Halacha also regulated other aspects of the Kohen Gadol's appearance. In these cases, as well, the purpose of the regulation was to assure a positive physical appearance. Our pasuk indicates that this attention to appearance was intended to assure that the Kohen Gadol would be treated with dignity and respect. This is surprising. Our Sages often taught the importance of not being impressed by superficial behaviors or appearances. Instead, we are to assess a person based upon the individual's inner self. Why does the Torah stress superficial aspects of the Kohen Gadol? More shocking is the prohibition against the Kohen Gadol's marriage to a widow. This prohibition is also designed to protect the public image of the High Priest. Why should the Torah acknowledge a shallow prejudice against the widow? Would it not be preferable for the Torah to allow this marriage? Such a policy would counter any social stigma attached to the widow.

    These laws demonstrate one of the unique qualities of the Torah. Torah takes human weakness seriously. The Torah was created to govern an actual society. In the real world, prejudice and superficiality exist. The Torah recognizes these faults. At the same time, it attempts to correct human behavior. Both measures are essential. Failure to recognize human frailty would result in a system poorly equipped to deal with an actual human being.

    The Torah also attempts to improve upon these human limitations. The garments of the Kohen Gadol are an excellent illustration of the Torah's method of dealing with this dilemma. The Torah requires that the Kohen Gadol wear beautiful garments. However, these garments are more than attractive vestments. Every detail of design is guided by an intricate system of halacha. The observer is attracted to the beauty of the garments, and hopefully, this initial interest leads to contemplation of the ingenious laws. The observer comes to recognize that the greatest beauty is not in the superficial material dimension. Instead, true beauty is found in the world of knowledge.

And you shall make sacred garments for Ahron your brother for dignity and glory. (Shemot 27:2)

The Purpose of the Kohen Gadol's Vestments

    The garments of the *Kohen Gadol* were designed to create an impressive visual effect. Other aspects of the *Kohen Gadol's* appearance were also regulated by *halachah*. For example, he was required to trim his hair every week.[1] In the above passage, Moshe is command to instruct Bnai Yisrael in the creation of these garments. The *pasuk* says that these garments are designed for honor and glory. However, the *pasuk* is vague. Whom— or what— do these garments glorify?

    The commentaries offer a number of responses to this question. Rabbaynu Avraham ibn Ezra suggests that these beautiful and impressive garments glorify Ahron or the *Kohen Gadol*

---

[1] Rabbaynu Moshe ben Maimon (Rambam) *Mishne Torah*, Hilchot K'lai Mikdash 5:6.

who wears them.² In other words, the purpose of the *Kohen Gadol's* garments and the regulations governing his grooming was to assure a positive physical appearance. Our *pasuk* indicates that this attention to appearance was intended to assure that the *Kohen Gadol* would be treated with dignity and respect.

This is surprising. Our Sages admonish us to "not look upon the container but at its contents."³ Their message is that we should not be impressed by superficial behaviors or appearances. Instead, we are to assess a person based upon the individual's inner-self. Why does the Torah stress superficial aspects of the *Kohen Gadol*?

More shocking than the Torah's emphasis on physical appearance is the prohibition against the *Kohen Gadol's* marriage to a widow. This prohibition is also designed to protect the public image of the High Priest.⁴ The Torah admonishes us to treat the widow with compassion and justice. The Torah commands us: "You shall not oppress the any widow or orphan."⁵ Why does the Torah prohibit the *Kohen Gadol's* marriage to a widow and thereby accommodate a shallow prejudice against the widow? Would it not be preferable for the Torah to allow this marriage? Such a policy would counter any social stigma attached to the widow.

These laws demonstrate one of the unique qualities of the Torah. Torah takes human weakness seriously. The Torah was created to govern an actual society. In the real world, prejudice and superficiality exist. These prejudices will undermine respect for the *Kohen Gadol* if he is married to a widow. The Torah recognizes these faults as forces in society. It prohibits the marriage. But, at the same time, the Torah attempts to correct human behavior. The Torah's approach to confronting prejudice is balanced. It legislates commandments to protect the rights of those likely to be oppressed or subject to prejudice. But it also recognizes the tenacity of these prejudices. Both measures are essential. The Torah also attempts to improve upon these human limitations. However, failure to recognize human frailty would result in a system poorly equipped to deal with and accommodate actual human beings.

The garments of the *Kohen Gadol* are an excellent illustration of the Torah's method of dealing with this dilemma. The Torah requires that the *Kohen Gadol* wear beautiful garments. However, these garments are more than attractive vestments. Every detail of design is guided by an intricate system of *halachah*. The observer is attracted to the beauty of the garments, and hopefully, this initial interest leads to contemplation of the ingenious laws which govern their design and structure. The observer comes to recognize that the greatest beauty is not in the superficial material dimension. Instead, true beauty is found in the world of knowledge.

Nachmanides acknowledges Ibn Ezra's interpretation of the *pasuk* as a reasonable possibility. He also suggests an alternative explanation. He proposes that the garments honor and glorify Hashem.⁶ Apparently, Nachmanides reasons that the *Kohen Gadol* serves Hashem. Performing his duties in these wondrous vestments glorifies the service and Hashem.

---

² Rabbaynu Avraham ibn Ezra, *Commentary on Sefer Shemot*, 28:2.
³ Mesechet Avot 4:20.
⁴ Rabbaynu Levi ben Gershon (Ralbag / Gershonides), *Commentary on Sefer VaYikra*, (Mosad HaRav Kook, 1997), pp. 353-4.
⁵ Shemot 22:21.
⁶ Rabbaynu Moshe ben Nachman (Ramban), *Commentary on Sefer* Shemot 28:2.

Rabbaynu Ovadia Sforno suggests that the garments serve *both* purposes. They honor Hashem and glorify the *Kohen Gadol*.[7]

This dispute regarding the function of the vestments of the *Kohen Gadol,* and presumably also the vestments of the *Kohen,* is the underlying basis for another disagreement.

There is another dispute among the Sages regarding the requirement that the *kohanim* wear special vestments. Maimonides, in his Sefer HaMitzvot, writes that our passage communicates a positive command. The *kohen* and the *Kohen Gadol* must wear their assigned vestments when serving in the sanctuary.[8] Halachot Gedolot disagrees with Maimonides. He does not derive a commandment from our passage. He maintains that there is no separate commandment directing the *Kohen Gadol* or the other *kohanim* to wear these garments.

Of course, this creates a problem. The *Kohen Gadol* and the *kohanim* are not permitted to perform service in the Temple without these garments. How can Halachot Gedolot contend that there is no specific commandment directing the Priests to wear these garments, and also acknowledge that the *kohanim* are not permitted to serve without their vestments?

Nachmanides responds to this question. He explains that Halachot Gedolot certainly acknowledges that a *kohen* cannot serve without the proper vestments. However, according to Halachot Gedolot, the vestments are a requirement for the proper performance of the service. They are a prerequisite for the performance of the *mitzvah* of service in the Temple. As a prerequisite for another command – the performance of the service—the requirement to wear the vestments does not merit to be classified as an independent commandment.[9]

Another example from *halachah* illustrates Nachmanides' argument. All males are required to wear *tefillin*. Wearing *tefillin* is a *mitzvah*. Now, in order to wear *tefillin,* one first must acquire them. Yet, the procurement of *tefillin* is not a separate *mitzvah*. It is merely a prerequisite for the fulfillment of the commandment to wear them. Nachmanides argues that similarly the garments worn by the *kohen* are a prerequisite for the proper performance of the Temple service. As a prerequisite, the wearing of these garments does not qualify as a separate *mitzvah*.

How would Maimonides respond to Nachmanides' position? Nachmanides is seemingly offering a compelling argument for not counting the wearing of the vestments as a separate *mitzvah*. Maimonides agrees that the procurement of *tefillin* is not a separate *mitzvah*. Why does he consider the requirement for the *kohen* to wear his special attire a separate *mitzvah*?

In order to answer this question, we must consider the order in which Maimonides organizes the various commandments concerning the *kohanim*. In his Sefer HaMitzvot, Maimonides states that the requirement of the *kohanim* to wear their garments is the thirty-third positive commandment of the Torah. According to Maimonides' enumeration of the commandments, the thirty-second positive commandment is to honor the *kohanim* – the descendants of Ahron. The close association of these two commandments suggests that they are related. What is this relationship?

---

[7] Rabbaynu Ovadia Sforno, *Commentary on Sefer Shemot* 28:2.
[8] Rabbaynu Moshe ben Maimon (Rambam) *Sefer HaMitzvot, Mitzvat Aseh* 33.
[9] R' Moshe ben Nachman (Ramban), *Critique on Maimonides' Sefer HaMitzvot, M. A.* 33.

Apparently, Maimonides adopts the position of Ibn Ezra: the garments are designed to honor and glorify the *kohanim*. He communicates his position by ordering this *mitzvah* directly after the commandment to honor the *kohanim*. These vestments distinguish the *kohanim* and assign to them special status. It is true that a *kohen* cannot serve in the Temple without his vestments. But according to Maimonides, this is not because the vestments are a prerequisite for the service. The garments are required in order to confer honor and glory upon the *kohen*. Only when wearing the vestments is he qualified for service. In other words, without the garments, the *kohen* is not the person permitted to perform the service.

The pivotal issue of contention between Maimonides and Nachmanides can now be identified. According to Nachmanides, the garments are a prerequisite for performance of the service. They are tied to, and enhance, the service. This interpretation reflects Nachmanides' interpretation of the above passage. The vestments glorify the Temple service and Hashem. Therefore, wearing this special attire is a prerequisite for proper performance of the service but does not constitute a separate *mitzvah*. In contrast, Maimonides maintains that the garments glorify and honor the *Kohanim*. They confer full honor and status upon the *kohen*. As a result, the wearing of the garments is a separate *mitzvah* within Taryag – the 613 Commandments.

And you should command Bnai Yisrael and they should bring to you pure olive oil, hand crushed for illumination to keep a lamp constantly burning. (Shemot 27:20)

The Oil for the Menorah

1. Only the purest olive oil can be used in the Menorah

In Parshat Tetzaveh the instructions for the construction of the Tabernacle – the Mishcan continue. This parasha primarily deals with the garments of the Kohanim – the priests – and Kohen Gadol – the High Priest. However, the opening passage of the parasha deals with the oil used in the Menorah – the candelabra of the Mishcan.

Only the purest oil is used in the Menorah. The Mishne in Tractate Menachot describes the production of this oil. The olives are hand crushed. The crushed olives are placed in the basket. The oil that drains from these olives is extremely pure. This is the only oil used in the Menorah.[10]

2. Filtered oil is not acceptable

There is another means of producing pure oil. This is through filtering. This method is not acceptable. Even if the filtered oil is perfectly pure, it may not be used for the Menorah. Of course, this raises a question. The requirement to use in the Menorah only oil from hand-crushed olives is intended to assure the purity of the oil.[11] A similar grade of purity could be assured through filtering. However, filtering is unacceptable! Why can filtering not be used?

In order to answer this question, we must further analyze the Torah's requirement for the oil of the Menorah. As our passage indicates, the oil must be pure. What is the definition of pure? Apparently, pure means that the oil should not contain solids. However, the oil must also be complete or whole. None of its components can be missing.

---

[10] Mesechet Menachot 8:4-5.
[11] Rabbaynu Shlomo ben Yitzchak (Rashi), Commentary on Sefer Shemot 27:20.

We can now understand the reason filtered oil cannot be used. There is a significant difference between pure oil derived from hand crushed olives and filtered oil. Oil derived from hand-crushed olives is innately pure. Without removing any component from the oil it is pure. Oil that is purified by filtering is not pure innately. Instead, the filtering removes the solids, leaving a purer oil. This answers our question. The oil used for the Menorah must be pure. It must also contain all of its components. These two requirements can only be met through hand-crushing the olives. Hand-crushing the olives produces pure oil without the removing any components. These requirements cannot be met through filtering.

3. The oil used for the Minchah offering

A Minchah – a grain offering – is also accompanied by oil. What grade of oil is required for a Minchah? The Torah, in describing this oil, mentions the same grade as required for the Menorah.[12] However, our Sages explain that the Minchah does not require this highest grade of oil. Even inferior grades are suitable. The passage merely indicates that the highest grade is not exclusively reserved for the Menorah. It can also be offered with the Minchah.[13] Maimonides adds that, although various grades of oil can be brought with the Minchah, one should bring the highest grade available. He explains that in performing any mitzvah one should always use the best materials.[14]

4. Fuels acceptable for Shabbat lights

Why is the highest grade of oil required for the Menorah but not absolutely required for the Minchah? The Midrash Tanchuma seems to answer this question. In order to understand the comments of the Midrash, an introduction is required. The Talmud discusses the types of fuels that may be used on Shabbat. There are two general considerations that determine the suitability of any fuel for the Shabbat lights. First, it must burn evenly. If the oil does not burn evenly, one might adjust the wick in order to improve the light. This adjustment is prohibited on Shabbat. Second, the fuel cannot burn with an unpleasant odor. The Shabbat lights are intended to provide useful light. If they produce an unpleasant odor, the members of the household will distance themselves from the Shabbat lights. These lights will not serve their intended purpose. The Mishne in Tractate Shabbat discusses various fuels that cannot be used for the Shabbat lights because of these two considerations. However, Rebbe Tarfon posits that it is not adequate for a fuel to burn well and not be unpleasant. He maintains that only olive oil may be used.[15] Tiferet Yisrael explains that the reason for Rebbe Tarfon's position is that olive oil burns best.[16]

Rebbe Tarfon's position is discussed at length in Midrash Tanchuma. There, the Sages argue with Rebbe Tarfon. They explain that olive oil is not readily available in all communities. Rebbe Tarfon's insistence on olive oil will pose a hardship in such communities! Rebbe Tarfon responds that the Torah insists on olive oil for the Menorah. This demonstrates the superiority of its flame. Rebbe Tarfon also seems to indicate that this is the reason for requiring the highest grade of oil. Extremely pure oil produces a better flame.[17]

---

[12] Sefer Shemot 29:40.
[13] Sifra Parshat Emor, chapter 13.
[14] Rabbaynu Moshe ben Maimon (Rambam) Mishne Torah, Hilchot Esurai Mizbayach 7:11.
[15] Mesechet Shabbat 2:1-2.
[16] Rav Yisrael Lipshitz, Tiferet Yisrael Commentary on Mesechet Shabbat 2:2, note 25.
[17] Midrash Tanchuma, Parshat BeHaatotecha, chapter 1.

We can now answer our question. The highest grade of oil is superior in two ways. First, it is the choicest oil. As Maimonides explains, we should use the most choice materials in performing any mitzvah. However, this requirement is not absolute. If it is not satisfied the mitzvah is nonetheless fulfilled. This means that both for the Minchah and the Menorah the purest oil is preferred. However, this consideration alone does not disqualify oil of a lower grade. Indeed, a lower grade may be brought with a Minchah offering.

The highest grade oil is superior in a second way. As Rebbe Tarfon explains, it produces a better flame than any other grade. This aspect of superiority is irrelevant to the Minchah offering. That oil is not intended to fuel a light. However, it is relevant to the Menorah. The Menorah requires the best flame. This requirement is absolute and can only be achieved with the purest oil.

In short, the Menorah is designed to produce light. The highest grade olive oil produces the best light. Therefore, it is required for the Menorah. This consideration is irrelevant to the Minchah offering. Therefore, although choice materials are always best in performing a mitzvah, lower grades of oil are not disqualified.

And make sacred vestments for Aharon, your brother, for honor and glory. (Shemot 28:2)

Balancing Diversity with Unity

The Jewish community at the local, national, and international level is composed of various sub-communities. The sub-communities may be defined by their affiliations with religious movements within Judaism – for example, Orthodox, Conservative, Reform, and others. The sub-communities are sometimes differentiated by the origins and religious practices of their members – for example, the Ashkenazic and Sephardic communities. Certainly, geography also creates sub-communities – for example, the community of Jews living in Israel and the community of those in the Diaspora. We are each members of multiple sub-communities. One person may be an Ashkenazic, Orthodox, Jew living in the United States and out of town (i.e. not in the New York metropolitan area). Along with membership in these many sub-communities each of us is also a member of the Jewish people. In other words, the members of our people are united by their shared Jewish identity and yet differentiated by their various sub-communities.

The result is that we often perceive our differences more keenly than we appreciate our shared identity. When we become intently aware of our differences, our identification with one another can deteriorate, distrust can develop, and alienation emerges.

This is particularly relevant to Jewish communal trends in the United States. Nationally, we have moved toward ever-greater segmentation or specialization of community services. Communities that were served by a single school or synagogue a decade ago have created multiple schools and synagogues. Each is distinct from the other and each is designed to serve a specific sub-community within the overall community.

The advantage of this trend is that sub-communities may be better served by these more specialized schools and synagogues. However, the trade-off is that the overall unity of the community is challenged. A paradox emerges. We may better serve our sub-communities through specialization but only at the cost of diminished unity.

In the discussion that follows, we will not attempt to resolve this paradox. Instead, we will consider an important paradigm from which it should be evaluated. Once that paradigm is identified, it will suggest – not a solution to the paradox – but a clearer path toward creating a healthy balance.

The *Kohen Gadol* had special vestments

Last week's *parasha* described the *Mishcan* – the tabernacle of the wilderness – and many of its most fundamental components. This week's *parasha* continues that discussion. It opens with a description of the special vestments of the *Kohen Gadol* – the high priest. One of these vestments was the *Choshen* – the breastplate. This vestment was fastened to a sort of apron worn by the *Kohen Gadol* and he bore it upon his chest. The main feature of the *Choshen* was the four rows of precious stones that occupied its center. Each of the four rows contained three stones, combining to a total of twelve stones. On each stone was inscribed the name of one of the tribes of Bnai Yisrael. On the first stone was inscribed Reuven, on the second Shimon, and so forth, through Binyamin.

> *And the stones should be according to the names of Bnai Yisrael – twelve according to their names. They should be engraved, each with its name for the twelve tribes. (Shemot 28:21)*

The *Choshen* and its inscriptions

The *Choshen* had two functions. As explained above, it was one of the vestments of the *Kohen Gadol*. He could perform his service in the *Mishcan* only when attired in all of his vestments – including the *Choshen*. The *Choshen* had a second function. It was a vehicle for prophecy. Through the agency of the *Choshen* the nation could secure prophetic responses to questions that could not be otherwise resolved. For example, the nation could ask whether it should engage in war against an enemy or avoid confrontation. Maimonides provides a description of how the *Choshen* was utilized. The king or an individual acting on behalf of the entire nation would pose the question to the *Kohen Gadol*. The *Kohen Gadol* would experience a prophetic vision in which the answer to the question would be provided through the letters inscribed on the *Choshen*. In his vision the letters forming the answer would appear to protrude. The *Kohen Gadol* would then report the response provided in his vision.

Maimonides further explains that because the response in the vision was presented through its inscribed letters, it was necessary for all of the letters of the Hebrew alphabet to be included on the *Choshen*. The names of the tribes do not encompass the entire alphabet. Rather than inscribing the missing letters in som arbitrary manner on the *Choshen*, a phrase was added above the first name inscribed on the *Choshen* and another after the last name. Above the name Reuven was inscribed "Avraham Yitzchak, and Yaakov". After Binyamin was inscribed "tribes of Hashem". With the addition of these two phrases the full complement of Hebrew letters was inscribed upon the *Choshen*.

The selection of these two phrases and their positions are of note. First, surely, these phrases were not selected randomly. They must have had some relevance to the *Choshen*. Second, these two phrases bracketed the names of the tribes. The names of the forefathers were above the name of the very first tribe and the phrase "tribes of Hashem" followed the name of the last tribe. The positioning of the names of the tribes between these two phrases suggests that these phrases referred to and commented upon the tribes. What was the message intended by these phrases and what was the relevance of that message to the names of the tribes?

And make a band of gold and engrave upon it "sanctified for Hashem". (Shemot 28:36)

The headband of the *Kohen Gadol* and its inscription

Let us consider another of the *Kohen Gadol*'s vestments. On his forehead, the *Kohen Gadol* wore a gold band. On this band was inscribed the phrase "sanctified for Hashem". The phrase refers to the *Kohen Gadol* and comments upon him. It declares that he is sanctified to Hashem. It is reasonable to assume that the names on the *Choshen* also comment on the *Kohen Gadol*. They declare that he is the representative of the nation – of all of the tribes of Israel. Together, these two inscriptions describe the *Kohen Gadol* as sanctified to serve Hashem as the representative of the nation.

Now, we can better appreciate the inscriptions on the *Choshen*. The people of Israel are described on the *Choshen* as a conglomeration of tribes. In other words, the *Choshen* recognizes or acknowledges that we are a nation composed of sub-communities. In turn, this suggests that these sub-communities – the tribes – are an important aspect of the structure of our nation. Why are these tribes so important?

The tribes of Israel contribute to the cohesiveness of the community

The strength of any community is built upon the connectedness of its members. When the members of a community identify with one another and feel this connectedness, then they will work for each other's welfare and care for one another. Furthermore, the members of the community are capable of engaging in collective activities for the welfare of their overall community. The sense of connectedness is the cement that holds together the structure of the community and if it is absent the community disintegrates. A corollary of this principle is that the more diverse a community, the more difficult for the community to engage in collctive activities. In other words, as communities become larger and naturally more diverse, they tend to become less effective as working units. The capacity of a community to engage in sustained cooperative activities is compromised by the degree of its diversity.

This consideration is addressed in Bnai Yisrael through the system of tribes. These tribes were functional sub-communities. The tribes were further divided into clans. The clans were further divided into families. These sub-communities of various sizes and degrees of diversity created a functional nation. The *Choshen* acknowledged and even promoted tribal identity. It expressed the importance of sub-communities for effective collective action.

Nurturing unity among the tribes of Israel

However, the names of the *Avot* – the forefathers – preceded the name of Reuven and the phrase "tribes of Hashem" followed the name of Binyamin. What do these two phrases communicate regarding the tribes? The *Avot* remind us that we all share a common ancestry. In fact, our existence is the fulfillment of the promise made by Hashem to the *Avot*. The phrase "tribes of Hashem" reminds us that we share a common mission and destiny. We have been selected for and consecrated to the service of Hashem. The *Choshen* communicates the overarching themes that must unite us.

In other words, the paradox described in the opening paragraphs of this discussion is embraced by the *Choshen* and even promoted by it. Sub-communities are effective operational units. In a diverse community they are a necessity. If they are sacrificed in pursuit of a vision of greater unity, the cohesion necessary for effective collective action may be destroyed. However, although sub-communities have an important function, they cannot be allowed to obscure the values that unite us. We must always remember that foremost we share the same *Avot* and an identical mission. We are consecrated to the service of Hashem. In other words, a careful balance must be maintained between the individuality of our specific community and the ever-awareness of our shared identity as Jews.

Creating a healthy balance within a community

This paradigm provides us with some guidelines that we can apply to our communities. It is healthy to feel a stronger connection with those who are members of one's sub-community. But this connection is destructive when it yields a sense of alienation from the other sub-communities that make us one people.

A city's Jewish community may be best served by multiple schools and synagogues – but only when the members of each also celebrate the successes of all the others. A strong sense of connectedness within our individual religious streams is healthy. But our love and compassion must also extend to those who are members of our other streams.

Without this balance, our individual sub-communities tear asunder our connectedness as Jews. Our shared identity as a people is replaced by distrust and alienation. When we achieve this balance, then our sub-communities are effective vehicles for collective action and our unity as a people is preserved and even nurtured.

"And you should make a Breast-plate of Judgment of a woven design. Like the design of the Ephod you shall make it. You shall make it of gold, blue, purple, scarlet wool and twisted linen." (Shemot 28:15)

The *Kohen Gadol* wore eight garments. These consisted of the four garments worn by every *kohen* and an additional four special vestments. One of the special vestments was the *Choshen Mishpat* – the Breast-plate of Judgment.

The *Choshen* hung from the shoulders of the *Kohen Gadol*. The vestment was made of woven cloth. Embedded into the *Choshen* were precious stones representing the *shevatim* – the tribes of Bnai Yisrael.

The *Choshen* had a unique function. Questions could be posed to the *Kohen Gadol*. He would respond by consulting the *Choshen*. Maimonides explains this process based upon the Talmud. The question would be brought to the *Kohen Gadol*. He would immediately be overcome with the spirit of prophecy. The *Kohen Gadol* would look at the *Choshen*. The response would be transmitted to him in a prophetic vision. The answer was expressed through the letters engraved upon the stones of the Breast-plate.[18]

According to Nachmanides the process of posing a question to the Kohen Gadol for a response from the Choshen is included in a positive command. What is this positive command?

In order to answer this question and understand Nachmanides' position, we must consider a set of *pesukim* at the end of Chapter 18 of Sefer Devarim. These passages begin with an admonition to not emulate the practices of the nations that lived in Canaan. The Torah then outlines various mystical practices and routines used by these nations to predict the future. Then, the Torah tells us that we must wholeheartedly follow Hashem. The section ends with laws

---

[18] Rabbaynu Moshe ben Maimon (Rambam) *Mishne Torah*, Hilchot Klai HaMikdash 10:11.

regarding prophets. We are commanded to obey true prophets and to punish false prophets.[19] The overall message of these passages is fairly clear. The people of Canaan had developed various primitive rituals and procedures for influencing their environment and predicting the future. Hashem commands Bnai Yisrael to not adopt these heathen customs. Hashem tells Bnai Yisrael that He will provide them with prophets. These prophets will communicate with Hashem and the people should rely on the prophets for guidance and leadership.

However, one passage is difficult to understand. After Hashem admonishes Bnai Yisrael against adopting the practices of the nations of Canaan and before commanding the people to obey His prophets there is a transitional *pasuk*. In this passage, Bnai Yisrael are told that they must wholeheartedly follow Hashem. What is the meaning of this passage?

Nachmanides contends that this passage is designed to connect the preceding and following passages. We are not to rely on fortune tellers and heathen rituals designed to predict the future. Instead, we are to follow Hashem wholeheartedly. How do we fulfill this requirement? We fulfill it though our obeying His prophets.

How is obedience to Hashem's prophets an expression of wholehearted commitment to Hashem? Nachmanides explains that all of the methods used the nations of Canaan to predict the future were based on the premise that this future is fixed and predetermined. He uses astrology and an example. Astrology is based in the assumption that the configuration of the stars appearing in the nighttime sky exercises an absolute casual influence on the event in this world. Astrology posits that by understanding this influence – or reading the stars – we can predict with certainty events in this world. If the predictions of astrologers are sometimes incorrect, this is because they have not correctly read the signs in the heavens. But the information is in the heavens for the astrologer that can properly unravel the message.

Nachmanides explains that this premise is inconsistent with the outlook of the Torah. According to the Torah, the events that occur in this world are not predetermined. Hashem is omnipotent. He rules over the universe and our world. He has the ability to suspend or disregard the laws of nature. According to Nachmanides, the astrologer does not fail simply because he has not correctly read the signs in the heavens. He fails because these signs are not absolute indications of the future. The stars may influence events in this world but they do not determine the future. Ultimately, only Hashem's will determines the future. No astrologer or fortune teller can know Hashem's will.

However, Hashem does reveal His will to His prophets. Therefore, only these prophets can actually know the future. If we must seek knowledge of the future, we are to turn to these prophets and not to astrologers and fortune tellers.

Based on this analysis, Nachmanides concludes that relying on astrology or other portents of the future is a denial of a fundamental tenet of the Torah. This is because reliance on these methods of predicting the further is predicated on the assumption that the future is fixed and that it is not ultimately determined by Hashem's will.

Now the meaning of the admonition to wholeheartedly follow Hashem emerges. We are required to accept the proposition that only Hashem's will determines the future and that only through His prophets can we truly know the future. According to Nachmanides this admonition

---

[19] Sefer Devarim 18:9-22.

to wholeheartedly follow Hashem – to accept the proposition that His will alone determines event in this world – is a positive command.[20] According to his reasoning it follows that by turning to Hashem's prophets or by posing our questions to the *Kohen Gadol* wearing the *Choshen*, we fulfill the *mitzvah* of wholeheartedly following Hashem.[21]

Maimonides does not regard this passage as a positive command. In other words, according to Maimonides, the admonition to wholeheartedly follow Hashem is not a *mitzvah*. Why did Maimonides not regard this instruction as a *mitzvah*? Nachmanides suggests a possible explanation. According to Maimonides, general admonitions to observe the commandments of the Torah are not in themselves *mitzvot*. In order for an admonition to be counted as a commandment, it must engender a specific obligation or prohibition. General admonishments do not meet this criterion and therefore cannot be counted among the 613 *mitzvot*.[22] Nachmanides suggests that according to Maimonides, the admonition to wholeheartedly follow Hashem is directing us to observe the commandments of the Torah. Because it is a general admonition, Maimonides does not include it in his enumeration of the 613 *mitzvot*.[23]

Meggilat Esther suggests a similar explanation for Maimonides' position. According to Meggilat Esther, the admonition to wholeheartedly follow Hashem is a positive formulation of the negative commandments in the preceding *pesukim*. As noted above, the preceding passages command Bnai Yisrael to not resort to and rely upon fortune-telling and other portents. These passages include a number of negative commandments that prohibit specific practices. The directive to wholeheartedly follow Hashem reiterates these prohibitions in a positive formulation. Maimonides maintains that in instances in which a positive directive merely reiterates the substance of a prohibition, the positive formulation is not generally counted as a separate *mitzvah*.[24] Meggilat Esther suggests that Maimonides applies this principle to the admonition to wholeheartedly follow Hashem and therefore, does not count it as a separate *mitzvah*.[25]

However a careful analysis of a related issue suggests an alternative explanation of Maimonides' position. In order to develop this explanation, it is necessary to return to Nachmanides' comments. As explained above, according to the Torah it is prohibited to rely on portents, fortune-tellers, and even astrology. According to Nachmanides, this prohibition is fundamentally an assertion that the events of this world are ultimately determined by Hashem. But Nachmanides is careful not to assert that astrology and other methods of predicting the future are baseless. Instead, he asserts that these methods are flawed. They are predicated on the belief that the future is solely controlled by the stars or natural forces. They assume that by understanding and "reading" these forces the future can be predicted. They do not acknowledge that such predictions are not absolute and can be overridden by Hashem. In other words, Nachmanides accepts that natural forces influence events in this world and that the affect of

---

[20] Rabbaynu Moshe ben Nachman (Ramban), *Commentary on Sefer Devarim* 18:13.
[21] Rabbaynu Moshe ben Nachman (Ramban), *Critique on Maimonides' Sefer HaMitzvot* -- Positive Commands that Maimonides Neglected to Include.
[22] Rabbaynu Moshe ben Maimon (Rambam) *Sefer HaMitzvot*, Principle 4.
[23] Rabbaynu Moshe ben Nachman (Ramban), *Critique on Maimonides' Sefer HaMitzvot* -- Positive Commands that Maimonides Neglected to Include.
[24] Rabbaynu Moshe ben Maimon (Rambam) *Sefer HaMitzvot*, Principle 9.
[25] Rabbaynu Yitzchak DeLeon, *Meggilat Esther, Commentary on Maimonides' Sefer Hamitzvot*, Comments on Nachmanides' Critique.

these forces can be predicted. However, he asserts that such predictions are not reliable because they do not account for Hashem's ability to override the natural laws.

In contrast, Maimonides contends that the methods utilized by the nations of Canaan were nonsensical and nothing more than superstitions. Maimonides asserts that one who believes that these methods have some validity and contain an element of truth is a fool. He does not attribute any credibility to these methods of predicting the future. Maimonides does not regard the study of portents and signs as a flawed approach to predicting the future. He emphatically declares that they are utter foolishness. It is this context the Maimonides makes reference to the admonition to wholeheartedly follow Hashem. According to Maimonides, this admonition tells us to be completely committed to the truth and to not revert to superstitions and their implicit primitive outlook.[26]

We can now appreciate Maimonides' decision to not count this admonition as a commandment. According to Maimonides, the admonition tells us to act intelligently and not regress to the superstitious and foolish beliefs of the heathen nations of Canaan. The admonition does not engender or prohibit a specific performance. Instead, it directs us to adopt a general outlook and to be completely faithful to this outlook. Accordingly, Maimonides does not count this general directive as a commandment.

"And you should make sacred garments for Ahron and your brother for honor and glory." (Shemot 28:2)

Our parasha discusses the garments of the Kohen Gadol. In the above passage, Moshe is command to instruct Bnai Yisrael in the creation of these garments. The pasuk says that these garments are designed for honor and glory. However, the pasuk is vague. The garments glorify whom or what?

The commentaries offer a number of responses to this question. Rabbaynu Avraham ibn Ezra suggests that these beautiful and impressive garments glorify Ahron or the Kohen Gadol who wears them.[27] Nachmanides acknowledges this possible interpretation of the pasuk. He also suggests an alternative explanation. He proposes that the garments honor and glorify Hashem.[28] Apparently, Nachmanides reasons that the Kohen Gadol serves Hashem. Performing his duties in these wondrous vestments glorifies the service and the Almighty.

Sforno suggests that the garments serve both purposes. They honor Hashem and glorify the Kohen Gadol.[29]

There is another dispute among the Sages regarding the requirement that Kohanim wear special vestments. Maimonides, in his Sefer HaMitzvot, writes that our passage communicates a positive command. The Kohen and the Kohen Gadol must wear their assigned vestments when serving in the sanctuary.[30] Halachot Gedolot disagrees with Maimonides. He does not derive a

---

[26] Rabbaynu Moshe ben Maimon (Rambam) *Mishne Torah*, Hilchot Avodah Zarah 11:16.
[27] Rabbaynu Avraham ibn Ezra, *Commentary on Sefer Shemot*, 28:2.
[28] Rabbaynu Moshe ben Nachman (Ramban), *Commentary on Sefer* Shemot 28:2.
[29] Rabbaynu Ovadia Sforno, *Commentary on Sefer Shemot* 28:2.
[30] Rabbaynu Moshe ben Maimon (Rambam) *Sefer HaMitzvot, Mitzvat Aseh* 33.

commandment from our passage. He maintains that there is no separate command that directs the Kohen Gadol or the other Kohanim to wear these garments.

Of course, this creates a problem. The Kohen Gadol and the Kohanim are not permitted to perform service in the Temple without these garments. How can Halachot Gedolot contend that there is no specific command directing the Priests to wear these garments, and also acknowledge that the Kohanim are not permitted to serve without their vestments?

Nachmanides responds to this question. He explains that the Halachot Gedolot certainly acknowledges that a Kohen cannot serve without the proper vestments. However, according to Halachot Gedolot, the vestments are a requirement for the proper performance of the service. They are a prerequisite for the performance of the mitzvah of service in the Temple. As a prerequisite for another command – the performance of the service, the requirement to wear the vestments does not merit to be classified as an independent commandment.[31] Let us consider another example from halacha that illustrates Nachmanides' argument. All males are required to wear Tefillin. Wearing Tefillin is a mitzvah. Now, in order to wear Tefillin one first must acquire the Tefillin. Yet, clearly the procurement of Tefillin is not a separate mitzvah. It is merely a prerequisite for the fulfillment of the commandment of wearing Tefillin. Nachmanides argues that similarly the garments worn by the Kohen are a prerequisite for the proper performance of the Temple service. As a prerequisite, the wearing of these garments does not qualify as a separate mitzvah.

How would Maimonides respond to Nachmanides' position? Nachmanides is seemingly offering a compelling argument for not counting the wearing of the vestments as a separate mitzvah. Maimonides agrees that the procurement of Tefillin is not a separate mitzvah. Why does he consider the requirement for the Kohen to wear his special attire a separate mitzvah?

In order to answer this question, we must consider the order in which Maimonides places the various commandments concerning the Kohanim. Maimonides states that the requirement of the Kohanim to wear their garments is the thirty-third positive command. According to Maimonides' enumeration of the commandments, the thirty-second positive commandment is to honor the Kohanim – the descendants of Ahron. It seems from the close association of these two commandments that they are related. What is this relationship?

Apparently, Maimonides maintains that the garments are designed to honor and glorify the Kohanim. These vestments distinguish the Kohanim and defer special status upon them. It is true that a Kohen cannot serve in the Temple without his vestments. But according to Maimonides, this is not because the vestments are a prerequisite for the service. The garments complete the status of the Kohen. The vestments qualify him for service. In other words, without the garments, the Kohen is not the person permitted to perform the service.

Let us now focus on identifying the pivotal issue of contention between Maimonides and Nachmanides. According to Nachmanides, the garments are designed to glorify the service in the Temple. They are a prerequisite for service. Therefore, wearing this special attire is not a separate mitzvah. In contrast, Maimonides maintains that the garments glorify and honor the Kohanim. They confer full status on the Kohen. As a result, the wearing of the garments is a separate mitzvah within Taryag --- the 613 commandments.

---

[31] Rabbaynu Moshe ben Nachman (Ramban), *Critique on Maimonides' Sefer HaMitzvot, Mitzvat Aseh* 33.

And these are the garments that they shall make: a breastplate, an apron, a jacket, a patterned tunic, a turban, and a belt. And they shall make sacred garments for Ahron your brother and for his sons so that they will serve as priests to me. (Shemot 28:4)

The Golden Garments of the Kohen Gadol

Parshat Tetzaveh discusses the garment worn by the *Kohen Gadol*—the High Priest. In total, the *Kohen Gadol* wore eight garments. Maimonides comments that the eight golden garments of the *Kohen Gadol* consisted of the four worn by the common priest, plus the jacket, apron, breastplate and headband.[32]

The *Kesef Mishne* is troubled by this statement. In fact, only the four special garments included gold thread. The other garments worn by both the *Kohen Gadol* and the common *kohen* did not include gold thread. Why, then, does Maimonides refer to all eight of the *Kohen Gadol*'s garments as "golden"?

Perhaps, Maimonides wishes to teach an important lesson. The eight garments of the *Kohen Gadol* are not individual, isolated items. Instead, they merge into a single vestment. The four common garments join with the four woven with gold to create a single, integrated entity. This integrated garment is the "golden vestments" of the *Kohen Gadol*. Therefore, it is not necessary for each individual garment to contain gold thread to be referred to as "golden". Instead, they are referred to as "golden" through inclusion in the overall entity of the "golden garments".

And you should make a Breast-plate of Judgment of a woven design. Like the design of the Ephod, you shall make it. You shall make it of gold, blue, purple, scarlet wool, and twisted linen. (Shemot 28:15)

The Function of Prophecy in the Resolution of Issues in Halachah

The *Kohen Gadol* wore eight garments. These consisted of the four garments worn by every *kohen* and an additional four special vestments. One of the special vestments was the *Choshen Mishpat* – the Breast-plate of Judgment. The *Choshen* hung from the shoulders of the *Kohen Gadol*. The vestment was made of woven cloth. Embedded into the *Choshen* were precious stones representing the *Shevatim* – the Tribes of Israel. The *Choshen* had a unique function. Questions could be posed to the *Kohen Gadol*. He would respond by consulting the *Choshen*. Maimonides describes this process based upon the comments of Talmud. The proposed question would be brought to the *Kohen Gadol*. He would immediately be overcome with the spirit of prophecy. The *Kohen Gadol* would look at the *Choshen*. The response would be transmitted to him in a prophetic vision. The answer was expressed through the illumination of the letters engraved upon the stones of the Breast-plate.[33]

What type of questions could be addressed to the *Choshen*? In the Prophets we find that the Choshen was consulted on national issues. A king might refer to the *Choshen* for guidance regarding a military campaign. However, Rashi comments in Tractate Eruvin that questions of

---

[32] Rabbaynu Moshe ben Maimon (Rambam) Mishne Torah, Hilchot Klai HaMikdash 10:11.
[33] Rabbaynu Moshe ben Maimon (Rambam) *Mishne Torah*, Hilchot Klai HaMikdash 10:11.

halachah were not addressed in this manner. This limitation upon the use of the *Choshen* reflects an important principle of the Torah. Prophecy cannot be used to resolve issues of *halachah*. Such questions are the responsibility of the Sages and the courts. They must address these issues using the standards of *halachah* and their own intellects.

Rabbaynu Yonatan ben Uziel makes an amazing comment that seems to contradict this principle. In our *pasuk*, The *Choshen* is referred to as the Breast-plate of Judgment. What is the relationship between the *Choshen* and judgment? Rabbaynu Yonatan ben Uziel explains that the *Choshen* could be consulted over legal issues! This seems to contradict the principle that issues of *halachah* cannot be resolved through prophecy.

A similar contradiction is suggested by the last mishna in Tractate Edyot. Our Sages teach us that the Messianic era will be preceded by the reappearance of, Eliyahu, the prophet. The mishna explains that Eliyahu will help prepare the path for the Moshiach. Raban Yochanan ben Zakai posits that one of Eliyahu's functions will be to clarify issues of lineage. Maimonides explains the meaning of this statement. Through prophecy, Eliyahu will identify those individuals who have become completely alienated from their Jewish roots. They will be welcomed back into Bnai Yisrael. In addition, impostors whose lineage is imperfect will be identified and excluded from the Jewish people. This would seem to be another example of prophecy used as a means to resolve an issue of *halachah*.

Rav Tzvi Hirsch Chayutz *Zt"l*, based upon a careful analysis of Maimonides' comments, offers a brilliant response. He explains that the limitation of prophecy as a means of resolving questions of *halachah* needs to be more fully understood. This limitation excludes prophecy from being used to determine the proper formulation of the law. For example, in order for a person to be punished by the courts for eating a prohibited substance, a minimum quantity must be ingested. Assume a person consumes less than this amount. Certainly, the person cannot be punished by the courts. But is this activity included in the Torah prohibition or is the consumption prohibited by only an injunction of the Sages? This issue is disputed by Rebbe Yochanan and Rebbe Shimon ben Lakish. The dispute revolves around the formulation of the Torah prohibition. Such an issue cannot be resolved through prophecy.

Sometimes a question of *halachah* develops in a case in which the formulation of the law is clear but the facts of the case are unknown. The questions of lineage to be resolved by Eliyahu are an example of this type of case. The laws governing lineage are not in question. Their formulation is known. However, the application of these laws is hindered by our ignorance of the actual lineage of the individual.

Rav Chayutz suggests that prophecy is not excluded as a means for resolving these factual questions. This explains the mishna in Tractate Edyot. Eliyahu, the prophet, will not resolve issues of lineage through altering the formulation of the law. This would indeed constitute a violation of the principle excluding prophecy from matters of *halachah*. Eliyahu will deal with factual issues. He will divine the true family history of the individual and determine the true facts in the case. This approach can also explain the comments of RabbaynuYonatan ben Uziel. There is a place in *halachah* for prophecy and the *Choshen*. This is the area identified by Rav Chayutz. Questions which are factual and not related to the formulation of the *halachah* could be referred to the *Choshen*.

The stones shall contain the names of Bnai Yisrael, one for each of the twelve stones. Each one shall be engraved as on a signet ring to represent the twelve tribes. (Shemot 28:21)

The Lettering on the Stones of the Choshen

One of the special garments worn by the *Kohen Gadol* was the *Choshen* – the breastplate. Upon the *Choshen* were mounted twelve stones. The stones were arranged in four rows. Three stones were in each row. On these stones were engraved the names of the tribes of Bnai Yisrael. One name was featured on each stone.

Maimonides explains that the first and last stones contained additional words. The first stone in the series was engraved with the name Reuven. Above the name were the names, "Avraham" and "Yitzchak VeYaakov" – the names of the forefathers. On the last stone in the series, the name "Binyamin" was engraved. Below the name were the words, "Shivtai Kah" – the tribes of G-d. Through the inclusion of these additional words, every letter of the Hebrew alphabet was contained within the engravings on the stones.[34]

This raises an interesting question. How did the first and last stones accommodate the additional words or names? Rabbaynu Avraham ben HaRambam offers two possibilities. The first possibility is that these stones were larger than the others; the larger-sized stones accommodating the additional lettering. The second possibility is that all the stones were of uniform size; additional words and names were engraved in smaller letters. Through reducing the size of the lettering the stones could contain the larger text.[35]

Rabbaynu Avraham seems to acknowledge the legitimacy of both solutions. However, he favors the second solution. He explains that is seems appropriate for all of the stones of the *Choshen* to be uniform in size. It seems that Maimonides agrees that the size was uniform.[36]

Through analyzing the basis for these two solutions we can gain an important insight into the nature of the *Choshen*. We will also better understand Rabbaynu Avraham's conclusion.

What was the function of the *Choshen*? The *Choshen* was one of the special garments of the *Kohen Gadol*. He was required to wear these garments when performing service in the *Mishcan*.

The *Choshen* had a second function. Through the letters on the *Choshen*, the *Kohen Gadol* received prophetic messages. A question was addressed to Hashem. Hashem provided a response to the *Kohen Gadol* through a prophetic vision. This vision utilized the letters engraved on the stones of the Choshen as the medium for communication. The response would be spelled out for the *Kohen Gadol* using these letters.[37] This second function was crucial in the design of the *Choshen*. The extra letters engraved at the top of the first stone and the bottom of the last completed the alphabet. This provided all letters needed to communicate the response.[38]

What was the relationship between these two functions? Let us consider two possibilities. The first possibility is that the *Choshen* was primarily an instrument designed to communicate prophecy. The *Choshen's* function as an essential garment of the *Kohen Gadol* was subsidiary.

---

[34] Rabbaynu Moshe ben Maimon (Rambam) *Mishne Torah*, Hilchot K'lai Mikdash 9:7.
[35] Rabbaynu Avraham ben HaRambam, *Commentary on Sefer Shemot* 28:21.
[36] Rabbaynu Moshe ben Maimon (Rambam) *Mishne Torah*, Hilchot K'lai Mikdash 9:7.
[37] Rabbaynu Moshe ben Maimon (Rambam) *Mishne Torah*, Hilchot K'lai Mikdash 10:11.
[38] Rabbaynu Moshe ben Maimon (Rambam) *Mishne Torah*, Hilchot K'lai Mikdash 9:7.

This means that the stones and the letters engraved upon them were the main element of the *Choshen*. The breastplate was fundamentally a garment designed to display the stones which featured these engravings. If this possibility is accepted, then it follows that the size of the stones and the lettering was dictated by the primary function – communicating prophecy. All letters were equally essential. All should have been the same size. This would require using larger stones for the first and last positions. In other words, this interpretation of the *Choshen's* design supports Rabbaynu Avraham's first solution.

The second possibility is that the primary function of the *Choshen* was to serve as an honorific garment of the *Kohen Gadol*. The *Choshen's* function as a vehicle in communicating prophecy was secondary. If we assume this interpretation, the overall beauty and appearance of the *Choshen* was a primary concern. This appearance would be enhanced through using stones of uniform size. The additional letters on the first and last stones would be reduced to accommodate the size of the stones. This is apparently the interpretation underlying Rabbaynu Avraham's second solution.

We can now understand Rabbaynu Avraham's reason for favoring this second solution. Rabbaynu Avraham preferred this solution because it is based upon a more reasonable interpretation of the *Choshen*. In other words, Rabbaynu Avraham was convinced that the *Choshen* primarily functioned as a garment glorifying the *Kohen Gadol*. What convinced Rabbaynu Avraham of the legitimacy of this interpretation?

In Parshat Terumah the Torah describes the items required for the construction of the *Mishcan* and its components. The stones of the *Choshen* are included in the list. The Torah describes these as *"avnai miluim"*. Most commentaries translate this term as "stones meant to be set". This is a strange appellation for these stones. Why did the Torah not merely describe them as stones for adornment of the *Kohen Gadol's* garments? What message is the Torah communicating by referring to the stones as *avnai miluim*?

Gershonides responds to this question. He explains that the *Choshen* featured gold settings. The stones were required in order to fill these gold settings.[39] This is an odd way to describe the relationship between the stones and the *Choshen*. The simpler, more straightforward description would be that the settings were required to accommodate the stones.

A simple example will illustrate this point. What is the relationship between the diamond in an engagement ring and its setting? It would be incorrect to describe the diamond as "required to fill", or complement, the setting (thus suggesting that the diamond is *secondary* to the setting). The setting is designed to hold the diamond! Why does Gershonides describe the stones as "required" to fill the gold settings?

Gershonides' point is that the stones were designated to adorn and complete the *Choshen*. According to Gershonides, the Torah describes the stones as *"avnai miluim"* in order to communicate that their essential function is to adorn the *Choshen* by filling its settings. This means that the *Choshen* was not merely a garment intended to carry the stones. This supports Rabbaynu Avraham ben HaRambam's conclusion that the *Choshen* was primarily designed as a garment of the *Kohen Gadol*. The stones were chosen for, and part of, this garment. Therefore, uniformity in size was appropriate.

---

[39] Rabbaynu Levi ben Gershon (Ralbag / Gershonides), *Commentary on Sefer Shemot*, (Mosad HaRav Kook, 1994), p 339.

And it shall be upon Aharon when he serves. And its sound will be heard when he comes to the sanctuary before Hashem, and when he goes out, he shall not die. (Shemot 28:35)

The Function of the Bells that Adorned the Jacket of the Kohen Gadol

Our *pasuk* discusses the jacket worn by the *Kohen Gadol*. This jacket is of unusual design. A series of gold bells hang from the jacket. What was the purpose of these bells? Most of the commentaries agree that our *pasuk* is addressing this question. However, they differ on the answer the passage is providing.

Nachmanides comments that the bells announce the *Kohen Gadol's* entry and exit from the sanctuary. Why is this notice required? Nachmanides explains that it is inappropriate to enter the presence of the King without announcing oneself. It is also disrespectful to leave the King's presence without first providing notice. The sanctuary must be treated with the same respect that is accorded a human king. Therefore, his entry and egress from the sanctuary must be announced by the sounding of the bells affixed to the *Kohen Gadol's* jacket.[40]

Rabbaynu Avraham ibn Ezra takes a very different approach to explaining our *pasuk*. He suggests that the proper translation of the *pasuk* is that "his – the *Kohen Gadol's* – voice will be heard when he comes to the sanctuary before Hashem." In other words his prayer and petitions will be heard by Hashem. According to Ibn Ezra, the bells, as well as the other garments, are designed to distinguish the *Kohen Gadol* from the other *kohanim*. Through wearing his special vestments, the *Kohen Gadol* distinguishes himself as the leader of the *kohanim* and the people. Because he represents the entire nation, the prayers *Kohen Gadol* have special significance. The passage assures that when the *Kohen Gadol* is adorned in the vestments of his office and is acting as his people's representative, then his sincere prayers will be heard.[41]

Gershonides offers a unique approach to explaining the bells of the jacket and the meaning of our passage. He explains that the *Kohen Gadol's* garments are not merely designed for visual beauty. These vestments also communicate important ideas. These various messages motivate the *Kohen Gadol* to concentrate exclusively on his spiritual mission. For example, the *Choshen* – the breastplate – worn by the *Kohen Gadol* includes a series of stones. Engraved on these stones are the names of the *Shevatim* – the Tribes of Israel. The *Choshen* conveys to and reminds the *Kohen Gadol* that he represents the entire nation. However, these various messages can only be communicated to the *Kohen Gadol* when he is aware of his special vestments. His attention must be drawn to them. The bells call the *Kohen Gadol's* attention to his garments. This, in turn, allows the vestments to convey their messages to him. Based on this interpretation of the bells, Gershonides explains our passage. The *Kohen Gadol* hears the ringing of bells adorning his vestments. This focuses his attention upon his garments and their special messages. His focus on these messages raises him to an elevated spiritual plane. As a result of his spiritual ascent, Hashem hears his voice and prayers.[42]

---

[40] Rabbaynu Moshe ben Nachman (Ramban), *Commentary on Sefer Shemot* 28:35.
[41] Rabbaynu Avraham ibn Ezra, *Abbreviated Commentary on Sefer Shemot*, 28:35.
[42] Rabbaynu Levi ben Gershon (Ralbag/Gershonides), *Commentary on Sefer Shemot*, (Mosad HaRav Kook, 1994), p 382.

It is noteworthy that Ibn Ezra's interpretation of the bells is consistent with his overall perspective on the vestments of the *Kohen Gadol*. Ibn Ezra maintains that the garments of the *kohanim* are designed to bestow honor and glory upon them. He interprets the bells as one of the elements of the vestments that distinguish the *Kohen Gadol*.

Nachmanides contends that the vestments are designed to glorify Hashem. His understanding of the bells is consistent with this perspective. He explains that the bells are required in order to show proper reverence when entering before Hashem and leaving His presence.

Gershonides' understanding of the bells is somewhat unique. He contends that the vestments are designed to communicate to the *Kohen Gadol*. The bells facilitate this communication. They focus the *Kohen Gadol's* attention of the garments. The bells are not a fundamental element of the vestments. They do not communicate any idea. However, they enhance the performance of the other vestments.

And you should make a Head-plate of pure gold. And you should engrave upon it as the engraving of a signet ring, "Sanctified to Hashem". (Shemot 28:36)
The Message of the Kohen Gadol's Head-Plate

One of the eight garments of the *Kohen Gadol* was the *Tzitz* – the golden head-plate. This band was worn on the forehead. Engraved upon the *Tzitz* were the words, *"kodesh laHashem"* – "sanctified to Hashem".

The message of the *Tzitz* seems difficult to unravel. The *Tzitz* is obviously declaring the sanctity of some object or person. However, the specific entity to which the *Tzitz* refers is not clear. Furthermore, we would expect the message of the *Tzitz* to be self-evident. The *Tzitz* is making the overt assertion that it—or someone—is "sanctified to G-d." Such a message should be easy to grasp!

This issue can perhaps be resolved from the comments of the Sefer HaChinuch. Sefer HaChinuch explains the garments of the *kohanim* and the *Kohen Gadol* were designed to reinforce an important impression. The *kohanim* and the *Kohen Gadol* were charged with the duty of serving in the Temple on behalf of the nation. This was a weighty responsibility. These individuals were required to be completely devoted to their duties. In order to reinforce this message, they were given special garments. These vestments were to remind the priests of their responsibilities.

This suggests the phrase, "sanctified to Hashem" refers to the *Kohen Gadol*. He is sanctified to Hashem. The *Tzitz* reminds the High Priest of his position and his duties. He must conduct himself in accordance with his responsibilities.[43]

Rabbaynu Shemuel ben Meir – Rashbam – offers an alternative explanation of the message of the *Tzitz*. The High Priest was required to wear all eight of his garments when serving in the *Mishcan*. If any garment was absent during the performance of a service, the service was invalidated. As explained above, the vestments of the *Kohen Gadol* were connected through *halachah* and formed a single entity. Rashbam suggests that in order to understand the

---

[43] Rav Ahron HaLeyve, *Sefer HaChinuch*, Mitzvah 99.

message of the *Tzitz*, it is essential to evaluate it as part of the entire set of vestments. The garments of the *Kohen Gadol* must be considered as a whole.

The *Tzitz* was not the only vestment featuring words. The *Ephod* – the apron – and the *Choshen* also featured words. On the stones of the *Ephod* and *Choshen* the names of the tribes were engraved. Rashbam suggests that the message of the *Tzitz* emerges when considered in relation to these other vestments and their engravings. Rashbam explains the *Tzitz* refers to the *shevatim* -- the tribes whose names were engraved on the stones of the *Ephod* and *Choshen*. The *Tzitz* refers to these *shevatim* as sanctified to Hashem.[44]

"And for the sons of Ahron you should make tunics. And you should make for them sashes. And hats you should make for them, for honor and glory." (Shemot 28:40)

This pasuk enumerates three of the garments worn by the kohen. The Jerusalem Talmud in Tractate Yoma notes that the plural is used in reference to the tunics. The Talmud explains that this alludes to the requirement to make two tunics for each kohen. These comments are difficult to understand. All of the garments in the passage are described in the plural. Yet, there was no requirement for the kohen to have two sashes or two hats. The plural is apparently used in agreement with the subject of the pasuk. The pasuk is describing the garments of the sons of Ahron. The subject the sons of Ahron is plural. Accordingly, the reference to each garment is in the plural!

Rashi, in his commentary on Tractate Yoma, discusses of the two tunics of the kohen. The Talmud explains that one of these tunics was of lesser quality. Rashi comments that each tunic had a specific function. The garment of lesser quality was worn when removing the ashes from the altar. This garment was then removed. The kohen dressed himself in the better tunic to perform his other services. This practice was designed as an expression of respect. The garment used to remove the ashes from the altar became soiled. It was henceforth unfit for the more elevated priestly services. Rashi's comments explain the need for two tunics. However, why must the first tunic be of lesser quality? Rashi apparently maintains that the requirement for two tunics was not merely practical. The first tunic was specifically of lower quality in order to distinguish it from the primary tunic. The primary tunic was worn during the offering of sacrifices. In order to emphasize the special significance of the primary tunic and the service associated with the garment, a secondary tunic was created. Its lower quality emphasized the sacredness of the primary tunic. In other words, it would have been inappropriate for the two garments to be of equal quality. This would fail to emphasize the elevated status of the primary tunic. From this perspective, it appears that the two tunics were not independent garments. Instead, they functioned as a single unit. The secondary tunic alluded to the sanctity of the primary garment. The two tunics are really one entity consisting of a primary and secondary element.

Now the comments of the Jerusalem Talmud can be better appreciated. The pasuk refers to this single entity of the tunic. However, the Sages created an allusion to the dual components of this entity through reinterpreting the pasuk in a non-literal sense. The passage now has a twofold meaning that accurately describes the tunic as a single unit composed of two parts.

---

[44] Rabbaynu Shemuel ben Meir (Rashbam) *Commentary on Sefer Shemot* 28:36.

"And they shall be on Ahron and his sons when they enter the Ohel Moed or when they approach the altar to serve in sanctity. And they shall not be guilty of sin and die. It is an eternal law for him and his descendants after him". (Shemot 28:43)

Rav Yitzchak Zev Soloveitchik Ztl explained that there is a crucial difference between the utensils of the Mishcan and the garments of the Kohen Gadol. The design of the garments was strictly governed by the law. If any garment was lost or damaged, it was replaced by an exact duplicate. The description of the garments was binding for all generations.

In contrast, the design of the utensils was not permanently binding in all of its details. The design described in the Chumash was intended for the Mishcan. These utensils were also essential components of the Bait HaMikdash. However, the utensils in the Holy Temple were not required to meet the description of the Chumash in every detail. Deviation was permitted.

Why is the law of the garments different from the law of the utensils? The Mizbeyach Menorah, Shulchan and other utensils were part of the Mishcan. They were as essential as the tent itself. The Mishcan was only one model of the institution of sanctuary. These utensils were designed for this model. Other models could have utensils designed in a different manner. However, the garments were not a part of this institution of sanctuary. They were an expression of the sanctity of the Kohen Gadol. This sanctity did not change with the various forms of sanctuary. Therefore, the garments were not altered. The Kohen Gadol of the Mishcan had the same sanctify as the individual serving in Shlomo's Temple. The garments of both High Priests were therefore identical.

And you should make an altar for the burning of incense. You should make it of acacia wood. (Shemot 30:1)

A Disjointed Torah Portion

1. An unexpected encounter with wisdom.

Many students of the Torah struggle with Parshat Terumah and Parshat Tetzaveh. These sections of the Torah deal exclusively with the construction of the *Mishcan* – the Tabernacle – and the garment of its priests. These are all described at a level of detail that is unusual for the Torah. The student is confronted with an extensive narrative devoted exclusively to a rather obtuse area of *halachah*.

These sections do have beauty and grandeur. Their splendor is not to be found in the drama of the narrative or in the tension within the plot. Their magnificence is expressed in the glimpses they provide into wonders of the world of *halachah* – Jewish law. Each detail and every nuance has a message and provides insight into the *Mishcan* and its components. Sometimes an important lesson is communicated through the details of the construction of a component of the *Mishcan*. Other times the organizational scheme in which the material is presented provides an unexpected insight. Let us consider an example.

2. The placement of the instructions for design of the incense altar.

Parshat Tetzaveh concludes Hashem's instructions to Moshe regarding the basic design of the *Mishcan* – the Tabernacle. This *parasha* focuses upon the design of the garments worn by the *kohen gadol* – the high priest. Also described, are the garments worn by the other *kohanim* – priests.

After completion of the instructions related to the design of the *Mishcan* and the garments of the *kohanim*, Hashem instructs Moshe on the consecration of the *kohen gadol*, the other *kohanim*, and the *Mishcan*. The above passage appears in the *parasha* after the completion of these instructions. This passage introduces the instructions for the design of the altar upon which incense was offered. The burning of incense on this altar was a component of the daily service in the *Mishcan*.

The Sages and the commentators note the passages describing the incense altar are out of place. As explained above, the design of the *Mishcan* and its components is divided between Parshat Terumah and Parshat Tetzaveh. The first *parasha* focuses upon the structure and its components. The second parasha focuses upon the garments of the *kohanim*. The incense altar was one of the components of the *Mishcan*. Its design should have been described in Parshat Terumah along with the instructions for the design of the *menorah* and *shulchan* – the candelabra and the table upon which the shew-bread was placed. Instead, after completing the instructions for the *Mishcan*, its components, the garments of the *kohanim*, and the instructions for consecration of the *Mishcan* and the *kohanim*, the Torah describes the design for the incense altar.

And make Me a sanctuary and I will dwell among them. (Shemot 25:8)

And I will dwell among Bnai Yisrael. I will be G-d to them. They will know that I am Hashem their G-d that took them forth from the land of Egypt to dwell among them. I am Hashem their G-d. (Shemot 29:45-46)

3. The instructions for the altar are treated as a postscript.

The second set of passages above appears immediately before the instructions for the design of the incense altar. These passages are the last in a series in which Hashem tells Moshe that Hashem will communicate to the nation through the *Mishcan* and it will be an expression of His presence among the people.

These passages communicate the same message that Hashem gave to Moshe when He introduced the instructions for the creation of the *Mishcan*. These instructions are introduced by the first passage above. In other words, the discussion of the instructions for the creation and consecration of the *Mishcan* begin and end with the same message. The *Mishcan* will represent the presence of Hashem within the nation. This format suggests that, in some sense, the second set of passages above brings to closure the instructions for the *Mishcan*'s creation and consecration. If this is correct, then why does the Torah place instructions for one of the *Mishcan*'s most significant components – the incense altar – after it has brought to closure the instructions for the design and consecration of the *Mishcan*?

In short, the specific placement of the instructions for the design of the incense altar presents two problems. First, why is the design of this component not placed alongside the instructions for the design of the other similar components? Second, why are the instructions for this component placed after the Torah has brought to closure its discussion of the design and consecration of the *Mishcan*?

4. Two types of *Mishcan* components.

The Sages and commentators have suggested a number of responses to these questions. One of the most interesting explanations is provided by Rabbaynu Ovadia Sforno. He explains that the function of the incense altar was fundamentally different from the function of the other components of the *Mishcan*.

Hashem commanded Bnai Yisrael to create a *Mishcan* and He will dwell among the people. The *Mishcan* and its basic components were designed to bring about this outcome. The *aron* – the ark, the *menorah*, the *shulchan*, and the sanctified domains of the *Mishcan* functioned as an "abode" for expression of Hashem's presence. Sacrifices were offered on the large copper-covered altar located in the *Mishcan*'s courtyard. These sacrifices combined with the sanctity of the abode of the *Mishcan* to "secure" expression of Hashem's presence.

The function of the incense altar was not to secure Hashem's presence. Instead, it was a response to His presence. The incense offered on the altar was a demonstration of honor and respect in response to the expression of Hashem's presence.[45]

An analogy will clarify Sforno's meaning. I am planning to invite a very important guest to my home. I want the guest to come to my home and feel welcome and comfortable. After all, I don't want him to enter my home, take a look around and bolt for the door. So, I clean and organize the house. I prepare a wonderful meal. I carefully set the table. If my plans are successful, the guest will come, enjoy his visit, and stay for a time.

Now, after the guest arrives, I am very appreciative of his presence. How do I express this appreciation? The meal that I prepared is not an expression of appreciation. I prepared the meal to entertain the guest. The carefully set table and the clean, organized appearance of the home are also not demonstrations of appreciation. They also are components of my strategy to entertain the guest. I want to do something that demonstrates my appreciation. So, maybe, before the guest leaves I offer him something to take home with him – some token that demonstrates my appreciation.

My efforts on behalf of the guest can be divided into two groups. Some were components of the plan to entertain the guest and to make him feel comfortable in my home. In addition, I also identified a measure that would demonstrate my appreciation.

Sforno suggests that the same distinction must be made when considering the elements of the *Mishcan*. Most were designed to secure Hashem's presence. These are analogous to the measure I take to entertain my guest. The incense altar is not one of these components. Instead, its function is to demonstrate appreciation though the incense offered upon it. It is the equivalent to the token I give to my guest before he leaves.

Sforno's comments respond to both of the questions above. The design of the incense altar is not included alongside the designs of the other components of the *Mishcan*. These other components were fundamental to the function of the *Mishcan*. These components secured the expression of Hashem's presence. The incense altar did not secure His presence. Therefore, description of its design is segregated from the descriptions of the *Mishcan*'s other components.

The proper place for the description of the design of the incense altar is after the *Mishcan*'s fundamental components have been described and the consecration of the *Mishcan* and the *kohanim* has been discussed. Hashem tells Moshe that through the execution of these instructions the Divine presence will be manifested in the *Mishcan*. The Torah then describes the

---

[45] Rabbaynu Ovadia Sforno, *Commentary on Sefer Shemot*, 30:1.

design of the incense altar. This is because the expression of Hashem's presence demands acknowledgement and a demonstration of respect. The incense offered on the incense altar is the required demonstration.

Ki Tisa

"This they shall give, everyone who goes through the counting: half a *shekel* according to the sacred *shekel*. Twenty gerahs equal one *shekel*; half of [such] a *shekel* shall be an offering to Hashem." (Shemot 30:13)

Watch Your Language

1. The census of the Jewish people

In the opening passages of Parshat Ki Tisa, Moshe is commanded to conduct a census of the nation. He is provided specific directions. These instructions deal with two issues: who is to be counted and how to conduct the census. The census is to include all males over the age of twenty. The method is unusual. Moshe is not to directly count the people. Instead, he is to instruct each male over the age of twenty to contribute a half of a sacred shekel to the Mishcan – the Tabernacle. These coins will be counted and the sum of the coins will correspond with the number of males over the age of twenty.

Ramban – Nachmanides – asks two interesting questions. First, the instructions refer to a coin called a "shekel." "Shekel" means "measurement." Why is the coin referred to by this name? Second, the amount to be contributed is half of a sacred shekel. What made these coins sacred?

Ramban begins with a key premise. He suggests that Moshe minted his own coins. He named his coin "shekel". Why did he give it the name "shekel" or "measurement"? Ramban explains, that Moshe was scrupulous in minting this coin. He made sure that each coin contained exactly twenty gerah of silver. The coin was named "shekel," or "measure," because each coin was a full measure of silver.

2. The sanctity of the shekel

Why was the coin referred to as a "sacred" shekel? Ramban explains that the coin was created to be used for various mitzvot. It was to be used for the redemption of the first born and the payment of various other amounts due to the Mishcan. Because of the coin's role in the fulfillment of mitzvot, it is referred to as the sacred shekel.

3. The sanctity of the Hebrew language

Ramban notes the Sages refer to Ivrit – Hebrew – as the "sacred language." Why is Ivrit sacred? He responds that Ivrit is the language in which the Torah, the Prophets, and other sacred works are composed. Because it is the language in which their messages are communicated, Ivrit is a sacred language. Ramban also notes other reasons for referring to Ivrit as sacred.[1]

Ramban acknowledges that his position differs from that of Rambam – Maimonides. Rambam explains that Ivrit is not sacred because it is the language of the Jewish people. Instead, the language is described as sacred because of an important characteristic. Classical Ivrit lacks explicit terms for the sexual organs, the sexual act, and for human waste; all are referred to though euphemisms. Rambam reasons that the exclusion of terminology for these items elevates Ivrit. This characteristic is the basis of its sanctity.[2]

---

[1] Rabbaynu Moshe ben Nachman (Ramban), Commentary on Sefer Shemot 30:13.
[2] Rabbaynu Moshe ben Maimon (Rambam) Moreh Nevuchim, volume 3, chapter 8.

Rambam seems to suggest that it is improper to directly refer to the sexual organs and basic bodily functions. Ivrit accommodates this ethic and the proscription of these terms endows Ivrit with its sanctity. Rambam's position seems prudish. This is not consistent with Rambam's general treatment of sexual issues which is straightforward and unabashed.[3] It seems strange that he should adopt a seemingly pedantic attitude towards sexuality and basic bodily functions.

4. Creating balance

In order to understand Rambam's position it is necessary to consider his comment more carefully. He explains that Ivrit is sacred because of the structure of the language. It employs euphemisms when referring to the sexual organs, the sexual act and bodily wastes. What does this characteristic tell us about the design and objective of the language? Apparently, although the language is remarkably precise and effective for the communication of ideas, it is ill-adapted for a discussion of sexuality and human waste. In other words, the language facilitates the exchange of most ideas but hinders communication focused on sexuality and waste.

How does this characteristic endow the language with sanctity? The Torah favors a healthy and balanced attitude towards sexuality. It recognizes that sexuality is a basic component of human nature. It should not be repressed or governed by primitive and unhealthy taboos. The Torah also recognizes the power of the sexual drive, its capacity to capture one's attention and to dominate one's thoughts and interests. It discourages preoccupation with the sexual. A balance is required. The structure of Ivrit reflects this balance. It is well-suited for the communication of ideas and this should be our focus – the pursuit of wisdom and knowledge. It is ill-suited for discussion of the sexual. This is an area in which we must maintain balance. It cannot become the focus of our attention.[4]

5. Living a balanced life

This concept of balance is reflected in an interesting comment by Rabbaynu Bachya. He asks why we are commanded to provide half of a shekel to the Mishcan. Why not provide a full shekel? There are many well-known answers to this question, but Rabbaynu Bachya's response is one of the most unique. He explains that the use of half of a shekel is intended to communicate a message. We cannot completely give ourselves over to the sacred. We must balance our devotion to the sacred with a regard for the material world.

This seems to be a remarkable statement! Should we not wholly devote ourselves to striving for the highest possible spiritual level? Should we not make every effort to escape our attachment to the temporal, material world? Rabbaynu Bachya responds that this attitude is oversimplified; we are material creatures and we cannot neglect, ignore or deny the material element of our nature. If we attempt to focus exclusively on our spiritual needs and neglect our

---

[3] See, for example, Rabbaynu Moshe ben Maimon (Rambam) Mishne Torah, Hilchot Essurai Bee'ah 21:9.

[4] This explanation of Rambam's position addresses one of Ramban's objections. Ramban notes that the Talmud describes the Torah's avoidance of "inappropriate" terms as use of "clean" language. He argues that according to Rambam, Ivrit should be called a "clean language" and not a "sacred language". One can respond that the term "sacred language" is not directly derived from the absence of words that explicitly describe the sexual organs, acts, and waste. Instead, the absence of these terms renders the language more suitable for discussion of the sacred rather than the sexual and associated areas. Because of this suitability the language is sacred.

material needs and desires, then we will secure neither. We cannot elevate ourselves spiritually unless we adequately address our material needs.

Rabbaynu Bachya explains that this idea is reflected in the manner in which we observe our festivals. Halachah requires that we apportion the day between spiritual and material endeavors. We are to spend half of the day in prayer, study and spiritual pursuits. The other half of the day is to be devoted to the festival meal and material indulgences.[5] It is strange that the festival – a sacred day – is to be used for material pursuits! Rabbaynu Bachya responds that addressing our material needs and desires does not detract from the spiritual element of the festival day. On the contrary, when our material needs and desires are addressed, we are better prepared to pursue spiritual ends.[6]

6. Preparing our children

Rabbaynu Bachya's comments have important implications. Let us identify one of these. We must give our children an education that prepares them for adulthood and independence. We execute this responsibility by giving them with an education that will enable them to support themselves. If, as adults, our children can provide for their material needs, then they can develop their spiritual potential.

"And you, take for yourself spices of the finest sort: of pure myrrh five hundred [shekel weights]; of fragrant cinnamon half of it two hundred and fifty [shekel weights]; of fragrant cane two hundred and fifty [shekel weights]." (Shemot 30:23)

The laws regarding the construction of the *Mishcan* – the Tabernacle – compose one of the most fascinating areas of *halacha* – Jewish law. This week's portion discusses the creation of the *Shemen HaMishchah* – the oil of anointing. The process of appointing a *Kohen Gadol* – a high priest – included being anointed with this oil. The original components created for the *Mishcan* were anointed with this oil. Some of the kings of Bnai Yisrael were anointed with this oil. In our *pasuk*, Moshe is commanded to create this oil. The *pasuk* also lists various ingredients that are included in this fragrant oil.

The Torah is an immense system of law that impacts virtually every aspect of personal, communal and national life. However, the multitude of individual laws is subsumed within *Taryag mitzvot* – six-hundred thirteen commandments. For example, the Torah tells us that we must honor our parents. This is a commandment. There are many laws that define the manner in which we are obligated to express this honor. These laws are all subsumed within the single *mitzvah* to honor our parents. The Torah does not expressly provide a list of the *Taryag mitzvot*. However, various scholars have suggested possible lists of the 613 commandments. It is not easy to compose such a list. The scholar must first develop a set of criteria for defining a *mitzvah*. Only after these criteria have been delineated, can the scholar develop a list of commandments.

One of the most famous lists of the 613 *mitzvot* was developed by Maimonides. His list is the subject of his Sefer HaMitzvot. Maimonides provides an extensive introduction to his list. In this introduction, he identifies fourteen criteria for defining *mitzvot*. For example, one criterion is that *Taryag mitzvot* only includes those commandments that are specifically included in the

---

[5] Mesechet Pesachim 68b.
[6] Rabbaynu Bachya, Commentary on Sefer Shemot 30:13.

Torah. Any obligations or prohibitions established by the Sages are not included in the list.[7] Therefore, the obligation to observe Purim cannot be included. Another criterion is that only obligations that apply for all generations are included in the 613 commandments. But obligations or prohibitions that were commanded by Hashem for a specific moment in history are not included in *Taryag mitzvot*. Although, at Revelation, only Moshe was commanded to ascend Sinai and the rest of the nation was forbidden from ascending or approaching the mountain, these instructions cannot be included in *Taryag mitzvot*. These instructions were intended for a specific moment in time – Revelation.[8]

Maimonides' tenth principle is that it is not appropriate to count as *mitzvot* obligations that are prerequisites or preliminary steps in the fulfillment of some greater objective. Maimonides offers a number of examples that illustrate the application of this principle. One example deals with our passage. Maimonides explains that Hashem's instructions to Moshe regarding the creation of the *Shemen HaMishchah* cannot be counted as one of the 613 commandments. This is because the *Shemen HaMishchah* is only created in order to accomplish a more fundamental objective. This objective is the actual anointing of the *Kohen Gadol*, the original components of the *Mishcan* and some kings. The *mitzvah* of *Shemen HaMishchah* is to anoint the appropriate individuals and the components of the *Mishcan*. The instructions to Moshe for the creating of the *Shemen HaMishchah* should be regarded as a prerequisite, or preliminary step, to this *mitzvah*.

There are a number of problems with these comments. The most obvious of these difficulties is identified by Kinat Soferim. In his code of law – Mishne Torah – Maimonides introduces each section with a brief list of the *mitzvot* that will be discussed in the section. The first *mitzvah* listed in his introduction to the laws regarding the vessels of the *Bait HaMikdash* is "to create *Shemen HaMishchah*." Kinat Soferim objects that this formulation of the commandment regarding *Shemen HaMishchah* directly contradicts Maimonides' comments in his Sefer HaMitzvot. There, Maimonides argues that the sole commandment regarding the *Shemen* is to use it for anointing. Creation of the oil is regarded as a prerequisite to this objective. However, in his Mishne Torah, Maimonides identifies the creation of the *Shemen* as the fundamental element of its *mitzvah*.[9]

There is an even more obvious question that Kinat Soferim does not ask. In his tenth principle, Maimonides explains that the *mitzvah* regarding the *Shemen HaMishchah* is to use it for anointing. However, in the actual list of commandments in Sefer HaMitzvot, Maimonides suggests an alternative definition for the *mitzvah* regarding the *Shemen*. He writes that the *mitzvah* regarding the *Shemen* is to have it available for use when needed.[10]

In short, Maimonides offers three different formulations of the *mitzvah* regarding *Shemen HaMishchah*. In the discussion of his tenth principle, he explains that the commandment is to use the oil for anointing. He insists that the creation of the *Shemen HaMishchah* cannot be the fundamental element of the *mitzvah*. In his Mishne Torah, Maimonides defines the *mitzvah* as the creation of the *Shemen*. Finally, in his actual enumeration of the *mitzvot* in Sefer HaMitzvot, he

---

[7] Rabbaynu Moshe ben Maimon (Rambam) *Sefer HaMitzvot,* Principle 1.
[8] Rabbaynu Moshe ben Maimon (Rambam) *Sefer HaMitzvot,* Principle 3.
[9] Rav Chanaya Kazis, *Kinat Soferim, Commen. on Maimonides' Sefer Hamitzvot,* Principle 10.
[10] Rabbaynu Moshe ben Maimon (Rambam) *Sefer HaMitzvot, Mitzvat Aseh* 34.

states that the commandment regarding the *Shemen* is that it should be available for use as needed.

Kinat Soferim does not note the discrepancy in Sefer HaMitzvot between the definition of the *mitzvah* of the *Shemen* suggested in the tenth principle and the definition offered in the actual enumeration of the commandments. This suggests an important inference. Kinat Soferim does not acknowledge the difference between these two definitions. He maintains that the two formulations are really alternative expressions of the same idea; they are the same idea viewed from two perspectives. This is difficult to understand. Anointing with the oil and having the *Shemen* available for anointing seem to be different ideas. How can Kinat Soferim regard these two formulations as alternative expressions of the same idea?

Kinat Soferim is suggesting an important subtlety in Maimonides' position. An object can be defined by its physical characteristics. It can also be defined by its objective or purpose. For example, we can define a pencil as an object that is composed of a thin stick of graphite encased in a tube of wood. Alternatively, we can define an object by its purpose. A pencil can be defined as an implement designed for writing. Sometimes, both of these methods can be combined to define an object. According to Maimonides, *Shemen HaMishcheh* is defined by both of these means. It is a material substance. Its ingredients are essential to its definition. But, this oil is referred to *Shemen HaMishchah* – oil of anointing. This name is not just a convenient means of identification. The name communicates that the oil is designated for a specific purpose and that this purpose is part of the fundamental definition of the oil. The oil must be used for the anointing. If it is not used for this purpose, it does not meet the definition of *Shemen HaMishcheh*.

This formulation has important ramifications. Assume a *Kohen Gadol* is appointed and the available *Shemen HaMishchah* is not used. What *mitzvah* is violated through this omission? Obviously, the *Kohen* has not been properly appointed. But according to Maimonides, there is an additional issue. The *mitzvah* of *Shemen HaMishchah* has been violated. The *Shemen* has not been used for its designated purpose. Therefore, the commandment to have the *Shemen* available for anointing can be described as an obligation to use the oil for anointing. This purpose is an essential element of the definition of the *Shemen*! In other words, the use of the oil does not fulfill an independent commandment to appoint people properly. It is a fulfillment of the commandment to have the *Shemen HaMishchah* available for its proper and designated use. When the oil is used, the *mitzvah* of *Shemen HaMishchah* is fulfilled. With its use, the *Shemen* fulfills its design and purpose.

This insight resolves explains another nuance on Maimonides' treatment of the *Shemen HaMishchah*. Part of the process of appointing a *Kohen Gadol* is his anointing with *Shemen HaMishchah*. We would expect Maimonides to explain the process of anointing the *Kohen Gadol* in his discussion of his appointment. However, in discussing the appointment of the *Kohen Gadol*, Maimonides merely mentions that anointing is required. The details of the process are not mentioned. Where does Maimonides discuss the details of the process? This discussion is included in the laws regarding the *Shemen HaMishchah*. Why does Maimonides discuss these details in this context? Maimonides maintains that the details of how the *Shemen* is used are part of the *mitzvah* of *Shemen HaMishchah*. The oil – by definition – is designated specifically for anointing. When the anointing is performed properly, the *mitzvah* of *Shemen HaMishchah* is fulfilled. Therefore, the details of the process of anointing are included in the laws of the *Shemen HaMishchah*.

One question remains. How can Maimonides state in his Mishne Torah that the *mitzvah* of the *Shemen* is its creation? In Sefer HaMitzvot, Maimonides explicitly rejected this formulation!

Kinat Soferim suggests an interesting interpretation of the tenth principle. Maimonides explains that instructions that are prerequisites for the fulfillment of a *mitzvah* are not to be counted as a *mitzvah*. But what is the status of these instructions? After all, they are legal requirements. Are they merely practical measures that must be undertaken to fulfill a *mitzvah* or are they subsumed within the *mitzvah* they facilitate? Kinat Soferim suggests that a prerequisite is not a separate *mitzvah*. But it may be part of the *mitzvah* that it facilitates. In our instance, the creation of the *Shemen HaMishchah* is part of the commandment to have the *Shemen* available. In his Mishne Torah, Maimonides is not stating that the commandment of the *Shemen* is merely to make it. The commandment is to bring it into existence so that it will be available.[11] In other words, Maimonides consistently maintains that the fundamental *mitzvah* regarding the *Shemen* is that it should be available. But, in Mishne Torah, he is explaining that part of the *mitzvah* is the process of creating this availability.

Kinat Soferim's comments do resolve the apparent contradiction between Mishne Torah and Sefer HaMitzvot. Nonetheless, it is interesting that in his Mishne Torah, Maimonides focuses on an element of the *mitzvah* that is de-emphasized in his Sefer HaMitzvot. Kinat Soferim does not address this issue.

In short, the *mitzvah* of *Shemen HaMishchah* has three components: an action, an outcome, and a purpose. These are all components of the *mitzvah*. The action is the creation of the *Shemen* -- creating the state of availability. Maimonides explains that this action cannot be counted as a separate *mitzvah*. It is performed in order to produce an outcome – the state of availability. The required outcome is that *Shemen* must be available. Finally, this *Shemen* has a purpose that is fundamental to its definition. It is designated to be used for all required anointing.

"And make of it sacred oil for anointing as made by a skilled perfumer. It shall be sacred oil for anointing." (Shemot 30:25)

The Mishcan, its utensils, Ahron and the other Kohanim were anointed with special oil. The anointing was a component of the process by which each was sanctified.

The Shemen HaMishcha – the Oil of Anointing – was created using two ingredients. These were olive oil and various fragrant spices. Maimonides explains that the spices were not added directly to the oil. Instead the spices were soaked in water. The water absorbed the fragrance of the spices. The oil was then added to the fragrant water. The water was boiled away leaving only the pure oil. However in the process of boiling off the water, the oil absorbed the fragrant odor of the spices.[12]

Why were the spices not ground and added directly to the oil? This would have been a simpler procedure! Rav Yosef Dov Soloveitchik Ztl explained that the Torah is very specific in its terminology. In this case, the Torah requires that Oil of Anointing be created. This implies that the substance used for anointing be an oil. It must consist of this single ingredient. It may not

---

[11] Rav Chanaya Kazis, *Kinat Soferim, Commen. on Maimonides' Sefer Hamitzvot,* Principle 10.
[12] Rabbaynu Moshe ben Maimon (Rambam) *Mishne Torah*, Hilchot Klai Mikdash 1:2.

be composed of various ingredients joined in a compound. However the Torah also requires that fragrant spices be used in creating the oil. How can these two opposing laws be fulfilled? The unique production process met both requirements. The Oil of Anointing was composed solely of the oil. The fragrance was added without adding an additional substance.[13]

"Between Me and Bnai Yisrael it is an eternal sign that in six days Hashem made the heavens and the earth. And on the seventh day he ceased and rested." (Shemot 31:17)

Hashem commands Bnai Yisrael to observe Shabbat. Even the construction of the Mishcan cannot take place on Shabbat. Shabbat represents the creation of the universe in six days and the cessation of that process with the entry of the seventh day. This symbol of the creation was entrusted to the Jewish people.

The Talmud explains it is prohibited for a non-Jew to observe the Shabbat.[14] This prohibition seems odd. Shabbat represents one the most important truths. It would seem reasonable for the no-Jew to be encouraged to observe Shabbat. Through observance the non-Jew would confirm that the Almighty created the universe! What is the reason for this prohibition?

Rashi offers an interesting explanation. Through our labors we contribute to society. An idle person does not support or cultivate the world. Idleness should be avoided and constructive endeavors should be pursued. The non-Jew is not commanded to observe Shabbat. Therefore, the moral obligation to occupy oneself in constructive activities applies throughout the week.[15] This does not mean that it is immoral to enjoy an occasional vacation or period of relaxation. The prohibition is to set aide a specific day of the week which is regularly excluded from useful endeavor.

A different explanation is suggested by the Shabbat liturgy. The section of Chumash that includes our pasuk is included in the Shabbat morning Amidah. This section is followed by an explanatory paragraph. "And Hashem our God did not give it to the peoples of the land. And our King did not bequeath it to those worshipping idols. In addition, the uncircumcised may not take part in our day of rest. Rather to Israel, His nation, He gave it, with love." What is the message of this paragraph?

Shabbat was created as a constant reminder of creation. However, the responsibility of observing Shabbat and demonstrating the truth of creation was not placed upon all of humanity. The Almighty chose Bnai Yisrael. The Jewish people was given the Torah and the duty of Shabbat observance. We are to teach humanity through our actions and observances. This selection of the Jewish people is the essence of our covenant with Hashem. This is a special relationship with Hashem that does not extent to the other peoples of the world.

Viewed from this perspective, Shabbat does not only represents creation. It is symbolic of the covenant between Hashem and Bnai Yisrael. This seems to be the message of the Amidah.

Now let us return to our original question. Why can the non-Jew not observe Shabbat? The Amidah suggests an important consideration. Observance of Shabbat is an expression of the

---

[13] Rav Yosef Dov Soloveitchik, Lectures on Mesechet Keritut.
[14] Mesechet Sanhedrin 58b.
[15] Rabbaynu Shlomo ben Yitzchak (Rashi), *Commentary on the Talmud,* Mes. Sanhedrin 58b.

unique relationship between Bnai Yisrael and Hashem. This association does not extend to the non-Jew. The non-Jew observing Shabbat is assuming a responsibility assigned to the Jewish people and denying the distinct role of the Jewish nation.

And Bnai Yisrael will observe the Shabbat to perform the Shabbat for their generation as an eternal covenant. Between Me and Bnai Yisrael it is an eternal sign that Hashem created the heavens and earth in six days and on the seventh day He ceased and He rested. (Shemot 31:16-17)

The Shabbat morning *Amidah's* reference to Shabbat

Parshat Ki Tisa reviews again the commandment of the Shabbat. The above passages are the final two passages of this section of *pesukim*. They were selected by our Sages for inclusion in the Shabbat morning *Amidah*. There are two ideas expressed in these passages:

Shabbat commemorates that Hashem created the universe in six days and rested on the seventh day.

Through observance of Shabbat, we fulfill a covenant between Hashem and Bnai Yisrael.

It is interesting that our Sages selected these two passages for inclusion in the Shabbat morning *Amidah*. In selecting these passages, the Sages skipped over a prior set of passages that are the Torah's initial commandment regarding Shabbat. These prior passages are in the Decalogue – the *Aseret HaDibrot*. In the Decalogue, Hashem commanded Bnai Yisrael to observe the Shabbat.

> *Remember the day of the Shabbat to sanctify it. Six days you should labor and perform all of your work. And the seventh day is Shabbat to Hashem your G-d. Do not perform any work – you, your son, your daughter, your servant, your maid servant, and your convert in your gates. For in six days Hashem made the heavens, the earth, the sea, and all within them. And He rested on the seventh day. Therefore, Hashem blessed the Shabbat day and sanctified it.* (Shemot 20:8-11)

The message of these passages is similar to the message of the *pesukim* in our *parasha*. Shabbat was given to us in order to commemorate the creation of the universe from the void. Why did the Sages pass over the Decalogue's passages in favor of those in our *parasha*?

If we consider the sentences in the Shabbat morning *Amidah* that precede the Torah passages, the Sages choice of *pesukim* is even more perplexing.

> *Moshe will rejoice with his gift-portion. For a trusted servant You called him. A crown of glory You gave when he stood before You on Mount Sinai. Two stone tablets he brought down in his hand. And written in them is observance of Shabbat and similarly it is written in Your Torah.*
> *(Shabbat morning Amidah)*

This introduction emphasizes that the commandment to observe Shabbat was inscribed by Hashem upon the Tablets of the Decalogue given to Moshe. We would expect these introductory remarks to be followed by the recitation of the Decalogue's commandment to observe Shabbat. But instead, after noting the inclusion of Shabbat upon the Tablets, we are directed – almost apologetically – to the passages in our *parasha*![16]

---

[16] Avudraham notes that the Sages reluctance to insert the *pesukim* from the Decalogue into the

The commentary *Iyun Tefilah* explains that although the Sages are noting the centrality of Shabbat through emphasizing its inclusion in the Decalogue, their selection of passages from the Torah for inclusion in the morning *Amidah* was dictated by the message following these *pesukim*.

> *And Hashem our G-d did not give it to the nations of the land. Our King did not give it as a portion to those who serve false gods. Neither do the uncircumcised dwell in its rest. Rather, to Your nation Israel You gave it in love – to the descendants of Yaakov that You selected. (Shabbat morning Amidah)*

The exclusivity of the relationship between Shabbat and Bnai Yisrael

The message of these sentences from the *Amidah* is that although the message of Shabbat is universal – that the universe and all within it are the creations of Hashem – the observance of Shabbat is given exclusively to Bnai Yisrael. The passages from our *parasha* are the perfect segue into this message. These *pesukim* focus upon the exclusive relationship between Bnai Yisrael and Shabbat. Shabbat was given to us alone as an expression of our covenantal relationship with Hashem. The passages in the Decalogue do not make reference to this exclusivity. [17]

The exclusivity of this relationship between Bnai Yisrael and Shabbat is not merely an abstraction. It is expressed in specific form in *halacha*. The Talmud explains that it is prohibited for a non-Jew to observe Shabbat.[18] There are a number of reasons for this restriction. But one reason is the message expressed by the passages in our *parasha*. Shabbat is given exclusively to Bnai Yisrael. By adopting Shabbat observance, the non-Jew lays claim to a legacy given exclusively to Bnai Yisrael.

The difference between *Taryag* and the Seven *mitzvot* given to the rest of humankind

But why was Shabbat given only to Bnai Yisrael? Its message is universal and relevant to all humankind. Possibly part of the answer lies in a fundamental difference between the system of *mitzvot* given to Bnai Yisrael and the system assigned to the rest of humanity. The Torah tells us that Hashem provided humankind with two sets of *mitzvot*. The Torah and its 613 commandments – the *Taryag Mitzvot* – were revealed to Bnai Yisrael at Sinai. For the rest of humanity – the descendants of Noach – Hashem provided seven general *mitzvot*. This system is comprised of six prohibitions and one positive commandment. The prohibitions are against stealing, murder, idolatry, blasphemy, removing and eating the limb of an animal that has not

---

Amidah may reflect the same concern that led the Sages to object to the recitation of the Decalogue within the daily prayers. The Sages feared that this practice would lend credence to a frivolous claim of the Torah's detractors. These detractors claimed that the Decalogue is the only authentic revelation and that the remainder of the Torah is not a revealed law. (Tractate Berachot 12a and Commentary of Rashi). Perhaps, this same concern led the Sages to acknowledge that the *mitzvah* of Shabbat is included in the Decalogue but in demonstrating that Shabbat observance is a Torah level commandment, the Sages selected a set of *pesukim* that are not from the Decalogue. In this manner, they not only avoided giving undue preference to the Decalogue, but they also affirmed that there is no distinction between the binding nature of these passages and those in the Decalogue as all passages in the Torah are revealed truth.

[17] Rav Aryeh Lev Gorden, *Siddur Avodus HaLev, Commentary Iyun Tefilah*.
[18] Tractate Sanhedrin 58b.

first been slaughtered, and various forms of incest and adultery. The positive commandment is to establish as judicial system. These *mitzvot* have a very specific focus and function. Their observance assures the existence of a functional, meaningful society. The society that results from these laws is just; it promotes monotheism, and its members accept some limits upon their pursuit of pleasure and gratification.

However, the Torah includes an entire additional class of *mitzvot*. These *mitzvot* are often referred to as *Chukot* (plural of *Chok*) or Divine decrees. The Torah often provides an explanation for *Chukot*. In general, these explanations share a common theme. The *Chok* is designed to communicate or reinforce some fundamental message or attitude. For example, one of the central themes of the Torah is our redemption by Hashem from Egypt. This theme is communicated and reinforced through a number of *mitzvot*. Among these *mitzvot* is the celebration of Pesach with all of its various aspects. The *mitzvah* of mezuzah is another example of a *Chok* designed to communicate and reinforce a specific message. We are required to place a mezuzah on the doorway in order to remind ourselves of the commandments. *Chukot* are designed to educate us, refine our habits, and to encourage the integration of the fundamental truths of the Torah into our outlook. Shabbat is another of the *Chukot* of the Torah. It is designed as a regular reminder of Hashem's creation of the universe and all that exists within it.

The system of commandments that Hashem assigned to the descendents of Noach does not include commandments that are designed to educate and promote ideas and attitudes. Consequently, it is understandable that the non-Jew is excluded from observing Shabbat. In other words, although the message of Shabbat is universal, this entire class and type of educational commandments is limited to the system of *Taryag Mitzvot* and is not included in the seven laws provided to the rest of humanity.[19]

Chukot are an innovation of the Torah

The *Chok*ot of the Torah — *mitzvot* with an educational aim, is one of the Torah's greatest innovations. It communicates that the Torah is not merely a set of behavioral expectations. Instead, it addresses every aspect of our lives – our homes, our work, our interpersonal relationships, and even our most inner convictions, perceptions and attitudes. The *Chukot* are designed to impact our world view, to refine our behaviors, and to integrate fundamental Torah truths into the innermost aspects of our thinking.

We must open our minds and respond to and embrace the messages communicated through the *Chukot* of the Torah. If we restrict our observance of the Torah to guiding our actions but do not embraced it as a personal perspective and world view, it loses much of its meaning and purpose. But when Torah extends beyond informing our behaviors and enters into the entirety of our lives and our very thinking, then it transforms us. We become enlightened and our innermost thoughts and feeling reflect the truths of Torah. It illuminates our existence and endows even the most mundane aspects of our lives meaning and sanctity.

---

[19] This is only a partial explanation. It explains the absence of a Shabbat commandment from the seven commandments given to all of humanity. However, other commandments – including Chukot – may be adopted and observed by a non-Jew without penalty. Therefore, it is clear that other considerations are relevant to the prohibition upon the non-Jew regarding Shabbat observance.

And when the people saw that Moshe delayed to come down from the mount, the people gathered themselves together unto Aharon, and said to him: Arise, make us a god who shall go before us; for as for this Moshe, the man who brought us up out of the Land of Egypt, we know not what has become of him. (Shemot 32:1)

Respect for the Torah

1. The creation and purpose of the Golden Calf

Parshat Ki Tisa describes the sin of the *Egel HaZahav* – the Golden Calf. This is one of the most troubling incidents in the Torah. All of Bnai Yisrael stood at Sinai and heard Hashem command them to not create other gods. Yet, with the passage of a few weeks, they violated this fundamental commandment and created and worshiped the *Egel*. Previously in *Thoughts* some of the factors that contributed to this failing were discussed. In this edition the focus will be upon the intellectual errors that underlay the sin.

As an introduction to this issue, it is essential to understand the nation's beliefs regarding the *Egel*. The people were not so primitive as to believe that the *Egel* – a product of their own design – was an actual deity. Instead, their intent was to create an idol that would function as an intermediary between themselves and Hashem. Their aspiration was that the *Egel* would become the focus of Hashem's providential presence and the He would perhaps animate the *Egel* or that, at least, it would function as an icon. As an icon, Hashem would communicate messages of guidance and inspiration through it.[20]

As explained in the above passage, the sin of the *Egel* was precipitated by Moshe's delay in descending from Mount Sinai. Why did the delay in Moshe's descent cause such intense panic? In order to understand the manner in which the people interpreted this delay, it is important to return to an earlier point in the Torah's account of Revelation.

And all the people perceived the thunder, and the lightning, and the voice of the horn, and the mountain smoking. And when the people saw it, they trembled, and stood afar off. They said unto Moshe: You speak with us, and we will hear; but let not G-d speak with us, lest we die. (Shemot 20:15-16)

2. The Jewish people's frightening encounter with prophecy

The Torah explains that Bnai Yisrael heard some or all of the statements of the Decalogue directly from Hashem. The people responded to this experience by insisting that Moshe intervene between them and Hashem. They did not wish to receive the rest of the Torah directly from Hashem. Instead, Moshe should be the direct recipient of the rest of the Torah and he should relate it to the people. What was the reason for this request?

Rabbeinu Ovadia Sforno explains that Bnai Yisrael did not merely hear a material voice declare the statements of the Decalogue. Each member of the nation experienced prophecy. For those moments the entire nation participated in a prophetic communion with Hashem. Their response to the experience reflects the overwhelming power and intensity of the prophetic encounter. They were awed and frightened. They declared that they could not continue the encounter.[21] They could not envision that a typical mortal could endure the intensity of a prolonged prophetic encounter. Ideally, they would have remained in prophetic communion with

---

[20] Rabbeinu Yehuda HaLevi, *Sefer HaKuzari*, part I, section 97.
[21] Rabbeinu Ovadia Sforno, *Commentary on Sefer Shemot*, 20:14-16.

Hashem and received the entire Torah directly from Him. However, they beseeched Moshe to stand in their stead. He should receive balance of the Torah from Hashem and transmit it to them.

In short, Bnai Yisrael concluded that the prolonged prophetic experience required to receive the Torah from Hashem could only be endured by an exceptional human being. They relied upon Moshe to assume this role.

Moshe did not descend from the mountain at the anticipated hour. The conclusion of Bnai Yisrael is now understandable. They had themselves experienced an intimate prophetic encounter. They had felt that the encounter bordered upon the unendurable. A prolonged encounter would require an exceptional individual. They had hoped that Moshe could serve as their representative. Moshe's failure to descend from the mountain pointed to a single interpretation. Moshe had not survived his extended encounter with Hashem.

When I was gone up to the mount to receive the tablets of stone, even the tablets of the covenant which Hashem made with you, then I abode in the mount forty days and forty nights. I did neither eat bread nor drink water. (Devarim 9:9)

3. Moshe's unique status among prophets

Moshe himself confirmed that this conclusion was partially accurate. He explains that during the forty days that he was upon the mountain he did not eat or drink. The implication of Moshe's statement is that he actually existed during those forty days of prophetic engagement in a state that was super-mortal. Only because of his unique capacity to achieve this state was he capable of enduring the prophetic communion of Revelation.

Maimonides explains that among the fundamental principles of the Torah is that Moshe is the greatest of all prophets. No prophet before Moshe and no prophet who will succeed him are his equal.[22] Why is the differentiation of Moshe from other prophets an essential principle of the Torah? There are a number of reasons. One is reflected in the above discussion. The communication of the entire Torah to a Moshe was a super-mortal experience. Acknowledgment of the Torah as a Divinely revealed truth is predicated upon accepting that Moshe achieved a qualitatively different prophetic state than any other prophet. He was not merely a greater prophet than his peers by a degree. He was distinguished from his peers by an order of magnitude.

Bnai Yisrael's decision to create an idol to replace Moshe was consistent with their outlook. They believed that Moshe had been taken from them. This confirmed their fear that a human being could not endure ongoing communion with Hashem. Therefore, they sought to create a different type of intermediary – one not subject to the frailties of a mortal being. This is reflected in the opening passages above. The people demanded that Aharon create an idol for them because Moshe – a mortal – had been taken from them.

And it came to pass, when Moshe came down from Mount Sinai with the two tablets of the testimony in Moshe's hand, when he came down from the mount, that Moshe knew not that the skin of his face sent forth beams while He talked with him. When Aharon and all the children of Israel saw Moshe, behold, the skin of his face sent forth beams. And they were afraid to come nigh to him. (Shemot 34:29-30)

---

[22] Rabbeinu Moshe ben Maimon (Rambam) *Commen. on the Mishna*, Mesechet Sanhedrin 10:1.

4. The message of Moshe's radiance

The final passages of the *parasha* describe Moshe's radiance. The Torah explains that when Moshe descended from Sinai with the second *Lucot* – the Tablets of the Decalogue – a strange radiance emanated from his face. Why was Moshe granted this unusual attribute? Based on the events described in the *parasha*, a possible reason emerges.

The people feared that Moshe had died. The basis for this fear was their underestimation of Moshe's prophetic gift and capacity. They had experienced a brief prophetic encounter. The encounter had overwhelmed them. When Moshe failed to descend from the mountain, they extrapolated from their own experience and concluded that the extended prophetic encounter required to receive the entire Torah was beyond mortal reach. They did not understand that Moshe's capacity for prophecy was differentiated from theirs by an order of magnitude. The light that flowed from Moshe's face was testimony to his unique and singular greatness. He was not to be compared to any other person.

Perhaps more importantly, the light that emanated from Moshe also testified to the Divine authorship of the Torah. It communicated that a very special human being did enter into a prolonged communion with Hashem and received from Him the Torah.

And Ezra opened the book in the sight of all the people – for he was above all the people – and when he opened it, all the people stood up. (Sefer Nechemyah 8:5)

5. The message communicated through demonstrating respect for the Torah

Maimonides explains that when the Torah is read in front of the congregation it is prohibited to speak.[23] Rabbaynu Manoach explains that this requirement is not merely to assure that at least a quorum of participants is attentive. In other words, even if there are ten members of the congregation who are attentive to the reading of the Torah, all other members must be silent.[24] What is the basis for this requirement?

Maimonides' ruling is based upon the Talmud. The Talmud cites as its source the record in the Book of Nechemyah of Ezra's reading of the Torah before the people. The passage explains that when Ezra opened the Torah the people stood. The Talmud explains that the passage means that they stopped speaking and became attentive. However, Rabbaynu Avraham Ibn Ezra comments that the simple meaning of the passage is also true. The people arose and stood in respect for the Torah.[25]

When the Torah is read in the congregation our silence communicates our deep reverence for the Torah and its contents. This respect reflects our recognition that the contents of the Torah are the words of Hashem, revealed to Bnai Yisrael and humanity through Moshe. Even if ten others are attentively listening to every word of the Torah reading, every member of the congregation must be silent. Our silence is our affirmation of the divinity of the Torah's sacred words.

And he took it from their hand and he formed it with a tool and they made it into a molten image of a calf. And they said: This is your god Yisrael that brought you up from Egypt. (Shemot 32:4)

---

[23] Rabbeinu Moshe ben Maimon (Rambam) *Mishna Torah*, Hilchot Tefillah 12:9.
[24] Rabbeinu Manoach of Narbonne, *Commentary on Mishne Torah*, Hilchot Tefilah 12:9.
[25] Rabbeinu Avraham ibn Ezra, *Commentary on Sefer Nechemyah*, 8:5.

Make Up Your Mind!

1. The incident of the golden calf

Parshat Ki Tisa describes the incident of the *egel* – the golden calf. Moshe had ascended the Mountain of Sinai to receive from Hashem the Torah and the tablets of the Decalogue. He remained on the mountain for forty days and nights. The people believed that Moshe had not returned to them because he had died on the barren mountain. They were overcome with panic and appealed to Aharon to make an idol for them that would replace Moshe. This idol would lead them forward. Aharon did not refuse the people and the *egel* was created. In the above passage the people adopt it as a replacement for Moshe and prepare to worship it.

The narrative continues and explains that Hashem sent Moshe back to the people. Before departing, Moshe beseeched Hashem to not destroy the people. Hashem agreed and Moshe descended from the mountain. Moshe carried with him the tablets of the Decalogue. He approached the camp and observed the *egel*. He shattered the tablets. Moshe then destroyed the idol and punished those who had worshiped it.

And now send and gather to me all of Israel at the Mountain of Karmel and the four hundred and fifty prophets of the Baal and the four hundred and fifty prophets of the Asheyrah who eat at the table of Ezevel. (Sefer Melachim I 18:19)

2. Eliyahu and the priests of the Ba'al

Each week, the reading of the Torah portion is accompanied by a short reading from the Neve'im – the Prophets. This reading is referred to as the *haftarah*. The reading is related to the Torah portion that it accompanies. The *haftarah* for Parsaht Ki Tisa discusses Eliyahu's challenge to the priests of the Ba'al.

Eliyahu was a contemporary of Achav, the king of Israel. During Achav's reign and with his approval, worship of the deity Ba'al was widely adopted by the people of Israel. Hashem brought a prolonged drought upon the land and terrible famine afflicted the nation. Achav sought out Eliyahu. Eliyahu confronted Achav. He told the king that the famine and suffering of the people was the result of his abandonment of Hashem and promotion of the worship of the Ba'al.

Eliyahu then proposed to Achav that they gather the priests of the Ba'al to the Mountain of Karmel. There Eliyahu would challenge them to a test.

Eliyahu and the priests of the Ba'al erected altars. Each placed a bull upon their respective altars. Neither set their altar aflame. Instead, each prayed to his deity and asked that a flame descend from the heavens and consume the sacrifice.

The priests of the Ba'al placed their sacrifice upon their altar. They cried out to the Ba'al but no flame came forth. Eliyahu ridiculed the priests of the Ba'al. He suggested that they pray louder. Perhaps, their god was sleeping. The priests of the Ba'al became ever-more frantic in their petitions but no response was evoked from their god.

Then Eliyahu prepared his altar. After placing wood upon it and his sacrifice, he thoroughly soaked the fuel with water. In front of the nation, Eliyahu prayed to Hashem. A flame descended from the heavens and consumed the sacrifice, the wood on the altar, and scorched the altar's stones and mortar. The people were awed by this wonder. They fell upon their faces and acknowledged that Hashem is the only G-d.

> *And Eliyahui approached the entire nation and he said: Until when will you continue to skip between two views? If Hashem is G-d, then go after Him. If the Ba'al, then go after him. And the nation did not answer him a word. (Sefer Melachim I 18:21)*

3. Eliyahu's strange criticism

The above passage introduces Eliyahu's challenge to the priests of the Ba'al. He asks the people to choose between worship of Hashem, and worship of the Ba'al. He then proposes his contest and the nation agrees to the challenge.

The commentators are disturbed by Eliyahu's message to the people. He criticizes them for wavering between the worship of Hashem and service to the Ba'al. He demands that they choose one or the other. It seems that he is criticizing their inconsistency and not their worship of the Ba'al. The implication of his criticism is that it would be satisfied by their wholehearted devotion to the Ba'al!

The Targum – the Aramaic translation of the text – suggests that Eliyahu was engaging in rhetoric. He was not actually proposing that wholehearted acceptance of the Ba'al was a reasonable response. He was saying to the people, "Is not Hashem, the only true G-d? Why do you stray after the Ba'al?"

4. Strange combinations

Malbim disagrees. In order to understand his interpretation of Eliyahu's rebuke of the people, we must understand the practices of the time. Many of the commentators suggest that the people of Eliyahu's time had not completely replaced worship of Hashem with service to the Ba'al. They could not ignore the drought and famine that were ravaging their land. The drought had been brought upon the land with the pronouncement of Eliyahu. He announced that it was a punishment for their idolatry. However, the priest of the Ba'al assured them that their loyalty to the Ba'al would bring an end to the drought.[26] They were confused. They were torn between worship of Hashem and service to the Ba'al. According to Malbim, they believed that these two perspectives could co-exist. In other words, rather than choosing between Hashem and the Ba'al, they believed they could worship both.

Malbim explains that Eliyahu criticized the people for combining two forms of worship that are exclusive of one another. The Torah teaches us that Hashem is the only G-d and that He is worthy of worship. It is impossible to combine this perspective with the worship of another deity. Eliyahu was not actually suggesting that the people adopt the worship of the Ba'al and abandon worship of Hashem. He was explaining to the people that the compromise they had adopted was nonsensical. Combined worship of Hashem and the Ba'al was indistinguishable from abandonment of Hashem. We serve Hashem as an expression of our recognition of His omnipotence and as acknowledgment that no other power can act contrary to His will. Service to Ba'al assumes that this deity acts independent of Hashem or in His stead. These two perspectives cannot be reconciled or co-exist.[27]

5. The tenets of Judasim are inseparable from one another

Another interpretation of Eliyahu's message is suggested by Rav Chaim Soloveitchik *Zt"l*. Rav Chaim's interpretation has two components. First, he suggests that

---

[26] Rabbaynu David Kimchi (Radak), *Commentary on Sefer Melachim I* 18:21.
[27] Rabbaynu Meir Libush (Malbim), *Commentary on Sefer Melachim I* 18:21.

Eliyahu told the people that their merging of worship of Hashem with service to the Ba'al was the same as wholehearted worship of the Ba'al. Second, Rav Chaim explains why this merger is undistinguishable from simply completely adopting worship of the Ba'al. He suggests that the Torah's fundamental tenets are inseparable. These tenets comprise a single system of theological outlook. The rejection of any one compromises the entirety. Therefore, if one accepts Hashem as creator and sustainer of the universe, but believes it appropriate to worship other deities, he has rejected the Torah's system of tenets. His acceptance of Hashem is rendered meaningless.[28]

6. Belief co-existing with doubt?

Rav Chaim's first point is that Eliyahu told the people that their merging of worship of Hashem with service to the Ba'al was the same as wholehearted worship of the Ba'al. His second point is an explanation for this equivalency. There is another, perhaps simpler, explanation for this equivalency.

There is a fundamental difference between a physical performance and an obligation of the heart and mind. A physical performance can sustain and retain its meaning even when its motives are compromised. If a person gives charity to one in need moved by selfish motives, the recipient has been provided with support. Of course, the *mitzvah* of assisting one in need has been performed in a less than ideal manner. But the charity retains some virtue and has a positive effect.

An obligation of the heart and mind cannot be executed in a partial manner. A person is either convinced that a belief is true or the person has doubts. Obligations of the heart and mind require that we fully subscribe to a tenet. If we accept the tenet, but retain some doubt, we have not fulfilled the obligation and must strive to eliminate that doubt.

This interpretation of Eliyahu's comment seems to be supported by Rashi. Rashi explains that Eliyahu said to the people, "You cannot choose between your two perspectives!"[29] This seems to be an odd criticism. If they could not choose, then they acted properly in following both perspectives!

However, as explained above, this is not an option in respect to an obligation of the heart and mind. One cannot believe that Hashem is the only G-d and yet harbor some doubt. If that doubt exists, then the obligation has not been properly executed. The obligation is to believe in Hashem wholeheartedly. Belief and doubt are incompatible.

7. Working on our convictions

We understand that we must work toward improving our performance of *mitzvot*. In the case of *mitzvot* that are accomplished through actions, the method for improving our performance is self evident. We study the *halachot* that guide us in the performance and we execute the *mitzvah* more scrupulously. If we wish to improve our observance of Shabbat, we study its *halachot* and we carefully observe them.

However, obligations of the heart and mind also deserve our attention and our commitment to their performance. In a sense, their demand upon our attention is even more urgent. These obligations are severely compromised when accompanied by doubt. The

---

[28] Rav Y. Hershkowitz, *Torat Chaim on TaNach*, p 203.
[29] Rabbaynu Shlomo ben Yitzchak (Rashi), *Commentary on Sefer Melachim I* 18:21.

appropriate execution of these obligations is achieved only through elimination of doubt and ambivalence.

"And now leave me and my anger will be expressed towards them and I will destroy them. And I will make you into a great nation." (Shemot 32:10)

Parshat Ki Tisa relates the incident of the Egel HaZahav – the Golden Calf. The basic outline of the incident is very clear. The Torah explains that Moshe ascended Sinai. Moshe was on the mountain for forty days. The people became alarmed that he had not returned and assumed that he would not come back. They turned to Aharon and pleaded with him to create a deity that would lead them. Aharon created the Egel and the nation immediately initiated worship of this figure. Hashem tells Moshe that He will destroy Bnai Yisrael and create a new nation from Moshe's descendants. Moshe prays on behalf of Bnai Yisrael and succeeds in saving the nation.

It is not clear from the Torah exactly how many members of the nation were involved in the sin of the Egel. However, Malbim argues that only three thousand members of Bnai Yisrael actually participated in this sin. His argument is based an interesting problem in the pesukim.

"And the children of Leyve did as Moshe had directed. And on that day, three thousand men fell from the nation." (Shemot 32:28)

Moshe descends from Sinai. He breaks the Luchot – the Tablets. He asks those who remain faithful to Hashem, to rally around him. Shevet Leyve responds to Moshe's call. He instructs the members of Shevet Leyve to execute those who have sinned by worshipping the Egel. The members of Shevet Leyve execute three thousand people. However, these are not the only people that were killed in response to the sin of the Egel.

"And Hashem struck the nation because they served the Egel that Aharon had made." (Shemot 32:35)

The Torah tells us that in addition to those who were executed by Shevet Leyve, others died in a plague that Hashem brought upon the nation. It is interesting that the Torah does not specify the number of people that died in the plague. This contrasts sharply with the account of the executions performed by Shevet Leyve. In that instance, the Torah indicates that three thousand people were executed.

There is a further question. Presumably Shevet Leyve killed those members of the nation that participated in the sin. Yet, a plague was necessary. Who did Hashem kill with the plague?

Rashi suggests that Shevet Leyve were only empowered to execute those members of the nation who were forewarned to not participate in the sin and then were seen worshipping the Egel. Therefore, they could not execute all of the members of the nation involved in the sin. Some of the sinner had not been forewarned or were not seen participating in worship. Shevet Leyve was not empowered to judge and execute these people. The plague addressed this problem.[30] Malbim notes that the Sages suggest that those sinners, who were not executed by Shevet Leyve, were struck down by the plague.[31]

---

[30] Rabbaynu Shlomo ben Yitzchak (Rashi), *Commentary on Sefer Shemot* 32:20.
[31] Rabbaynu Meir Libush (Malbim), *Commentary on Sefer Shemot* 32:35.

This explains why the plague was needed. However, the Sages' comments do not explain why the Torah does not reveal the number of people killed in this plague. Malbim raises another issue. The Torah describes the worship of the Egel as a public event. It seems unlikely that a significant number of people participated in this event and were not seen by witnesses. Although the Torah does not indicate how many people died in the plague, the very term plague indicates the number must have been significant. How is it possible that a substantial number of people participated in the sin and were not seen by witnesses?

Malbim answers these questions based in an earlier pasuk. The Torah tells us that when Bnai Yisrael left Egypt they were accompanied by a mixed group of people from other nations.[32] This group was composed of individual who were not members of Bnai Yisrael. However, they were impressed by the wonders they had witnessed Hashem perform on Bnai Yisrael's behalf. They decided to join Bnai Yisrael and follow them out of Egypt. The Torah does not explicitly tell us of the fate of the group – the Erev Rav. However, they quickly disappear from the narrative of the Torah.

Malbim suggests that although only a small portion of Bnai Yisrael participated in the sin of the Egel, a large portion of the Erev Rav were involved in the sin. Therefore, among Bnai Yisrael there were many innocent people that forewarned their neighbors to not worship the Egel. If their forewarning was disregarded these same individuals were available to serve as witnesses of the sin. Shevet Leyve relied on these innocent people in order to judge and execute those who were guilty of worshipping the Egel.

In contrast, among the Erev Rav there were few if any innocents who forewarned their neighbors. And there were few members of the Erev Rav who were untainted by the sin of the Egel and qualified to testify against others. Therefore, Shevet Leyve was not empowered to punish members of the Erev Rav who had participated in the sin.

Malbim suggests that these members of the Erev Rav who went unpunished by Shevet Leyve were killed by the plague.[33] Malbim's insight explains why the Torah does not indicate the number of people killed by the plague. The Torah indicates the number of members of Bnai Yisrael executed by Shevet Leyve because this information is relevant to the narrative of the Torah. The Torah is describing the development of the Jewish nation. However, the Erev Rav was not part of Bnai Yisrael. After this incident, the Erev Rav was decimated and no longer significant. Therefore, the number of members of the Erev Rav killed by the plague is not treated as a significant element of the narrative.

Malbim's position raises an important question. According to Malbim, the three thousand people executed by Shevet Leyve represent the entire portion of the nation that worshiped the Egel. Yet, Hashem tells Moshe that because of this sin He wishes to destroy Bnai Yisrael. This seems like a remarkably harsh punishment. How could Hashem destroy an entire nation because of the sin of a relatively small minority of its members?

Sforno addresses this question through a remarkable analysis of another issue.

"And he said to them, "So says Hashem the G-d of Israel: Each man should place his sword on his thigh and pass back and froth from one gate to the other in the camp. Each man should kill

---

[32] Sefer Shemot 12:38.
[33] Rabbaynu Meir Libush (Malbim), *Commentary on Sefer Shemot* 32:35.

his brother; each man should kill his friend and each man should kill his relative." (Shemot 32:27)

Moshe addresses the members of Shevet Leyve. He tells them that Hashem expects them to act as executioners. They are to execute all those guilty of the sin of worshipping the Egel. They may not show mercy to brothers, friends or relatives. Any person who is judged to be guilty must be executed.

Sforno is bothered by a problem in this passage. Moshe begins by instructing the members of Shevet Leyve to pass back and forth through the camp. Why did Moshe add this detail to his instructions? Sforno suggests that Moshe was instructing Shevet Leyve to perform its task as publicly as possible. The sinners were to be judged and then executed in the open. The actions of Shevet Leyve should be observed by the entire nation.

Why was Moshe concerned with creating a public display? Sforno suggest that this was a fundamental element of the punishment! How?

Sforno is bothered by another problem. He assumes that only a portion of Bnai Yisrael were involved in the worship of the Egel. What was the attitude of the rest of the nation? Why did the rest of the nation not take action to prevent the creation of the Egel and its worship? He concludes that although only a small portion of the nation actually worshipped the Egel, many others stood by passively and did little to prevent their neighbors from violating the prohibition against idolatry – one of the most important injunctions of the Torah. They could have acted responsibly and forcibly prevented the sin from taking place. But they could not bring themselves to take aggressive action. As a result, the sin of the Egel took place. In other words, the sin was the result of the actions of the few and the passivity of the majority.

Hashem wanted to punish both those who sinned actively by worshipping the Egel and those who sinned through their passivity – by not taking the action necessary to prevent the sin. The sinners were punished by death. Those who failed to act were punished by being forced to watch the executions. They had been unable to take action against their friends. They would not watch the executions of these same friends.[34]

Sforno's insight explains Hashem's response to the sin of the Egel. It is true that only a small portion of the nation was actively involved in the sin. However, the Egel could not have been created a worshipped without the passive acquiescence of the many others. Hashem suggested to Moshe that the nation deserved to be destroyed. They deserved this punishment because of the sin of the few and the passivity of the majority.

And it was when he approached the camp and he saw the Calf and drums, Moshe was angered. He threw the Tablets from his hands and shattered them at the foot of the mountain. (Shemot 32:19)

Acceptable Anger

1. **The shattering of the Luchot**

---

[34] Rabbaynu Ovadia Sforno, *Commentary on Sefer Shemot*, 32:27.

Parshat Ki Tisa describes the sin of the Egel – the Golden Calf. Moshe ascended Mount Sinai to receive the Torah and the Luchot – the Tablets of the Decalogue. He did not return at the expected time. The people panicked. They feared Moshe, their leader, had perished on the mountain. They demanded of Aharon that he fashion a figure to replace Moshe. This figure will lead them through the wilderness. Aharon fashioned the Golden Calf. He told them that the next day they will convene a celebration for Hashem. The next day arrived. The people celebrated offering sacrifices. The celebration devolved into meaningless frivolity.

Hashem described to Moshe these events and told him that He will extinguish the nation. Moshe interceded; Hashem would not immediately destroy Bnai Yisrael.

Moshe descended the mountain. He approached the camp and observed the Egel and the celebration. He threw the Luchot to the ground and shattered them at the foot of the mountain.

Why did Moshe shatter the Luchot? Our commentators offer various explanations.

And the Tablets were the work of the L-rd and the script was the script of the L-rd engraved upon the Tablets. (Shemot 32:16)

2. The Luchot were Hashem's work

The above passage describes the Luchot as the work of Hashem. He created the Tablets and He engraved upon them the Decalogue. The passage appears immediately before the Moshe approaches the camp of Bnai Yisrael. Ramban – Nachmanides – notes that the passage seems out of place. The Torah previously recorded Hashem giving the Luchot to Moshe.[35] At that point in the narrative, the Torah should have provided its description of the Tablets. It did not. Instead, the description was postponed and first appears in the above passage.

Ramban explains that the Torah provides the description at this point to emphasize Moshe's decisiveness. Hashem gave him these Luchot that He had created. Yet, Moshe concluded that they should be shattered rather than given to the people. He did not hesitate. He threw the Tablets to the ground, shattering them. This required remarkable decisiveness and courage.[36]

3. Unfit to receive the Luchot

Why did Moshe feel it necessary to shatter the Luchot? The commentators have different responses. Rabbaynu Ovadia Sforno explains that Moshe observed the people's celebration and recognized that they could not be rehabilitated adequately to deserve these Luchot.[37]

There are three important aspects to Sforno's explanation. First, it answers a question. Hashem told Moshe that the people had committed a horrendous sin, engaged in idolatry, and that they deserved to be annihilated. Yet, Moshe descended the mountain with the Luchot. Apparently, he believed the people could be redeemed and receive the Luchot. What caused him to revise his judgement? Sforno responds that when he observed their celebration Moshe concluded the people could not receive these Luchot.

Second, Sforno maintains that the people's celebration added a new dimension to their sin. What was this dimension and why did it convince Moshe that the people could not receive

---

[35] Sefer Shemot 31:18.
[36] Rabbaynu Moshe ben Nachman (Ramban), Commentary on Sefer Shemot 32:16.
[37] Rabbaynu Ovadia Sforno, Commentary on Sefer Shemot 32:19.

the Luchot? Apparently, Moshe hoped to observe ambivalence. He expected that although the people were engaged in idolatry, they would feel some doubt and discomfort with their behavior. Moshe planned to appeal to this voice of reason. He encountered the people rejoicing in their idolatry. They were wholeheartedly given-over to their sin. His observation of this abandonment of reason and good-sense persuaded him that he would not completely rehabilitate the nation.[38]

And Hashem said to Moshe, "Chisel for yourself two stone tablets like the first and I will write on the tablets the words that were on the first tablets that you shattered." (Shemot 34:1)

4. The second Tablets

The third aspect of Sforno's position becomes evident when another question is considered. Moshe destroyed the Luchot because he believed the people did not and would never deserve them. Yet, Hashem commanded Moshe to create a second set of Luchot and He inscribed them with the Decalogue. Was Moshe mistaken in his assessment of the people? Did they exceed his expectations and completely redeem themselves?

Sforno explains that the second set of Tablets differed significantly from the first. The first was created entirely by Hashem. He fashioned the stone tablets and He recorded upon them the Decalogue. The second set of tablets was chiseled by Moshe. He ascended the mountain with them and there Hashem inscribed upon them the words of the Decalogue. The first Tablets were, in their entirety, the work of Hashem. The second set was created through a partnership between Hashem and Moshe.[39]

This indicates that Moshe was not mistaken in his assessment. Bnai Yisrael did receive a second Luchot. However, these were not the "work of the L-rd". They were the product of a partnership. The second Luchot were not the equivalent of the first.

5. Moshe's outrage

Ramban offers a different explanation of Moshe's decision to shatter the Luchot. He comments that when he observed the behavior of the people he was angered. He could not restrain himself.[40] It seems that according to Ramban, Moshe responded in anger. He shattered the Luchot in response to his outrage.

This is a difficult explanation to accept. Rambam – Maimonides – comments on acting out of anger:

> "Anger is a very evil trait. It is fitting that a person should distance oneself from it to the extreme. One should train oneself to not anger even in response to something it is fitting to anger over." (Rambam, Mishne Torah, Hilchot Deyot 2:3)

Rambam continues to explain that our Sages warn us that losing oneself to one's anger is equivalent to idolatry.

How can Ramban suggest that Moshe shattered the Luchot in rage? Would this not mean that his actions were as reprehensible as those of the people. They engaged in idolatry; he was overtaken by his anger – a sin the Sages equate with idolatry.

---

[38] See notes of Rav Yehuda Kuperman on Sforno ad loc.
[39] Rabbaynu Ovadia Sforno, Commentary on Sefer Shemot 34:27.
[40] Rabbaynu Moshe ben Nachman (Ramban), Commentary on Sefer Shemot 32:16.

6. Appropriate anger

To answer this question, we must more carefully consider Rambam's comments. Rambam acknowledged that sometimes anger is appropriate. Yet, it is prohibited to anger. If anger is appropriate in a situation, why is it prohibited? Rambam's further comments respond to this issue.

> "If one wishes to instill fear in one's children or members of the household, or if a leader [wishes to inspire fear in] the community, and one wishes to anger toward them to motivate their improvement, then one should act before them as if angry to chastise them and remain internally calm." (Rambam, Mishne Torah, Hilchot Deyot 2:3)

There is a difference between demonstrating anger and being in a state of anger. A demonstration of anger is a tool we use in our interactions with others. Sometimes, this tool is appropriate and even necessary. Rambam explains that in such circumstances one may and perhaps, should demonstrate anger.

The state of anger is a state of mind. One is enraged and overcome by anger. The state of anger is prohibited without qualification. When anger is a requisite and appropriate response, one demonstrates anger but remains internally calm.

And I took hold of the two Tablets and I sent them forth from upon my hands. I shattered them before your eyes. (Devarim 9:17)

7. Moshe makes a statement

In the above passage, Moshe reviews with the people the episode of the Egel and the shattering of the Luchot. Moshe adds two elements to his description that are not included in the initial narrative in our parasha. First, he says, "I took hold of the two Tablets". Moshe descended the mountain carrying the Luchot. What does he mean by saying he took hold of the Luchot and then shattered them? He means that he modified his grasp to prepare to throw the Luchot. Why does he mention this seemingly insignificant detail? Let's consider his second addition to the narrative.

Moshe says, "I shattered them before your eyes". In other words, he shattered them with the intention that the people observe the event – the destruction of the Luchot. Now, Moshe's message in noting that he modified his grasp on the Luchot in preparation of destroying them emerges. Moshe is explaining to the people that he acted with intention. His breaking of the Luchot was intended to communicate a message to the people. It was not a spontaneous reactive impulse. It was a carefully considered response to the people's behavior. Moshe repositioned his hands, altering his grasp, to hurl the Luchot before the people.

Now, Ramban's position is clarified. He is not suggesting that Moshe became lost in his rage and acted without thinking. Moshe recognized that he needed to shock the people and immediately and drastically alter their mood. He used the Luchot to accomplish this. He demonstrated to them that they no longer deserved the Luchot created by Hashem. He shattered them before the people, communicating to them the severity of their sin and its terrible consequences.

8. Justified anger

This discussion of Ramban's position has obvious implications. First, the distinction between demonstrating anger and experiencing anger is very important and relevant to our lives.

We may encounter situations in which a demonstration of anger is appropriate. However, we are not permitted to succumb to our anger and be moved by it. Demonstration of anger is a communication tool. Like any tool, it is only effective when used sensibly. Therefore, especially when we are demonstrating anger, it is essential to maintain our internal calm so that we fashion and execute our demonstration effectively.

Second, our culture treats demonstration of anger as virtually taboo. Moshe did not accept this. He identified a situation requiring a demonstration of anger and he created and executed a very dramatic one.

Now it came to pass when he drew closer to the camp and saw the calf and the dances, that Moshe's anger was kindled, and he flung the tablets from his hands, shattering them at the foot of the mountain. (Shemot 32:19)

Moshe's Self-Promotion

Moshe shatters the Tablets

Parshat Ki Tisa describes one of the most perplexing incidents in the Torah. Moshe shatters the *Luchot* – the Tablets of the Decalogue. Hashem tells Moshe that the people have created the *Egel* – the Golden Calf. Hashem expresses His intention to destroy the nation. Moshe intercedes and Hashem reverses His position. He will not immediately destroy the Jewish people. Moshe descends from the mountain with the *Luchot* in his hands. These *Luchot* are the wondrous work of Hashem. Moshe approaches the camp of Bnai Yisrael. He observes the *Egel* and the festivities in which the people are engaged. He is angered and throws forth the *Luchot*, shattering them. How are we to understand Moshe's behavior? What right did he have to break the *Luchot*?

Moshe as a passive actor

The commentators are troubled by Moshe's behavior and adopt three basic approaches to explain it. The simplest approach suggests that Moshe did not make a decision. He was directed or forced to break the *Luchot*. Many commentators explain the incident using this approach. Rabbaynu Avraham ibn Ezra notes an opinion that Moshe was directed by Hashem to throw down the Tablets.[41] Rashbam explains that Moshe was overwhelmed at observing the behavior of the people. He lost his strength and could no longer support the weight of the Tablets. He threw the *Luchot* away from himself to avoid injury. In these interpretations Moshe does not make a decision. He is forced to shatter the Tablets.

Perhaps, the most intriguing application of this approach is found in the midrash and quoted widely among the commentaries. When Moshe entered the camp, the letters engraved upon the *Luchot* departed. Moshe was now carrying blank tablets. There are two versions of the ensuing event. According to Midrash Rabbah, Moshe broke the blank stone tablets.[42] According to Tanchuma, the blank stone tablets suddenly became unbearably heavy. Moshe could not support their weight and he dropped them.[43] According to both variants, Moshe did not did not decide to shatter the *Luchot*. According to Midrash Rabba's version of the events, the tablets

---

[41] Rabbeinu Avraham ibn Ezra, *Abbreviated Commentary on Sefer Shemot*, 32:19. Ibn Ezra does not favor this explanation. However, it is adopted and developed by Netziv.
[42] Midrash Rabba, Sefer Shemot 46:1.
[43] Midrash Tanchuma, Parshat Ki Tisa, Chapter 32.

were no longer the *Luchot* when Moshe threw them to the ground. According to Tanchuma's version, once the letters departed from the *Luchot*, Moshe was unable to support their weight.[44]

The common element shared by the responses adopting this approach is that Moshe did not have the right to decide to break the *Luchot*. He broke the *Luchot*, either because Hashem directed him, he was overwhelmed by the events, or the *Luchot* were deprived of their sacred character and Moshe shattered mere stone tablets.

Moshe applied established principles

The second approach acknowledges that Moshe made the decision to break the *Luchot*. He based his decision upon clear, self-evident principles. Rashi suggests that Moshe deduced from the laws of the Pesach sacrifice that the people were unfit to receive the *Luchot*. The Torah teaches that one who is an idolator is not fit to participate in the Pesach sacrifice. Moshe reasoned that one who is disqualified from the Pesach sacrifice is certainly not fit to receive the entire Torah.[45]

Ralbag – Gersonides – develops this answer more extensively. He explains that the *Luchot* represented the covenant between Hashem and Bnai Yisrael. Through entering into this covenant the Jewish people accepted the responsibility to observe the commandments. Acceptance of Hashem as the L-rd is the fundamental foundation of the Torah. Idolatry is a rejection of that foundation. With their repudiation of this most fundamental of principles, the people were rendered unfit to receive the *Luchot* that represented the covenant.[46]

Moshe created a new role for himself

The third approach also acknowledges that Moshe exercised his own authority in shattering the *Luchot*. However, he did not base his action upon established principles. This approach is found in Midrash Rabba[47] and adopted by Ramban – Nachmanides. Moshe understood the *Luchot* as the equivalent of a marriage contract between Hashem and Bnai Yisrael. Moshe was Hashem's – the groom's – agent, charged with the responsibility of delivering this contract. He reasoned that if this contract would be executed, then the idolatry of Bnai Yisrael would be analogous to adultery. He destroyed the *Luchot* – the marriage contract – in order to diminish the severity of the nation's sin.[48] Ramban adds that Moshe demonstrated enormous courage. He could not be certain that he had the authority to destroy Hashem's *Luchot* or that the behavior he contemplated was consistent with Hashem's will. Moshe risked his own life for the welfare of the Jewish people.[49]

Three interpretations of Moshe's role

---

[44] Etz Yosef, commenting on Tanchuma, suggests that the letters of the *Luchot* did not actually disappear. They lost their sanctity. Moshe was able to support the weight of the *Luchot* only when they were endowed with sanctity. Once this sanctity departed, their true material weight asserted itself and Moshe was overwhelmed.
[45] Rabbeinu Shlomo ben Yitzchak (Rashi), *Commentary on Sefer Shemot* 32:19.
[46] Rabbeinu Levi ben Gershon (Ralbag / Gersonides), *Commentary on Sefer Shemot* 32:19.
[47] Midrash Rabba, Sefer Shemot 46:1.
[48] Rabbeinu Moshe ben Nachman (Ramban), *Commentary on Sefer Shemot* 32:17.
[49] Rabbeinu Moshe ben Nachman (Ramban), *Commentary on Sefer Devarim* 9:17.

These three approaches to understanding Moshe's behavior differ in their understanding of Moshe's role in this incident and as the leader of the nation. The first approach treats Moshe as a passive actor in the incident. Hashem did not assign to him authority to exercise a significant degree of discretion. This approach absolves Moshe from any responsibility for shattering the *Luchot*. He was responding to irresistible forces.

The second approach understands Moshe as an active participant in these events. He decided to shatter the *Luchot* based upon clear and sound principles. He was not a passive player. However, neither did he have a creative role. He was permitted only to apply established principles to the present situation. He acted as a judge applying the relevant principles to the real-time events. He came down from Sinai carrying *Luchot* created by Hashem. His decision to destroy this most sacred object demonstrates his wisdom, confidence, and remarkable capacity to make an objective judgment in an unimaginably difficult situation. However, he acted in a role that was familiar to him. Also, he believed that his actions were consistent with the role assigned to him by Hashem.

The final approach, championed by Ramban, ascribes a remarkable role to Moshe. At his own initiative, he acted creatively and assumed a role that had not been clearly assigned to him. He became the arbitrator of the relationship between Hashem and Bnai Yisrael. He assumed responsibility for managing this relationship. He postponed the conclusion of the covenant – the marriage – between Hashem and Bnai Yisrael in order to save his people from more severe punishment.

Moshe's behavior required enormous courage. He did not know that he had the right to assume this role. He did not know whether his action would be accepted by Hashem as heroic or rejected as presumptuous. He knew only that his action was required in order to preserve the Jewish people.

The uniqueness of Moshe

Rambam – Maimonides – explains that Moshe was the greatest of all prophets. According to Rambam, Moshe's superiority over other prophets was not a matter of degree. In other words, it is not correct to say he was a better, more gifted, or more accomplished prophet. His prophecy was qualitatively different from all others.[50] Ramban is asserting that Moshe was also unique in regards to his relationship with Hashem. Other prophets spoke for Hashem. They appealed to Hashem on behalf of the Jewish people. Moshe was devoted to these activities. However, he also achieved a unique relationship with Hashem in which he became a creative actor developing a role for himself that Hashem had not clearly assigned to him.

A leader must determine the extent of his authority

All three of these approaches are reasonable. The diverse perspectives that they encompass provide an insight into the one of the greatest challenges of leadership. Every leader is confronted with the question of how far to extend one's authority. A leader must distinguish between exercising authority appropriately and acting presumptuously. A leader must balance appreciation for the boundaries of one's authority with the creativity to imagine and shape new roles for oneself. How does a righteous, ethical leader resolve these difficult challenges?

---

[50] Rabbeinu Moshe ben Maimon (Rambam) *Mishnah Torah*, Hilchot Yesodei HaTorah 6:6.

An important response emerges from this discussion. Ramban emphasizes it. Moshe did not know whether his action would be accepted by Hashem. He believed his behavior was consistent with Hashem's will but he was not certain. He realized that he was placing his own life at risk to save the Jewish people. In other words, Moshe did not act for his own benefit. He focused completely on Hashem's will and the needs of Bnai Yisrael.

The exercising of authority is often challenging. It may not be clear whether a specific initiative is an appropriate use of authority or overreaches. The challenge is often made far greater because our egos or our desire for control and authority assert themselves. Alternatively, sometimes, timidity or under-confidence may cause us to refrain from acting boldly. Moshe's model provides a framework for responding to the challenge. One must assess the situation based upon an analysis of right and wrong and with the objective of benefiting those whom one leads. This requires self-awareness and giving diligent attention to evaluating one's true motives.[51]

And Moshe returned to Hashem and he said: I beseech You! This nation has committed a terrible sin. They have created for themselves a god of gold. (Shemot 32:31)

Deep Pockets Need Long Arms

Hashem shares responsibility for the golden calf

This week's *parasha* describes the sin of the *egel ha'zahav* – the golden calf. Moshe ascended Mount Sinai to receive the Torah. He remained there for forty days and nights. The people feared that their leader had perished upon the mountain. They were seized by panic. In their state of dismay, a movement arose to create a new, more durable leader – an idol that would lead them. The product of this initiative was the golden calf. It was created by Aharon and then worshiped by a segment of the nation.

---

[51] There is an interesting story that reflects this issue. Rav Chaim Volozhin decided that before moving forward with the establishment of the Volozhin Yeshiva he must consult with and secure the blessing of his rebbe, the Gaon of Vilna. He made the trip from Volozhin to Vilna and with great enthusiasm and excitement he presented his plan and vision to his rebbe. The Gaon did not approve the project and suggested that Rav Chaim postpone the ambitious endeavor for the time-being.

Some years later, Rav Chaim again approached his teacher and systematically and calmly argued for the establishment of the yeshiva. This time, the Goan gave his immediate approval. Rav Chaim was pleased to receive his teacher's blessing but perplexed by the change in his position. He asked the Goan to explain why he now immediately approved of the same project he had dismissed a few years earlier.

The Goan responded that he rejected the initial proposal because of the intense excitement that Rav Chaim exhibited in that presentation. Rav Chaim's deep personal identification with the project was obvious. This gave the Goan reason to suspect that Rav Chaim might not have carefully and objectively evaluated his initiative but instead, was driven by personal motivations. In contrast, the second presentation was calm and systematic. When the Goan observed that Rav Chaim was now able to evaluate the initiative in an objective and detached manner, he felt confident in his student's assessment of the project and gave it his blessing.

Hashem threatened to destroy Bnai Yisrael in response to this infidelity. Moshe interceded and succeeded in postponing Hashem's immediate punishment of his people. Moshe descended from the mountain, destroyed the *egel*, rebuked the nation, and punished the most egregious of the sinners. Then, Moshe again ascended the mountain to seek Hashem's forgiveness for the nation. In the above passage, Moshe acknowledges and recounts the sin. The people made a god of gold. Why did Moshe note that their idol was made of gold?

In his comments on this passage, Rashi explains that Moshe was communicating an implicit message to Hashem. The idol the people fashioned was made of gold. From where did a company of escaped slaves secure this gold? Moshe is reminding Hashem that He had commanded the people to take with them the wealth of Egypt as they emerged from bondage. Their possession of the great wealth He provided led them to create the golden calf.

Rashi's comments are difficult to understand. He seems to contend that the wealth with which Hashem blessed Bnai Yisrael was responsible for their retreat into idolatry. How did their wealth lead to, or moderate, their responsibility for creating and worshiping an idol? It is true that the gold that they used was provided by Hashem. But is Moshe suggesting that if the people had not had this gold they would not have made their idol? This is not a credible contention. Certainly, they would have used some other material that was at hand to create their idol! In order to understand Moshe's argument, we must consider the capacities and limitations of human imagination.

And Hashem commanded us to observe all of these laws in order to fear Hashem our L-rd for our benefit all of the days and to give us life as on this day. (Devarim 6:24)

The impossibility of envisioning the afterlife

According to our Torah, the ultimate reward for observance of the Torah is *olam ha'bah* – the afterlife. This is eternal existence of the immortal human soul after the demise of the mortal body. Remarkably, the afterlife is not clearly discussed in the Torah. When it is noted in the Torah, it is referred to vaguely, as in the above passage. In the passage, Moshe tells the people that their observance of the commandments will be rewarded "all of the days." Commenting on the passage, Chizkuni suggests that this phrase refers to our reward in the afterlife. Instead of explicitly discussing the afterlife, the Torah promises us reward in the material world for our faithful observance of the Torah. Why is the afterlife not clearly discussed and identified as the ultimate reward for observance?

Maimonides explains in the introduction to his commentary on the tenth chapter of Tractate Sanhedrin that we do not have the capacity to grasp or appreciate the afterlife. It is beyond the capacity of our imaginations. He explains that because we are material creatures our physicality prevents us from conceiving and imagining the nature of an existence divorced from physical expression. He provides a wonderful analogy to the obstacle we encounter when we attempt to imagine the afterlife. Consider a person who was born sightless. Can one explain to this person the meaning of color? It is impossible! We describe to a person something he or she has not experienced by comparing the new object to others that the person has experienced. But something that is unlike anything else in a person's inventory of experiences cannot be explained to that person. Just as the sightless person cannot conceive color, we cannot truly imagine a completely non-material existence.

Chizkuni and others draw upon Miamonindes' comments to explain the Torah's relative neglect of the topic of *olam ha'bah*. Chizkuni continues his comments on the above passage and notes that the Torah focuses on those rewards that are the most powerful motivators. It selects rewards which appeal to our imaginations and inspire us to observe the commandments. *Olam ha'bah* presented truthfully and frankly will not be a motivator for most individuals. It cannot be imagined and appreciated. Therefore, it is given little attention in the Torah.

This discussion of the Torah's treatment of *olam ha'bah* illustrates that the imagination is not boundless. It has absolute limits. These limits constitute boundaries that cannot be passed through. In addition to this absolute limitation, imagination sometimes struggles to grasp concepts that are at the edges of these boundaries. These concepts are accessible but not readily, and not at all times.

And Hashem spoke to you from within the conflagration. You heard the sound of words but you did not see any image– only a voice. (Devarim 4:12)

The struggle to relate to Hashem as a non-corporeal being

In the above passage Moshe reminds Bnai Yisrael of their experience at Sinai. He describes their encounter with Hashem. They heard a voice; they saw no form or image. Moshe understands that our concept of Hashem challenges our imagination. We conceive of Hashem as a non-material being. He is divorced from any material aspect. Yet, we know Him through our encounter with His actions in our material world. He redeemed us from bondage, destroyed our oppressors; we heard His commandments. One's imagination, challenged by the demand of conceiving of such a being, stretched to its limits, may seek to retreat from the challenge. One may anthropomorphize Hashem – give Him physical form or attributes so that one can more easily imagine Him. Moshe warns the people to not surrender or this temptation, to recall the words that they heard at Sinai – disembodied from any material form.

To this point, we have discovered that imagination has absolute limits. We have also recognized that even concepts within these limits can be difficult to grasp and integrate into our personal reality. Let's take one more step in our exploration of the imagination.

The impact of lifestyle on the capacity to imagine the non-corporeal

In essence, imagination gives us the capacity to envision that which we cannot observe or may not even be observable. It requires one to embrace that which is not here and now – that which is not concrete. Because imagination is a capacity to grasp, manipulate, and integrate abstractions, the vitality of one's imagination is sensitive to one's attachment to material possessions and endeavors. Why is this so? Imagination requires one to rise above the material, concrete reality. If one's whole being is devoted to living in that concrete reality, the challenge of imagining abstractions that are not part of that reality is daunting. In other words, our capacity to imagine and to embrace abstractions is proportionate to our capacity to rise above the concrete reality that surrounds us. The more one is immersed in the corporeal, the more difficult it is to rise above it.

Wealth stunted Bnai Yisrael's capacity to relate to Hashem

Now that we have studied the workings of imagination, we can return to Rashi's comments. He remarked that the great wealth and the gold that the Jewish people brought with them into the wilderness contributed to creating and worshiping the *egel*. Hashem gave them this wealth. Therefore, He shares responsibility for the sins engendered by these riches. We can now understand how wealth undermined Bnai Yisrael and encouraged Bnai Yisrael's retreat into idolatry.

Moshe does not mean that without this gold Bnai Yisrael would not have had the materials to create an idol. As noted above, they could easily have created some other idol. They could have carved an idol from stone hewn from the mountain. Moshe is saying that Bnai Yisrael responded to their crisis with an idol because of the destructive impact of their wealth. How did wealth corrupt Bnai Yisrael?

In order to answer this question, let us consider Bnai Yisrael's behavior. Why was Bnai Yisrael overcome with panic when they believed Moshe had been taken? Moshe was flesh and blood. He was corporeal. One did not need to stretch one's imagination to relate to Moshe and to integrate him into perceptual reality. But when the people concluded that Moshe had perished on the mountain, they were suddenly deprived of this corporeal manifestation of Hashem's presence and influence. They replaced Moshe with an idol.

Rashi is explaining that the decision to resort to an idol as a replacement for Moshe represents a failure of the imagination. Seeking a representation of the Divine presence through the fabrication of a golden calf evidences a weakness in the people's capacity to relate to a non-corporeal reality. Rashi is explaining that this stunting of the imagination and the people's incapacity to embrace the non-corporeal was a result of their newfound wealth.

The people were enraptured by their riches. They had been transformed from destitute slaves into individuals of great wealth and stature. But this joy represented an immersion in the concrete, corporeal world. And this world became their only reality. Wealth became an emotional and intellectual entrapment from which they could not escape. Their fascination with their wealth drew then into and tied them to the material reality. And as a result, their capacity to imagine and embrace the reality of the non-corporeal was undermined. They could not relate to a Divine presence without a material representation. They replaced Moshe with the *egel*.

We think of sharing our wealth as an act of self-sacrifice. We sacrifice in response to our compassion for others. Rashi's comments challenge this perspective. Our attachment to our wealth expresses a self-deception. Our true self – our spiritual souls – only pass through this material world on the journey to eternity. More real than the concrete reality with which we interact with our senses, is the spiritual values and ideals that we embrace with our minds and souls. What's more real; the gold coin on the table or the ideals of the Torah? Frankly, the coin is much easier to embrace as real. Appreciating that the coin is far less significant or real than the spiritual ideal of the Torah takes imagination. Developing and maintaining that imagination requires moderating our attitude toward the corporeal reality. We practice this moderation when we give of our wealth – when we use it to support spiritual goals.

Our decision to give charity and to share our blessings is an expression of compassion toward others. It is also an act of compassion toward our own souls – toward our true selves. We should feel profound sadness for those who cannot give. These individuals are trapped by their possessions. They believe in a delusion – that they are the master of these possessions. But they are manipulated by their riches. Their souls are entrapped; they live only in the temporal.

We do not want to be one of these woeful individuals. Our participation in charity saves us; it transforms us. It provides us with the opportunity to rise above the reality of the corporeal and to embrace values that are eternal and truly real!

"And I will remove My hand and you will see My back. And My face will not be seen." (Shemot 33:23)

Moshe ascends Mount Sinai. He asks the Almighty to reveal to him His essential nature. Hashem responds that a material being is not capable of grasping the Divine essence. However, Hashem agrees to allow Moshe to see His back. This apparently means that although we cannot attain an absolute understanding of the Almighty, we are capable of some lower level of comprehension. This more mundane understanding is represented as seeing the Almighty's back.

The Talmud in Tractate Berachot comments on this episode.[52] The Talmud explains that Moshe saw the knot of the teffillin worn by the Almighty on His head. These comments present two obvious difficulties. First, Hashem is not physical. He cannot be conceived as a being wearing teffillin. Second, Maimonides explains that Moshe achieved the highest possible understanding of the Almighty. It did not involve any corporeal element.[53] It is possible that a less perfect individual might attribute some physicality to the Almighty. But how could our Sages claim that Moshe perceived Hashem wearing teffillin?

Rashi, in his commentary on the Talmud, provides some direction in interpreting the Sages' comments. He refers us to a previous text. In this text the Talmud explains that Hashem wears teffillin.[54] The Talmud also deals with the contents of the Almighty's teffillin. The Talmud explains that these teffillin contain the passage, "Who is like Your nation Israel? They are a singular people in the land".[55] This text is also difficult to understand. However, it provides an essential element needed to explain Moshe's vision. In order to appreciate the message of the Talmud, we must place Moshe's vision in context.

Bnai Yisrael had committed the sin of creating and worshiping the egel – the golden calf. This sin altered the relationship between the Almighty and His nation. Moshe wished to reestablish the intimate connection between Hashem and Bnai Yisrael. In this context, Moshe asked Hashem for a revelation of His nature. The Almighty responded by showing Moshe the knot of His teffillin. This vision gave Moshe the knowledge he needed. With this new understanding, he was able to reestablish the relationship damaged by the sin of the egel. In this context, let us reconsider the comments of the Talmud. The Sages explain that the Almighty's teffillin contain a passage that affirm the unique relationship between the Almighty and Bnai Yisrael. In other words, the teffillin represent the bond between Hashem and His people. Moshe could not see the front of Hashem. He could not fully understand the nature of Hashem. He also could not view the front of Hashem's teffillin. This means that the relationship between the Almighty and Bnai Yisrael is a consequence of the Divine essence. Moshe's understanding of the relationship was necessarily limited. Without full understanding of Hashem's nature, he could not fully grasp the relationship. However, he could see the knot of the teffillin. He was able to study the relationship as an emanation or effect of the Divine essence. An analogy will help illustrate this concept.

---

[52] Mesechet Berachot 7a.
[53] Rabbaynu Moshe ben Maimon (Rambam) Moreh Nevuchim, volume 1, chapter 5.
[54] Mesechet Berachot 6a.
[55] Divrai HaYamim I, 17:21.

Let us compare the Almighty to fire. When the ancient human discovered fire, this unsophisticated individual could not understand the scientific nature of combustion. However, our ancestors could study the effect of fire and heat on different substances. The study of these phenomena did not require a complete comprehension of fire itself. Similarly, Moshe could not understand the ultimate nature of the Almighty. Yet, he could contemplate the relationship between the Almighty and Bnai Yisrael. This understanding enabled Moshe to appeal properly to Hashem and beseech Him for forgiveness for His nation. We now understand that Moshe's vision did not involve any corporeal element. Our Sages are utilizing imagery to communicate an important message regarding Moshe's experience at Sinai.

> *"And when Moshe came before Hashen to speak with Him, he would remove the covering until he went out. And he would go out and speak to Bnai Yisrael telling them what had been commanded. And the nation saw that the skin of Moshe's face glowed. And Moshe would restore the covering over his face until he came to speak with Him." (Shemot 34:34-35)*

Moshe ascended Mount Sinai a final time. On this occasion he achieved a profound understanding of the Almighty and His ways. This knowledge is the most advanced understanding of the Almighty that can be acquired by a human being. The Torah explains that when Moshe descended from the mountain his face glowed. At first, Ahron and the people were afraid to approach Moshe. However, Moshe called to Ahron and Bnai Yisrael to approach him. He then spoke with Ahron, the leaders and the nation. Upon completion of this address, Moshe placed a covering over his face.[56] This covering hid the light that glowed from his face. Our passages explain the role of this covering. Whenever Moshe communicated with the Almighty he removed this covering. Most commentaries maintain that the covering remained removed while Moshe delivered Hashem's message to the people. After Moshe completed his presentation, he restored the covering. Moshe's face remained covered until he next communicated with Hashem.[57]

Gershonides seems to differ on the use of the covering.[58] According to his opinion, the covering was restored as soon as Moshe finished speaking with Hashem. When Moshe spoke with the people, his face was covered. The commentaries offer various interpretations of the glow and the covering. Most understand the Torah's account literally. Moshe's face actually beamed with light. The covering is also understood in the literal sense. However, Gershonides takes a different approach to explaining this narrative. He suggests that neither the beams of light or the covering should be interpreted literally. Instead, they are to be understood figuratively. In order to understand Gershonides' interpretation it is important to remember that he maintains that the covering was only removed during Moshe's communication with Hashem. During his address to Bnai Yisrael, the covering was restored. Gershonides begins by explaining that Moshe achieved the highest possible level of prophecy. He explains that Moshe's prophetic ability developed over time. At Sinai, Hashem revealed to Moshe the most profound truths a human being can grasp. This implies that Sinai represented the full maturation of Moshe as a prophet. He was at the zenith of his prophetic powers.

Moshe's advanced level of prophecy expressed itself in various ways. Maimonides outlines the differences between Moshe and other prophets in his Mishne Torah.[59] One of these

---

[56] Rabbaynu Shlomo ben Yitzchak (Rashi), Commentary on Sefer Shemot 34:33.

[57] See, for example, Rabbaynu Avraham ibn Ezra, Commentary on Sefer Shemot, 34:33.

[58] Rabbaynu Levi ben Gershon (Ralbag / Gershonides), Commentary on Sefer Shemot, (Mosad HaRav Kook, 1994), p 440.

differences is that other prophets can only receive prophecy after adequate preparation. The prophet must enter into an appropriate state. In this state the individual sheds all attachment with the material world. An inner peace and calm must also be reached. This is not an easily achieved state. The difficulty of attaining and maintaining this state limits the opportunity of the prophet to receive prophecy. Moshe could achieve prophecy at any time. He was always in the state requisite for prophecy. He possessed a super-human ability to detach himself from the material world and focus on the Almighty.[60] Gershonides asserts that this distinction can be expressed in an even more basic manner. Other prophets are basically focused on the material world. In order to achieve prophecy, they force themselves to refocus their orientation. Through tremendous effort, they shed their material orientation and focus on the spiritual. In contrast, Moshe ultimately altered his basic orientation. When Moshe descended from Sinai, he was no longer similar to other human beings or prophets. He was completely focused on the spiritual.[61] He was entirely detached from the material world. In other words, Moshe was innately focused on the spiritual.

We can now understand Gershonides' interpretation of Moshe's glow and his covering. Moshe descended from Sinai. He was no longer like other human beings. He was an essentially spiritual being. Ahron and the Bnai Yisrael sensed Moshe's complete detachment from the material world. The "glow" that emanated from Moshe was this super-human spiritual focus. Ahron and the nation reacted with awe. They could not approach Moshe. Neither could Moshe easily communicate with the material world and its inhabitants. This created a problem. Moshe was the Almighty's prophet. His responsibility was to deliver the Divine message to the people. Yet, a barrier now existed between Moshe and the nation. His very perfection, interfered with his relationship with Bnai Yisrael. The people were in awe of Moshe and could not approach him. Moshe, not longer related to the world he was commanded to instruct. In order for Moshe to communicate with the people, he was forced to reenter the material realm. For Moshe, this required an act of will. He was required to suspend some element of his spiritual orientation. This reorientation to the material is described as a covering. The covering symbolizes Moshe hiding his true nature. Moshe hid an element of his spiritual self in order to communicate with the nation.

"And Hashem passed before him and He proclaimed, "Hashem, Hashem Omnipotent, merciful and kind. He is slow to anger and is abundant in kindness and truth." (Shemot 34:6)

Our pasuk introduces one of the most profound prophecies revealed to Moshe. In this prophecy, Hashem reveals to Moshe His thirteen midot – attributes. Among these attributes is that Hashem is merciful and slow to anger.

This pasuk presents an apparent problem. One of the fundamental principles of the Torah is that Hashem is an absolute unity. Every day we declare our acceptance of this principle in the

---

[59] Rabbaynu Moshe ben Maimon (Rambam) Mishne Torah, Hilchot Yesodai HaTorah, chp. 7.
[60] Rabbaynu Moshe ben Maimon (Rambam) Mishne Torah, Hilchot Yesodai HaTorah, 7:4-6
[61] Rabbaynu Levi ben Gershon (Ralbag / Gershonides), Commentary on Sefer Shemot, (Mosad HaRav Kook, 1994), p 440.

Shema. We say that Hashem is one. This does not merely mean that there is only one G-d. This statement means that Hashem is an absolute unity. He has no parts.

It is inadequate to merely enunciate this principle. This is a basic principle of our Torah. We cannot claim affinity to this truth without understanding its meaning. We must appreciate the meaning of Hashem's absolute unity.

Maimonides discusses the meaning of this unity in his commentary on the Mishne. He explains that Hashem's unity is unique. There is no other example of absolute unity. He cannot be compared to a single entity that is a compound. A compound has components or elements that join to create the whole. He cannot be compared to an elemental unit. This unit has dimensions or aspects. Imagine a block of pure metal. The block has a back and front.[62] In his Mishne Torah, Maimonides adds that this concept of unity precludes attribution of any characteristic to the Almighty. The attribution of any characteristic compromises the absolute unity of Hashem. This is because Hahsem would possess the characteristic. By definition, a distinction would exist between Hashem and the characteristic He possesses. This is impossible.[63]

An example will help illustrate the problem. Let us assume that a certain individual – Reuven – is merciful. This means that Reuven possesses the characteristic of mercy. Reuven is not mercy. Mercy is a characteristic that Reuven possesses. Reuven and the characteristic are separate. In the same sense, it seems impossible to ascribe the characteristic of mercy to Hashem and simultaneously declare His absolute unity!

We can now identify the problem presented by our passage and the thirteen midot. The term midot is translated as characteristics. How can the Torah attribute characteristics to the Almighty? How can the Torah describe Hashem as merciful or slow to anger? This contradicts the assertion that the Almighty is an absolute unity.

Our Sages provide a solution to this problem. Maimonides, in his Moreh Nevuchim, discusses the solution thoroughly. He explains that it is not the Torah's intent to ascribe actual attributes or characteristics to the Almighty. Hashem is an absolute unity. He does not posses attributes or characteristics. Instead, the Torah is describing the various patterns of behavior that we observe.[64] A simple example will illustrate this concept. Imagine a flame. A chip of ice is passed before the flame and it melts. A piece of thin paper is passed before the flame and it ignites. A hand hovers over the flame and it senses heat or even pain. These various outcomes are not the consequence of different characteristics of the flame. Instead, the effect of the single flame varies. The material that is passed before the flame determines the effect. In a similar sense, the Almighty is a single absolute unity. However, under various circumstances, different patterns of action emerge from this entity.[65] The Torah is describing these patterns of behavior. In other words, the Torah is describing our perceptions. The Torah is not defining the nature of Hashem.

It is important to note that there is an alternative approach to resolving the contradiction between absolute unity and characteristics. One might be tempted to resolve this problem through asserting that Hashem is an absolute unity but, in some unfathomable manner, He

---

[62] R' Moshe ben Maimon (Rambam) *Commentary on the Mishne*, Mesechet Sanhedrin, 10:1.
[63] Rabbaynu Moshe ben Maimon (Rambam) *Mishne Torah*, Hilchot Yesodai HaTorah 1:7.
[64] Rabbaynu Moshe ben Maimon (Rambam) *Moreh Nevuchim*, volume 1, chapter 54.
[65] Illustration provided by Rav Yisroel Chait.

possesses attributes. Nachmanides deals with this issue. He explains that this approach is fundamentally flawed. It is not acceptable. We are required to do more than pronounce Hashem's unity. We must adopt this conviction. It is impossible for a person to actually accept the concept of absolute unity and simultaneously assert that Hashem has characteristics. Such a paradoxical set of convictions is meaningless. The concept of unity is reduced to a meaningless phrase. Instead, we must understand the concept of unity and dismiss any attribution of characteristics as alien to this concept. Nachmanides succinctly states that one cannot affirm that which is not understood![66]

---

[66] Rabbaynu Moshe ben Nachman (Ramban), *Vikuach / Milchamot Hashem*, chps 105-107.

VaYakhel

And Moshe assembled all the congregation of Bnai Yisrael and he said to them: These are the things that Hashem commanded that they be done. (Shemot 35:1)

Responding to the Presence of Hashem

1. The *Mishcan* was a place for sacrifices

In Parshat Terumah and Parshat Tetzaveh Hashem commands Moshe to create the *Mishcan* – the Tabernacle. He communicates to Moshe the design of the *Mishcan* and of the garments for the priests and the *kohen gadol* – the high priest. In Parshat VaYakhel and Parshat Pekuday Moshe transmits the commandment and the specific instructions he received to Bnai Yisrael. The fabrication of the *Mishcan* and the garments is described. Parshat Pekuday concludes with a description of the *Mishcan*'s assembly.

Sefer VaYikra begins with the dedication of the *Mishcan* and the sacrifices that were to be offered on its altars. The Torah's presentation of the *Mishcan* suggests that its purpose was to serve as a place for the offering of sacrifices. Fixed daily sacrifices were to be offered in the morning and afternoon. Additional sacrifices were to be offered on festivals. Individuals also offered personal sacrifices as expressions of thanks or as part of the process of atonement.

After Bnai Yisrael conquered and settled the Land of Israel, the *Mishcan* continued to serve as the spiritual center of the nation. Eventually, the *Mishcan* was destroyed. King Shlomo replaced the *Mishcan* with the *Bait HaMikdash* – the Sacred Temple. The *Bait HaMikdash* became the permanent sanctuary of Bnai Yisrael and the center of national spiritual life.

> *Yet have respect unto the prayer of your servant, and to his supplication, O LORD my God, to hearken unto the cry and to the prayer, which Your servant prays before You today. That Your eyes may be open toward this house night and day, even toward the place of which you have said, "My name shall be there". That You may hearken unto the prayer which Your servant shall make toward this place. (Sefer Melachim I 8:28-29)*

2. The *Bait HaMikdash* as a place of prayer

In its dedication, King Shlomo spoke to the nation about the function of the *Bait HaMikdash*. We would expect him to describe the Temple as a place for the offering of the nation's sacrifices. However, King Shlomo makes no mention of the sacrifices offered in the *Bait HaMikdash*. Instead, he describes the Temple as a place of prayer. Why does King Shlomo not expound upon the Temple's sacrifices? Why does he instead describe the *Bait HaMikdash* as a place of prayer? In order to resolve this discrepancy between these two treatments of the *Mishcan* and *Bait HaMikdash* another incident must be reviewed.

> *And Moshe took the tent and pitched it outside of the camp, far off from the camp; and he called it the Tent of Meeting. And it came to pass, that everyone who sought Hashem went out unto the Tent of Meeting, which was outside of the camp. And it was that when Moshe went out unto the tent, all the people rose up, and stood, every man at his tent door, and looked after Moshe, until he came into the tent. And it was that when Moshe entered into the tent, the pillar of cloud descended, and stood at the door of the tent; and Hashem spoke with Moshe. (Shemot 33:7-9)*

3. Hashem's estrangement from Bnai Yisrael

The passages above describe events that took place after Bnai Yisrael created and worshiped the *egel* – the golden calf. Moshe succeeded in his intervention with Hashem and He did not destroy the people for their terrible sin. However, the sin did have consequences. Moshe took a tent and he removed it from the camp. It seems from the narrative that in this tent Moshe received his prophecies. When Moshe sought prophecy, he traveled to this tent – now located far from the people's encampment. Moshe would stand at the tent and a cloud would descend. This cloud expressed the influence of Hashem[1] and communicated that Moshe was prophesying.

What was Moshe's objective in removing this tent and relocating it from the nation's encampment? Rashbam explains that the tent's removal communicated Hashem's estrangement from the people. Hashem would not communicate with Moshe while he was in the camp. He could only receive prophecy by removing himself from the camp and traveling to the distant tent.[2]

Then the cloud covered the Tent of Meeting, and the glory of Hashem filled the Tabernacle. And Moshe was not able to enter into the Tent of Meeting, because the cloud abode thereon, and the glory of Hashem filled the Tabernacle. (Shemot 40:34-35)

4. The establishment of the *Mishcan* and Hashem's return to the camp

Parshat Pekuday concludes with a description of the assembly of the *Mishcan*. The *Mishcan* was assembled within the midst of the camp. The above passages describe the cloud that expressed the Divine presence descending upon the *Mishcan*. Moshe would no longer travel to a tent far outside of the camp in order to communicate with Hashem. Instead, he would seek the *Mishcan* – located in the center of the camp. There, he would encounter the presence of Hashem and receive prophecy.

And let them make Me a sanctuary, that I may dwell among them. (Shemot 25:8)

5. The *Mishcan* was designed as a place for expression of Hashem's presence

The return of Hashem's presence within the midst of the camp of Bnai Yisrael fulfilled the objective of the *Mishcan*. This objective was described to Moshe when Hashem communicated to him the commandment to create the Tabernacle. He told Moshe that the nation should create the Tabernacle so that Hashem might dwell within the nation. It is in this context that the Torah so strongly associates the *Mishcan* with sacrificial service.

We can now understand the Torah's emphasis upon the sacrifices offered in the *Mishcan*. The *Mishcan* was designed as a place that expressed the Divine presence. The sacrifices offered to Hashem in the *Mishcan* contributed to creating a place in which the Divine influence was evident. The Torah is asserting that the Temple in which Hashem's presence is expressed must feature sacrificial service.

Personal sacrifices were also brought to the *Mishcan*. This was a consequence of Hashem's presence within the *Mishcan*. No other place could be more fit for offering sacrifices than this unique place in which the presence of Hashem was manifested.

---

[1] Throughout this presentation, references are made to the presence of Hashem. These are not intended to be understood in their literal sense. Hashem in not associated with space or place. However, in the *Mishcan* and the *Bait HaMikdash* His influence was more clearly expressed or evidenced.

[2] Rabbaynu Shemuel ben Meir (Rashbam) *Commentary on Sefer Shemot* 33:7.

Nonetheless, King Shlomo did not focus on the sacrifices offered in the *Bait HaMikdash*. He described the prayers that would be offered in the Temple. Why did King Shlomo focus on these prayers?

6. Responding to the presence of Hashem

Maimonides' Sefer HaMItzvot – Book of Commandments – provides a listing and a brief description of each of the 613 commandments. He first lists and describes the positive commandments and then he lists and describes the negative commandments. Maimonides' overall organizational scheme is not easily identified. However, it seems that his order communicates connections between individual commandments and sets of commandments. He begins his positive commandments with the obligation to accept the existence of Hashem. The second commandment is to accept Hashem's oneness or unity. The third and forth commandments are to love and fear Hashem. The fifth positive commandment is to worship Hashem. Maimonides understands this reference to worship as a directive to engage in prayer. Why does Maimonides give the commandment to pray such prominence in his compilation of the Torah's commandments?

It seems that Maimonides maintains that prayer is our response to awareness of Hashem. We acknowledge His existence and unity. This leads to our love and fear of Him. This love and fear achieves expression in the prayer that it inspires.

Let us return to King Shlomo's treatment of the *Bait HaMikdash*. It seems that King Shlomo understood that sacrifices are crucial in establishing a place for expression of the presence of Hashem. However, he was concerned with a different issue. Once the presence of Hashem is among us, how should we respond? King Shlomo communicated to the people that we respond with prayer. In other words, sacrifices are essential in creating a place in which the presence of Hashem is expressed. Prayers are the activity in which we engage in response to that presence. King Shlomo was not instructing the people in how to create a house for Hashem. He was teaching them what to do with that house.

Six days work should be performed and the seventh day should be sacred for you as a sabbatical day to Hashem. Anyone who performs work on it should die. (Shemot 35:2)

And Moshe said to all the congregation of Bnai Yisrael, "This is the thing that Hashem has commanded you saying: Take from yourselves an offering to Hashem. Every person inspired by his heart should bring the offering of Hashem – gold, silver, and copper." (Shemot 35:4-5)

The Relationship between the Tabernacle and Shabbat

1. Two lessons derived from the association of the Mishcan with Shabbat

The Parshiyot of Vayakhel and Pekudai conclude the Torah's discussion of the fabrication of the Mishcan – the Tabernacle. Parshat VaYakhel opens with a reiteration of the commandment to observe Shabbat. Shabbat is to be a day of rest. Work is not to be performed on that day. After a brief discussion of Shabbat, the Torah returns to its discussion of the fabrication of the Mishcan. Why is this discussion of Shabbat inserted into the narrative concerning the creation of the Mishcan? Rashi comments, based upon the Talmud and Midrash, that the Torah specifically reiterates the directive to observe Shabbat at this juncture in order to communicate an important message regarding the creation of the Mishcan. The tasks involved in the manufacturing of the Mishcan cannot be performed on Shabbat.[3] In other words, despite the sanctity of the Mishcan, the imperative of its creation does not supersede Shabbat.

The Talmud derives another principle from the insertion of the Shabbat directive into the narrative of the Mishcan. In order to understand this second principle a brief introduction is required. The directive to observe Shabbat is mentioned in the Torah in twelve locations.[4] The most basic element of Shabbat observance is to rest and not perform melachah – loosely translated as "work". However, despite the Torah's frequent reference to Shabbat and its key element, the Torah does not provide a definition of the term melachah. In other words, the Torah does not precisely define what specific activities are included within the perimeters of melachah.

The Sages explain that the Torah alludes to the definition of melachah through juxtaposing the commandment to observe Shabbat with the narrative of the Mishcan. The message of the juxtaposition is that the process of creating the Mishcan serves as the model from which the perimeters of melachah are derived. This means that the basic forms of melachah are derived from the Mishcan's fabrication process. This process included thirty-nine significant components. These thirty-nine activities constitute the basic forms of melachah. One is to abstain from these activities on Shabbat. In practice, halachah treats each of these thirty-nine activities as the heading of a general category of materially creative activity. Each category contains other subsidiary activities that are akin to the heading. However, the important point is that the perimeters of melachah are derived from the manufacture of the Mishcan. This suggests an important question. Why does the Mishcan provide the model for defining melachah?

Because Hashem made the heavens, the earth, the sea, and all that is in them in six days and He rested on the seventh. Therefore, He blessed the Shabbat day and sanctified it. (Shemot 20:11)

And you should remember that you were a slave in the Land of Egypt and Hashem, your G-d, took you forth from there with a mighty hand and an outstretched arm. Therefore, Hashem, your G-d, commanded you to observe the Shabbat day. (Devarim 5:15)

2. Two rationales for Shabbbat

In order to fully appreciate this problem, the rationale for Shabbat must be considered. The Torah provides two rationales for the observance of Shabbat. The first is that Hashem created the universe in six days and "rested" on the seventh day. We observe Shabbat to recall the creation and in order to acknowledge that Hashem is the creator and master of the universe. The second rationale is that Shabbat reminds us that we were slaves in Egypt and that Hashem redeemed us from bondage. Through our obedience to His command to observe Shabbat, we acknowledge that we were redeemed in order to submit to the Divine will. We would expect that melachah should be defined in some manner that is relevant to one or both of these two rationales.

In fact, our commentators were sensitive to this issue. Tosefot quotes the Midrash as suggesting that the thirty-nine major forms of melachah do correspond with the various forms of intense labor that the Egyptians imposed upon Bnai Yisrael.[5]

---

[3] Rabbaynu Shlomo ben Yitzchak (Rashi), Commentary on Sefer Shemot 35:2.
[4] Rav Avraham of Sochetshav, Eglai Tal, p 1.
[5] Tosefot, Mesechet Pesachim 117b.

Rav Eliyahu – the Gaon of Vilna identified an ancient source that relates the thirty-nine melachot (plural of melachah) with the activities in which Hashem engaged in the creation of the universe. The source is a liturgical poem that some Ashkenzic communities insert into the morning Amidah on Shabbat Shekalim.[6] The poem opens with a lengthy list of verbs – exactly thirty-nine. The Goan suggested that this list of verbs is intended to correspond with the thirty-nine activities in which Hashem engaged in creating the universe. Upon completion of creation, He rested from these activities and therefore, we are required to abstain from the thirty-nine melachot of Shabbat.[7]

In short, our commentators searched for some relationship between the thirty-nine melachot and the rationales provided by the Torah for Shabbat. However, it is clear from the Talmud that the actual specific identity of the melachot is not derived from either of these rationales but from the construction of the Mishcan.

And the one who offered his sacrifice on the first day was Nachshon the son of Aminadav of the tribe of Yehudah. (BeMidbar 7:12)

And G-d called the light day and the dark He called night. And it was evening and morning (constituting) one day. (Beresheit 1:5)

3. The completion of the Mishcan as an element of creation

Upon the completion of the Mishcan and its dedication, an inauguration period followed. On each day of this inauguration the leader of one of the twelve tribes provided a set of offerings. The above passage explains that the first day was assigned to the leader of the tribe of Yehudah – Nachshon the son of Aminadav. The Sages note an anomaly in the Hebrew wording of passage. The passage could have identified the first day as yom rishon. Instead, the passage identifies the day as yom ha'rishon. The addition of the "ha" prefix suggests that the first day of the inauguration corresponded with a date that had some other pre-existing significance. What was this preexisting significance?

The Sages explain that there is another related anomaly in the Torah's description of a "first day." In its description of the six days of the creation, all days after the first are referred to by an ordinal number. In other words, the Torah refers to the second, third, fourth, fifth and sixth day of creation. For some reason the first day is not described in this way. The Torah calls this day "one day" not the first day. The Sages explain that the Torah intends to communicate an important message by using the cardinal number one in reference to this day. The message is that the day was deficient and that the deficiency of this day persisted throughout the days and ages that followed.

What was the deficiency initiated at the very beginning of creation? The Sages explain that there did not yet exist any nation or society in which Hashem could dwell.[8] This deficiency

---

[6] Shabbat Shekalim is the Shabbat on which the Parshat Shekalim is read from the Torah. Parshat Shekalim is one of four special Torah readings that are added to the Shabbat reading in the weeks leading up to Pesach.

[7] Rav Aryeh Lev Gordon, Etz Yosef – Commentary on Siddur Otzer HaTeffilot, vol 2, p154.

[8] The term "dwell" is not to be understood literally. Hashem is not material and does not dwell in material space. The idea expressed by the description of Hashem dwelling among Bnai Yisrael is that He makes His providence evident. The reality of this providence is so intense and impressive

was finally addressed with the establishment of the Mishcan. The Mishcan became His abode or the symbol of His Divine providential influence.

For this reason the Torah refers to the first day of the inauguration as yom ha'rishon. This was the true first day of creation. In other words, creation had finally overcome its deficiency and now the created universe could truly have meaning and significance. This first day was the replacement for, or the fulfillment of the very first day of creation.

The Sages are communicating a profound message through their comments. The universe's highest and only meaningful function is as an expression of Hashem's will. Only when His existence and providence are evident and palpable does the universe achieve meaning and true significance. The establishment of the Mishcan represented a great achievement in the development of humanity and the universe. For the first time, Hashem made His presence or influence tangibly evident within humanity on an ongoing basis.

Before this point, the Patriarchs observe the presence of Hashem in the natural world. On occasion, Hashem manifested His providence through minor miracles or even wonders. However, all demonstrations of Hashem's existence and influence were either sporadic – as in the case of miracles – or only subtle – as in the case of nature's revelation of Hashem as its designer and sustainer. The Mishcan changed this. Now, Hashem's providential presence was evident and incorporated into the very structure of the nation. The nation encamped around the Mishcan. Hashem's cloud was present. His flame descended from the heavens and consumed the daily sacrifices. He communicated with Moshe through a voice that he perceived as emanating from between the cherubs of the Ark Cover. Before, Hashem was like a relative living far away who made occasional visits. Now, He was the center of the household. This relationship between Hashem and humanity represents the highest achievement of humankind and the most meaningful outcome of creation.

Now, the relationship between the melachot and the Mishcan can be understood. The melachot are derived from the Mishcan in order to communicate to us that the establishment of the Mishcan was the completion of creation. The universe fashioned and formed in the first six days was deficient of meaning and purpose. This creation of the Mishcan completed the creation process. Therefore, the activities that were significant components in the process of the Mishcan's construction are truly the highest expression of creation. Shabbat recalls creation of the universe. We observe Shabbat and remind ourselves of His six days of creation followed by the seventh day of rest by imitating him. On the seventh day – our Shabbat – we too refrain from those activities that were the components of humanity's highest creative expression.

You should not kindle a fire in any of your dwellings on the Shabbat. (Shemot 35:3)

The Prohibition against Melachah on Shabbat and Yom Tov

This pasuk tells us that one may not kindle a fire on Shabbat. In other words, this pasuk informs us that creating fire – havarah – is one of the thirty-nine forms of melachah – creative work – prohibited on Shabbat. It is odd that the Torah finds it necessary to specify this melachah. The thirty-nine melachot are not enumerated in the Torah. Instead, they are derived from the Mishcan – the Tabernacle. Those functions that were fundamental to the construction of the

---

that the people have a sense of His presence in their midst.

Mishcan are included among the melachot. Havarah is one of these functions. Therefore, it seems reasonable that the kindling of fire should be one of the melachot. We should not need a special passage to inform us that havarah is a melachah. Why does the Torah specifically prohibit this melachah?

The commentaries offer a number of responses to this question. Rabbaynu Ovadia Sforno suggests that havarah lacks one of the basic requirements necessary for an activity to be defined as a melachah. All melachot are creative activities. For example, the melachah of writing results in written letters. The melachah of sewing produces stitches. Kindling a flame is fundamentally destructive. The fuel is burned and consumed by the fire. It is not at all obvious that havarah should be included among the melachot. Therefore, the Torah specifies that creating fire is melachah.[9]

Nachmanides offers a different explanation for our pasuk. In order to understand his comments, some background is required. Shabbat is not the only occasion on which melachah is prohibited. It is also prohibited to perform melachah on Yom Tov – a festival. However, the prohibition on Yom Tov does not include all of the thirty-nine melachot. Those melachot that are related to ochel nefesh – those melachot that provide personal pleasure – are permitted. For example, it is permitted to cook on Yom Tov. This is because food provides personal enjoyment. Havarah is permitted on Yom Tov. This activity also is performed for the purpose of personal pleasure and is considered a melachah of ochel nefesh. Why are melachot of ochel nefesh permitted on Yom Tov? One of the fundamental differences between Shabbat and Yom Tov is that the observance of Yom Tov includes a requirement simchah – happiness. In order to enable us to achieve this state of simchah, the melachot of ochel nefesh are permitted. The observance of Shabbat does not include an obligation of simchah. Nachmanides explains that our passage tells us that kindling fire is prohibited on Shabbat. This pronouncement teaches that the prohibition of melachah on Shabbat differs from the Yom Tov prohibition. On Shabbat, all thirty-nine melachot are prohibited. Even the melachot of ochel nefesh are included in the Shabbat prohibition.

Nachmanides further explains that it is not obvious that melachot of ochel nefesh should be included in the prohibition against melachah on Shabbat. Although the obligation of simchah does not extend to Shabbat, we are obligated in oneg – experiencing joy – on Shabbat. It is reasonable to assume that this obligation of oneg on Shabbat has a similar impact as the obligation of simchah on Yom Tov. We would expect the obligation of oneg to dictate that melachot of ochel nefesh should be permitted on Shabbat. This is the lesson of our passage. Despite the obligation of oneg on Shabbat, all thirty-nine melachot are prohibited – even those of ochel nefesh.[10]

Nachmanides does not discuss one important question. As explained above, the obligation of oneg on Shabbat is similar to the requirement of simchah on Yom Tov. Because of the obligation of simchah, those melachot related to ochel nefesh are not prohibited on Yom Tov. Why does not the obligation of oneg on Shabbat have the same impact? Why are the melachot of ochel nefesh prohibited on Shabbat?

---

[9] Rabbaynu Ovadia Sforno, *Commentary on Sefer Shemot* 35:3.
[10] Rabbaynu Moshe ben Nachman (Ramban), *Commentary on Sefer Shemot* 35:3.

Before answering this question, it is important to note that the sanctity of Yom Tov and Shabbat is expressed through the prohibition against melachah. All occasions that the Torah describes as sacred are characterized by this prohibition. Therefore, the melachah prohibition is elemental to the definition and character of these days. Our question suggests that there is a basic difference between the obligation of simchah on Yom Tov and oneg on Shabbat. Simchah is not merely an activity in which we engage on Yom Tov. The obligation of simchah – like the melachah prohibition – is part of the definition or character of Yom Tov. Yom Tov is defined as a period of simchah. The requirement to refrain from the performance of melachah must be formulated in a manner that is consistent with and accommodates the simchah element of Yom Tov observance. Therefore, it is impossible for the Yom Tov prohibition of melachah to include the melachot of ochel nefesh. The inclusion of these melachot would be result in an inconsistency in the fundamental character of the Yom Tov.

Oneg is an obligation on Shabbat. However, it is not part of the basic definition or character of the day. In other words, oneg is an activity that we perform on Shabbat. It is not elemental to the character of Shabbat. Therefore, the prohibition on Shabbat of the melachot of ochel nefesh does not contradict the nature or definition of Shabbat. Instead, the obligation of oneg must be fulfilled in a manner that accommodates the sanctity and character to Shabbat. It must be fulfilled without performance of those melachot associated with ochel nefesh.

An analogy will help understand this distinction. A clothing designer is considering fabrics and colors for a suit under design. He envisions a man's suit that will be worn on formal occasions. He chooses a dark wool fabric for the basic design. He then decides he should bring another subtle color into the design and adds a maroon windowpane pattern. Notice that the basic color for the suit was selected based upon the function for which the suit was designed. The second color was selected to enhance the primary one. Similarly, oneg – like the maroon of the suit – is an enhancement; it is not elemental. Therefore, it is observed in a manner that is consistent with the melachah prohibition. In contrast, the obligation of simchah on Yom Tov is comparable to the designer's vision of the suit's use. This purpose is fundamental to the suit's design; its color is selected to accommodate this objective. So too, the Yom Tov melachah prohibition is designed to accommodate the requirement of simchah.

And Moshe spoke to the entire congregation of Bnai Yisrael saying: This is that which Hashem has commanded saying, "Take from you an offering to Hashem. Every person whose heart moves him should bring the offering to Hashem – gold, silver, and brass." (Shemot 35:4-5)

Details, Details, Details!

1. The Written and Oral Laws

The Torah includes 613 commandments. In many instances a commandment is presented by the Torah in a single passage. For example, we are commanded to recite *kiddush* with the entry of Shabbat. *Kiddush* is a short pronouncement that acknowledges the sanctity of Shabbat. This commandment is derived from a single passage in the Decalogue. The passage does not provide any details regarding the manner in which the commandment is to be preformed. It merely sets forth a very general instruction to "recall Shabbat". The content of the *kiddush* is not indicated by the Torah. Neither does the Torah reveal that *kiddush* should be recited with the entrance of Shabbat. From where are these essential details derived?

Many of the details are provided by the Oral Law. What is the Oral Law? Moshe received at Sinai the Written Law and the Oral Law. The Written Law composes the text of the Torah. Hashem dictated this text word-by-word to Moshe and he precisely recorded Hashem's communication. What is the relationship between the Written and Oral Laws?

Most of the *mitzvot* are presented in the Torah without detail or specific instructions. We are commanded to perform the commandment. Yet, the essential details required to execute the commandment are missing from the Torah's presentation. How, then, are we to fulfill our obligation?

The Written Law was given to Moshe with an oral commentary. This commentary is the Oral Law. The commentary provides the essential details needed to fulfill the *mitzvot*. In general, the Written Law recorded in the Torah provides a brief reference to each *mitzvah* and the Oral Law provides the essential details required to perform the commandment.

Moshe was directed to preserve the oral character of the Oral Law. He was forbidden from recording it. Instead, the Oral Law was to be a verbal tradition that would be transmitted throughout the generations from teacher to student. Eventually, the preservation of the Oral Law required that it too be given written form. The process of committing the Oral Law to writing began with the recording of the Mishne. This was followed by the recording of the Gemara.

In short, generally, the *mitzvot* of the Torah are only briefly referenced in the Torah. The details are provided by the Oral Law.

2. The detail in the Torah's treatment of the *mishcan*

The Torah's treatment of the *mishcan* – the tabernacle – is an exception to this format. The *mitzvah* to create the *mishcan* is outlined by the Torah in detail. In Parshat Terumah and Parshat Tetzaveh, the Torah describes the instructions given to Moshe. The design of the structure, its components, and the garments of the *kohen gadol* – the high priest – are all presented with elaborate detail. In Parshat VaYakhel the Torah describes the execution of these instructions. This narrative is introduced by the above passage. In other words, the Torah does not merely state that the *mishcan*, its components, and the vestments of the *kohen gadol* were created as prescribed. The Torah provides a detailed description of the fabrication and repeats many of the details that were previously enumerated. What is the message in this detailed and repetitive treatment of the *mitzvah*?

The impression that is communicated by all of this detail is that these details are enormously important. The message can be simply stated: The *mishcan* is all about attention to an elaborate system of details.

This raises a basic and important question. Why are all of these details necessary? We are commanded to create a *mishcan*. Why is it necessary for the Torah to dictate every detail of this commandment? Why could not the Torah command us to create the *mishcan* and leave to us the details of its design?

This issue is not limited to the commandment to build the *mishcan*. Many other commandments are also formulated with an astounding level of detail. An obvious example is the obligation to pray to Hashem. In order to fully perform this commandment, we must follow an elaborate system of prayer that is composed by the Torah and the Sages. One cannot perform this commandment by simply addressing Hashem and petitioning Him for one's needs and desires.

> *And he made the sacred oil of anointing and the pure incense – the product of a perfumer.*
> *(Shemot 37:29)*

3. The specific formulation of the incense offered in the *mishcan*

Two altars were located in the in the *mishcan*. The larger altar was located in the courtyard of the *mishcan*. This courtyard was an area in front of the entrance of the *mishcan* that was enclosed by curtains. This larger altar was used for almost all of the sacrifices. The second altar was much smaller. It was located inside the *mishcan*. This altar was used exclusively for burning incense.

The above passage states that the incense was formulated as required. These requirements are very detailed. The Torah provides some of the details of its formulation. The Oral Torah provides additional detail. The specific ingredients and their quantities are stipulated by *halachah*. No deviation from this precise formulation is acceptable.

Gershonides asks two important questions. What is special about this formulation? Why does the Torah prescribe this specific formulation and no other? His response to this question is fascinating. He explains that we should not assume that this specific formulation has some unique characteristic. He acknowledges that – in theory – the Torah could have specified an alternative set of ingredients and proportions. This alternative formulation would have been as satisfactory as the one that is specified by the Torah. The Torah's objective is simply to require a single specific appropriate formulation. The specific formulation that the Torah has selected for the incense may be completely arbitrary.

An example will help explain Gershonides' view. A few moments ago I opened the fruit bin in our refrigerator and selected an apple. The bin held a number of apples. I could have selected any one of them. Why did I select this apple and not one of the others? Well, I had no reason for selecting this apple from among the others. I wanted one apple. So, arbitrarily I selected one. Similarly, the Torah's objective was to establish a specific formulation for the incense. Its selection of one specific formulation from among all the possible appropriate formulations does not suggest that it has special meaning and significance.

4. A novel perspective on the importance of details

Of course, this leads to Gershonides' second question. Why did the Torah specify any formulation? Why did the Torah not leave to our discretion the specific formulation? Could not the Torah have instructed us to offer the incense and leave it to us to determine the formulation?

In response to this question, Gershonides offers an important observation and novel solution. He suggests that the more exalted an object or an activity, the more specific it is in its details. Before considering the application of this principle to *halachah*, let's consider an example from everyday life.

A person is considering two restaurants for his dinner. Both have varied menus and share some selections. One is an elegant restaurant. In the other restaurant the customers pick up their food from the counter and find a table in the seating area. Setting aside the differences in ambiance, how do these two establishments differ? The chef in the elegant restaurant considers each main course and selects a few appropriate side-dishes that enhance the patron's experience. He places the elements of the meal on the diner's plate with care. He gives consideration to the placement of each item and even to the combinations of colors. It is this attention to detail that distinguishes the two establishments.

Gershonides suggests that a similar dynamic exists in *halachah*. Every *mitzvah* is a sacred activity. We should expect it to be characterized by a degree of detail consistent with the exalted nature of a sacred activity. The attention to detail assures that the *mitzvah*-activity is performed in precisely the manner that fulfills the objective of the commandment.

Let us return to the example of prayer. The attention to detail assures that the activity accomplishes its goals and objectives. When these details are carefully observed the activity is transformed. It is no longer a simplistic or even primitive encounter with the supernatural. It becomes a moving encounter with the Creator. The petitioner is reminded of the most fundamental elements of our relationship with Hashem and approaches Hashem from a humble and enlightened perspective.

Now, the detailed requirements for the formulation of the incense are explained. Perhaps, some other formulation would also provide an appropriate fragrance. Nonetheless, some specific formulation is dictated by *halachah*. The incense is offered upon the altar to Hashem. We should expect this sacred activity to be characterized by attention to detail. This detail assures that the activity achieves its goals and objectives.

5. Reconsidering the details of the *mishcan's* design

Why does the Torah place enormous emphasis upon the details of the *mishcan's* design? According to Gershonides this emphasis is to be expected. The *mishcan* was to serve as the sanctuary of Hashem. His presence would be expressed in the *mishcan*. It was to be the most sacred and exalted structure created by humanity. The details are a reflection of this exalted nature and sacred character. These details transform the *mishcan*. The careful design of each element renders it uniquely fit for its function.

6. *Halachah's* many details

The details of *halachah* are sometimes a challenge for us. The proper performance of a *mitzvah* requires attention to its details. As explained, it is often the most important *mitzvot* that are the most detailed in their requirements. We have occasionally experienced frustration in our quest to meet the numerous requirements for the proper performance of a *mitzvah*. However, as Gershonides explains, these details are a reflection of the special nature of the *mitzvah*-act. It expresses its exalted nature and sacredness.

Take for yourselves an offering for Hashem. Every person who is moved by his heart should bring it – an offering before Hashem – gold, silver and copper. (Shemot 35:5)

Judging one another's Beliefs

The meaning of the name "Tabernacle of the Testimony"

The Parshiyot of Vayakel and Pekudai complete the Torah's account to the creation of the *Mishcan* – the Tabernacle. These final two Torah portions discuss the actual fabrication of the *Mishcan*'s components, the manufacture of the garments of the *Kohen Gadol* and *Kohanim*, the High Priest and the other Priests, and the assembly of the *Mishcan*. In the above passage Moshe invites the people to contribute materials for the project. He describes the project as the construction of the *Mishcan*. However, the term *Mishcan* seems to be an abbreviation of the full name of the structure. The full name of the *Mischan* is *Mishcan HaEydut* – the Tabernacle of the Testimony. The name associates the *Mishcan* with testimony. However, testimony must be about some event or fact. What is the event or fact to which the *Mishcan* testifies?

Many commentators suggest that the term *Mishcan HaEydut* does not mean that the Tabernacle provides testimony. Instead, the term means that the *Mishcan* contains or is the home of the *Luchot*– the Tablets of the Decalogue. These Tablets are referred to in the Torah as the *Luchot HaEydut* – the Tablets of the Testimony. The *Luchot* provide testimony to the Revelation. Therefore, the *Mishcan* that contains the Tablets is referred to as the Tabernacle of the Testimony. However, Rashi disagrees with this interpretation. He suggests that the term *Mishcan HaEydut* means that the *Mishcan* provides testimony. Therefore, Rashi must identify the event or fact to which the *Mishcan* testifies.

Rashi explains that the *Mishcan* testifies that Hashem indulged or excused Bnai Yisrael after the sin of the Golden Calf. He further explains that when the *Mishcan* was assembled, the cloud of Hashem descended upon it and the glory of Hashem filled the *Mishcan*. This expression of Hashem's presence within the encampment of Bnai Yisrael demonstrated that the sin of the *Egel HaZahav* – the Golden Calf had been excused or indulged.

Rashi's phrasing is notable. He does not say that the sin was forgiven or that the nation had adequately atoned for the sin. Instead, he explains that Hashem decided to excuse or to indulge the nation. Rashi seems to suggest that although Hashem restored His presence in the midst of the nation, this restoration represented something less than total forgiveness.[11] An example will help explain this distinction. If a person harms me, and apologizes, I may decide to forgive the person. This means I completely disregard the act of harm done to me. I have decided to treat this person as if the action never occurred. It is erased and no longer a factor in our relationship. However, I may decide that I can excuse the person or that I am willing to indulge him but that I am not prepared to forgive the person. In this case, I am willing to overlook the action. I do feel a need to exact retribution. But I am not satisfied that the person truly regrets his behavior and accepts full responsibility for his wrongdoing. In other words, forgiveness is secured through a change in the wrongdoer. Indulgence or being excused is a unilateral decision made by the wronged party and does not necessarily reflect any change in the wrongdoer's attitude.

Rashi's interpretation raises two issues:

- According to Rashi, Hashem did not forgive the sin of the *Egel*; He excused it. Why were Bnai Yisrael not worthy of forgiveness?
- If Bnai Yisrael did not deserve to be forgiven, then why were they excused? They had committed a very serious transgression and did not deserve forgiveness. Yet, they were excused! How can this be explained?

And Hashem said to Moshe: I have seen this nation and it is a stiff-necked nation. (Shemot 32:9)

---

[11] See Rabbaynu Shlomo ben Yitzchak (Rashi), *Commentary on Sefer Devarim* 9:18. [Ed.]

Various interpretations of "stiff-necked"

After the sin of the *Egel*, Hashem describes Bnai Yisrael as a stiff-necked nation. What is the meaning of this term? The commentators offer a number of explanations. The consensus is that the term communicates that the nation is stubborn and not likely to repent. However, their interpretations differ in significant aspects. Rabbaynu Ovadia Sforno explains that the term communicates a resistance to learning and adopting new practices and ideas. The generation that worshipped the *Egel* was the product of a pagan, idolatrous society. It had assimilated many of the attitudes, beliefs, and values of this society. The nation was certainly capable of moments of absolute clarity. At these moments, the people understood the folly of their preconceptions and embraced the truths of the Torah. However, they were not capable of completely uprooting and abandoning all remnants of the worldview that they had developed in Egypt. As a result, at moments of extreme stress, the nation was capable of reverting to idolatrous behaviors. The sin of the *Egel* was such a moment. The stress and anxiety caused by Moshe's failure to descend from Sinai developed into a fear of abandonment. The nation responded to this fear by reverting to the false, but familiar, sense of security provided by idolatrous practices.

Rashi disagrees. He does not understand the term as describing an inability to learn and adopt new and novel outlooks. Instead, he explains that the term describes an unwillingness or inability to respond positively to criticism. Rashi does not explain the source or cause of this resistance to accepting criticism. In general, this character flaw is a consequence of poor self-image or weak ego. In order to accept criticism, a strong ego is helpful. A person lacking this degree of self-assuredness struggles to maintain a positive self-image. Therefore, he resists all criticism. Conversely, a strong self-image allows a person to accept that he or she has a flaw without feeling that this flaw is a threat to his self-respect. A nation of freed slaves can be expected to struggle with self-image issues. The members of the nation are likely to have weak self-images and egos. Accepting criticism will, be difficult, if not impossible.

According to both of these explanations, it was unlikely that the generation redeemed from Egypt could fully repent. According to Sforno, the nation could achieve moments of complete clarity. However, the absolute abandonment of the views, beliefs, and behaviors learned in Egypt was beyond its grasp. As a result, they remained susceptible to reverting to these beliefs and behaviors. According to Rashi, the people lacked the ego strength to accept criticism and learn from mistakes. Therefore, they lacked the ability to engage in the introspection needed to completely shed the remnants of idolatry from their perspectives and behaviors. Consequently, Bnai Yisrael was not forgiven for the sin of the *Egel*. Forgiveness would have required a level of repentance that was beyond the capacity of the nation. Nonetheless, Hashem did excuse the nation. Why did He excuse them?

The Torah's minimal standards for beliefs and convictions

Maimonides explains that there are certain beliefs regarding Hashem that every Jew must adopt. For example, every member of Bnai Yisrael must acknowledge that Hashem is incorporeal and He is an absolute unity not subject to any form of division. He explains that these fundamental ideas must be taught to every Jew at his or her level. Maimonides limits this list of fundamentals to very few elements, and also, prescribes a minimal degree of understanding as being adequate for those who are either uneducated or incapable of a more thorough, broad, and definitive understanding of the Torah's fundamental principles. This is an amazing concession. Maimonides often stresses the importance of a proper understanding of

Hashem and devotes much of his *Moreh Nevuchim* to developing this understanding. How can Maimonides' emphasis upon the importance of a proper understanding of Hashem be reconciled with the minimal standard he proposes for the uneducated or less capable?

Maimonides is suggesting that although these unfortunate individuals have not secured the level of understanding for which we are all required to strive, nonetheless, they are excused for their shortcoming. In other words, the Torah establishes a minimum set of beliefs and an ideal. We are all required to strive for the ideal. But if we achieve only the minimum, we are excused. In short, a person who, as a consequence of ignorance or incapacity, has developed an incomplete or not completely accurate understanding of the Torah's fundamentals, is excused for this shortcoming.

Forgiveness vs. indulgence

Based upon Maimonides' comments, Rav Yisrael Chait suggests an explanation of Hashem's response to Bnai Yisrael's failure to fully repent from the sin of the *Egel*. The nation accepted the fundamentals of the Torah. The people were not completely immune from beliefs and attitudes that if carefully considered, would be seen to be inconsistent with the Torah. Also, this lack of introspection and study resulted in some ambiguity and occasional ambivalence. However, the nation accepted the fundamentals at a level consistent with its capacity. Therefore, the nation's failings were not forgiven. Forgiveness requires a level of repentance that was beyond the capacity of the generation that left Egypt. However, they were indulged or excused.

Tolerance for others

This suggests that we also should exercise care in judging one another's beliefs. Even if they are not completely consistent with the Torah, we should try to educate and avoid condemning these individuals. Certainly, there are a few very basic beliefs that should be taught rigorously and extensively to all Jews. But beyond this short list, we should exercise the same behavior demonstrated by Hashem toward the generation that created and worshipped the *Egel*.

Every talented individual among you shall come and make all that Hashem has commanded. (Shemot 35:10)

Each Craftsman Was Required To Grasp the Entire Project of Fabricating the Mishcan

Beginning with Parshat Terumah, the Torah deals with the construction of the *Mishcan*. However, Parshat VaYakhel represents a transition in the discussion. To this point, the Torah describes instructions that Hashem gave to Moshe. Now, the Torah changes the focus of the discussion. The Torah describes Moshe's presentation of the instructions to Bnai Yisrael and the actual construction and assembly of the *Mishcan*.

In our *pasuk*, Moshe addresses the nation. He calls on all the talented craftsmen to join in this endeavor. In the following passages, Moshe provides a general description of the project. He lists the components that will be created and assembled. Why does Moshe provide this inventory of the items to be created? It would seem more appropriate for Moshe to list the skills that will be required!

Nachmanides offers an interesting response. He explains that Moshe was commanded to describe the items to be fabricated. The individual craftsmen were not qualified to participate in the project until each knew the breadth of the project and its various components. Each was required to understand the entire project and perceive the manner in which it would be accomplished.[12]

This seems to be a strange requirement. Most of these participants had a specific role in the construction of the *Mishcan*: some craftsmen created the curtains; others fashioned the upright boards that supported the tent; the metal workers fashioned the sockets into which these boards were fitted. It is reasonable that each worker should understand his specified task. However, why should each be required to grasp the *entire* project?

In order to explain Nachmanides' comments, it is important to appreciate that the *Mishcan* was constructed as an integrated whole. The identity of *Mishcan* did not emerge with the assembly of the components. Instead, each component was created as part of the entity of *Mishcan*. This entity includes the structure of the *Mishcan* and the vessels within. Therefore, in creating a socket, the craftsman was not fashioning a mere insignificant item that, upon assembly, would become part of the *Mishcan*. At the time of creation, he was fashioning a portion of the integrated *Mishcan*.

We can now understand Nachmanides' observation. It is obvious that in order for a craftsman to participate in this project, he must be qualified to execute his responsibility. His responsibility was not to merely create a socket or weave a curtain. His job was to create the socket or curtain as part of the *Mishcan*. There is a major difference between these two responsibilities. In order to create a socket, the craftsman need only understand the design specifications of the socket. He does not need to understand or appreciate the entire project and the role of his socket within the whole. However, to create a socket that is an integrated component of a *Mishcan*, a far more imposing qualification is requisite. The craftsman must understand the entire project and the role of the socket within the entirety. With this broader and more comprehensive knowledge, he can execute his task with a vision of his component's significance in the overall project; he can create a socket that is part of the integrated whole. This is the reason Moshe described the entire project to the craftsmen. Only after the craftsmen had conceptualized the entire "blueprint" were they qualified to participate in the project.

Nachmanides observes that this insight explains another set of passages. In Parshat Pekudey, the Torah describes the presentation of the components of the *Mishcan* to Moshe. The Torah recounts, in detail, the order in which the components were presented. What is the purpose of this elaborate account? Nachmanides explains that the account of the presentation demonstrates that the craftsmen understood the relationship of the various components within the whole of the *Mishcan*.[13] Each component was presented in the proper order in relation to the other parts. In other words, this account demonstrates that the craftsmen succeeded in fashioning the components as part of an integrated whole.

"Every man whose heart lifted him came forward. And every person whose heart moved him brought the offering of Hashem for the creating of the Ohel Moed, all of its components and the sacred garments." (Shemot 35:21)

Exact Measurements in Jewish Law

---

[12] Rabbaynu Moshe ben Nachman (Ramban), *Commentary on Sefer Shemot* 36:8.
[13] Rabbaynu Moshe ben Nachman (Ramban), *Commentary on Sefer Shemot* 36:8.

Hashem commanded Bnai Yisrael to build a Mishcan – a Tabernacle. The Mishcan was constructed from materials provided and contributed by Bnai Yisrael. Our pasuk describes the response of the nation to Moshe's request to supply these materials. In his comments on this passage, Rabbaynu Yonatan ben Uziel explains that the craft-people who build the Mishcan were guided by the spirit of prophecy.[14] Why did they require this spirit of prophecy to perform their tasks? In order to answer this question, we must identify and understand a fundamental paradox within the commandment to build the Mishcan.

One of the interesting issues that is discussed repeatedly in the Talmud is whether we can rely on the accuracy of measurements. Let us consider a simple case that illustrates this issue. On Succot we are required to live in a succah. The most fundamental element of a succah is its roof. The roof must be composed of branches or a similar substance. We cannot use a metal poles or even wooden poles that have been manufactured to the extent that they are regarded as vessels. The Mishne discusses a succah whose sechach – roof is composed of a combination of suitable and unsuitable material. The two materials are place on the roof in an alternating pattern so that the quantity of the suitable material is exactly equal to the unsuitable material. The Mishne rules that this succah is acceptable. The Talmud observes that according to some authorities in order for a structure to be regarded as a succah only half of its roof must be covered with suitable sechach. A majority of the roof need not be covered with suitable sechach. Apparently, the Mishne supports this position. The implication of this discussion is that if we assume that we cannot relay on the exactness of the measurements of the two substances, the structure could not be regarded decisively as a suitable succah. This is because we could not be sure that the suitable sechach is exactly equal in quantity to the unsuitable material.[15]

In short, the Sages disagree as to whether we can assume that measurements are exact. Some Sages maintain that we can make this assumption. Others argue that we cannot make such an assumption. If we assume that measurements can be exact, then the structure described in the Mishne is a suitable succah, without qualification. However, if we assume that measurements cannot be regarded as exact, then the structure would not be suitable unless a marginal quantity of sechach is added. This additional quantity of sechach would assure that – in fact – the sechach was at least equal to the unsuitable substance.

The same dispute extends to the measurement of events as being simultaneous. The Sages that contend that measurements can be regarded as exact, also assert that we can assume that two events that appear simultaneous actually have occurred at the same moment. The Sages that do not accept measurements as being exact, also deny that two apparently simultaneous events can be regarded as truly having occurred at the same moment.

At first glance, this dispute seems difficult to understand. It is empirically evident that it is remarkably difficult to exactly measure any quantity. Even if a measurement seems to be exact, more careful examination will indicate that it is not. Certainly, it is nearly impossible to conclude that two events are precisely simultaneous. Therefore, it would seem that the more reasonable position is to assume that measurements are not exact.

We can gain an insight into this dispute through another discussion in the Talmud. The Talmud in Tractate Bechorot attempts to resolve the dispute between the Sages on this issue. The

---

[14] Rabbaynu Yonatan ben Uziel, *Tirgum on Sefer Shemot* 35:21.
[15] Mesechet *Succah* 15a – 15b.

Talmud suggests that the dispute can be resolved through considering the Torah's commandment to build a Mishcan. The Torah provides exact measurements for each of the elements of the Mishcan. Precise dimensions are delineated for the Aron – the ark, the Shulchan – the Table that held the Shew Bread, and every other component of the Mishcan. The builders of the Mishcan were required to build the components to these exact specifications. They could not deviate from any of the specified dimensions. The Talmud asserts that this proves that we can rely on the precision of measurements! However, the Talmud rejects this proof. It explains that it is true that the Torah commands us to build a Mishcan and provides exact dimensions. However, the dimensions described by the Torah were not precisely achieved. Instead, the builders did their best to construct the Mishcan and its components according to these dimensions. However, because of the innate imperfection of any human measurement, they were not successful.[16]

This discussion is difficult to understand. The Talmud's discussion begins by assuming that the Torah required the Mishcan to be built to precise measurements. This is offered as a proof to the opinion that measurements can be regarded a precise. However, as explained above, it is virtually impossible to make an exact measurement. How can the Torah command us to perform the impossible?

This question suggests an important insight into the Sages' dispute regarding the precision of measurements. As we have explained, the Mishcan presents a paradox. We were required to build the Mishcan according to exact specifications. Yet, precise measurement is virtually impossible! There are two obvious approaches to resolving this paradox.

One possibility is that the dimensions outlined in the Torah represent targets. They are impossible to precisely achieve but in constructing the Mishcan the builders were provided with a model towards which they were required to strive. The actual Mishcan was not an exact embodiment of this model. It is the closest possible actualization of the model.

The second possible resolution of this paradox is that the specifications must be achieved. An approximation is not adequate. However, the Torah accepts an empirical standard for all measurements. In other words, if a measurement is empirically met, the Torah regards the measurement as precise.

Let us now return to the discussion in the Talmud. The Talmud initially asserts that the requirement to build the Mishcan and its components to exact specifications indicates that we can rely on the precision of measurements. This proof can now be understood. The proof is based upon the assumption that the Torah's standard of measurement is empirical. If the builders of the Mishcan carefully measured their work and all of their empirical measurements indicated that the design specifications had been met, then the standard of measurement was satisfied. In other word, if empirical measurement indicated that the Mishcan had been build exactly to specification, then according to the Torah's standards the Mishcan was regarded as built exactly according to its specifications.

However, the Talmud rejects this argument. It suggests that – in fact – empirical measurements are not regarded as precise. Instead, in providing exact specifications for the Mishcan, the Torah created design targets. The Torah recognizes that these targets cannot be precisely achieved. However, it is not necessary to precisely achieve these specifications. They

---

[16] Mesechet Bechorot 17b.

are a target. The Mishcan was acceptable because it was the closes possible embodiment of the required dimensions.

This analysis provides an explanation of the dispute between the Sages. The Sages recognize that it is virtually impossible to achieve precise measurements. The Sages that contend that measurements can be regarded as exact do not dispute this issue. However, they contend that in establishing measurements the Torah only requires that the measurements be met to an empirical level of precision. When the measurement has been empirically achieved, the Torah's requirement is satisfied. However, the Sages who maintain that precision is impossible, argue that the measurements of the Torah are exact requirements that cannot be satisfied at an empirical level of precision. If this is the case, they must assume that Torah's specifications for the Mishcan are intended as design targets but not absolute standards.

The Talmud offers another resolution of the paradox of the Mishcan. The resolution is quite enigmatic. It consists of a passage from Divrei HaYamim – Chronicles. King David instructed his son Shlomo to build the Bait HaMikdash – the Temple. He provided Shlomo with precise instructions. He explained to Shlomo that he was providing him with precise written instructions that he – David – had received from Hashem through prophecy.[17],[18]

The Talmud does not comment on the passage or explain its relevance to the paradox. However, Rav Yitzchak Zev Soloveitchik – the GRI"Z – offers an interesting explanation of the Talmud's comments. He suggests that although it is virtually impossible to make a measurement with exact precision, it is innately impossible. In attempting to make a precise measurement we are typically defeated by the imprecision of our measuring tools and the limitations of the human senses. However, if these limitations can be overcome, a precise measurement is possible. Based on this assertion, the GRI"Z explains the Talmud's comments. David told Shlomo that he had received through prophecy exact specifications for the Bait HaMikdash. He assured Shlomo that the building of the Bait HaMikdash would be guided by the same Divine inspiration. Through this inspiration they would achieve a level of perfect precision not normally possible.

According to the GRI"Z, the Talmud is suggesting that even the Sages that maintain that exact precision is normally impossible to achieve would acknowledge that the Mishcan and its components were built with exact precision. They too were guided in their efforts by Divine inspiration. This guidance enabled them to achieve a level of precision that is normally not attainable.

We can now understand Rabbaynu Yonatan ben Uziel's comments on our passage. The crafts-people who build the Mishcan required the spirit of prophecy in order to complete their task. This spirit of prophecy guided them and assured their success in achieving the precise specifications required for the Mishcan and its components.[19]

---

[17] Sefer Divrei HaYamim I, 28:19.
[18] Mesechet Bechorot 17b.
[19] Rav Y. Hershkowitz, *Netivit Rabotaynu* (Jerusalem 5762), volume 1, pp. 415-416.

"And the men came with the women. Every charitable person brought bracelets, earrings, rings, and body ornaments. All were objects of gold. There were also all those who brought offerings of gold to Hashem." (Shemot 35:22)

This is a difficult pasuk to translate. The above translation interprets the passage to mean that their husbands accompanied the women. Why was this necessary? Rav Naftali Tzvi Yehudah Berlin ZTL (Netziv) explains that the property donated by the women often required the acquiescence of the husband. In order to assure that both parties agreed to the donation, the husband came with his wife.

Meshech Chachmah offers another explanation. His comments are based upon a more literal interpretation of the pasuk. Literally translated, the pasuk indicates that the jewelry was brought while still worn by the women. The procedure used for donating this jewelry was unusual. A woman would come to the collection point wearing her jewelry. When the woman arrived, the jewelry would be removed and donated to the construction of the Mishcan. Why was this odd procedure required?

Meshech Chachmah begins by explaining that these contributions were collected after the sin of the Egel HaZahav – the creation and worship of the golden calf. A review of that incident will help answer our question.

Bnai Yisrael were distraught with the fear that Moshe had died on Mount Sinai. The people came to Ahron and asked him to create an idol. The idol would act as an intermediary between the nation and Hashem. Rashi explains that Ahron knew that Moshe would return. He hoped to delay the people until Moshe descended. He told the people to bring him the jewelry from their wives and children. Ahron reasoned that the owners of these valuables would resist. This was a miscalculation. Our Sages explain that the women did not willingly contribute their jewelry. But their husbands forcibly removed these valuables from their wives. The gold was quickly collected and donated for the creation of the Egel.

An object that has been consecrated to idolatry becomes prohibited. It can no longer be used for any purpose. This prohibition applies once some act has been performed upon the object to associate it with idolatry. A verbal declaration has no effect in prohibiting the object. However, the Meshech Chachmah maintains that a verbal declaration will render the object unfit for use in the Mishcan.

This law created a problem. How could Moshe accept any jewelry for the Mishcan? The possibility existed that this jewelry had previously been committed to be used in creating the Egel. Even a verbal declaration would disqualify the object for use in the Mishcan!

The solution required identifying those women who had successfully resisted their husbands. This was done by requiring the jewelry to be brought while still worn. A woman came to the donation point wearing the valuable she wished to donate. This indicated that her husband had not been successful in securing the object for use in creating the Egel.

And the materials were sufficient for all of the work that was to be done and there was extra. (Shemot 36:7)

An Exact Inventory Was Kept of the Collections for the Mishcan

The *Mishcan* was constructed from materials donated by the people. The exuberance of the nation was so great that the contributions exceeded the needs. Moshe notified the people that more than enough materials had been received. There was no need for additional donations.

The *pasuk* indicates that Moshe did not suspend donations when the exact amount of material required for the project had been received. Instead, allowed the donations to continue until a surplus of materials was created. It might be assumed that this was unintentional. Moshe needed to be sure that adequate supplies were available. He monitored the inventory of the collected materials but realized that his computation of the collection might not be perfectly accurate. The actual inventory of some materials might have exceeded his reckoning of the amount collected. In some instances, the inventory might have been slightly overestimated. In order to be certain that the inventory of materials was adequate, he allowed collections to continue until he felt the precise requirements were exceeded. He wanted to allow for a margin of error in the tally of the collections.

Rabbaynu Ovadia Sforno comments that this was *not* the reason for accumulating excess materials. Moshe was not uncertain of the accuracy of his accounts. He intentionally allowed supplies to be collected that he knew were in excess of the amount needed. Why did Moshe collect more than was necessary? Sforno responds that he did not want the craftsmen constructing the *Mishcan* to be frugal in the use of the materials. Frugality might diminish the quality of the final product.

Sforno is teaching a practical lesson. Parsimony is likely to result in a less-than-optimal product. To create something special, we must be ready to pay the price. However, there is possibly another concept implicit in Sforno's comments.

Sforno explains that the sacredness of the *Mishcan* was enhanced by the unique attention given to its construction. The craftsmen were totally committed to the fulfillment of Hashem's will. Therefore, every component of the *Mishcan* was a perfect reflection of the will of Hashem.

This concept suggests an additional meaning to Moshe's determination to avoid frugality. The command to construct the *Mishcan* required strict adherence to the specifications. The craftsmen were permitted to consider no other factor. Had the craftsman given any thought to the adequacy of the supply of materials, and how he might compensate for its deficiency, the notion of "compromise" would have invariably entered into the design. Therefore, the legal requirements of the command required that the materials exceed the actual needs.

Although the above passage indicates that Moshe did not end the collection of donations until a slight surplus was collected, the commentaries remark that an *exact* tally was kept of the donations. The purpose of this accounting was twofold: first, it was essential to secure sufficient materials; second, Moshe did not wish to collect more than was reasonably needed for the project. A slight surplus was necessary, but not an unjustified excess.

The importance of collecting sufficient materials is obvious. However, the Chumash emphasizes that Moshe was equally concerned with not collecting an unnecessary excess of materials. Once the needed materials were donated and the necessary surplus reserve had been created, Moshe immediately directed Bnai Yisrael to stop bringing donations. Why was this issue so crucial? Why was Moshe so deeply concerned with not accepting additional donations?

The commentaries offer various explanations. We will consider one of these responses. Gershonides explains that Moshe's concern was based on a principle found in the Talmud. In

Tractate Ketubot, the Talmud explains that a person should not donate more than one-fifth of one's assets to charity.[20] Maimonides extends this principle to the performance of all *mitzvot*. A person should not spend more than one-fifth of his wealth on the performance of any *mitzvah*. For example, this limit applies in purchasing an animal for sacrifice. Maimonides' explanation for this restriction is that a person should avoid being dependent on others for support. Therefore, one should not risk impoverishing himself.[21]

Gershonides explains that Moshe's concern was based on this principle. He did not want the people to bring more than was needed. He did not want anyone to become impoverished out of zeal to contribute to the *Mishcan*.

Gershonides offers an important insight into the restriction against spending an excess of one-fifth of one's wealth in the performance of a *mitzvah*. He agrees with Maimonides' explanation of the restriction that one should not risk poverty and loss of independence in performing a mitzvah. However, Gershonides asserts that there is a more fundamental explanation of the restriction. He explains that the Torah prohibits the performance of a *mitzvah* in a manner that leads to evil. Becoming impoverished through contributing to charity, or performing a *mitzvah,* is a negative—or evil—outcome. Gershonides further explains that such an evil outcome discourages others from performing the *mitzvah*.[22]

The men came with the women; every generous hearted person brought bracelets and earrings and rings and buckles, all kinds of golden objects, and every man who waved a waving of gold to Hashem. (Shemot 35:22)

Everyone who set aside an offering of silver or copper brought the offering for Hashem, and everyone with whom acacia wood was found for any work of the service, brought it. (Shemot 35:24)

Two Motifs of Tzedakah

1. The special treatment of offerings of gold

Parshat VaYakhel Perkuday completes the Torah's discussion of the construction of the Mishcan – the Tabernacle. In the above passages, the Torah describes the donations of gold, silver, and copper. Ramban – Nachmanides – notes that the Torah describes the donations of gold as tenufah – a waved offering. The contribution of silver and copper are described as terumah – an offering. Why is the gold a tenufah?

Ramban explains that silver and copper were more abundant than gold. Its scarcity gave contributions of gold special significance. The name tenufah is derived from the process implemented for giving and receiving donations of gold. When one donated gold, he or she would wave it. Apparently, this was done to publicize the contribution. Another explanation is that the donation was waved by the one receiving it. This was done to draw attention to the donor and to praise his or her generosity. Because only contributions of gold received this treatment they are described as tenufah offerings.[23,24]

---

[20] Mesechet Ketubot 50a.
[21] Rabbaynu Moshe ben Maimon (Rambam) *Mishne Torah*, Hilchot Erchin VeCharamin 8:13.
[22] Rabbaynu Levi ben Gershon (Ralbag / Gershonides), *Commentary on Sefer Beresheit*, (Mosad HaRav Kook, 1994), p. 444.

2. Anonymous charity

According to Ramban, it is appropriate for one who donates to draw attention to one's generosity. It is also fitting for the recipient to publicly acknowledge the gift. This seems to contradict a well-known teaching of Rambam – Maimonides. He explains that it is best to give charity anonymously and through an intermediary. Ideally, the donor should not know who receives the gift and the recipient should not know the identity of his benefactor.[25] According to Ramban, rather than encouraging anonymity, the donations of gold to the Mishcan were given and/or received with fanfare designed to draw attention to the donor.

3. Empathy for the less fortunate

The solution to this problem is provided by another comment of Rambam:

Any person who gives charity to a poor person with reluctance and with his face to the ground, even if he gives him a thousand gold pieces, he has lost his merit or diminished it. Rather one should give willingly, and with joy. He should mourn with him (the poor person) over his suffering… He should speak to him words of comfort and consolation…[26]

Rambam is explaining that we are obligated to not only provide the poor with sustenance; we must also treat them with compassion and sensitivity. We are not permitted to embarrass the recipient of charity. We are obligated to comfort the poor. In short, we must provide material support and demonstrate empathy.

4. Tzedakah to the needy vs. to the Mishcan

The reason that anonymous gifts are preferable is because of our obligation to act with empathy and sensitivity toward the less fortunate. The donor does not know to whom his charity has been distributed and the recipient does not know his benefactor. This arrangement helps preserve the dignity of the person forced to survive through the generosity of others.

This consideration did not apply to the donations made to the Mishcan. In this process another consideration took precedence – inspiring the community to participate in the project. Those who donated gold waved it in front of the community. They challenged others to emulate their generosity. Gifts of gold were acknowledged with fanfare. This was intended to inspire others to participate in the project.

In short, charity to the poor should be given with anonymity. Charity to the Mishcan was well publicized. One assumes that Ramban would extend this principle to our support for charitable organizations in our communities. Donors should give openly and their gifts should be publicly acknowledged. Hopefully, this inspires others to participate in supporting our institutions.

"And they made the upright beams of the Mishcan out of acacia wood." (Shemot 36:20)

---

[23] Ramban acknowledges that in Sefer Shemot 38:29 the term tenufah is used to describe offerings of copper and offers a number of explanations.

[24] Rabbaynu Moshe ben Nachman (Ramban), Commentary on Sefer Shemot 35:24.

[25] Rabbaynu Moshe ben Maimon (Rambam) Mishne Torah, Hilchot Matnot Aniyim 10:8.

[26] Rabbaynu Moshe ben Maimon (Rambam) Mishne Torah, Hilchot Matnot Aniyim 10:8.

Parshat VaYakhel includes a discussion of the fabrication of the components of the Mishcan. This process began with the fabrication of the tent and its coverings. This was followed by the fashioning of the upright boards or beams that supported the tent. This same order was followed in the instructions provided to Moshe for the creation of the Mishcan.[27] The instructions for the tent and its coverings preceded the instructions for these beams. Gershonides discusses this order.[28] He explains that the function of the boards was to support the tent. Therefore, it was appropriate to construct the tent and then the supporting boards. It is difficult to understand Gershonides' comments. First, Gershonides bases his explanation for the order of manufacture on the relationship between the boards and the tent. Based on the same relationship, an argument can be made for first constructing the boards. The tent cannot be erected until after the boards are fashioned. This suggests that the boards should be fashioned first and then the curtains and the coverings for the tent! Second, Gershonides' position would be more comprehensible were the Mishcan assembled piecemeal. Under such circumstances, the argument could be made that the components should be fashioned in the order they were needed. However, the Mishcan was not erected piecemeal. It was assembled only after all of the components were fashioned. At the time of assembly, all of the components were present and put in place. The boards and the tent were needed virtually simultaneously!

In order to explain Gershonides' comments, we must identify an important concept regarding the Mishcan. The Mishcan was composed of various components. Examples of these components are the tent, the boards, the Menorah, and the Ark. However, these components were not of the same nature. Some components were complete in themselves. Others were merely prerequisites for other components. This distinction is evident through comparing the tent and the boards. The tent was a complete component in itself. In this sense it was similar to the Ark and the Menorah. However, the boards were only a requisite for the function of the tent. The boards supported the tent. We can now understand Gershonides' comments. The tent was innately a complete component. It did not require the boards in order to be complete. Therefore, the tent could be fashioned before, and independent of, the boards. In contrast, the boards were merely a prerequisite for the curtains of the tent. Therefore, they had no function or significance prior to the existence of the tent. It follows that the boards could be formed only after the tent was manufactured.

And Bezalel made the Ark of acacia-wood: two cubits and a half was the length of it, and a cubit and a half the breadth of it, and a cubit and a half the height of it... And he cast for it four rings of gold, in the four feet thereof: even two rings on the one side of it, and two rings on the other side of it. And he made staves of acacia-wood, and overlaid them with gold. And he put the staves into the rings on the sides of the Ark, to bear the Ark. (Shemot 37:1-5)

And he made the Table of acacia-wood: two cubits was the length thereof, and a cubit the breadth thereof, and a cubit and a half the height thereof.... And he cast for it four rings of gold, and put the rings in the four corners that were on the four feet thereof. Close by the border were the rings, the holders for the staves to bear the Table. (Shemot 37:10-14)

---

[27] Sefer Shemot 26:1-30.
[28] Rabbaynu Levi ben Gershon (Ralbag / Gershonides), Commentary on Sefer Beresheit, (Mosad HaRav Kook, 1994), pp. 444-445.

And he made the Altar of Incense of acacia-wood: a cubit was the length thereof, and a cubit the breadth thereof, four-square; and two cubits was the height thereof; the horns thereof were of one piece with it…. And he made for it two golden rings under the crown thereof, upon the two ribs thereof, upon the two sides of it, for holders for staves wherewith to bear it. (Shemot 37:25-27)

And he made the Altar of Burnt-offering of acacia-wood: five cubits was the length thereof, and five cubits the breadth thereof, four-square, and three cubits the height thereof…. And he made for the altar a grating of network of brass, under the ledge round it beneath, reaching halfway up. And he cast four rings for the four ends of the grating of brass, to be holders for the staves. (Shemot 38:1-5)

The Ark's Unique Design

1. The staves and their holders

Parshat VaYakhel describes the actual fabrication of the Mishcan – the Tabernacle – and its components. The Mishcan accompanied Bnai Yisrael during their travels in the wilderness. The Mishcan was designed as a transportable structure. Each time Bnai Yisrael was instructed to embark upon the next stage of their journey, the Mishcan was disassembled. Upon reaching their destination, the Mishcan was reassembled. The function of the Mishcan as a transportable structure was reflected in its basic design and in the design of many of its internal components. The structure was composed of curtains draped over upright boards. Its courtyard was also composed of curtains. These were hung from poles. Many of the internal components included in their design integrated rings. Staves were inserted into these rings. These staves were used to carry the components when Bnai Yisrael traveled from one encampment to the next.

The above passages describe four of the Mishcan's components that include in their design these integrated rings. These components are the Aron – the Ark, the Shulchan – the Table upon which the Shew Bread was displayed, theMizbe'ach HaKetoret – the Incense Altar, and the Mizbe'ach HeNechoshet – the Brass Alter – upon which sacrifices were offered. In describing the Shulchan, Mizbe'ach HaKetoret, and Mizbe'ach HaNechoset, these rings are consistently described as batim la'vadim – holders for the staves. However, in describing the rings that were included in the design of the Aron, this description is omitted. Instead, the Torah describes the placement of the rings at the four corners of the Aron and the insertion of the staves into the rings. These rings are not described as holders for the staves. Why does the Torah carefully describe the function of the rings of the Shulchan, Mizbe'ach HaKetoret, and Mizbe'ach HaNechoset as holders for the staves and not include this description in its discussion of the fabrication of the Aron?

And you should bring the staves into the rings on the sides of the Aron to carry the Aron with them. In the rings of the Aron should be the staves. They should not be removed from it. (Shemot 25:14-15)

2. The unusual design of the Aron's staves

The above passages describe the staves that were inserted through rings of the Aron. Chizkuni suggests that the above passages seem to contain a contradiction. The Torah explains that the staves were inserted through the rings. This implies that the staves were fashioned so that they could be inserted through the rings but they were not fixed to the rings. However, the Torah then states: In the rings of the Aron should be the staves. This statement implies that they were permanently fixed to the rings and could not be removed. Based on the comments of the Talmud, Chizkuni explains that the two statements can be reconciled. The staves were fashioned with thick ends which tapered toward the center. The diameters of the staves at their ends were nearly the same as the inner diameters of the rings. The staves were forced through the rings. Once the thick ends of the staves were forced through the rings, the staves were able to move freely within the rings.[29] In short, the staves of the Aron were uniquely designed. They were fashioned so that once inserted into the rings of the Aron, they could not easily be removed. This design feature was not applied to the staves of any of the other components of the Mishcan. Why did the staves of the Aron require this unique design?

The answer to this question is provided by the above passages. The Torah explains that the staves are not to be removed from the Aron. Chinkuni explains that the simplest interpretation of this statement is that the Torah is telling us that the staves of the Aron need not be removed when the Mishcan is erected. In contrast, the staves of the other components should be removed. Chizkuni explains the reason for this distinction. The other objects that featured staves were located in parts of the Mishcan or its courtyard to which access was allowed. The nation offered its sacrifices upon the Mizbe'ach HaNechoset situated in the Mishcan's courtyard. The Kohanim were allowed access and performed services in the outer compartment of the Mishcan. The Shulchan and the Mizbe'ach HaKetoret were located in this compartment. The staves were removed from the components located in these areas in order to facilitate the movement of the people who were provided with access to these areas. The Aron was located in the inner compartment of the Mishcan. This compartment was the Kodesh HaKadashim – the Most Sacred. Only the Kohen Gadol – the High Priest – was allowed access to this area and only on Yom Kippur. Because access to the area containing the Aron was so limited, it was not necessary to remove the staves from the Aron.

3. The prohibition against removing the staves from the Aron

However, as Chizkuni acknowledges, the Sages provided a different interpretation of the passage. According to the Sages, the closing phrase in the above passages is an admonition. Hashem commands Bnai Yisrael to not remove the staves from the Aron. In other words, the removal of the staves is prohibited.[30]

This explains the unique design of the Aron's staves. The staves of the other components were intended to be removed when the objects were set into their proper place in the Mishcan. Therefore, the staves of these objects were designed for easy removal. The staves of the Aron were not to be removed. Their removal was prohibited. Therefore, these staves had a unique design. Once inserted into their rings, the Aron's staves could not be easily removed.

The commentaries offer a number of interesting explanations for the prohibition against removing the staves from the Aron. Many are related to another unique law of the Aron. Unlike the other components of the Mishcan which could be transported by wagon, the Aron was carried by the Leveyim.[31] In other words, whereas the staves attached to the other components of the Mishcan were used only to move and lift these objects onto wagons the Aron was transported through the wilderness by the Leveyim who carried it by its staves.

---

[29] Rabbaynu Chizkiya ben Manoach (Chizkuni), Commentary on Sefer Shemot, 25:15.
[30] Rabbaynu Moshe ben Maimon (Rambam) Mishne Torah, Hilchot Klai HaMikdash 2:12.
[31] Rabbaynu Moshe ben Maimon (Rambam) Mishne Torah, Hilchot Klai HaMikdash 2:12.

Maimonides explains that because the staves were essential to the Aron's transport, they could not be removed. The Aron was designed to be transportable and the staves were essential to this function. If removed, the Aron would be incomplete.[32]

Rabbaynu Yosef Bechor Shur offers a similar explanation. He explains that because of its sanctity, we are commanded to treat the Aron with extreme respect. We are not to handle it unnecessarily but only to the extent absolutely required. Therefore, in order to limit contact with the Aron – as is consistent with its sanctity – the Torah prohibits removal of its staves. The Torah is preventing the unnecessary contact that would occur if the staves were removed with each encampment and then reinserted with each new stage of the journey through the wilderness.[33]

Don Isaac Abravanel provides one of the most interesting explanations for the prohibition.[34] He suggests that the staves of the Aron were not merely a feature included in the Aron's design in order to facilitate its transport. Instead, the staves were included in the Aron's design because it is prohibited to make direct contact with the Aron. The admonition against removing the staves reinforces the prohibition against making direct contact with the Aron.

4. The relationship of the Aron to its staves

Each of these Sages is explaining the prohibition against removal of the staves from the Aron. However, they do not share the same perspective on the relationship between the staves and the Aron. According to Maimonides, the staves are an integral component of the Aron. Their removal renders the Aron incomplete. Bechor Shur and Abravanel do not agree with this position. According to both, the prohibition against removal of the staves is predicated upon the staves separate identity from the Aron. Abravanel argues that the staves may not be removed because the Aron may not be touched. The staves – which are not part of the Aron – make it possible to move and transport the Aron. Bechor Shur's position is similar. He seems to agree that the staves are not an integral component of the Aron. He does not contend that their removal would render the Aron incomplete. Instead, he argues that the staves may not be removed because their removal would result in unnecessary contact with the Aron.

Now, the Torah's description of the rings holding the staves of each component can be explained. In discussion the Shulchan, Mizbe'ach HaKetoret, and the Mizbe'ach HaNechoset, the Torah refers to the rings as holders for the staves. This description is appropriate because the staves were not intended to be a permanent component of these objects. In other words, this description implies that the rings are designed to hold the staves which are not themselves part of the component. The staves are inserted into their rings – which act as their holders – and then removed.

This description is not appropriate for the rings of the Aron. The Aron's staves are a permanent element of its design. They are never removed. Therefore, the Torah does not describe the rings as holders for the staves. Instead, the Torah describes the Aron, its rings, and staves as a single integrate whole.

It is notable that Maimonides' position, described above, most accords with this description of the rings. According to Maimonides, the Aron, its rings, and staves are quite

---

[32] Rabbaynu Moshe ben Maimon (Rambam) Moreh Nevuchim, volume 3, chapter 45.
[33] Rabbaynu Yosef Bechor Shur, Commentary on Sefer Shemot 25:15.
[34] Don Yitzchak Abravanel, Commentary on Sefer Shemot, 25:15.

literally a single integrated entity. According to Maimonides, removal of the staves actually renders the Aron incomplete. However, According to Bechor Shur and Abravanel, the staves are technically not a part of the Aron. They may not be removed and there exists a very high degree of integration between the staves and the Aron. However, the staves are not an actual component of the Aron.

And he made the sacred oil for anointing and the pure incense using the technique of a perfumer. (Shemot 37:29)

The Detailed Description of the Construction of the Mishcan

In VaYakel and Pekuday the Torah retells the construction of the *Mishcan* and the vestments of *Kohanim* and the *Kohen Gadol*. Virtually every element is described in specific detail. However, there are two notable exceptions. These two items are mentioned in our *pasuk*.

The *Shemen HaMishchah* was the oil used for anointing the *kohanim* and the *Mishcan*. This anointing was part of the process of conferring sanctity on these individuals and the *Mishcan*. The instructions for creating the oil are outlined in Parshat Ki Tisa. There, the Torah explains that the *Shemen HaMishchah* was created through introducing specific fragrances into pure olive oil.[35]

The *Ketoret* was the incense burned in the *Mishcan*. In Parshat Ki Tisa, the Torah discusses the compounding of the *Ketoret*. The Torah lists the elements contained in the *Ketoret* and their proportions. The *parasha* also describes the preparation of the incense.[36]

In Parshat VaYakhel, the manufacture of these two items is not recounted at length. The quoted above passage contains the entire discussion. The Torah merely states that these items were created as required.

VaYakel and *Pekuday* discuss the manufacture of the *Mishcan* and the garments of the *kohanim*. The Torah, in previous chapters, also provides details on the construction of these items. Although *VaYakel* and *Pekuday* meticulously describe the actual manufacture of the *Mishcan* and the garments, the *Ketoret* and the *Shemen HaMishchah* are excluded from this intensive review! The question is obvious. Why are these items not reviewed in our Torah portion?

Rabbaynu Avraham ben HaRambam offers a fascinating response. He explains that the *Shemen HaMishchah* and the *Ketoret* differed from the other items described in the *parasha*. They required a high level of processing and, once produced, did not resemble their original components. The *Shemen HaMishchah* was created through burning various fragrances. The oil then absorbed the smoke from the fragrances. The final product did not include the substance of the original aromatic elements. Only their fragrance remained in the oil. The *Ketoret* was created through thoroughly grinding the original elements. The individual elements could not be identified in the final compound. Rabbaynu Avraham posits that because the original elements of these two items were not identifiable in the final product, their manufacture is not described in detail.[37]

---

[35] Sefer Shemot 30:22-33.
[36] Sefer Shemot 30:34-36.
[37] Rabbaynu Avraham ben HaRambam, *Commentary on Sefer Shemot* 37:29.

Rabbaynu Avraham's response requires analysis. He presents a fundamental distinction between the *Shemen HaMishchah* and the *Ketoret* as compared with the other elements of the *Mishcan* and the garments. However, a question still remains: Why is this distinction important? Why does the Torah only review the manufacture of items in which the constituent components remain evident?

It seems that the purpose of our Torah portion is to communicate a visual image of the components of the *Mishcan* and the garments of the *Kohanim*. This is accomplished through describing their manufacture. Describing the manufacture of the *Ketoret* and the *Shemen HaMishchah* would not contribute to creating a visual image of these items in their final form. Therefore, the creation of these items is not discussed in detail.

This insight helps resolve another issue. The Torah describes the construction of the *Mishcan* and the garments in excruciating detail. We now know that this was done to create a visual image. Why is this image necessary?

The Torah includes six-hundred thirteen *mitzvot*. Most apply at all times. However, the *mitzvot* relating to the *Mishcan* are an exception. The *Mishcan* and the Temple do not currently exist. Exile from the Land of Israel and the destruction of the Temple deprived these *mitzvot* of their physical expression. As a consequence of exile, an important portion of the content in the Torah does not exist in material form. These *mitzvot* will not be fulfilled again until the rebuilding of the Temple.

This creates a paradox. The *taryag mitzvot* – the six-hundred thirteen commandments – are eternal. They must be real to every generation. How can the *mitzvot* related to the *Mishcan* remain alive even when there is no *Bait HaMikdash*? The Torah addresses this problem. These *mitzvot* are preserved through creating a detailed visualization. The *Mishcan* does not exist in physical form. However, it is still real to the student reading the Torah. In this manner these *mitzvot* are preserved for all time.

"And he made a copper washbasin and its copper base from the mirrors of the women that came to pray at opening of the Mishcan." (Shemot 38:8)

Sforno explains that these mirrors were not among the original donations to the Mishcan. He also comments that it is not at all obvious that the mirrors should have been accepted. Mirrors are designed for use in indulging fascination with personal appearance. Therefore, they are identified with the instinctual component of the personality. It might be concluded that this identification would disqualify the mirrors from use in the Mishcan. Why were the mirrors accepted? Sforno explains that these women had devoted themselves to the study of Torah. They congregated at the Mishcan to hear the Torah lessons taught there. Their decision to contribute their mirror reflected their personal values. They had determined that the instinctual habits represented by the mirrors were not worthy of their attention. Therefore, they abandoned the mirrors. These mirrors did not represent the instinctual. They represented the conquest of these individuals over the yetzer harah.

Rashi provides a different perspective on this donation. He comments that Moshe was reluctant to accept this contribution. Hashem instructed Moshe to reverse his decision. Moshe was concerned with the mirrors' association with the yetzer harah. Why did Hashem want this donation? Rashi explains that one of the reasons the Egyptians afflicted Bnai Yisrael with intense physical labor was to slow down the population growth. Paroh wanted to work the men to the point of exhaustion. He reasoned that this would undermine relations between man and wife. The women defeated Paroh's plan. They would travel out to the men. They would bring food. And they brought their mirrors. Man and wife would share a meal. Then the wife would hold her mirror in front of herself and her husband. Jokingly the wife would brag of her greater beauty. A relaxed banter would develop. The rigor of the work would be temporarily forgotten. Marital life was maintained.

The washbasin in the Mishcan was designed entirely from these mirrors. What is the lesson that the Torah wishes to teach through this utensil? Perhaps, the washbasin is designed to represent an important aspect of the Torah's perspective on the yetzer harah the human instincts. The instinctual component of the personality is responsible for sin. Greed, lust, hatred and every other lowly personality trait are derived from the instincts. For this reason, our Sages refer to this component of the personality as the yetzer harah. However, the Torah does not maintain that the instincts are inherently evil.

Rav Eliyahu of Vilna the Vilna Gaon explains that the yetzer harah is responsible for many essential human functions. Procreation would not be possible without the drive of the yetzer harah. He argues that we would not even eat were we not instinctually motivated. These are a few examples of the many important functions of human instinct. Only if the pursuit of instinctual pleasure is an end within itself, do these drives become evil. So, although sin is derived from the yetzer harah, the instincts are not innately sinful. The mirrors reflect this concept. Although the mirrors are tools of the instincts, they are not evil or unfit for use in the Mishcan. The suitability of the mirrors depends upon the manner in which they are used. If used towards a proper end, the instincts and the mirrors belong in the sacred Mishcan. Only when misused are the mirrors and instincts tainted.

"And he made a copper washbasin and its copper base from the mirrors of the women that came to pray at opening of the Mishcan." (Shemot 38:8)
Yetzer Hara

I remember first learning about the yetzer ha'rah and the yetzer ha'tov as a student in elementary school. We were told that the yetzer ha'rah is constantly urging us to do bad things. But the yetzer ha'tov gives us the proper guidance. It directs us to do good things and battles the evil council of the yetzer ha'rah. I remember the image evoked by this lesson. I imagined two little angels – one perched on each of my shoulders. The angel on one shoulder – the yetzer ha'rah – whispers evil council into my ear, while the other angel situated on the other shoulder – the yetzer ha'tov – advises me to ignore the tempting suggestion of its adversary. Of course, I do not attribute this simplistic characterization to my teachers – probably my first and second grade rabbayim. Instead, this was the manner in which I – the immature – student interpreted and adapted the sophisticated ideas that were beyond my immature level of understanding.

As I grew older I decided that this imagery – indeed my fundamental understanding of the yetzer ha'rah and the yetzer ha'tov – needed some reworking. I became disillusioned with this simplistic characterization on many levels. On the most basic level, I came to realize that the yetzer ha'rah and the yetzer ha'tov seemed to conform to forces with which I had some familiarity. These two terms seemed to accurately describe the battle I often experienced between urges that I identified as less than wholesome and my better judgment which recognized the folly in following these urges. So, although there was some attraction in clinging to the belief that there was some real internal me that acted as an arbitrator between these two external forces, I realized that in reality these forces were intimate elements of my internal nature.

On a more intellectual level, I was uncomfortable with the idea that Hashem had created some evil force whose sole purpose was to mislead and corrupt innocent individuals. So, the idea of a purely evil yetzer ha'rah was somewhat disturbing.

So, what is the yetzer ha'rah? Can it be a purely evil force? Does Hashem create in each of us an inclination to perform evil? How can such a concept be reconciled with the Torah's concept of a perfectly benevolent Creator who does no evil? An important insight into this issue is contained in this week's parasha.

Our parasha describes the actual fabrication and construction of the Mishcan. Each component is briefly describes and its place within the overall structure of the Mishcan is defined. In the above pasuk, the Torah discusses the washbasin which was located in the courtyard of the Mishcan and used by the Kohanim to wash their hands and feet prior to performing their service in the Mishcan. The pasuk tells us that this washbasin and its stand were manufactured from the mirrors of the women that would congregate to pray at the opening of the Mishcan.

Rashi comments that Moshe was reluctant to accept this contribution. What was Moshe's objection? In order to appreciate his objection, we must begin with a simple question. For what purpose are mirrors used? We look in mirrors to study our appearance. Mirrors are a tool that we use in order to indulge personal vanity. Vanity is an expression of the yetzer ha'rah. So, mirrors are one of the tools of the yetzer ha'rah. Moshe was concerned with this association between mirrors and the yetzer ha'rah. The Mishcan was designed for the service of Hashem. So, he concluded that it was inappropriate to build an element of the Mishcan from a material associated with the yetzer ha'rah.

Moshe's reasoning seems sound. But apparently Moshe was wrong. Hashem instructed Moshe to reverse his decision. Why did Hashem want this donation to be accepted? What was Moshe's error?

Rashi explains that one of the reasons the Egyptians afflicted Bnai Yisrael with intense physical labor was to slow down the population growth. Paroh wanted to work the men to the point of exhaustion. He reasoned that this would undermine relations between man and wife. The women defeated Paroh's plan. They would travel out to the men. They would bring food. And they brought their mirrors. Man and wife would share a meal. Then the wife would hold her mirror in front of herself and her husband. Jokingly the wife would brag of her greater beauty. A relaxed banter would develop. The rigor of the work would be temporarily forgotten. Marital life was maintained.[38]

On a superficial level, the comments of Rashi are difficult to understand. Moshe argues that these mirrors were the tool of the yetzer ha'rah. On this basis, he rejected them for use in the fabrication of an element of the Mishcan. Hashem responded by pointing out that the mirrors had been used for a positive end and for this reason they should be included in the materials for the

---

[38] Rabbaynu Shlomo ben Yitzchak (Rashi), *Commentary on Sefer Shemot* 38:8.

Mishcan. But if this is the meaning of Rashi's comments, then Moshe actually seems to be fully justified in his objection. It is true that in an isolated instance the mirrors were used for a positive end. But this does not refute Moshe's objection. Surely, Moshe was aware of this incident in which the mirrors had been used for a positive purpose. But Moshe's objection was that this isolated instance does not compensate for the overall nature of the mirrors. Despite this single instance in which the mirrors had served a positive end, their overall nature is clear and unchanged. They are a tool of the yetzer ha'rah! How can a single instance of this tool being employed for a positive end compensate for its overall nature?

But before we consider an alternative interpretation of Rashi's comments let us study another pasuk.

"And you should love Hashem your G-d with all of your heart and with all of your soul and with all of your resources." (Devarim 6:5)

This familiar pasuk is recited each day as part of the Shema. It instructs us in the commandment to love Hashem. It explains that this love must be all encompassing. It must reflect the feeling of our hearts, our souls and that all of our resources must be made available for the expression of our love of Hashem. The Mishna explains that the phrase "all of you heart" means with both the yetzer ha'tov and the yetzer ha'rah.[39] We can readily understand that we must love Hashem with our yetzer ha'tov. But the amazing element of this comment of the Sages is that we can and must love Hashem with our yetzer ha'rah! How does one do this?

Maimonides discusses this issue at length. The general message of Maimonides is that a person a person should serve Hashem in all of one's actions. He makes two points. First, he explains that ideally, a person should not eat in order to indulge desires. Instead, a person should eat in order to give oneself the strength to serve Hashem. Second, he explains the comments of the Talmud in Tractate Shabbat. The Talmud comments that a Torah scholar should seek to secure a pleasant marital life, a pleasant home, and pleasant clothing – for these elements of life aid the scholar in his studies.[40] According to Maimonides, a person is influenced by one's environment. This environment can either encourage a positive attitude or foster depression. A scholar will be most successful in his studies if his attitude and general outlook is positive. Therefore, the scholar should seek to secure a positive environment.

According to Maimonides, this is the meaning of serving Hashem with our yetzer ha'rah. We all have physical needs and material desires. In satisfying our physical needs we should set as our objective the service of Hashem. We should also not neglect our material desires. When these desires are addressed in a measured and realistic manner, we can achieve a state of internal peace that is essential in the study of Torah. When we neglect these desires, we encumber our efforts with frustration and depression.[41]

Apparently, Maimonides defines the yetzer ha'rah as our physical and material desires and urges. According to his interpretation, we do not actually directly serve Hashem with our yetzer ha'rah. But we must consider and develop an accommodation with our yetzer ha'rah in order to serve Hashem fully. We cannot overindulge our yetzer ha'rah and neither can we ignore

---

[39] Mesechet Berachot 9:5.
[40] Messechet Shabbat 25b, Mesechet Berachot 57b.
[41] Rabbaynu Moshe ben Maimon (Rambam) *Commentary on the Mishne*, Introduction to Mesechet Avot, chapter 5.

it. Instead, complete service of Hashem requires a balanced accommodation of human nature. Without this accommodation our service will be compromised.

In Maimonides' approach, the yetzer ha'rah is neither evil nor good. It is an element of basic human existence. We are physical, material creatures. Therefore, we are subject to desires that stem from this element of our nature. If we respond to these desires properly, the results will be positive. If we do not respond properly the outcome will be evil.

Now, let us return to Rashi's comments regarding the mirrors used for the washbasin. If we adopt Maimonides' approach to understanding the yetzer ha'rah, Rashi's comments can be readily understood. Moshe rejected the mirrors because they represented the yetzer ha'rah. But let us reconsider Hashem's refutation of Moshe's argument. Perhaps, the point that Hashem made to Moshe was that even though the mirrors represent the yetzer ha'rah, this does not disqualify them for use in the Mishcan. The yetzer ha'rah is neither evil nor good. The women of Bnai Yisrael used these mirrors in order to attract the attention of their husbands and to brighten their mood. They were evoking and appealing to the physical desires of their husbands. But they were not interested in awakening these desires simply as an expression of lust. Instead, their goal was to assure the future of Bnai Yisrael.

In summary, the yetzer ha'rah is neither good nor evil. If it is indulged as an end unto itself, it leads us away from Hashem. We are also diverted from the service of Hashem if we neglect the yetzer ha'rah. But if we respond to the urges of the yetzer ha'rah, we will be empowered to more fully serve Hashem. In addition, as Rashi points out, the yetzer ha'rah can even act as an ally in serving Hashem.

Pekudey

"And these are the accounts of the Mishcan -- the Tabernacle of the Testimony – that were calculated by Moshe. It was the service of the Leveyim under the authority of Itamar the son of Ahron the Kohen." (Shemot 38:21)

This *pasuk* introduces Parshat Pekudey. The *parasha* provides an account of the materials donated for the *Mishcan* and a description of the manner in which these materials were used.

The *pasuk* refers to the *Mishcan* as the Tabernacle of the Testimony. The simple meaning of this term is that the *Mishcan* housed the *Luchot* – the Tablets of the Decalogue. These *Luchot* provided testimony. They evidenced the authenticity of the Torah and the relationship between Hashem and His nation.

Rashi, based on Midrash Rabba, offers another interpretation of the testimony identified with the *Mishcan*. He explains that the Tabernacle indicated that Hashem had forgiven Bnai Yisrael for the sin of the *Egel HaZahav* – the Golden Calf. Upon the completion of the *Mishcan*, the Divine Presence descended upon the Tabernacle. This indicated that the relationship with Hashem was reestablished.

This interpretation of the midrash creates an interesting difficulty. The end of the *pasuk* explains that the service in the *Mishcan* was entrusted to the *Leveyim* and *Kohanim*. This was not the original design. Initially, service was commended to the first-born. However, the first-born became involved in the sin of the *Egel*. In contrast, the *Leveyim* and *Kohanim* withstood temptation and opposed the *Egel*. As a consequence, the responsibility for service in the *Mishcan* was transferred from the first-born to the *Leveyim* and *Kohanim*. The end of the *pasuk* confirms this change from the original plan.

According to the Midrash, the *pasuk* delivers a confusing message. The first part of the *pasuk* indicates that the *Mishcan* testified to Hashem's forgiveness. The second part of the *pasuk* seems to indicate the opposite. The service was not restored to the first-born. This seems to imply that the sin of the *Egel* had not been completely forgiven.

Meshech Chachmah offers an interesting answer to this question. Maimonides explains that a *Kohen* who practices or confirms idolatry may not serve in the Temple. This law applies even if the *Kohen* repents fully from his sin. Why can the repentant *Kohen* not return to service? Presumably, Hashem has forgiven him! It seems that once the *Kohen* becomes associated with idolatry he is permanently unfit for service in the *Mishcan*. Repentance and forgiveness do not remove this association.

Based on this law, the Meshech Chachmah explains the message of the *pasuk*. The *pasuk* explains that Bnai Yisrael had, indeed, been forgiven for the sin of the *Egel*. Nonetheless, the first-born were no longer qualified to serve. They had identified themselves with the idolatry of the *Egel* and were permanently disqualified from service in the *Mishcan*.

"And these are the accounts of the Mishcan -- the Tabernacle of the Testimony – that were calculated by Moshe. It was the service of the Leveyim under the authority of Itamar the son of Ahron the Kohen." (Shemot 38:21)

Parshat Pekuday completes the Torah's discussion of the construction of the Mishcan – the Tabernacle. The Mishcan was the central element of the camp of Bnai Yisrael during their travels in the wilderness. Once Bnai Yisrael entered the land of Israel, conquered, and settled the land, the Mishcan was replaced by the Bait HaMikdash – the Temple. King Shlomo built the first Bait HaMikdash. Shlomo's Bait HaMikdash was destroyed. Ezra initiated the construction of the second Bait HaMikdash. This Temple was also destroyed. Today, we do not have a Bait HaMikdash but we look forward to its rebuilding.

Although we do not presently have a Bait HaMikdash, the Talmud refers to the synagogues and study-halls that we construct in the places of our exile as minor versions of the Bait HaMikdash.[1] In what sense are these synagogues and study-halls minor versions of the Bait HaMikdash? In other words, what are the practical implications of the status?

The Talmud's observation is followed by an admonishment to not use the synagogue as a shortcut. This means that a person may not pass through a synagogue in order shorten his route to a destination. It seems from the Talmud's juxtaposition of these two discussions that the status of the synagogue as a minor Mikdash engenders an obligation to treat a synagogue with respect.

Maimonides seems to take the comparison of the synagogue to the Bait HaMikdash one step further. In his Sefer HaMitzvot, Maimonides explains that one of the negative commands of the Torah prohibits the destruction of the Bait HaMikdash, erasure of the name of Hashem or the destruction of any of the prophetic works.[2] Maimonides also provides a list of the 613 mitzvot in the introduction to his Mishne Torah. In that version of the 613 mitzvot, he explains that the prohibition against destroying the Bait HaMikdash includes an injunction against destroying a synagogue or study-hall. It seems that according to Maimonides, we are not only required to treat the synagogue with respect but that destroying a synagogue or study-hall is a Torah level violation of the prohibition against destroying the Bait HaMikdash or erasing Hashem's name.

In short, it seems that the Talmud's description of the synagogue and study-hall as minor version of the Mikdash is not merely a homily. This comparison actually expresses itself in specific laws regarding the manner in which we must treat these institutions.

However, if we investigate Maimonides' position more carefully a problem becomes evident. As we have explained, Maimonides seems to treat very literally the Talmud's assertion that a synagogue and study-hall have the status of a minor Mikdash. This implies that – in some sense – the synagogue and study-hall partake of the sanctity of the Bait HaMikdash.

Maimonides explains in his Mishne Torah and his Sefer HaMitzvot that the Bait HaMikdash is a place designated for the offering of sacrifices.[3] Furthermore, Maimonides explains that the Bait HaMikdash is composed of specific elements including the altars, Menorah, and Shulchan. The synagogue and study-hall do not meet either of these requirements. We cannot offer sacrifices in the synagogue or study-hall. Neither do these institutions have the components essential to the Bait HaMikdash. So, in what sense do the synagogue and study-hall partake of the sanctity of the Bait HaMikdash?

---

[1] Mesechet Meggilah 29a.
[2] Rabbaynu Moshe ben Maimon (Rambam) *Sefer HaMitzvot, Mitzvat Lo Ta'aseh* 65.
[3] Rabbaynu Moshe ben Maimon (Rambam) *Mishne Torah*, Hilchot Bait HaBechirah 1:1, *Sefer HaMitzvot, Mitzvat Aseh* 20.

The obvious response to this question is to recognize that in our time prayer takes the place of the sacrifices offered in the Bait HaMikdash.[4] However, it is unlikely that Maimonides' comparison the synagogue and study-hall to the Bait HaMikdash is based on this factor.

Maimonides explains that there is a positive mitzvah in the Torah to build a Bait HaMikdash. He discusses this commandment as length in his Sefer HaMitzvot and Mishne Torah. Nowhere in this discussion does he remotely indicate that this commandment includes building a synagogue or study-hall. However, in his discussion of the mitzvah of prayer he does acknowledge that we are obligated to build synagogues. He explains that any community composed of ten Jews is required to designate a structure to serve a synagogue. The structure must be available at all times for prayer. He adds that the members of the community may force one another to participate in the building of this synagogue.[5] Maimonides' placement of this obligation in his discussion of the laws of prayer, indicates that the obligation is somehow connected to the positive command to pray daily. The specific connection is apparent from two other requirements that Maimonides outlines. First, he explains that it is appropriate for a person to designate a regular place in which to pray. Each time the person prays he should do so from this designated place.[6] Second, explains that praying with a congregation is preferable to praying alone.[7] The synagogue is a place designated for the prayer of the community. It fulfills both of these requirements. This seems to be the basis for the obligation to build a synagogue.

It emerges from this discussion that the synagogue and the Bait HaMikdash are fundamentally different institutions. The Bait HaMikdash is a structure with a specific description that is designed and designated for the offering of sacrifices. The synagogue is an institution that is required in order for the mitzvah of prayer to be properly fulfilled. On a deeper level, the distinction between these two institutions is even more fundamental. The Bait HaMikdash is innately the subject and substance of a mitzvah – it is a cheftza shel mitzvah. The synagogue is not innately the subject or substance of a mitzvah. It is needed in order to perform the mitzvah of prayer properly. Apparently, this is the reason that Maimonides includes the requirement to build a synagogue in his discussion of the mitzvah of prayer and not in his discussion of the Bait HaMikdash. So, in what sense are the synagogue and study-hall a minor Mikdash?

It seems that according to Maimonides the synagogue and study-hall derive their sanctity from two different but related sources. He hints to one these sources in the end of his discussion regarding the synagogue. He comments that a public square that is used on occasion for community prayer is not endowed with sanctity. He explains that although this public square is used for prayer this is not its sole designation. Instead, it is generally used for secular purposes and is only used for prayer on occasion.[8] The implication of this explanation is that the synagogue and study-hall are endowed with sanctity because of their exclusive designations as places for prayer and Torah study. Maimonides further explains that in this sense there is a valid comparison that can be made between the synagogue and study-hall and the Bait HaMikdash. The Bait HaMikdash retains its sanctity even after its destruction. The place in which the Bait

---

[4] Rabbaynu Moshe ben Maimon (Rambam) *Mishne Torah*, Hilchot Tefillah 1:5-6.
[5] Rabbaynu Moshe ben Maimon (Rambam) *Mishne Torah*, Hilchot Tefillah 11:1.
[6] Rabbaynu Moshe ben Maimon (Rambam) *Mishne Torah*, Hilchot Tefillah 5:6.
[7] Rabbaynu Moshe ben Maimon (Rambam) *Mishne Torah*, Hilchot Tefillah 8:1.
[8] Rabbaynu Moshe ben Maimon (Rambam) *Mishne Torah*, Hilchot Tefillah 11:21.

HaMikdash stood is sacred even today. He explains that the same rule applies to a synagogue and study-hall. Even if they are destroyed, the place on which they stood retains its sanctity.[9] In other words, according to Maimonides, there is a valid comparison between the synagogue and study-hall and the Bait HaMikdash. All retain their sanctity even when destroyed. This common characteristic apparently is a result of the similar designation of these institutions. All are structures designated exclusively for the service of Hashem. This designation results in a residual sanctity even after the structures have been destroyed. In other words, as explained above, the sanctity of the Bait HaMikdash is innate, whereas the sanctity of the synagogue and study-hall is derived from the activities that are performed within their structures. Nonetheless, they share the common characteristic of being structures designated for the service of Hashem. As a result of this common characteristic, they retain their sanctity even when destroyed.

According to Maimonides, the sanctity of the synagogue and study-hall is also derived from a second source. As explained above, Maimonides maintains that the prohibition against destroying the Bait HaMikdash or erasing Hashem's name includes a prohibition against the destruction of a synagogue or study-hall. On what basis is the destruction of a synagogue or study-hall included in this prohibition.

It is interesting that Maimonides does not discuss this prohibition in his treatment of the laws regarding the Bait HaMikdash. Instead, it is placed in the opening chapters of his Mishne Torah. In these opening chapters, Maimonides describes the foundations of the Torah. There are two characteristics of Maimonides' discussion of this prohibition that are directly relevant to our question. First, Maimonides begins the discussion by explaining that it is prohibited to erase Hashem's name. Only after outlining the laws related to this element of the prohibition does he mention that the prohibition includes destroying the Bait HaMikdash.[10] Second, Maimonides discusses this prohibition directly after of our obligation to sanctify Hashem's name through our actions and behaviors and the prohibition against desecrating His name through our actions and behaviors.[11]

It seems that the prohibition against destroying the Bait HaMikdash or erasing Hashem's name is an extension of the prohibition against desecrating His name. Furthermore, although the mitzvah includes both destroying the Bait HaMikdash and erasing Hashem's name Maimonides seems to regard the erasure of Hashem's name as the primary element of the prohibition. The destruction of the Bait HaMikdash is included in the prohibition because this action is an expression of the same underlying theme. What is this unifying theme?

Apparently, according to Maimonides, the destruction of the Bait HaMikdash is comparable to the erasure of Hashem's name because the Bait HaMikdash is intimately associated with Hashem. As we have explained, it is a place designated for His worship. Therefore, one who destroys the Bait HaMikdash has desecrated Hashem's name in a manner that similar and on par with erasing His name.

We can now identify the reasoning that compelled Maimonides to include within this mitzvah a prohibition against destroying a synagogue or study-hall. As we have explained, these institutions are also designated for the service of Hashem. In this sense, they share a fundamental

---

[9] Rabbaynu Moshe ben Maimon (Rambam) *Mishne Torah*, Hilchot Tefillah 11:11.
[10] Rabbaynu Moshe ben Maimon (Rambam) *Mishne Torah*, Hilchot Yesodai HaTorah 6:1-7.
[11] Rabbaynu Moshe ben Maimon (Rambam) *Mishne Torah*, Hilchot Yesodai HaTorah 5.

characteristic of the Bait HaMikdash. Therefore, the mitzvah prohibiting the erasure of Hashem's name includes the prohibition against destroying the Bait HaMikdash and destroying a synagogue or study-hall.

These are the accounts of the Tabernacle, the Tabernacle of the Testimony, which were counted at Mohse's command; [this was] the work of the Levites under the direction of Itamar, the son of Aharon the Kohen. (Shemot 38:21)

The Golden Calf: The Rest of the Story

The "testimony" of the *Mishkan*

Parshat VaYakhel and Parshat Pekudei are often read on a single Shabbat. Parshat Pekudei opens with an account of the materials donated and used for the creation of the Tabernacle and for producing the garments of Aharon and his sons. The above passage introduces the *parsha*. In the passage the *Mishkan* is referred as the Tabernacle of the Testimony. What is the testimony associated with the *Mishkan*? Ramban – Nachmanides – provides the simplest response. He explains that the *Mishkan* would be created to house the Tablets of the Testimony – the *Luchot*. The *Luchot* are testimony to Revelation and the covenant between Bnai Yisrael and Hashem.[12]

Rashi disagrees with this interpretation of "Tabernacle of the Testimony". He explains that Hashem's Glory would reside in the *Mishkan*. The presence of His Glory testifies that Hashem has excused Bnai Yisrael for the sin of the *Egel* – the Golden Calf.[13] Rashi's comments are very difficult to understand. Before considering the problem that they present, an introduction is necessary.

For Hashem, your L-rd, is a consuming fire. He is a zealous L-rd. (Devarim 4:24)

Hashem does not excuse sins

We are commanded to walk in the path of Hashem. Rambam – Maimonides – explains that this commandment embodies the principle of *imitatio Dei*. It directs us to imitate Hashem in our behaviors. We are to study Hashem's behaviors and treat His behaviors as a guide and model for our own. However, this principle cannot be applied superficially. We must be thoughtful in its application. For example, in the above passage the Torah describes Hashem as a zealous G-d. This means that Hashem punishes those who sin against Him.[14] It does not follow that we should be unforgiving of those who wrong us. Rambam explains that we should insist that Hashem be obeyed and honored but be forgiving of those who transgress against ourselves. We should be slow to anger and quick to forgive those who harm us.[15] In short, we must be thoughtful in our imitation of Hashem and avail ourselves of the Torah's insights into how this commandment is to be fulfilled.

---

[12] Rabbeinu Moshe ben Nachman (Ramban), *Commentary on Sefer Shemot* 38:21.
[13] Rabbeinu Shlomo ben Yitzchak (Rashi), *Commentary on Sefer Shemot* 38:21.
[14] According to Rambam, this phrase and similar descriptions of Hashem's strict punishment of transgressors are related primarily to those who engage in idolatry. See *Moreh Nevuchim*, vol 1, chap 36.
[15] Rabbeinu Moshe ben Maimon (Rambam) *Mishne Torah*, Hilchot Deyot 7:7.

A corollary of this principle is that behaviors and attitudes that are appropriate for us are not necessarily those practiced by Hashem. We should excuse others for wrongs they commit against us. Hashem does not excuse those who sin against Him. This is emphasized by the Talmud and midrash. The Talmud comments that anyone who asserts that Hashem excuses our wrong-doings will be punished severely.[16] Commenting on this text, Rashi explains that this attitude encourages sin. One who believes that wrongdoings have no consequences will be less deterred from committing such acts.

Now, the problem with Rashi's comments on our *parasha* emerges. Rashi seems to be violating this principle of the Sages. The Sages declare that we should not assert that Hashem excuses sin. Rashi contends that Hashem's presence in the *Mishkan* testifies that He has excused us from the sin of the *Egel*!

And now go, lead the people to [the place] of which I have spoken to you. Behold, My angel will go before you. But on the day I make an accounting [of sins upon them], I will bring their sin to account against them. (Shemot 32:34)

The sin of the *Egel* was not forgiven

The first step in understanding Rashi's position is to more carefully evaluate the meaning of Hashem excusing the sin of the *Egel*. Does excusing the sin mean that Hashem forgave Bnai Yisrael? It is clear from the Torah that He did not. In the above passage, Hashem directs Moshe to resume the journey to the Land of Israel. Hashem will send His angel before the nation. He also tells Moshe that when He makes an accounting of their sins, the sin of the *Egel* will be considered and included in the accounting. What does this enigmatic statement mean? Rashi explains that Hashem is telling Moshe that He has accepted his prayer. The nation will be spared immediate destruction. However, the people will not escape punishment. When Hashem punishes them in the future for sins that they inevitably will commit, the punishment will include an additional degree of severity as punishment for the *Egel*.[17] In other words, the punishment for *Egel* will not be meted out immediately; it will be exacted from the people over the course of ages.

It is clear from the passage, as explained by Rashi, that the sin of the *Egel* was not forgiven. If it was not forgiven, then in what sense was it excused?

Now it came to pass when he drew closer to the camp and saw the calf and the dances, that Moshe's anger was kindled, and he flung the tablets from his hands, shattering them at the foot of the mountain. (Shemot 32:19)

The sin of the *Egel* rendered the people unfit to receive the *Luchot*

In order to understand Rashi's use of this term "excused", we must consider another comment of Rashi. The above passage describes Moshe's shattering of the *Luchot*. The commentators discuss Moshe's justification for destroying these *Luchot* that were created by Hashem. Rashi suggests that Moshe deduced from the laws of the Pesach sacrifice that the people were unfit to receive the *Luchot*. The Torah teaches that one who is an idolater is not fit to participate in the Pesach sacrifice. Moshe reasoned that one who is disqualified from the Pesach sacrifice is certainly not fit to receive the entire Torah.[18] Rashi elsewhere explains that through

---

[16] Mesechet Baba Kamma 50a.
[17] Rabbeinu Shlomo ben Yitzchak (Rashi), *Commentary on Sefer Shemot* 32:34.

breaking the *Luchot*, Moshe forestalled the consummation of relationship between Hashem and Bnai Yisrael.[19]

The above discussion reveals that Rashi maintains that the sin of the *Egel* had two consequences. The first was that the people were held accountable to Hashem for their sin and subject to severe punishment. As explained above, initially Hashem announced to Moshe that He would destroy the nation. Moshe interceded and Hashem revised the punishment. Rather than being destroyed, the nation's punishment would be distributed through the ages. The second, consequence was that the relationship between Hashem and Bnai Yisrael was suspended. Bnai Yisrael was unfit to receive Hashem's Torah. Without the Torah, Bnai Yisrael would not become the Chosen People; Hashem's Glory would not reside in the midst of the nation. This consequence was not a punishment. It was an inevitable and inherent outcome of the sin. Its association with idolatry rendered the nation unsuitable to receive the Torah and to be the *Am HaNivchar* – the Chosen People of Hashem.

An analogy will help illustrate these two consequences. Consider a person who shoplifts. He is apprehended, tried, and convicted. His sentence requires that he make restitution to the store from which he stole and perform community service. After making restitution and performing his community service, the sincerely contrite and repentant perpetrator appeals to the store-owner for a job. The store-owner assesses whether he should give this person a position. He decides that it not appropriate to withhold the position as punishment. A fair punishment was already administered by the court. But he considers whether he trusts this person. He must decide whether the shoplifting incident was an aberrant past behavior or an indication of a deep character flaw. He thoroughly interviews the applicant, considers the issue carefully, and decides to give this person the job.

Like the shoplifter, one consequence of Bnai Yisrael's sin was its punishment. This punishment would be administered over the course of ages. Like the shoplifter, the sin of the *Egel* also evinced a serious question about the character of the nation. The character issue intervened between Bnai Yisrael and Hashem. It prevented the advancement of their relationship.

Hashem did not define Bnai Yisrael's character by its sin

Now, we can understand Rashi's comment that the establishment of the *Mishkan* demonstrated that Hashem had excused the sin of the *Egel*. This does not mean that Hashem would not punish the nation. Instead, it means that He determined that the sin should be treated as an aberration and not as a fundamental character flaw. Through the creation of the *Mishkan*, Hashem's Glory would reside within the nation. The relationship that was suspended by the sin of the *Egel* would be fully established. The sin was excused in the sense that it no longer arrested the advancement of the relationship between Hashem and His *Am HaNivchar*. In the *Mishkan*, this relationship achieved its full expression.

Now, let's return to our original question. Does Hashem excuse sin as Rashi suggests? If He does how are we to understand the Talmud's assertion that Hashem does not excuse sin? The answer is that the Talmud is speaking of the inevitability of punishment. Hashem does not overlook or excuse sin. When we sin, we must either repent and seek forgiveness or endure the punishment. We cannot expect Hashem to pardon us. Rashi is not suggesting that Hashem

---

[18] Rabbeinu Shlomo ben Yitzchak (Rashi), *Commentary on Sefer Shemot* 32:19.
[19] Rabbeinu Shlomo ben Yitzchak (Rashi), *Commentary on Sefer Shemot* 34:1.

excused the sin of the *Egel* and did not punish us for it. He is explaining, the despite our sin, Hashem completed our selection as the *Am HaNivchar* and caused His Glory to reside in our midst.

Seeing more in others than their failings

There is an important personal message in the comments of Rashi. Moshe beseeched Hashem to not determine His relationship with us based on our trespass. He asked that Hashem not assess us exclusively based upon our terrible sin. He should regard the sin as an aberration in our behavior and not as defining our character. Hashem granted Moshe's request and accepted us as His *Am HaNivchar*.

We should consider this model in our own personal relationships. We should strive to imitate Hashem. We each experience harm and hurt at the hands of others. We often define those who have acted wrongly toward us by these acts. The result is that we sever our relationship with these individuals. If we follow Hashem's model, we will look beyond the wrong done to us and consider the overall character of the individual. This will allow us to find good even in those who have acted wrongly toward us and preserve our relationship with them.

These are the accounts of the Tabernacle – the Tabernacle of the Testimony – that were compiled at Moshe's direction, the service of the Leveyim under the supervision of Etamar the son of Aharon the Kohen. (Shemot 38:21)

Judging one another's Beliefs
The meaning of the name "Tabernacle of the Testimony"

The Parshiyot of Vayakel and Pekuday complete the Torah's account to the creation of the Mishcan – the Tabernacle. These final two Torah portions discuss the actual fabrication of the Mishcan's components, the manufacture of the garments of the Kohen Gadol and Kohanim the High Priest and the other Priests, and the assembly of the Mishcan. The above passage introduces the Torah portion of Pekuday. In the passage, the Mishcan is referred to as Mishcan HaEydut – the Tabernacle of the Testimony. The name associates the Mishcan with testimony. However, testimony must be about some event or fact. What is the event or fact to which the Mishcan testifies?

Many commentators suggest that the term Mishcan HaEydut does not mean that the Tabernacle provides testimony. Instead, the term means that the Mishcan contains or is the home of the Luchot – the Tablets of the Decalogue. These Tablets are referred to in the Torah as the Luchot HaEydut – the Tablets of the Testimony[20]. The Luchot provide testimony to the Revelation. Therefore, the Mishcan that contains the Tablets is referred to as the Tabernacle of the Testimony. [21] However, Rashi disagrees with this interpretation. He suggests that the term Mishcan HaEydut means that the Mishcan provides testimony. Therefore, Rashi must identify the event or fact to which the Mishcan testifies.

Rashi explains that the Mishcan testifies that Hashem indulged or excused Bnai Yisrael after the sin of the Golden Calf. He further explains that when the Mishcan was assembled, the

---

[20] E.g. Shemot 31:18
[21] E.g. Rabbaynu Avraham ibn Ezra, Commentary on Sefer BeMidbar 1:50.

cloud of Hashem descended upon it and the glory of Hashem filled the Mishcan. This expression of Hashem's presence within the encampment of Bnai Yisrael demonstrated that the sin of the Egel HaZahav – the Golden Calf had been excused or indulged.

Rashi's phrasing is notable. He does not say that the sin was forgiven or that the nation had adequately atoned for the sin. Instead, he explains that Hashem decided to excuse or to indulge the nation. Rashi seems to suggest that although Hashem restored His presence in the midst of the nation, this restoration represented something less that total forgiveness. An example will help explain this distinction. If a person harms me, and apologizes, I may decide to forgive the person. This means I completely disregard the act of harm done to me. I have decided to treat this person as if the action never occurred. It is erased and no longer a factor in our relationship. However, I may decide that I can excuse the person or that I am willing to indulge him but that I am not prepared to forgive the person. In this case, I am willing to overlook the action. I do feel a need to exact retribution. But I am not satisfied that the person truly regrets his behavior and accepts full responsibility for his wrongdoing. In other words, forgiveness is secured through a change in the wrongdoer. Indulgence or being excused is a unilateral decision made by the wronged party and does not necessarily reflect any change in the wrongdoer's attitude.[22]

Rashi's interpretation raises two issues:

According to Rashi, Hashem did not forgive the sin of the Egel; He excused it. Why were Bnai Yisrael not worthy of forgiveness?

If Bnai Yisrael did not deserve to be forgiven, then why were they excused? They had committed a very serious transgression and did not deserve forgiveness. Yet, they were excused! How can this be explained?

Various interpretations of "stiff-necked"

And Hashem said to Moshe: I have seen this nation and it is a stiff-necked nation. (Shemot 32:9)

After the sin of the Egel, Hashem describes Bnai Yisrael as a stiff-necked nation. What is the meaning of this term? The commentators offer a number of explanations. The consensus is that the term communicates that the nation is stubborn and not likely to repent. However, their interpretations differ in significant aspects. Rabbaynu Ovadia Sforno explains that the term communicates a resistance to learning an adopting new practices and ideas. The generation that worshipped the Egel was the product of a pagan, idolatrous society. It had assimilated many of the attitudes, beliefs, and values of this society. The nation was certainly capable of moments of absolute clarity. At these moments, the people understood the folly of their preconceptions and embraced the truths of the Torah. However, they were not capable of completely uprooting abandoning all remnants of the worldview that they had developed in Egypt. As a result at moments of extreme stress, the nation was capable of reverting to idolatrous behaviors. The sin of the Egel was such a moment. The stress and anxiety caused by Moshe's failure to descend from Sinai developed into a fear of abandonment. The nation responded to this fear by reverting to the false but familiar sense of security provided by idolatrous practices.

---

[22] Rashi's comments are based upon the Midrash quoted by Yalkut Shimoni, BeMidbar 10:723. However, a similar Midrash is found in Midrash Rabbah, Shemot 51:4. In the Midrash Rabba version, Hashem does forgive the nation for the sin of the *Egel*.

Rashi disagrees. He does not understand the term as describing an inability to learn and adopt new and novel outlooks. Instead, he explains that the term describes an unwillingness or inability to respond positively to criticism. Rashi does not explain the source or cause of this resistance to accepting criticism. In general, this character flaw is a consequence of poor self-image or weak ego. In order to accept criticism, a strong ego is helpful. A person with lacking this degree of self-assuredness struggles to maintain a positive self-image. Therefore, he resists all criticism. Conversely, a strong self-image allows a person to accept that he or she has a flaw without feeling that this flaw is a threat to his self-respect. A nation of freed slaves can be expected to struggle with self-image issues. The members of the nation are likely to have weak self-images and egos. Accepting criticism will difficult if not impossible.

According to both of these explanations, it was unlikely that the generation redeemed from Egypt could fully repent. According to Sforno, the nation could achieve moments of complete clarity. However, the absolute abandonment of the views, beliefs, and behaviors learned in Egypt was beyond its grasp. As a result, they remained susceptible to reverting to these beliefs and behaviors. According to Rashi, the people lacked the ego strength to accept criticism and learn from mistakes. Therefore, they lacked the ability to engage in the introspection needed to completely shed the remnants of idolatry from their perspectives and behaviors. Consequently, Bnai Yisrael was not forgiven for the sin of the Egel. Forgiveness would have required a level of repentance that was beyond the capacity of the nation. Nonetheless, Hashem did excuse the nation. Why did He excuse them?

The Torah's minimal standards for beliefs and convictions

Maimonides explains that there are certain beliefs regarding Hashem that every Jew must adopt. For example, every member of Bnai Yisrael must acknowledge that Hashem is incorporeal and He is an absolute unity not subject to any form of division. He explains that these fundamental ideas must be taught to every Jew at his or her level. Maimonides limits this list of fundamentals to very few elements and also, prescribes a minimal degree of understanding as being adequate for those who are either uneducated or incapable of a more thorough, broad, and definitive understanding of the Torah's fundamental principles. [23] This is an amazing concession. Maimonides often stresses the importance of a proper understanding of Hashem[24] and devotes much of his Moreh Nevuchim to developing this understanding. How can Maimonides' emphasis upon the importance of a proper understanding of Hashem be reconciled with the minimal standard he proposes for the uneducated or less capable?[25]

Maimonides is suggesting that although these unfortunate individuals have not secured the level of understanding for which we are all required to strive, nonetheless, they are excused for their shortcoming. In other words, the Torah establishes a minimum set of beliefs and an ideal. We are all required to strive for the ideal. But if we achieve only the minimum, we are excused. In short, a person who, as a consequence of ignorance or incapacity, has developed an

---

[23] Rabbaynu Moshe ben Maimon (Rambam) *Moreh Nevuchim*, volume 1, chapter 34.
[24] E.g. Rabbaynu Moshe ben Maimon (Rambam) *Moreh Nevuchim*, volume 1, chapter 36.
[25] It should not be assumed that Maimonides is merely exercising pragmatic compassion for those less fortunate – those who lack either the wit or opportunity to secure a proper education. Maimonides is famously unsympathetic for those who err in their grasp of the fundamentals as a result of the misfortune of their upbringing or their incapacity to grasp these principles. See for example *Moreh Nevuchim* volume 1, chapter 36.

incomplete or not completely accurate understanding of the Torah's fundamentals, is excused for this shortcoming.

Forgiveness vs. indulgence

Based upon Maimonides' comments, Rav Yisrael Chait suggested an explanation of Hashem's response to Bnai Yisrael's failure to fully repent from the sin of the Egel. The nation accepted the fundamentals of the Torah. The people were not completely immune from beliefs and attitudes that if carefully considered would be seen to be inconsistent with the Torah. Also, this lack of introspection and study resulted in some ambiguity and occasional ambivalence. However, the nation accepted the fundamentals at a level consistent with its capacity. Therefore, the nation's failings were not forgiven. Forgiveness requires a level of repentance that was beyond the capacity of the generation that left Egypt. However, they were indulged or excused.

Tolerance for others

This suggests that we also should exercise care in judging one another's beliefs. Even if they are not completely consistent with the Torah, we should try to educate and avoid condemning these individuals. Certainly, there are a few very basic beliefs that should be taught rigorously and extensively to all Jews. But beyond this short list, we should exercise the same behavior demonstrated by Hashem towards the generation that created and worshipped the Egel. [26]

And out of the blue, purple, and crimson wool they made the packing cloths for sacred use, and they made Aharon's sacred garments, as Hashem commanded Moshe. (Shemot 39:1)

Clothes Makes the Man

The vestments of the *kohen gadol* are for his honor and glory

Parshat Pekudai completes the Torah's discussion of the fabrication of the *Mishcan*. Included in the *parasha* is a description of the garments to the *kohen gadol* – the high priest. The *kohen gadol*'s vestments include eight components. These are his shirt, pants, headdress, belt, jacket, an apron-like garment, his breast-plate, and a gold band worn on the forehead.

What is the purpose of these elaborate vestments? It should be noted that on the most sacred day of the year – *Yom Kippur* – the *kohen gadol* performs the services that are unique to that day in simple garments of white linen. Why during the rest of the year are those simple garments replaced by elaborate vestments?

The beautiful and detailed garments of the *kohen gadol* are first described in Parshat Tetzaveh. There, the Torah explains that the vestments of the *kohen gadol* are designed for his honor and glory. Nachmanides explains that they are the vestments typical of royalty. Assigning these vestments to him communicates the elevated status within the nation of the *kohen gadol*. Rabbaynu Avraham ibn Ezra adds that these vestments are assigned exclusively to the *Kohen gadol* and no other member of the nation may wear such garments. Ibn Ezra may be referring to the cloth used for the *kohengadol's* vestments. These garments include combinations of wool and linen. This combination of materials is typically prohibited. The exception to this prohibition is the vestments of the *kohengadol,* and to a lesser extent, this combination is also included in the garments of the common *kohen*.

---

[26] Rav Yisrael Chait, TTL Library, *The Tabernacle of Testimony* D-346.

Sefer HaChinuch suggests that these vestments are not intended to glorify and elevate the status of the *kohen gadol*. Instead, the objective in designating these beautiful and elaborate vestments to the *kohen gadol* is to emphasize the importance of the *Mishcan*. The *kohen gadol* is assigned these vestments because of his role in the service in the *Mishcan* and in securing atonement for the sins of the people. Therefore, the vestments do not honor the *kohen gadol* but rather communicate the awesome sacredness of the *Mishcan*.

The vestments also communicate a message to the *kohen gadol*

Sefer HaChinuch suggests, that although the vestments communicate the exalted sanctity of the *Mishcan*, they have another more immediate function. His position is based upon a study of these vestments and upon his understanding of human behavior.

Sefer HaChinuch notes, that not only are the vestments detailed in design, they are also considerable in their extent and mass. They cover the *kohen gadol* from head to foot. Some of the vestments are voluminous. The belt is so long as to require that it be wound around the *kohen gadol* multiple times. The headdress is similarly extensive. This characteristic of the vestments leads Sefer HaChinuch to conclude that the vestments' design is not solely aimed at impressing the observer. The design suggests that the *kohen gadol* is to also be very aware of his vestments. Their weight, extent, and sheer mass are intended to attract and retain his attention. What message do these vestments communicate to the *kohen gadol*?

Before addressing this question, we must consider an insight of Sefer HaChinuch into human behavior. We understand that our actions reflect our attitudes. For example, when I speak respectfully to another person, my behavior reflects my regard for the person whom I am addressing. When I recite the daily prayers, my actions reflect my faith in Hashem. Actions are expressions of our internal attitudes, beliefs, and opinions. However, Sefer HaChinuch asserts that it is also true that our behaviors exercise an influence on our internal attitudes and beliefs. If I treat others with respect, my actions will shape or re-enforce my respect for others. Through my praise of Hashem, I re-enforce my sense of His grandeur.

Now, we are prepared to address our question. What is the message communicated to the *kohengadol* by his vestments? Sefer HaChinuch responds that the vestments remind the *kohen gadol* that he is the servant of Hashem, and that to Him, he offers his service. By wearing his vestments, the *kohen gadol* is constantly reminded of these messages and they become more thoroughly integrated into his thinking and outlook.

In summary, his vestments are designed to not only bring honor to the *kohen gadol*; they also serve as an ongoing reminder to him that he is acting in the service of Hashem and that it is He whom he worships. Through this ongoing reminder, these messages are constantly re-enforced and become integrated into the *kohen gadol's* thinking and perspective.

Our clothing impacts our perception of ourselves and our values

This insight of Sefer HaChinuch has implications beyond our understanding of the vestments of the *kohen gadol*. Sefer HaChinuch's insight suggests an approach to understanding the Torah's attitude toward how we should dress. The Torah requires that we dress modestly and not in a revealing manner. The Torah also has other standards for dress. Maimonides explains that a Torah scholar should wear clean and attractive garments. A scholar should wear neither extravagantly expensive nor tawdry clothing, but instead, clothing that reflects the mean standard.

Unfortunately, when these expectations are considered most attention is given to the requirement for modest dress, and more specifically, to imputing from these standards attitudes toward gender and sexuality. Approached from this perspective, the Torah's standards for modesty in dress are critically interpreted, as at best, expressing an antiquated prudishness.

Let us apply Sefer HaChinuch's insight to the Torah's expectations. According to Sefer HaChinuch, our clothing communicates a message to others and also to ourselves. Let's focus on the message we communicate to ourselves through our manner of dress. Moderate garments remind the Torah scholar to be moderate in the pursuit of one's desires and in one's behaviors. Clean, appealing clothing remind the scholar to behave with the self-respect that is demanded by the scholar's role in representing the Torah. The Torah scholar's moderate garments are also a reminder of the importance balancing this self-respect with humility. By consistently dressing according to the Torah's standards, these messages are constantly re-enforced and integrated.

Modesty in our attire also communicates a message to us. It reminds us that we are more than our physical bodies. Through resisting the tendency to reveal or accentuate our most attractive physical features, we remind ourselves that our inner-self is far more significant than our superficial physical endowments. Again, consistent adherence to the Torah's standard provides on-going re-enforcement of this message.

Perhaps, this is also the message that modest dress is intended to communicate to the observer. The message expressed is that the true distinction of a human being is never to be found in the person's outward attractiveness. Our virtue is derived from our spiritual endowments.

An April 2012 article in the New York Times discusses the scientific field of embodied cognition. The article describes various studies that support the hypothesis that our clothing impacts our attitudes and behaviors. As Sefer HaChinuch suggests, how we act and how we dress does have impact upon how we think.

And he made the Eyfode. [He made it from] gold thread, blue techelet thread, purple thread, scarlet thread, and spun wool. (Shemot 39:2)

A Neglected Torah Portion

1. **Part I. The Eyfode and Choshen - A further review of the Mishcan**

    The Torah's discussion of the Mishcan – the Tabernacle – extends through five consecutive portions. Parshat Pekuday is the final portion in the series. The parasha opens reporting the tally of some of the materials donated for the Mishcan's construction and how these materials were used. The parasha continues with a description of the actual fabrication of the Mishcan and the vestments of the Kohen Gadol and Kohanim. The parasha concludes with Moshe's assembly of the Mishcan. Most of the material is covered in the preceding portions. First, these present the commandment for the construction of the Mishcan and the vestments. Then, they record Moshe's instruction to Betzalel and his workers. Because the parasha does not seem to include new material, it is somewhat neglected. However, the parasha provides interesting insights into the Mishcan and the vestments. Let us consider a few of these.

2. **The Eyfode's design**

    This passage introduces the account of the manufacture of the Kohen Gadol's – the High Priest's – vestments.

The first vestment described is the Eyfode. There are different opinions regarding the specific design of the garments. The above image reflects Rashi's position.[27] The Eyfode was a cloth panel worn like an apron and opening in the front. Sewn into the Eyfode were a cloth belt – the cheshev – and two cloth shoulder straps – ketayfote. The belt was sewn into the top of the Eyfode and tied at the Kohen Gadol's waist.[28] The ketayfote straps were sewn into cheshev behind the Kohen Gadol. They extended up and over his shoulders, hanging down in front of him.

The ketayfote had two functions. First, on the top of each shoulder was a shohum stone. On each stone was engraved the names of six Shevatim – tribes. Together, these stones bore the names of all twelve tribes. Second, the breastplate of the Kohen Gadol – the Choshen – hung from the ketayfote.

Rashi explains that the cheshev and ketayfote of the Eyfode were parts of the Eyfode. In other words, the Eyfode was composed of three parts – the panel, the cheshev that bound it to the Kohen Gadol, and the ketayfote straps whose functions are described above.[29] Because they combined to create a single vestment, they shared the same thread combination. What about the Eyfode and the Choshen that was suspended from it? Were these a single vestment or separate vestments? From the first time they are described, the Torah consistently refers to these are separate vestments.[30] This raises a question. What is the relationship between these two vestments? Was the Choshen the more significant vestment and the Eyfode supported it? Was the Eyfode the more fundamental vestment and the Choshen adorned it?

And he made the Choshen, the work of a craftsman, like the design of the Eyfode – [made of] gold thread, blue thread, purple thread, scarlet thread, and spun wool. (Shemot 39:8)

---

[27] Rabbaynu Shlomo ben Yitzchak (Rashi), Commentary on Sefer Shemot 28:6.
[28] In the above image, the cheshev is tied in the front. Rashi 28:6 explains that the cheshev was tied behind the Kohen Gadol.
[29] Rabbaynu Shlomo ben Yitzchak (Rashi), Commentary on Sefer Shemot 28:6.
[30] Sefer Shemot 28:4.

3. The Choshen – Eyfode relationship

The above passage describes the design of the Choshen. It was made of the same thread combination as the Eyfode. However, the Torah adds that its design should be like that of the Eyfode. The implication is that its design is determined by the Eyfode. This suggests that the Eyfode was the more fundamental vestment and that the Choshen's design was dictated by it.

This seems odd. The Choshen was a very important vestment. It was encrusted with gems that were engraved with the names of the Shevatim. It was certainly visually more prominent than the Eyfode. Also, it had important functions. These included playing a central role in the Kohen Gadol's prophetic pronouncements.[31]

Rabbaynu Bachya responds to this issue. He explains that we must consider the relationship between these two vestments from two perspectives. An illustration will help explain his insight.

I purchase a beautiful tie. I decide I will wear it this Shabbat. I select a suit to wear that complements the tie. I dress in the suit and the tie. Which garment is more fundamental to the outfit – the suit or the tie? The answer depends on perspective. A tie is an accent element. It is not a fundamental garment. From the perspective of the inherent relationship between the garments, the suit is more fundamental than the tie. However, my objective in selecting the suit was to accommodate the tie. From the perspective of purpose and objective, the tie is more fundamental in the creation of the outfit.

Rabbaynu Bachya explains that viewed from the perspective of the inherent relationship between components, the Eyfode was more the fundamental vestment of the Kohen Gadol. It was the central component of the ensemble of vestments. The Choshen was an adornment. However, from the perspective of function, the Choshen is the more prominent. In other words, the prominent vestment – the Choshen – was worn as an adornment of the Eyfode.[32]

Part II. The placement of the objects in the Mishcan

And he brought the Aron to the Mishcan. He placed the Parochet curtain and covered the Aron of Testimony as Hashem commanded Moshe. He put the Shulchan table in the Ohel Moed on the north side of the Mishcan, outside of the Parochet. .... He placed the Menorah candelabra in the Ohel Moed opposite the Shulchan, on the south side of the Mishcan. ... He placed the entry-curtain of the Mishcan. He placed the Gold Altar... The Olah Altar he placed.... He placed the Laver... (Shemot 40:22-30)

1. Moshe assembles the Mishcan

Moshe assembles the Mishcan. He places its contents in their proper places. The above passages describe the placement of the various components and the contents. The verses use three different verbs to describe the placement of the components and contents. The Aron – the Ark – is brought (hayvee) into the Mishcan. The Shulchan – table – is put (natan) in its place by the north side of the Mishcan. All other objects are placed (sum). Why are these first elements brought or put into the Mishcan and the others placed?

---

[31] The Kohen Gadol received prophetic messages in a visual form. The names of the tribes were engraved upon the Choshen's gems. The prophetic communication appeared to him in these letters.

[32] Rabbaynu Bachya ben Asher ibn Halawa, Commentary on Sefer Shemot 28:6.

2. The role of the Aron and Shulchan

The Aron was brought into the Mishcan; the Shulchan was put in the Mishcan. These two objects were unique. The Aron and Shulchan were assigned unique, inherent places in the Mishcan. Their placements directly or indirectly determined the placements of every other object in the above passages. With the installation of the Aron and Shulchan, the positions of all the other objects were determined. This is reflected in the choice of verbs used to describe in object's installation. The verb "place" is used to communicate that the object was installed into its predetermined position in relation to another object. They were installed in positions in relationship to and determined by the Aron and Shulchan. Moshe filled each spot with its appropriate object. In contrast to the Aron and Shulchan, the other objects in the passages did not have inherent positions.

3. The position of the Menorah

Let us consider the Menorah. Where did Moshe install it? He installed it on the south side of the Mishcan, opposite the Shulchan. When the Shulchan was installed, the position of the Menorah was determined. When Moshe installed the Menorah, he placed it in a specific spot in relation to the Shulchan. Its position was identified with with the installation of the Shulchan and the Menorah "filled" that spot.

4. The placement of the other objects

Each use of the verb "place" communicates this same phenomenon. The object was placed in a spot determined by the placement of a preceding object. The object fills this spot. The installation of the Aron determined the placement of the Parochet curtain. It must be positioned before the Aron. The installation of the Parochet curtain determined the placement of the Gold Altar. It must be "before the Parochet". The raising of the Mishcan determined the placement of the entry curtain – at the opening to the Mishcan. It also determined the placement of the Olah Altar – at its entrance. The Lavar's position was between the Olah Altar and Mishcan.

5. The beauty of the Mishcan

The parasha provides many more insights into the Mishcan and the vestments. The Torah is teaching us that a comprehensive system of halachah governs their design and use. An important message emerges from careful study of the five Torah portions that discuss the Mishcan and vestments. Their design and use are not dictated solely by aesthetic considerations. Halachah plays a prominent role in their design and use. Their beauty is not only superficial and aesthetic; it was also found in the pervasive system of underlying halachah.

The Torah's treatment of the Mishcan and the vestments illuminates the nature of the authentic religious experience. It is not the aesthetic aspect of the experience that endows it with meaning. Beautiful melodies, sung in an impressive sanctuary do not themselves create an authentic religious experience. The Torah requires that the experience be based upon and give expression to a system of underlying halachah.

"And they beat the gold into thin plates and cut them into threads, which they included in the blue, dark red, crimson wool, and fine linen as patterned brocade." *(Shemot 39:3)*

The garments of the *Kohen Gadol* contain a number of materials. The basic threads are blue wool, dark red wool, crimson wool, and fine linen. The vestments also contain gold threads. However, the gold threads are interwoven into the other threads. How is this accomplished? Each thread of blue wool, dark red wool, crimson wool and fine linen is composed of seven strands woven together. Six of the stands are of the basic material of the thread. The seventh strand is gold. For example, a thread of blue wool in composed of seven individual strands woven together to create a single thread. Six of these strands are blue wool. The seventh strand is gold. In this manner, gold is included in each of the threads of the garment.

Our *pasuk* describes the process through which these gold threads are created. A quantity of gold is beaten into a thin plate or foil. Then, this foil is cut into fine threads.

The Torah does not provide many details regarding the manufacturing processes used in creating the *Mishcan* and the vestments of the *Kohanim*. For example, the craftsmen created silver sockets. The boards that supported the curtains of the *Mishcan* were inserted into these sockets. The Torah does not describe the process by which these sockets were fabricated. These details of the manufacturing process are not included in the Torah's narrative.

The only detail that the Torah does provide is the method by which these gold threads were fashioned. It is odd that this detail should be mentioned. Why does this detail deserve special attention?

Nachmanides offers an answer to this question. He explains that the Torah did not dictate the specific manufacturing processes. The Torah described the elements of the *Mishcan* and the vestments of the *Kohanim*. However, the Torah did not command the craftsmen to manufacture these items in any specific manner. The craftsmen were free to rely on their own ingenuity to fashion these items. For this reason, the specific manufacturing processes are not included in the Torah. These processes were not part of the commandments to create a *Mishcan* and vestments for the *Kohanim*.

This presented the craftsmen with a dilemma. They understood the description of the *Kohen Gadol*'s garments. They realized that the individual threads of the garments must contain a gold strand. However, they were not familiar with a process through which gold thread could be manufactured. This challenge exceeded their experience and knowledge. They were required to invent some novel process for manufacturing these gold strands. The Torah is describing the manufacturing process invented by the craftsmen of the *Mishcan*. This process is described in order to demonstrate the wisdom of these craftsmen. They invented a completely new process.[33]

And they brought the Tabernacle to Moshe – the tent and its vessels, its clasps, its planks, its bars, its pillars and its sockets. (Shemot 39:33)

And he made fifty golden clasps. He joined together the curtains, one to another, with the clasps. And it was one Mishcan. (Shemot 37:13)

The Components of the Mishkan and their Relationships

1. The golden clasps and the curtains of the *Mishcan*

Parshat Pekudai includes a description of the actual assembly of the *Mishcan* – the Tabernacle. This description provides important insights into the relationships between the various elements of the *Mishcan*. After the components of the *Mishcan* were fabricated, they were brought to Moshe for assembly. The first passage enumerates the components of the actual

---

[33] Rabbaynu Moshe ben Nachman (Ramban), *Commentary on Sefer Shemot* 39:3.

basic structure. The components were the planks that supported the structure and the sockets into which these planks were inserted. These planks were held together by horizontal wooden bars that ran the length of the supporting walls. Pillars were used to hold up curtains. Clasps joined together the curtains that were supported by the planks.

The second passage above is from Parshat VaYakhel. This passage describes the assembly of the curtain of the *Mishcan*. The *Mishcan*'s most inner covering was composed of ten curtains of identical dimensions. These curtains were divided into two groups – each composed of five curtains. The five curtains of each group were sewn together. The outer edge of the outer curtain of each set included fifty loops. The two sets of curtains were laid-out with the loops of each set aligned with those of the other set. The two sets were then joined together using golden clasps. The entire assembly – all ten curtains was draped over the upright planks. The curtains created a covered inner space and extended down the sides of the planks.

The design of this covering is somewhat odd. The five curtains in each group were joined together with stitching. However, the two resultant groups of five curtains were connected to one another by a series of golden clasps. Why was this combination of methods used to join together the curtains? Why were clasps used only to join together the two groups of curtains but not to join the curtains within the groups?

And you should place the Parochet under the claps. And you should bring there – inside of the Parochet – the Ark of Testimony. The Parochet should separate for you between the Sacred and the Most Sacred. (Shemot 26:33)

2. The *Parochet* separated the Sacred from the Most Sacred

The above passage is from Parshat Terumah. In this passage, the Torah explains that the *Mishcan* was divided into two areas – the Sacred and the Most Sacred. The Most Sacred was the area in which the *Aron* – the Ark – and the Ark Covering were placed. The Sacred was the area in which the *Mizbeach HaKetoret*, the *Menorah*, and the *Shulchan* – the Golden Altar, the Candelabra, and the Table of the Shew Bread – were placed. These two domains were of unequal areas. The Most Sacred measured 10X10 cubits and the Sacred measured 10X20 cubits. The two areas were separated by a curtain – the *Parochet*.

The above passage explains that the *Parochet* should be placed directly under the clasps that held together the two sets of curtains. In other words, the curtains were draped over the planks so that the clasps that joined the two sets were ten cubits forward from the rear or western wall. The *Parochet* was then placed directly under these clasps. The placement of the *Parochet* under the clasps set off an inner area – the Most Sacred – of 10X10 cubits. The passage above implies that the correspondence between the location of the clasps and the position of the *Parochet* was not accidental. It was a significant aspect of the *Mishcan*'s design. Why was this correspondence important?

And you should make the planks for the Mishcan – upright acacia wood. (Shemot 36:20)

3. The upright planks of the *Mishcan*

The above passage from Parshat VaYakhel describes the planks that held up the *Mishcan*'s curtains. The passage is understood by the Sages to require that the planks be arranged in an upright position. In other words, the planks could not be arranged horizontally and piled upon one another to create a wall.[34] Upright planks were inserted into metal sockets for the planks of the *Mishcan*. The planks were held together by horizontal bars.

What is the reason for this requirement? This requirement implies that the function of the planks was not to form a wall. The planks were intended to support the curtains. The placement of the planks in their upright position demonstrated that they served as a continuous series of pillars which supported the covering curtains. In other words, the *Mishcan* was not composed of wooden walls covered by tapestry. It was a set of curtains supported by wooden planks. This means that the curtains were the more fundamental component of the structure and the planks were merely intended to support and give form to these curtains.

4. The function of the clasps and their relationship to the *Parochet*

Now the function of the clasps and their placement in correspondence with the *Parochet* can be understood. The curtains were the more fundamental structural element of the *Mishcan*. The clasps that brought together the two sets of curtains reflected a fundamental element of the *Mishcan*'s design. This fundamental element was the existence within structure of two discreet areas – the Sacred and the Most Sacred. This requirement – the creation of two separate areas – was so fundamental to the *Mishcan*'s design that it was incorporated into the design of the curtains. The curtains themselves were composed to two separate sets. One set was designated to cover the Most Sacred and the other set was designated to cover the Sacred.[35] The placement of the *Parochet* under the clasps, actualized the separation of the two areas suggested and designated by the golden clasps.

And Moshe brought the Ark to the Mishcan and put in place the covering Parochet. He covered the Ark of Testimony as Hashem commanded Moshe. (Shemot 40:21)

5. The *Parochet* was hung after the *Aron* was positioned

Parshat Pekudai describes the order in which Moshe assembled the *Mishcan* and arranged its vessels. The above passage explains that Moshe first placed the *Aron* into the Most Sacred. After placing the *Aron* in its assigned position, he erected the *Parochet*. This seems odd. The Most Sacred was the inner portion of the *Mishcan*. It was separated from the outer portion by the *Parochet*. Why did Moshe place the *Aron* in the inner area of the *Mishcan* before completing its separation from the outer portion with the erection of the *Parochet*?

The passage above describes the *Parochet* as the "covering" *Parochet*. This means that the *Parochet* served a dual purpose. It separated the Sacred from the Most Sacred. It also covered or shielded the *Aron*. The order followed by Moshe suggests that *Parochet* could only be erected when it could fulfill both functions. Before Moshe placed the *Aron* in its designated area, the *Parochet* could not function as its cover or shield. Therefore, Moshe first placed the *Aron* in its position and then he erected the *Parochet* as the *Aron*'s cover or shield.

And you should bring the Shulchan and arrange upon it its assembly (of loaves). You should bring the Menorah and ignite its candles. (Shemot 40:4)

And you should place the Shulchan outside of the Parochet and the Menorah opposite the Shulchan – on the south side of the Mishcan. And the Shulchan should be on the north side. (Shemot 26:35)

6. The *Shulchan*'s relationship to the *Parochet*

---

[34] Rashi 27:15.
[35] See Rashbam 27:33.

The first of the above passages is from Parshat Pekudai. It explains that after Moshe placed the *Parochet* in its place, he placed the *Shulchan* and *Menorah* in their respective positions. The passage does not provide an explanation for the order in which Moshe positioned these items. However, the rationale for the order is evident from the passages in Parshat Terumah in which Hashem instructs Bnai Yisrael to create the *Mishcan*. The second above passage is from these instructions. In this passage, the location of the *Shulchan* is described as "outside of the *Parochet*" – meaning facing the outer-side of the *Parochet*. The *Parochet* created an inner area of the *Mishcan* – the Most Sacred and an outer area – the Sacred. The passage instructs Bnai Yisrael to place the *Shulchan* in this outer area. However, it is important to note the position of the *Shulchan* is described relative to the *Parochet*. Therefore, the *Shulchan* could not be put in place until the *Parochet* was erected. It was only possible to position the *Shulchan* opposite the *Parochet* after the *Parochet* was hung in place.

7. The relationship between the *Shulchan* and *Menorah*

The first passage explains that Moshe first placed the *Shulchan* in its proper place and then the *Menorah* was placed in its proper position. Again, this order was not arbitrary. Instead, Moshe's order reflects the instructions provided earlier in Parshat Terumah. There, the position of the *Menorah* is described as opposite the *Shulchan*. In other words, the *Menorah*'s position was determined by and relative to the *Shulchan*. Only after placing the *Shulchan* in its proper place was it possible to place the *Menorah* in position.

"And Hashem spoke to Moshe, saying: On the first day of the first month you shall erect Tabernacle, the Tent of Meeting." (Shemot 40:1-2)

Bnai Yisrael were commanded to construct a sanctuary that would accompany them in the wilderness. The Chumash provides a detailed description of this sanctuary and its contents. In the above passage, Moshe is commanded to assemble and erect the completed sanctuary. The passage employs two terms in referring to this sanctuary. It is referred to it as *Mishcan* – Tabernacle – and as *Ohel Moed* – Tent of Meeting. What is the difference between these two terms? Both seem to refer to the single sanctuary! Why are both terms needed?

"And Moshe erected the Tabernacle, and laid its sockets, and set up its planks, and put in its bars, and reared up its pillars. And he spread the tent over the Tabernacle, and put the covering of the tent above upon it; as Hashem commanded Moshe." (Shemot 40:18-19)

This *pasuk* describes Moshe's activities in erecting the sanctuary. It is clear from this passage that the sanctuary includes three coverings. The *Mishcan* is composed of a series of curtains. These curtains are spread over a skeletal structure of boards. The curtains create a ceiling or covering over the area within the boards and extend over most of the outer area of the boards. The result is a box-like structure of curtains supported by the skeletal boards. Over the *Mishcan* is spread a second series of curtains. Our passage refers to this second set of curtains as a tent. These curtains cover the entire surface of the *Mishcan*. Finally, a third covering is placed over the roof of the tent curtains. According to some opinions, this covering is composed of two layers. Therefore, three layers of coverings are suspended over the inner area of the sanctuary. The curtains of the *Mishcan* are the inner surface, or ceiling. Lying atop this ceiling are the curtains of the tent. These curtains are covered by a third covering of a single or double layer.

Each of the layers has its own name. The innermost layer is the *Mishcan*. The middle layer is referred to as the tent. The outer layer is referred to as a covering. What is the significance of these three terms? All three of the terms seem applicable to each layer. The innermost layer is part of the *Mishcan*. It creates a tent over the inner area, and it covers this area. The same can be said regarding the middle and outer layers. Yet, the Torah never interchanges these names. The inner layer is always refereed to a *Mishcan*. The middle is the tent. The outer layer is the covering.

Rabbaynu Ovadia Sforno deals with this question. Before we consider his explanation some background information is helpful. The inner curtains are woven. The design of the weave is intricate. Shapes of cherubs are interwoven into the fabric. These cherubs are visible on both sides of the curtains.

Sforno explains that the inner curtains of the sanctuary are referred to as *Mishcan* because they are designed to surround with cherubs the *aron, shulchan* and *menorah* – the ark, table, and candelabra.[36] He further explains that the middle layer of curtains is described as a tent because their purpose is to create a tent over the inner curtains. However, the inner curtains are not referred to as a tent. This is because their purpose is not to serve as a tent. Their purpose is solely to impose the figures of the cherubs above and surrounding the *aron, shulchan,* and *menorah*.[37]

In these comments, Sforno is explaining the meaning of the term *Mishcan* and tent. Sforno is proposing that these two terms have very different meanings. The term 'tent' refers to a structure designed to create an inner space. It demarks the inner space, separates it, and shields it from the surrounding. The term *'Mishcan'* refers to walls and a ceiling that are not designed to create a space. Instead, they are designed to create a specific appearance or environment within a space.

An analogy will be helpful. Consider a house. A house has outer walls and a roof. These outer walls and the roof are designed to separate the space within from the outside and to protect this space from the elements outside. These outer walls may be made of brick, stone, wood, or some other substance. The roof will be composed of shingle, tile or some other substance. The substance will be selected to correspond with the design and function of the outer walls and roof. They will not be composed of plaster or wood paneling. These materials are not appropriate for the function of these outer walls and roof. But plaster is appropriate for the inner walls and ceiling. The inner walls and ceiling are not designed to protect the space from the outside. They create the living area within. Their appearance, form, and texture should complement this space and give it character. In fact, we use different terms to refer to the overhead surfaces on the outside and inside. The outside surface is a roof; the inner surface is a ceiling. These two terms communicate their different functions. Although we do not have different terms to refer to the inner and outer walls, these two surfaces are distinguished in function and design in the same manner as a roof and ceiling.

Sforno is suggesting that the inner *Mishcan* curtains are designed to surround with cherubs the essential components of the sanctuary. They provide character and environment. In other words, they create an environment of surrounding cherubs within which the *aron,*

---

[36] Rabbaynu Ovadia Sforno, *Commentary on Sefer Shemot,* 26:1.
[37] Rabbaynu Ovadia Sforno, *Commentary on Sefer Shemot,* 26:7.

shulchan, and *menorah* are placed. The middle layer of curtains – the tent – is designed to separate and protect the inner space from the outer area.

In order to fully appreciate the meaning of these comments, it is important to visualize an outcome of the design of the sanctuary. The inner curtains – the *Mishcan* – include the cherub figures. However, these figures are only visible to an observer standing inside the sanctuary and looking overhead. The figures woven into the curtains that hung down to form walls are not visible from the inside or outside of the sanctuary. On the inside, they are obscured by the boards that hold up the curtains. On the outside, they are completely covered by the tent curtains that descend over them. It seems odd that the essential feature of the *Mishcan* curtains – the cherubs – are only visible to a person inside looking up!

Sforno is suggesting that although these cherubs are not readily visible from within or without, they nonetheless are the essential feature of the environment of the *Mishcan*. They create an environment of surrounding cherubs. Their effect-- or the creation of this environment -- is not dependent on their visibility. Their existence as figures woven into the fabric of the curtains creates the required environment.

Now, we can understand the term used to refer to the outer curtains. These curtains are placed atop the roof of the tent. They are referred to as a covering. The term 'covering' has a very literal meaning in our context. These curtains are not designed to create a space or to create an environment. They serve as a covering to protect the surface of the middle tent curtains.

Based on Sforno's comments, we can appreciate the lack of interchangeability of the terms '*Mishcan*', 'tent', and 'covering'. The inner *Mishcan* curtains cannot be referred to as a tent. They are not designed to create an inner space and separate and protect the inner space from the outer area. Neither are these curtains a covering. The middle curtains are a tent. They do not create the inner environment. They are not a covering. The outermost covering of curtains is not a tent. Also, they do not create an inner space and they do not create an environment.

"And you shall make the planks for the Mishcan of acacia wood, upright." (Shemot 26:15)

As noted above, the *Mishcan* curtains are supported by a skeletal structure of planks. Our passage explains that these planks are to be placed upright. Each plank is placed immediately adjacent to its neighbor. In this manner a continuous surface is created. The commentaries explain that the planks must be upright. They cannot be positioned horizontally upon one another.[38] This is an interesting requirement. It would seem that whether placed upright to create a continual surface or placed horizontally upon one another, the same outcome is achieved. Why must the planks be placed in an upright position?

According to Sforno, we can understand this requirement. These planks are not intended to create an inner wall. The inner wall of the *Mishcan* is the curtains of the *Mishcan*. The sole function of these planks is to support the curtains. In other words, the planks support the curtains; the curtains do not cover and adorn the planks. The positioning of the planks communicates their function. Horizontally placed planks placed atop one another creates the impression of an inner wall. Such an inner wall contradicts the function of the *Mishcan* curtains. It is these curtains that

---

[38] Rabbaynu Shlomo ben Yitzchak (Rashi), *Commentary on Sefer Shemot* 26:15.

create the inner environment of the *Mishcan*. The upright position of the planks contributes to communicating their purpose – the support of the *Mishcan* curtains.

Now, our original question is easily answered. The terms *Mishcan* and *Ohel Moed* both refer to the sanctuary. However, these terms refer to different aspects of the structure. *Mishcan* is the innermost structure. The innermost curtains create this structure. *Ohel Moed* – tent of meeting – refers to the middle curtains that create the tent within, where the *Mishcan* is situated.

And you should place there the Ark of Testimony. And you should shield the Aron with the curtain. (Shemot 40:3)

The Curtain in front of the Ark

Our *pasuk* discusses the *Parochet*. This was a curtain suspended in the *Mishcan*, in front of the *Aron*. According to our *pasuk*, the function of the *Parochet* was to shield the *Aron*.

The *Mishcan* was composed of two areas. These two areas were the *Kodesh* – the Holy – and the *Kodesh HaKadashim* – the Holy of the Holy. The *Aron* was placed in the *Kodesh HaKadashim*. The *Parochet* separated these two areas. The Chumash, in Parshat Terumah, indicates that the purpose of the *Parochet* was to separate the *Kodesh* from the *Kodesh HaKadashim*.

It seems that the Chumash is offering two different characterizations of the function of the *Parochet*. Our *parasha* indicates that the function of the *Parochet* was to shield the *Aron*. In Parshat Terumah, the Chumash indicates that the function of the *Parochet* was to separate the *Kodesh* from the *Kodesh HaKadashim*. How can we reconcile the two conflicting characterizations?

In reality, these two sources are not contradictory. The *Parochet* was essentially a shield in front of the *Aron*. The Chumash, in Parshat Terumah, does not contradict this function. The Chumash is merely requiring that this shield be extended beyond the dimensions of the *Aron*, in order to create two areas within the *Mishcan*. In other words, the shielding function defines the *Parochet*. Once the *Parochet* meets this essential qualification, it can be extended to create a separation between the *Kodesh* and the *Kodesh HaKadashim*.

There are various laws that support this understanding of the *Parochet*. The Talmud, in Tractate Yoma, comments that the staves of the *Aron* actually protruded into the *Parochet*. One who observed the *Parochet* from the *Kodesh* saw two projections pushing out the curtain. This strange requirement can be understood based upon our knowledge of the *Parochet*. The essential function of the *Parochet* was to shield the *Aron*. In order to demonstrate this function – that the *Parochet* was a shield for the Aron – the staves protruded into the *Parochet*.

This also explains another interesting *halachah*. The *Parochet* played a role in the service associated with certain sacrifices. A portion of the blood of these sacrifices was sprinkled, by the *kohen*, in the direction of the *Parochet*. This law is expressly stated in the Chumash. The midrash Torat Kohanim comments that the blood could not be sprinkled toward any portion of the *Parochet*. The sprinkling must be directed specifically towards the portion of the *Parochet* into which the staves of the *Aron* protruded. Why was this portion of the *Parochet* special? Based on the above discussion, this *halachah* can be appreciated. The *Parochet* was, in essence, a shield for the *Aron*. Therefore, the essential portion of the *Parochet* was the portion directly in front of the staves. The blood was to be sprinkled on this portion of the *Parochet*.

This role of the *Parochet* is evident in today's synagogues. It is customary to hang a curtain in front of the *Aron*. Rav Yosef Dov Soloveitchik *Zt"l* explained that this practice is based upon the *halachah* in our *pasuk*. We are duplicating the practice in the *Mishcan*. Our Ark represents the *Aron* of the *Mishcan*. Therefore, our Ark requires a curtain. It is fitting that we call this curtain a *Parochet*.

"And place the sacrificial altar before the opening of the Mishcan the Ohel Moed. And place the laver between the Ohel Moed and the altar and fill it with water." (Shemot 40:6-7)

Parshat Pekuday includes a detailed discussion of the actual assembly of the Mishcan. A careful analysis of the details of this account reveals many interesting aspects of the Mishcan. In particular, the relationship of the various components can be defined through these details. Our passage provides a beautiful example.

The first step in assembling the Mishcan was erecting the tent. The central element of the Mishcan was the Ark the Aron. Therefore, once the tent was erected, the Aron was placed inside. Generally, the other components were added in a specific order. This order corresponded to the distance of the component from the Aron. In other words, the objects closest to the Aron were installed first. These were the Menorah (the candelabra), the Shulchan (the table), and the incense altar. The sacrificial altar was located in the courtyard of the Mishcan. It was farther away from the Aron than the previous items. Therefore, the sacrificial altar was installed after the Menorah, Shulchan and incense altar. However, there is an exception to this order. The laver was located in the courtyard. It was placed between the sacrificial altar and the Mishcan. It was closer to the Aron than the sacrificial altar. Therefore, we would expect it to be installed before the sacrificial altar. Yet, the installation of the sacrificial altar preceded the placement of the laver!

Rav Chaim Soloveitchik Ztl explains that in order to answer this question, we must review the command regarding the laver. This command is found in the beginning of Parshat Ki Tisa. There, Hashem commands Moshe to construct the laver and place it between the Mishcan and the sacrificial altar. Rav Chaim points out that this command defines the location of the laver in relation to the Mishcan and the altar. This location emerges only after the Mishcan and altar are in place. In other words, no point can be defined as "between the Mishcan and the sacrificial altar", until the Mishcan and altar are in place. This answers our question. The laver could not be installed until after the altar. This is because the location of the laver is defined relative to the altar and the Mishcan. This location only emerges after the altar is installed.[39]

And it was that in the first month of the second year, on the first day of that month the Mishcan was erected. (Shemot 40:17)

---

[39] Rav Yitzchak Zev Soloveitchik, Chidushai HaGRIZ on T'NaCH and Aggadah, Parshat Pekuday.

Moshe's Service in the Mishcan

The *Mishcan* was completed and brought to Moshe. Moshe erected the *Mishcan* on the first day of Nisan, in the second year of the sojourn in the wilderness.

This was the eighth day of the inauguration of the *Mishcan*. On this day, the service in the *Mishcan* was performed by Moshe together with the *kohanim*. After this day, all service would be performed by the *kohanim* alone. Moshe would no longer serve in the *Mishcan*.

Moshe was not a *kohen*. Yet, during the eight days of the inauguration, Moshe served as a priest. Why was Moshe appointed for this task? The service was assigned to Aharon and his sons. How could Moshe serve in the place of the *kohanim*?

The commentaries offer various answers to this question. One of the most interesting solutions is provided by Gershonides. He explains that Moshe was selected and qualified to serve on these days because he was "the father of the priesthood and had given birth to it".[40] What is Gershonides telling us? Moshe was not Aharon's father! He was Aharon's brother. He had not given birth to the *kohanim*; they were not his children!

It is clear that Gershonides' statement is not to be understood literally. Instead, Gershonides is explaining an important concept underlying the selection of the *kohanim* to serve in the Temple. The *kohanim* were not chosen simply because they are the descendants of Aharon. Neither was Aharon selected purely on the basis of his own merit. Aharon was chosen because he was Moshe's brother. Similarly, Aharon's descendants are *kohanim* not merely because Aharon is their ancestor. They are descendants of Moshe's brother. This relationship is essential to their status as priests.

Gershonides is explaining that Moshe is the father of the institution of priesthood. Without him, Aharon would not have merited to be selected as *Kohen Gadol*. Neither would his children be *kohanim*. This explains the basis of Moshe's qualification to serve as a *kohen*. He was the source of the *kohanim*'s sanctity. If the *kohanim* served by virtue of their relationship to Moshe, it follows that Moshe could serve.

"And he burned incense on it as Hashem had commanded Moshe." (Shemot 40:26)

After the craftsmen completed the *Mishcan*, they brought it to Moshe for assembly. There is a difference of opinion regarding the date of this event. Many authorities maintain that the *Mishcan* was first assembled on the twenty-third of Adar. On this date, a seven-day period of initiation began. Moshe assembled and took down the *Mishcan* every day. According to some Sages, Moshe repeated this process as many as three times daily. Ahron and the *Kohanim* did not perform the services during this seven-day initiation. Instead, Moshe acted as the *Kohen Gadol* and theonly *Kohen*. On the eighth day – the first of Nissan – the *Mishcan* was again assembled. However, on this day it was not disassembled. Ahron and his sons began to assume the duties of the *Kohen Gadol* and the *Kohanim*.

Our passage states that, as one of his duties, Moshe burned incense on the altar. It is not at all clear from the Torah whether this service was only performed on the eighth day, or whether

---

[40] Rabbahynu Levi ben Gershon (Ralbag / Gershonides), *Commentary on Sefer Beresheit*, (Mosad HaRav Kook, 1994), p 457.

it was also performed during the seven-day initiation period. Nachmanides takes the position that Moshe offered the incense each of the seven days of the initiation.[41]

This position presents a problem. In Parshat Tetzaveh, Hashem commands Moshe to conduct the seven-day initiation. The Torah describes the sacrifices that Moshe was commanded to offer. In our *parasha*, Hahsem commands Moshe on the procedure he was to follow in erecting the *Mishcan*. Hashem tells Moshe that he should place the *Mishcan*'s vessels in their proper place. He also tells Moshe to light the Menorah and place the bread on the *Shulchan* – the table. However, no mention is made of offering incense. In short, in neither instance in which Hashem instructs Moshe on the procedures of the seven-day initiation is any mention made of offering incense. Why did Moshe perform a service not commanded by Hashem?

In order to answer this question, we must resolve another difficult issue. Why does the Torah divide the instructions for the initiation period between Parshat Tetzaveh and our *parasha*? Why are some instructions provided to Moshe in Parshat Tetzaveh and other instructions included in our *parasha* within the directions for the assembly of the *Mishcan*?

The answer is that these two sections are dealing with completely different aspects of the initiation process. Parshat Tetzaveh deals with the special offerings required to initiate Ahron, the *Kohanim*, and the altar. This *parasha* does not include the lighting of the Menorah or the placing of the bread on the *Shulchan*. These activities were not special services performed to initiate the *Mishcan* and the *Kohanim*.

Our *parasha* deals with a different aspect of the initiation period. During this period, Moshe performed the daily activities that are fundamental to the *Mishcan*. These activities include the lighting of the Menorah and the display of the bread on *Shulchan*. This section does not mention the special sacrifices offered as initiation. These sacrifices were not among the daily activities fundamental to the *Mishcan*.

It is noteworthy that the offering of the *Tamid* sacrifice is mentioned in both sections. The *Tamid* sacrifice is a daily offering made in the morning and afternoon. Why is the *Tamid* included in both sections? The answer is that apparently the *Tamid* serves two purposes. First, it is one of the fundamental daily activities of the *Mishcan*. For this reason, it is included in the instructions in our *parasha*. Second, all other sacrifices are offered after the morning *Tamid* service and before the afternoon *Tamid*. Therefore, the special offerings of the initiation period could only be sacrificed in conjunction with the *Tamid*. The requirement to sacrifice these special offerings generated an obligation to offer the *Tamid* sacrifice in the morning and afternoon. Therefore, the discussion of the special sacrifices in Parshat Tetzaveh includes mention of the *Tamid*.

We can now answer our question. Why did Moshe offer the incense during the seven-day initiation period? The answer is that our *parasha* clearly indicates that those services that are fundamental to the operation of the *Mishcan* were required during these seven days. For this reason, the lights of the Menorah were kindled and the bread was displayed on the *Shulchan*. Moshe recognized that the offering of incense is also a fundamental performance.

He concluded that the commands to light the Menorah, display the bread on the *Shulchan,* and offer the *Tamid* were only examples of a more general obligation to perform all services

---

[41] Rabbaynu Moshe ben Nachman (Ramban), *Commentary on Sefer Shemot* 40:27.

fundamental to the *Mishcan*. Therefore, he included in his daily service the offering of the incense. He realized that this service is included in the general obligation of performing all of the fundamental services.42

---

42 See comments of Nachmanides *Sefer Shemot* 40:27.

Made in the USA
Middletown, DE
27 December 2021